L'EUROPE

Le français est la langue officielle

Le français est une des langues officielles

NORVÈGE
GRANDE-BRETAGNE
IRLANDE
Mer du Nord
ESTONIE
SUÈDE
DANEMARK
LETTONIE
RUSSIE
LITUANIE
RUSSIE
BIÉLORUSSIE
PAYS-BAS
ALLEMAGNE
POLOGNE
BELGIQUE
LUXEMBOURG
OCÉAN ATLANTIQUE
RÉPUBLIQUE TCHÈQUE
UKRAINE
FRANCE
SLOVAQUIE
SUISSE
AUTRICHE
MOLDAVIE
HONGRIE
SLOVÉNIE
CROATIE
ROUMANIE
ANDORRE
PORTUGAL
ESPAGNE
Mer Méditerranée
CORSE
ITALIE
BOSNIE-HERZÉGOVINE
YOUGOSLAVIE
BULGARIE
MACÉDOINE
ALBANIE
GRÈCE
TURQUIE

0 100 200 milles
0 100 200 kilomètres

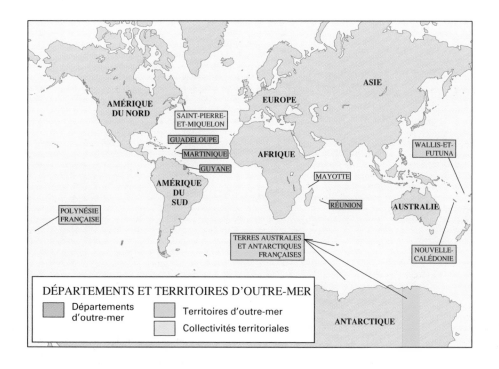

AMÉRIQUE DU NORD
EUROPE
ASIE
SAINT-PIERRE-ET-MIQUELON
GUADELOUPE
MARTINIQUE
GUYANE
AFRIQUE
WALLIS-ET-FUTUNA
MAYOTTE
AMÉRIQUE DU SUD
RÉUNION
AUSTRALIE
POLYNÉSIE FRANÇAISE
TERRES AUSTRALES ET ANTARCTIQUES FRANÇAISES
NOUVELLE-CALÉDONIE
ANTARCTIQUE

DÉPARTEMENTS ET TERRITOIRES D'OUTRE-MER

Départements d'outre-mer

Territoires d'outre-mer

Collectivités territoriales

ENTRE AMIS

ENTRE AMIS

An Interactive Approach

Fifth Edition

Michael D. Oates

Emeritus, University of Northern Iowa

Larbi Oukada

Indiana University, Indianapolis

Houghton Mifflin Company   Boston   New York

Components of *Entre amis*, Fifth Edition

■ **Student Text with In-Text Audio CDs**

■ **Instructor's Annotated Edition with In-Text Audio CDs**

■ **Student Activities Manual (SAM)** (*Cahier d'activités*)

■ **SAM Audio CDs**

■ **E-SAM powered by Quia**

■ **Instructor's HM Class Prep CD with HM Testing**

■ *Pas de problème!* **Video**

■ *Entre amis* **Student CD-ROM**

■ *Entre amis* **Student Companion Web Site**

■ *Entre amis* **Instructor's Companion Web Site**

Publisher: Roland Hernández
Sponsoring Editor: Van Strength
Development Manager: Glenn A. Wilson
Executive Marketing Director: Eileen Bernadette Moran
Associate Marketing Manager: Claudia Martínez
Development Editor: Katherine Gilbert
Senior Project Editor: Florence Kilgo
Production Editorial Assistant: Kristen Truncellito
Art and Design Manager: Gary Crespo
Photo Editor: Jennifer Meyer-Dare
Composition Buyer: Sarah Ambrose
Senior Manufacturing Manager: Chuck Dutton

Cover photo: ©Photodisc Royalty Free

Credits for text, photos, realia and illustrations appear on the last pages of this book, which constitute an extension of the copyright page.

Printed in the U.S.A.

Library of Congress Catalog Card Number: 2004117617

Student Text ISBN: 0-618-50691-8

Instructor's Annotated Edition ISBN: 0-618-50692-6

1 2 3 4 5 6 7 8 9-**DOW**-09 08 07 06 05

ENTRE AMIS

Key for the SAM. For information about the Oral Test Audio CD packaged with Class Prep, please see p. IAE-9.

■ ***Négociations*** activities provide task-based, student-to-student interaction and an active review of grammar and vocabulary. They constitute a capstone activity and, in the fifth edition of ***Entre amis,*** are located in the *Intégration* section of each chapter and in Appendix D. These activities provide valuable practice prior to oral and written testing. Suggestions for preparation and follow-up for each *Négociations* activity are found on the Instructor's HM Class Prep CD.

■ **E-SAM powered by Quia.** The Student Activities Manual, containing Workbook, Lab Manual, and Video Worksheets, is now available in an electronic, interactive format.

■ **Seven new *Lectures*** have been added and other *Lectures* have been updated.

Chapter Organization

Each of the fifteen chapters of ***Entre amis*** has three main parts: *Coup d'envoi, Buts communicatifs*, and *Intégration*. The following chart illustrates the organization of the chapters and the purpose of each section.

Section	Purpose
Chapter opener	Identification of functions, structures, and cultural content of the chapter Sets the scene
Coup d'envoi	Conceptualized introduction to some of the vocabulary and grammar
*Prise de contact**	Preparation phase to familiarize students with context and content
*Conversation/Lettre**	Model for interaction Role-playing
À propos	Insights into the cultural content of the chapter
À vous!	Initial personalization
Entre amis	Paired activity
*Prononciation**	Explanation and practice to build correct speech
Buts communicatifs	Function-based organizing principle
Introduction*	Preparation phase to familiarize students with context and content
Grammar	Structures related to the targeted function
Vocabulary	Theme-related vocabulary introduced as needed
Activities	Meaningful practice in communication
Entre amis	Paired activity at the end of each *But communicatif*
Intégration	Review and development of reading skill
Révision	Additional practice to build control and fluency *Début de rédaction* pre-writing activity *Négociations* (Information Gap) activity
Lecture(s)	Reading(s) with pre- and post-reading activities
Vocabulaire actif	List for review
* Recorded on the In-Text (Student) Audio CDs packaged with the textbook	

Other Program Components

■ **The Instructor's Annotated Edition with In-Text Audio CDs** contains the student text with marginal annotations providing cultural and phonetic information, suggestions for follow-up activities, and other teaching tips.

■ **The In-Text (Student) Audio CDs** are free with each copy of the student textbook. Cued by an icon in the text, recordings include all oral presentation material (*Prise de contact, Conversations/Lettres*, introductions to the *Buts communicatifs*), pronunciation sections, and poetry readings from the *Intégration* section.

■ **The Student Activities Manual (*Cahier d'activités*)**

1. **Workbook:** The Workbook activities provide students with additional practice of vocabulary and grammar. One or more activities reinforce what has been taught in each section of the chapter. The final activity, *Rédaction*, provides detailed instructions and suggestions for the writing process and content.

2. **Lab Manual and SAM (Lab) Audio CDs:** Activities in the Lab Manual are divided into three sections: A. *Prononciation*, B. *Compréhension*, C. *En contexte*. Section C is new to the fifth edition and features contextualized listening comprehension and self-testing. Recordings are available on the SAM Audio CDs.

3. **Video Worksheets** provide lexical and cultural preparation for the *Pas de problème!* Video. Students complete worksheets, referring as needed to the *Vocabulaire à reconnaître* that lists expressions used in the Video and their meaning. Each set of activities ends with a cultural comparison (*Réflexion*). Doing these activities should take no more than fifteen minutes.

   The Video worksheets in the Student Activities Manual reinforce the tie between text and video by drawing students' attention to specific cultural components of ***Entre amis.*** Examples include gestures and body language, greetings, communicative strategies, technology, transportation, shopping, and ordering food. The worksheet activities are based on the following correlation chart of text chapters and video modules.

Entre amis	*Pas de problème!* Video	*Entre amis*	*Pas de problème!* Video
Chapter 1	Introduction	Chapter 9	Module 6
Chapter 2	Module 1	Chapter 10	Module 7
Chapter 3	Module 1	Chapter 11	Module 8
Chapter 4	Module 2	Chapter 12	Module 9
Chapter 5	Module 2	Chapter 13	Module 10
Chapter 6	Module 3	Chapter 14	Module 11
Chapter 7	Module 4	Chapter 15	Module 12
Chapter 8	Module 5		

■ ***Entre amis* Student Companion Web Site.** This Student Web Site has been updated and includes:

1. **ACE Practice Tests** that practice grammar and vocabulary for each *Coup d'envoi* and *But communicatif* in the text. Each chapter also contains a listening-comprehension video activity based on a short segment drawn from the *Pas de problème!* Video. Students receive immediate feedback so that they can monitor their own progress. The tests can also be printed or e-mailed to the instructor upon completion.

To the Instructor

Entre amis, Fifth Edition, uses a functional, integrated skills approach to teach French to beginning students. The primary objective of the program is to give students an opportunity to acquire communication skills through interaction with the teacher and with each other in paired activities. Students also develop an awareness of language structure as it relates to French culture. The two are closely integrated throughout each chapter. The use of French gestures to facilitate the presentation and retention of vocabulary is but one illustration of the way that language and culture are interwoven in *Entre amis.* Students compare French grammar and culture to their own and personalize what they practice in their activities.

Main Features

Integration of language and culture.   Cultural content is interwoven in language practice throughout the textbook. Culture is an integral part of what students learn, helping to develop their strategic competence and sociolinguistic accuracy.

Functional organization.   Each chapter is divided into several *Buts communicatifs,* focusing students on meaningful interaction from the start.

Student-centered approach.   The functions and activities of *Entre amis* equip students to exchange information about their own lives. The focus is on the learner's needs: describing personal tastes, activities, possessions, etc.

Interactive activities that work.   While personalization is the goal of all of the interactive activities in *Entre amis,* students are never required to use expressions that they have not yet practiced. Grammar and vocabulary are presented in clear contexts before students are required to put them to use.

Manageable grammar and vocabulary.   Each chapter introduces structures and expressions related to the targeted functions. The grammar syllabus and vocabulary load are then expanded and reinforced through recycling in subsequent chapters.

Reading as a process.   Authentic *Lectures* feature pre-reading and post-reading activities. Students are trained to use cognates, context, and their own experience to comprehend material that is above their level of production.

Writing as a process.   The *Intégration* section of each chapter of *Entre amis* includes a *Début de rédaction* activity. This constitutes the first step of a writing process that culminates with the *Rédaction* in the corresponding chapter of the Workbook. An instructor's annotation in the text serves as a reminder of this process and adds suggestions for incorporating one or more of the national *Standards for Foreign Language Learning* in the process.

Francophone culture.   Many of the *Lectures,* as well as the *Réalités culturelles* notes in each chapter, familarize students with the French-speaking world.

New and Revised in the Fifth Edition

■ **Réalités culturelles.** Throughout the text, concise sections have been included to help students appreciate various aspects of French culture, as well as the extent and diversity of the French-speaking world. There is a corresponding entry on the ***Entre amis*** Web Site to facilitate further research into each of these topics. These new sections replace the *Escale* sections of previous editions of the text. Their content is closely tied to that of the chapter in which they appear.

■ **The grammar sequence,** in response to user feedback, now includes earlier introduction of the verb **aller,** clearer explanations of the comparative and the superlative, and a streamlined presentation of the subjunctive.

■ **Self-testing.** The fifth edition of ***Entre amis*** includes a number of specific activities through which students can check their own readiness for tests, both oral and written. These include practice tests found both on the Web Site and in the Student Activities Manual (*Cahier d'activités*/Workbook/Lab Manual/Video Worksheets).

  1. The ACE Practice Tests on the ***Entre amis*** Student Companion Web Site allow students to check their retention of vocabulary and grammar. There is a practice test for each *Coup d'envoi* and *But communicatif* found in the 15 chapters of ***Entre amis.*** We suggest that instructors include in their quizzes one or more of the questions from the Web Site and inform students that they will do so.
  2. Similarly, the Flashcards on the ***Entre amis*** Student Companion Web Site offer a rapid review of basic verb forms and of the *Vocabulaire actif* list at the end of each chapter.
  3. In the Student Activities Manual (SAM), Part C of the Lab Manual, there is a *Vignette* (partial dictation) activity. Instructors who would like students to check their own answers can duplicate the script of the *Vignette,* found in the Answer Key on the Instructor's HM Class Prep CD.
  4. Also in the SAM, Part C of the Lab Manual, there is a practice test that corresponds to the *À vous* activity in the *Intégration* section of each chapter of the text. Students are instructed to respond orally and in writing to the questions that they hear. A similar oral-question, written-answer activity is part of each chapter test in the ***Entre amis*** Test Bank. Once students complete this activity, they are referred to a specific page of the text to check their comprehension of the questions. The Answer Key on the Instructor's HM Class Prep CD includes suggestions for responses to these *À vous* questions.

■ **A consistent alignment with the national Standards for Foreign Language Learning.** The tie between learning strategies and the national Standards has been reinforced and enhanced in the fifth edition of ***Entre amis.*** Throughout the text, instructor annotations suggest procedures that closely align specific activities with one or more of the goals of Communication, Cultures, Connections, Comparisons, and Communities.

■ **Instructor's HM Class Prep CD with HM Testing.** This CD-ROM contains the instructor's resource material, including a step-by-step guide for instructors and teaching assistants, suggestions and directions for the text-based *Négociations* (Information Gap) activities, the Test and Quiz Bank, the SAM Audioscript, the Video Transcript, Transparencies, and the Answer

Key for the SAM. For information about the Oral Test Audio CD packaged with Class Prep, please see p. IAE-9.

■ *Négociations* activities provide task-based, student-to-student interaction and an active review of grammar and vocabulary. They constitute a capstone activity and, in the fifth edition of *Entre amis,* are located in the *Intégration* section of each chapter and in Appendix D. These activities provide valuable practice prior to oral and written testing. Suggestions for preparation and follow-up for each *Négociations* activity are found on the Instructor's HM Class Prep CD.

■ **E-SAM powered by Quia.** The Student Activities Manual, containing Workbook, Lab Manual, and Video Worksheets, is now available in an electronic, interactive format.

■ **Seven new *Lectures*** have been added and other *Lectures* have been updated.

Chapter Organization

Each of the fifteen chapters of **Entre amis** has three main parts: *Coup d'envoi, Buts communicatifs*, and *Intégration*. The following chart illustrates the organization of the chapters and the purpose of each section.

Section	Purpose
Chapter opener	Identification of functions, structures, and cultural content of the chapter Sets the scene
Coup d'envoi	Conceptualized introduction to some of the vocabulary and grammar
Prise de contact*	Preparation phase to familiarize students with context and content
Conversation/Lettre*	Model for interaction Role-playing
À propos	Insights into the cultural content of the chapter
À vous!	Initial personalization
Entre amis	Paired activity
Prononciation*	Explanation and practice to build correct speech
Buts communicatifs	Function-based organizing principle
Introduction*	Preparation phase to familiarize students with context and content
Grammar	Structures related to the targeted function
Vocabulary	Theme-related vocabulary introduced as needed
Activities	Meaningful practice in communication
Entre amis	Paired activity at the end of each *But communicatif*
Intégration	Review and development of reading skill
Révision	Additional practice to build control and fluency *Début de rédaction* pre-writing activity *Négociations* (Information Gap) activity
Lecture(s)	Reading(s) with pre- and post-reading activities
Vocabulaire actif	List for review
* Recorded on the In-Text (Student) Audio CDs packaged with the textbook	

Other Program Components

- **The Instructor's Annotated Edition with In-Text Audio CDs** contains the student text with marginal annotations providing cultural and phonetic information, suggestions for follow-up activities, and other teaching tips.

- **The In-Text (Student) Audio CDs** are free with each copy of the student textbook. Cued by an icon in the text, recordings include all oral presentation material (*Prise de contact, Conversations/Lettres*, introductions to the *Buts communicatifs*), pronunciation sections, and poetry readings from the *Intégration* section.

- **The Student Activities Manual (*Cahier d'activités*)**

  1. **Workbook:** The Workbook activities provide students with additional practice of vocabulary and grammar. One or more activities reinforce what has been taught in each section of the chapter. The final activity, *Rédaction*, provides detailed instructions and suggestions for the writing process and content.

  2. **Lab Manual and SAM (Lab) Audio CDs:** Activities in the Lab Manual are divided into three sections: A. *Prononciation*, B. *Compréhension*, C. *En contexte*. Section C is new to the fifth edition and features contextualized listening comprehension and self-testing. Recordings are available on the SAM Audio CDs.

  3. **Video Worksheets** provide lexical and cultural preparation for the *Pas de problème!* Video. Students complete worksheets, referring as needed to the *Vocabulaire à reconnaître* that lists expressions used in the Video and their meaning. Each set of activities ends with a cultural comparison (*Réflexion*). Doing these activities should take no more than fifteen minutes.

     The Video worksheets in the Student Activities Manual reinforce the tie between text and video by drawing students' attention to specific cultural components of **Entre amis.** Examples include gestures and body language, greetings, communicative strategies, technology, transportation, shopping, and ordering food. The worksheet activities are based on the following correlation chart of text chapters and video modules.

Entre amis	*Pas de problème!* Video	*Entre amis*	*Pas de problème!* Video
Chapter 1	Introduction	Chapter 9	Module 6
Chapter 2	Module 1	Chapter 10	Module 7
Chapter 3	Module 1	Chapter 11	Module 8
Chapter 4	Module 2	Chapter 12	Module 9
Chapter 5	Module 2	Chapter 13	Module 10
Chapter 6	Module 3	Chapter 14	Module 11
Chapter 7	Module 4	Chapter 15	Module 12
Chapter 8	Module 5		

- ***Entre amis* Student Companion Web Site.** This Student Web Site has been updated and includes:

  1. **ACE Practice Tests** that practice grammar and vocabulary for each *Coup d'envoi* and *But communicatif* in the text. Each chapter also contains a listening-comprehension video activity based on a short segment drawn from the *Pas de problème!* Video. Students receive immediate feedback so that they can monitor their own progress. The tests can also be printed or e-mailed to the instructor upon completion.

2. **Web-Search activities,** cued by an icon in the *Intégration* section of the text. These require students to access web links in order to answer questions closely related to the chapter topics. Student answers can also be printed or e-mailed to the instructor.
3. **Flashcards** that offer a quick review of the active vocabulary of each chapter.
4. *Réalités culturelles* links to sites that provide additional background for topics addressed in each of the thirty *Réalités culturelles* notes found throughout the text.

■ **A revised *Entre amis* Student CD-ROM** provides interactive language practice for the conversations, vocabulary, and grammar of each of the fifteen chapters of the textbook. This CD-ROM also includes a grammar reference, a verb conjugation reference, a glossary of grammatical terms, and bilingual French-English and English-French glossaries. A progress report is provided for each chapter as well as a means of sending open-ended exercises to the instructor via e-mail. The CD-ROM also contains clips from the *Pas de problème!* Video.

■ **Instructor's Companion Web Site.** A password-protected web site for instructors, this includes the Instructor's Guide, the SAM Audioscript, and the Video Transcript. For the sake of security, it does not include the Test and Quiz Bank or the Answer Keys (found on the Instructor's HM Class Prep CD). The site will be updated on a regular basis.

■ **Oral Test Audio CD,** packaged with the Instructor's HM Class Prep CD, allows instructors who so desire to test many students at one time in a language laboratory. There are five different levels of speaking tests corresponding to Chapters 3, 6, 9, 12, & 15 in *Entre amis*. These tests are separate from the written chapter tests. The Class Prep includes a script and directions.

Teaching with the *Entre amis* Program

THE INSTRUCTOR AS MODEL, FACILITATOR, AND JUDGE

Comme Maître Jacques dans l'Avare, nous jouons tous plusieurs rôles.

■ **Model.** Presenting a clear model for our students is the first of our roles. In addition to introducing the contextualized material that students will practice *(Prise de contact, Conversation,* and *Buts communicatifs),* we also have many opportunities to "model" attentive listening, patience, enthusiasm, and an ability to laugh at ourselves. Our students will "catch" our attitude toward learning and communicating in French. The Instructor's HM Class Prep CD and the Instructor's Companion Web Site have suggestions for presenting new material.

■ **Facilitator.** With an interactive approach, we spend most of our time involving students in the learning process. In a learner-centered classroom, the accent is on personalization and sharing. The exercises in *Entre amis* were written to facilitate student-to-student interaction. Well-primed, paired activities, followed by a brief closed-book check (follow up), will pay dividends in student progress and enthusiasm. The Instructor's HM Class Prep CD and the Instructor's Companion Web Site have suggestions for planning your class time, warm-up, and follow-up activities.

■ **Judge.**   Anticipating possible errors and giving feedback are an integral part of our role as judge. The most appropriate time to invite student questions and to provide correction is immediately following short personalized interaction, e.g., after a communicative activity and before the follow-up. On the Instructor's HM Class Prep CD, there are written tests and quizzes for each chapter in *Entre amis,* as well as detailed suggestions for oral testing.

ENTRE AMIS AND THE NATIONAL STANDARDS[1]

Communication

Communities   Cultures

Comparisons   Connections

Communication.   *This is at the heart of second language study. Students get many opportunities to communicate face-to-face, in writing, and through reading.*

Interpersonal.   Contextualized pair practice is an integral part of the *Entre amis* interactive approach. Specific activities include *Prise de contact* (8)[2], *Jouez ces rôles* (9), *À vous* (11), *Entre amis* (11, 51, 105), and *Trouvez quelqu'un qui ...* (51). Students have many chances to provide and obtain personal information, to express feelings, and to exchange opinions. Activities in this text have truth value, i.e., students are never forced to say, "I love spinach," if they really don't.

Interpretive.   Students have numerous opportunities to hear and read French. Listening comprehension includes instructor modeling in the *Prise de contact* (8, 29) and initial presentations in the *Buts communicatifs* (13, 18), student-to-student negotiating of meaning in the *Négociations* activities (25, 52), taped material (In-Text Audio and SAM Audio), and video activities (Video Worksheets and ACE Practice Test Video). Authentic readings in each chapter feature pre- and follow-up learning strategies that involve students in reading, re-reading, and interpreting the selections (25–26, 52–53, 83–86).

Presentational.   Students share personal information and ideas in contextualized writing assignments in both the text and the workbook portion of the SAM. A process approach to writing is used in the *Début de rédaction* (24, 51) and *Rédaction,* at the end of each chapter in the workbook, and in specific activities in the text, e.g., *Un test de votre personnalité* (98). Instructor annotations in the text suggest numerous opportunities for oral presentations by students (8, 40, 47).

> Throughout this instructor's edition, annotations suggest procedures that closely align specific activities with one or more of the national standards. Because most of the activities in *Entre amis* are already interpersonal, there is no annotation for the *Communication (Interpersonal)* sub-category.

---

[1]   From the National Standards in Foreign Language Education project: *Standards for Foreign Language Learning: Preparing for the 21st Century,* © 1996. All rights reserved.

[2]   Page numbers refer to examples in the text.

Cultures. *Students gain knowledge and understanding of the cultural contexts in which language occurs.*

The *Conversations* and *À propos* sections integrate language and culture. They help students understand the cultural context in which their language practice takes place. Likewise, many of the activities of ***Entre amis*** are designed to help students put to use their growing knowledge of the target culture (17, 21, 23, 37, 40). Web-Search activities, the *Pas de problème!* Video and accompanying Video Worksheets, the ***Entre amis*** Student CD-ROM, and the *Il y a un geste, Réalités culturelles,* and *Notes culturelles* sections all reinforce the cultural component of ***Entre amis.***

Connections. *Students use their language to access additional knowledge, sometimes unavailable to the monolingual English speaker.*

The ***Entre amis*** Student Companion Web Site expands upon students' knowledge base. Closely tied to the themes of each chapter, the Web-Search activities enable students to access up-to-date information about France and the French-speaking world (24, 53). These activities require students to use the Internet to examine a variety of sources intended for native speakers and to extract specific information.

Comparisons. *Students compare and contrast the target language and culture with their own.*

Included in the *À propos* section of each chapter in the Instructor's Annotated Edition of ***Entre amis*** are specific suggestions to involve students in reflecting on their own culture in light of what they are learning about the target culture (2, 23). Students are also required to compare and contrast French and English through the grammar sections of the text as well as in marginal student annotations that refer to previously studied material and serve as reminders of grammatical (50, 144, 181) or lexical (25, 52, 173) usage. Similarly, each *Pas de problème!* Video Worksheet includes a *Réflexion* activity.

Communities. *Students have contact with multilingual communities in a variety of contexts and in culturally appropriate ways.*

The *Réalités culturelles* sections and their web links (15, 20, 34) are meant to whet students' appetite for knowledge about a number of areas of the world where French is spoken. Internet activities associated with each chapter put students in contact with several francophone communities (24, 51), including the opportunity to interact with other speakers of French beyond their campus.

Suggested Syllabi

The following schedules are meant only as general guidelines. Instructors who wish to make full use of the rich ancillary package that accompanies ***Entre amis*** are likely to spend more time with each chapter, especially if they wish students to participate more fully in classroom interaction.

Please consult the Instructor's HM Class Prep CD for chapter activities, including detailed lesson plans for the *First Ten Days* and the Test Bank.

Two semesters, meeting 5 days per week

	Semester 1				
Week	Day 1	Day 2	Day 3	Day 4	Day 5
1	1st day	Prelim.	Prelim.	Quiz	Chap. 1
2	*But* 1	*But* 1/2	*But* 2	*But* 3	*Intég.*
3	WWW	Test	Chap. 2	*But* 1	*But* 2
4	*But* 2/3	*But* 3	*But* 4	*But* 4	*Intég.*
5	WWW	Test	Chap. 3	*But* 1	*But* 2
6	*But* 2	*But* 3	*But* 3	*Intég.*	WWW
7	Review	Oral	Test	Chap. 4	*But* 1
8	*But* 1/2	*But* 2	*But* 3	*But* 4	*But* 5
9	*Intég.*	WWW	Test	Chap. 5	*But* 1
10	*But* 1/2	*But* 2	*But* 3	*But* 3/4	*But* 4
11	*Intég.*	WWW	Test	Chap. 6	*But* 1
12	*But* 1	*But* 2	*But* 2/3	*But* 3	*But* 3
13	*Intég.*	WWW	Test	Chap. 7	*But* 1
14	*But* 1	*But* 2	*But* 2	*But* 2/3	*But* 3
15	*Intég.*	WWW	Review	Oral	Test

	Semester 2				
Week	Day 1	Day 2	Day 3	Day 4	Day 5
1	Review	Chap. 8	*But* 1	*But* 1	*But* 2
2	*But* 3	*But* 4	*Intég.*	WWW	Test
3	Chap. 9	*But* 1	*But* 1/2	*But* 2	*But* 3
4	*But* 3	*Intég.*	WWW	Test	Chap. 10
5	*But* 1	*But* 2	*But* 3	*But* 3	*But* 4
6	*Intég.*	Test	Chap. 11	*But* 1	*But* 1/2
7	*But* 2	*But* 3	*But* 3	*Intég.*	WWW
8	Review	Oral	Test	Chap. 12	*But* 1
9	*But* 1/2	*But* 2	*But* 3	*But* 3	*Intég.*
10	WWW	Test	Chap. 13	*But* 1	*But* 2
11	*But* 3	*But* 3/4	*But* 4	*Intég.*	WWW
12	Test	Chap. 14	*But* 1	*But* 1	*But* 2
13	*But* 2/3	*But* 3	*Intég.*	WWW	Test
14	Chap. 15	*But* 1	*But* 1	*But* 2	*But* 2
15	*Intég.*	WWW	Review	Oral	Test

Two semesters, meeting 4 days per week

	Semester 1			
Week	Day 1	Day 2	Day 3	Day 4
1	1st day	Prelim.	Prelim.	Quiz
2	Chap. 1	*But* 1	*But* 1/2	*But* 2
3	*But* 3	*Intég.*	Test	Chap. 2
4	*But* 1	*But* 2	*But* 3	*But* 3/4
5	*But* 4	*Intég.*	Test	Chap. 3
6	*But* 1	*But* 2	*But* 2	*But* 3
7	*But* 3	*Intég.*	Test	Chap. 4
8	*But* 1	*But* 1/2	*But* 2	*But* 3
9	*But* 4	*But* 5	*Intég.*	Test
10	Chap. 5	*But* 1	*But* 2	*But* 3
11	*But* 3/4	*But* 4	*Intég.*	Test
12	Chap. 6	*But* 1	*But* 1/2	*But* 2
13	*But* 3	*But* 3	*Intég.*	Test
14	Chap. 7	*But* 1	*But* 1/2	*But* 2
15	*But* 3	*Intég.*	Oral	Test

	Semester 2			
Week	Day 1	Day 2	Day 3	Day 4
1	Chap. 8	*But* 1	*But* 1	*But* 2
2	*But* 3	*But* 4	*Intég.*	Test
3	Chap. 9	*But* 1	*But* 1/2	*But* 2
4	*But* 3	*But* 3	*Intég.*	Test
5	Chap. 10	*But* 1	*But* 2	*But* 3
6	*But* 3	*But* 4	*Intég.*	Test
7	Chap. 11	*But* 1	*But* 1/2	*But* 2
8	*But* 3	*But* 3	*Intég.*	Test
9	Chap. 12	*But* 1	*But* 1/2	*But* 2
10	*But* 3	*But* 3	*Intég.*	Test
11	Chap. 13	*But* 1	*But* 2	*But* 3
12	*But* 4	*Intég.*	Test	Chap. 14
13	*But* 1	*But* 1	*But* 2	*But* 3
14	*Intég.*	Test	Chap. 15	*But* 1
15	*But* 2	*Intég.*	Oral	Test

2. **Web-Search activities,** cued by an icon in the *Intégration* section of the text. These require students to access web links in order to answer questions closely related to the chapter topics. Student answers can also be printed or e-mailed to the instructor.
3. **Flashcards** that offer a quick review of the active vocabulary of each chapter.
4. *Réalités culturelles* links to sites that provide additional background for topics addressed in each of the thirty *Réalités culturelles* notes found throughout the text.

- **A revised *Entre amis* Student CD-ROM** provides interactive language practice for the conversations, vocabulary, and grammar of each of the fifteen chapters of the textbook. This CD-ROM also includes a grammar reference, a verb conjugation reference, a glossary of grammatical terms, and bilingual French-English and English-French glossaries. A progress report is provided for each chapter as well as a means of sending open-ended exercises to the instructor via e-mail. The CD-ROM also contains clips from the *Pas de problème!* Video.

- **Instructor's Companion Web Site.** A password-protected web site for instructors, this includes the Instructor's Guide, the SAM Audioscript, and the Video Transcript. For the sake of security, it does not include the Test and Quiz Bank or the Answer Keys (found on the Instructor's HM Class Prep CD). The site will be updated on a regular basis.

- **Oral Test Audio CD,** packaged with the Instructor's HM Class Prep CD, allows instructors who so desire to test many students at one time in a language laboratory. There are five different levels of speaking tests corresponding to Chapters 3, 6, 9, 12, & 15 in *Entre amis*. These tests are separate from the written chapter tests. The Class Prep includes a script and directions.

Teaching with the *Entre amis* Program

THE INSTRUCTOR AS MODEL, FACILITATOR, AND JUDGE

Comme Maître Jacques dans l'Avare, nous jouons tous plusieurs rôles.

- **Model.**   Presenting a clear model for our students is the first of our roles. In addition to introducing the contextualized material that students will practice *(Prise de contact, Conversation,* and *Buts communicatifs)*, we also have many opportunities to "model" attentive listening, patience, enthusiasm, and an ability to laugh at ourselves. Our students will "catch" our attitude toward learning and communicating in French. The Instructor's HM Class Prep CD and the Instructor's Companion Web Site have suggestions for presenting new material.

- **Facilitator.**   With an interactive approach, we spend most of our time involving students in the learning process. In a learner-centered classroom, the accent is on personalization and sharing. The exercises in *Entre amis* were written to facilitate student-to-student interaction. Well-primed, paired activities, followed by a brief closed-book check (follow up), will pay dividends in student progress and enthusiasm. The Instructor's HM Class Prep CD and the Instructor's Companion Web Site have suggestions for planning your class time, warm-up, and follow-up activities.

■ **Judge.**   Anticipating possible errors and giving feedback are an integral part of our role as judge. The most appropriate time to invite student questions and to provide correction is immediately following short personalized interaction, e.g., after a communicative activity and before the follow-up. On the Instructor's HM Class Prep CD, there are written tests and quizzes for each chapter in *Entre amis,* as well as detailed suggestions for oral testing.

ENTRE AMIS AND THE NATIONAL STANDARDS[1]

Communication

Communities

Cultures

Comparisons

Connections

Communication.   *This is at the heart of second language study. Students get many opportunities to communicate face-to-face, in writing, and through reading.*

Interpersonal.   Contextualized pair practice is an integral part of the *Entre amis* interactive approach. Specific activities include *Prise de contact* (8)[2], *Jouez ces rôles* (9), *À vous* (11), *Entre amis* (11, 51, 105), and *Trouvez quelqu'un qui …* (51). Students have many chances to provide and obtain personal information, to express feelings, and to exchange opinions. Activities in this text have truth value, i.e., students are never forced to say, "I love spinach," if they really don't.

Interpretive.   Students have numerous opportunities to hear and read French. Listening comprehension includes instructor modeling in the *Prise de contact* (8, 29) and initial presentations in the *Buts communicatifs* (13, 18), student-to-student negotiating of meaning in the *Négociations* activities (25, 52), taped material (In-Text Audio and SAM Audio), and video activities (Video Worksheets and ACE Practice Test Video). Authentic readings in each chapter feature pre- and follow-up learning strategies that involve students in reading, re-reading, and interpreting the selections (25–26, 52–53, 83–86).

Presentational.   Students share personal information and ideas in contextualized writing assignments in both the text and the workbook portion of the SAM. A process approach to writing is used in the *Début de rédaction* (24, 51) and *Rédaction*, at the end of each chapter in the workbook, and in specific activities in the text, e.g., *Un test de votre personnalité* (98). Instructor annotations in the text suggest numerous opportunities for oral presentations by students (8, 40, 47).

> Throughout this instructor's edition, annotations suggest procedures that closely align specific activities with one or more of the national standards. Because most of the activities in *Entre amis* are already interpersonal, there is no annotation for the *Communication (Interpersonal)* sub-category.

---

[1]   From the National Standards in Foreign Language Education project: *Standards for Foreign Language Learning: Preparing for the 21st Century,* © 1996. All rights reserved.

[2]   Page numbers refer to examples in the text.

Three 10-week quarters, meeting 5 days per week

First quarter:	Second quarter:	Third quarter:
1 day for beginning	8 days for chapters 6 to 10	8 days each for chapters 11 to 15
3 days for the *Chapitre préliminaire*	2 days for Web-Search activities	2 days for Web-Search activities
7–8 days each for chapters 1 to 5	2 days for review	2 days for review
2 days for Web-Search activities	5 days for testing	5 days for testing
1 day for review		
5 days for testing		

Three 10-week quarters, meeting 3 days per week

First quarter:	Second quarter:	Third quarter:
1 day for beginning	7 days each for chapters 4 to 7	7 days each for chapters 8 to 11
3 days for the *Chapitre préliminaire*	2 days for testing	2 days for testing
8 days each for chapters 1 to 3		
2 days for testing		

High Beginners

Some students in first-semester French already have had exposure to the French language. They often have a background in grammar but need opportunities to develop their oral skills. Instructors who tailor a course to this type of student are encouraged to use classroom time for personalized interactive practice of French and assign grammar and culture study for out-of-class preparation. Since a copy of the In-Text Audio CDs is bound with each copy of the text, and grammar is presented in English, **Entre amis** is suited for use with *faux débutants* as well as with true beginners.

Three semesters, meeting 3 days per week*

At some institutions, the introductory-level curriculum covers three semesters. *Entre amis,* with its numerous student-centered interactive activities and process approach to reading and writing, is also ideally suited for use in an extended program. If a student's study of French begins at the college level, we suggest that *Entre amis* be used in conjunction with an intermediate text with a communicative approach, such as *Personnages,* in a four-or-five-semester sequence.

Semester 1			
Week	**Day 1**	**Day 2**	**Day 3**
1	1st day	Prelim.	Prelim.
2	Quiz	Chap. 1	*But* 1
3	*But* 1/2	*But* 2	*But* 3
4	*Intég.*	Test	Chap. 2
5	*But* 1	*But* 2	*But* 3
6	*But* 3	*But* 4	*Intég.*
7	Test	Chap. 3	*But* 1
8	*But* 2	*But* 2	*But* 3
9	*But* 3	*Intég.*	Test
10	Chap. 4	*But* 1	*But* 1/2
11	*But* 2	*But* 3	*But* 4
12	*But* 5	*Intég.*	Test
13	Chap. 5	*But* 1	*But* 2
14	*But* 3	*But* 4	*Intég.*
15	Review	Oral	Test

Semester 2			
Week	**Day 1**	**Day 2**	**Day 3**
1	Review	Chap. 6	*But* 1
2	*But* 1	*But* 2	*But* 2/3
3	*But* 3	*But* 3	*Intég.*
4	Test	Chap. 7	*But* 1
5	*But* 1	*But* 2	*But* 2/3
6	*But* 3	*Intég.*	Oral
7	Test	Chap. 8	*But* 1
8	*But* 1	*But* 2	*But* 3
9	*But* 4	*Intég.*	Test
10	Chap. 9	*But* 1	*But* 1/2
11	*But* 2	*But* 3	*But* 3
12	*Intég.*	Test	Chap. 10
13	*But* 1	*But* 2	*But* 3
14	*But* 3	*But* 4	*Intég.*
15	Review	Oral	Test

Semester 3			
Week	**Day 1**	**Day 2**	**Day 3**
1	Review	Chap. 11	*But* 1
2	*But* 1/2	*But* 2	*But* 3
3	*But* 3	*Intég.*	Test
4	Chap. 12	*But* 1	*But* 1/2
5	*But* 2	*But* 3	*But* 3
6	*Intég.*	Oral	Test
7	Chap. 13	*But* 1	*But* 2
8	*But* 3	*But* 3/4	*But* 4
9	*Intég.*	Test	Chap. 14
10	*But* 1	*But* 1	*But* 2
11	*But* 2/3	*But* 3	*Intég.*
12	Test	Chap. 15	*But* 1
13	*But* 1	*But* 2	*But* 2
14	*Intég.*	Test	Review
15	Review	Oral	Test

* For a two-semester, three-days-per-week syllabus, see the *Entre amis* Instructor's Companion Web Site.

Three quarters, meeting 4 days per week

Quarter 1				
Week	Day 1	Day 2	Day 3	Day 4
1	1st day	Prelim.	Prelim.	Quiz
2	Chap. 1	*But* 1	*But* 1/2	*But* 2
3	*But* 3	*Intég.*	Test	Chap. 2
4	*But* 1	*But* 2	*But* 2/3	*But* 3
5	*But* 4	*But* 4	*Intég.*	Test
6	Chap. 3	*But* 1	*But* 2	*But* 2
7	*But* 3	*But* 3	*Intég.*	Test
8	Chap. 4	*But* 1	*But* 1	*But* 2
9	*But* 2	*But* 3	*But* 4	*But* 5
10	*Intég.*	Review	Oral	Test

Quarter 2				
Week	Day 1	Day 2	Day 3	Day 4
1	Chap. 5	*But* 1	*But* 2	*But* 3
2	*But* 3/4	*But* 4	*Intég.*	Test
3	Chap. 6	*But* 1	*But* 2	*But* 3
4	*But* 3	*Intég.*	Test	Chap. 7
5	*But* 1	*But* 1/2	*But* 2	*But* 3
6	*Intég.*	Test	Chap. 8	*But* 1
7	*But* 1	*But* 2	*But* 3	*But* 4
8	*Intég.*	Test	Chap. 9	*But* 1
9	*But* 1/2	*But* 2	*But* 3	*But* 3
10	*Intég.*	Review	Oral	Test

Quarter 3				
Week	Day 1	Day 2	Day 3	Day 4
1	Chap. 10	*But* 1	*But* 2	*But* 2/3
2	*But* 3	*But* 4	*Intég.*	Test
3	Chap. 11	*But* 1	*But* 1/2	*But* 2
4	*But* 3	*But* 3	*Intég.*	Test
5	Chap. 12	*But* 1	*But* 1/2	*But* 2
6	*But* 3	*But* 3	*Intég.*	Test
7	Chap. 13	*But* 1	*But* 2	*But* 3
8	*But* 4	*Intég.*	Test	Chap. 14
9	*But* 1	*But* 1	*But* 2	*But* 2/3
10	*But* 3	*Intég.*	Oral	Test

Three 10-week quarters, meeting 5 days per week

First quarter:	Second quarter:	Third quarter:
1 day for beginning	8 days for chapters 6 to 10	8 days each for chapters 11 to 15
3 days for the *Chapitre préliminaire*	2 days for Web-Search activities	2 days for Web-Search activities
7–8 days each for chapters 1 to 5	2 days for review	2 days for review
2 days for Web-Search activities	5 days for testing	5 days for testing
1 day for review		
5 days for testing		

Three 10-week quarters, meeting 3 days per week

First quarter:	Second quarter:	Third quarter:
1 day for beginning	7 days each for chapters 4 to 7	7 days each for chapters 8 to 11
3 days for the *Chapitre préliminaire*	2 days for testing	2 days for testing
8 days each for chapters 1 to 3		
2 days for testing		

High Beginners

Some students in first-semester French already have had exposure to the French language. They often have a background in grammar but need opportunities to develop their oral skills. Instructors who tailor a course to this type of student are encouraged to use classroom time for personalized interactive practice of French and assign grammar and culture study for out-of-class preparation. Since a copy of the In-Text Audio CDs is bound with each copy of the text, and grammar is presented in English, **Entre amis** is suited for use with *faux débutants* as well as with true beginners.

ENTRE AMIS

ENTRE AMIS

An Interactive Approach

Fifth Edition

Michael D. Oates

Emeritus, University of Northern Iowa

Larbi Oukada

Indiana University, Indianapolis

Houghton Mifflin Company   Boston   New York

Components of *Entre amis*, Fifth Edition

- **Student Text with In-text Audio CDs**
- **Student Activities Manual (SAM) (*Cahier d'activités*)**
- **SAM Audio CDs**
- **E-SAM powered by Quia**
- ***Pas de problème!* Video**
- ***Entre amis* Student CD-ROM**
- ***Entre amis* Student Companion Web Site**

Publisher: Roland Hernández
Sponsoring Editor: Van Strength
Development Manager: Glenn A. Wilson
Executive Marketing Director: Eileen Bernadette Moran
Associate Marketing Manager: Claudia Martínez
Development Editor: Katherine Gilbert
Senior Project Editor: Florence Kilgo
Production Editorial Assistant: Kristen Truncellito
Art and Design Manager: Gary Crespo
Photo Editor: Jennifer Meyer-Dare
Composition Buyer: Sarah Ambrose
Senior Manufacturing Manager: Chuck Dutton

Cover photo: ©Photodisc Royalty Free

Credits for text, photos, realia and illustrations appear on the last pages of this book, which constitute an extension of the copyright page.

Printed in the U.S.A.

Library of Congress Catalog Card Number: 2004117617

Student Text ISBN: 0-618-50691-8

Instructor's Annotated Edition ISBN: 0-618-50692-6

1 2 3 4 5 6 7 8 9-**DOW**-09 08 07 06 05

Table des matières

Chapitre 4 *L'identité* 89

Chapitre 5 *Quoi de neuf?* 122

Chapitre 6   *Vos activités*   **154**

Chapitre 7   *Où êtes-vous allé(e)?*   **183**

Chapitre 15 *Qu'est-ce que je devrais faire?*   **407**

Références

To the Student

Entre amis is a first-year college French program centered around the needs of a language learner like you. Among these needs is the ability to communicate in French and to develop insights into French culture and language. You will have many opportunities to hear French spoken and to interact with your instructor and classmates. Your ability to read and write French will improve with practice. The functions and exercises are designed to enable you to share information about your life—your interests, your family, your tastes, your plans.

Helpful Hints

While you will want to experiment with different ways of studying the material you will learn, a few hints, taken from successful language learners, are in order:

En français, s'il vous plaît!   Try to use what you are learning with anyone who is able to converse in French. Greet fellow students in French and see how far you can go in conversing with each other.

Enjoy it.   Be willing to take off the "wise-adult" mask and even to appear silly to keep the communication going. Everybody makes mistakes. Try out new words, use new gestures, and paraphrase, if it helps. Laugh at yourself; it helps.

Bring as many senses into play as possible.   Study out loud, listen to the taped materials, use a pencil and paper to test your recall of the expressions you are studying. Anticipate conversations you will have and prepare a few French sentences in advance. Then try to work them into your conversations.

Nothing ventured, nothing gained.   One must go through lower-level stages before reaching a confident mastery of the language. Study and practice, including attentive listening, combined with meaningful interaction with others will result in an ability to use French to communicate.

Where there's a will, there's a way.   Be resourceful in your attempt to communicate. Seek alternative ways of expressing the same idea. For instance, if you are stuck in trying to say, «*Comment vous appelez-vous?*» ("What is your name?"), don't give up your attempt and end the conversation. Look for other ways of finding out that person's name. You may want to say, «*Je m'appelle John/Jane Doe. Et vous?*» or «John/Jane Doe» (pointing to yourself). «*Et vous?*» (pointing to the other person). There are often numerous possibilities!

Use your imagination.   Some of the exercises will encourage you to play a new role. Add imaginary details to these situations, to your life story, etc., to enliven the activities.

Organization of the Text

The text is divided into fifteen chapters, plus a brief preliminary chapter. Each chapter is organized around a central cultural theme with three major divisions: *Coup d'envoi*, *Buts communicatifs*, and *Intégration*.

All presentation material—the *Prise de contact* and the *Conversation* or *Lettre* in the *Coup d'envoi*, plus the introduction to each *But communicatif*—are recorded on the In-Text (Student) Audio CDs shrink-wrapped with your text. Listen to these to prepare for your French class or to review by yourself afterwards.

Coup d'envoi = *Kickoff.*
Prise de contact = *Initial Contact.* See pp. 8, 29, etc.
Buts communicatifs = *Communicative goals.* See pp. 13, 34, etc

Coup d'envoi

This section starts the cycle of listening, practicing, and personalizing which will make your learning both rewarding and enjoyable. You will often be asked to reflect and to compare French culture to your own culture.

Prise de contact is a short illustrated presentation of key phrases. In this section you are encouraged to participate and to respond to simple questions about your family, your life, or your recent activities.

*Conversation (*or *Lettre)* typically shows a language learner in France adapting to French culture. You will often find this person in situations with which you can identify: introducing him- or herself or asking for directions, for example. Then you will be asked what you would do or say in a similar situation.

The *À propos* section describes particular aspects of French culture closely tied to the *Conversation* or *Lettre*. These cultural sections will help you understand why, for example, the French do not usually say "thank you" when responding to a compliment or how meals are structured in France.

The *Il y a un geste* section is a special feature of *Entre amis* and an integral part of every chapter. It consists of photos and descriptions of common French gestures. The primary purpose of the gestures is to reinforce the meaning of the expressions associated with them that you will learn and use throughout the year.

The *À vous* and *Entre amis* activities in the *Coup d'envoi* provide initial opportunities for personalized practice with another student.

The *Prononciation* section helps you to imitate correctly general features of French pronunciation as well as specific sounds. It is important that your speech be readily understandable so that you can communicate more easily with people in French. The In-Text Audio CDs also practice the pronunciation lesson for each chapter.

Buts communicatifs

As is the case in the *Coup d'envoi* section, each of the *Buts communicatifs* sections begins with a presentation that includes key phrases that you will use to interact with your instructor and classmates. Material from the *Coup d'envoi* is recycled in the *Buts communicatifs*. The section is divided according to specific tasks, such as asking for directions, describing your weekend activities, or finding out where things are sold. Within this context, there are grammar explanations, exercises, vocabulary, and role-play activities. The vocabulary is taught in groups of words directly related to each of the functions you are learning. All of these words are then listed at the end of each chapter in the *Vocabulaire actif* section.

Each section of the *Buts communicatifs* ends with an *Entre amis* activity that encourages you to put to use what you have just learned. These *Entre amis* activities involve negotiating a real-life situation (ordering a meal, discussing your schedule, finding out what your partner did) and practicing it until you are comfortable with your performance. Your spoken French will improve by preparing for and participating in this type of interaction.

Intégration

This final section provides an opportunity to review vocabulary and grammar studied in the chapter. It features a *Début de rédaction* (initial composition) activity that is the first step in a writing process that culminates in the *Rédaction* activity found in the Workbook portion of the Student Activities Manual (SAM). It also features a *Négociations* (Information Gap) activity, which encourages students to work together, exchanging information to complete a task. Finally, it includes one or more reading selections (*Lectures*). These readings are from authentic French materials, such as excerpts from newspapers, magazines, literary texts, or poems. (The poems are recorded on your In-Text Audio CDs.) There are activities both before and after each reading to relate the material to your own experience and to help increase your understanding. A list of all the active vocabulary of the chapter (*Vocabulaire actif*) is included at the end of this section.

Réalités culturelles

Throughout the text, an effort has been made to provide you with an appreciation of French culture and the extent and diversity of the French-speaking world in the twenty-first century. In English during the first part of the text, the *Réalités culturelles* will increase your cultural literacy with respect to the places where French is spoken, the achievements of French-speaking people, and why French is relevant to your daily life.

Appendices

The reference section contains verb conjugations, an appendix of phonetic symbols, a list of professions, a glossary of grammatical terms, the "Student B" information for the *Négociations* activities, French-English and English-French glossaries, and an index.

Ancillaries

Student Activities Manual (*Cahier d'activités*)

The Student Activities Manual includes the Workbook, Lab Manual, and Video Worksheets.

The Workbook activities provide you with additional practice for each section of vocabulary and grammar. A final activity, *Rédaction*, is part of the writing process that begins in the *Intégration* section of the text.

The Lab Manual and SAM Audio CDs combine to help you practice your pronunciation and your listening and speaking skills. You will listen to the recordings and instructions of the SAM Audio CDs. The Lab Manual will provide you with cues to answer the questions. Each chapter of the Lab Manual includes activities *(Vignettes, À vous)* that allow you to check your readiness for tests.

The Video Worksheets help you to understand the *Pas de problème!* Video (see below). A *Vocabulaire à reconnaître* lists new words spoken in the Video and their meanings. The worksheets provide simple activities that reinforce the links between the Video and what you learned in your textbook.

Pas de problème! Video

The video *Pas de problème!* was filmed in France. Each module introduces young people—French native speakers from different countries—living in France, interacting with each other, and encountering everyday problems that you might experience if you visit France. Between the modules, the video includes *Impressions,* short sections shot in France and in Guadeloupe, that provide insights into the culture and way of life of people in these countries. The themes presented expand on topics addressed in the video or in the textbook. In Guadeloupe, native speakers express their opinion or talk about their own experience as it applies to the chosen themes.

Entre amis Student CD-ROM

This multimedia CD-ROM provides immediate feedback while helping you to practice each chapter's vocabulary and grammar. It offers a grammar reference and French-English glossary. Each chapter includes art- and listening-based activities to help you develop your reading, writing, listening, and speaking skills. The CD-ROM also contains clips from the *Pas de problème!* Video.

Entre amis Student Companion Web Site

You can access this site through the Houghton Mifflin web site. Icons in the textbook will direct you to the site. At the beginning of the *Intégration* section, an icon indicates Web-Search activities you can do by accessing the links described. Likewise, links are provided for all of the *Réalités culturelles* notes found in the text that allow you to locate quickly additional information on the web. In addition, the web site offers interactive ACE Practice Tests that will enable you to check your understanding of the chapter grammar and vocabulary, as well as vocabulary Flashcards and other helpful resources.

Acknowledgments

We, the authors, are indebted to the editorial staff of Houghton Mifflin for giving us the opportunity to develop and produce the text. Their encouragement and guidance made **Entre amis,** Fifth Edition possible. We are especially grateful for the guidance and friendship of our developmental editor, Katherine Gilbert, our project editor, Florence Kilgo, and our native reader, Micheline Moussavi.

Michael Oates specifically wishes to thank his wife, Maureen O'Leary Oates, for her patience during the development and editing of **Entre amis.** He is grateful for the support of Joye Lore-Lawson, of Indian Hills CC, Linda Quinn Allen of Iowa State University, Jean-Marie Salien, of Fort Hays State University, and Deirdre Bucher Heistad and Lowell Hoeft of the University of Northern Iowa. Larbi Oukada also wishes to express his gratitude to the following individuals:

Rosalie Vermette
France Agnew
Liz Barnard

We would also like to express our sincere appreciation to the following people for their thoughtful reviews of *Entre amis.*

Patricia Han, Skidmore College
Dori Seider, Mercer County College
Catherine Dowling, USDA
Maura Nelson, Des Moines Area Community College
Moses Hardin, Valdosta State University
Marion Yudow (Language Lab), Rutgers University
S. Pascale Dewey, Kutztown University
Katherine Kurk, Northern Kentucky University
Sylvie Vanbaelen, Butler University
Tim Wilkerson, Wittenberg University
Eileen McDonald, Marquette University
Marion Hines, Howard University
Jacqueline Klaassen, Laney College
Elizabeth Emery, Montclair State University
Leanne Wierenga, Wittenberg University
Anne Carlson, Utah State University
Elizabeth Guthrie, University of California-Irvine
Hedwige Meyer, University of Washington
Marian Brodman, University of Central Arkansas
Claude Fouillarde, New Mexico State University
Nathalie Porter, Vanderbilt University
Sarah Dodson, Colorado State University
Juliette Parnell-Smith, University of Nebraska at Omaha
Annie Duménil, University of South Carolina

ENTRE AMIS

Au départ

Buts communicatifs
Understanding basic
classroom commands
Understanding numbers
Understanding basic
expressions of time
Understanding basic
weather expressions

Culture
• *Il y a un geste*
Frapper à la porte
Compter avec les
doigts
Comment? Pardon?

Buts communicatifs

See the suggestions for teaching this lesson on the Class Prep CD-ROM.

This material is recorded on the Student Audio that accompanies your text. Practice with the recording as part of your homework.

Grasping the meaning of spoken French is fundamental to learning to communicate in French. Developing this skill will require patience and perseverance, but your success will be enhanced if you associate a mental image (e.g., of a picture, an object, a gesture, an action, the written word) with the expressions you hear. This preliminary chapter will focus on establishing the association of sound and symbol in a few basic contexts: classroom expressions, numbers, time, and weather.

1. Understanding Basic Classroom Commands

Dans la salle de classe

 ■ Listen carefully and watch the physical response of your teacher to each command. Once you have learned to associate the actions with the French sentences, you may be asked to practice them.

Point out that accents are part of spelling in French, but that they may be omitted on capital letters.

Levez-vous!
Allez à la porte!
Ouvrez la porte!
Sortez!
Frappez à la porte!
Entrez!
Fermez la porte!

Allez au tableau!
Prenez la craie!
Écrivez votre nom!
Mettez la craie sur la table!
Donnez la craie à ... !
Donnez-moi la craie!
Asseyez-vous!

This gesture is used in the *Pas de problème* video, *Module 2*.

Comparison: Have students describe how people knock on a door in their country.

Il y a un geste

Frapper à la porte. When knocking on a door (**toc, toc, toc**), the French often use the back of the hand (open or closed).

2. Understanding Numbers

 0 1 2 3 4 5 6 7 8 9

Il y a un geste

Les nombres

0 zéro	16 seize
1 un	17 dix-sept
2 deux	18 dix-huit
3 trois	19 dix-neuf
4 quatre	20 vingt
5 cinq	21 vingt et un
6 six	22 vingt-deux
7 sept	23 vingt-trois
8 huit	24 vingt-quatre
9 neuf	25 vingt-cinq
10 dix	26 vingt-six
11 onze	27 vingt-sept
12 douze	28 vingt-huit
13 treize	29 vingt-neuf
14 quatorze	30 trente
15 quinze	

Teach students to associate the numbers 1–10 with the gestures for counting on the fingers in French. Numbers above 30 are taught in Ch. 3.

The gesture on the right is used in the *Pas de problème* video, *Module 4.*

Compter avec les doigts. When counting, the French normally begin with the thumb, then the index finger, etc. For instance, the thumb, index, and middle fingers are held up to indicate the number three, as a child might indicate when asked his/her age.

3. Understanding Basic Expressions of Time

Quelle heure est-il?

Il est une heure.

Il est une heure dix.

Il est une heure quinze.

Il est une heure trente.

Il est deux heures moins vingt.

Il est deux heures moins dix.

Il est deux heures.

Il est trois heures.

Time is taught in Ch. 5.

Prononciation

This material is recorded on the Student Audio that accompanies your text. Use it to practice pronunciation.

Comparison: Have students identify the words as masculine (left hand) or feminine (right hand). The same phonetic principle will be used for the adjectives in Chs. 1, 3, & 4.

It is normally easier for students to learn the feminine first and to emphasize the pronunciation of the final consonant. The masculine can often be derived by dropping the final consonant sound.

Practice the French alphabet with the expressions you have learned so far. Read an expression out loud; spell it in French; close your book and try to write it from memory.

Model the alphabet several times for students. Dictate students' names using the French Alphabet; ask the class to try to identify the names you spell in French. Follow up by having individuals spell their own names in French.

The alphabet is reviewed and accents are taught in Ch. 2.

Masculin ou féminin?

■ Nouns do not have gender in English, but they do in French. You will learn to identify nouns and adjectives as masculine or feminine.

Often, the feminine form ends in a consonant sound while the masculine form ends in a vowel sound.

▶ **Listen and repeat:**

Féminins		*Masculins*	
Françoise	Louise	François	Louis
Jeanne	Martine	Jean	Martin
Laurence	Simone	Laurent	Simon
chaude	froide	chaud	froid
française	intelligente	français	intelligent
anglaise	petite	anglais	petit

L'alphabet français

	prononciation
A	*ah*
B	*bé*
C	*sé*
D	*dé*
E	*euh*
F	*effe*
G	*jé*
H	*ashe*
I	*i*
J	*ji*
K	*ka*
L	*elle*
M	*emme*
N	*enne*
O	*oh*
P	*pé*
Q	*ku*
R	*erre*
S	*esse*
T	*té*
U	*u*
V	*vé*
W	*double vé*
X	*iks*
Y	*i grec*
Z	*zed*

Comment est-ce qu'on écrit **merci?**   *How do you spell "merci"?*
Merci s'écrit M-E-R-C-I.   *"Merci" is spelled M-E-R-C-I.*

4. Understanding Basic Weather Expressions

Weather is taught in Ch. 7.

Quel temps fait-il?

Il fait beau.
Il fait du soleil.

Il fait du vent.

Il fait froid.

Il fait chaud.

Il pleut.

Il neige.

www Réalités culturelles

Le français: la langue de toutes les saisons

When we think of where the French language is spoken, we often think of France. But actually, France's territory extends beyond **l'Hexagone** (the hexagon-shaped mainland of France). In the forthcoming chapters, we will examine many French-speaking countries, but for now, here are some selected French-speaking regions from around the world, representing various climate zones during the month of October.

À Tahiti (en Polynésie), il pleut.
À Bruxelles (en Belgique), il fait du vent.
En Antarctique, il neige.
En Guyane (en Amérique du Sud), il fait du soleil.
À Québec (au Canada), il fait froid.
À Port-au-Prince (en Haïti), il fait beau.
À Dakar (au Sénégal), il fait chaud.

Source: www.meteo.fr

Il y a un geste

Comment? Pardon? An open hand, cupped behind the ear, indicates that the message has not been heard and should be repeated.

Practice the expressions **Comment dit-on ... ?** and **Que veut dire ... ?** to check on the meaning of words already introduced.

VOCABULAIRE

Quelques expressions pour la salle de classe

Pardon? *Pardon?*
Comment? *What (did you say)?*
Répétez, s'il vous plaît. *Please repeat.*
Encore. *Again.*
En français. *In French.*
Ensemble. *Together.*
Tout le monde. *Everybody, everyone.*

Fermez le livre. *Close the book.*
Écoutez. *Listen.*
Répondez. *Answer.*

Comment dit-on «*the teacher*»? *How do you say "the teacher"?*
On dit «le professeur». *You say **"le professeur."***

Que veut dire «le tableau»? *What does **"le tableau"** mean?*
Ça veut dire «*the chalkboard*». *It means "the chalkboard."*

Je ne sais pas. *I don't know.*
Je ne comprends pas. *I don't understand.*

www Réalités culturelles

La France

"Every man has two countries: his own and France." (Thomas Jefferson)

Official name	**République française**
Capital	**Paris**
Area (continental France)	**544,435 square kilometers**
Area (with other territories)	**639,761 square kilometers**
Population (continental France)	**59,500,000**
Population (including overseas territories)	**61,000,000**
Monetary unit	**Euro**
Official religion	**None**
National holiday	**July 14**

Bonjour!

Coup d'envoi

Prise de contact   Les présentations

This material is recorded on the Student Audio that accompanies your text. Practice with the recording as part of your homework.

See the Class Prep CD-ROM for detailed suggestions on how to teach this lesson.

Mademoiselle Becker

Je m'appelle°
   Lori Becker.
J'habite à° Boston.
Je suis° américaine.
Je suis célibataire°.

Monsieur Davidson

Je m'appelle
   James Davidson.
J'habite à San Francisco.
Je suis américain.
Je suis célibataire.

My name is

I live in
I am
single

Review the Helpful Hints found in the *To the Student* section in the front of your text.

Be sure to learn the vocabulary on the first two pages of each chapter.

Madame Martin

Je m'appelle
   Anne Martin.
J'habite à Angers.
Je suis française.
Je suis mariée°.

Monsieur Martin

Je m'appelle
   Pierre Martin.
J'habite à Angers.
Je suis français.
Je suis marié.

married

Communication (Presentational): Once the *Prise de contact* has been practiced, have students present themselves in French to the class.

▶ **Et vous?**   Qui êtes-vous?°

And you? Who are you?

Conversation

Dans un hôtel à Paris

The *Conversation* is recorded on the Student Audio that accompanies your text.

Listen carefully to your instructor and/or the Student Audio. Will you be able to recall any words immediately after the presentation?

Suggestions for modeling and student practice are found in the Class Prep CD-ROM.

In the **hôtel Ibis** there is a buffet system for meals, with self-seating. The main desk is near the restaurant.

After practicing the *Conversation*, have students complete ex. A in the Workbook.

Deux hommes sont au restaurant de l'hôtel Ibis à Paris.

PIERRE MARTIN:	Bonjour°, Monsieur! Excusez-moi de vous déranger.°	*Hello* *Excuse me for bothering you.*
JAMES DAVIDSON:	Bonjour. Pas de problème.°	*No problem.*
PIERRE MARTIN:	Vous permettez?° *(He touches the empty chair.)*	*May I?*
JAMES DAVIDSON:	Certainement. Asseyez-vous là°.	*there; here*
PIERRE MARTIN:	Vous êtes anglais?°	*Are you English?*
JAMES DAVIDSON:	Non, je suis américain. Permettez-moi de me présenter.° Je m'appelle James Davidson. *(They stand up and shake hands.)*	*Let me introduce myself.*
PIERRE MARTIN:	Martin, Pierre Martin. *(A receptionist comes into the room.)*	
LA RÉCEPTIONNISTE:	Le téléphone, Monsieur Davidson. C'est pour vous.° Votre communication de Californie.°	*It's for you.* *Your call from California.*
JAMES DAVIDSON:	Excusez-moi, s'il vous plaît, Monsieur.	
PIERRE MARTIN:	Oui, certainement. Au revoir, Monsieur. *(They shake hands again.)*	
JAMES DAVIDSON:	Bonne journée°, Monsieur.	*Have a good day*
PIERRE MARTIN:	Merci°, vous aussi°.	*Thank you / also; too*

▶ **Jouez ces rôles.** Role-play the conversation with a partner. Use your own identities.

10 *dix*

Comparison: Have students describe how they break the ice with a new acquaintance.

À propos

Why does Pierre Martin say Bonjour, Monsieur instead of just Bonjour?

a. He likes variety; either expression will do.
b. **Bonjour** alone is a bit less formal than **Bonjour, Monsieur.**
c. He is trying to impress James Davidson.

Only one answer is culturally accurate. Read the information below to find out which one.

Monsieur, Madame et Mademoiselle

A certain amount of formality is in order when initial contact is made with French speakers. It is more polite to add **Monsieur, Madame,** or **Mademoiselle** when addressing someone than simply to say **Bonjour.** James Davidson catches on toward the end of the conversation when he remembers to say **Bonne journée, Monsieur.**

Le premier contact (Breaking the ice)

Pierre Martin asks if he can sit at the empty seat. However, the French are usually more reticent than Americans to "break the ice." This may present a challenge to the language learner who wishes to meet others, but as long as you are polite, you should not hesitate to begin a conversation.

La politesse

See the *Entre amis* web site for additional information.

According to Polly Platt, the five most important words in French are **Excusez-moi de vous déranger.** This is a polite way to interrupt someone in France and a valuable formula for students and tourists who need to ask for directions or get permission to do something.

Remaining polite, even in the face of adversity, is an important survival technique.

Le prénom (first name)

It is not unusual to have the French give their last name first, especially in professional situations. Americans are generally much quicker than the French to begin to use another's first name. Rather than instantly condemning the French as "colder" than Americans, the wise strategy would be to refrain from using the first name when you meet someone. It is important to adapt your language usage to fit the culture. "When in Rome, do as the Romans do."

VOCABULAIRE

La politesse

Au revoir, Monsieur. *Good-bye, sir.*
Bonjour, Madame. *Hello, ma'am.*
Bonne journée, Madame. *Have a good day, ma'am.*
Enchanté(e). *Delighted (to meet you).*
Excusez-moi. *Excuse me.*
Excusez-moi de vous déranger. *Excuse me for bothering you.*
Je vous demande pardon … *I beg your pardon …*
Merci. Vous aussi. *Thanks. You too.*
Pardon. *Pardon me.*
Permettez-moi de me présenter … *Please allow me to introduce myself …*
S'il vous plaît. *Please.*
Vous permettez? *May I?*

Il y a un geste

These gestures are used in the *Pas de problème* video. For the handshake, see video, *Module 1*. See video, *Modules 8 & 12* for **le téléphone**.

Le contact physique. James Davidson and Pierre Martin shake hands during their conversation, a normal gesture for both North Americans and the French when meeting someone. However, the French would normally shake hands with friends, colleagues, and their neighbors each time they meet and, if they chat for a while, at the end of their conversation as well. Physical contact plays a very important role in French culture and forgetting to shake hands with a friend would be rude.

Le téléphone. The French indicate that there is a telephone call by spreading the thumb and little finger of one hand and holding that hand near the ear.

▶ **À vous.** How would you respond to the following?

1. Je m'appelle Alissa. Et vous?
2. Vous êtes français(e)?
3. J'habite à Paris. Et vous?
4. Excusez-moi, s'il vous plaît.
5. Bonne journée.

Model the *Entre amis* activity with a student first. Then have students stand and interact.

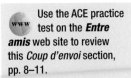

Use the ACE practice test on the *Entre amis* web site to review this *Coup d'envoi* section, pp. 8–11.

ENTRE AMIS

Permettez-moi de me présenter.

1. Greet your partner.
2. Find out if s/he is French.
3. Give your name and tell where you live.
4. Can you say anything else? (Be sure to shake hands when you say good-bye.)

Prononciation

This pronunciation lesson is recorded on the Student Audio that accompanies your text. Use it to practice pronunciation at home.

In 1066, the duke of Normandy (William the Conqueror) and his army defeated the English at the Battle of Hastings. A French aristocracy ruled England for the next several centuries.

Comparison: Review these basic principles often to reduce the influence of English.

L'accent et le rythme

■ There is an enormous number of related words in English and French. We inherited most of these after the Norman Conquest, but many are recent borrowings. With respect to pronunciation, these are the words that tend to reveal an English accent the most quickly.

▶ **Compare:**

Anglais	Français	Anglais	Français
CER-tain	cer-TAIN	MAR-tin	Mar-TIN
CER-tain-ly	cer-taine-MENT	a-MER-i-can	a-mé-ri-CAIN

■ Even more important than mastering any particular sound is the development of correct habits in three areas of French intonation.

1. *Rhythm:* French words are spoken in groups, and each syllable but the last is said very evenly.
2. *Accent:* In each group of words, the last syllable is lengthened, thus making it the only accented syllable in the group.
3. *Syllable formation:* Spoken French syllables end in a vowel sound much more often than English ones do.

▶ Counting is an excellent way to develop proper French rhythm and accent. Repeat after your instructor:

un DEUX	un deux TROIS	un deux trois QUATRE
mon-SIEUR	s'il vous PLAÎT	le té-lé-PHONE
mer-CI	cer-taine-MENT	A-sse-yez-VOUS
fran-ÇAIS	té-lé-PHONE	Mon-sieur Mar-TIN

Les consonnes finales

■ A final (written) consonant is normally not pronounced in French.

François	permettez	s'il vous plaît
Georges	français	trois
Il fait froid	américain	deux

■ There are some words whose final consonant is always pronounced (many words ending in **c, f, l,** or **r,** for instance).

Frédéric   neuf   Michel   bonjour

These are the same as the consonants in the English word CaReFuL.

■ When a consonant is followed by **-e** within the same word, the consonant is always pronounced. A single **-s-** followed by **-e** is pronounced as [z]. Two **-ss-** followed by **-e** are pronounced [s].

française   suisse   américaine   j'habite   je m'appelle

The rules governing obligatory liaison will be summarized in Ch. 5.

■ When a final silent consonant is followed by a word beginning with a vowel, it is often pronounced with the next word. This is called **liaison.**

vous *(silent)*   vous [z]êtes
deux *(silent)*   deux [z]hommes

Buts communicatifs

1. Exchanging Personal Information

Learn all the words in each *But communicatif*.

Comment vous appelez-vous?°   *What is your name?*
    Je m'appelle Nathalie Lachance.

Où habitez-vous?°   *Where do you live?*
    J'habite à Laval. J'habite près de° Montréal.   *near*

Êtes-vous célibataire?
    Non, je suis mariée.

Pronounce **appelle** [apɛl] and **appelez** [aple]. Practice with the Student Audio at home.

▶ **Et vous, Monsieur (Madame, Mademoiselle)?**

Remind students to look up the phonetic symbols in App. A.

REMARQUES

1. **Je m'appelle** and **Comment vous appelez-vous?** should be memo-rized for now. Note that in **Comment vous appelez-vous?** there is only one **l**, while in **Je m'appelle,** there are two.
2. Use **J'habite à** to identify the city in which you live.
3. Use **J'habite près de** to identify the city you live *near.*
4. **M., Mme,** and **Mlle** are the abbreviations for **Monsieur, Madame,** and **Mademoiselle.**

Students will learn in Ch. 5 which prepositions to use with countries.

I **Les inscriptions** *(Registration).* You are working at a conference in Geneva. Greet the following people and find out their names and the city where they live. Your partner will provide the answers.

MODÈLE: M. Robert Perrin (Lyon)

    —**Bonjour, Monsieur. Comment vous appelez-vous?**
    —**Je m'appelle Perrin, Robert Perrin.**
    —**Où habitez-vous?**
    —**J'habite à Lyon.**

On the *Entre amis* web site there is a practice test for each *But communicatif* in this text.

1. Mlle Marie Dupont (Metz)
2. Mme Anne Vermette (Montréal)
3. M. Joseph Guy (Lausanne)
4. Mlle Jeanne Delon (Paris)

5. le professeur de français
6. le président français
7. le président américain
8. le premier ministre canadien

A. Les pronoms sujets

See Appendix C, *Glossary of Grammatical Terms,* for an explanation of any terms with which you are not familiar.

■ The subject pronouns in French are:

singular forms		plural forms	
je (j')	*I*	**nous**	*we*
tu	*you*		
vous	*you*	**vous**	*you*
il	*he; it*	**ils**	*they*
elle	*she; it*	**elles**	*they*
on	*one; someone; people; we*		

Teachers may choose to explain the difference between **h muet** and **h aspiré.** Words beginning with **h aspiré** are noted with an asterisk in the French-English Vocabulary at the end of the book.

See Ch. 3 for a more complete explanation of **tu** and **vous.**

■ Before a vowel sound at the beginning of the next word, **je** becomes **j'.** This happens with words that begin with a vowel, but also with most words that begin with **h-,** which is silent.

J'adore Québec, mais **j'**habite à New York.

■ **Tu** is informal. It is used to address one person with whom you have a close relationship. **Vous** is the singular form used in other cases. To address more than one person, one always uses **vous.**

Tu es à Paris, Michel?
Vous êtes à Lyon, Monsieur?
Marie! Paul! **Vous** êtes à Bordeaux!

NOTE — Whether **vous** is singular or plural, the verb form is always plural.

Gender is explained further with the article **le** in Ch. 2.

■ There are two genders in French: masculine and feminine. All nouns have gender, whether they designate people or things. **Il** stands for a masculine person or thing, **elle** for a feminine person or thing. The plural **ils** stands for a group of masculine persons or things, and **elles** stands for a group of feminine persons or things.

le tableau = **il**
la porte = **elle**
les tables = **elles**
les téléphones = **ils**

■ For a group that includes both masculine and feminine nouns **(Nathalie, Karine, Paul et Marie), ils** is used, even if only one of the nouns is masculine.

Karine et Éric? **Ils** sont à Marseille.

■ **On** is a subject pronoun used to express generalities or unknowns, much as do the English forms *one, someone, you, people.* In informal situations, **on** can sometimes be used to mean *we.*

On est à San Francisco.   *We are in San Francisco.*
On est riche en Amérique?   *Are people in America rich?*

B. Le verbe *être*

Il est à Québec.
Je suis à Strasbourg.
Nous sommes à Besançon.

■ The most frequently used verb in French is **être** *(to be).*

je	**suis**	*I am*	nous	**sommes**	*we are*
tu	**es**	*you are*	vous	**êtes**	*you are*
il	**est**	*he is; it is*	ils	**sont**	*they are (m. or m. + f.)*
elle	**est**	*she is; it is*	elles	**sont**	*they are (f.)*
on	**est**	*one is; people are; we are*			

Review the use of **liaison** on p. 12.

■ Before a vowel sound at the beginning of the next word, the silent final consonant of many words (but not all!) is pronounced and is spoken with the next word. This is called **liaison. Liaison** is necessary between a pronoun and a verb.

Vous [z]êtes à Montréal.   On [n]est où?

Point out that this is also true of **nous, ils,** and **elles** if they are used before a verb that begins with a vowel sound (see Ch. 2).

■ **Liaison** is possible after all forms of **être,** but is common *only* with **est** and **sont.**

Il est [t]à Paris.   Elles sont [t]à Marseille.

2 **Où sont-ils?** *(Where are they?)* Identify the cities where the following people are. Use a subject pronoun in your answer.

MODÈLES: tu (Los Angeles) **Tu es à Los Angeles.**
vous (Québec) **Vous êtes à Québec.**

1. Lori (Boston)
2. Lise et Elsa (Bruxelles)
3. Thierry (Monte Carlo)
4. je (...)
5. Pierre et Anne (Angers)
6. nous (...)
7. Sylvie (Paris)

www Réalités culturelles

Paris

Paris, the "city of lights," has always been a crossroads of ideas, a large financial center, and a tourist destination of choice. Paris is home to some of the most renowned art museums of the world. A visit to Paris would not be complete without a visit to the **Louvre,** the largest museum in the world. In addition, there are 101 other museums in Paris, from the medieval **Cluny** to the ultra-modern **Centre Georges-Pompidou.** Paris has been and continues to be home to large numbers of artists, many of whom display their works on the banks of the Seine or in front of the **Sacré-Cœur** basilica.

Paris offers an amazing array of things to see and do: there are large public squares, such as the **Place Beaubourg,** where singers, jugglers, dancers, and mimes entertain audiences; large avenues, such as the **Champs-Élysées** and the **Boulevard Saint-Michel,** where shops, theaters, and cafes keep people strolling through the night; open-air markets, where Parisians buy flowers, fresh vegetables, meat, and cheese; and extensively landscaped parks, such as the **jardin du Luxembourg,** where people of all ages can escape from the hectic pace of life in a busy city. A visitor can also take a ride on a **bateau-mouche,** explore student life in the **Quartier latin,** or simply observe the great diversity of people who live, study, and work in Paris.

C. L'accord des adjectifs

Review *Prononciation*, p. 4.

■ Most adjectives have two pronunciations: one when they refer to a feminine noun and one when they refer to a masculine noun. From an oral point of view, it is usually better to learn the feminine form first. The masculine pronunciation can often be found by dropping the last consonant *sound* of the feminine.

Point out the nasal vowel at the end of **américain.**

Choose famous people. Have students make up sentences using **il, elle,** etc.

Barbara est **américaine.**   Bob est **américain** aussi.
Christine est **française.**   David est **français** aussi.

■ Almost all adjectives change their spelling depending on whether the nouns they refer to are masculine or feminine, singular or plural. These spelling changes may or may not affect pronunciation.

Il est américain.   Elle est américain**e.**
Ils sont américain**s.**   Elles sont américain**es.**

Il est marié.   Elle est marié**e.**
Ils sont marié**s.**   Elles sont marié**es.**

■ The feminine adjective almost always ends in a written **-e.** A number of masculine adjectives end in **-e** also. In this case, masculine and feminine forms are identical in pronunciation and spelling.

célibataire   fantastique   optimiste

■ The plural is usually formed by adding a written **-s** to the singular. However, since the final **-s** of the plural is silent, the singular and the plural are pronounced in the same way.

américain   américain**s**
américaine   américaine**s**

NOTE — If the masculine singular ends in **-s,** the masculine plural is identical.
un homme français   deux hommes français

■ Adjectives that describe a group of both masculine and feminine nouns take the masculine plural form.

Bill et Judy sont **mariés.**

VOCABULAIRE

Fiancé(e) is not legally a marital status.

L'état civil *(marital status)*

Femmes	Hommes	Women/men
célibataire(s)	célibataire(s)	*single*
mariée(s)	marié(s)	*married*
fiancée(s)	fiancé(s)	*engaged*
divorcée(s)	divorcé(s)	*divorced*
veuve(s)	veuf(s)	*widowed*

With the exception of **veuve(s)** [vœv] and **veuf(s)** [vœf], the spelling changes in the adjectives listed to the right do not affect pronunciation.

3 **Quelle coïncidence!** *(What a coincidence!)* State that the marital status of the second person or group is the same as that of the first.

MODÈLES: Léa est fiancée. Et Marc?   Pierre est marié. Et Zoé et Max?
Il est fiancé aussi.   **Ils sont mariés aussi.**

1. Anne et Paul sont fiancés. Et Marie?
2. Nous sommes mariés. Et Monique?
3. Nicolas est divorcé. Et Sophie et Thérèse?
4. Je suis célibataire. Et Georges et Sylvie?
5. Madame Beaufort est veuve. Et Monsieur Dupont?

4 **Qui est-ce?** *(Who is it?)* Answer the following questions. Try to identify real people or famous fictional characters. Can you name more than one person? Make sure that the verbs and adjectives agree with the subjects.

MODÈLE: Qui est fiancé?
Olive Oyl est fiancée.   ou
Olive Oyl et Popeye sont fiancés.

Communication (Interpretive): Have students ask you the questions first; then (books closed) ask them the questions.

1. Qui est célibataire?   5. Qui est veuf?
2. Qui est fiancé?   6. Qui est français?
3. Qui est marié?   7. Qui est américain?
4. Qui est divorcé?

5 **Carte de débarquement** *(Arrival form).* When you travel overseas you are usually given an arrival form to fill out. Identify yourself by providing the information requested in the form below in French.

Communication (Interpretive and Presentational): Give students time to try to interpret the form before having them fill it out.

Carte de débarquement

Nom de famille: _____

Prénom(s): _____

Âge: _____ ans

Nationalité: _____

État civil: _____

Adresse: _____

_____

_____

Code postal: _____

Numéro de passeport: _____

Motif du voyage: ❏ touristique   ❏ professionnel
                   ❏ transit   ❏ visite privée

ENTRE AMIS

Model the *Entre amis* activity with a student first. Then have students stand and interact.

Dans un avion *(In an airplane)*

Complete the following interaction with as many members of the class as possible.

1. Greet your neighbor in a culturally appropriate way.
2. Find out if s/he is French.
3. Find out each other's name.
4. Find out the city in which s/he lives.
5. What else can you say?

2. Identifying Nationality

Learn all the words in each *But communicatif.*

 Quelle est votre nationalité?°

Moi, je suis canadienne.

What is your nationality?

▶ **Et vous?** Vous êtes chinois(e)°?

Pas du tout!° Je suis ...

Chinese

Not at all!

Remember to pronounce the final consonant in the feminine (see p. 4).

Culture: The signs are those used by the **Fédération internationale de l'automobile.** Ask students if they have ever seen one of these symbols on a car.

	Féminin	**Masculin**	
GB	anglaise	anglais	*English*
F	française	français	*French*
J	japonaise	japonais	*Japanese*
SN	sénégalaise	sénégalais	*Senegalese*
USA	américaine	américain	*American*
MA	marocaine	marocain	*Moroccan*
MEX	mexicaine	mexicain	*Mexican*
CDN	canadienne	canadien	*Canadian*
I	italienne	italien	*Italian*
S	suédoise	suédois	*Swedish*
D	allemande	allemand	*German*
E	espagnole	espagnol	*Spanish*
B	belge	belge	*Belgian*
CH	suisse	suisse	*Swiss*
RUS	russe	russe	*Russian*

REMARQUE

In written French, some feminine adjectives are distinguishable from their masculine form not only by a final **-e,** but also by a doubled final consonant.

un homme canadien *a Canadian man*
une femme canadie**nne** *a Canadian woman*

Communication (Interpretive):
Tell students to pick a nationality.
The instructor and/or the class
will try to guess it.

6 **Quelle est votre nationalité?** The customs agent needs to know each person's nationality. Your partner will play the role of the customs agent and ask the question. You take the role of each of the following people, and answer.

MODÈLES: Madame Jones et Mademoiselle Jones (GB)
    —Quelle est votre nationalité?
    —Nous sommes anglaises.

    Maria Gomez (MEX)
    —Quelle est votre nationalité?
    —Je suis mexicaine.

  1. Jean-François (CDN)
  2. Monsieur et Madame Smith (USA)
  3. Mademoiselle Nakasone (J)
  4. Madame Colon et Mademoiselle Colon (E)
  5. Mademoiselle Balke (D)

  6. Bruno (SN)
  7. Madame Volaro (I)
  8. Marie-Christine (F)
  9. votre professeur de français
  10. vous

Ces trois amis habitent à Paris.

7   **Qui êtes-vous?** *(Who are you?)* Assume the identity of each one of the following people and introduce yourself, indicating your name, your nationality, and the city you are from.

MODÈLE: Mademoiselle Brigitte Lapointe/Paris (F)
Je m'appelle Brigitte et je suis française. J'habite à Paris.

Extension: Students give their last names first: **Je m'appelle Lapointe, Brigitte Lapointe.**

1. Monsieur Pierre La Vigne/Québec (CDN)
2. Madame Margaret Jones/Manchester (GB)
3. Madame Anne Martin/Angers (F)
4. Monsieur Yasuhiro Saya/Tokyo (J)
5. Madame Mary O'Leary/Boston (USA)
6. Monsieur Ahmed Zoubir/Casablanca (MA)
7. votre professeur de français
8. vous

www Réalités culturelles

L'Agence de la francophonie

The French language is spoken on all the continents of the globe. In 1970, several French-speaking countries created the **Agence de la francophonie** *(Agency for French-speaking communities).* The word **francophonie** was coined in 1880 by geographer Onésime Reclus to describe the areas of the world where French is spoken by a significant part of the population. The chief purpose of the **Agence de la francophonie** is to use the universality of the French language in the service of peace and to promote cultural and economic cooperation among French-speaking countries. Today, the agency, which consists of some fifty states and governments, focuses its efforts on the promotion of the French language. It sponsors a French-language television station, **TV5,** which those living in North America can subscribe to through cable. It has also created a French-speaking university, **l'université Senghor,** in Alexandria, Egypt.

D. La négation

James Davidson **n'**est **pas** français. Il est américain.
Il **n'**habite **pas** à Paris. Il habite à San Francisco.

■ Two words, **ne** and **pas,** are used to make a sentence negative: **ne** precedes the conjugated verb and **pas** follows it.

Guy et Zoé **ne** sont **pas** mariés.   *Guy and Zoé aren't married.*
Il **ne** fait **pas** très beau.   *It's not very nice out.*

■ Remember that both **ne** and **pas** are necessary in standard French to make a sentence negative.

ne + conjugated verb + **pas**

■ **Ne** becomes **n'** before a vowel sound.

Je **n'**habite **pas** à Paris.   *I don't live in Paris.*
Nathalie **n'**est **pas** française.   *Nathalie is not French.*

Suggestion: Elicit the questions
for #1–8 before pairing students.

8 **Ils sont français?** Ask your partner whether the following people are French. Choose the correct form of **être** and make sure that the adjective agrees. Your partner will first respond with a negative, and then state the correct information.

MODÈLE: —**Elles sont françaises?**
     —**Non, elles ne sont pas françaises. Elles sont anglaises.**

1.

2.

3.

4.

5.

6.

7.

8.

ENTRE AMIS

Je ne suis pas suisse.

Pick a new nationality (from the list on page 18), but don't tell your partner which one you have chosen.

Remind students in step 1 to
choose adjectives that match
their partner's gender.

1. Your partner will try to guess your new nationality by asking you questions.
2. Respond **"Pas du tout! Je ne suis pas ..."** if the guess is incorrect.
3. Once your partner has guessed your nationality, switch roles.

3. Describing Physical Appearance

Learn all the words in each *But communicatif.*

Try to use **assez** and, in the case of a negative, **pas très** to avoid being overly categorical when describing people.

Voilà° Christine.
Elle est jeune°.
Elle est assez grande°.
Elle n'est pas grosse°.
Elle est assez jolie°.

Voilà le Père Noël.
Il est assez° vieux°.
Il est assez petit°.
Il n'est pas très° mince°.

There is; Here is
young / rather / old
tall / short; small
fat / very / thin
pretty

Suggestions for the presentation of this material are found on the Class Prep CD-ROM.

▶ **Et vous?** Vous êtes …

jeune	*ou*	vieux (vieille)?
petit(e)	*ou*	grand(e)?
gros(se)	*ou*	mince?
beau (belle)	*ou*	laid(e)?°

Décrivez votre meilleur(e) ami(e).°

attractive or ugly?
Describe your best friend.

This gesture is closely related to the gesture for **Ça va (comme ci, comme ça)** taught in Ch. 2.

Il y a un geste

Assez *(sort of, rather; enough).* The gesture for **assez** is an open hand rotated back and forth (palm down).

E. L'accord des adjectifs (*suite*)

Adjective placement and the special masculine forms **bel** and **vieil** are taught in Ch. 4. Until Ch. 4, students use adjectives as predicate adjectives only.

■ The masculine forms of some adjectives are not like their feminine forms in either pronunciation or spelling, and so they must be memorized.

belle **beau** vieille **vieux**

■ The masculine plural of some adjectives is formed by adding **-x.** Pronunciation of the plural form remains the same as the singular.

Robert et Paul sont très **beaux.**

Some nouns form the plural in the same way: **le tableau, les tableaux.**

■ Masculine singular adjectives that end in **-s** or **-x** keep the same form (and pronunciation) for the masculine plural.

Bill est **gros.** Roseanne et John sont **gros** aussi.
Je suis **vieux.** Georges et Robert sont très **vieux.**

Synthèse: l'accord des adjectifs

féminin		*masculin*	
singulier	*pluriel*	*singulier*	*pluriel*
petite	petites	petit	petits
grande	grandes	grand	grands
jolie	jolies	joli	jolis
belle	belles	beau	beaux
laide	laides	laid	laids
jeune	jeunes	jeune	jeunes
vieille	vieilles	vieux	vieux
mince	minces	mince	minces
grosse	grosses	gros	gros

Culture & Comparison: Ask students if they or their friends ever express themselves in this fashion.

9 **Oui, il n'est pas très grand.** The French often tone down what they wish to say by stating the opposite with a negative and the word **très**. Agree with each of the following descriptions by saying the opposite in a negative sentence.

MODÈLE: Michael J. Fox est petit.
Oui, il n'est pas très grand.

1. Abraham et Sarah sont vieux.
2. Marie-Christine est mince.
3. Goofy est laid.
4. Alissa est petite.
5. Dumbo l'éléphant est gros.
6. L'oncle Sam est vieux.
7. James et Lori sont jeunes.

10 **Décrivez ...** Describe the following people. If you don't know what they look like, guess. Pay close attention to adjective agreement.

MODÈLE: Décrivez James Davidson.　　**Il est grand, jeune et assez beau.**

Culture: Remind students that **assez** is useful when making a judgment. Remind students to use the gesture for **assez.** Also suggest that they can use a negative with **très** if they wish.

1. Décrivez votre meilleur(e) ami(e).
2. Décrivez votre professeur de français.
3. Décrivez une actrice.
4. Décrivez un acteur.
5. Décrivez Minnie Mouse et Daisy Duck.
6. Décrivez le (la) président(e) de votre université.
7. Décrivez-vous.

ENTRE AMIS

Une personne célèbre

1. Choose a famous person and describe him/her.
2. If your partner agrees with each description s/he will say so.
3. If your partner disagrees, s/he will correct you.

Intégration

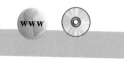

Connections & Communities: The web search activities for this chapter expose students to several French-language newspapers.

Révision

Suggestion: Encourage students to use the Student Audio and listen once more to the conversation for Ch. 1. This will give them a feeling of confidence and will provide an additional model for timing and fluency.

A **Il y a plus d'une façon** *(There's more than one way).*

1. Give two ways to break the ice in French.
2. Give two ways to find out someone's name.
3. Give two ways to find out where someone lives.
4. Give two ways to find out someone's nationality.

B **L'Inspecteur Clouseau.** A bumbling inspector is asking all the wrong questions. Correct him. Invent the correct answer if you wish. Use subject pronouns.

MODÈLES: Vous êtes Madame Perrin?
Non, pas du tout, je ne suis pas Madame Perrin; je suis Mademoiselle Smith.

Madame Perrin est française?
Non, pas du tout, elle n'est pas française; elle est canadienne.

Notice that #1 & 2 are plural. Use **nous** in your answer.

1. Vous êtes Monsieur et Madame Martin?
2. Vous *(pl.)* êtes belges?
3. Madame Martin est veuve?
4. Monsieur et Madame Martin sont divorcés?
5. James et Lori sont mariés?
6. Lori est italienne?
7. James est français?

Communication (Presentational): Have students present their descriptions to the class. If names are omitted, other students can be asked to try to identify the people described. Suggestion: Assign the **Rédaction** at the end of Ch. 1 in the Workbook.

C **Début de rédaction.** Choose three people and give as complete a description as you can of each of them. Include at least one famous person.

MODÈLE: **James Davidson est grand, jeune et assez beau. Il est aussi célibataire. Il est américain et il habite à San Francisco.**

Communication (Interpretive): Encourage students to use the practice test on the Lab Audio Program.

D **À vous.** How would you respond to the following?

1. Bonjour, Monsieur (Madame, Mademoiselle).
2. Excusez-moi de vous déranger.
3. Vous êtes Monsieur (Madame, Mademoiselle) Dupont?
4. Comment vous appelez-vous?
5. Vous n'êtes pas français(e)?
6. Quelle est votre nationalité?
7. Vous habitez près d'Angers?
8. Où habitez-vous?
9. Vous êtes marié(e)?
10. Bonne journée!

Négociations:

Identifications. Work with your partner to prepare a new identity. First, decide with your partner whether you are describing a man or a woman. Then, complete the first half of the following form; your partner will complete the second half, using the form in Appendix D. Each will ask questions in French to complete the form.

MODÈLE: **Comment vous appelez-vous? Quel est votre nom de famille? Êtes-vous français(e)? Êtes-vous jeune?**

For complete instructions on how to prepare for and use this activity, see *Négociations* on the Class Prep CD-ROM.

Video for Chapter 1: A. Video worksheets (Cahier); B. ACE Video practice test (WWW); C. CD-ROM.

A

Nom de famille: _____

Prénom: _____

Nationalité: _____

B

État civil: _____

Description 1: _____

_____

Description 2: _____

_____

Lecture

This first reading is a series of headlines (**manchettes**) taken from the French-language media. It is not vital that you understand every word in order to grasp the general meaning of what you read. The context will often help you guess the meaning.

Comparison: Ask students to identify cognates they already know before reading the headlines.

A **Trouvez les mots apparentés (cognates).** In French and English, many words with similar meanings have the same or nearly identical spelling. These words are called cognates. Scan the headlines that follow and find at least fifteen cognates.

Comparison: Ask students to identify acronyms used in their country.

B **Sigles (Acronyms).** Acronyms are used frequently in French. They are abbreviations made of the first letter of each word in a title and may involve the same letters in their French and English forms. However, the order of the letters is normally different because in French, adjectives usually follow a noun, e.g., **la Croix-Rouge** (*the Red Cross*). Can you guess the meaning of the following French acronyms?

MODÈLE: ONU (a group of countries)
UN, the United Nations (Organization)

1. NATO 2. AIDS 3. EU (European Union) 4. Value-added tax 5. DNA 6. In-vitro fertilization 7. International Monetary Fund 8. HIV 9. MRI 10. Severe Acute Respiratory Syndrome

1. OTAN (an alliance)
2. SIDA (a disease)
3. UE (a group of European countries)
4. TVA (a special tax)
5. ADN (a way to identify)
6. FIV (a way to conceive)
7. FMI (lends money to poor countries)
8. VIH (a virus)
9. IRM (a body scan to detect illness)
10. SRAS (a type of pneumonia)

Give students 2–3 minutes. Tell them to keep rereading the headlines until you stop them.

Manchettes

1.
Le traité d'Athènes: ratification de l'élargissement de l'UE

2.
Un homme innocenté par des tests d'ADN

3.
Washington a l'ambition de reconstruire l'Irak en un an

4.
Un Allemand pour remplacer le Français à la tête du FMI?

5.
Le Conseil de sécurité, unanime, réactive «Pétrole contre nourriture»

6.
Mise au point aux États-Unis d'un test prédicatif pour le cancer héréditaire

7.
Un nouveau président français pour Euro Disney en difficultés

8.
Un observatoire national du SIDA va être mis en place

9.
Ottawa a entrepris de renforcer son dispositif de défense dans le Grand Nord

10.
Le camp de la paix ne renonce pas

C **Les manchettes.** Read the above headlines and decide which ones apply to any of the following categories.

1. Canada
2. the United States
3. Europe
4. health and medicine
5. war and peace
6. the United Nations

D **Dans ces contextes (In these contexts).** Study the above headlines to help you guess the meaning of the following expressions.

1. élargissement
2. homme
3. reconstruire
4. tête
5. nourriture
6. pour
7. nouveau
8. mis en place
9. renforcer
10. paix

VOCABULAIRE ACTIF

Pour identifier les personnes
Noms
un acteur / une actrice *actor / actress*
une femme *woman*
un homme *man*
un(e) meilleur(e) ami(e) *best friend*
le Père Noël *Santa Claus*
une personne *person (male or female)*
un professeur *teacher (male or female)*
la nationalité *nationality*
un nom *name*
un nom de famille *family name*
un prénom *first name*

Description physique
beau (belle) *handsome (beautiful)*
grand(e) *big; tall*
gros(se) *fat; large*
jeune *young*
joli(e) *pretty*
laid(e) *ugly*
mince *thin*
petit(e) *small; short*
vieux (vieille) *old*

D'autres noms
un hôtel *hotel*
une porte *door*
un restaurant *restaurant*
une table *table*
un tableau *chalkboard*
un téléphone *telephone*
l'université f. *university*

Prépositions
à *at; in; to*
de *from, of*
en *in*
près de *near*

Adjectifs de nationalité
allemand(e) *German*
américain(e) *American*
anglais(e) *English*

belge *Belgian*
canadien(ne) *Canadian*
chinois(e) *Chinese*
espagnol(e) *Spanish*
français(e) *French*
italien(ne) *Italian*
japonais(e) *Japanese*
marocain(e) *Moroccan*
mexicain(e) *Mexican*
russe *Russian*
sénégalais(e) *Senegalese*
suédois(e) *Swedish*
suisse *Swiss*

Pronoms sujets
je *I*
tu *you*
il *he, it*
elle *she, it*
on *one, people, we, they*
nous *we*
vous *you*
ils *they*
elles *they*

État civil
célibataire *single*
divorcé(e) *divorced*
fiancé(e) *engaged*
marié(e) *married*
veuf (veuve) *widowed*

Nombres
un *one*
deux *two*
trois *three*
quatre *four*

À propos de l'identité
Comment vous appelez-vous? *What is your name?*
Je m'appelle ... *My name is ...*
Madame (Mme) *Mrs.*
Mademoiselle (Mlle) *Miss*
Monsieur (M.) *Mr.; sir*
Permettez-moi de me présenter. *Allow me to introduce myself.*
Quelle est votre nationalité? *What is your nationality?*

Vous habitez ... *You live, you reside ...*
Où habitez-vous? *Where do you live?*
J'habite ... *I live, I reside ...*

La politesse
Au revoir. *Goodbye.*
Bonjour. *Hello.*
Bonne journée. *Have a good day.*
Enchanté(e). *Delighted (to meet you).*
Excusez-moi. *Excuse me.*
Excusez-moi de vous déranger. *Excuse me for bothering you.*
Je vous demande pardon ... *I beg your pardon ...*
Merci. Vous aussi. *Thanks. You too.*
Pardon. *Pardon me.*
S'il vous plaît. *Please.*
Vous permettez? *May I?*

Verbe
être *to be*

Adverbes
assez *sort of, rather; enough*
aussi *also, too*
certainement *surely, of course*
là *there; here*
ne ... pas *not*
où *where*
très *very*

D'autres expressions utiles
Asseyez-vous. *Sit down.*
C'est ... *It is ...; This is ...*
C'est pour vous. *It's for you.*
entre amis *between friends*
Et moi? *And me?*
Oui ou non? *Yes or no?*
Pas du tout! *Not at all!*
qui *who*
Voilà ... *There is (are) ...; Here is (are) ...*
votre communication de ... *your call from ...*

Qu'est-ce que vous aimez?

Buts communicatifs

Asking and responding to "How are you?"

Giving and responding to compliments

Offering, accepting, and refusing

Expressing likes and dislikes

Structures utiles

Le verbe **aller**

Les verbes en **-er**

L'article défini: **le, la, l'** et **les**

Les questions avec réponse **oui** ou **non**

Culture

• *À propos*

Les compliments

Merci

Le kir

• *Il y a un geste*

À votre santé

Non, merci

Ça va

• *Lecture*

Seul(e) et las(se) de l'être

Coup d'envoi

Quelque chose à boire?

Est-ce que vous aimez ...°   *Do you like ...*

   le café? le coca? le vin? le thé?°   *coffee? Coca-Cola? wine? tea?*

J'aime° le coca.   *I like (love)*
J'aime beaucoup° le thé.   *very much; a lot*
Je n'aime pas le café.

Voulez-vous boire quelque chose?°   *Do you want to drink something?*

Non, merci.
Oui, je veux bien.°   *Gladly; Yes, thanks.*

Je voudrais ...°   *I'd like ...*
   une tasse° de café.   *a cup*
   une tasse de thé.
   un verre° de coca.   *a glass*
   un verre de vin.

▶ **Et vous?**   Voulez-vous boire quelque chose?
         Qu'est-ce que vous voulez?°   *What do you want?*

Est-ce que is often placed at the start of a sentence to make it a question.

See the suggestions for teaching this lesson in the Class Prep CD-ROM.

Conversation

Listen carefully to your instructor and/or the Student Audio while the conversation is presented. As soon as the presentation has ended, try to recall as many words as you can.

Communication (Interpretive): Use the gestures below when presenting this material.

Une soirée à Besançon

James Davidson étudie le français à Besançon. Mais il vient de° San Francisco. Au cours d'une soirée°, il aperçoit° Karine Aspel, qui est assistante au laboratoire de langues.

        he comes from / During a party / notices

JAMES: Bonsoir.° Quelle° bonne surprise! Comment allez-vous?°

        Good evening. / What a / How are you?

KARINE: Ça va bien°, merci. Et vous-même°?

        Fine / yourself

JAMES: Très bien ... Votre prénom, c'est Karine, n'est-ce pas?°

        isn't it?

KARINE: Oui, je m'appelle Karine Aspel.

JAMES: Et moi, James Davidson.

KARINE: Est-ce que vous êtes américain? Votre français est excellent.

JAMES: Merci beaucoup.

KARINE: Mais c'est vrai!° Vous êtes d'où?°

        But it's true! / Where are you from?

JAMES: Je viens de° San Francisco. Au fait°, voulez-vous boire quelque chose? Un coca?

        I come from / By the way

KARINE: Merci°, je n'aime pas beaucoup le coca.

        No thanks

JAMES: Alors°, un kir, peut-être°?

        Then / perhaps

KARINE: Je veux bien. Un petit kir, pourquoi pas°? *(James hands a glass of kir to Karine.)*

        why not

JAMES: À votre santé°, Karine.

        To your health

KARINE: À la vôtre°. Et merci, James.

        To yours

After practicing the *Conversation*, have students complete ex. A in the Workbook.

▶ **Jouez ces rôles.** Role-play the above conversation with a partner. Use your own identities. Choose something else to drink.

Il y a un geste

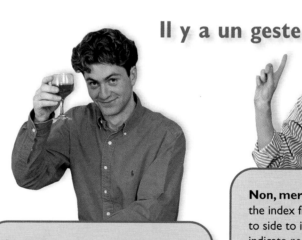

The French often say **Tchin-tchin** as their glasses touch.

À votre santé. The glass is raised when saying *To your health.* Among friends, the glasses are lightly touched as well.

Non, merci. The French often raise the index finger and move it from side to side to indicate *no.* They also may indicate *no* by raising a hand, palm outward, or by shaking their heads as do English speakers. In France, however, the lips are usually well rounded and often are pursed when making these gestures.

À propos

Why does Karine say Mais c'est vrai! when James says Merci beaucoup?

a. She misunderstood what he said.
b. She doesn't mean what she said.
c. She feels that James doesn't really believe her when she tells him his French is good.

Les compliments

While certainly not averse to being complimented, the French may respond by playing down a compliment, which may be a way of encouraging more of the same. While Americans are taught from an early age to accept and respond *thank you* to compliments, **merci,** when used in response to a compliment, is often perceived by the French as saying "you don't mean it." It is for this reason that Karine Aspel responds **Mais c'est vrai!,** insisting that her compliment was true. It is culturally more accurate, therefore, and linguistically enjoyable, to develop a few rejoinders such as **Oh, vraiment?** *(Really?)* or **Vous trouvez?** *(Do you think so?),* which one can employ in similar situations. In this case, a really French response on James's part might be **Mais non! Je ne parle pas vraiment bien. Mon accent n'est pas très bon.** *(Oh, no! I don't speak really well. My accent's not very good.)*

Merci

The word **merci** is, of course, one of the best ways of conveying politeness, and its use is, by all means, to be encouraged. Its usage, however, differs from that of English in at least one important way: when one is offered something to eat, to drink, etc., the response **merci** is somewhat ambiguous and is often a way of saying *no, thank you.* One would generally say **je veux bien** or **s'il vous plaît** to convey the meaning *yes, thanks.* **Merci** is, however, the proper polite response once the food, the drink, etc., has actually been served.

Le kir

A popular drink in France, four parts white wine and one part black currant liqueur, **kir** owes its name to **le Chanoine Kir,** a French priest and former mayor of Dijon. It is often served as an **apéritif** *(before-dinner drink).*

Use the ACE practice test on the *Entre amis* web site to review this *Coup d'envoi* section, pp. 29–31.

 À vous. How would you respond to the following questions?

1. Comment allez-vous?
2. Est-ce que vous êtes français(e)?
3. Votre prénom, c'est … ?
4. Vous êtes d'où?
5. Voulez-vous boire quelque chose?

ENTRE AMIS

À une soirée (*At a party*)

1. Greet another "invited guest."
2. Find out his/her name.
3. Find out his/her nationality.
4. Find out where s/he comes from.
5. What else can you say?

Prononciation

Review the alphabet on p. 4 before doing this activity.

Review what was said about **l'accent et le rythme,** p. 12.

TGV = Train à grande vitesse, a very fast French train; **La SNCF = La Société nationale des chemins de fer français,** the French railroad system.

L'alphabet français (*suite*)

■ English and French share the same 26-letter Latin alphabet, and although this is useful, it is also potentially troublesome.

■ First, French and English cognates may not be spelled the same. French spellings must, therefore, be memorized.

adresse   personne   appartement

■ Second, because the alphabet is the same, it is tempting to pronounce French words as if they were English. Be very careful, especially when pronouncing cognates, not to transfer English pronunciation to the French words.

téléphone   conversation   professeur

■ Knowing how to say the French alphabet is not only important in spelling out loud. It is also essential when saying the many acronyms used in the French language.

le TGV   les USA   la SNCF

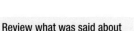 **Quelques sigles.** Read out loud the letters that make up the following acronyms.

1. **SVP**   S'il vous plaît
2. **RSVP**   Répondez, s'il vous plaît
3. **La SNCF**   La Société nationale des chemins de fer français
                  (*French railroad system*)
4. **La RATP**   La Régie autonome des transports parisiens (*Paris subway and bus system*)
5. **Les BD**   Les bandes dessinées (*comic strips*)
6. **Les USA**   Les United States of America (= Les États-Unis)
7. **La BNP**   La Banque nationale de Paris
8. **La CGT**   La Confédération générale du travail (*a French labor union*)
9. **BCBG**   Bon chic bon genre (*a French yuppy*)
10. **Le RER**   Le Réseau Express Régional (*a train to the suburbs*)

Les accents

■ French accents are part of spelling and must be learned. They can serve:

1. to indicate how a word is pronounced

ç → [s]: français

é → [e]: marié

è → [ɛ]: très

ê → [ɛ]: être

ë → [ɛ]: Noël

2. or to distinguish between meanings

ou	*or*	la	*the (feminine)*
où	*where*	là	*there*

French names		Examples
´	**accent aigu**	am**é**ricain; t**é**l**é**phone
`	**accent grave**	**à**; tr**è**s; o**ù**
^	**accent circonflexe**	**â**ge; **ê**tes; s'il vous pla**î**t; h**ô**tel; s**û**r
¨	**tréma**	No**ë**l; co**ï**ncidence
¸	**cédille**	fran**ç**ais
-	**trait d'union**	Jean-Luc
'	**apostrophe**	J'aime

Ç is explained on p. 214.

Crème s'écrit C–R–E accent grave–M–E.

▶ **Comment est-ce qu'on écrit … ?** Your partner will ask you to spell the words below. Give the correct spelling.

MODÈLE: être

VOTRE PARTENAIRE: **Comment est-ce qu'on écrit «être»?**

VOUS: **«Être» s'écrit E accent circonflexe–T–R–E.**

1. français
2. monsieur
3. belge
4. mademoiselle
5. professeur
6. vieux
7. hôtel
8. très
9. téléphone
10. j'habite
11. canadienne
12. asseyez-vous

www Réalités culturelles

Besançon

Besançon, the capital of the Franche-Comté region, is located in the eastern part of France. It is an important industrial town, two and a half hours from Paris by the TGV. Besançon is home to the **Université de Franche-Comté,** which is noted for its applied sciences program and for its center for applied linguistics.

Besançon has historical significance for France. In 58 B.C., recognizing its strategic importance, Julius Caesar captured the city, and during the five-century-long Roman occupation, Besançon became a cross-roads for travel from Switzerland and Italy to Paris. **La Porte noire,** an old Roman archway, is a favorite of tourists who visit the city. Besançon was heav-

ily bombed by the German forces during World War II. **La Citadelle,** a fort built by the architect Vauban during the reign of Louis XIV in the seventeenth century, is a note-worthy historical sight and has a museum dedicated to the World War II Resistance.

Today, Besançon has a population of about 120,000. It is France's clock- and watch-making capital and has a high-tech chronometry center that designed and manufactured resonators for the *Voyager* space probe. It also has research centers in microtechnology and biomedical engineering.

Buts communicatifs

1. Asking and Responding to "How are you?"

Salutations et questions

more formal
Bonjour, Madame (Monsieur, Mademoiselle).
Comment allez-vous?
Vous allez bien?

first-name basis
Salut°, Lori (James, etc.).
Comment ça va?°
Ça va?

Hi
How's it going?

Learn all the words in each *But communicatif.*

Point out that **je vais** is used with adverbs and **je suis** is used with adjectives.

Réponses

Je vais très bien°, merci.	*Very well; I'm fine*
Ça va bien.	
Ça ne va pas mal°.	*Not bad.*
Oh! Comme ci, comme ça.°	*So-so.*
Oh! Pas trop bien.°	*Not too great.*
Je suis assez fatigué(e).°	*I'm rather tired.*
Je suis un peu malade.°	*I'm a little sick.*

▶ **Et vous?** Comment allez-vous?

REMARQUES

1. It is very important to try to tailor your language to fit the situation. For example, with a friend or another student, you would normally ask **Ça va?** or **Comment ça va?** For someone whom you address as **Monsieur, Madame,** or **Mademoiselle,** you would normally say **Comment allez-vous?**
2. **Bonjour** and **bonsoir** are used for both formal **(Monsieur, Madame,** etc.**)** and first-name relationships.
3. The family name **(le nom de famille)** is not used in a greeting. For example, when saying hello to Madame Martin, one says **Bonjour, Madame.**
4. **Salut** is used only in first-name relationships.

Il y a un geste

The gesture for **assez** is explained in Ch. 1, p. 22.

This gesture is used in video, *Module 3.*

Ça va. This gesture implies "so-so" and is very similar to **assez.** Open one or both hands, palms down, and slightly rotate them. This is often accompanied by a slight shrug, and the lips are pursed. One may also say **comme ci, comme ça.**

V O C A B U L A I R E

À quel moment de la journée? *(At what time of day?)*

le jour	*day, daytime*
le matin	*morning, in the morning*
l'après-midi	*afternoon, in the afternoon*
le soir	*evening, in the evening*
la nuit	*night, at night*

Have students work with partners and practice responses as well.

1 **Attention au style.** Greet the following people at the indicated time of day and find out how they are. Adapt your choice of words to fit the time and the person being greeted. Be careful not to be overly familiar. If there is more than one response possible, give both.

MODÈLES: M. Talbot (le matin à 8 h)
Bonjour, Monsieur. Comment allez-vous?

Anne (le soir à 7 h)
Salut, Anne. Comment ça va?   ou
Bonsoir, Anne. Comment ça va?

1. Paul (le soir à 7 h)
2. Mademoiselle Monot (le matin à 9 h 30)
3. Monsieur Talbot (l'après-midi à 4 h)
4. le professeur de français (le matin à 11 h)
5. votre meilleur(e) ami(e) (le soir à 10 h)
6. le (la) président(e) de votre université (l'après-midi à 1 h)

2 **Vous allez bien?** Ask the following people how they are doing. Be careful to choose between the familiar and the formal questions. Your partner will provide the other person's answer.

MODÈLE: Marie (a little sick)
VOUS: **Comment ça va, Marie?**
MARIE: **Oh! je suis un peu malade.**

1. Mme Philippe (tired)
2. Paul (not too great)
3. M. Dupont (sick)
4. Mlle Bernard (very well)
5. Anne (so-so)
6. votre professeur de français (...)
7. votre meilleur(e) ami(e) (...)
8. le (la) président(e) de l'université (...)

A. Le verbe *aller*

■ One of the uses of the verb **aller** *(to go)* is to talk about one's health.

Nous **allons** bien.	*We are fine.*
Comment **vont** vos parents?	*How are your parents?*

aller *(to go)*			
je	**vais**	nous	**allons**
tu	**vas**	vous	**allez**
il/elle/on	**va**	ils/elles	**vont**

See Appendix C, *Glossary of Grammatical Terms,* for an explanation of any terms with which you are not familiar.

■ You will study the verb **aller** again in Chapter 5. It is used, for example, with the infinitive to express the future.

Je **vais boire** une tasse de café.	*I am going to drink a cup of coffee.*

3 **À vous.** Respond.

MODÈLE: Comment vont vos parents?
Ils vont bien. ou
Ils ne vont pas trop bien.

1. Comment va votre professeur?
2. Comment vont les étudiants?
3. Comment allez-vous?
4. Comment va votre meilleur(e) ami(e)?

ENTRE AMIS

Au café

Practice the following situation with as many members of the class as possible.
You are in a sidewalk café at one o'clock in the afternoon.

1. Greet your partner in a culturally appropriate manner.
2. Inquire how s/he is doing.
3. Offer him/her something to drink.
4. What else can you say?

2. Giving and Responding to Compliments

Quelques° compliments   *A few*

Vous parlez très bien le français.°   *You speak French very well.*
Vous dansez très bien.
Vous chantez° bien.   *sing*
Vous skiez vraiment° bien.   *really*
Vous nagez comme un poisson.°   *You swim like a fish.*

Quelques réponses

Examples of the **Vous**
trouvez? response are in
Module 4 and *Module 7* of the
video.

Vous trouvez?°   *Do you think so?*
Pas encore.°   *Not yet.*
Oh! pas vraiment.°   *Not really.*
Oh! je ne sais pas.°   *I don't know.*
C'est gentil mais vous exagérez.°   *That's nice but you're exaggerating.*
Je commence seulement.°   *I'm only beginning.*
Je n'ai pas beaucoup d'expérience.°   *I don't have a lot of experience.*

REMARQUE

There are several ways to express an idea. For instance, there are at least
three ways to compliment someone's French:

Votre français est excellent.   *Your French is excellent.*
Vous parlez bien le français.   *You speak French well.*
Vous êtes bon (bonne) en français.   *You are good in French.*

4 **Un compliment.** Give a compliment to each of the people pictured below. Another student will take the role of the person in the drawing and will provide a culturally appropriate rejoinder.

MODÈLE: —**Vous parlez bien le français.**
—**Vous trouvez? Oh! je ne sais pas.**

1.   2.   3.   4.

B. Les verbes en -er

■ All verb infinitives are made up of a **stem** and an **ending.** To use verbs in the present tense, one removes the ending from the infinitive and adds new endings to the resulting stem. Verbs that use the same endings are often classified according to the last two letters of their infinitive. By far the most common class of verbs is the group ending in **-er.**

parler *(to speak)*	*stem*	*endings*
je	parl	**e**
tu	parl	**es**
il/elle/on	parl	**e**
nous	parl	**ons**
vous	parl	**ez**
ils/elles	parl	**ent**

tomber *(to fall)*	*stem*	*endings*
je	tomb	**e**
tu	tomb	**es**
il/elle/on	tomb	**e**
nous	tomb	**ons**
vous	tomb	**ez**
ils/elles	tomb	**ent**

■ Whether you are talking to a friend (**tu**), or about yourself (**je**), or about one or more other persons (**il, elle, ils, elles**), the verb is pronounced the same because the endings are silent.

Est-ce que tu **patines** bien?	*Do you skate well?*
Non, je ne **patine** pas du tout.	*No, I don't skate at all.*
Anne et Pierre **patinent** bien, n'est-ce pas?	*Anne and Pierre skate well, don't they?*
Elle **patine** bien.	*She skates well.*
Mais Pierre **tombe** souvent.	*But Pierre falls often.*

■ If you are using the **nous** or **vous** form, the verb is pronounced differently. The **-ez** ending is pronounced [e] and the **-ons** ending is pronounced [ɔ̃].

Vous **dansez** avec Marc?	*Do you dance with Marc?*
Nous ne **dansons** pas très souvent.	*We don't dance very often.*

■ Remember that the present tense has only *one* form in French, while it has several forms in English.

*Remember to change **je** to **j'** before a vowel sound. See p. 14.*

je **danse**	*I dance, I do dance, I am dancing*
j'**habite**	*I live, I do live, I am living*

■ Before a vowel sound, the final **-n** of **on** and the final **-s** of **nous, vous, ils,** and **elles** are pronounced and linked to the next word.

On [n]écoute la radio?	*Is someone listening to the radio?*
Nous [z]étudions le français.	*We are studying French.*
Vous [z]habitez ici?	*Do you live here?*

VOCABULAIRE

Suggestion: Have students translate a few expressions, e.g., *She dances well, He is watching TV.*

Activités

chanter (une chanson)	*to sing (a song)*
chercher (mes amis)	*to look for (my friends)*
danser (avec mes amis)	*to dance (with my friends)*
écouter (la radio)	*to listen to (the radio)*
enseigner (le français)	*to teach (French)*
étudier (le français)	*to study (French)*
jouer (au tennis)	*to play (tennis)*
manger	*to eat*
nager	*to swim*
parler (français)	*to speak (French)*
patiner	*to skate*
pleurer	*to cry*
regarder (la télé)	*to watch, to look at (TV)*
skier	*to ski*
travailler (beaucoup)	*to work (a lot)*
voyager (souvent)	*to travel (often)*

NOTE Verbs ending in **-ger** add an **-e-** before the ending in the form used with **nous: nous mangeons, nous nageons, nous voyageons.**

5 **Comparaisons.** Tell what the following people do and then compare yourself to them. Use **Et moi aussi, ...** or **Mais moi, ...** to tell whether or not the statement is also true for you.

MODÈLE: Pierre et Anne/habiter à Angers
Ils habitent à Angers. Mais moi, je n'habite pas à Angers.

1. vous/nager comme un poisson
2. James/parler bien le français
3. Monsieur et Madame Dupont/danser très bien
4. tu/étudier le français
5. vous/chanter vraiment bien
6. tu/regarder souvent la télévision
7. le professeur/enseigner le français
8. Karine et James/travailler beaucoup
9. Sébastien/patiner/mais/il/tomber souvent

6 **Non, pas du tout.** Respond to each question with a negative and follow up with an affirmative answer using the words in parentheses. Supply your own responses for items 5 and 6.

MODÈLES: Je danse *mal*, n'est-ce pas? (bien)
Non, pas du tout. Vous ne dansez pas mal; vous dansez bien.

Vous *écoutez la radio?* (regarder la télé)
Non, pas du tout. Je n'écoute pas la radio; je regarde la télé.

1. Vous *enseignez* le français? (étudier)
2. Le professeur *voyage* beaucoup? (travailler)
3. Est-ce que je chante *très mal?* (assez bien)
4. Vous *chantez* avec le professeur? (parler français)
5. Vous habitez *à Paris?* (...)
6. Est-ce que nous étudions *l'espagnol?* (...)

VOCABULAIRE

Des gens que je connais bien (People that I know well)

mon ami	*my (male) friend*
mon amie	*my (female) friend*
mes amis	*my friends*
ma mère	*my mother*
mon père	*my father*
le professeur	*the (male or female) teacher*
les étudiants	*the students*
ma camarade de chambre	*my (female) roommate*
mon camarade de chambre	*my (male) roommate*
ma petite amie	*my girlfriend*
mon petit ami	*my boyfriend*

Suggestion: Follow up with a stand-up drill; see the Class Prep CD-ROM.

7 **Mes connaissances.** Tell about your family and your acquaintances by choosing an item from each list to create as many factual sentences as you can. You may make any of them negative.

MODÈLES: **Nous ne dansons pas mal.**
Mon amie Mary n'étudie pas le français.

	chanter bien
les étudiants	travailler beaucoup
le professeur	écouter souvent la radio
je	étudier le français
nous	skier bien
ma mère	danser mal
mon père	patiner beaucoup
mes amis	habiter en France
mon ami(e) _____	parler français
mon petit ami	nager comme un poisson
ma petite amie	voyager souvent
	pleurer souvent
	regarder souvent la télévision

Culture: Explain that, although it is not being practiced here, it is also possible to have a first-name relationship with some people and still use the pronoun **vous.** This will be explained in Ch. 3, p. 58.

8 **Tu parles bien le français!** Pay compliments to the following friends. Use **tu** for each individual; use **vous** for more than one person.

MODÈLES: Éric skie bien.
Tu skies bien!

Yann et Sophie dansent bien.
Vous dansez bien!

1. Alissa est très jolie.
2. Christophe parle très bien l'espagnol.
3. David est bon en français.
4. François et Michel parlent bien l'anglais.
5. Ils travaillent beaucoup aussi.
6. Anne et Marie sont vraiment bonnes en maths.
7. Elles chantent bien aussi.
8. Olivier est vraiment très beau.
9. Luc skie comme un champion olympique.

9 **Identification.** Answer the following questions as factually as possible.

MODÈLE: Qui parle bien le français?
Le professeur parle bien le français.
Mes amis parlent bien le français.

Communication (Interpretive): Have students ask you the questions first; then (books closed) ask them the questions.

1. Qui étudie le français?
2. Qui enseigne le français?
3. Qui ne skie pas du tout?
4. Qui chante très bien?
5. Qui joue mal au tennis?
6. Qui regarde souvent la télévision?
7. Qui écoute souvent la radio?

ENTRE AMIS

Suggestion: Follow up with a chain drill; see the Class Prep CD-ROM.

Avec un(e) ami(e)

Practice the following situation with as many members of the class as possible.

1. Pay your partner a compliment.
2. Your partner will give a culturally appropriate response to the compliment and then pay you a compliment in return.
3. Give an appropriate response.

3. Offering, Accepting, and Refusing

Point out the pronunciation of **eau** [o] in the Wisconsin city *Eau Claire.*

NOTE CULTURELLE
Les jeunes Américains aiment beaucoup le lait. Mais, en général, les jeunes Français n'aiment pas le lait.

Pour offrir une boisson°	*To offer a drink*
Voulez-vous boire quelque chose?	
Voulez-vous un verre d'orangina°?	*orange soda*
Voulez-vous un verre de (d') ... ?	
bière°?	*beer*
eau°?	*water*
jus d'orange°?	*orange juice*
lait°?	*milk*
Voulez-vous une tasse de ... ?	
café?	
chocolat chaud°?	*hot chocolate*
Qu'est-ce que° vous voulez?	*What*

Pour accepter ou refuser quelque chose°	*To accept or refuse something*
Je veux bien.	
Volontiers.°	*Gladly.*
S'il vous plaît.	
Oui, avec plaisir.°	*Yes, with pleasure.*
Oui, c'est gentil à vous.°	*Yes, that's nice of you.*
Merci.	
Non, merci.	

Review the gesture for **Non, merci** on p. 30.

▶ **Et vous?** Est-ce que vous voulez boire quelque chose?

10 **Voulez-vous boire quelque chose?** Use the list of words below to create a dialogue in which one person offers a glass or a cup of something to drink and the other responds appropriately.

MODÈLES: Coca-Cola
—**Voulez-vous un verre de coca?**
—**Volontiers.**

coffee
—**Voulez-vous une tasse de café?**
—**Non, merci.**

1. water	4. wine	7. hot chocolate
2. tea	5. milk	8. beer
3. orange soda	6. orange juice	

www Réalités culturelles

Le café

A time-honored tradition in France is the outdoor café, a place with small tables on the sidewalk (**la terrasse**) where friends spend time talking and having drinks. Others come to the café to read their newspaper, write letters, or just watch people passing by. The French cafés are like mini-restaurants. You can order a drink and sometimes a sandwich or snack, but usually not a full meal. The cafés are open from early morning to very late in the evening. In the winter, large cafés enclose the **terrasse** in glass partitions so that one can still enjoy watching life on the street.

For the French, especially Parisians, the cultural tradition of meeting others at the café is most likely due to the cramped nature of urban living in Paris, where apartments are usually small, and the privacy the French reserve for their homes. Often even friends may not be invited "inside," but are met in cafés instead.

Le Procope, founded in 1686, is reputed to be the oldest café in Paris, having served such well-known figures as Voltaire, Balzac, Victor Hugo, and Benjamin Franklin. Other cafés popular with tourists are **Café de Flore** and **Deux Magots**, gathering spots in the early twentieth century for intellectuals and poets.

Pronounce the items on the menu for students before they begin.

11 **Qu'est-ce que vous voulez?** Examine the drink menu of **La Bague d'or** *(The Golden Ring)* and order something.

MODÈLES: **Je voudrais une tasse de thé.**
Je voudrais un verre de coca-cola, s'il vous plaît.

Comparison: Have students compare this with a typical list of drinks in their country.

La Bague d'or
BRASSERIE ALSACIENNE

Boissons

Vin rouge

Riesling (Vin d'Alsace)

Jus de fruits

Bière (pression)

Café

Thé

Chocolat chaud

Coca-cola

Orangina

Eau minérale (Perrier)

C. L'article défini: *le, la, l'* et *les*

■ You have already learned that all nouns in French have gender — that is, they are classified grammatically as either masculine or feminine. You also know that you need to remember the gender for each noun you learn. One of the functions of French articles is to mark the gender (masculine or feminine) and the number (singular or plural) of a noun.

forms of the definite article	when to use	examples
le (l')	before a masculine singular noun	**le** thé
la (l')	before a feminine singular noun	**la** bière
les	before all plural nouns, masculine or feminine	**les** boissons

■ **Le** and **la** become **l'** when followed by a word that begins with a vowel sound. This includes many words that begin with the letter **h.**

le professeur
 but **l'**étudiant, **l'**ami, **l'**homme
la femme
 but **l'**étudiante, **l'**amie

■ When they are used to refer to specific things or persons known to both the speaker and the listener, **le, la, l',** and **les** all correspond to the English definite article *the.*

Le professeur écoute **les** étudiants. *The teacher listens to the students.*
L'université de Paris est excellente. *The University of Paris is excellent.*

■ **Le, la, l',** and **les** are also used before nouns that have a generic meaning, even when in English the word *the* would not be used.

Le lait est bon pour **la** santé. *Milk is good for your health.*
Elle regarde souvent **la** télé. *She often watches TV.*
J'étudie **le** chinois. *I'm studying Chinese.*

Review nationalities, p. 18.

■ All languages are masculine. Many are derived from the adjective of nationality. All verbs except **parler** require **le** before the name of a language. With **parler, le** is normally kept if there is an adverb directly after the verb, but is normally omitted if there is no adverb directly after the verb.

Ils **étudient le** russe. *They are studying Russian.*
Ma mère **parle bien le** français. *My mother speaks French well.*
Mon père **parle** français **aussi.** *My father speaks French too.*

VOCABULAIRE

Pour répondre à Comment? *(How?)*

très bien	*very well*
(vraiment) bien	*(really) well*
assez bien	*rather well*
un peu	*a bit*
assez mal	*rather poorly*
(vraiment) mal	*(really) poorly*
ne ... pas du tout	*not at all*

12 **Parlez-vous bien le français?** For each language, describe how well you and a friend of yours (**mon ami(e) ____**) speak it.

MODÈLE: l'allemand
Je ne parle pas du tout l'allemand mais mon ami Hans parle très bien l'allemand.

*Remind students to use **mais** or **et** when comparing themselves and a friend.*

1. le russe   2. l'espagnol   3. l'anglais   4. le français

13 **À vous.** Practice asking and answering the following questions with your partners.

*Remember that **Est-ce que ...?** just signals a question; **Qu'est-ce que ...?** means What ...?*

1. Qu'est-ce que vous étudiez?
2. Étudiez-vous le français le matin, l'après-midi ou le soir?
3. Étudiez-vous aussi l'anglais?
4. Parlez-vous souvent avec le professeur de français?
5. Est-ce que le professeur chante avec la classe?
6. Est-ce que le professeur de français parle anglais?
7. Parlez-vous bien le français?
8. Parlez-vous un peu l'espagnol?

ENTRE AMIS

Une réception

You are at a reception at the French consulate.

1. Greet your partner and inquire how s/he is.
2. Offer him/her something to drink.
3. S/he will accept appropriately.
4. Toast each other.
5. Compliment each other on your ability in French.
6. Respond appropriately to the compliment.

4. Expressing Likes and Dislikes

Qu'est-ce que tu aimes, Sophie?
  J'aime beaucoup le vin blanc°. *white wine*
  J'adore voyager.
  J'aime bien danser.
Moi aussi°, j'aime voyager et danser. *Me too*
Et qu'est-ce que tu n'aimes pas?
  Je n'aime pas le vin rosé.
  Je déteste le coca.
  Je n'aime pas chanter.
  Je n'aime pas beaucoup travailler.
Moi non plus°, je n'aime pas travailler. *Me neither*

Communication (Presentational): Follow up pair practice by having several students share their responses with the class.

▶ **Et vous?** Qu'est-ce que vous aimez?
  Qu'est-ce que vous n'aimez pas?

REMARQUES

1. When there are two verbs in succession, the second is not conjugated. It remains in the infinitive form.

Mon ami **déteste nager** dans l'eau froide. *My friend hates to swim in cold water.*
Les étudiants **aiment parler** français. *The students like to speak French.*
Francis **désire danser.** *Francis wants to dance.*

2. The use of **le, la, l',** and **les** to express a generality occurs particularly after verbs expressing preferences.

Marie adore **le** chocolat chaud. *Marie loves hot chocolate.*
Elle aime **les** boissons chaudes. *She likes hot drinks.*
Mais elle déteste **la** bière. *But she hates beer.*
Et elle n'aime pas **l'**eau minérale. *And she doesn't like mineral water.*

3. Be careful to distinguish between **j'aime** and **je voudrais.** Use **je voudrais** (*I would like*) when choosing something. Use **j'aime** or **je n'aime pas** to express whether or not you like it.

Je **voudrais** une tasse de thé. *I'd like a cup of tea.*
Je n'**aime** pas le café. *I don't like coffee.*

Prime this by having students "predict" your tastes, e.g., **Le professeur adore skier.** Respond **oui** or **non.**

14 **Qu'est-ce qu'ils aiment?** Tell, as truthfully as possible, what the following people like and don't like by combining items from each of the three lists. Guess, if you don't know for certain. How many sentences can you create?

MODÈLES: **Mes amis détestent le lait.**
  Je n'aime pas du tout skier.

		skier
		travailler
		la bière
		le français
	adorer	la télévision
mes amis	aimer beaucoup	chanter
le professeur	ne pas aimer vraiment	patiner
je	ne pas aimer du tout	danser
nous	détester	le lait
		l'université
		voyager
		nager
		enseigner

15 **Vous aimez danser?** Use the words below to interview the person sitting next to you. Find out if s/he likes to dance, to swim, etc. Use **aimer** in every question.

MODÈLE: dance

> VOUS: **Vous aimez danser?**
> VOTRE PARTENAIRE: **Oui, j'aime (beaucoup) danser.** ou
> **Non, je n'aime pas (beaucoup) danser.**

Communication (Presentational): Follow up by asking students to share what they learned about their partner, e.g., **Elle aime beaucoup étudier le français.**

1. sing
2. swim
3. watch television
4. ski
5. study
6. study French
7. work
8. travel
9. play tennis
10. speak French

VOCABULAIRE

Popular mineral waters are **Vichy, Évian, Vittel, Perrier. Coca** and **orangina** are brand names often used generically.

NOTE CULTURELLE
La limonade française ressemble beaucoup à la boisson *7-Up.* La boisson américaine *lemonade* est **le citron pressé** en France.

Le café au lait est moitié *(half)* café, moitié lait chaud.

Quelques boissons populaires

le café	*coffee*	le coca	*cola*
le café au lait	*coffee with milk*	la limonade	*lemon-lime soda*
le café crème	*coffee with cream*	l'orangina *m.*	*orangina (an orange soda)*
le chocolat chaud	*hot chocolate*		
le citron pressé	*lemonade*	la bière	*beer*
l'eau minérale *f.*	*mineral water*	le kir	*kir*
le jus d'orange	*orange juice*	le vin	*wine*
le thé	*tea*		

16 **Vous aimez le café?** First use the preceding list of **boissons populaires** to order something. Then take an (imaginary) sip. Finally, your partner will ask if you like it. Respond.

MODÈLE:

> le café
> VOUS: **Je voudrais une tasse de café.**
> VOTRE PARTENAIRE: **Est-ce que vous aimez le café?**
> VOUS: **Oui, j'aime le café.** ou
> **Non, je n'aime pas le café.**

Remember to distinguish between **un verre** and **une tasse.**

17 **En général, les étudiants ...** Decide whether you agree (**C'est vrai**) or disagree (**C'est faux**) with the following statements. If you disagree, correct the statement.

MODÈLE: En général, les étudiants détestent voyager.
C'est faux. En général, ils aiment beaucoup voyager.

1. En général, les étudiants n'aiment pas du tout danser.
2. En général, les étudiants détestent la pizza.
3. En général, les étudiants aiment beaucoup étudier.
4. En général, les étudiants n'aiment pas beaucoup regarder la télévision.
5. En général, les étudiants aiment nager.
6. En général, les étudiants aiment skier.
7. En général, les étudiants aiment beaucoup patiner.
8. En général, les étudiants détestent chanter.
9. En général, les étudiants aiment parler français avec le professeur.
10. En général, les étudiants désirent habiter à New York.

18 **Comment trouvez-vous le café français?** (*What do you think of French coffee?*) Your partner will ask you to give your opinion about something you have tasted. Use **aimer, adorer,** or **détester** in an answer that reflects your own opinion. Or make up an imaginary opinion. You might also say **Je ne sais pas, mais ...** and offer an opinion about something else that is related, instead.

MODÈLE: les tamalis mexicains
VOTRE PARTENAIRE: **Comment trouvez-vous les tamalis mexicains?**
VOUS: **J'aime beaucoup les tamalis mexicains.** ou
Je ne sais pas, mais j'adore les enchiladas.

Encourage students to respond **Moi aussi** or **Moi non plus** if they agree with their partner's opinion.

Culture & Comparison: Ask students which of these associations are the same in their country.

1. le thé anglais
2. le chocolat suisse
3. la pizza italienne
4. l'eau minérale française
5. le jus d'orange de Floride
6. le café de Colombie
7. la limonade française
8. la bière allemande
9. le vin français

D. Les questions avec réponse *oui* ou *non*

■ In spoken French, by far the most frequently used way of asking a question that can be answered *yes* or *no* is by simply raising the voice at the end of the sentence.

Vous parlez français?   *Do you speak French?*

Lori est américaine?   *Is Lori American?*

Hélène danse bien?   *Does Hélène dance well?*

■ **Est-ce que** is often placed at the beginning of a sentence to form a question. It becomes **Est-ce qu'** before a vowel sound.

Est-ce que vous parlez français?	*Do you speak French?*
Est-ce que Lori est américaine?	*Is Lori American?*
Est-ce qu'Hélène danse bien?	*Does Hélène dance well?*

Have students give the probable response to these questions: **Mais oui, je parle français,** etc.

■ The phrase **n'est-ce pas?** (*right?, aren't you?, doesn't he?,* etc.), added at the end of a sentence, expects an affirmative answer.

Vous parlez français, **n'est-ce pas?**	*You speak French, don't you?*
Lori est américaine, **n'est-ce pas?**	*Lori is American, isn't she?*
Hélène danse bien, **n'est-ce pas?**	*Hélène dances well, doesn't she?*

■ Another question form, which is used more often in written French than in speech and which is characteristic of a more formal speech style, is *inversion* of the verb and its *pronoun* subject. When inversion is used, there is a hyphen between the verb and the pronoun.

Parlez-vous français?	*Do you speak French?*
Aimez-vous chanter?	*Do you like to sing?*
Êtes-vous américain(e)?	*Are you American?*

NOTE — If the third person (**il, elle, on, ils, elles**) is used in inversion, there is always a **[t]** sound between the verb and the subject pronoun. If the verb ends in a vowel, a written **-t-** is added between the final vowel of the verb and the initial vowel of the pronoun. If the verb ends in **-t,** no extra **-t-** is necessary.

	Enseigne-**t-**il le français?	*Does he teach French?*
	Aime-**t-**elle voyager?	*Does she like to travel?*
But:	Aimen**t-**ils voyager?	*Do they like to travel?*
	Es**t-**elle française?	*Is she French?*
	Son**t-**ils américains?	*Are they American?*

FOR RECOGNITION ONLY

Some material is taught initially for recognition only. Inversion with a noun is made active in Ch. 5.

If the subject is a noun, the inversion form can be produced by adding the pronoun of the same number and gender after the verb.

noun + verb + pronoun

Karen est-elle américaine?	*Is Karen American?*
Thierry aime-t-il la bière?	*Does Thierry like beer?*
Nathalie et Stéphane aiment-ils danser?	*Do Nathalie and Stéphane like to dance?*

Review the gesture for
Comment?, p. 6.

19 **Comment?** *(What did you say?)* We are often obliged to repeat a question when someone doesn't hear or understand us. For each question with inversion, ask a question beginning with **Est-ce que** and a question ending with **n'est-ce pas.**

MODÈLES: James habite-t-il à San Francisco?
   VOTRE PARTENAIRE: **Comment?**
   VOUS: **Est-ce que James habite à San Francisco?**
   VOTRE PARTENAIRE: **Comment?**
   VOUS: **James habite à San Francisco, n'est-ce pas?**

1. James est-il américain?
2. Étudie-t-il le français?
3. Parle-t-il bien le français?
4. Aime-t-il Karine Aspel?
5. Karine est-elle française?
6. Allez-vous bien?

20 **Une enquête entre amis** *(A survey among friends).* Use the following list to determine the likes and dislikes of two classmates. Be prepared to report back the results of your "survey" to the class. Are there any items on which all the students agree completely?

MODÈLES: skier   —**Est-ce que tu aimes skier?**
                  —**Oui, j'adore skier.**

   le jogging   —**Est-ce que tu aimes le jogging?**
                  —**Non, je n'aime pas le jogging.**   ou
                      Non, je déteste le jogging. Je n'aime pas les sports.

1. parler français
2. parler avec le professeur de français
3. voyager
4. regarder la télévision
5. chanter en français
6. la politique
7. l'université
8. étudier le français
9. nager dans l'eau froide
10. travailler beaucoup

21 **Les Dupont.*** Here are a few facts about the Dupont family. Interview a classmate to find out if this information is also true for him/her.

MODÈLES: Les Dupont habitent à Marseille.
   VOUS: **Habites-tu à Marseille aussi?**
   VOTRE PARTENAIRE: **Non, je n'habite pas à Marseille.**

Review the verb **être,** p. 14,
and **-er** verbs, p. 38.

   Gérard et Martine sont mariés.
   VOUS: **Es-tu marié(e) aussi?**
   VOTRE PARTENAIRE: **Non, je ne suis pas marié(e).**   ou
                      Oui, je suis marié(e) aussi.

1. Martine adore voyager.
2. Gérard Dupont aime la limonade.
3. Les Dupont sont malades.
4. Martine Dupont parle un peu l'espagnol.
5. Monsieur et Madame Dupont aiment beaucoup danser.
6. Les Dupont voyagent beaucoup.

An **-s is not added to family names in French; the article **les** indicates the plural.*

ENTRE AMIS

À un bal

Practice the following situation with as many members of the class as possible. You are at a dance and are meeting people for the first time. Use **vous.**

1. Say good evening and introduce yourself.
2. Find out if your partner likes to dance.
3. Ask your partner if s/he wants to dance. (S/he does.)
4. Tell your partner that s/he dances well.
5. Offer your partner something to drink.
6. Toast each other.
7. Compliment each other on your ability in French.
8. Respond appropriately to the compliment.

Intégration

Communication & Communities: The web search activities for this chapter will expose students to several topics, including museums, movies, and shopping.

Révision

A **Trouvez quelqu'un qui ... (*Find someone who ... *).** Interview your classmates in French to find someone who ...

Prime for this activity by eliciting questions. Then have students move about interviewing classmates. Allow 5 minutes, then check to see who has the most answers.

MODÈLE: speaks French **Est-ce que tu parles français?**

1. likes coffee
2. swims often
3. doesn't like beer
4. sings poorly
5. studies a lot
6. doesn't ski
7. is tired
8. hates to work
9. likes to travel
10. cries often
11. skates

Communication (Presentational): Have students present their descriptions to the class. Suggestion: Assign the *Rédaction* at the end of Ch. 2 in the Workbook.

B **Début de rédaction.** Choose three people you know. Tell where they live (city), describe their language ability, and indicate their likes and dislikes.

MODÈLE: **Mon amie Barbara habite à Chicago. Elle étudie le français et elle parle un peu l'espagnol. Elle adore voyager, mais elle n'aime pas beaucoup travailler. Elle déteste la bière.**

Communication (Interpretive): Encourage students to use the practice test on the Lab Audio Program.

C **À vous.** How would you respond to the following questions and comments?

1. Parlez-vous français?
2. Comment allez-vous?
3. Où habitez-vous?
4. Voulez-vous boire quelque chose?
5. Si oui, qu'est-ce que vous désirez boire?
6. Vous parlez très bien le français!
7. Vous étudiez l'espagnol, n'est-ce pas?
8. Aimez-vous voyager?
9. Est-ce que vous aimez danser?
10. Qu'est-ce que vous n'aimez pas?

Remind students of the difference between **Est-ce que** and **Qu'est-ce que**, pp. 45 & 49.

Négociations:

For complete instructions on how to prepare for and to use this activity, see *Négociations* on the Class Prep CD-ROM.

Video for Chapter 2: A. Video worksheets (*Cahier*); B. ACE Video practice test (WWW); C. CD-ROM

Les activités. Use the form below to interview as many students as possible. Other students will use one of the forms in Appendix D. Try to find people who answer the questions affirmatively, then write their initials in the appropriate boxes. No student's initials should be used more than twice.

MODÈLE: **Est-ce que tu détestes les hot-dogs?**

A		
écouter la radio le matin	jouer au tennis	parler espagnol
chanter une chanson française	aimer patiner	étudier l'anglais
tomber quelquefois	détester les hot-dogs	être célibataire
adorer skier	pleurer quelquefois	aimer étudier le français

Lecture

Comparison: Have students list the cognates they find in the ad. Be sure they do not include false cognates.

The following reading selection is taken directly from the *Gab,* a weekly newspaper published in Besançon. It is not vital that you understand every word.

A **Étude du vocabulaire.** There are words in French that we refer to as **faux amis** *(false friends, false cognates),* since they mean something different from the English word they seem to resemble. Study the following sentences and match the **faux ami,** in bold print, with the correct meaning in English: *understanding, reading, sensitive.*

La lecture est mon passe-temps préféré.
Florence est timide et très **sensible.**
Nous aimons les professeurs **compréhensifs.**

B **Familles de mots** *(Word families).* Can you guess the meanings of the following words? One member of each word family is found in the reading.

1. comprendre, compréhensif, compréhensive, la compréhension
2. recevoir, une réception
3. sortir, une sortie
4. lire, un lecteur, une lectrice, la lecture

Connections: Readers can often anticipate information they will read by using their knowledge of a topic to help predict some of the content. This reading deals with a dating service.

SEUL(E) ET LAS(SE) DE L'ÊTRE*

VOUS ASPIREZ À NOUER UNE RELATION SENTIMENTALE DURABLE

Simplement, facilement, vous pouvez connaître quelqu'un
qui comme vous est motivé par une vie de couple stable.

Depuis 1975
ANDRÉE MOUGENOT CONSEILLÈRE DIPLÔMÉE
10 RUE DE LA RÉPUBLIQUE BESANÇON

fait des heureux

Retournez tout simplement le bon ci-dessous, vous recevrez gratuitement sans aucune marque extérieure un exemple de proposition de mise en relation.

JE SUIS

Nom et prénom..   Célibataire ☐ Veuf(ve) ☐ Divorcé(e) ☐
Adresse   J'aime recevoir ☐ Sortir ☐ Danser ☐
                                                           Le sport ☐ La nature ☐ Bricoler ☐
....
Âge .... Taille ....   Jardiner ☐ Voyager ☐ La lecture ☐
Profession .... La musique ☐

JE CHERCHE

Célibataire ☐ Veuf(ve) ☐ Divorcé(e) ☐   Simple ☐ Gai(e) ☐ Loyal(e) ☐ Calme ☐
Âgé(e) de........ à........ans   Amusant(e) ☐ Tendre ☐ Sensible ☐
Études souhaitées ....   Compréhensif(ve) ☐ Affectueux(se) ☐
Profession souhaitée   Sincère ☐ Tolérant(e) ☐ Conciliant(e) ☐
                                                           Passionné(e) ☐ Dynamique ☐
....

Autres caractéristiques ....
....

*Alone and tired of it.   Le Gab n° 648 (Besançon)

Communication (Presentational): Ask a few students to present their descriptions to the class.

C **Autoportrait** *(Self-portrait).* Describe *yourself* using five adjectives from the **Je cherche** section of the reading.

MODÈLE: célibataire, loyal(e), …

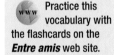 **Practice this vocabulary with the flashcards on the *Entre amis* web site.**

VOCABULAIRE ACTIF

Quelque chose à boire
la bière *beer*
une boisson *drink*
le café *coffee*
le café au lait *coffee with milk*
le café crème *coffee with cream*
le chocolat chaud *hot chocolate*
le citron pressé *lemonade*
le coca *cola*
l'eau *f.* (minérale) *(mineral) water*
le jus d'orange *orange juice*
le kir *kir*
le lait *milk*
la limonade *lemon-lime soda*
l'orangina *m.* orangina *(an orange soda)*

le thé *tea*
le vin (rouge, blanc, rosé) *(red, white, rosé) wine*

Des gens que je connais bien
les étudiants *the students*
ma camarade de chambre *my (female) roommate*
ma mère *my mother*
ma petite amie *my girlfriend*
mes amis *my friends*
mon ami(e) *my friend*
mon camarade de chambre *my (male) roommate*
mon père *my father*
mon petit ami *my boyfriend*

D'autres noms et pronoms
une chanson *song*
le jogging *jogging*
la pizza *pizza*
un poisson *fish*
la politique *politics*
quelque chose *something*
quelqu'un *someone*
la radio *radio*
une soirée *an evening party*
une tasse *cup*
la télévision (la télé) *television (TV)*
un verre *glass*

Adjectifs

bon (bonne) *good*
chaud(e) *hot*
cher (chère) *dear*
excellent(e) *excellent*
fatigué(e) *tired*
faux (fausse) *false; wrong*
froid(e) *cold*
malade *sick*
vrai(e) *true*

Pour répondre à un compliment

Vous trouvez? *Do you think so?*
Pas encore. *Not yet.*
Oh! Pas vraiment. *Not really.*
Je ne sais pas. *I don't know.*
C'est gentil mais vous exagérez.
   That's nice but you're exaggerating.
Je commence seulement. *I'm only beginning.*
Je n'ai pas beaucoup d'expéri-ence. *I don't have a lot of experience.*

Articles définis

le, la, l', les *the*

Verbes

aller *to go; to be + adverb (health)*
chanter *to sing*
chercher *to look for*
danser *to dance*
désirer *to want*
écouter *to listen to*
enseigner *to teach*
étudier *to study*
habiter *to live; to reside*
jouer (au tennis) *to play (tennis)*
manger *to eat*
nager *to swim*
parler *to speak*
patiner *to skate*
pleurer *to cry*
regarder *to watch; to look at*
skier *to ski*
tomber *to fall*
travailler *to work*
trouver *to find; to be of the opinion*
voyager *to travel*

Mots invariables

alors *then, therefore, so*
avec *with*
beaucoup *a lot*
bien *well; fine*
comme *like*
en général *in general*
ensemble *together*
mais *but*
mal *poorly; badly*
peut-être *maybe; perhaps*
pour *for; in order to*
pourquoi *why*
seulement *only*
souvent *often*
un peu *a little bit*
vraiment *really*

À quel moment de la journée?

à ... heure(s) *at ... o'clock*
le jour *day, daytime*
le matin *morning, in the morning*
l'après-midi *afternoon, in the afternoon*
le soir *evening, in the evening*
la nuit *night, at night*

Pour demander à quelqu'un comment il va

Comment allez-vous? *How are you?*
Vous allez bien? *Are you well?*
(Comment) ça va? *How is it going?*
Je vais très bien. *Very well.*
Ça va bien. *(I'm) fine.*
Comme ci, comme ça. *So-so.*
Assez bien. *Fairly well.*
Je suis fatigué(e). *I am tired.*
Je suis un peu malade. *I am a little sick.*
Pas trop bien. *Not too well.*
Ça ne va pas mal. *I'm not feeling bad.*

Pour offrir, accepter et refuser quelque chose

Voulez-vous boire quelque chose? *Do you want to drink something?*
Je veux bien. *Gladly. Yes, thanks.*
Volontiers. *Gladly.*
S'il vous plaît. *Please.*
Oui, avec plaisir. *Yes, with pleasure.*
Oui, c'est gentil à vous. *Yes, that's nice of you.*
Merci. *No, thank you.*
Non, merci. *No, thank you.*
Je voudrais ... *I would like ...*

Verbes de préférence

adorer *to adore; to love*
aimer *to like; to love*
détester *to hate; to detest*

D'autres expressions utiles

Bonsoir. *Good evening.*
Comment? *What (did you say)?*
est-ce que ... ? *(question marker)*
n'est-ce pas? *right? are you? don't they? etc.*
Comment est-ce qu'on écrit ... ? *How do you spell ... ?*
Comment trouvez-vous ... ? *What do you think of ... ?*
Qu'est-ce que vous aimez? *What do you like?*
Qu'est-ce que vous voulez? *What do you want?*
Vous êtes d'où? *Where are you from?*
Quelle bonne surprise! *What a good surprise!*
À votre santé! *(Here's) to your health!*
À la vôtre! *(Here's) to yours!*
Au fait ... *By the way ...*
Je ne sais pas. *I don't know.*
Je viens de ... *I come from ...*
... s'écrit ... ... *is spelled ...*
même(s) *-self (-selves)*
moi aussi *me too*
moi non plus *me neither*
Salut! *Hi!; Bye!*

Chez nous

Coup d'envoi

Prise de contact   **Une photo de ma famille**

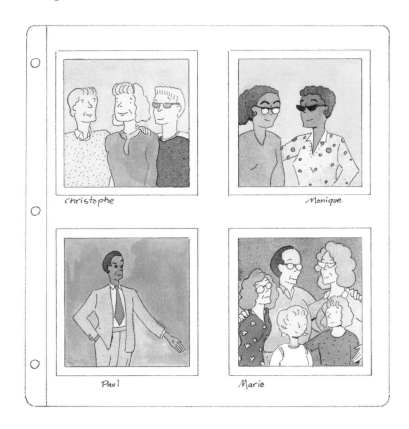

MARIE:	Avez-vous des frères ou des sœurs?°
CHRISTOPHE:	J'ai° un frère et une sœur.
MONIQUE:	J'ai une sœur, mais je n'ai pas de° frère.
PAUL:	Moi, je n'ai pas de frère ou de sœur.
MARIE:	Dans° ma famille il y a° cinq personnes. Il y a trois enfants°, deux filles° et un garçon°. Ma sœur s'appelle° Chantal et mon frère s'appelle Robert. Mes parents s'appellent Bernard et Sophie.

Do you have any brothers or sisters? / I have

I don't have any

In / there are
children / girls
boy / My sister's name is

▶ **Et vous?** Avez-vous des frères ou des sœurs?
Avez-vous une photo de votre famille?
Qui est sur la photo?°

Who is in the picture?

Communication (Presentational): Once the **Prise de contact** has been practiced, have students present real or imaginary photos to their classmates.

Conversation

L'arrivée à la gare

Lori Becker est une étudiante américaine qui vient en France pour passer un an° dans une famille française. Elle descend du train à la gare° Saint-Laud à Angers. Anne Martin et sa fille°, Émilie, attendent° son arrivée.

year
railroad station
daughter / are waiting for

MME MARTIN:	Mademoiselle Becker?
LORI:	Oui. Bonjour, Madame. Vous êtes bien Madame Martin?°
MME MARTIN:	Oui. Bonjour et bienvenue°, Mademoiselle. Vous êtes très fatiguée, sans doute°?
LORI:	Pas trop°. J'ai dormi° un peu dans le train.
MME MARTIN:	Mademoiselle Becker, voilà ma fille.
LORI:	Bonjour, tu t'appelles comment?
LA PETITE FILLE:	Émilie.
LORI:	Et tu as quel âge?° *The child holds up her thumb and two fingers.*
MME MARTIN:	Elle a trois ans.
LORI:	Elle est charmante.° Vous avez d'autres enfants°, Madame Martin?
MME MARTIN:	Oui, nous avons six enfants.
LORI:	Comment? Combien dites-vous?°
MME MARTIN:	Six.
LORI:	Mon Dieu°! Vraiment?
MME MARTIN:	Pourquoi? Qu'est-ce qu'il y a?°
LORI:	Euh ... rien°. J'aime beaucoup les enfants.

You're Mme Martin, aren't you?
welcome

probably
too much / I slept

And how old are you?

She's charming.
other children

How many do you say?

God
What's the matter?
nothing

▶ Jouez ces rôles. Role-play the conversation exactly as if you were Lori Becker and Mme Martin. Once you have practiced it several times, role-play the conversation using one partner's identity in place of Lori's.

After practicing the *Conversation,* have students complete ex. A in the Workbook.

Il y a un geste

This gesture is used at the start of the *Pas de problème* video, *Module 1,* and again in *Module 4.*

Voilà. The open hand is extended, palm up, to emphasize that some fact is evident. **Voilà** is also used to conclude something that has been said or to express that that's how things are.

À propos

Why does Lori say "Mon Dieu!"?

a. She is swearing.
b. She is praying.
c. She is expressing surprise.

Why does Lori use **tu** with Émilie Martin?

a. They have met before and are good friends.
b. She is speaking to a child.
c. Lori considers Émilie an inferior.

La langue et la culture

Each language has its own unique way of expressing reality. The fact that French uses the verb **avoir** *(to have)* when expressing age, whereas English uses the verb *to be,* is only one of many examples that prove that languages are not copies of each other. Similarly, the expression **Mon Dieu!** *(Wow!)* is milder in French than its literal English equivalent *My God!* The French way is not right or wrong, nor is it more or less logical than its English counterpart. In addition, one language may have separate expressions to convey two concepts, while another language uses the same expression for both.

English	French
girl/daughter	**fille** (see pp. 56–57)
there are	**voilà/il y a** (see p. 70)

Les pronoms *tu et vous*

French has two ways of saying *you.* The choice reflects the nature of the relationship, including degree of formality and respect. **Tu** is typically used when speaking to one's family and relatives as well as to close friends, fellow students, children, and animals. **Vous** is normally used when speaking to someone who does not meet the above criteria (e.g., in-laws, employers, teachers, or business acquaintances). It expresses a more formal relationship or a greater social distance than **tu.** In addition, **vous** is always used to refer to more than one person.

Visitors to French-speaking countries would be well advised to use **vous** even if first names are being used, unless they are invited to use the **tu** form. In the *Conversation,* Lori correctly uses **vous** with Madame Martin and **tu** with Émilie.

La famille et les amis

Very attached to home, family, and friends, the French are usually fond of family reunions, picnics, and gatherings with close friends, which provide an opportunity to nurture these relationships. They are often equally attached to the region in which they live. It is common to find homes that have been lived in by successive generations of the same family.

Pour gagner du temps *(To stall for time)*

A helpful strategy for the language learner is to acquire and use certain expressions and gestures that allow him or her to "buy time" to think without destroying the conversational flow or without resorting to English. Like the cup of coffee we sip during a conversation to give us a chance to organize our thoughts, there are a number of useful expressions for "buying time" in French. The number one gap-filler is **euh,** which is the French equivalent of the English *uh* or *umm.* Some useful expressions follow.

continued

VOCABULAIRE

Euh rhymes with **deux. Ben** [bɛ̃] is derived from **bien**.

Students hear many of these expressions in the video.

Pour gagner du temps *(To stall for time)*

alors	*then; therefore, so*	euh	*uh; umm*
ben	*well*	hein?	*huh?*
bon	*good*	mais ...	*but ...*
comment?	*what (did you say)?*	oui ...	*yes ...*
eh bien	*well then*	tiens!	*well, well!*
et ...	*and ...*	voyons	*let's see*

▶ **À vous.** How would you respond to the following?

1. Comment s'appellent vos parents?
2. Vous avez des frères ou des sœurs?
3. (Si oui) Comment s'appellent-ils (elles)?
4. Où habitent-ils (elles)?

ENTRE AMIS

Des frères ou des sœurs?

1. Introduce yourself and tell what you can about yourself.
2. Find out what you can about your partner.
3. Find out if your partner has brothers or sisters.
4. If so, find out their names.

Prononciation

L'accent et le rythme (*suite*)

■ Remember: When pronouncing French sentences, it is good practice to pay particular attention to the facts that: (1) French rhythm is even (just like counting), (2) syllables normally end in a vowel sound, and (3) the final syllable of a group of words is lengthened.

▶ Count before repeating each of the following expressions.

Review the *Prononciation* section of Ch. 1.

un, deux, trois, quatre, cinq, SIX

Je suis a-mé-ri-CAIN.
Elle est cé-li-ba-TAIRE.
Vous tra-va-illez beau-COUP?

un, deux, trois, quatre, cinq, six, SEPT

Je m'a-ppelle Ka-rine As-PEL.
Vous ha-bi-tez à Pa-RIS?
Je n'aime pas beau-coup le VIN.

Les sons [e], [ɛ], [ə], [a] et [wa]

■ The following words contain some important and very common vowel sounds.

▶ Practice saying these words after your instructor, paying particular attention to the highlighted vowel sound.

[e]   • **é**crivez, z**é**ro, r**é**p**é**tez, **é**coutez, nationalit**é,** t**é**l**é**phone, divorc**é**

   • ouvr**ez,** entr**ez,** ferm**ez,** ass**ez,** assey**ez**-vous, excus**ez**-moi

   • présent**er,** habit**er,** écout**er,** arrêt**er,** commenc**er,** continu**er**

   • **et**

Words with [ɛ] in open syllables are omitted, e.g., **est, très, sais.** Instructors can decide whether they wish to stress the [e]/[ɛ] contrast in open syllables.

[ɛ]   • p**e**rsonne, prof**e**sseur, hôt**e**l, univ**e**rsité, **e**spagnol, **e**lle, canadi**e**nne

   • cr**è**me, fr**è**re, ch**è**re, discr**è**te

   • **ê**tre, **ê**tes

   • angl**ai**se, franç**ai**se, célibat**ai**re, l**ai**de, cert**ai**nement

[ə]   • l**e,** l**e**vez-vous, pr**e**nez, r**e**gardez, qu**e,** d**e,** j**e,** n**e,** votr**e** santé, m**e**

──(NOTE)──┌─ encor~~e~~, heur~~e~~, femm~~e~~, homm~~e~~, un~~e~~, ami~~e~~, famill~~e~~, entr~~e~~ amis

[a]   • l**a, a**llez, **a**mie, **a**méric**a**in, **a**ssez, m**a**tin, c**a**n**a**dien, qu**a**tre, s**a**lut, d'**a**ccord

   • **à,** voil**à**

[wa]   • Franç**oi**s, m**oi**, tr**oi**s, v**oi**là, Madem**oi**selle, au rev**oi**r, bons**oi**r

   • v**oy**age

▶ Now go back and look at how these sounds are spelled and in what kinds of letter combinations they appear. What patterns do you notice?

▶ It is always particularly important to pronounce **la** [la] and **le** [lə] correctly since each marks a different gender, and the meaning of a word may depend on which is used. Listen and repeat:

la tour=*tower*
la tour Eiffel

le tour=*tour, turn*
le Tour de France

Buts communicatifs

1. Identifying Family and Friends

—Je vous présente° mon amie, Anne Martin.
    Elle a° une sœur qui habite près d'ici.
—Votre sœur, comment s'appelle-t-elle?
—Elle s'appelle Catherine.
—Et vous êtes d'où?
—Je suis de Nantes.
—Tiens! J'ai des cousins à Nantes.
—Comment s'appellent-ils?
—Ils s'appellent Dubois.

I introduce to you
has

Point out that the singular **s'appelle-t-il (elle)** and the plural **s'appellent-ils (elles)** are pronounced the same way.

Communication (Presentational): Have students practice this in pairs and then follow up by having two students introduce each other to the class.

▶ **Et vous?** Présentez un(e) ami(e).

REMARQUE

When you use **qui,** the verb that follows agrees with the person(s) to whom **qui** refers.

Elle a des cousins **qui habitent** à Nantes.

Communication (Interpretive): Use the drawing to help present the relationships. Then ask students **Comment s'appelle la femme de Pierre Martin?**, etc.

Arbre généalogique d'une famille française

Jean et Monique Martin — Marie et Georges Duhamel

Éric Bernard et Chantal — Michel — Pierre et Anne — Catherine et Alain Dubois

Christophe — Céline — David — Sylvie — Amélie — Benoît — Émilie — Nathalie — Stéphane

VOCABULAIRE

Une famille française

des parents	*parents; relatives*
un mari et une femme	*a husband and a wife*
un père et une mère	*a father and a mother*
un(e) enfant	*a child (male or female)*
un fils et une fille	*a son and a daughter*
un frère et une sœur	*a brother and a sister*
des grands-parents	*grandparents*
un grand-père	*a grandfather*
une grand-mère	*a grandmother*
des petits-enfants	*grandchildren*
un petit-fils et une petite-fille	*a grandson and a granddaughter*
un oncle et une tante	*an uncle and an aunt*
un neveu et une nièce	*a nephew and a niece*
un(e) cousin(e)	*a cousin (male or female)*
des beaux-parents	*stepparents (or in-laws)*
un beau-père	*a stepfather (or father-in-law)*
une belle-mère	*a stepmother (or mother-in-law)*
un beau-frère	*a brother-in-law*
une belle-sœur	*a sister-in-law*
un demi-frère	*a stepbrother*
une demi-sœur	*a stepsister*

Contrast the pronunciation of **fils** [fis] and **fille** [fij].

Add **arrière-** before **petit** or **grand** to convey the meaning *great:* **un arrière-petit-fils; une arrière-grand-mère.**

Point out that there is no **-e** on **grand** in the word **grand-mère.**

NOTES

1. Most plurals of nouns are formed by adding **-s.** In compound words for family members, an **-s** is added to both parts of the term: **des grands-pères, des belles-mères.**
2. The words **neveu** and **beau** form their plurals with an **-x: des neveux, des beaux-frères.**
3. The word **fils** is invariable in the plural: **des fils, des petits-fils.**
4. **C'est** (*He/She/It is*) and **Ce sont** (*They are/These are*) are often used with a noun phrase to identify someone or something.

> **C'est** la grand-mère d'Amélie. *It's (She's) Amélie's grandmother.*
> **Ce sont** les grands-parents de Stéphane. *They're Stéphane's grandparents.*

■ Ce sont les parents de Pierre. Study the genealogical chart on p. 61 and then use **C'est** and **Ce sont** to explain how the following people are related to Pierre.

MODÈLE: David?
C'est le fils de Pierre.

1. Anne?
2. Jean et Monique Martin?
3. Christophe?
4. Céline et Sylvie?
5. Marie et Georges Duhamel?

A. L'article indéfini: *un, une* et *des*

■ The French equivalent of the English article *a (an)* is **un** for masculine nouns and **une** for feminine nouns.

un frère	**un** train	**un** orangina
une sœur	**une** table	**une** limonade

By now, students should know the meaning of the word **liaison**; that is, when a silent final consonant is pronounced and linked to a vowel sound that follows it.

The rules governing obligatory **liaison** will be summarized in Ch. 5.

■ The final **-n** of **un** is normally silent. Liaison is required when **un** precedes a vowel sound.

un [n]étudiant

■ The consonant **-n-** is always pronounced in the word **une**. If it precedes a vowel sound, it is linked to that vowel.

une femme   [yn fam]
But: une étudiante   [y ne ty djãt]

■ The plural of **un** and **une** is **des**.

singulier: un frère   une sœur
pluriel: **des** frères   **des** sœurs

■ **Des** corresponds to the English *some* or *any*. However, these words are often omitted in English. **Des** is not omitted in French.

J'ai **des** amis à Paris.   *I have (some) friends in Paris.*

■ Liaison is required when an article precedes a vowel sound.

un [n]enfant	un [n]étudiant	un [n]homme
des [z]enfants	des [z]étudiants	des [z]hommes

■ In a series, the article *must* be repeated before each noun.

un homme et **une** femme   *a man and (a) woman*
une mère et **des** enfants   *a mother and (some) children*

2 **Présentations.** How would you introduce the following people?

MODÈLE: Mademoiselle Blondel / F / frère à New York
Je vous présente Mademoiselle Blondel.
Elle est française.
Elle a un frère qui habite à New York.

Review nationalities on p. 18.

1. Madame Brooks / GB / sœur à Toronto
2. Mademoiselle Jones / USA / parents près de Chicago
3. Monsieur Callahan / CDN / frère à Milwaukee
4. Monsieur Lefont / B / fils près d'ici
5. Madame Perez / MEX / petits-enfants près d'El Paso
6. Mademoiselle Keita / SN / cousins à New York
7. un ami
8. une amie
9. votre père ou votre mère

Communication (Presentational): Have students present #7, 8, & 9 to the class.

3 **Quelque chose à boire?** Order the following items.

MODÈLE: citron pressé
Je voudrais un citron pressé, s'il vous plaît.

Review the list of **boissons** on p. 47.

1. thé
2. café
3. bière
4. verre d'eau
5. jus d'orange
6. chocolat
7. coca
8. limonade
9. orangina
10. café crème

B. Le verbe *avoir*

J'ai des cousins à Marseille.   *I have cousins in Marseille.*
Tu as un(e) camarade de chambre?   *Do you have a roommate?*
Nous avons un neveu qui habite   *We have a nephew who lives near*
près de Chicago.   *Chicago.*

avoir (to have)	
j'	**ai**
tu	**as**
il/elle/on	**a**
nous	**avons**
vous	**avez**
ils/elles	**ont**

Liaison is summarized in the *Pronunciation* section of Ch. 5.

■ Liaison is required in **on a, nous avons, vous avez, ils ont,** and **elles ont.**

on [n]a

nous [z]avons

■ Do not confuse **ils ont** and **ils sont.** In liaison, the **-s** in **ils** is pronounced [z] and is linked to the following verb.

Ils [z]ont des enfants.   *They **have** children.*

But: **Ils sont** charmants.   *They **are** charming.*

After **pas de,** either the singular or the plural is acceptable. **Je n'ai pas de frère. /Je n'ai pas de frères.**

■ Use **Je n'ai pas de (d') ...** to say *I don't have a ...* or *I don't have any ...*

Je n'ai pas de père.   *I don't have a father.*

Je n'ai pas de frère.   *I don't have any brothers.*

Je n'ai pas d'enfants.   *I don't have any children.*

4 **Un recensement (*A census*).** These people are being interviewed by the census taker. Work with a partner to complete each interview, following the model.

MODÈLE: Mademoiselle Messin / 2 sœurs, 0 frère / Jeanne et Perrine (frères ou sœurs?)
LE RECENSEUR: **Avez-vous des frères ou des sœurs, Mademoiselle?**
MLLE MESSIN: **J'ai deux sœurs mais je n'ai pas de frère.**
LE RECENSEUR: **Comment s'appellent-elles?**
MLLE MESSIN: **Elles s'appellent Jeanne et Perrine.**

1. Monsieur Dubois / 2 frères, 0 sœur / Henri et Luc (frères ou sœurs?)
2. Madame Bernard / 1 enfant: 1 fils, 0 fille / Christophe (enfants?)
3. Monsieur Marot / 2 enfants: 1 fils, 1 fille / Pascal et Hélène (enfants?)
4. vos parents (enfants?)
5. votre meilleur(e) ami(e) (frères ou sœurs?)
6. vos grands-parents (petits-enfants?)
7. vous (?)

5 **La famille de David.** Use the genealogical chart on page 61 to create sentences describing David's family ties.

MODÈLE: **David a des parents qui s'appellent Pierre et Anne.**

ENTRE AMIS

Votre famille

1. Find out if your partner has brothers or sisters.
2. If so, find out their names.
3. Find out where they live.
4. Find out if your partner has children and, if so, what their names are.
5. Introduce your partner to another person and share the information you have just found out.

2. Sharing Numerical Information

Combien de personnes y a-t-il dans ta famille, Christelle?
Quel âge ont tes parents?
Quel âge a ta sœur?
Quel âge as-tu?
En quelle année es-tu née?

Il y a quatre personnes: mes parents, ma sœur et moi.
Ils ont cinquante ans et quarante-sept ans.
Elle a dix-huit ans.
J'ai vingt ans.
Je suis née° *I was born*
en mille neuf cent quatre-vingt-six.

▶ **Et vous?** Combien de personnes y a-t-il dans votre famille? Quel âge ont les membres de votre famille? Quel âge avez-vous?

REMARQUES

1. The verb **avoir** is used when asking or giving someone's age.

Quel âge **a** ta camarade de chambre? *How old is your roommate?*
Quel âge **a** ton petit ami? *How old is your boyfriend?*

2. In inversion, remember to insert a **-t-** before the singular forms **il, elle,** and **on.**

Quel âge ont-elles? *How old are they?*
But: Quel âge a**-t-**elle? *How old is she?*

3. The word **an(s)** must be used when giving someone's age.

J'ai vingt et un **ans.** *I am twenty-one.*

C. Les nombres (*suite*)

Review the numbers 0–29 on p. 3.

Have students count from 3 to 99 by 3s; have them try to guess the age of some famous people.

30	trente
31	trente et un
32	trente-deux
33	trente-trois
	etc.
40	quarante
41	quarante et un
42	quarante-deux
43	quarante-trois
	etc.
50	cinquante
51	cinquante et un
52	cinquante-deux
53	cinquante-trois
	etc.
60	soixante
61	soixante et un
62	soixante-deux
63	soixante-trois
	etc.

Numbers from 70 to 99 show a different pattern:
70 = 60 + 10;
80 = 4 × 20;
90 = 80 + 10.

70	soixante-dix
71	soixante et onze
72	soixante-douze
73	soixante-treize
74	soixante-quatorze

75	soixante-quinze
76	soixante-seize
77	soixante-dix-sept
78	soixante-dix-huit
79	soixante-dix-neuf
80	quatre-vingts
81	quatre-vingt-un
82	quatre-vingt-deux
83	quatre-vingt-trois
	etc.
90	quatre-vingt-dix
91	quatre-vingt-onze
92	quatre-vingt-douze
	etc.
100	cent
101	cent un

Numbers above 101 repeat the same pattern: **cent vingt *et* un, cent quatre-vingt-un, deux cent vingt *et* un,** etc.

200	deux cents
1.000	mille
1.999	mille neuf cent quatre-vingt-dix-neuf
2.000	deux mille
2.006	deux mille six
100.000	cent mille
1.000.000	un million
1.000.000.000	un milliard

■ All numbers are invariable except **un.** Remember to replace the number **un** with **une** before a feminine noun, even in a compound number.

un oncle	trois oncles	vingt et un cousins
une tante	trois tantes	**vingt et une** cousines

You may wish to point out that **quatre** may also be pronounced [kat] before a consonant. Students will hear this in the video.

■ When numbers from 1 to 10 stand alone, the final consonants of **un, deux,** and **trois** are silent, but all others are pronounced. The **-x** at the end of **six** and **dix** is pronounced [s].

un   deux   trois

But: quatre cinq six sept huit neuf dix

■ Certain numbers have a different pronunciation when they precede a noun:

- The final consonant of **six, huit,** and **dix** is not pronounced before a consonant.

  six personnes   huit jours   dix verres

- When the following noun begins with a vowel sound, the final consonant is always pronounced and linked to the noun. Note that with **quatre,** both final consonants are linked and the final **-e** is not pronounced.

un [n]homme	cinq [k]hommes	huit [t]hommes
deux [z]hommes	six [z]hommes	neuf [f]hommes
trois [z]hommes	sept [t]hommes	dix [z]hommes
quatre [tʀ]hommes		vingt [t]hommes

- The **-f** in **neuf** is pronounced as [v] only before the words **ans** *(years)* and **heures** *(hours).*

neuf [v]ans   neuf [v]heures

But: neuf [f]enfants   neuf [f]hommes

- The final **-t** in **vingt** is silent when the number stands alone, but is pronounced in the compound numbers built on it.

vingt	[vɛ̃]
vingt et un	[vɛ̃ te ɛ̃]
vingt-deux	[vɛ̃t dø]

■ For numbers ending in 1, from 21 to 71, **et** is used. From 81 to 101 **et** is not used.

vingt **et** un   *But:* quatre-vingt-un

You may wish to teach that **quatre-vingts** does not take an **-s** in the expression **page quatre-vingt.**

■ **Vingt** and **cent** do not add an **-s** if they are *followed* by a number.

quatre-vingt**s** personnes	*But:* quatre-vingt-un
trois cent**s** personnes	*But:* trois cent cinq

■ **Mille** never adds an **-s.**

mille personnes deux **mille** personnes

■ The words **million** and **milliard** are nouns and take an **s** in the plural. If they are followed by another noun, **de** is inserted between the nouns.

deux millions d'euros

> **NOTE**
>
> In France, commas and periods used with numbers are the reverse of the system used in North America.
>
> L'état a besoin de **2.000.000,00** d'euros. (deux millions)

Have students read this sentence out loud. Be sure they correctly identify this as **deux millions.**

■ There are five pairs of numbers in a French telephone number: **02.42.83.21.14.** The first pair indicates the general area of France.

6 **Les numéros de téléphone.** Pronounce the following phone numbers.

MODÈLE: 02.81.88.40.01

zéro deux / quatre-vingt-un / quatre-vingt-huit / quarante / zéro un

Culture & Comparison: Have students count to 100 by 5s; then have them dictate their phone numbers. When giving American or Canadian phone numbers, give the first 3 digits together, then the last 4 in pairs, e.g., 212-3240 **deux cent douze / trente-deux / quarante.**

1. 02.41.93.21.80
2. 04.77.63.06.97
3. 04.42.08.98.89
4. 02.31.86.15.96
5. 04.71.83.61.91
6. 04.67.85.76.90
7. 05.61.10.99.02
8. 02.51.81.95.12
9. 03.88.19.82.43
10. 04.78.87.03.92

7 **Parlez-moi de votre famille** *(Tell me about your family).* Describe the people listed below. Use the model as a guide. If you don't have a brother, etc., say so.

MODÈLE: un frère

J'ai un frère qui s'appelle Bill.
Il habite à Boston.
Il est grand et assez beau.
Il a vingt-trois ans.

1. une sœur
2. un frère
3. un oncle
4. une tante
5. des cousins
6. une cousine
7. un grand-père ou une grand-mère
8. des parents

www Réalités culturelles

Find the places mentioned in this section on the map on the inside front cover.

Les départements et les territoires d'outre-mer

France is divided into 100 **départements,** administrative units created by the revolutionary government in 1790 to replace the old provinces. Included in the 100 are four overseas departments: **la Guadeloupe** and **la Martinique** (both in the Caribbean), **la Guyane** (in South America), and **la Réunion** (in the Indian Ocean). These **départements d'outre-mer** (DOM) have the same legal status as the continental departments, and their inhabitants enjoy the same rights of French citizenship.

France also has a number of overseas possessions or territories, **les territoires d'outre-mer** (TOM), which do not have the same legal status as the departments. Their residents are, however, French citizens. These territories are **la Nouvelle-Calédonie, Wallis-et-Futuna,** and **la Polynésie** (all in the Pacific Ocean), **Mayotte** (off the eastern coast of Africa), **Saint-Pierre-et-Miquelon** (off the coast of Canada), and French Antarctica. Mayotte and Saint-Pierre-et-Miquelon have a special status that is close to that of a department.

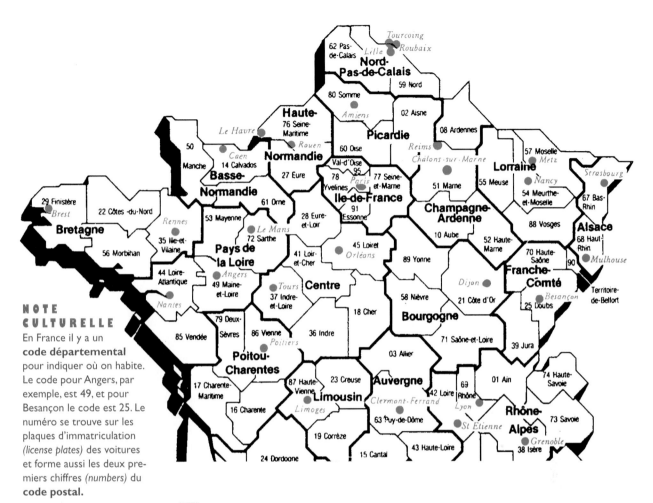

NOTE CULTURELLE

En France il y a un **code départemental** pour indiquer où on habite. Le code pour Angers, par exemple, est 49, et pour Besançon le code est 25. Le numéro se trouve sur les plaques d'immatriculation (*license plates*) des voitures et forme aussi les deux premiers chiffres (*numbers*) du **code postal**.

8 **Codes postaux.** The map above shows major cities and the first two numbers of the zip code for several French **départements.** Give the general zip code for the following cities.

MODÈLE: Nantes
Le code postal pour Nantes est quarante-quatre mille (44000).

Do this in pairs, assigning two or three cities to each team. Use **au nord, au sud, à l'est, à l'ouest de Paris,** to help students locate the cities.

1. Dijon
2. Amiens
3. Tours
4. Besançon
5. Angers
6. Le Mans
7. Orléans
8. Nantes
9. Paris
10. Brest
11. Rouen
12. Strasbourg

D. Les expressions *il y a* et *voilà*

Voilà la famille Laplante.

> **Il y a combien de** personnes dans la famille Laplante?
> **Il y a** quatre personnes.
>
> **Il y a combien de** garçons et **combien de** filles?
> **Il y a** deux filles mais **il n'y a pas de** garçon.

- ■ **Voilà** can mean either *there is (are)* or *here is (are)*. **Il y a** means *there is (are)*. While **voilà** and **il y a** are both translated *there is* or *there are* in English, they are used quite differently.

Voilà is often used in place of voici. Neither of them can be used in negative or interrogative sentences.

- ■ **Voilà** and **voici** *(here is, here are)* point something out. They bring it to another person's attention. There is usually an accompanying physical movement—a nod of the head, a gesture of the hand toward the person or object, or a pointing of the finger to identify a specific object.

Voici mon fils et ma fille.	*Here are my son and daughter.*
Voilà ma voiture.	*There's my car.*

- ■ **Il y a** simply states that something exists or tells how many there are.

Il y a un livre sur la table.	*There is a book on the table.*
Il y a quatre filles et deux garçons dans la famille Martin.	*There are four girls and two boys in the Martin family.*

- ■ The negative of **il y a un (une, des)** is **il n'y a pas de.**

Il n'y a pas de voiture ici.	*There aren't any cars here.*

> (ATTENTION) — Do not use **de** if **il n'y a pas** is followed by a number.
>
> | | |
> |---|---|
> | **Il n'y a pas trois** voitures dans le garage; il y a quatre voitures. | *There aren't three cars in the garage; there are four cars.* |

- ■ There are several ways to use **il y a** in a question.

Il y a un livre sur la table? **Est-ce qu'il y a** un livre sur la table? **Y a-t-il** un livre sur la table?	*Is there a book on the table?*

■ **Il y a** is often used with **combien de.**

Il y a combien de garçons?
Combien de garçons **est-ce qu'il y a?**
Combien de garçons **y a-t-il?**

9 **Lori parle avec Anne Martin.** Complete the following sentences using either **il y a** or **voilà.**

MODÈLE: <u>**Voilà**</u> ma fille Émilie.

1. _____ deux enfants dans votre famille?
2. Non, Mademoiselle, _____ six enfants.
3. _____ une photo de ma famille.
4. _____ ma mère. Elle est jolie, n'est-ce pas?
5. _____ combien de filles dans votre famille?
6. Où sont-elles? Ah! _____ vos filles!

10 **À vous.** Answer the following questions as factually as possible.

1. Quel âge avez-vous?
2. Combien de personnes y a-t-il dans votre famille?
3. Quel âge ont les membres de votre famille?
4. Combien d'étudiants y a-t-il dans votre classe de français? Combien d'hommes et combien de femmes y a-t-il?
5. Quel âge a votre professeur de français? (Imaginez!)
6. Combien d'oncles et combien de tantes avez-vous? Quel âge ont-ils?

E. Les adjectifs possessifs *mon, ton, notre* et *votre*

—Comment s'appellent **tes** parents?
—**Mes** parents s'appellent Marcel et Jacqueline.
—Combien d'enfants y a-t-il dans **ta** famille?
—Il y a trois enfants dans **ma** famille: deux garçons et une fille.
—Quel âge a **ton** frère? Quel âge a **ta** sœur?
—**Mon** frère a dix-huit ans et **ma** sœur a douze ans.
—Où habitent **vos** grands-parents?
—**Nos** grands-parents habitent à Saumur.

adjectifs possessifs

en anglais	*masculin*		*féminin*		*pluriel* (m. et f.)	
my	mon		ma		mes	
your	ton	père	ta	mère	tes	parents
our	notre		notre		nos	
your	votre		votre		vos	

■ Possessive adjectives agree in gender and number with the nouns they modify (the "possessions"). **Notre** and **votre** are used for both masculine and feminine singular nouns.

Denise, **ton** père est gentil.	*Denise, your father is nice.*
Alain, **ta** mère est gentille aussi!	*Alain, your mother is nice also!*
Nathalie, **tes** parents sont très gentils.	*Nathalie, your parents are very nice.*

■ In the singular, **ma** and **ta** become **mon** and **ton** when used directly before a feminine word beginning with a vowel sound.

	ma meilleure amie
But:	**mon** amie

	ta tante
But:	**ton** autre tante

■ Liaison occurs if the word following **mon, ton, mes, tes, nos,** or **vos** begins with a vowel sound.

mon̸ petit ami	vos̸ bons amis
But: mon [n]ami	vos [z]amis

■ As with **quatre,** the final **-e** of **notre** and **votre** is not pronounced before a vowel sound, but the final consonants are linked to the next word.

notr̸e [tR]ami

11 **Qui?** Try to identify people from among your friends and relatives who "fit" the following questions. Use possessive adjectives in each response. Be sure that verbs agree with subjects, and that adjectives agree with nouns.

MODÈLE: Qui chante bien?
Mes parents chantent bien. ou
Notre ami chante bien.

Communication (Interpretive): Have students ask you the questions first. Then (books closed) ask them the questions.

1. Qui est grand?
2. Qui parle français?
3. Qui ne skie pas?
4. Qui adore le sport?
5. Qui n'aime pas beaucoup la bière?
6. Qui aime être étudiant(e)?

Communication (Presentational): After students have practiced this, ask several of them to give a presentation to the class. In place of photos, students could draw stick figure caricatures.

12 **À vous.** Show a real (or imaginary) picture of your family and point out parents, brothers, sisters, cousins, uncles, and aunts. Give each person's age as well.

MODÈLE: **Voilà ma sœur, Kristen. Elle a seize ans.**

ENTRE AMIS

Dans ta famille

Use possessive adjectives whenever possible.

1. Ask your partner how many people there are in his/her family.
2. Find out the names of his/her brother, sister, etc.
3. Find out how old they are.
4. Find out where they live.
5. Ask if his/her brother, sister, etc. speaks French or studies French.
6. What else can you find out about his/her family members?

Suggest that students consult the list of activities on p. 39 when asking #6.

3. Talking about Your Home

Habitez-vous dans une maison° ou dans
  un appartement°, Lori?
    Nous habitons dans une maison.

house
apartment

Et combien de pièces° y a-t-il dans votre
  maison?
    Il y a sept pièces.

rooms

Et qu'est-ce qu'il y a chez vous°?
  Chez moi° il y a ...

at your house
at my house

Bureau can mean either *desk* or *office*. The teacher's office = **le bureau du professeur. Chambre** normally implies *bedroom*, not *room* in general.

... dans ma salle de séjour.

... dans ma chambre.

... dans ma cuisine.

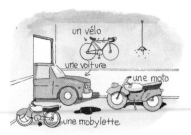

... dans mon garage.

 Et vous? Qu'est-ce qu'il y a chez vous?

13 **Les renseignements** *(Information).* Olivier is giving some information about people in his neighborhood. Help him to complete the sentences. Use the verb **avoir** and a number. Where no number is indicated, use **un, une,** or **des** as appropriate.

MODÈLE: Les Dufoix / deux enfants / chat
Les Dufoix ont deux enfants et un chat.

1. Charles / radio antique
2. Je / enfants extraordinaires
3. Les Dubois / trois télévisions / stéréo / ordinateur
4. Madame Martin / mari / six enfants
5. Nous / petit appartement / voiture
6. Mes grands-parents / grande maison / quatre chambres
7. Les Martin / chat / chien / deux réfrigérateurs / cuisinière à gaz / lave-vaisselle
8. Madame Davis / voiture japonaise / vélo français

F. La négation + *un (une, des)*

Review the negative of **il y a,**
p. 70.

After **pas de,** words may be singular or plural: **pas de frère(s).**

■ After a negation, indefinite articles *(un, une, des)* usually become *de (d').*

Vous avez **un** ordinateur?	Non, je n'ai pas **d'**ordinateur.
Vous avez **une** voiture?	Non, je n'ai pas **de** voiture.
Vous avez **des** frères ou **des** sœurs?	Non, je n'ai pas **de** frère ou **de** sœur.
Y a-t-il **un** lave-vaisselle?	Non, il n'y a pas **de** lave-vaisselle.

NOTE

You may wish to present the **ni ... ni ...** construction for recognition.

This rule does not apply after **être.**

Christophe n'est pas **un** enfant.	*Christophe isn't a child.*
La voiture n'est pas **une** Ford.	*The car is not a Ford.*
Ce ne sont pas **des** amis.	*They're not friends.*

■ Also, definite articles **(le, la, l', les)** and possessive adjectives **(mon, ma, mes,** etc.) do not change after a negation.

Je n'aime pas **le** thé.   Mon frère n'aime pas **notre** chien.

■ When contradicting a negative statement or question, use **si** instead of **oui.**

Il n'y a pas de sandwichs ici.	**Si,** il y a des sandwichs.
Vous n'avez pas d'ordinateur?	**Si,** j'ai un ordinateur.
Vous n'aimez pas le café?	**Si,** j'aime le café.

14 **Un riche et un pauvre.** Guy has everything, but Philippe has practically nothing. Explain how they differ.

MODÈLE: voiture
Guy a une voiture, mais Philippe n'a pas de voiture.

1. appartement
2. lave-linge
3. petite amie
4. ordinateur
5. amis
6. chien

15 **Bavardages** *(Gossip).* Someone has made up gossip about you and your neighbors. Correct these falsehoods.

MODÈLE: Monsieur Dupont a des filles.
Mais non! Il n'a pas de fille.

1. Marie a un petit ami.
2. Il y a une moto dans votre garage.
3. Vous détestez le café.
4. Jean-Yves a des enfants.
5. Christophe et Alice ont un chien.
6. Votre voiture est une Renault.

16 **As-tu ... ?** Your partner will interview you according to the model. If you really do have the item in question, say so. If not, give a negative answer and then name something that you do have.

MODÈLE: une voiture
VOTRE PARTENAIRE: **As-tu une voiture?**
VOUS: **Non, je n'ai pas de voiture mais j'ai une moto.**

1. une maison
2. un chien
3. un cousin à Lyon
4. un ordinateur
5. des amis qui habitent à Paris
6. un frère ou une sœur qui parle français

17 **Une diseuse de bonne aventure.** A fortune teller has made the following statements about you. Affirm or deny them. Be careful to use **si** if you wish to contradict a negative statement.

MODÈLE: Vous n'avez pas de frère.
Si, j'ai un frère (des frères). ou
Oui, c'est vrai, je n'ai pas de frère.

Communication (Interpretive):
Follow up by playing the role of a fortune teller. Students have to affirm or deny statements you make: **Vous avez trois sœurs et deux frères, Vous n'avez pas d'ordinateur.**.

1. Vous n'avez pas de sœur.
2. Vous n'habitez pas dans un appartement.
3. Vous n'avez pas de stéréo.
4. Vous n'étudiez pas beaucoup.
5. Le professeur n'est pas gentil.
6. Vous n'aimez pas étudier le français.

VOCABULAIRE

Les pièces d'une maison

You may wish to refer students to p. 157 for the distinction between **salle de bain** and **toilettes.**

un bureau	*office*	les toilettes	*restroom*
une chambre	*bedroom*	un salon	*living room*
une cuisine	*kitchen*	une salle de séjour	*den; living room*
une salle à manger	*dining room*	un sous-sol	*basement*
une salle de bain	*bathroom*	une véranda	*porch*

Communication (Presentational): Once students have practiced this with a partner (books open), have several of them give short presentations to the class (books closed).

18 **À vous.** Answer the following questions.

1. Où habitez-vous?
2. Combien de pièces y a-t-il chez vous?
3. Quelles pièces est-ce qu'il y a?
4. Y a-t-il un fauteuil dans votre chambre?
5. Combien de chaises y a-t-il dans votre chambre?
6. Y a-t-il un chien ou un chat dans votre maison?
7. Qu'est-ce qu'il y a dans votre chambre?
8. Qu'est-ce qu'il y a dans le garage du professeur? (Imaginez!)

G. La possession avec *de*

C'est le mari **de** Mme Martin.	*It's Mme Martin's husband.*
Ce n'est pas la maison **de** René.	*It's not René's house.*
C'est la maison **des** parents **de** René.	*It's René's parents' house.*

Drill **Marie a une sœur.** → **Voilà la sœur de Marie.** Other examples: **Alain a une voiture, Monique a un frère, Marc a des amis.**

■ The preposition **de (d')** is used to indicate possession or relationship. French has no possessive *-'s* ending: *Marie's sister* has to be expressed in French as *the sister of Marie.*

la sœur **de** Marie	*Marie's sister*
la voiture **d'**Alain	*Alain's car*

■ If the "owner" is indicated with a proper name, **de (d')** is used without article or possessive adjective. When the word referring to the "owner" is not a proper name, an article or a possessive adjective precedes it: *The grandmother's room* has to be expressed as *the room of the grandmother.*

la chambre de **la** grand-mère	*the grandmother's room*
la moto de **mon** ami	*my friend's motorcycle*

$$\text{possession} + \textbf{de} + \left\{ \begin{array}{c} \text{article} \\ \\ \text{possessive adjective} \end{array} \right\} + \text{"owner"}$$

■ The preposition **de** contracts with the articles **le** and **les,** but there is no contraction with the articles **la** and **l'**.

de + le	→	**du**	du professeur
de + les	→	**des**	des étudiants
de + la	→	**de la**	de la femme
de + l'	→	**de l'**	de l'enfant

Remember that **de l'** could be masculine or feminine.

C'est une photo **du** professeur.   *It's a picture of the teacher.*
C'est la maison **des** parents d'Éric.   *It's Éric's parents' house.*
C'est le chat **de la** mère de Céline.   *It's Céline's mother's cat.*
C'est la voiture **de l'**oncle de Pascal.   *It's Pascal's uncle's car.*

Check comprehension by having students translate a few expressions. E.g., *Bill's stereo, the teacher's car.*

Remember to use only **de (d')** with a proper name.

19 **J'ai trouvé une radio** *(I found a radio).* A number of objects have been found. Ask a question to try to identify the owners. Your partner will answer negatively and will decide who *is* the owner.

MODÈLE: J'ai trouvé une radio. (Jeanne)
VOUS: **J'ai trouvé une radio. C'est la radio de Jeanne?**
VOTRE PARTENAIRE: **Non, ce n'est pas la radio de Jeanne. C'est la radio de Kévin.**

Tell students to use names of students in class for the real owner

1. J'ai trouvé une voiture. (Madame Dufour)
2. J'ai trouvé une radio. (professeur)
3. J'ai trouvé un chat. (Karine)
4. J'ai trouvé une moto. (l'ami de Michèle)
5. J'ai trouvé un chien. (les parents de Denis)
6. J'ai trouvé une calculatrice. (Frédérique)
7. J'ai trouvé un vélo. (la sœur de Sophie)

20 **Nos possessions.** Complete the following sentences by filling in the blanks.

Ask students to explain the choices they make.

1. Le vélo _____ Laurence est dans le garage.
2. La voiture _____ père _____ Anne est bleue.
3. La photo _____ oncle et _____ tante _____ Guy est sur le bureau _____ grands-parents _____ Guy.
4. Le chat _____ frère _____ Chantal est sur le lit _____ parents _____ Chantal.
5. Où est la calculatrice _____ sœur _____ Sandrine?
6. C'est la stéréo _____ enfants _____ professeur.
7. La moto _____ mon frère est dans notre garage.

21 **Où est-ce?** Patrick's family has a number of possessions. Ask where each item is.

MODÈLE: La sœur de Patrick a un vélo.   **Où est le vélo de la sœur de Patrick?**

1. Les sœurs de Patrick ont une télévision.
2. Le frère de Patrick a une voiture.
3. L'oncle de Patrick a un chien.
4. Les cousins de Patrick ont une stéréo.
5. Les enfants de Patrick ont un ordinateur.
6. La cousine de Patrick a un appartement.
7. Les parents de Patrick ont une voiture allemande.
8. Le père de Patrick a un bureau.
9. La tante de Patrick a un petit chat.
10. Les parents de Patrick ont une belle maison.

H. Les adjectifs possessifs *son* et *leur*

As-tu une photo de la famille de Léa?	Voilà une photo de **sa** famille.
Où est le père de Léa?	Voilà **son** père.
Où est la mère de Léa?	Voilà **sa** mère.
Où sont les grands-parents de Léa?	Voilà **ses** grands-parents.
Où est la fille de M. et Mme Dupont?	Voilà **leur** fille. C'est Léa!
Où sont les cousins des Dupont?	Voilà **leurs** cousins.

Communication (Presentational): Suggestion for a warm-up: Pair students to show family pictures again: **Voilà ma sœur,** etc. Then have them describe their partner's pictures: **Voilà sa sœur,** etc.

■ **Son, sa,** and **ses** can mean either *his* or *her.* As with **mon, ma,** and **mes,** the choice of form depends on whether the "possession" is masculine or feminine, singular or plural. It makes no difference what the gender of the "owner" is.

son lit	*his bed* or *her bed*
sa chambre	*his room* or *her room*
ses chaises	*his chairs* or *her chairs*

■ **Leur** and **leurs** mean *their* and are used when there is more than one "owner." Both forms are used for either masculine or feminine "possessions."

leur lit	**leur** chambre
leurs lits	**leurs** chambres

NOTE

Be sure not to use **ses** when you mean **leurs.**

Communication (Interpretive): Use the drawing on p. 61 to ask questions about Pierre and his family, e.g., **Comment s'appelle sa femme, sa mère, son père, ses enfants? Comment s'appelle leur mère, leur cousine, leurs cousins?**

ses parents	*his parents* or *her parents*
leurs parents	*their parents*

■ In the singular, **sa** becomes **son** when used directly before a feminine word beginning with a vowel sound.

> **sa** meilleure amie

But: **son** amie

■ Liaison occurs if the word following **son, ses,** or **leurs** begins with a vowel sound.

> son petit ami   ses bons amis   leurs parents

But: son [n]ami   ses [z]amis   leurs [z]amis

■ Sometimes the identity of the "owner" would be unclear if a possessive adjective were used. In such cases, it is better to use the possessive construction with **de.**

Robert et Marie habitent avec **sa** mère.	*(Robert's mother? Marie's mother?)*
Robert et Marie habitent avec **la** mère **de Marie.**	*(clearly Marie's mother)*

Synthèse: les adjectifs possessifs

pronom	masculin	féminin	pluriel (m. et f.)	
je	**mon**	**ma**	**mes**	*my*
tu	**ton**	**ta**	**tes**	*your*
il/elle/on	**son**	**sa**	**ses**	*his/her*
nous	**notre**	**notre**	**nos**	*our*
vous	**votre**	**votre**	**vos**	*your*
ils/elles	**leur**	**leur**	**leurs**	*their*

22 **La chambre de qui?** Clarify the identity of the "owner" in each of the following phrases by completing the following expressions with the appropriate form of **de** + the definite article.

MODÈLE: sa chambre. La chambre de qui?   La chambre **du** frère de Marc.

*Follow-up: (1) Have students translate the possessive adjectives. (2) Close books and reverse the process: **La chambre du frère → sa chambre.***

1. leur photo. La photo de qui?   La photo _____ enfants de ma tante.
2. son nom. Le nom de qui?   Le nom _____ jeune fille.
3. sa moto. La moto de qui?   La moto _____ mari d'Anne.
4. leurs livres. Les livres de qui?   Les livres _____ étudiants.
5. son chien. Le chien de qui?   Le chien _____ oncle d'Isabelle.
6. sa maison. La maison de qui?   La maison _____ ami de Laurent.
7. ses amies. Les amies de qui?   Les amies _____ sœur de Denis.
8. son chat. Le chat de qui?   Le chat _____ petite amie de Jean-Luc.
9. son bureau. Le bureau de qui?   Le bureau _____ professeur.

23 **Comment s'appellent-ils?** Ask the names of the following people, using a possessive adjective in each question. Your partner will supply the answer.

*Be careful to distinguish between **son/sa/ses** and **leur(s)** when asking these questions.*

MODÈLES: le cousin de Nathalie? (Stéphane)
   VOUS: **Comment s'appelle son cousin?**
   VOTRE PARTENAIRE: **Il s'appelle Stéphane.**

les cousines de Nathalie? (Christelle et Sandrine)
   VOUS: **Comment s'appellent ses cousines?**
   VOTRE PARTENAIRE: **Elles s'appellent Christelle et Sandrine.**

1. le père de Nathalie? (Michel)
2. la sœur d'Éric? (Isabelle)
3. la mère d'Éric et d'Isabelle? (Monique)
4. les frères de Nathalie? (Christophe et Sébastien)
5. les sœurs de Nathalie? (Sylvie et Céline)
6. le chien de Nathalie? (Fidèle)
7. les grands-parents de Nathalie? (Marie et Pierre Coifard; Louis et Jeanne Dupuis)
8. les parents de votre meilleur(e) ami(e)?
9. les amis de vos parents?

24 **À vous.** Ask and answer the questions using possessive adjectives.

MODÈLE: Où est la maison de votre ami(e)?
Sa maison est à Denver.

Communication (Presentational): Follow up by having students report on their partner's best friend: **son/sa meilleur(e) ami(e) ...**

1. Comment s'appelle votre meilleur(e) ami(e)?
2. Quel âge a votre ami(e)?
3. Combien de personnes y a-t-il dans la famille de votre ami(e)?
4. Comment s'appellent les parents de votre ami(e)?
5. Où habitent les parents de votre ami(e)?
6. Qu'est-ce qu'il y a dans la maison des parents de votre ami(e)?

ENTRE AMIS

Dans ta chambre

Use **tu** with your partner in this interview.

1. Find out where your partner lives.
2. Find out if your partner has a TV in his/her room.
3. Find out two other items that s/he has in his/her room.
4. Find out two other items that s/he does not have.
5. Find out if your partner has a roommate.
6. If so, find out his/her name and two items of information about the roommate.
7. Turn to another person and share what you found out.

Comment s'appellent leurs filles?

Intégration

Connections & Communities: The web search activities for this chapter will familiarize students with Versailles and families who have lived there.

Révision

Have students interview you to verify their selections, e.g., **Il y a une moto dans votre garage, n'est-ce pas?**

Prime this activity by brainstorming with the class to elicit the questions first. See p. 51 for suggestions.

A **Chez mon professeur.** Imagine the home, garage, etc. of your French teacher. Make up five different sentences to state what s/he has or does not have.

MODÈLE: **Il y a une moto dans son garage.**

B **Trouvez quelqu'un qui ...** Interview your classmates in French to find someone who ...

MODÈLE: speaks French
Est-ce que tu parles français?

1. has a computer
2. has no brothers or sisters
3. has a dog or a cat or a fish
4. likes children a lot
5. is 21 or older
6. has a sister named Nicole
7. has a brother named Christopher
8. lives in an apartment
9. has grandparents who live in another state or province

Communication
(Presentational & Interpretive):
If students present their descriptions to the class, others can be asked to re-call information that was pre-sented. Suggestion: Assign the *Rédaction* at the end of Ch. 3 in the Workbook.

C **Début de rédaction.** Think of two people you know and, for each one, write a description of that person's room/house/apartment (all that apply). Where does s/he live? What items does s/he have or not have?

MODÈLE: **Lori Becker habite à Boston chez ses parents. Ils ont une petite maison. Dans la chambre de Lori il y a un lit, un bureau et un ordinateur. Il y a aussi une stéréo, mais il n'y a pas de radio ou de télévision. Lori regarde la télévision dans son salon.**

Communication *(Interpretive):*
Encourage students to use the practice test on the Lab Audio Program.

D **À vous.** Answer the following questions.

1. Combien de personnes y a-t-il dans votre famille?
2. Comment s'appellent deux de vos ami(e)s?
3. Où habitent-ils?
4. Quel âge ont-ils?
5. Sont-ils étudiants? Si oui, ont-ils une chambre à l'université? Étudient-ils le français ou une autre langue?
6. Avez-vous des amis qui ont un appartement? Si oui, qu'est-ce qu'il y a dans leur appartement?
7. Avez-vous un ami qui est marié? Si oui, comment s'appelle sa femme? Quel âge a-t-elle?
8. Avez-vous une amie qui est mariée? Si oui, comment s'appelle son mari? Quel âge a-t-il?
9. Avez-vous des amis qui ont des enfants? Si oui, combien d'enfants ont-ils? Comment s'appellent leurs enfants? Quel âge ont-ils?

Négociations: **C'est la voiture de son frère?** Work with your partner to complete the forms. Your partner's form is in Appendix D. Ask questions to determine the information that is missing.

MODÈLES: **C'est la voiture du frère de David?**
C'est le vélo de ses grands-parents?

For complete instructions on how to prepare for and to use this activity, see *Négociations* on the Class Prep CD-ROM.

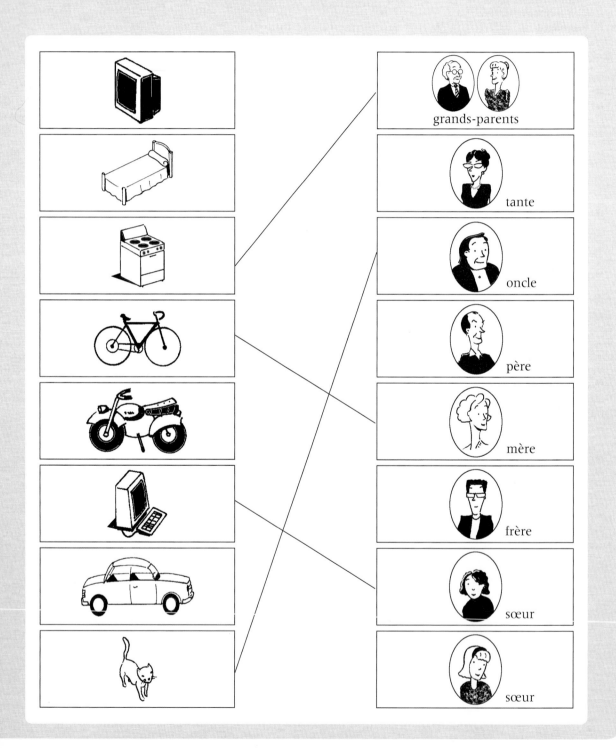

Lecture I

You may wish to consult the vocabulary on page 75 when labeling the rooms.

Video for Chapter 3: A. Video worksheets (Cahier); B. ACE Video practice test (WWW); C. CD-ROM

A **Ma maison idéale.** Draw a sketch of a home that would be ideal for you. Then label each of the rooms in French.

B **Étude du vocabulaire.** Study the following sentences and choose the English words that correspond to the French words in bold print: *square meters, fireplace, planted with trees, in new condition, winter, landscaped lot, approximately, stone, in good taste, on one level, roof, country, house, set up/ready-to-use.*

1. Le **pavillon** est situé à la **campagne** à **environ** 30 kilomètres de Paris.
2. Près de la maison il y a un jardin **arboré** et un beau **terrain paysager** de 300 **mètres carrés.**
3. En **hiver,** s'il fait froid, il y a une belle **cheminée** en **pierre** dans la salle de séjour.
4. La cuisine est **aménagée** et équipée **avec goût.**
5. La **toiture** de la maison est **à l'état neuf.**
6. Les personnes handicapées n'ont pas de problème avec une maison de **plain-pied.**

C **Les pièces.** Read the four ads in order to:
1. identify the number of rooms in each home, and
2. make a list of the rooms that are mentioned.

MAISONS À VENDRE

Quelques abréviations: m² (mètres carrés); mn (minutes); s. de b. (salle de bain)

CADRE EXCEPTIONNEL

Belle maison récente, agréable séjour-salon en L 45 m² environ, cuisine aménagée équipée, 3 chambres, belle salle de bain, garage et jardin, mérite votre visite !

ELLE VOUS SÉDUIRA

Aux portes de Cholet, agréable pavillon indépendant sur 500 m² de terrain, cuisine aménagée équipée, beau séjour-salon avec cheminée, 3 chambres, garage 2 voitures et jardin aménagé avec goût.

DE TOUTE BEAUTÉ

Le charme de la campagne à 10 mn de Cholet, belle cuisine aménagée équipée, vaste pièce de réception 90 m² avec superbe cheminée en pierre, salon d'hiver parfaitement exposé, 4 chambres, 2 s. de b., bureau, grand garage, 1 700 m² de terrain paysager, aménagement de goût et de qualité !

EXCEPTIONNELLE

Plain-pied indépendant, séjour-salon, 2 chambres, toiture état neuf, garage et jardin arboré. Affaire à saisir !

D **Inférence.** Reread the ads to try to determine the following information. Be ready to justify your answers by quoting the reading.

1. the newest home
2. the biggest home
3. the largest lot
4. the home that has been remodeled
5. the name of the closest French city
6. the home you would choose and why

E **À discuter.** Aimez-vous ces maisons? Pourquoi ou pourquoi pas?

Comparison & Culture: Have students compare these French housing ads with listings from your local newspaper. Do both cultures look for similar features in a home?

F **Comparaisons culturelles.** What similarities or differences between French homes and those of your country can you infer from what you have read?

www **Réalités culturelles**

Le Québec

Quebec is the largest of the ten Canadian provinces. The vast majority of people in **la belle province**, as the **Québécois** refer to it, speak French, while the majority language in the other provinces is English. However, sizable French-speaking minorities exist in Ontario and New Brunswick, and smaller French-speaking populations can be found in the other provinces. The history of Quebec goes back to the sixteenth century, when Jacques Cartier established a French colonial empire in North America called New France. In 1608, Samuel de Champlain founded the city of Quebec. In 1763, at the end of the Seven Years' War, England was granted possession of the whole province. Quebec's French-speaking population now faced the challenge of maintaining its distinct language and cultural heritage under British rule. Over the course of the next two centuries, the **Québécois'** tenacity has resulted in a vibrant French-speaking culture. By the beginning of the 1960s, French Canadians considered themselves not so much a *minority* in the Canadian Confederation as the Francophone *majority* in the province of Quebec. This situation culminated in the passage of the Charter of the French Language in 1997, which established French as the sole official language in the province of Quebec. Its goal was to "ensure the quality and influence of the French language" in North American civilization.

Lecture II

N O T E   L E X I C A L E

Les douze mois de l'année *(months of the year)* sont janvier, février, mars, avril, mai, juin, juillet, août, septembre, octobre, novembre et décembre.

Students will learn to use the months actively in Ch. 7. Have them skim the reading to find four months that are mentioned.

A **Étude du vocabulaire.** Study the following sentences and choose the English words that correspond to the French words in bold print: *for, already, takes place, birth, today, the most, later, illness, to stay, joy.*

1. La **naissance** d'un enfant est une **joie** pour sa famille.
2. **Aujourd'hui** le SIDA est la **maladie** la plus dangereuse et **la plus** mortelle.
3. Il est 4 heures. Tu étudies **déjà**, n'est-ce pas?
4. Non, j'étudie **plus tard**, à 7 heures.
5. Et je ne veux pas **rester** dans ma chambre **pendant** trois heures.
6. Mais le match de football **a lieu** à 7 heures!

B **Parcourez la lecture** *(Skim the reading).* Skim the following reading to identify:

1. the number of musical instruments played by members of Céline's family.
2. the number of people who were invited to her wedding.
3. two examples that confirm that English is not her native language.

Céline Dion et sa famille

La plus jeune d'une famille francophone modeste de quatorze enfants, Céline Dion est aujourd'hui une superstar internationale. Elle est nommée meilleure interprète Pop des années quatre-vingt-dix. Elle gagne tous les prix[1] musicaux imaginables: les Grammy Awards aux États-Unis, les Junos et les prix Félix au Canada et les World Music Awards en Europe.

Née le trente mars 1968 à Charlemagne, un petit village canadien près de Montréal, Céline a huit sœurs et cinq frères. Et tout le monde adore la musique. Son frère Jacques joue de la guitare, son autre frère Clément joue de la batterie[2] et un troisième, Daniel, joue de l'orgue. Sa mère, Thérèse, joue du violon et son père, Adhémar, joue de l'accordéon. À l'âge de 5 ans, Céline chante déjà avec ses frères et sœurs. C'est une véritable famille de musiciens.

Page suivante

---

1. *wins all the prizes*   2. *drums*

À l'âge de 12 ans, avec sa mère et un de ses frères, Céline compose une chanson en français et une cassette démo avec la chanson est envoyée[3] à René Angélil, un imprésario très respecté. René est captivé par la voix[4] de la jeune fille et décide de faire[5] de Céline une grande artiste. Son premier spectacle a lieu le trois mai à la place des Arts à Montréal et les bénéfices sont donnés directement à l'Association de la Fibrose Kystique. Sa nièce Karine Ménard, fille de sa sœur Liette, a la maladie de la fibrose kystique depuis[6] l'âge de neuf mois, une maladie héréditaire et incurable.

Pour avoir une carrière internationale, Céline étudie l'anglais. L'objectif de René Angélil est de propulser Céline dans la grande machine qui est le *show business* américain. Céline, la chanteuse francophone, devient[7] une chanteuse bilingue. Pendant dix-huit ans, elle voyage continuellement. Sa vie[8], c'est les studios d'enregistrement[9], les émissions de télévision, les journalistes, les interviews, les tournages[10] de clips, les promotions, les concerts et les fans. Céline Dion marque l'histoire de la musique avec ses soixante millions d'albums vendus[11]. Elle est aujourd'hui la chanteuse numéro un du monde.

Céline et René se marient le dix-sept décembre 1994, à la basilique Notre-Dame de Montréal. Leur mariage réunit les parents de Céline, ses treize frères et sœurs et cinq cents invités. Céline entre dans la basilique avec ses huit sœurs, Denise, Claudette, Liette, Louise, Ghislaine, Linda, Manon et Pauline.

La plus grande joie de Céline et René est l'arrivée de leur fils, René-Charles Angélil, né le vingt-cinq janvier 2001. Il est baptisé six mois plus tard, le vingt-cinq juillet, à la basilique Notre-Dame. Après la naissance de son fils, Céline décide de rester chez elle et de s'occuper[12] du bébé. Mais en mars 2003, elle signe un contrat avec Caesar's Palace à Las Vegas, une salle de quatre mille places.

D'après les sites web www.sonymusic.fr et www.celinedion.com

www The **Entre amis** web site includes a link with information about Céline Dion.

---

3. *sent*   4. *voice*   5. *to make*   6. *since*   7. *becomes*   8. *life*   9. *recording*   10. *filming*   11. *sold*
12. *to take care of*

C **Questions.** Answer the following questions in French.

1. Comment s'appelle le mari de Céline Dion?
2. Comment s'appelle leur fils?
3. Comment s'appellent les parents de Céline?
4. Combien d'enfants est-ce qu'il y a dans leur famille?
5. Où est-ce que Céline est née?
6. Qui est Karine?
7. À quel âge est-ce que la jeune Céline chante pour l'imprésario?
8. À quel âge est-ce qu'elle se marie?
9. Quel âge a-t-elle aujourd'hui?

D **Inférence.** Reread the passage to determine the following. Be ready to quote the reading to justify your answers.

1. Céline's love of family
2. Her strength of character

VOCABULAIRE ACTIF

Possessions

un bureau *desk*
une calculatrice *calculator*
une chaise *chair*
un chat *cat*
un chien *dog*
une cuisinière *stove*
un fauteuil *armchair*
un lave-linge *washing machine*
un lave-vaisselle *dishwasher*
un lit *bed*
un livre *book*
une mobylette *moped, motorized bicycle*
une moto *motorcycle*
un ordinateur *computer*
un réfrigérateur *refrigerator*
un sofa *sofa*
une stéréo *stereo*
un vélo *bicycle*
une voiture *automobile*

La maison ou l'appartement

un appartement *apartment*
un bureau *office*
une chambre *bedroom*
une cuisine *kitchen*
un garage *garage*
une maison *house*
une salle à manger *dining room*
une salle de bain *bathroom*
une salle de séjour *den; living room*
un salon *living room*
un sous-sol *basement*
les toilettes *restroom*
une véranda *porch*

La famille

un beau-père *stepfather (or father-in-law)*
des beaux-parents *(m. pl.) stepparents (or in-laws)*
une belle-mère *stepmother (or mother-in-law)*
une belle-sœur *sister-in-law*

un(e) cousin(e) *cousin*
un(e) enfant *child*
une famille *family*
une femme *wife*
une fille *daughter*
un fils *son*
un frère *brother*
un demi-frère *stepbrother*
une grand-mère *grandmother*
une arrière-grand-mère *great grandmother*
un grand-père *grandfather*
des grands-parents *(m. pl.) grandparents*
un mari *husband*
une mère *mother*
un neveu *nephew*
une nièce *niece*
un oncle *uncle*
des parents *(m. pl.) parents; relatives*
un père *father*
une petite-fille *granddaughter*
un petit-fils *grandson*
des petits-enfants *(m. pl.) grandchildren*
une sœur *sister*
une tante *aunt*

D'autres noms

l'âge *(m.) age*
un an *year*
un(e) étudiant(e) *student*
une fille *girl*
un garçon *boy*
la gare *(train) station*
un membre *member*
une photo *photograph*
un train *train*

Nombres

trente *thirty*
quarante *forty*
cinquante *fifty*
soixante *sixty*
soixante-dix *seventy*

soixante et onze *seventy-one*
soixante-douze *seventy-two*
quatre-vingts *eighty*
quatre-vingt-un *eighty-one*
quatre-vingt-dix *ninety*
quatre-vingt-onze *ninety-one*
cent *one hundred*
mille *one thousand*
un million *one million*
un milliard *one billion*

Adjectifs possessifs

mon, ma, mes *my*
ton, ta, tes *your*
son, sa, ses *his; her*
notre, nos *our*
votre, vos *your*
leur, leurs *their*

D'autres adjectifs

autre *other*
charmant(e) *charming*
gentil(le) *nice*

Verbes

avoir *to have*
passer (un an) *to spend (a year)*

Prépositions

chez *at the home of*
dans *in*
sur *on*

Conjonction

si *if*

Articles indéfinis

un/une *a, an*
des *some; any*

Adverbes

combien (de) *how many; how much*
comment *how; what*
encore *still; again; more*
trop (de) *too much; too many*

Expressions utiles

Bienvenue! *Welcome!*

C'est *He/she/it is*

Ce sont *They are/There are*

chez moi *at my house*

chez nous *at our house; back home*

chez vous *at your house*

Comment s'appelle-t-il (elle)?
What's his (her) name?

Comment s'appellent-ils (elles)?
What are their names?

Il (elle) s'appelle ... *His (her) name is ...*

Ils (elles) s'appellent ... *Their names are ...*

il y a *there is (are)*

Je suis né(e) *I was born*

Je vous présente ... *Let me introduce you to ...*

Qu'est-ce qu'il y a ... ? *What is there ... ?*

Qu'est-ce qu'il y a? *What's the matter?*

Quel âge avez-vous? (a-t-il?, etc.)
How old are you? (is he?, etc.)

sans doute *probably*

Si! *Yes!*

sur la photo *in the picture*

voici *here is; here are*

vous dites *you say*

L'identité

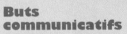

Buts communicatifs
Describing personal attributes
Describing clothing
Describing people and things
Describing what you do at home
Identifying someone's profession

Structures utiles
Quelques groupes d'adjectifs
Ne ... jamais
Les adjectifs de couleur
L'adjectif démonstratif
La place de l'adjectif
Le verbe **faire**
Les mots interrogatifs **qui**, **que** et **quel**

Culture
• *À propos*
Au pair
Le franglais
Les McDo et l'influence américaine
Les cartes postales

• *Il y a un geste*
Bravo!
Paresseux
Ennuyeux
Cher!

• *Lectures*
Offres d'emploi
«Familiale»

Coup d'envoi

Prise de contact

Qu'est-ce que c'est?
(Quel est ce vêtement?°)

What is this article of clothing?

 C'est ...

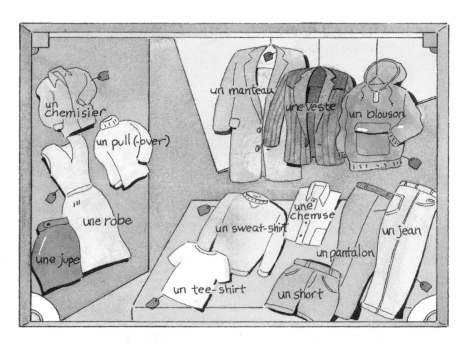

Ce sont...

**Communication
(Presentational):** Once the
Prise de contact has been
practiced, have students
describe what they are wearing
to their classmates.

▶ **Et vous?** Qu'est-ce que vous portez aujourd'hui?°
Moi, je porte ...

What are you wearing today?

Lettre

Une carte postale au professeur

Lori Becker adresse une carte postale à son professeur américain, Madame Walter.

> *Chère Madame,*   *Angers, le 2 Octobre*
>
> *Me voilà au pair chez les Martin. J'aime bien cette[1] famille! Je garde[2] deux des enfants et je fais quelquefois le ménage.[3] Ça me donne[4] beaucoup de travail mais c'est Mme Martin qui fait la cuisine.[5] Et puis[6] les enfants font la vaisselle[7] le soir.*
>
> *Quelle belle ville[8]! Et les gens[9] sont vraiment charmants! Comme chez nous, beaucoup d'étudiants portent un jean et un tee-shirt. Et il y a quatre McDo ici[10]! Je suis heureuse[11] d'être en France, mais il faut[12] étudier beaucoup! Avec mon meilleur souvenir[13],*
>
>   *Lori*

1. *this* 2. *look after* 3. *do housework sometimes* 4. *That gives me* 5. *who does the cooking* 6. *then*
7. *do the dishes* 8. *city* 9. *people* 10. *here* 11. *happy* 12. *it is necessary; I have to* 13. *Best regards,*

▶ **Compréhension.** Taking turns, read the following statements with your partner. Decide whether they are true (**C'est vrai**) or false (**C'est faux**). If a sentence is false, correct it.

1. Lori Becker habite à Angers.
2. Elle habite chez ses parents.
3. Elle travaille pour les Martin.
4. Elle fait la cuisine et la vaisselle.
5. Elle est contente d'être en France.
6. Les vêtements des jeunes Français sont très différents des vêtements des jeunes Américains.

After practicing the *Compréhension*, have students complete ex. A in the Workbook.

Il y a un geste

This gesture is used in the video, *Module 1*.

Bravo! The "thumbs up" gesture is used in French to signify approval.

À propos

Pourquoi est-ce que Lori fait le ménage et garde les enfants de Madame Martin?

a. Elle est masochiste.
b. Elle est très gentille et désire aider *(help)* la famille Martin.
c. Il y a souvent des jeunes filles qui habitent avec une famille française et qui travaillent pour payer leur chambre et leurs repas *(meals)*.

Au pair

Many young women from foreign countries work as **jeunes filles au pair** *(nannies)* in France. They are able to spend a year abroad by agreeing to work in a French home. In exchange for room and board, but only a token salary, they do some light housework and help to take care of the children. Lori is **au pair chez les Martin.**

Le franglais

Borrowing inevitably takes place when languages come in contact. The Norman conquest in 1066 introduced thousands of French words into English and many English words have been borrowed by the French. While some of these French cognates are obvious in meaning (**le chewing-gum, un tee-shirt, un sweat-shirt**), others may surprise you: **un smoking,** for instance, means a *tuxedo.* Official measures have been adopted in France to try to stem the flow of English expressions into the French language. Currently, for example, the term **le logiciel** is being encouraged rather than the English cognate **le software.**

Les McDo et l'influence américaine

Due in large part to the influence of movies and TV programs, there has been an undeniable "sharing" of popular culture among many countries. Some examples are to be found in the way people dress and in the spread of fast-food restaurants. In France, many claim that this is due to the influence of American culture. Decried by some and praised by others, these changes also reflect the fast-paced life of modern France.

Les cartes postales

When sending postcards, most French people will insert the card in an envelope and put stamp and address on the envelope. This perhaps speeds delivery and ensures privacy.

À vous. Describe to your partner what your classmates are wearing.

MODÈLE: VOTRE PARTENAIRE: **Qu'est-ce que Sean porte aujourd'hui?**
VOUS: **Il porte ...**

ENTRE AMIS

J'aime beaucoup vos chaussures. Elles sont très belles.

1. Compliment your partner on some article of clothing s/he is wearing.
2. S/he should respond in a culturally appropriate manner.
3. Point to two other articles of clothing and ask what they are.
4. If s/he doesn't know, s/he should say **Je ne sais pas.**
5. If s/he *is* able to name the articles, be sure to say that s/he speaks French well.

Prononciation

Les voyelles nasales: [ɛ̃], [ɑ̃] et [ɔ̃]

■ Note the pronunciation of the following words:

[ɛ̃]
- **im**possible, **im**probable, **in**telligent, ci**n**quante, vi**n**, vi**n**gt, mi**n**ce

- sy**m**pathique, sy**m**phonie, sy**n**thèse

- f**aim**, améric**ain**, maroc**ain**, mexic**ain**, tr**ain**

- h**ein**

- canadi**en**, itali**en**, bi**en**, je vi**en**s, chi**en**, combi**en**, ti**en**s

Some French speakers pronounce the nasal vowel in the words **un** and parf**um** as [ɛ̃]; others pronounce it as [œ̃]. The [œ̃] pronunciation is not being taught at this level.

[ɑ̃]
- cha**m**bre, **an**, fr**an**çais, ch**an**ter, m**an**ger, gr**an**d, pend**an**t, étudi**an**te, t**an**te, dem**an**dent

- **en**se**m**ble, me**m**bre, par ex**em**ple, **en**, **en**core, comm**en**t, souv**en**t

EXCEPTION — ex**am**en [ɛgzamɛ̃]

[ɔ̃]
- to**m**ber, co**m**bien, n**om**, prén**om**, **on**, **on**t, c**on**versati**on**, n**on**, **on**cle, **on**ze

▶ Now go back and look at how these sounds are spelled and in what kinds of letter combinations they appear. What patterns do you notice?

■ When **-m-** or **-n-** is followed by a consonant or is at the end of a word, it is usually not pronounced. It serves instead to indicate that the preceding vowel is nasal.

| ci**n**quante | **en**semble | co**m**bien | **im**possible |

■ When **-m-** or **-n-** is followed by a written vowel (pronounced or not pronounced), the preceding vowel is *not* nasal.

| ca**n**adien | crè**m**e | télép**h**one |
| bru**n**e | i**n**évitable | i**m**aginaire |

NOTE — The vowel preceding a written **-mm-** or **-nn-** is also not nasal.

| i**nn**ocent | i**mm**obile | co**mm**e | perso**nn**e |

Comparison: Be sure students pronounce nonnasal **i** as [i], not as a short English *i.*

▶ Practice saying the following words after your instructor, paying particular attention to the highlighted vowel sound. In these words, the highlighted vowel sound is *not* nasal.

a méricain	m**ê**me	lim**o**nade	c**o**mme	**u**ne
Mad**a**me	**ai**me	cous**i**ne	c**o**mment	lunettes
ex**a**men	améric**ai**ne	**i**nactif	pers**o**nne	f**u**me

▶ In each of the following pairs of words, one of the words contains a nasal vowel and one does not. Pronounce each word correctly.

1. impossible / immobile
2. minuit / mince
3. faim / aime
4. marocain / marocaine
5. canadienne / canadien
6. une / un
7. ambulance / ami
8. anglaise / année
9. crème / membre
10. dentiste / Denise
11. combien / comment
12. bonne / bon

Buts communicatifs

1. Describing Personal Attributes

Comment est votre meilleur(e) ami(e)? Est-il (elle) ...

calme	ou nerveux (nerveuse)?	
charmant(e)	ou désagréable?	
compréhensif (compréhensive)°	ou intolérant(e)°?	*understanding / intolerant*
discret (discrète)	ou bavard(e)°?	*talkative*
généreux (généreuse)	ou avare°?	*stingy*
gentil(le)	ou méchant(e)°?	*mean*
heureux (heureuse)	ou triste°?	*sad*
intelligent(e)	ou stupide?	
intéressant(e)	ou ennuyeux (ennuyeuse)°?	*boring*
optimiste	ou pessimiste?	
patient(e)	ou impatient(e)?	
travailleur (travailleuse)°	ou paresseux (paresseuse)°?	*hard-working / lazy*

▶ **Et vous?** Comment êtes-vous? Comment sont vos professeurs?

I **La famille de Sandrine.** Correct the following false impressions, beginning with **Mais pas du tout!** Make sure each adjective agrees with the noun it modifies.

MODÈLE: Le frère de Sandrine est désagréable.
Mais pas du tout! Il est charmant.

1. Sandrine est paresseuse.
2. Ses parents sont ennuyeux.
3. Leurs enfants sont très stupides.
4. La mère de Sandrine est triste et pessimiste.
5. Ses frères sont désagréables.
6. La sœur de Sandrine est méchante.
7. Son père est impatient.
8. Sa famille est bavarde.

You may also wish to teach the expressions **la barbe** and **Il a un poil dans la main.**

Il y a un geste

Paresseux. The thumb and index finger of one hand "caress" an imaginary hair in the palm of the other hand. This gesture signifies that someone is so lazy that a hair could grow in his/her palm.

Ennuyeux. The gesture for **ennuyeux** is made by rubbing the knuckles back and forth on the side of the jaw. This rubbing of the "beard" is used to indicate that something is so boring that one could grow a beard while it is happening.

A. Quelques groupes d'adjectifs

Remind students that adjectives ending in **-x** in the masculine singular keep the same form and pronunciation in the masculine plural.

Some feminine adjectives differ from the masculine by a double final consonant as well as by a final **-e**.

Final consonants **c, f, l,** & **r** are usually pronounced: **chic, sportif, intellectuel, travailleur.**

féminin	masculin
discrète(s)	discret(s)
ennuyeuse(s)	ennuyeux
généreuse(s)	généreux
heureuse(s)	heureux
nerveuse(s)	nerveux
paresseuse(s)	paresseux
travailleuse(s)	travailleur(s)
gentille(s)	gentil(s)
intellectuelle(s)	intellectuel(s)
active(s)	actif(s)
compréhensive(s)	compréhensif(s)
sportive(s)	sportif(s)
naïve(s)	naïf(s)
veuve(s)	veuf(s)

■ The **-l** in the masculine form **gentil** is not pronounced. The final consonant sound of the feminine form **gentille** is [j], like the English **y** in *yes*.

gentil   [ʒɑ̃ti]   gentille   [ʒɑ̃tij]

Comparison: Point out that while **cher** and **chère** sound alike, **discret** and **discrète** do not.

■ Many feminine adjectives in written French follow the pattern **-è-** + consonant + **-e**. Their masculine forms omit the final **-e** and the accent on the initial **e**. This may or may not affect pronunciation.

chère   cher *(no change in pronunciation)*
discrète   discret *(pronunciation varies)*

■ Some French adjectives are invariable. There is no change to indicate gender or number.

deux femmes **snob**   des chaussures **chic**

Communication (Interpretive): Have students ask you the questions first.

2 **Qui est comme ça?** Answer the following questions. Make sure each adjective agrees with the subject.

MODÈLE: Qui est patient dans votre famille?
Ma mère est patiente.
Mes sœurs sont patientes aussi.

If ex. 2 is assigned as written homework, remind students to add an **-s** in the plural, unless the word ends in **-s** or **-x**.

1. Qui est travailleur dans votre famille?
2. Qui est bavard dans votre cours de français?
3. Qui est quelquefois triste?
4. Qui est généreux et optimiste?
5. Qui est sportif?
6. Qui est discret?
7. Qui est snob?
8. Comment sont vos parents?
9. Avez-vous des amis qui sont naïfs?
10. Et vous? Comment êtes-vous?

B. *Ne ... jamais*

Review the formation of the negative in Ch. 1, p. 20.

Mon amie **n'**est **jamais** méchante.   *My friend is never mean.*
Mon petit ami **ne** porte **jamais**   *My boyfriend never wears socks.*
   de chaussettes.

■ **Ne ... jamais** *(never)* is placed around the conjugated verb just like **ne ... pas.** It is one of the possible answers to the question **Quand?** *(When?).*

Quand est-ce que tu étudies?   *When do you study?*
Je **n'**étudie **jamais!**   *I never study.*

NOTE

Jamais can be used alone to answer a question.

Quand est-ce que tu pleures?   *When do you cry?*
Jamais!   *Never!*

VOCABULAIRE

Quand? (Adverbes de fréquence)

toujours	*always*
d'habitude	*usually*
généralement	*generally*
souvent	*often*
quelquefois	*sometimes*
rarement	*rarely*
(ne ...) jamais	*never*

3 **Comment sont-ils?** Describe the following people with as many true sentences as you can create. Use items from the lists below (or their opposites). Make all necessary changes, paying special attention to the form of the adjectives.

MODÈLE: **Mes parents ne sont jamais impatients.**
         Ils sont toujours patients.

Follow up with a stand-up drill. Each student has to give an example: **Mon oncle est généreux; il n'est jamais avare.** See the Class Prep CD-ROM for a description of a stand-up drill.

mes parents		intolérant
je		méchant
mon petit ami	ne ... jamais	triste
ma petite amie	rarement	paresseux
mes amis	quelquefois	bavard
mon professeur	souvent	impatient
nous (les étudiants)	d'habitude	pessimiste
le (la) président(e) de l'université	toujours	ennuyeux
		désagréable
		avare

4 **Un test de votre personnalité.** Complete the questionnaire by answering **oui** or **non**. Then read the analysis that follows and write a paragraph to describe yourself.

	oui	non
1. Vous parlez beaucoup avec certaines personnes, mais vous refusez de parler avec tout le monde.	———	———
2. Vous aimez beaucoup les sports, mais vous détestez étudier et travailler.	———	———
3. Vous détestez jouer, danser ou chanter avec les autres, mais vous aimez bien étudier.	———	———
4. Vous avez beaucoup d'argent *(money)*, mais vous donnez rarement de l'argent à vos amis.	———	———
5. Vous n'avez pas d'argent, mais vous n'êtes jamais triste.	———	———
6. Votre conversation est toujours agréable et vous parlez avec tout le monde.	———	———
7. Vous étudiez beaucoup, vous aimez parler français et vous êtes certain(e) que votre professeur de français est charmant.	———	———

Une analyse de vos réponses

1. Si vous répondez **oui** au numéro 1, vous êtes extroverti(e) et bavard(e), mais vous êtes aussi un peu snob.
2. Si vous répondez **oui** au numéro 2, vous êtes sportif (sportive), mais aussi paresseux (paresseuse). Vous n'avez probablement pas de bonnes notes *(good grades)*.
3. Un **oui** au numéro 3, et vous êtes introverti(e), mais aussi travailleur (travailleuse). Vous avez probablement des notes excellentes.
4. Un **oui** au numéro 4, et vous êtes avare et pessimiste. Vous n'avez probablement pas beaucoup d'amis.
5. Si vous répondez **oui** au numéro 5, vous êtes d'habitude optimiste et heureux (heureuse), mais peut-être aussi un peu naïf (naïve).
6. Si vous répondez **oui** au numéro 6, vous n'êtes pas du tout ennuyeux (ennuyeuse). Vos amis sont contents d'être avec vous.
7. Enfin *(finally)*, si votre réponse est **oui** au numéro 7, vous êtes certainement très intelligent(e), charmant(e) et intéressant(e). Les professeurs de français adorent les étudiant(e)s comme vous.

Communication (Interpretive): As a warm-up after students have written the assignment, read one or more of the descriptions and see how many details students can remember.

5 **Cinq personnes que j'aime.** Write a description of five people you like. How much can you tell about each one?

MODÈLE: **Charles Thomas est mon ami.**
Charles est petit et un peu gros.
Il est très gentil et intelligent.
Mais il est aussi un peu paresseux.
Voilà pourquoi il n'est pas du tout sportif.

ENTRE AMIS

Qui est la personne sur la photo?

1. Show your partner a picture (real or imaginary) of someone.
2. Identify that person (name, age, address).
3. Describe his/her personality.
4. Give a physical description as well.
5. Your partner will try to recall what you have shared.

Suggestion: For #3, have students add *always, seldom,* etc. for each characteristic mentioned.

2. Describing Clothing

Voilà Jean-Pierre.	Voilà Marie-Claire.
Qu'est-ce qu'il porte?	Qu'est-ce qu'elle porte?
Il porte un complet, une chemise, une cravate, une montre, une ceinture, des chaussettes et des chaussures.	Elle porte un chapeau, un foulard, un imperméable, des gants et des bottes. Elle porte aussi des lunettes.

The plural of **chapeau** is **chapeaux**.

Communication (Presentational): Follow up pair practice by having several students describe to the class what they are wearing today.

 Et vous? Qu'est-ce que vous portez aujourd'hui?

6 **Qu'est-ce que c'est?** Identify the following items.

MODÈLES:

—Qu'est-ce que c'est?   —Qu'est-ce que c'est?
—C'est une ceinture.   —Ce sont des chaussures.

1.   2.   3.

4.   5.   6.

7.   8.   9.

7 **Qu'est-ce qu'ils portent?** Describe the clothing tastes of several people you know. What items of clothing do they wear often, rarely, never?

MODÈLES: **Mon professeur de français ne porte jamais de jean.**
Je porte souvent un tee-shirt mais je porte rarement un chapeau.

1. mon professeur de français
2. les étudiants de mon cours de français
3. une actrice/un acteur de Hollywood
4. mon/ma meilleur(e) ami(e)
5. les musiciens d'un groupe rock
6. les membres de ma famille
7. moi

www **Réalités culturelles**

Le foulard islamique

A heated debate in France has focused on the decision of a number of Muslim girls to wear the Islamic head scarf (**le foulard** or **le voile islamique**) while in school. According to a recent survey (ifop.com), sixty-five percent of the French questioned would be in favor of a law that would forbid any sign of religious belief in public schools. They cite the **principe de laïcité** (separation of church and state) as their main reason. Such a law was passed in March 2004. It forbids religious apparel and signs that "conspicuously show" a student's religious affiliation.

A number of girls have been suspended from school for covering their hair with the scarf while in class. Two sisters (Lila, 18, and Alma, 16), were expelled from their high school at Aubervilliers in the suburbs of Paris after repeatedly refusing to remove their head scarves.

Source: IFOP and Agence France Presse

C. Les adjectifs de couleur

Point out that **il est** often precedes an adjective and that **c'est** often precedes a noun.

De quelle couleur est le pantalon de Jean-Pierre?
Il est **gris**. C'est un pantalon **gris**.

De quelle couleur est sa chemise?
Elle est **bleue**. C'est une chemise **bleue**.

De quelle couleur sont ses chaussures?
Elles sont **noires**. Ce sont des chaussures **noires**.

▶ **Et vous?** De quelle couleur sont vos vêtements?

VOCABULAIRE

Quelques couleurs

You may wish to point out that **marron** = *brown*, not *maroon*.

Communication (Interpretive): As a warm-up to reinforce comprehension, say: **Levez-vous si vous portez des baskets noires,** etc.

	Féminin	Masculin		Féminin	Masculin
	blanche	blanc		marron	marron
	grise	gris		jaune	jaune
	verte	vert		orange	orange
	violette	violet		rose	rose
	bleue	bleu		rouge	rouge
	noire	noir		beige	beige

NOTE ⊢Plurals of colors are formed by adding **-s.** Exceptions in this list are **gris,** (which already ends in **-s**) and **marron** and **orange,** which are invariable: **des cheveux** *orange,* **des chaussettes** *marron.*

8 **De quelle couleur sont leurs vêtements?** Ask your partner about the color of the following articles of clothing.

MODÈLES: les chaussures de Jérôme (noir)

VOUS: **De quelle couleur sont ses chaussures?**
VOTRE PARTENAIRE: **Elles sont noires. Ce sont des chaussures noires.**

le pull de Martine (bleu)

VOUS: **De quelle couleur est son pull?**
VOTRE PARTENAIRE: **Il est bleu. C'est un pull bleu.**

Follow-up: Use real names and clothing of students in the class.

1. la cravate de Denis (jaune et bleu)
2. la robe de Françoise (vert)
3. la veste de Jean (gris)
4. l'imperméable d'Annette (blanc)
5. les chaussettes d'un(e) autre étudiant(e)
6. la chemise d'une autre personne
7. les chaussures de votre partenaire
8. les vêtements du professeur

VOCABULAIRE

Pour décrire *(to describe)* les vêtements

bon marché	*inexpensive*	ou	cher (chère)	*expensive*
chic	*stylish*	ou	confortable	*comfortable*
élégant(e)	*elegant*	ou	ordinaire	*ordinary, everyday*
propre	*clean*	ou	sale	*dirty*
simple	*simple, plain*	ou	bizarre	*weird, funny-looking*

 This gesture is used in video, *Module 7.*

Il y a un geste

An alternate gesture is to shake the open hand vigorously. See, for example, the gesture **Quelle histoire!,** Ch. 14.

Cher! Similar to its English equivalent, the gesture for **cher!** is made by rubbing the thumb, index, and middle fingers together.

NOTE ──┐ **Chic** and **bon marché** are invariable. They do not change in the feminine or in the plural: **Ce sont des chaussures *chic*, mais elles sont *bon marché*.**

Confortable is not used to describe how a person feels. It is used to describe *a thing:* **une chemise confortable, une vie confortable.**

Synthèse: les adjectifs invariables

bon marché   chic   marron   orange   snob

---

9 **Au contraire!** Your partner will make a series of statements with which you will disagree. Provide the corrections by following the model.

MODÈLE: la robe de Simone (cher)

VOTRE PARTENAIRE: **La robe de Simone est chère.**

VOUS: **Non, elle n'est pas chère. C'est une robe bon marché.**

1. la veste de Martin (élégant)
2. le sweat-shirt de Monsieur Dupont (propre)
3. la robe de Pascale (chic)
4. les chaussettes du professeur (?)
5. l'imperméable de l'inspecteur Colombo (?)
6. les vêtements de deux autres étudiants (?)

Supply the adjectives for #4–6.

10 **À vous.** Answer the following questions.

1. Qu'est-ce que vous portez aujourd'hui?
2. De quelle couleur sont vos vêtements?
3. Décrivez les vêtements que vous portez.
4. Décrivez les vêtements d'un(e) autre étudiant(e).
5. Qu'est-ce que le professeur porte d'habitude?
6. De quelle couleur sont ses vêtements?
7. Qui ne porte jamais de jean dans votre classe de français?
8. Qui porte rarement des chaussures bon marché?
9. Qu'est-ce qu'on porte quand il fait froid?

Suggestion: Have students describe the clothes of the characters in the video.

D. L'adjectif démonstratif

Cette femme est très intelligente. — *That (this) woman is very intelligent.*

Ce vin est excellent! — *This (that) wine is excellent!*

Vous aimez **cet** appartement? — *Do you like this (that) apartment?*

Qui sont **ces** deux personnes? — *Who are those (these) two people?*

	singulier	pluriel
masculin:	ce (cet)	ces
féminin:	cette	ces

■ The demonstrative adjectives are the equivalent of the English adjectives *this (that)* and *these (those)*.

ce garçon	*this boy*	or	*that boy*
cet ami	*this (male) friend*	or	*that (male) friend*
cette amie	*this (female) friend*	or	*that (female) friend*
ces amis	*these friends*	or	*those friends*
ces amies	*these (female) friends*	or	*those (female) friends*

■ **Cet** is used before masculine singular words that begin with a vowel sound. It is pronounced exactly like **cette**.

cet homme	*this man*	or	*that man*
cet autre professeur	*this other teacher*	or	*that other teacher*

■ If the context does not distinguish between the meanings *this* and *that* or *these* and *those*, it is possible to make the distinction by adding **-ci** (for *this/these*) or **-là** (for *that/those*) to the noun.

J'aime beaucoup cette chemise-**ci**.	*I like this shirt a lot.*
Ces femmes-**là** sont françaises.	*Those women are French.*

■ **Au grand magasin (At the department store).** While shopping, you overhear a number of comments but are unable to make out all the words. Try to complete the following sentences using one of the demonstrative adjectives **ce, cet, cette,** or **ces,** as appropriate.

1. Vous aimez _____ chaussures? Oui, mais je déteste _____ chemise.
2. _____ pantalon est beau. Mais _____ jupes sont très chères.
3. _____ jean est trop petit pour _____ homme-là.
4. Je ne sais pas comment s'appelle _____ vêtement-là.
5. _____ robes sont jolies, mais _____ sweat-shirt est laid.
6. J'aime beaucoup _____ pull-là, mais je trouve _____ veste trop longue.

Brainstorm with the class for possible reasons for disliking items before putting students in pairs.

■ **Non, je n'aime pas ça.** Your shopping has made you tired and grouchy. Respond to your friend's questions or comments by saying that you dislike the item(s) in question. Use a demonstrative adjective in each response and invent a reason for your disapproval.

Modèle: Voilà une robe rouge.
Je n'aime pas beaucoup cette robe; elle est bizarre.

1. Voilà une belle cravate.
2. Voilà un ordinateur!
3. Oh! la petite calculatrice!
4. C'est un beau chapeau!
5. Tu aimes les chaussures vertes?
6. Voilà des chaussettes blanches intéressantes.
7. J'adore le chemisier bleu.
8. Tu aimes la veste de ce monsieur?

13 **Qui est-ce?** Describe as completely as possible the clothing of a fellow classmate.

MODÈLE: **Cette personne porte un pull jaune et un pantalon vert. Elle porte des chaussures marron. Elle ne porte pas de chaussettes. Ses vêtements ne sont peut-être pas très élégants mais ils sont confortables.**

ENTRE AMIS

Au téléphone

You are meeting a friend for dinner in twenty minutes.

1. Call to find out what s/he is wearing.
2. Find out the colors of his/her clothing.
3. Describe what you are wearing as completely as possible.

3. Describing People and Things

De quelle couleur sont les yeux° et les cheveux° de Michèle?   *eyes / hair*

Elle a les yeux bleus.

Elle a les cheveux blonds.

De quelle couleur sont les yeux et les cheveux de Thierry?

Il a les yeux verts et les cheveux roux°.   *red*

De quelle couleur sont les yeux et les cheveux de Monsieur Monot?

Il a les yeux noirs, mais il n'a pas de cheveux.

Il est chauve°.   *bald*

▶ **Et vous?** De quelle couleur sont vos yeux et vos cheveux?

(REMARQUES)

1. Use the definite article **les** with the verb **avoir** to describe the color of a person's hair and eyes.

   Thierry **a les** yeux verts et **les** cheveux roux.

2. The word **cheveu** is almost always used in the plural, which is formed by adding **-x.**

   Michèle a **les cheveux** blonds.

3. Note that the adjective used to describe red hair is **roux** (**rousse**), never **rouge.**

   Il a les cheveux **roux.**

   Notre petite-fille est **rousse.**

4. Use the adjective **brun(e)** to describe brown hair, never **marron.**

   Alissa a les cheveux **bruns.**

   Elle est **brune.**

Remember that the masculine plural adjective is used with the words **yeux** and **cheveux: les yeux bleus, les cheveux noirs.**

The singular **cheveu** refers to a single strand of hair.

14 **Leurs yeux et leurs cheveux.** Complete the following sentences with a form of the verb **être** or **avoir,** as appropriate.

1. Mon père _____ les yeux bleus. Il _____ chauve.
2. Brigitte et Virginie _____ les cheveux roux.
3. Vous _____ les yeux noirs.
4. De quelle couleur _____ les yeux de votre mère?
5. Elle _____ les yeux verts.
6. Mes oncles _____ les cheveux blonds, mais ils _____ aussi un peu chauves.

15 **De quelle couleur ... ?** Ask and answer questions with a partner based on the list below. If you don't know the answer, guess.

MODÈLES: vos yeux

VOUS: **De quelle couleur sont vos yeux?**
VOTRE PARTENAIRE: **J'ai les yeux verts.**

les cheveux de votre oncle

VOUS: **De quelle couleur sont ses cheveux?**
VOTRE PARTENAIRE: **Il n'a pas de cheveux. Il est chauve.**

Communication (Presentational): Follow-up: Have students report as many of their partner's answers as they can.

1. vos yeux
2. vos cheveux
3. les yeux de votre meilleur(e) ami(e)
4. les cheveux de votre meilleur(e) ami(e)
5. les yeux et les cheveux d'un(e) autre étudiant(e)
6. les cheveux de vos grands-parents
7. les yeux et les cheveux de vos frères et sœurs (ou de vos amis)

E. La place de l'adjectif

un livre **intéressant**	*an interesting book*
une femme **charmante**	*a charming woman*
un **bon** livre	*a good book*
l'**autre** professeur	*the other teacher*

■ Most adjectives (including colors and nationalities) follow the noun they modify.

un homme **charmant**	un garçon **bavard**
une femme **intelligente**	une fille **sportive**
une robe **bleue**	une voiture **française**

■ Certain very common adjectives, however, normally precede the noun.

1. Some that you already know are:

autre	grand	joli
beau	gros	petit
bon	jeune	vieux

2. Two others that usually precede the noun are:

masculin singulier	féminin singulier	masculin pluriel	féminin pluriel	équivalent anglais
mauvais	**mauvaise**	**mauvais**	**mauvaises**	*bad*
nouveau	**nouvelle**	**nouveaux**	**nouvelles**	*new*

> Remember that **nouveau,** like **beau** and **chapeau,** forms the plural by adding **-x.**

> Point out that students have already learned the special form **cet** to replace **ce** before a noun beginning with a vowel sound.

3. **Beau, vieux,** and **nouveau** each have a special masculine singular form (**bel, vieil, nouvel**) for use when they precede a noun beginning with a vowel sound. These special forms are pronounced exactly like the feminine forms.

un **bel** homme   un **vieil** ami   un **nouvel** appartement

> The rules governing **obligatory liaison** will be summarized in Ch. 5.

4. Adjectives ending in a silent consonant are linked by liaison to words beginning with a vowel sound. When linked, a final **-s** or **-x** is pronounced [z] and a final **-d** is pronounced [t].

un mauvais [z]hôtel   deux vieux [z]amis   un grand [t]hôtel

5. A few adjectives can be used either before or after the noun. Their position determines the exact meaning of the adjective.

un **ancien** professeur	*a former teacher*
un château **ancien**	*an ancient castle*

le **pauvre** garçon	*the unfortunate boy*
le garçon **pauvre**	*the boy who has no money*

In formal spoken and written French, **des** is replaced by **de** if a plural adjective comes *before* the noun:

des professeurs intelligents	**des** voitures françaises

Mais: **de** bons professeurs intelligents   **d**'autres voitures françaises

---

16   **C'est vrai.** Restate the following sentence.

MODÈLES: Les chaussures de Monsieur Masselot sont sales.
C'est vrai. Il a des chaussures sales.

L'appartement de Monsieur Masselot est vieux.
C'est vrai. Il a un vieil appartement.

1. L'appartement de Monsieur Masselot est beau.
2. Les enfants de Monsieur Masselot sont jeunes.
3. La femme de Monsieur Masselot est intelligente.
4. Les parents de Monsieur Masselot sont charmants.
5. Le chat de Monsieur Masselot est gros.
6. Le chien de Monsieur Masselot est méchant.
7. La voiture de Monsieur Masselot est mauvaise.
8. L'ordinateur de Monsieur Masselot est nouveau.
9. L'appartement de Monsieur Masselot est grand.
10. Le réfrigérateur de Monsieur Masselot est petit.
11. La cravate de Monsieur Masselot est bleue.
12. Les chaussettes de Monsieur Masselot sont bizarres.

17   **Quelques compliments.** Select items from each of the lists to pay a few compliments. How many compliments can you create? Make all necessary changes.

MODÈLES: **C'est une jolie robe.**
Tu as des chaussures chic.

Remind students of the French reaction to compliments (see Ch. 2, p. 37). As an extension, have them respond to their partner's compliments.

You may require students to use **de** instead of **des** before plural adjectives that precede nouns. If you do, remind them that this is a more formal style.

		robe	joli
		maison	élégant
		appartement	bon
tu as	un	vêtements	magnifique
c'est	une	chemise	intéressant
ce sont	des	chemisier	superbe
		chaussettes	beau
		chaussures	chic
		jean	

Review pp. 22, 94 & 105.

18 **Une identité secrète.** Choose the name of someone famous that everyone will recognize. The other students will attempt to guess the identity of this person by asking questions. Answer only **oui** or **non.**

MODÈLE: **C'est une femme?**
Est-ce qu'elle est belle?
A-t-elle les cheveux roux?
Est-ce qu'elle porte souvent des vêtements élégants? etc.

ENTRE AMIS

Warm-up: Describe a student (clothing, hair, eyes, etc.) and ask the class to guess his/her identity.

Mon ami(e)

1. Find out the name and age of your partner's best friend.
2. Find out that friend's hair and eye color.
3. Inquire about the clothing that that friend usually wears.
4. What else can you find out about that friend?
5. Repeat the information you obtained in order to verify it.

4. Describing What You Do at Home

Que fais°-tu chez toi°, Catherine?   *do / at home*
    Je regarde la télé ou j'écoute la radio.
    J'étudie et je fais mes devoirs°.   *homework*
    Je fais souvent la cuisine°.   *the cooking*
    Je parle avec mes parents.
    Je fais quelquefois la vaisselle°.   *the dishes*
    Je fais rarement le ménage°.   *housework*

▶ **Et vous?** Que faites-vous chez vous?

V O C A B U L A I R E

Des choses qu'on fait
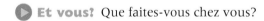

les courses	*errands; shopping*	une promenade	*walk; ride*
la cuisine	*cooking; food*	les provisions	*groceries*
les devoirs	*homework*	la sieste	*nap*
la lessive	*wash; laundry*	la vaisselle	*dishes*
le ménage	*housework*		

F. Le verbe *faire*

Je déteste **faire** les courses, mais j'aime **faire** la liste.	*I hate doing the shopping, but I like making the list.*
Ma mère **fait** des provisions.	*My mother does the grocery shopping.*
Mes sœurs **font** la cuisine.	*My sisters do the cooking.*
Et c'est moi qui **fais** la vaisselle.	*And I'm the one who does the dishes.*
Nous **faisons** tous la lessive.	*We all do the wash.*

Idiomatic uses of **faire** to describe the weather will be studied again in Ch. 7.

faire *(to do; to make)*

je	**fais**	nous	**faisons**
tu	**fais**	vous	**faites**
il/elle/on	**fait**	ils/elles	**font**

■ The **-ai-** in **nous faisons** is pronounced [ə] as in **le, de,** etc.

■ The plural **les devoirs** means *homework*. The singular **la vaisselle** means *the dishes*. The plural **les courses** means *the shopping*.

Je fais **mes devoirs.**	*I do my homework.*
Qui aime faire **la vaisselle?**	*Who likes to do the dishes?*
Nous faisons **nos courses** ensemble.	*We do our shopping together.*

Idiomatic uses of **faire** to describe the weather will be studied again in Ch. 7.

■ There are a number of idiomatic uses of the verb **faire.**

Je ne **fais** jamais **la sieste.**	*I never take a nap.*
Veux-tu **faire une promenade?**	*Would you like to take a walk?*
Quel temps fait-il?	*What is the weather like?*
Il fait chaud.	*It's hot out.*
Faites attention!	*Pay attention!* or *Watch out!*

■ A question using **faire** does not necessarily require the verb **faire** in the response.

Que **faites**-vous?
Je *patine*, je *chante*, je *regarde* la télé, j'*écoute* la radio, etc.

19 **Nous faisons beaucoup de choses.** Use the list below to create as many factual sentences as you can.

MODÈLES: **Mon petit ami ne fait jamais de promenade.**
Ma mère ne fait jamais la sieste.
Nous faisons souvent les courses.

mes amis			la lessive
mon petit ami		toujours	la vaisselle
ma petite amie		d'habitude	la sieste
ma mère	faire	souvent	les courses
mon père		quelquefois	la cuisine
nous (ma famille)		rarement	une promenade
je		ne ... jamais	le ménage
			des provisions
			attention

20 **À vous.** Answer the following questions.

1. Faites-vous toujours vos devoirs?
2. Faites-vous la sieste l'après-midi?
3. Faites-vous souvent des promenades?
4. Faites-vous quelquefois la cuisine pour vos amis?
5. Est-ce que vous aimez la cuisine italienne?
6. Qui fait le ménage d'habitude dans votre famille?
7. Qui fait généralement la lessive?

Communication (Presentational):
Follow-up: Have several
students tell what they found out
about their partners.

ENTRE AMIS

Chez toi

1. Find out where your partner lives.
2. Find out who does the grocery shopping and who does the cooking at his/her house.
3. How much can you find out about what your partner does or does not do at home?

*Communication
(Presentational):* Follow-up:
Have several students tell what
they found out about their
partners.

En France, on aime faire ses
courses au marché.

5. Identifying Someone's Profession

—Chantal, qu'est-ce que tu veux faire dans la vie?°   *what do you want to do in life?*
—Je voudrais être journaliste. Et toi?
—Je ne sais pas encore.°   *I don't know yet.*

A more extensive list of professions can be found in Appendix B at the end of this book.

▶ **Et vous?** Qu'est-ce que vous voulez faire dans la vie?

V O C A B U L A I R E

Quelques professions

architecte		*ingénieur	*engineer*
artiste		interprète	
assistant(e) social(e)	*social worker*	journaliste	
athlète		*médecin	*doctor*
avocat(e)	*lawyer*	ménagère	*housewife*
*cadre	*executive*	*militaire	*serviceman (-woman)*
comptable	*accountant*	ouvrier (ouvrière)	*laborer*
cuisinier (cuisinière)	*cook*	patron(ne)	*boss*
*écrivain	*writer*	pharmacien(ne)	
employé(e)		*professeur	
fermier (fermière)	*farmer*	programmeur	
fonctionnaire	*civil servant*	(programmeuse)	
homme (femme) d'affaires	*businessman (-woman)*	secrétaire	
homme (femme) politique	*politician*	vendeur (vendeuse)	*salesperson*
infirmier (infirmière)	*nurse*		

*Certain professions are used only with masculine articles and adjectives **(un, mon, ce)** for a woman, as well as a man:** **Elle est médecin. C'est un médecin.**

Nouns of profession, nationality, and religion all act like adjectives when used this way.

Communication (Presentational): Ask students to tell which professions they think are the most interesting: **À mon avis, les professions les plus intéressantes sont ...**

REMARQUES

1. There are two ways to identify someone's profession:

   • One can use a name or a subject pronoun + **être** + profession, without any article.

Céline **est artiste.**	*Céline is an artist.*
Je **suis pharmacienne.**	*I am a pharmacist.*
Il **est ouvrier.**	*He is a factory worker.*

   • For *he*, *she*, and *they*, one can also say **c'est** (**ce sont**) + indefinite article + profession.

C'est un professeur.	*He (she) is a teacher.*
Ce n'est pas un employé; c'est le patron.	*He isn't an employee; he's the boss.*
Ce sont des fonctionnaires.	*They are civil servants.*

2. To give more detail, one can use a possessive adjective or an article with an adjective. **C'est (ce sont)**, not **il/elle est (ils/elles sont)**, is used.

C'est ton secrétaire?	*Is he your secretary?*
Monique est une athlète **excellente.**	*Monique is an excellent athlete.*
Ce sont des cuisiniers **français.**	*They are French cooks.*

21 **Que voulez-vous faire?** Use the vocabulary list above to select professions that you would like and professions that you would not like.

MODÈLE: **Je voudrais être journaliste mais je ne voudrais pas être écrivain.**

22 **Qu'est-ce qu'il faut faire?** *(What do you have to do?)* The following sentences tell what preparation is needed for different careers. Complete the sentences with the name of the appropriate career(s).

MODÈLE: Il faut étudier la biologie pour être **médecin, dentiste** ou **infirmier.**

1. Il faut étudier la pédagogie pour être ...
2. Il faut étudier la comptabilité pour être ...
3. Il faut étudier le commerce pour être ...
4. Il faut étudier le journalisme pour être ...
5. Il faut étudier l'agriculture pour être ...
6. Il faut parler deux ou trois langues pour être ...
7. Il faut désirer aider les autres pour être ...
8. Il faut avoir une personnalité agréable pour être ...
9. Il faut faire très bien la cuisine pour être ...

www Réalités culturelles

Jean Piaget, psychologue et pédagogue suisse

Jean Piaget, well-known researcher in cognitive psychology, was born in the French-speaking part of Switzerland on August 9, 1896. While still in secondary school, he wrote a short paper on an albino sparrow that started him on a brilliant scientific career. He later obtained a doctorate in natural science from the University of Neuchâtel and moved to France, where he developed an interest in psychoanalysis and standardized intelligence tests.

Piaget wrote over sixty books and several hundred articles. Among Piaget's contributions is his attempt to map out the various cognitive stages through which children move as they transition from childhood to adolescence. For instance, Piaget noticed that during the first years of children's cognitive development, they do not realize that an object still exists if it moves out of sight ("object permanence"); that they see things only from their own perspectives ("egocentrism"); and that prior to the age of seven, children fail the "conservation" test and believe that, for instance, a liter of water increases in quantity if it is poured into a skinny, tall container and loses quantity if it is poured into a flat, larger container. Piaget's keen observations have contributed immensely to our understanding of child psychology. Educators in Europe and the United States have used his research to build effective and responsive primary education curricula. Jean Piaget died in Geneva on September 16, 1980.

G. Les mots interrogatifs *qui, que* et *quel*

Qui and que will be studied in detail in Ch. 15. For the present, students need only make the distinctions explained here.

Qui fait la cuisine dans votre famille?	*Who does the cooking in your family?*
Que faites-vous après le dîner?	*What do you do after dinner?*
À **quelle** heure dînez-vous?	*At what time do you eat dinner?*

■ **Qui** *(who, whom)* is a pronoun. Use it in questions as the subject of a verb or as the object of a verb or preposition.

Point out that **qui** never drops the **i** in front of a vowel.

Qui est-ce?	*Who is it?*
Qui regardez-vous?	*At whom are you looking?*
Avec **qui** parlez-vous?	*With whom are you talking?*

■ **Que** *(what)* is also a pronoun. Use it in questions as the object of a verb. It will be followed either by inversion of the verb and subject or by **est-ce que.** There are therefore two forms of this question: **Que ... ?** and **Qu'est-ce que ... ?**

Que font-ils? **Qu'est-ce qu'**ils font?	*What do they do?*

■ Don't confuse **Est-ce que ... ?** (simple question) and **Qu'est-ce que ... ?** *(What?)*.

Est-ce que vous voulez danser?	*Do you want to dance?*
Qu'est-ce que vous voulez faire?	*What do you want to do?*
Qu'est-ce qu'il y a?	*What is it? What's the matter?*

■ **Quel** *(which, what)* is an adjective. It is always used with a noun and agrees with the noun.

Quel temps fait-il?	*What is the weather like?*
Quelles actrices aimez-vous?	*Which actresses do you like?*

Comparison: Be sure students understand that translating English expressions literally may get them into trouble. Point out that it is better to memorize certain common expressions such as **Quel âge avez-vous?** and **Comment vous appelez-vous?**

	singulier	pluriel
masculin	**quel**	**quels**
féminin	**quelle**	**quelles**

NOTE

The noun may either follow **quel** or be separated from it by the verb **être.**

Quels vêtements portez-vous?	*Which clothes are you wearing?*
Quelle est votre **adresse?**	*What is your address?*

Suggestion: Elicit the questions from the class before pairing students.

23 **Quelles questions!** Ask questions using the appropriate form of **quel** with the words provided below.

MODÈLE: votre profession
Quelle est votre profession?

1. heure/il est
2. à/heure/vous mangez
3. temps/il fait
4. votre nationalité
5. âge/vous avez
6. vêtements/vous portez/quand il fait chaud
7. votre numéro *(m.)* de téléphone
8. de/couleur/vos yeux

24 *Qui, que ou quel?* Complete the following sentences.

1. _____ fait le ménage chez toi?
2. _____ font tes parents?
3. _____ âge ont tes amis?
4. De _____ couleur sont les cheveux du professeur?
5. Avec _____ parles-tu français?
6. À _____ heure dînes-tu d'habitude?
7. _____ désires-tu faire dans la vie?
8. _____ fais-tu après le dîner?

25 **À vous.** Answer the following questions.

1. Avez-vous des frères ou des sœurs? Si oui, que font-ils à la maison? Qu'est-ce qu'ils désirent faire dans la vie?
2. Que voulez-vous faire dans la vie?
3. Qu'est-ce que vous étudiez ce semestre?
4. Qu'est-ce que votre meilleur(e) ami(e) désire faire dans la vie?
5. Qui fait la cuisine chez vous?
6. À quelle heure faites-vous vos devoirs d'habitude?
7. Que font vos amis après le dîner?
8. Qui ne fait jamais la vaisselle?

ENTRE AMIS

Dans un avion *(In an airplane)*

1. Greet the person sitting next to you on the plane.
2. Find out his/her name and address.
3. Find out what s/he does.
4. What can you find out about his/her family?
5. Find out what the family members do.

Intégration www ◎

Révision

A Portraits personnels. Provide the information requested below.

1. Décrivez les membres de votre famille.
2. Décrivez votre meilleur(e) ami(e).
3. Décrivez une personne dans la salle de classe. Demandez à votre partenaire de deviner *(guess)* l'identité de cette personne.

B Trouvez quelqu'un qui ... Interview your classmates in French to find someone who ...

Prime this activity by eliciting the questions first. See p. 51 for suggestions.

MODÈLE: wants to be a doctor
Est-ce que tu désires être médecin?

1. likes to wear jeans and a sweatshirt
2. is wearing white socks
3. never wears a hat
4. has green eyes
5. likes to cook
6. likes French food
7. hates to do housework
8. wants to be a teacher
9. takes a nap in the afternoon

Communication (Presentational & Interpretive): If students present their descriptions to the class, others can be asked to recall information that was presented. Assign the *Rédaction* at the end of Ch. 4 in the Workbook.

C Début de rédaction. Write a description of two people you know. Describe their personality, hair and eye color, and taste in clothing. Indicate what they like to do. Can you also describe their (future) profession?

MODÈLE: **Anne Smith est étudiante. C'est une jeune fille travailleuse et très gentille. Elle est assez grande et elle a les cheveux bruns et les yeux noirs. Anne porte d'habitude des vêtements simples et confortables. Elle fait bien la cuisine et elle adore la cuisine française. Elle désire être femme d'affaires.**

Communication (Interpretive): Encourage students to use the practice test on the Lab Audio Program.

3: Remind students of the idiomatic use of **faire** in weather expressions: **Il fait chaud.** This will be taught in more detail in Ch. 7.

Video for Chapter 4: A. Video worksheets (Cahier); B. ACE Video practice test (WWW); C. CD-ROM

D À vous. Answer the following questions.

1. De quelle couleur sont les vêtements que vous portez aujourd'hui?
2. Qu'est-ce que vos amis portent en classe d'habitude?
3. Quels vêtements aimez-vous porter quand il fait chaud?
4. De quelle couleur sont les yeux de votre meilleur(e) ami(e)?
5. De quelle couleur sont les cheveux de votre meilleur(e) ami(e)?
6. Que faites-vous à la maison?
7. Que font les autres membres de votre famille chez vous?
8. Que voulez-vous faire dans la vie?
9. Qu'est-ce que votre meilleur(e) ami(e) désire faire?

Négociations:

Nos amis. Work with your partner to complete the forms. Your partner's form is in Appendix D. Ask questions to determine the information that is missing.

MODÈLE: **Est-ce que Marie a les yeux bleus?**

For complete instructions on how to prepare for and to use this activity, see *Négociations* on the Class Prep CD-ROM.

A

nom	yeux	cheveux	description	à la maison	dans la vie	vêtement
Marie	verts			vaisselle	avocate	
Alain		bruns	calme		professeur	cravate
Chantal	marron		extrovertie			lunettes
Éric		chauve		cuisine		veste
Karine		blonds				
Pierre	bleus		sportif	ménage	vendeur	
Sylvie	gris					chaussures
Jean		noirs	travailleur	sieste	ingénieur	

Lecture I

A **Parcourez les petites annonces.** Glance at the classified ads below to find out what kind of job each one is advertising. Guess which one would pay the most. Which ones require a car? Which ones do not require experience? Which ones are for summer employment only?

Typical salaries in euros per month:
(1) 100 euros
(2) 1,000 euros
(3) 1,000–1,500 euros
(4) 0 euros
(5) 2,000–3,000 euros
(6) 2,000–3,000 euros

Offres d'emploi

1 _____
Bébé, un an et demi, cherche fille au pair de nationalité américaine ou canadienne, expérience avec enfants. Appelez Cunin en fin de matinée 02.43.07.47.26.

2 _____
Nous recherchons des secrétaires bilingues. Appelez l'Agence bilingue Paul Grassin au 02.42.76.10.14.

3 _____
Professeurs anglophones pour enseigner l'anglais aux lycéens étrangers en France, école internationale, château. Deux sessions: du 30 juin au 21 juillet; du 25 juillet au 14 août. Tél. 02.41.93.21.62.

4 _____
Famille offre logement et repas en échange de baby-sitting le soir et certains week-ends. Les journées sont libres. Écrivez BP 749, 49000 Angers.

5 _____
Opportunité de carrière. Compagnie internationale, établie depuis 71 ans, est à la recherche de jeunes personnes ambitieuses pour compléter son équipe commerciale. Si vous avez une apparence soignée, si vous êtes positif(ve), si vous possédez une voiture, appelez-nous au 02.41.43.00.22.

6 _____
Vous cherchez un job d'été (juillet et août) bien rémunéré, vous aimez discuter et vous possédez une voiture: venez rejoindre notre équipe de commerciaux. Formation assurée. Débutants acceptés. Tél. 02.41.43.15.80.

You may want students to give
their reasons in English to check
their comprehension.

B **Cela vous intéresse?** *(Does this interest you?)* Reorder the classified
ads above according to how much they appeal to you (which ones you
would apply for and in what order). Be prepared to explain your reasons.

C **Votre petite annonce.** Write a classified ad to say you are looking
for work in France. Mention your personal description and experience and
include the fact that you speak French. Be sure to tell how you can be
contacted.

Lecture II

A **Étude du vocabulaire.** Study the following sentences and choose
the English words that correspond to the French words in bold print: *knits,
killed, no more, war, nothing.*

1. Cet étudiant paresseux **ne** travaille **plus**.
2. Oui, il **ne** fait **rien**.
3. Ma grand-mère **tricote** souvent des vêtements. Elle **fait du tricot**
   quand elle regarde la télévision.
4. Il y a des militaires qui sont **tués** pendant la **guerre**.

Comparison: Explain that
tricoter and **faire du tricot**
have the same meaning.

B **Correspondances.** The poet associates each of the family members
with specific activities. Read the poem and then identify the person(s) that
the poet associates with the activities in the right-hand column.

	___ fait la guerre
	___ fait des affaires
a. le fils	___ fait du tricot
b. la mère	___ est tué
c. le père	___ est ménagère
	___ est homme d'affaires
	___ est militaire
	___ vont au cimetière

Familiale

La mère fait du tricot
Le fils fait la guerre
Elle trouve ça tout naturel la mère
Et le père qu'est-ce qu'il fait le père?
Il fait des affaires
Sa femme fait du tricot
Son fils la guerre
Lui[1] des affaires
Il trouve ça tout naturel le père

---

1. *him*

Et le fils et le fils

Qu'est-ce qu'il trouve le fils?

Il ne trouve rien absolument rien le fils

Le fils sa mère fait du tricot son père des affaires lui la guerre

Quand il aura fini[2] la guerre

Il fera[3] des affaires avec son père

La guerre continue la mère continue elle tricote

Le père continue il fait des affaires

Le fils est tué il ne continue plus

Le père et la mère vont au cimetière

Ils trouvent ça naturel le père et la mère

La vie continue la vie avec le tricot la guerre les affaires

Les affaires la guerre le tricot la guerre

Les affaires les affaires et les affaires

La vie avec le cimetière.

Jacques Prévert, Éditions Gallimard

---

2. *will have finished*   3. *will do*

C **Questions.** Answer the following questions in French.

1. Qui sont les personnages du poème?
2. Quel est le rôle de chaque personnage?
3. Qu'est-ce que le père et la mère trouvent naturel?

D **Discussion.**

1. Prévert wrote this poem shortly after the Second World War. What does the poem reveal about his experience of war?
2. What words are repeated in the poem? How does the poet use repetition to reinforce his message?

E **Familles de mots.** Can you guess the meaning of the following words? At least one member of each word family is found in the reading.

1. tricoter, le tricot, un tricoteur, une tricoteuse
2. vivre, vivant(e), la vie
3. la nature, naturel, naturelle, naturellement

VOCABULAIRE ACTIF

Quelques professions

un(e) assistant(e) social(e) *social worker*
un(e) avocat(e) *lawyer*
un cadre *executive*
un(e) comptable *accountant*
un cuisinier/une cuisinière *cook*
un écrivain *writer*
un(e) employé(e) *employee*
un fermier/une fermière *farmer*
un(e) fonctionnaire *civil servant*
un homme d'affaires/une femme d'affaires *businessman/business-woman*
un homme politique/une femme politique *politician*
un infirmier/une infirmière *nurse*
un ingénieur *engineer*
un médecin *doctor*
une ménagère *housewife*
un(e) militaire *serviceman (-woman)*
un ouvrier/une ouvrière *laborer*
un(e) patron(ne) *boss*
un vendeur/une vendeuse *salesman/saleswoman*

Description personnelle

avare *miserly; stingy*
bavard(e) *talkative*
calme *calm*
chauve *bald*
compréhensif (compréhensive) *understanding*
désagréable *disagreeable*
discret (discrète) *discreet; reserved*
ennuyeux (ennuyeuse) *boring*
extroverti(e) *outgoing*
généreux (généreuse) *generous*
gentil (gentille) *nice*
heureux (heureuse) *happy*
impatient(e) *impatient*
intellectuel (intellectuelle) *intellectual*
intelligent(e) *intelligent*
intéressant(e) *interesting*
intolérant(e) *intolerant*
méchant(e) *nasty; mean*
naïf (naïve) *naive*
nerveux (nerveuse) *nervous*

optimiste *optimistic*
paresseux (paresseuse) *lazy*
patient(e) *patient*
pessimiste *pessimistic*
sportif (sportive) *athletic*
stupide *stupid*
travailleur (travailleuse) *hard-working*
triste *sad*

Des choses qu'on fait

les courses *(f. pl.) errands; shopping*
la cuisine *cooking; food*
les devoirs *(m. pl.) homework*
la lessive *wash; laundry*
le ménage *housework*
une promenade *walk; ride*
les provisions *(f. pl.) groceries*
la sieste *nap*
la vaisselle *dishes*

D'autres noms

une adresse *address*
une carte postale *postcard*
les cheveux *(m. pl.) hair*
une chose *thing*
une couleur *color*
le dîner *dinner*
les gens *people*
un magasin *store*
une note *note; grade, mark*
un numéro de téléphone *telephone number*
un souvenir *memory, recollection; regards*
le temps *weather*
la vie *life*
une ville *city*
les yeux *(m. pl.) eyes*

Adjectifs de couleur

beige *beige*
blanc (blanche) *white*
bleu(e) *blue*
blond(e) *blond*
brun(e) *brown(-haired)*
gris(e) *grey*
jaune *yellow*
marron *brown*

noir(e) *black*
orange *orange*
rose *pink*
rouge *red*
roux (rousse) *red(-haired)*
vert(e) *green*
violet(te) *purple*

Pour décrire les vêtements

bizarre *weird, funny-looking*
bon marché *inexpensive*
cher (chère) *dear; expensive*
chic *chic; stylish*
confortable *comfortable*
élégant(e) *elegant*
ordinaire *ordinary, everyday*
propre *clean*
sale *dirty*
simple *simple, plain*

Vêtements

des baskets *(f.) high-top sneakers*
un blouson *windbreaker, jacket*
des bottes *(f.) boots*
une ceinture *belt*
un chapeau *hat*
des chaussettes *(f.) socks*
des chaussures *(f.) shoes*
une chemise *shirt*
un chemisier *blouse*
un complet *suit*
une cravate *tie*
un foulard *scarf*
des gants *(m.) gloves*
un imperméable *raincoat*
un jean *(pair of) jeans*
une jupe *skirt*
des lunettes *(f. pl.) eyeglasses*
un manteau *coat*
une montre *watch*
un pantalon *(pair of) pants*
un pull-over (un pull) *sweater*
une robe *dress*
un short *(pair of) shorts*
un sweat-shirt *sweatshirt*
un tee-shirt *tee-shirt*
des tennis *(f.) tennis shoes*
une veste *sportcoat*
un vêtement *an article of clothing*

D'autres adjectifs

ce/cet (cette) *this; that*
ces *these; those*
mauvais(e) *bad*
nouveau/nouvel (nouvelle) *new*

Pronoms

cela (ça) *that*
toi *you*
tous (*m. pl.*) *all*

Verbes

dîner *to eat dinner*
donner *to give*
faire *to do; to make*
garder *to keep; to look after*
porter *to wear; to carry*

Quand? (Adverbes de fréquence)

aujourd'hui *today*
d'habitude *usually*
généralement *generally*
jamais (ne ... jamais) *never*
quand *when*
quelquefois *sometimes*
rarement *rarely*
toujours *always*

Mots invariables

ici *here*
puis *then; next*

Mots interrogatifs

que ... ? *what ... ?*
qu'est-ce que ... ? *what ... ?*
quel(le) ... ? *which ... ? what ... ?*

Expressions utiles

Au contraire! *On the contrary!*
avec mon meilleur souvenir *with my best regards*
Comment est (sont) ... ? *What is (are) ... like?*
De quelle couleur est (sont) ... ? *What color is (are) ... ?*
en classe *in class; to class*
faire attention *to pay attention*
Il fait chaud. *It's hot out.*
Il faut ... *It is necessary ...*
Quel temps fait-il? *What is the weather like?*
Qu'est-ce que c'est? *What is this?*

Quoi de neuf?

Buts communicatifs
Expressing future time
Telling time
Explaining your schedule
Telling where to find
  places

Structures utiles
À + article défini
Le verbe **aller** (suite)
L'heure
Les jours de la semaine
Le verbe **devoir**
Quelques prépositions de
  lieu
L'impératif
Les prépositions de lieu
  avec une ville ou un pays
Les mots interrogatifs **où**
  et **quand**

Culture
• *À propos*
Quelques malentendus
  culturels

• *Il y a un geste*
Au revoir/Salut
La bise

• *Lectures*
Vos vacances à Angers
«Village natal»

Coup d'envoi

Prise de contact

Qu'est-ce que vous allez faire?

Qu'est-ce que tu vas faire° le week-end
prochain°, Sylvie?

What are you going to do
next weekend

    Je vais sortir vendredi° soir.

I'm going to go out on Friday

    Je vais danser parce que j'adore danser.

    Je vais déjeuner dimanche° avec mes amis.

    Je vais aller à la bibliothèque.°

I'm going to have lunch on
Sunday / I'm going to go
to the library.

    Je vais étudier et faire mes devoirs.

    Mais je ne vais pas rester° dans ma
      chambre tout le week-end°.

to stay
the whole weekend

▶ **Et vous?** Qu'est-ce que vous allez faire le week-end prochain? Où allez-vous étudier?

***Communication
(Presentational):*** Once the
Prise de contact has been
practiced in pairs, have 2 or
3 students give a short
presentation about their
weekend.

Conversation

Une sortie

C'est vendredi après-midi. Lori rencontre° son amie Denise après° son cours de littérature française.

     meets
     after

LORI: Salut, Denise. Comment vas-tu?

DENISE: Bien, Lori. Quoi de neuf?°
(Elles s'embrassent° trois fois°.)

     What's new?
     kiss / times

LORI: Pas grand-chose°, mais c'est vendredi et je n'ai pas l'habitude de passer° tout le week-end dans ma chambre. Tu as envie d'aller au cinéma?°

     Not much
     I'm not used to spending
     Do you feel like going to the movies?

DENISE: Quand ça?

LORI: Ce soir ou demain° soir?

     tomorrow

DENISE: Ce soir je ne suis pas libre°. Mais demain peut-être. Tu vas voir° quel film?

     free
     to see

LORI: Ça m'est égal.° Il y a toujours un bon film au cinéma Variétés.

     I don't care.

DENISE: D'accord°, très bien. À quelle heure?

     Okay

LORI: Vers 7 heures et demie°. Ça va?° Rendez-vous devant° le cinéma?

     Around 7:30 / Okay?
     in front of

DENISE: C'est parfait°.

     perfect

LORI: Bonne soirée, Denise, et à demain soir.

After practicing the *Conversation*, have students complete ex. A in the Workbook.

▶ **Jouez ces rôles.** Répétez la conversation avec votre partenaire. Utilisez vos noms et le nom d'un cinéma près de chez vous.

Il y a un geste

Au revoir/Salut. When waving good-bye, the open palm, held at about ear level, is normally turned toward the person to whom one is waving. It is often moved toward the other person.

La bise. The French kiss their friends and relatives on both cheeks. This is referred to as **faire la bise.** The number of times that their cheeks touch varies, however, from one region to another: twice in Besançon, three or four times in Angers, and four times in Quimper! In Paris, the number varies from two to four, most likely because people have moved to the capital from different regions.

À propos

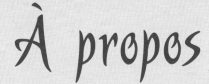

Pourquoi est-ce que Lori et Denise s'embrassent trois fois?

a. Elles sont superstitieuses.
b. Denise habite à Angers et elle a l'habitude d'embrasser ses amis trois fois.
c. En France on embrasse tout le monde.

Quelques malentendus culturels

A possible misunderstanding may result from the use of expressions that seem to be equivalent in two languages. In the United States, for example, the expression *see you later* is often used as an alternate to *goodbye,* without necessarily implying any real meeting in the near future. This has proven to be frustrating for French visitors, for whom *see you later* is interpreted as meaning *see you soon.* Likewise, any North American who uses the French expression **À tout à l'heure** should realize that this implies that the people in question will be meeting again very soon.

This example is perhaps a useful springboard to understanding one of the basic differences between North Americans and the French: while typically more hesitant to extend an invitation to their home and certainly more reluctant to chat with strangers, once an invitation is extended or a conversation begun, the French take it seriously. North Americans may complain about not being invited to French homes right away, but they themselves have readily and casually extended invitations to "come and see us" and have then been surprised when French acquaintances write to say they are actually coming.

Another source of error for English speakers is the attempt to translate expressions such as *good morning* and *good afternoon* literally when greeting someone. **Bon**

après-midi is used only when taking leave of someone. When saying hello, the only common expressions in French are **bonjour, bonsoir,** and **salut.** When saying good-bye, however, the range of possible expressions is much more extensive, as can be seen in the list below.

VOCABULAIRE

Pour dire *au revoir*

à bientôt	*see you soon*	bon après-midi	*have a good afternoon*
à demain	*see you tomorrow*	bonne journée	*have a good day*
à la prochaine	*until next time, be seeing you*	bonne nuit	*pleasant dreams* (lit. *good night*)
à tout à l'heure	*see you in a little while*	bonne soirée	*have a good evening*
au plaisir (de vous revoir)	*(I hope to) see you again*	bonsoir	*good evening, good night*
		salut	*bye(-bye)* (fam.)
au revoir	*goodbye, see you again*	tchao	*bye* (fam.)

▶ **À vous.** Répondez.

1. Comment allez-vous?
2. Allez-vous rester dans votre chambre ce soir?
3. À quelle heure allez-vous faire vos devoirs?
4. Qu'est-ce que vous allez faire demain soir?
5. Avez-vous envie d'aller au cinéma?

ENTRE AMIS

Le week-end prochain

1. Greet your partner.
2. Find out how s/he is doing.
3. Find out what s/he is going to do this weekend.
4. Find out if s/he wants to go to a movie.
5. If so, agree on a time.
6. Be sure to vary the way you say goodbye.

Prononciation

Les syllabes ouvertes

■ There is a strong tendency in French to end spoken syllables with a vowel sound. It is therefore important to learn to link a pronounced consonant to the vowel that follows it.

| il a | [i la] | votre ami | [vɔ tʀa mi] |
| elle a | [ɛ la] | femme américaine | [fa ma me ʀi kɛn] |

■ The above is also true in the case of liaison. Liaison must occur in the following situations.

Synthèse: les liaisons obligatoires

		Alone	**With liaison**
1.	when a pronoun is followed by a verb	nous vous	nous [z]a vons vous [z]êtes
2.	when a verb and pronoun are inverted	est ont sont	est-[t]elle ont-[t]ils sont-[t]ils
3.	when an article or adjective is followed by a noun	un des deux trois mon petit	un [n]homme des [z]en fants deux [z]heures trois [z]ans mon [n]a mi petit [t]a mi
4.	after one-syllable adverbs or prepositions	très en dans	très [z]im por tant en [n]A mé rique dans [z]une fa mille

Buts communicatifs

1. Expressing Future Time

Qu'est-ce que tu vas faire samedi° prochain,
Julien?   *Saturday*

> D'abord° je vais jouer au tennis avec
> mes amis.   *First (of all)*
>
> Ensuite° nous allons étudier° à la
> bibliothèque.   *Next / we're going to study*
>
> Je n'aime pas manger seul°, alors après°,   *alone / so after(wards)*
> nous allons dîner ensemble au restaurant
> universitaire.
>
> Enfin°, nous allons regarder la télé.   *Finally*

NOTE CULTURELLE
Le restaurant universitaire, qu'on appelle d'habitude **le Resto U,** est très bon marché. C'est parce qu'en France on subventionne *(subsidizes)* en partie les repas *(meals)* des étudiants. Si on a une carte d'étudiant, on bénéficie d'une réduction du prix des repas.

▶ **Et vous?** Qu'est-ce que vous allez faire?

A. À + article défini

Remember to consult Appendix C, the Glossary of Grammatical Terms, at the end of the book to review any terms with which you are not familiar.

Céline ne travaille pas **à la** bibliothèque.   *Céline doesn't work at the library.*

Elle travaille **au** restaurant universitaire.   *She works in the dining hall.*

■ The preposition **à** can mean *to, at,* or *in,* depending on the context. When used with the articles **la** and **l'**, it does not change, but when used with the articles **le** and **les,** it is contracted to **au** and **aux.**

à	+	le	**au**	au restaurant
à	+	les	**aux**	aux toilettes
à	+	la	**à la**	à la maison
à	+	l'	**à l'**	à l'hôtel

■ Liaison occurs when **aux** precedes a vowel sound:

aux [z]États-Unis.

VOCABULAIRE

Quelques endroits *(A few places)*

Sur le campus

un bâtiment	*building*	une librairie	*bookstore*
une bibliothèque	*library*	un parking	*parking lot, garage*
une cafétéria	*cafeteria*	une piscine	*swimming pool*
un campus	*campus*	une résidence	
un couloir	*hall, corridor*	(universitaire)	*dormitory*
un cours	*course, class*	une salle de classe	*classroom*
un gymnase	*gymnasium*	les toilettes *(f. pl.)*	*restroom*

Culture & comparison:
Have students study the places **en ville** to determine which would not be found in their city.

Do not pronounce the **c** in the word **tabac**.

En ville

un aéroport	*airport*	une école	*school*
une banque	*bank*	une église	*church*
un bistro	*bar and café*	une épicerie	*grocery store*
une boulangerie	*bakery*	une gare	*railroad station*
un bureau de poste	*post office*	un hôtel	*hotel*
un bureau de tabac	*tobacco shop*	un musée	*museum*
un centre	*shopping center,*	une pharmacie	*pharmacy*
commercial	*mall*	un restaurant	*restaurant*
un château	*chateau, castle*	une ville	*city*
un cinéma	*movie theater*		

█ Qu'est-ce que c'est? Identifiez les endroits suivants.

MODÈLE: C'est une église.

1.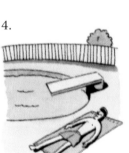

2.

3.

4.

5.

6.

2 **Où vas-tu?** Posez la question. Votre partenaire va répondre d'après le modèle *(according to the model)*.

MODÈLE: restaurant (bibliothèque)
—Tu vas au restaurant?
—Non, je ne vais pas au restaurant; je vais à la bibliothèque.

1. bureau de poste (pharmacie)
2. église (centre commercial)
3. restaurant (cinéma)
4. librairie (bibliothèque)
5. hôtel (appartement de ma sœur)
6. gare (aéroport)

3 **Qu'est-ce que vous allez faire?** Indiquez vos projets avec **Je vais à** + article défini et les mots donnés *(given)*. Utilisez aussi les mots **d'abord,** **ensuite** et **après**.

MODÈLE: banque, centre commercial, épicerie
D'abord je vais à la banque, ensuite je vais au centre commercial et après je vais à l'épicerie.

1. école, bibliothèque, librairie
2. banque, restaurant, aéroport
3. bureau de poste, pharmacie, cinéma
4. église, campus, résidence

ENTRE AMIS

D'abord, ensuite, après

1. Tell your partner that you are going to go out.
2. S/he will try to guess three places where you are going.
3. S/he will try to guess in what order you are going to the three places.

B. Le verbe *aller* *(suite)*

Je vais en classe à 8 heures.	*I go to class at eight o'clock.*
Allez-vous en ville ce soir?	*Are you going into town this evening?*
Où **allons-nous** dîner?	*Where are we going to eat dinner?*
Les petits Français ne **vont** pas à l'école le mercredi.	*French children don't go to school on Wednesday.*

Review the conjugation of
aller on p. 36.

■ The fundamental meaning of **aller** is *to go.*

Où **vas-tu?**   *Where are you going?*

■ As you have already learned, the verb **aller** is also used to discuss health and well-being.

Comment allez-vous?	*How are you?*
Je vais bien, merci.	*I'm fine, thanks.*
Ça va, merci.	*Fine, thanks.*

■ The verb **aller** is also very often used with an infinitive to indicate the future, especially the near future.

Qu'est-ce que **tu vas faire** ce soir?   *What are you going to do this evening?*
Je vais étudier, comme d'habitude.   *I'm going to study, as usual.*
Nous allons passer un test demain.   *We are going to take a test tomorrow.*
Thierry **ne va pas déjeuner** demain.   *Thierry won't eat lunch tomorrow.*

Point out the idiomatic expression **passer un test** in the third example.

4   **Comment vont-ils?** Utilisez le verbe **aller** pour poser des questions. Votre partenaire va répondre.

MODÈLE: ton frère
VOUS: **Comment va ton frère?**
VOTRE PARTENAIRE: **Il va très bien, merci.**   ou
Quel frère? Je n'ai pas de frère.

Review the possible answers (taught in Ch. 2, p. 35) before doing the exercise.

Remind students that if they don't have a niece, etc., they should say so.

1. tes amis du cours de français
2. tu
3. ton professeur de français
4. ta sœur
5. ton ami(e) qui s'appelle _____
6. tes grands-parents
7. ta nièce
8. tes neveux

VOCABULAIRE

Quelques expressions de temps (futur)

tout à l'heure	*in a little while*
dans une heure	*one hour from now*
ce soir	*tonight*
avant (après) le dîner	*before (after) dinner*
demain (matin, soir)	*tomorrow (morning, evening)*
dans trois jours	*three days from now*
le week-end prochain	*next weekend*
la semaine prochaine	*next week*
la semaine suivante	*the following week*

Several of these expressions can be preceded by **à** to mean *"See you ..."* or *"Until ...,"* e.g., **à ce soir, au week-end prochain.**

5   **Que vont-ils faire ce soir?** Qu'est-ce qu'ils vont faire et qu'est-ce qu'ils ne vont pas faire? Si vous ne savez pas, devinez. *(If you don't know, guess.)*

MODÈLE: mes parents / jouer au tennis ou regarder la télévision
Ce soir, ils vont regarder la télévision; ils ne vont pas jouer au tennis.

1. je / sortir ou rester dans ma chambre
2. le professeur / dîner au restaurant ou dîner à la maison
3. mes amis / étudier à la bibliothèque ou étudier dans leur chambre
4. je / regarder la télévision ou faire mes devoirs
5. mon ami(e) _____ / travailler sur ordinateur ou aller au centre commercial
6. les étudiants / rester sur le campus ou aller au bistro

6 **À vous.** Répondez.

1. Qu'est-ce que vous allez faire ce soir?
2. Qu'est-ce que vos amis vont faire?
3. Qui va passer un test cette semaine?
4. Où allez-vous déjeuner demain midi?
5. Où et à quelle heure allez-vous dîner demain soir?
6. Allez-vous dîner seul(e) ou avec une autre personne?
7. Quand allez-vous étudier? Avec qui?
8. Qu'est-ce que vous allez faire samedi prochain?
9. Qu'est-ce que vous allez faire dimanche après-midi?

ENTRE AMIS

Communication
(Presentational): Before putting
students in pairs, have them
write 3 things they are going to
do this weekend.

Est-ce que tu vas jouer au tennis?

1. Tell your partner that you are not going to stay in your room this weekend.
2. S/he will try to guess three things you are going to do.
3. S/he will try to guess in what order you will do them.

2. Telling Time

Quelle heure est-il maintenant?°   *What time is it now?*
    Il est 10 heures et demie.°   *It's half past ten.*
    Je vais au cours de français à 11 heures.
    Je déjeune à midi.°   *I eat lunch at noon.*
    Je vais à la bibliothèque à une heure.
    Je vais au gymnase à 4 heures.
    J'étudie de 7 heures à 10 heures du soir.
    J'étudie au moins° trois heures par jour°.   *at least / per day*

> -- cours de français 11 h
> -- déjeuner 12 h avec Étienne
> -- bibliothèque 13 h
> -- gymnase 16 h

▶ **Et vous?** À quelle heure déjeunez-vous?
    À quelle heure allez-vous à la bibliothèque?
    À quelle heure allez-vous au gymnase?
    À quelle heure allez-vous au cours de français?
    Quelle heure est-il maintenant?

(REMARQUE)

The distinction between **heure,**
temps, and **fois** will be
explained in Ch. 6.

The word **heure** has more than one meaning.

J'étudie trois **heures** par jour.   *I study three hours a day.*
De quelle **heure** à quelle **heure?**   *From what time to what time?*
De 15 **heures** à 18 **heures.**   *From three until six o'clock.*

C. L'heure

■ You have already learned to tell time in a general way. Now that you know how to count to 60, you can be more precise. There are two methods of telling time. The first is an official 24-hour system, which can be thought of as a digital watch on which the hour is always followed by the minutes. The other is an informal 12-hour system that includes the expressions **et quart** *(quarter past, quarter after),* **et demi(e)** *(half past),* **moins le quart** *(quarter to, quarter till),* **midi,** and **minuit** *(midnight).*

Review *Understanding Basic Expressions of Time*, p. 3, and numbers, pp. 3, 66.

The word **heure(s)** is usually represented as **h** (without a period) on schedules, e.g., **5 h 30.**

	Système officiel	*Système ordinaire*
9 h 01	neuf heures une	neuf heures une
9 h 15	neuf heures quinze	neuf heures et quart
9 h 30	neuf heures trente	neuf heures et demie
9 h 45	neuf heures quarante-cinq	dix heures moins le quart
12 h 30	douze heures trente	midi et demi
13 h 30	treize heures trente	une heure et demie
18 h 51	dix-huit heures cinquante et une	sept heures moins neuf
23 h 45	vingt-trois heures quarante-cinq	minuit moins le quart

■ In both systems, the feminine number **une** is used to refer to hours and minutes because both **heure** and **minute** are feminine.

1 h 21   **une** heure vingt et **une**

Point out the plural **-s** on all times except **une heure.**

■ In the 12-hour system, **moins** is used to give the time from 1 to 29 minutes *before* the hour. For 15 minutes *before* or *after* the hour, the expressions **moins le quart** and **et quart,** respectively, are used. For 30 minutes past the hour, one says **et demie.**

9 h 40   dix heures **moins** vingt

9 h 45   dix heures **moins le quart**

10 h 15   dix heures **et quart**

10 h 30   dix heures **et demie**

NOTE — After **midi** and **minuit,** which are both masculine, **et demi** is spelled without a final **-e:** midi **et demi.**

■ The phrases **du matin, de l'après-midi,** and **du soir** are commonly used in the 12-hour system to specify A.M. or P.M. when it is not otherwise clear from the context.

trois heures **du matin** (3 h)

trois heures **de l'après-midi** (15 h)

dix heures **du matin** (10 h)

dix heures **du soir** (22 h)

7 **Quelle heure est-il?** Donnez les heures suivantes. Indiquez l'heure officielle et l'heure ordinaire s'il y a une différence.

Have students count from 1 to 24 with the word **heure(s): une heure, deux heures,** etc.

MODÈLE: 13 h 35
système officiel: **Il est treize heures trente-cinq.**
système ordinaire: **Il est deux heures moins vingt-cinq de l'après-midi.**

Remember that these numbers are based on a 24-hour system.

1. 2 h 20   6. 1 h 33
2. 4 h 10   7. 22 h 05
3. 15 h 41   8. 3 h 45
4. 1 h 17   9. 11 h 15
5. 6 h 55   10. 10 h 30

Culture: Have students review the country abbreviations in Ch. 1, p. 18.

8 **Décalages horaires** (*Differences in time*). Vous êtes à Paris et vous voulez téléphoner à des amis. Mais quelle heure est-il chez vos amis? Demandez à votre partenaire.

Use the maps on the inside covers of this book to locate as many of these places as possible.

Décalages horaires
(calculés par rapport à l'heure de Paris)

Anchorage (USA)	− 10	Montréal (CDN)	− 6
Athènes (Grèce)	+ 1	Mexico (MEX)	− 7
Bangkok (Thaïlande)	+ 6	Nouméa	
Casablanca (MA)	− 1	(Nouvelle-Calédonie)	+ 10
Chicago (USA)	− 7	New York (USA)	− 6
Dakar (SN)	− 1	Papeete (Polynésie)	− 11
Denver (USA)	− 8	Saint-Denis (Réunion)	+ 3
Fort-de-France		San Francisco (USA)	− 9
(Martinique)	− 5	Sydney (Australie)	+ 9
Halifax (CDN)	− 5	Tokyo (J)	+ 8
Le Caire (Égypte)	+ 1	Tunis (Tunisie)	0
Londres (GB)	− 1		

Suggestion: Drill the model and do one or two sentences before putting students in pairs.

Follow up (books closed) by redoing several sentences.

MODÈLE: 3 h à Paris/Bangkok?
VOUS: **S'il est trois heures à Paris, quelle heure est-il à Bangkok?**
VOTRE PARTENAIRE: **Il est neuf heures à Bangkok.**

1. 23 h à Paris/Anchorage?   5. 12 h à Paris/Mexico?
2. 6 h à Paris/Montréal?   6. 3 h 20 à Paris/Chicago?
3. 14 h à Paris/Londres?   7. 15 h 45 à Paris/Saint-Denis?
4. 18 h 30 à Paris/Fort-de-France?   8. 11 h à Paris/Tokyo?

9 **À vous.** Répondez.

1. Quelle heure est-il maintenant?
2. À quelle heure déjeunez-vous d'habitude?
3. Allez-vous faire vos devoirs ce soir? Si oui, de quelle heure à quelle heure?
4. Combien d'heures étudiez-vous par jour?
5. À quelle heure allez-vous dîner ce soir?
6. Allez-vous sortir ce soir? Si oui, à quelle heure? Avec qui?
7. Allez-vous regarder la télévision ce soir? Si oui, de quelle heure à quelle heure? Qu'est-ce que vous allez regarder?

ENTRE AMIS

À l'aéroport

1. Ask your partner what time it is.
2. Ask if s/he is going to Paris. (S/he is.)
3. Ask what time it is in Paris now.
4. Ask at what time s/he is going to arrive in Paris.
5. Find out what s/he is going to do in Paris.

3. Explaining Your Schedule

Quel jour est-ce aujourd'hui?
C'est ...

lundi°	*Monday*
mardi°	*Tuesday*
mercredi	
jeudi°	*Thursday*
vendredi	
samedi	
dimanche	

Quel jour est-ce demain?
Quel est votre jour préféré°?   *favorite*

D. Les jours de la semaine

■ Days of the week are not capitalized in French.

■ The calendar week begins on Monday and ends on Sunday.

❄	janvier					❄
lundi	mardi	mercredi	jeudi	vendredi	samedi	dimanche
		1	2	3	4	5
6	7	8	9	10	11	12
13	14	15	16	17	18	19
20	21	22	23	24	25	26
27	28	29	30	31		

■ When referring to a specific day, neither an article nor a preposition is used.

Demain, c'est **vendredi.**	*Tomorrow is Friday.*
C'est **vendredi** demain.	*Tomorrow is Friday.*
J'ai envie de sortir **vendredi** soir.	*I feel like going out Friday evening.*
J'ai l'intention d'étudier **samedi.**	*I plan to study Saturday.*

> Review the verb **avoir,** p. 64. It is used with **envie, l'intention,** and **l'habitude.** Remember to use **de** + infinitive after these expressions.

■ To express the meaning *Saturdays, every Saturday, on Saturdays*, etc., the article **le** is used with the name of the day.

Je n'ai pas de cours **le samedi.**	*I don't have class on Saturdays.*
Le mardi, mon premier cours est à 10 heures.	*On Tuesdays, my first class is at ten o'clock.*
Le vendredi soir, j'ai l'habitude de sortir avec mes amis.	*On Friday nights, I usually go out with my friends.*

■ Similarly, to express the meaning *mornings, every morning, in the morning*, etc., with parts of the day, **le** or **la** is used before the noun.

Le matin, je vais au cours de français.	*Every morning, I go to French class.*
L'après-midi, je vais à la bibliothèque.	*Afternoons, I go to the library.*
Le soir, je fais mes devoirs.	*In the evening, I do my homework.*
La nuit, je suis au lit.	*At night, I'm in bed.*

10 **Le samedi soir.** Utilisez l'expression **avoir envie de** ou **avoir l'habitude de,** d'après les modèles.

MODÈLES: les étudiants / envie / sortir ou rester dans leur chambre
Le samedi soir, ils ont envie de sortir; ils n'ont pas envie de rester dans leur chambre.

ma sœur / l'habitude / aller au cinéma ou faire ses devoirs
Le samedi soir, elle a l'habitude d'aller au cinéma; elle n'a pas l'habitude de faire ses devoirs.

1. les étudiants / envie / rester sur le campus ou aller au cinéma
2. je / l'habitude / voir un film ou faire mes devoirs
3. le professeur / l'habitude / préparer ses cours ou regarder la télévision
4. mes amis et moi, nous / envie / dîner entre amis ou dîner seuls
5. mon ami(e) _____ / l'habitude / sortir avec moi ou rester dans sa chambre

11 **À vous.** Répondez.

1. Quels sont les jours où vous allez au cours de français?
2. À quelle heure est votre cours?
3. Quels sont les jours où vous n'avez pas de cours?
4. Qu'est-ce que vous avez l'intention de faire le week-end prochain?
5. Avez-vous l'habitude d'aller au gymnase? Si oui, quels jours et à quelle heure?
6. À quelle heure avez-vous votre premier cours le mardi?
7. Quand est-ce que vous allez à la bibliothèque?
8. Quand écoutez-vous la radio?
9. Quand avez-vous envie de regarder la télévision?

VOCABULAIRE

Quelques cours

l'art *(m.)*	*art*	la musique	*music*
la chimie	*chemistry*	la pédagogie	*education, teacher*
le commerce	*business*		*preparation*
la comptabilité	*accounting*	la philosophie	*philosophy*
la gestion	*management*	la psychologie	*psychology*
la gymnastique	*gymnastics*	les sciences *(f. pl.)*	*science*
l'histoire *(f.)*	*history*	les sciences	
l'informatique *(f.)*	*computer science*	économiques *(f. pl.)*	*economics*
la littérature	*literature*	les sciences	
les mathématiques		politiques *(f. pl.)*	*political science*
(f. pl.)	*math*		

12 **Mon emploi du temps** *(My schedule).* Indiquez votre emploi du temps pour ce semestre. Indiquez le jour, l'heure et le cours.

MODÈLE: **Le lundi à dix heures, j'ai un cours de français.**
Le lundi à onze heures, j'ai un cours de mathématiques.
Le lundi à une heure, j'ai un cours d'histoire.

Communication (Interpretive):
Follow up by putting an individual student in front of the class. Others must ask questions about his/her schedule.

13 **As-tu un cours de commerce?** Essayez de deviner *(try to guess)* deux des cours de votre partenaire. Demandez ensuite quels jours et à quelle heure votre partenaire va à ces cours. Votre partenaire va répondre à vos questions.

MODÈLE: **As-tu un cours d'histoire?**
Quels jours vas-tu à ce cours?
À quelle heure vas-tu à ce cours?

www Réalités culturelles

For more information about Angers, see the *Lecture,* p. 149. To learn more about the **TGV**, see the *À propos* section, Ch. 7, p. 186.

Angers

Set in the heart of the **Pays de la Loire** and located ninety minutes from Paris by the **TGV (le train à grande vitesse)**, Angers is a city of approximately 160,000 inhabitants. It has a rich history as the seat of the counts of Anjou and attracts over 400,000 visitors annually. There is a massive **château fort**, built by Saint Louis (Louis IX) in the thirteenth century, that serves as a museum of Apocalypse tapestry.

Angers offers visitors numerous museums, gardens, restaurants, art and film festivals, and an international festival of journalism that takes place each November. Angers hosts the National Center for Contemporary Dance, the National Drama Center, and a regional center for textile design. With its network of 5,500 companies and groups of international stature, Angers combines respect for the environment with high-tech business. Large international companies like Bosch, Thomson Multimedia, and Motorola have selected Angers as the site of their manufacturing centers. In addition, the **Université d'Angers** and the **Université Catholique de l'Ouest** run several agricultural, biotechnological, and business research institutes. A dynamic and rapidly growing city, Angers seems to be striking a good balance between modernization and the preservation of its culture and environment.

E. Le verbe *devoir*

Les étudiants doivent beaucoup travailler.	*Students have to work a lot.*
Vous devez être fatigués.	*You must be tired.*

devoir *(to have to, must; to owe)*	
je	**dois**
tu	**dois**
il/elle/on	**doit**
nous	**devons**
vous	**devez**
ils/elles	**doivent**

■ **Devoir** is often used with the infinitive to express an obligation or a probability.

Vous **devez faire** attention! *(obligation)*	*You must pay attention!*
Lori **doit avoir** vingt ans. *(probability)*	*Lori must be twenty.*

■ **Devoir** plus a noun means *to owe.*

Je dois vingt dollars à mes parents.	*I owe my parents twenty dollars.*

Synthèse: révision des verbes

	parler	être	avoir	faire	aller	devoir
je	**parle**	**suis**	**ai**	**fais**	**vais**	**dois**
tu	**parles**	**es**	**as**	**fais**	**vas**	**dois**
il/elle/on	**parle**	**est**	**a**	**fait**	**va**	**doit**
nous	**parlons**	**sommes**	**avons**	**faisons**	**allons**	**devons**
vous	**parlez**	**êtes**	**avez**	**faites**	**allez**	**devez**
ils/elles	**parlent**	**sont**	**ont**	**font**	**vont**	**doivent**

14 **Mais qu'est-ce qu'on doit faire?** Utilisez l'expression entre parenthèses pour indiquer ce que chaque personne doit faire.

MODÈLE: Gérard a envie d'aller au cinéma. (étudier)
Gérard a envie d'aller au cinéma mais il doit étudier.

1. Nous avons envie de sortir ce soir. (préparer un examen)
2. Les étudiants ont envie de regarder la télévision. (étudier)
3. Tu as envie de danser ce soir. (faire tes devoirs)
4. J'ai envie de rester au lit. (aller aux cours)
5. Le professeur a envie de faire un voyage. (enseigner)
6. Tes amis ont envie d'aller en ville. (faire la lessive)

15 **Je dois faire ça cette semaine.** Faites une liste de sept choses que vous devez faire cette semaine (une chose pour chaque jour).

Communication (Presentational & Interpretive):
Follow up by pairing students who will try to guess three items on their partner's list.

MODÈLE: **Samedi, je dois faire le ménage.**

16 **Et alors?** Pour chaque phrase, inventez une ou deux conclusions logiques.

MODÈLE: Lori n'a pas envie de passer le week-end dans sa chambre.
Qu'est-ce qu'elle va faire?
Elle va sortir. ou **Elle a l'intention d'aller au cinéma.**

Follow-up (books closed): Read the questions and brainstorm with students to suggest as many answers as possible.

1. Lori a envie de sortir ce soir. Où va-t-elle? Que fait-elle?
2. Mais son amie Denise n'est pas libre. Qu'est-ce qu'elle doit faire?
3. Lori et Denise font souvent les courses ensemble. Où vont-elles?
4. Aujourd'hui Denise reste dans sa chambre. Pourquoi? Comment va-t-elle?
5. Lori téléphone à Denise. Pourquoi? De quoi parle-t-elle?

ENTRE AMIS

Ton emploi du temps

1. Find out what time it is.
2. Find out what day it is today.
3. Find out what classes your partner has today.
4. Find out when your partner goes to the library.
5. Find out if your partner has to work and, if so, on what days.
6. Find out if your partner feels like going to the movies tonight.

Je dois aller à la librairie.

4. Telling Where to Find Places

 Où se trouve° la souris?   *is located*

La souris est loin
du fromage.

La souris est près
du fromage.

La souris est devant
le fromage.

La souris est derrière
le fromage.

La souris est sur
le fromage.

La souris est sous
le fromage.

La souris est dans
le fromage.

Où se trouve le
fromage? Le fromage
est dans la souris.

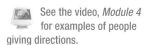
See the video, *Module 4*
for examples of people
giving directions.

F. Quelques prépositions de lieu

Les toilettes se trouvent **dans** le couloir.   *The restroom is in the hall.*
Les toilettes sont **à côté de** la salle   *The restroom is next to the*
   de classe.   *classroom.*
Le cinéma se trouve **au** centre   *The movie theater is at*
   commercial.   *the mall.*
La banque est **à droite** ou **à gauche**   *Is the bank on the right or on the*
   du parking?   *left of the parking lot?*
Allez **tout droit** et ensuite tournez   *Go straight ahead and then*
   à droite.   *turn to the right.*

à	*at; in; to*		**dans**	*in*
à côté de	*beside*		**entre**	*between; among*
à droite de	*on the right of*	≠	**à gauche de**	*on the left of*
derrière	*behind*	≠	**devant**	*in front of*
loin de	*far from*	≠	**près de**	*near*
sous	*under*	≠	**sur**	*on*

Remember that **à droite** means *to (on) the right*, while **tout droit** means *straight ahead*.

■ **À côté, à droite, à gauche, loin,** and **près** can all drop the **de** and stand alone.

> Nous habitons **à côté d'**une église.   *We live next to a church.*
> *But:* **L'église est à côté.**   *The church is next door.*

17 **Où se trouvent ces endroits?** Répondez à la question posée par *(asked by)* votre partenaire.

MODÈLE: La bibliothèque (près / bâtiment des sciences)
VOTRE PARTENAIRE: **Où se trouve la bibliothèque?**
VOUS: **Elle est près du bâtiment des sciences.**

Review contractions with **de**, p. 76.

1. le bâtiment administratif (près / bibliothèque)
2. la pharmacie (à côté / église)
3. les résidences universitaires (sur / campus)
4. le restaurant universitaire (dans / résidence)
5. le cinéma (à / centre commercial)
6. le bureau de poste (derrière / pharmacie)
7. le centre commercial (loin / campus)
8. les toilettes (devant / salle de classe)
9. le parking (à gauche / banque)

Connection & Communication (Presentational): Follow up by telling students you are a French-speaking visitor to campus. Have them give directions to specific places.

18 **Votre campus.** Faites rapidement le plan *(Draw a map)* de votre campus. Expliquez où se trouvent cinq endroits différents.

MODÈLE: **Voilà la résidence qui s'appelle Brown Hall. Elle est près de la bibliothèque.**

G. L'impératif

You already learned a number of imperatives in the Preliminary Chapter, p. 2.

Regarde!	*Look!*
Regardez!	*Look!*
Regardons!	*Let's look!*
Tourne à gauche!	*Turn to the left!*
Tournez à gauche!	*Turn to the left!*
Tournons à gauche!	*Let's turn to the left!*

The imperatives of **avoir** and **être** will be learned in Ch. 10.

■ The imperative is used to give commands and to make suggestions. The forms are usually the same as the present tense for **tu, vous,** and **nous.**

■ If the infinitive ends in **-er,** the final **-s** is omitted from the form that corresponds to **tu.**

| parler français | tu parle**s** français | But: | **Parle** français! |
| aller aux cours | tu va**s** aux cours | But: | **Va** aux cours! |

■ For negative commands, **ne** precedes the verb and **pas** follows it.

Ne regardez **pas** la télévision!
Ne fais **pas** attention à Papa!

19 **En ville.** Regardez le plan (*map*) de la ville. Demandez où se trouvent les endroits suivants. Votre partenaire va expliquer où ils se trouvent.

MODÈLE: cinéma

VOUS: **Où se trouve le cinéma, s'il vous plaît?**
VOTRE PARTENAIRE: **Il est à côté du café. Allez tout droit et tournez à gauche. Il est à droite.**

1. café
2. épicerie
3. église
4. boulangerie
5. bureau de poste
6. bureau de tabac
7. banque
8. cinéma
9. pharmacie
10. hôtel

Vous êtes ici.

20 **Qu'est-ce que les bons étudiants doivent faire?** Utilisez l'impératif pour répondre à la question. Décidez ce qu'un bon étudiant doit ou ne doit pas faire.

Suggestion: Have students redo this activity using the **tu** form of the imperative.

MODÈLE: Est-ce que je dois passer tout le week-end dans ma chambre?
Ne passez pas tout le week-end dans votre chambre! ou
Oui, passez tout le week-end dans votre chambre!

1. Est-ce que je dois habiter dans une résidence universitaire?
2. Est-ce que je dois manger à la cafétéria?
3. Est-ce que je dois faire mes devoirs dans ma chambre?
4. Est-ce que je dois étudier à la bibliothèque?
5. Est-ce que je ne dois pas aller au bistro?
6. Est-ce que je ne dois pas parler anglais au cours de français?

Review the contractions in this chapter on p. 127.

H. Les prépositions de lieu avec une ville ou un pays

■ Use **à** to say that you are in a city or are going to a city.

NOTE

In cases where the name of a city contains the definite article **(Le Mans, Le Caire, La Nouvelle-Orléans),** the article is retained and the normal contractions occur where necessary.

Emmanuelle habite **à La Nouvelle-Orléans.** Nous allons **au Mans.** Je suis **à Paris.** Je vais **à New York.**

■ Most countries, states, and provinces ending in **-e** are feminine. An exception is **le Mexique.**

la Belgiqu**e**	**la** Colombi**e** Britannique
la Virgini**e**	**la** Californi**e**

But: **le Mexique**

■ To say you are in or going to a *country,* the preposition varies. Use **en** before feminine countries or those that begin with a vowel sound. Use **au** before masculine countries which begin with a consonant. Use **aux** when the name of the country is plural.

en France	**au** Canada	**aux** États-Unis
en Israël	**au** Mexique	**aux** Pays-Bas

■ To say you are in or going to an American *state* or a Canadian *province,* **en** is normally used before those that are feminine or that begin with a vowel sound. The preposition **au** is often used with masculine provinces that begin with a consonant and with the states of Texas and New Mexico.

en Virginie	**en** Ontario	**au** Manitoba
en Nouvelle-Écosse	**en** Ohio	**au** Nouveau-Mexique

The use of the preposition **de** with countries is introduced in Ch. 7.

■ **Dans l'état de** or **dans la province de** can be used with any state or province, masculine or feminine

dans l'état de New York.

dans la province d'Alberta.

dans l'état de Californie.

Review the adjectives of nationality in Ch. 1, p. 18. The adjective corresponding to **Irak** is **irakien(ne).**

See how many of the countries listed you can find on the maps on the inside covers of your text.

Connection & Comparison: Remind students that all languages are masculine and therefore most will be like the masculine form of the adjective.

Quelques langues et quelques pays

On parle ...		**en** ...	
	allemand		Allemagne
	anglais		Angleterre
	français et flamand		Belgique
	chinois		Chine
	espagnol		Espagne
	français		France
	arabe		Irak
	anglais et irlandais		Irlande
	italien		Italie
	russe		Russie
	suédois		Suède
	français, allemand et italien		Suisse
On parle ...	français et anglais	**au** ...	Canada
	japonais		Japon
	français et arabe		Maroc
	espagnol		Mexique
	portugais		Portugal
	français et wolof		Sénégal
On parle ...	anglais, espagnol et français	**aux** ...	États-Unis
	hollandais		Pays-Bas

■ When talking about more than one country, use a preposition before each one.

On parle français **en** France, **en** Belgique, **au** Canada, **au** Maroc, **au** Sénégal, etc.

■ When there is no preposition with a country, state, or province, the definite article must be used.

La France est un beau pays.
J'adore **le Canada.**

NOTE — **Israël** is an exception.

Israël est à côté de la Syrie.

21 **Où habitent-ils?** Dans quel pays les personnes suivantes habitent-elles?

MODÈLE: Vous êtes français.
Vous habitez en France.

1. Lucie est canadienne.
2. Les Dewonck sont belges.
3. Phoebe est anglaise.
4. Pepe et María sont mexicains.
5. Yuko est japonaise.

6. Yolande est sénégalaise.
7. Sean et Deirdre sont irlandais.
8. Caterina est italienne.
9. Hassan est marocain.
10. Nous sommes américains.

22 Qui sont ces personnes? Où habitent-elles? Vous êtes à l'aéroport d'Orly et vous écoutez des touristes de divers pays. Devinez leur nationalité et où ils vont.

MODÈLE: Il y a deux hommes qui parlent espagnol.
Ils doivent être espagnols ou mexicains.
Ils vont probablement en Espagne ou au Mexique.

1. Il y a un homme et une femme qui parlent français.
2. Il y a deux enfants qui parlent anglais.
3. Il y a une jeune fille qui parle russe.
4. Il y a trois garçons qui parlent arabe.
5. Il y a une personne qui parle suédois.
6. Il y a un homme qui parle allemand.
7. Il y a deux couples qui parlent flamand.
8. Il y a deux jeunes filles qui parlent italien.
9. Il y a un homme et une femme qui parlent japonais.

I. Les mots interrogatifs *où* et *quand*

Remind students that if a third-person verb ends in a vowel, a **-t-** is added between the verb and the pronoun (Ch. 2).

■ A question using **quand** or **où** is formed like any other question, using inversion or **est-ce que.**

Où habitent-ils?   Quand arrive-t-elle?
Où est-ce qu'ils habitent?   Quand est-ce qu'elle arrive?

NOTE ── In **Quand est-ce que,** the **-d** is pronounced [t]. When **quand** is followed by inversion, there is no liaison.

Review interrogative forms, pp. 48–49.

■ With a *noun* subject, the inversion order is *noun + verb + subject pronoun.*

Où **tes parents habitent-ils?**   Quand **ta sœur arrive-t-elle?**

Be sure that students understand that noun inversion is quite limited in speech.

■ In addition, if there is only one verb and no object, the noun subject and the verb may be inverted.

Où **habitent tes parents?**   Quand **arrive ta sœur?**

23 Où et quand? Pour chaque phrase, posez une question avec **où.** Votre partenaire va inventer une réponse. Ensuite, posez une question avec **quand.** Votre partenaire va inventer une réponse à cette question aussi.

MODÈLE: Mon frère fait un voyage.
VOUS: **Où est-ce qu'il fait un voyage?**
VOTRE PARTENAIRE: **Il fait un voyage en France.**
VOUS: **Quand est-ce qu'il fait ce voyage?**
VOTRE PARTENAIRE: **Il fait ce voyage la semaine prochaine.**

1. Mon amie a envie de faire des courses.
2. Nous avons l'intention de déjeuner ensemble.
3. Je vais au cinéma.
4. Mon cousin travaille.
5. Mes amis étudient.

24 **À vous.** Répondez.

1. Où les étudiants de votre université habitent-ils?
2. Où se trouve la bibliothèque sur votre campus?
3. Quels bâtiments se trouvent près de la bibliothèque?
4. Où se trouve la salle de classe pour le cours de français?
5. Quand avez-vous votre cours de français?
6. Où les étudiants dînent-ils d'habitude le dimanche soir?
7. Où allez-vous vendredi prochain? Pourquoi?

ENTRE AMIS

Vous êtes un(e) nouvel(le) étudiant(e).

Choose a new name and a new country of origin from among the French-speaking countries.

1. Greet your partner and find out if s/he speaks French. (S/he does.)
2. Identify your new name and tell where you live.
3. Say that you are a new student.
4. Find out where the library is.
5. Get directions to a shopping center.
6. Thank your partner and say goodbye.

www Réalités culturelles

L'immigration

France has always welcomed citizens of other countries who wish to live within its borders for political, economic, or cultural reasons. In recent years, the presence of a growing number of immigrants has caused bitter ideological disputes between those who deem immigration to be a threat to the French identity and those who consider immigration as a positive factor that contributes to France's prosperity. Some go as far as wishing to deport all immigrants (legal as well as illegal), create a separate social security office for immigrants, allow social benefits only for French citizens, change the requirements for refugee status, and make citizenship dependent on a "blood right." Others see the anti-immigration movement as racist, xenophobic, and discriminatory and feel that while immigration causes serious complications and challenges, immigrants are a valuable asset to France.

Intégration

Révision

A **Au revoir.** Quels sont cinq synonymes de l'expression **au revoir?**

B **Les pays.** Répondez.

1. Mentionnez cinq pays où on parle français.
2. Nommez deux pays en Europe, deux pays en Asie et deux pays en Afrique.
3. Dans quels pays se trouvent ces villes: Dakar? Genève? Trois-Rivières? Lyon? Montréal? Prairie du Chien? Rabat? Bruxelles? Des Moines? Bâton Rouge?

C **Trouvez quelqu'un qui ...** Interviewez les autres étudiants pour trouver quelqu'un qui …

MODÈLE: joue au tennis
Est-ce que tu joues au tennis?

1. étudie l'informatique
2. va rarement à la bibliothèque
3. a envie d'aller au Sénégal, au Maroc ou en Suisse
4. doit travailler ce soir
5. va au cinéma vendredi soir prochain
6. a l'habitude d'étudier dans sa chambre
7. n'a pas de cours le mardi matin
8. aime manger seul
9. étudie au moins trois heures par jour

Suggestion: Assign the *Rédaction* at the end of Ch. 5 in the Workbook.

D **Début de rédaction.** Faites une liste de cinq endroits où vous allez la semaine prochaine. Indiquez le jour, l'heure et pourquoi vous allez à ces endroits. Expliquez aussi où ces endroits se trouvent.

MODÈLE: **Lundi je vais au cinéma à sept heures du soir. J'ai envie de voir un film. Le cinéma se trouve au centre commercial.**

Communication (Interpretive): Encourage students to use the practice test on the Lab Audio Program.

E **À vous.** Répondez.

1. Qu'est-ce que vous avez envie de faire ce week-end?
2. Qu'est-ce que vous devez faire?
3. Qu'est-ce que vos amis aiment faire le samedi soir?
4. Qu'est-ce que vous faites le lundi? (trois choses)
5. Quels sont les jours où vous allez à votre cours de français?
6. À quelle heure allez-vous à ce cours?
7. Dans quel bâtiment avez-vous ce cours? Où se trouve ce bâtiment?
8. Quel est votre jour préféré? Pourquoi?

Négociations:

L'emploi du temps de Sahibou. Interviewez votre partenaire pour trouver les renseignements qui manquent (*missing information*). La copie de votre partenaire est dans l'appendice D.

Video for Chapter 5: A. Video worksheets (*Cahier*); B. ACE Video practice test (WWW); C. CD-ROM

MODÈLE: Est-ce qu'il a un cours le mercredi à onze heures?
Est-ce que c'est un cours de mathématiques?

For complete instructions on how to prepare for and to use this activity, see *Négociations* on the Class Prep CD-ROM.

A

	lundi	mardi	mercredi	jeudi	vendredi	samedi	dimanche
9h	histoire		histoire		histoire		
10h						gymnase	
11h		sciences économiques		sciences économiques		gymnase	
12h		philosophie		philosophie			
1h	chimie		chimie		chimie		
2h	travail	travail	travail	travail	banque		sieste
7h						restaurant	
8h						chez des amis	

Lecture I

A **Étude du vocabulaire.** Étudiez les phrases suivantes et choisissez (*choose*) les mots anglais qui correspondent aux mots français en caractères gras (*bold print*): *river, friendly, winter, foreigners, summer, holiday, king, team, schedule.*

Before reading, have students locate Anjou, Angers, and the Loire on the map on the inside front cover of the text.

1. Le 14 juillet est un **jour férié** parce que c'est la fête nationale française.
2. Il faut consulter l'**horaire** des trains avant d'aller à la gare.
3. La Loire est le **fleuve** le plus long de France.
4. Les Angevins sont très **accueillants.** Ils vous invitent souvent.
5. L'**équipe** canadienne a gagné le match de hockey.
6. Un **roi** est le monarque d'un pays.
7. En **hiver** il fait d'habitude froid et en **été** il fait souvent très chaud.
8. À Paris on rencontre toujours beaucoup d'**étrangers:** des touristes allemands, américains, anglais et des immigrés aussi.

B **Parcourez la publicité.** Lisez rapidement la lecture pour trouver l'adresse et le numéro de téléphone de l'Office de Tourisme.

Vos vacances à Angers

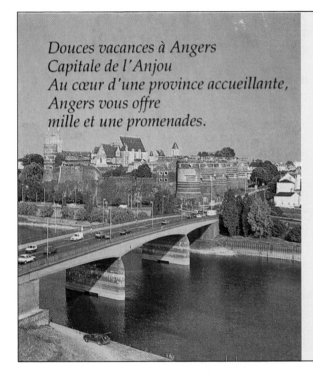

Douces vacances à Angers
Capitale de l'Anjou
Au cœur d'une province accueillante,
Angers vous offre
mille et une promenades.

Angers
Capitale de l'Anjou

Il y a en France, le long d'un fleuve majestueux qu'on appelle la Loire, une vallée célèbre par ses richesses, son climat et sa beauté. C'est dans cette région que les seigneurs, les princes et les rois de France ont fait construire les plus beaux châteaux, les plus belles maisons. C'est dans cette vallée de la Loire que se trouve l'Anjou et la capitale de l'Anjou s'appelle Angers. Angers est située à égale distance de Paris (à 2 h 30 par l'autoroute et à 1 h 30 en TGV) et de l'océan Atlantique. C'est la 16e ville de France, avec 160.000 habitants, située dans une agglomération de 260.000 habitants. Angers est avant tout une ville jeune avec plus de 30.000 étudiants.

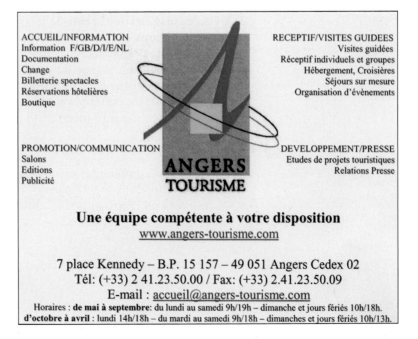

ACCUEIL/INFORMATION
Information F/GB/D/I/E/NL
Documentation
Change
Billetterie spectacles
Réservations hôtelières
Boutique

RECEPTIF/VISITES GUIDEES
Visites guidées
Réceptif individuels et groupes
Hébergement, Croisières
Séjours sur mesure
Organisation d'évènements

PROMOTION/COMMUNICATION
Salons
Editions
Publicité

DEVELOPPEMENT/PRESSE
Etudes de projets touristiques
Relations Presse

ANGERS
TOURISME

Une équipe compétente à votre disposition
www.angers-tourisme.com

7 place Kennedy – B.P. 15 157 – 49 051 Angers Cedex 02
Tél : (+33) 2 41.23.50.00 / Fax : (+33) 2.41.23.50.09
E-mail : accueil@angers-tourisme.com
Horaires : **de mai à septembre**: du lundi au samedi 9h/19h – dimanche et jours fériés 10h/18h.
d'octobre à avril : lundi 14h/18h – du mardi au samedi 9h/18h – dimanches et jours fériés 10h/13h.

C Questions. Relisez toute la lecture et ensuite répondez aux questions suivantes.

1. Où se trouve la ville d'Angers?
2. Qu'est-ce que c'est que la Loire?
3. Pourquoi la vallée de la Loire est-elle célèbre?
4. À quelle heure l'Office de Tourisme ouvre-t-il le dimanche?
5. À quelle heure l'Office de Tourisme ferme-t-il le samedi en été?
6. À quelle heure ferme-t-il le 14 juillet? Pourquoi?
7. Combien d'heures faut-il pour aller de Paris à Angers par le train?

D Familles de mots. Essayez de deviner le sens *(try to guess the meaning)* des mots suivants.

1. accueillir, un accueil, accueillant(e)
2. célébrer, une célébrité, célèbre
3. construire, la construction, constructif, constructive
4. offrir, une offre, offert(e)
5. simplifier, la simplification, simple

Connection: Have a team of students write or fax the Office de Tourisme in Angers to request information.

Lecture II

A Trouvez le Cameroun. Cherchez le Cameroun sur la carte à l'intérieur de la couverture de ce livre. Sur quel continent se trouve ce pays? Quelle est la capitale du Cameroun? Quels sont les pays qui se trouvent près du Cameroun?

B Étude du vocabulaire. Étudiez les phrases suivantes et choisissez les mots anglais qui correspondent aux mots français en caractères gras: *birds, against, a cooking utensil, I see, each one, I hear, people, a popular African food, mine, peace, bark, roof.*

1. **J'entends** quelquefois des chiens qui **aboient** quand une voiture passe.
2. Il y a des **oiseaux** sur le **toit** de la maison.
3. **Je vois** des **gens** qui portent des vêtements africains.
4. **Chacun** porte des sandales.
5. Dans leur village on mange du **taro**.
6. On prépare la cuisine avec un **pilon**.
7. Êtes-vous pour ou **contre** la **paix** dans ce pauvre pays?
8. Voilà ton livre; où est **le mien**?

C Discussion. Répondez en anglais ou en français.

1. Cherchez les exemples dans le poème qui prouvent que le poète est heureux d'être dans son village.
2. Quelles ressemblances et quelles différences y a-t-il entre le poète et vous?

Village natal

Ici je suis chez moi,
Je suis vraiment chez moi.
Les hommes que je vois,
Les femmes que je croise[1]
M'appellent leur fils
Et les enfants leur frère.
Le patois qu'on parle est le mien,
Les chants que j'entends expriment[2]
Des joies et des peines qui sont
  miennes.
L'herbe que je foule reconnaît mes
  pas[3].
Les chiens n'aboient pas contre moi,
Mais ils remuent la queue[4]
En signe de reconnaissance.
Les oiseaux me saluent au passage
Par des chants affectueux.
Des coups de pilon m'invitent

À me régaler de[5] taro
Si mon ventre est creux[6].
Sous chacun de ces toits qui
  fument
Lentement dans la paix du soir
On voudra m'accueillir[7].
Bientôt c'est la fête, la fête de
  chaque soir:
Chants et danses autour du feu[8],
Au rythme du tam-tam, du
  tambour, du balafon[9].
Nos gens sont pauvres
Mais très simples, très heureux;
Je suis simple comme eux[10]
Content comme eux,
Heureux comme eux.
Ici je suis chez moi,
Je suis vraiment chez moi.

Jean-Louis Dongmo, *Neuf poètes camerounais*, Éditions Clé

---

1. *that I meet*   2. *express*   3. *the grass I walk on recognizes my steps*   4. *wag their tails*   5. *have a delicious meal of*   6. *stomach is empty*   7. *people will welcome me*   8. *around the fire*   9. *musical instruments*   10. *them*

Réalités culturelles

Le Cameroun

Located in Central Africa along the continent's western coast, **le Cameroun** is composed of sweltering rain forests, densely populated cities, and isolated beaches. Cameroon also includes stretches of savannah and arid desert regions in the north, volcanoes, wildlife parks, and mountain ranges. The Waza national park is one of Central Africa's best, hosting several wildlife and bird species.

Cameroon's population is ethnically diverse, speaking twenty-four different African languages. English and French, reminiscent of Cameroon's colonial past, are its official languages. Christianity, Islam, and several indigenous religions are practiced. The cuisine of Cameroon is considered among the best in Central Africa, and its **macossa** music is popular in other African countries. Yaoundé, the capital, and Douala host several museums on African culture and colonial influences. Foumban is the center of African art and home to the **musée des Arts et des Traditions Bamoun**.

> Practice this vocabulary with the flashcards on the *Entre amis* web site.

VOCABULAIRE ACTIF

Adverbes
après *after*
au moins *at least*
avant *before*
d'abord *at first*
demain *tomorrow*
enfin *finally*
ensuite *next, then*
maintenant *now*

Jours de la semaine
lundi *(m.) Monday*
mardi *(m.) Tuesday*
mercredi *(m.) Wednesday*
jeudi *(m.) Thursday*
vendredi *(m.) Friday*
samedi *(m.) Saturday*
dimanche *(m.) Sunday*

Adjectifs
libre *free*
parfait(e) *perfect*
préféré(e) *favorite*
premier (première) *first*
prochain(e) *next*
seul(e) *alone; only*
suivant(e) *following*

Expressions de lieu
à côté *next door; to the side*
à côté de *next to, beside*
derrière *behind*
devant *in front of*
à droite *on (to) the right*
à gauche *on (to) the left*
entre *between, among*
loin *far*
sous *under*
tout droit *straight ahead*

Pays
l'Allemagne *(f.) Germany*
l'Angleterre *(f.) England*
la Belgique *Belgium*
le Canada *Canada*
la Chine *China*
l'Espagne *(f.) Spain*
les États-Unis *(m. pl.) United States*
la France *France*
l'Irlande *(f.) Ireland*
Israël *(m.) Israel*
l'Italie *(f.) Italy*
le Japon *Japan*
le Maroc *Morocco*
le Mexique *Mexico*
les Pays-Bas *(m. pl.) Netherlands*
le Portugal *Portugal*
la Russie *Russia*
le Sénégal *Senegal*
la Suède *Sweden*
la Suisse *Switzerland*

Verbes

aller *to go*
aller en ville *to go into town*
avoir envie de *to want to; to feel like*
avoir l'habitude de *to usually; to be in the habit of*
avoir l'intention de *to plan to*
déjeuner *to have lunch*
devoir *to have to, must; to owe*
faire un voyage *to take a trip*
passer un test *to take a test*
rester *to stay*
tourner *to turn*

Cours

la chimie *chemistry*
le commerce *business*
la comptabilité *accounting*
la gestion *management*
la gymnastique *gymnastics*
l'informatique (f.) *computer science*
la littérature *literature*
la pédagogie *education, teacher preparation*
les sciences (f.) *science*
les sciences économiques (f.) *economics*

Autres prépositions

par *per; by; through*
vers (8 heures) *approximately, around (8 o'clock)*

Expressions de temps

Quelle heure est-il? *What time is it?*
Quel jour est-ce? *What day is it?*
Il est ... heure(s). *It is ... o'clock.*

Il est midi (minuit). *It is noon (midnight).*
et demi(e) *half past*
et quart *quarter past, quarter after*
moins le quart *quarter to, quarter till*
ce soir *tonight*
dans une heure (trois jours, etc.) *one hour (three days, etc.) from now*
une minute *minute*
une semaine *week*
tout à l'heure *in a little while*
tout le week-end *all weekend (long)*

D'autres expressions utiles

Cela (ça) m'est égal. *I don't care.*
D'accord. *Okay.*
Je vais sortir. *I'm going to go out.*
Où se trouve (se trouvent) ... ? *Where is (are) ... ?*
pas grand-chose *not much*
Quoi de neuf? *What's new?*
Ça va? *Okay?*
Tu vas voir. *You are going to see.*

D'autres noms

une bise *kiss*
un emploi du temps *schedule*
un film *film, movie*
le fromage *cheese*
un rendez-vous *appointment; date*
une souris *mouse*
un voyage *trip, voyage*

l'arabe *Arabic*
le flamand *Flemish*
le portugais *Portuguese*
le wolof *Wolof*

Endroits

un aéroport *airport*
une banque *bank*
un bâtiment *building*
une bibliothèque *library*
un bistro *bar and café; bistro*
une boulangerie *bakery*
un bureau de poste *post office*
un bureau de tabac *tobacco shop*
une cafétéria *cafeteria*
un campus *campus*
un centre commercial *shopping center, mall*
un château *chateau; castle*
un cinéma *movie theater*
un couloir *hall; corridor*
un cours *course; class*
une école *school*
une église *church*
un endroit *place*
une épicerie *grocery store*
un état *state*
un gymnase *gymnasium*
une librairie *bookstore*
un musée *museum*
un parking *parking lot, garage*
un pays *country*
une pharmacie *pharmacy*
une piscine *swimming pool*
une province *province*
une résidence (universitaire) *dormitory*
un restaurant *restaurant*
une salle de classe *classroom*
les toilettes (f. pl.) *restroom*
une ville *city*

Chapitre 6

Vos activités

Coup d'envoi

Prise de contact

Qu'est-ce que tu as fait hier?

Point out the use of **à** before an object with **téléphoner.**

Sébastien, qu'est-ce que tu as fait hier?°   *What did you do yesterday?*

　　J'ai téléphoné à deux amis.
　　J'ai envoyé des messages électroniques°.   *sent e-mail*
　　J'ai fait mes devoirs.
　　J'ai étudié pendant° trois heures.   *for*
　　J'ai déjeuné à midi et j'ai dîné à 7 heures du soir.
　　J'ai regardé un peu la télévision.
　　Mais je n'ai pas fait le ménage.
　　Et je n'ai pas passé d'examen°.   *test*

▶ **Et vous?**   Qu'est-ce que vous avez fait?

Lettre

This letter is recorded on the Student Audio included with your text.

Communication (Interpretive): Allow students to keep their books open the first time you read this letter, then reread it (books closed). Can they remember any words? You may wish to play the recording for the class on the Student Audio.

Une lettre à des amis

Lori a écrit une lettre à deux de ses camarades du cours de français aux États-Unis.

Chers John et Cathy,   Angers, le 15 décembre

Merci beaucoup de vos lettres. Que le temps passe vite![1] Je suis en France depuis déjà trois mois.[2] Vous avez demandé si j'ai le temps de voyager. Oui, mais la plupart[3] du temps je suis très active et très occupée parce qu'[4]il y a toujours tant de[5] choses à faire chaque[6] jour. C'est la vie, n'est-ce pas?

Dimanche dernier[7], j'ai accompagné ma famille française au Mans chez les parents de Mme Martin. Nous avons passé trois heures à table! Cette semaine, j'ai lu une pièce[8] de Molière pour mon cours de littérature et j'ai écrit une dissertation[9]. J'ai aussi fait le ménage et j'ai gardé[10] les enfants pour Mme Martin. Heureusement, je ne me lève pas tôt[11] le samedi.

Vous avez demandé si j'ai remarqué[12] des différences entre la France et les États-Unis. Eh bien, oui. Chez les Martin, par exemple, les portes à l'intérieur de la maison sont toujours fermées[13], les toilettes ne sont pas dans la salle de bain et les robinets[14] sont marqués «C» et «F». J'ai déjà oublié[15] deux fois[16] que «C» ne veut pas dire «cold». Aïe![17]

Dites bonjour[18] pour moi à Madame Walter, s.v.p. Écrivez-moi à lbecker@wanadoo.fr

Bonnes vacances!

Votre amie «française»,
Lori

---

1. *How time flies!* 2. *I've already been in France for three months.* 3. *most* 4. *because* 5. *so many*
6. *each; every* 7. *last* 8. *I read a play* 9. *I wrote a (term) paper* 10. *watched, looked after*
11. *Fortunately, I don't get up early* 12. *I noticed* 13. *closed* 14. *faucets* 15. *I already forgot* 16. *times*
17. *Ouch!* 18. *Say hello*

After practicing the *Compréhension*, have students complete ex. A in the Workbook.

▶ **Compréhension.** Décidez si les phrases suivantes sont vraies ou fausses. Si une phrase est fausse, corrigez-la.

1. Lori a déjà passé trois mois en France.
2. En France on passe beaucoup de temps à table.
3. Lori n'a pas passé d'examen.
4. Lori a beaucoup de temps libre.
5. On ferme les portes dans une maison française.
6. «C» sur un robinet veut dire «chaud».
7. «F» sur un robinet veut dire «français».

À propos

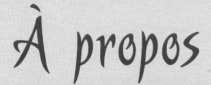

La maison

Living in France has meant more to Lori than just learning the French language. She has also had the opportunity to become part of a French family and has had to learn to cope with a number of cultural differences. There is no need in French for a separate word to distinguish between *house* and *home*. Both are **la maison,** and **la maison** is seen as a refuge from the storm of the world outside, a place to find comfort and solace and to put order into one's existence. Given the French attitude about **la maison,** it is not surprising to find social and architectural indications of that need for order. There is a set time for meals, and family members are expected to be there. There is an order to a French meal that is quite different from the everything-on-one-plate-at-one-time eating style prevalent in English-speaking North America. The walls around French houses, the shutters on the windows, and the closing of the doors inside the home are other examples of the French desire for order and clearly established boundaries.

Relativité culturelle: La maison

The home is undoubtedly the scene of the greatest number of cultural contrasts. There are, therefore, some potentially troublesome adjustments, some of which are described in the chart below.

Pourquoi est-ce que les portes sont fermées à l'intérieur d'une maison française?

a. Les Français ne désirent pas tomber malades.
b. Les Français préfèrent l'ordre et l'intimité *(privacy)*.
c. Les Français ont peur des voleurs *(are afraid of thieves)*.

In France	In North America
Doors are closed, especially the bathroom door, even when no one is in the room. Fear of drafts **(des courants d'air)** is often mentioned as a reason for keeping doors closed inside of a home.	Doors inside a house are often left open.
Since the toilet, tub, and shower are all in the bathroom, be more specific about whether one is looking for **la salle de bain** or **les toilettes.**	Since the toilet, tub, and shower are all in the bathroom, one person may inconvenience the rest of the family.
Hands can be scalded trying to test "cold" water from a faucet marked "C."	Turning on a faucet marked "C" will not make the water get hot **(chaud)** no matter how long one waits.
There are no screens on windows to keep out insects.	Screens on windows don't allow the wide-open feeling one gets from French windows.
There are almost always walls or a hedge to ensure privacy and clearly mark the limits of one's property. See, for example, p. 83.	In many neighborhoods there are no walls to separate houses.

The **C'est la vie** gesture is used in the video, *Module 11.*

Il y a un geste

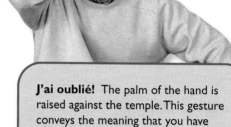

C'est la vie. A gesture often accompanies the expression **C'est la vie:** the shoulders are shrugged, and the head is slightly tilted to one side. Sometimes the lips are pursed as well, and the palms are upturned. The idea is *That's life and I can't do anything about it.*

J'ai oublié! The palm of the hand is raised against the temple. This gesture conveys the meaning that you have forgotten something or have made a mistake.

▶ **À vous.** Donnez une réponse personnelle.

1. Où avez-vous dîné hier soir?
2. Combien de temps avez-vous passé à table?
3. Qu'est-ce que vous avez fait après le dîner?

ENTRE AMIS

Hier

1. Ask what your partner did yesterday.
2. S/he will tell you at least two things.
3. Choose one of the things s/he did and find out as much as you can about it (at what time, where, etc.).

Prononciation

Use the Student Audio to help practice pronunciation.

Les sons [u] et [y]

■ Because of differences in meaning in words such as **tout** and **tu,** it is very important to distinguish between the vowel sounds [u] and [y]. The following words contain these two important vowel sounds. Practice saying these words after your teacher, paying particular attention to the highlighted vowel sound.

[u] • bonj**ou**r, r**ou**ge, c**ou**rs, éc**ou**ter, j**ou**er, tr**ou**ver, v**ou**lez, je v**ou**drais, t**ou**jours, beau**cou**p, **pou**rquoi, **sou**vent, **cou**sin, d**ou**te, **ou**vrier, bl**ou**son, **cou**leur, **cou**rse, n**ou**veau, auj**ou**rd'hui, **cou**loir, s**ou**s, t**ou**t, **ou**blié

• **où**

[y] • j**u**s, **u**ne, ét**u**dier, ét**u**diants, t**u**, b**u**reau, calc**u**latrice, voit**u**re, s**u**r, j**u**pe, l**u**nettes, p**u**ll-over, n**u**méro, diffic**u**lté, br**u**ne, st**u**pide, camp**u**s, **u**niversitaire, m**u**sique, R**u**ssie, min**u**te, d**u**, occ**u**pé, j'ai l**u**, littérat**u**re

■ The [u] sound, represented by written **ou** or **où,** is close to the sound in the English word *tooth.*

n**ou**s   r**ou**ge   **où**

■ The [y] sound is represented by a single written **-u-.** There is, however, no English "equivalent" for this French sound. To produce it, round your lips as if drinking through a straw; then, without moving your lips, pronounce the vowel in the word **ici.**

d**u**   **u**ne   sal**u**t   v**u**e

▶ In each of the following pairs of words, one of the words contains the [u] sound, the other the [y] sound. Pronounce each word correctly.

Be sure students pronounce [u] and not [ɔ] or [ə] in closed syllables, especially before an **-r.** If necessary, have them pronounce the vowel in open syllables first: **tout, tour; joue, jour; pou, pour.**

1. sur / sous
2. jour / jupe
3. vous / vu
4. pure / pour
5. cours / cure
6. russe / rousse
7. roux / rue
8. ou / eu
9. tout / tu

Buts communicatifs

1. Relating Past Events

Tell students to follow the model when interviewing each other.

Avez-vous déjà[1] nettoyé[2] votre chambre ce semestre?

Oui, j'ai déjà nettoyé ma chambre.
Non, je n'ai pas encore nettoyé ma chambre.

	oui	non
Avez-vous déjà chanté en français?	_____	_____
Avez-vous déjà dansé la valse?	_____	_____
Avez-vous déjà mangé des crêpes?	_____	_____
Avez-vous déjà joué au tennis?	_____	_____
Avez-vous déjà travaillé dans un restaurant?	_____	_____
Avez-vous déjà fumé[3] un cigare?	_____	_____
Avez-vous déjà été absent(e) ce semestre?	_____	_____
Avez-vous déjà eu un accident?	_____	_____
Avez-vous déjà fait vos devoirs pour demain?	_____	_____
Avez-vous déjà eu la grippe[4]?	_____	_____

---

1. *already*   2. *cleaned*   3. *smoked*   4. *flu*

A. Le passé composé avec *avoir*

Remember to consult Appendix C at the end of the book to review any grammatical terms with which you are not familiar.

Hier soir, **Michel a regardé** la télévision.
Et puis **il a fait** ses devoirs.
Pendant combien de temps **a-t-il étudié?**
Il a étudié pendant deux heures.

Last night, Michel watched television.
And then he did his homework.
How long did he study?
He studied for two hours.

■ The passé composé *(compound past)* is used to tell about or narrate specific events that have already taken place. Depending on the context, its English translation may be any one of several possibilities.

J'ai mangé une pomme. $\begin{cases} \textit{I ate an apple.} \\ \textit{I did eat an apple.} \\ \textit{I have eaten an apple.} \end{cases}$

Verbs taking the auxiliary **être** will be studied in Ch. 7.

■ The passé composé is formed with the present tense of an auxiliary verb (normally **avoir**) and a past participle.

manger *(au passé composé)*			
j'ai	**mangé**	nous avons	**mangé**
tu as	**mangé**	vous avez	**mangé**
il/elle/on a	**mangé**	ils/elles ont	**mangé**

The conjugation of regular **-re** and **-ir** verbs will be taught in Chs. 9 and 12, respectively.

■ The past participles of all **-er** verbs are pronounced the same as the infinitive. They are spelled by replacing the **-er** ending of the infinitive with **-é.**

étudi~~er~~	+	-é	$\longrightarrow$	**étudié**
mang~~er~~	+	-é	$\longrightarrow$	**mangé**
jou~~er~~	+	-é	$\longrightarrow$	**joué**

In the expression **j'ai eu** *(I had)* the word **eu** is pronounced [y].

■ The past participles of many verbs that *don't* end in **-er** must be memorized.

eu (avoir)	**été** (être)	**fait** (faire)	**dû** (devoir)

J'**ai eu** la grippe pendant trois jours!
Anne et Guy **ont fait** la cuisine ensemble.
Ils ont **dû** dîner à la maison.

I had the flu for three days!
Anne and Guy did the cooking together.
They must have eaten at home.
They had to eat at home.

Remind students that **devoir** can imply either obligation or probability (see p. 138).

■ In the negative, **ne ... pas (ne ... jamais)** is placed around the auxiliary verb.

> **ne (n')** + auxiliary verb + **pas (jamais)** + past participle

Point out that **la plupart de** is usually used with plural nouns and takes a plural verb. The only common exception is **la plupart du temps.**

Review the formation of questions in Ch. 2, pp. 48–49.

Il **n'a pas** écouté la radio.	*He didn't listen to the radio.*
Nous **n'avons pas** fait de promenade.	*We didn't take a walk.*
La plupart des étudiants **n'ont jamais** fumé de cigare.	*Most students have never smoked a cigar.*

■ Questions in the passé composé are formed the way they are in the present tense. Note, however, that in all cases of inversion, only the auxiliary verb and the subject pronoun are involved. The past participle follows the inverted pronoun.

Il a fait ses devoirs?	
Est-ce qu'il a fait ses devoirs?	*Has he (Marc) done his homework?*
A-t-il fait ses devoirs?	
Marc a-t-il fait ses devoirs?	

1   **Mais il a fait ça hier.** Demandez si David fait les choses suivantes aujourd'hui. Votre partenaire va répondre que David a fait ces choses hier.

MODÈLE: travailler
> VOUS: **Est-ce que David travaille aujourd'hui?**
> VOTRE PARTENAIRE: **Non, mais il a travaillé hier.**

1. jouer au tennis
2. être absent
3. avoir une lettre de ses grands-parents
4. dîner avec Véronique
5. manger une pizza
6. faire la vaisselle
7. regarder la télé

2   **Véronique.** Pierre aime Véronique et il vous pose des questions parce qu'elle a dîné avec David hier soir. Répondez à ses questions d'après le modèle.

MODÈLE: Véronique a-t-elle dîné seule? (avec David)
> **Non, elle n'a pas dîné seule; elle a dîné avec David.**

1. Ont-ils dîné au restaurant? (chez David)
2. David a-t-il fait la cuisine? (la vaisselle)
3. Ont-ils mangé un sandwich? (une pizza)
4. Véronique a-t-elle détesté la pizza? (aimé)
5. Ont-ils dansé après le dîner? (regardé la télévision)

3 **La plupart des étudiants.** Qu'est-ce que la plupart des étudiants ont fait hier? Décidez.

> Be sure to use plural verb forms with **la plupart des.**

MODÈLE: fumer une cigarette

> VOTRE PARTENAIRE: **Est-ce que la plupart des étudiants ont fumé une cigarette hier?**
>
> VOUS: **Non, la plupart des étudiants n'ont pas fumé de cigarette.**

> Add the question: **Et vous? Avez-vous fumé une cigarette hier?** Have students answer **Moi aussi** or **Moi non plus** if the answer is the same for them.

1. étudier à la bibliothèque
2. faire leurs devoirs
3. passer un test
4. avoir une bonne note
5. déjeuner avec leurs professeurs
6. travailler après les cours

VOCABULAIRE

Expressions de temps (passé)

> Remember that **tout à l'heure** can also refer to the future: *in a little while.* The expression **à tout à l'heure** means *see you soon.*

tout à l'heure	*a little while ago*
ce matin	*this morning*
hier soir	*last night*
hier	*yesterday*
hier matin	*yesterday morning*
lundi dernier	*last Monday*
le week-end dernier	*last weekend*
la semaine dernière	*last week*
le mois dernier	*last month*
l'année dernière	*last year*
récemment	*recently*
il y a deux (trois, etc.) ans	*two (three, etc.) years ago*
il y a longtemps	*a long time ago*
la dernière fois	*the last time*
pendant les vacances	*during vacation*

NOTES

1. **Il y a,** used with an expression of time, means *ago:* **il y a deux mois** *(two months ago);* **il y a trois ans** *(three years ago).*

2. In general, the word **an** is used when counting the number of years: **un an, deux ans,** etc. The word **année** is normally used when referring to a specific year: **cette année, l'année dernière,** etc. The same distinction is made between **jour** and **journée: Il y a trois jours; une belle journée.**

4 **Il y a combien de temps?** Qu'avons-nous fait? Que n'avons-nous pas fait? Utilisez un élément de chaque colonne pour composer des phrases affirmatives ou négatives.

MODÈLES: **Mes parents ont fait un voyage il y a deux ans.**
Mes parents n'ont jamais parlé français.

	faire un voyage	ne ... jamais
je	avoir des vacances	il y a ...
mes parents	dîner au restaurant	... dernier (dernière)
mon meilleur ami	avoir une lettre	pendant les vacances
ma meilleure amie	être absent(e)(s)	hier (...)
nous	faire la vaisselle	ce matin
	parler français	tout à l'heure
	étudier pendant trois heures	récemment

Do this exercise in pairs. Follow up by having the class interview the instructor.

5 **La dernière fois.** Demandez à votre partenaire quand il (elle) a fait ces choses pour la dernière fois. Il (elle) va répondre.

MODÈLE: être absent(e)

VOUS: **Quelle est la dernière fois que vous avez été absent(e) ce semestre?**

VOTRE PARTENAIRE: **J'ai été absent(e) la semaine dernière.** ou **Je n'ai jamais été absent(e).**

1. étudier seul(e)
2. fumer
3. devoir passer un examen
4. être malade
5. téléphoner à un ami
6. avoir «A» à l'examen
7. passer trois heures à table
8. nager à la piscine
9. manger une pizza

6 **À vous.** Répondez.

1. Pendant combien de temps avez-vous étudié hier soir?
2. Pendant combien de temps avez-vous regardé la télévision?
3. Quelle est la dernière fois que vous avez téléphoné à un(e) ami(e)? Pendant combien de temps avez-vous parlé au téléphone?
4. Quelle est la dernière fois que vous avez eu la grippe? Pendant combien de temps avez-vous été malade?
5. Quelle est la dernière fois que vous avez été absent(e)?
6. Pendant combien de jours avez-vous été absent(e) ce semestre?

Communication (Interpretive): Follow up (books closed) by using these questions to poll the class, then summarize the answers.

ENTRE AMIS

Hier soir

1. Find out where your partner ate last night.
2. Find out if s/he watched TV or listened to the radio.
3. If so, find out what s/he watched or listened to.
4. Find out if s/he did his/her homework.
5. If so, find out where.
6. If so, find out how long s/he studied.

2. Describing Your Study Habits

	vrai	faux
J'aime étudier seul(e).	____	____
Je fais mes devoirs à la bibliothèque.	____	____
J'écris[1] souvent des dissertations.	____	____
Je ne passe pas beaucoup de temps à faire mes devoirs.	____	____
Je passe au moins[2] trois heures à étudier par jour.	____	____
Je lis[3] au moins un livre par semaine.	____	____
J'écoute la radio pendant que[4] j'étudie.	____	____
Je regarde la télé pendant que j'étudie.	____	____

1. *write*   2. *at least*   3. *read*   4. *while*

REMARQUE

Use **passer** + unit(s) of time + **à** + infinitive to express how long you spend doing something.

Nous **avons passé deux heures à manger.**

We spent two hours eating.

D'habitude, Marc **passe quatre heures à faire** ses devoirs.

Marc usually spends four hours doing his homework.

B. Les verbes *écrire* et *lire*

J'aime **lire** des romans policiers.
J'ai passé trois heures à **lire** hier soir.

I like to read detective stories.
I spent three hours reading last night.

Quelles langues **lisez-vous?**
Éric lit le journal pendant qu'il mange.

What languages do you read?
Éric reads the newspaper while he eats.

Mes parents n'**écrivent** pas souvent.
À qui **écrivez-vous?**
Comment est-ce qu'**on écrit** le mot «lisent»?

My parents don't write often.
Who are you writing to?
How do you spell the word "lisent"?

écrire *(to write)*	
j'	**écris**
tu	**écris**
il/elle/on	**écrit**
nous	**écrivons**
vous	**écrivez**
ils/elles	**écrivent**
passé composé: j'**ai écrit**	

lire *(to read)*	
je	**lis**
tu	**lis**
il/elle/on	**lit**
nous	**lisons**
vous	**lisez**
ils/elles	**lisent**
passé composé: j'**ai lu**	

■ Note the pronunciation distinction between the third person singular and plural forms.

il écrit [ekRi]   ils [z]écrivent [ekRiv]   elle lit [li]   elles lisent [liz]

■ The verb **décrire** *(to describe)* is conjugated like **écrire.**

Nous **décrivons** nos familles au professeur.

VOCABULAIRE

Des choses à lire ou à écrire

une bande dessinée	*comic strip*	un message	*e-mail message*
une carte postale	*postcard*	électronique	
une dissertation	*(term) paper*	une pièce	*play*
un journal	*newspaper*	un poème	*poem*
une lettre	*letter*	un roman	*novel*
un livre	*book*	un roman policier	*detective story*
un magazine	*magazine*		

See p. 22. The plural of **journal** is **journaux**.

7 **Qu'est-ce qu'ils lisent? Qu'est-ce qu'ils écrivent?** Répondez aux questions. Si vous ne savez pas la réponse, devinez.

1. Combien de livres lisez-vous par semestre?
2. Vos parents écrivent-ils beaucoup de lettres?
3. À qui écrivez-vous des messages électroniques?
4. Qui, dans votre famille, lit des bandes dessinées?
5. Combien de dissertations un étudiant écrit-il par an?
6. Avez-vous déjà écrit une dissertation ce semestre? Si oui, pour quel(s) cours?
7. Avez-vous lu un journal ou un magazine cette semaine? Si non, pourquoi pas?
8. Combien d'heures passez-vous à lire par semaine? par mois?

C. *Ne ... rien*

■ The opposite of **quelque chose** is **ne ... rien** *(nothing, not anything)*.

Mangez-vous **quelque chose?** *Are you eating something?*

Non, je **ne** mange **rien.** *No, I am not eating anything.*

Connection: Point out Édith Piaf's **Non, je ne regrette rien** at the end of this chapter. Play a recording of this song for the class.

■ **Ne ... rien** works like **ne ... pas** and **ne ... jamais;** that is, **ne** and **rien** are placed around the conjugated verb. This means that in the passé composé, **ne** and **rien** surround the auxiliary verb and the past participle follows **rien.**

Je **ne** vais **rien** écrire. *I'm not going to write anything.*

Je **n'**ai **rien** écrit hier soir. *I didn't write anything last night.*

■ **Rien** can follow a preposition.

Je **ne** parle **de rien.** *I'm not talking about anything.*

Je **n'**ai parlé **de rien.** *I didn't talk about anything.*

Review the use of ne ... jamais, p. 97.

■ Unlike English, French allows the use of more than one negative word in a sentence.

Il **ne** fait **jamais rien!** *He never does anything!*

The use of **rien** as a subject will be studied in Ch. 15.

■ Like **jamais**, **rien** can be used alone to answer a question.

Qu'est-ce que tu as lu? **Rien.**

FOR RECOGNITION ONLY

Quelque chose and **rien** can be made slightly more specific by the addition of **de** + *masculine adjective* or of **à** + *infinitive*. The two constructions can even be combined.

Jean lit **quelque chose** *d'intéressant.*   Éric **ne** lit **rien** *d'intéressant.*
Il a **quelque chose** *à lire.*   Il **n'**a **rien** *à lire.*
Il a **quelque chose** *d'intéressant à lire.*   Il **n'**a **rien** *d'intéressant à lire.*

---

8 **Une personne paresseuse.** Éric ne fait rien. Répondez aux questions suivantes avec le mot **rien**.

MODÈLES: Qu'est-ce qu'il fait le vendredi soir?   **Il ne fait rien.**
Qu'est-ce qu'il a fait vendredi dernier?   **Il n'a rien fait.**
Qu'est-ce qu'il va faire vendredi prochain?   **Il ne va rien faire.**

1. Qu'est-ce qu'il étudie à la bibliothèque?
2. Qu'est-ce qu'il lit pendant le week-end?
3. Qu'est-ce qu'il va faire cet après-midi?
4. Qu'est-ce qu'il va lire pour ses cours?
5. Qu'est-ce qu'il a écrit pendant les vacances?
6. Qu'est-ce qu'il a lu l'année dernière?

9 **Ces travailleurs.** Sylvie et David sont très travailleurs et la semaine dernière, ils n'ont pas eu le temps de faire des choses amusantes. Posez une question à leur sujet au passé composé. Votre partenaire va utiliser **rien** dans sa réponse.

MODÈLE: regarder quelque chose à la télé
VOUS: **Est-ce qu'ils ont regardé quelque chose à la télé?**
VOTRE PARTENAIRE: **Non, ils n'ont rien regardé.**

Redo ex. 9 in the near future with **aller: Est-ce qu'ils vont regarder quelque chose? Non, ils ne vont rien regarder.**

1. écouter quelque chose à la radio
2. écrire des poèmes
3. chanter quelque chose ensemble
4. lire un roman policier
5. faire quelque chose en ville

10 **À vous.** Répondez.

1. D'habitude qu'est-ce que vous lisez le matin?
2. À qui avez-vous écrit la semaine dernière?
3. Qu'avez-vous lu hier soir?
4. Avez-vous écouté la radio ce matin? Si oui, qu'est-ce que vous avez écouté?
5. Avez-vous des amis qui regardent la télé pendant qu'ils étudient?
6. Qu'est-ce que vous regardez à la télévision pendant que vous étudiez?
7. Combien de temps passez-vous d'habitude à préparer vos cours?
8. Lisez-vous souvent des magazines? Si oui, quels magazines?
9. Combien de dissertations écrivez-vous par semestre?

D. *Temps, heure* et *fois*

■ Depending on the context, the French use different words to express what, in English, could always be expressed by the word *time*.

- **L'heure,** as you already know, means *clock time.*

Quelle **heure** est-il?   *What time is it?*

REMINDER

Heure can also mean *hour* or *o'clock.*

J'ai étudié pendant trois **heures.**   *I studied for three hours.*

Il est deux **heures.**   *It is two o'clock.*

- **La fois** means *time* in a countable or repeated sense.

Combien de **fois** par an?   *How many times per year?*

la dernière **fois**   *the last time*

chaque **fois**   *each time*

- **Le temps** means *time* in a general sense.

Remember that **temps** can also mean *weather:* **Quel temps fait-il aujourd'hui?**

Je n'ai pas **le temps** d'étudier.   *I don't have time to study.*

Avez-vous **le temps** de voyager?   *Do you have time to travel?*

Combien de **temps** avez-vous?   *How much time do you have?*

11 **Hier soir.** Utilisez **temps, heure** ou **fois** pour compléter ce dialogue.

1. Hier soir j'ai étudié pendant quatre _____.
2. Avez-vous eu assez de _____ pour regarder la télévision?
3. Non, parce que mes parents ont téléphoné trois _____.
4. À quelle _____ ont-ils téléphoné la première _____?
5. À six _____.
6. Combien de _____ par mois allez-vous chez vos parents?
7. Trois ou quatre _____.
8. Quand avez-vous dîné hier soir? À sept _____.
9. Combien de _____ avez-vous passé à table?
10. Une _____.

12 **À vous.** Répondez.

1. D'habitude combien de temps passez-vous à faire vos devoirs?
2. Pendant combien d'heures avez-vous étudié hier soir? Combien de temps avez-vous passé à faire vos devoirs pour le cours de français?
3. À quelle heure avez-vous dîné? Combien de temps avez-vous passé à table?
4. Combien de temps par semaine passez-vous avec votre meilleur(e) ami(e)?
5. Combien de fois par mois allez-vous au cinéma?
6. Combien de temps avez-vous passé à la bibliothèque la semaine dernière?

ENTRE AMIS

Es-tu un(e) bon(ne) étudiant(e)?

1. Find out if your partner spends a lot of time studying.
2. Ask if s/he watches TV while s/he studies.
3. Find out how long s/he studied last night.
4. Ask what s/he read for your French course.
5. Ask your partner how to spell some word in French.
6. Compliment your partner on his/her French.

3. Describing Your Weekend Activities

Qu'est-ce que vous faites pendant le week-end?

	oui	non
Je pars[1] du campus chaque week-end.	_____	_____
Je sors[2] avec mes amis.	_____	_____
Je m'amuse[3] bien.	_____	_____
Je vais au cinéma.	_____	_____
Je joue du piano.	_____	_____
Je joue au golf.	_____	_____
Je fais du vélo.	_____	_____
Je fais beaucoup de sport.	_____	_____
Je dors[4] beaucoup.	_____	_____
Je me lève tard[5].	_____	_____
Je ne me couche[6] pas tôt.	_____	_____
Je nettoie[7] ma chambre.	_____	_____

1. *leave*   2. *go out*   3. *have fun*   4. *sleep*   5. *late*   6. *go to bed*   7. *clean*

E. Les verbes pronominaux

■ Reflexive verbs **(les verbes pronominaux)** are those whose subject and object are the same. English examples of reflexive verbs are *he cut himself* or *she bought herself a dress.*

■ You have already learned a number of expressions that use reflexive verbs in French.

Comment vous appelez-vous?	*What is your name?*
Je m'appelle ...	*My name is ...*
Comment s'appellent vos amis?	*What are your friends' names?*
Asseyez-vous là!	*Sit there!*

■ Reflexive verbs use an object pronoun (**me, te, se, nous, vous**) in addition to the subject. With the exception of affirmative commands, this pronoun is always placed directly in front of the verb.

s'amuser		se lever	
je	**m'**amuse	je	**me** lève
tu	**t'**amuses	tu	**te** lèves
il/elle/on	**s'**amuse	il/elle/on	**se** lève
nous	**nous** amusons	nous	**nous** levons
vous	**vous** amusez	vous	**vous** levez
ils/elles	**s'**amusent	ils/elles	**se** lèvent

■ Use **est-ce que** or a rising intonation to ask a yes/no question.

Est-ce que tu te lèves tôt le matin?   *Do you get up early in the morning?*

Tu t'amuses au cours de français?   *Do you have fun in French class?*

■ In the negative, **ne** is placed before the object pronoun and **pas** after the verb.

Je **ne** me lève **pas** tôt.   *I don't get up early.*

Mes professeurs **ne** s'amusent **pas**.   *My teachers don't have fun.*

Vous **ne** vous couchez **pas** avant minuit?   *Don't you go to bed before midnight?*

■ When the reflexive verb is used in the infinitive form after another verb, the reflexive pronoun agrees with the subject of the sentence.

À quelle heure vas-**tu te** coucher?   *At what time are you going to go to bed?*

Je n'aime pas **me** lever tôt.   *I don't like to get up early.*

Les étudiants ont l'habitude de **s'**amuser le samedi soir.   *Students are used to having fun on Saturday night.*

Communication (Presentational): Pair students to complete this activity. Then (books closed) have students share as many examples as they can remember from the activity.

13 Identifications. Identifiez, si possible, des personnes qui correspondent aux descriptions suivantes.

MODÈLE: une personne qui se lève très tôt le dimanche matin
Mon père se lève très tôt le dimanche matin.

1. une personne qui se couche tôt le dimanche soir
2. une personne qui ne se couche pas s'il y a quelque chose d'intéressant à la télévision
3. deux étudiants qui se couchent tard s'ils ont un examen
4. deux personnes qui s'amusent beaucoup au cours de français
5. deux de vos amis qui ne se lèvent pas tôt le samedi matin
6. une personne qui ne va pas s'amuser pendant les vacances
7. une personne qui se lève quelquefois trop tard pour le cours de français

14 **À vous.** Répondez.

1. Comment vous appelez-vous et comment s'appelle votre meilleur(e) ami(e)?
2. Quel jour est-ce que vous vous couchez tard?
3. Est-ce que vous vous levez tôt ou tard le samedi matin? Expliquez votre réponse.
4. Avez-vous des amis qui ne s'amusent pas beaucoup? Si oui, comment s'appellent-ils?
5. Est-ce que vos professeurs aiment s'amuser en classe?
6. Est-ce que vous vous amusez au cours de français? Pourquoi ou pourquoi pas?
7. À quelle heure est-ce que vous vous levez le lundi matin? Pourquoi?
8. À quelle heure est-ce que vous allez vous coucher ce soir? Expliquez votre réponse.

F. *Jouer de* et *jouer à*

■ *To play a musical instrument* is expressed by **jouer de** + definite article + musical instrument. The definite article is retained in the negative before the name of the instrument.

Mon frère **joue du** saxophone, mais il ne **joue** pas **de la** guitare.	*My brother plays the saxophone but he doesn't play the guitar.*
De quoi **jouez**-vous?	*What (instrument) do you play?*
Moi, je ne **joue de** rien.	*I don't play any (instrument).*

VOCABULAIRE

Review **de** + article, p. 76, and **à** + article, p. 127.

Quelques instruments de musique

un accordéon	*accordion*	un piano	*piano*
une batterie	*drums*	un saxophone	*saxophone*
une flûte	*flute*	une trompette	*trumpet*
une guitare	*guitar*	un violon	*violin*

Point out that in **le hockey** the article does not change to **l'**. The **h aspiré** is explained in the pronunciation section of Ch. 10.

■ To *play a game* is expressed by **jouer à** + definite article + game.

— Mon amie **joue au** golf le lundi, elle **joue à la** pétanque le mercredi et elle **joue aux** cartes le vendredi soir. Mais elle ne **joue** jamais **aux** échecs.
— **À** quoi **jouez**-vous?
— Moi, je ne **joue à** rien.

Connections: **La pétanque** can be seen in the video, *Modules 1 & 11.* **La pétanque** is also called **les boules.** Point out the photo on p. 154.

NOTE CULTURELLE
La pétanque est un jeu de boules très populaire en France. On joue à la pétanque à l'extérieur, par exemple près des cafés. Pour marquer des points, il faut placer les boules le plus près possible du co-chonnet *(small wooden ball).*

VOCABULAIRE

Quelques jeux *(Several games)*

le basket-ball (le basket)	*basketball*	le football américain	*football*
le bridge	*bridge*	le golf	*golf*
les cartes *(f. pl.)*	*cards*	le hockey	*hockey*
les dames *(f. pl.)*	*checkers*	la pétanque	*lawn bowling (bocce)*
les échecs *(m. pl.)*	*chess*	le rugby	*rugby*
le football (le foot)	*soccer*	le tennis	*tennis*

15 **Tout le monde joue.** À quoi jouent-ils? De quoi jouent-ils? Faites des phrases complètes avec les éléments donnés.

MODÈLES: **Les Canadiens jouent au hockey.**
Ma sœur ne joue pas de l'accordéon.

Communication (Interpretive): Follow up by creating "illogical" sentences, e.g., **Tiger Woods joue du violon.** Have students correct them.

les Français			la pétanque
Tiger Woods			l'accordéon
Shaquille O'Neal			le piano
ma sœur			les cartes
mon frère		de	le saxophone
les violonistes	(ne ... pas) jouer	à	le basket-ball
les Américains			la guitare
les Canadiens			les échecs
les sœurs Williams			le violon
je			le golf
mon ami(e) ...			le hockey
...			le tennis

16 **À vous.** Répondez.

1. Quel est votre instrument de musique préféré?
2. Quel est votre sport préféré?
3. Jouez-vous d'un instrument de musique? Si oui, de quoi jouez-vous?
4. Êtes-vous sportif (sportive)? Si oui, à quoi jouez-vous?
5. Avez-vous des amis qui jouent aux cartes? Si oui, à quel jeu de cartes jouent-ils?
6. Avez-vous des amis qui jouent d'un instrument de musique? Si oui, de quoi jouent-ils?

G. Les pronoms accentués

Students will learn in Ch. 11 to use stress pronouns in comparisons: **Il est plus grand que** *moi.*

■ *Stress pronouns* **(les pronoms accentués)** are used in certain circumstances where a subject pronoun cannot be used. Each stress pronoun has a corresponding subject pronoun.

The use of **moi, toi,** etc., after a verb will be presented on pp. 283 and 357.

je	→	**moi**	nous	→	**nous**
tu	→	**toi**	vous	→	**vous**
il	→	**lui**	ils	→	**eux**
elle	→	**elle**	elles	→	**elles**
on	→	**soi**			

■ Stress pronouns are used in the following circumstances:

• to stress the subject of a sentence

Moi, je n'aime pas le café.　　*I don't like coffee.*
Ils aiment le thé, **eux.**　　***They** like tea.*

• in a compound subject

Point out the use of the first person plural when **moi** is one of the compound subjects.

Mes parents et **moi,** nous habitons ici.　　*My parents and I live here.*
Monsieur Martin a des enfants?
Oui, sa femme et **lui** ont six enfants.　　*Yes, he and his wife have six children.*

• after a preposition

chez **soi**　　*at one's house*　　pour **lui**　　*for him*
entre **nous**　　*between us*　　sans **elles**　　*without them*

> **NOTE**　A stress pronoun after the expression **être à** indicates possession.
>
> Ce livre est **à moi.**　　*This book belongs to me.*
> Il est **à toi,** ce pull?　　*Is this sweater yours?*

• after **c'est** and **ce sont**

C'est **moi.**　　*It is I (me).*　　Ce n'est pas **elle.**　　*It is not she (her).*

> **NOTE**　**C'est** is used with **nous** and **vous**. **Ce sont** is used only with **eux** and **elles**.
>
> **C'est** nous.　　*It is we (us).*　　**Ce sont** eux.　　*It is they (them).*

• alone or in phrases without a verb

Lui!　　*Him!*
Et **toi?**　　*And you?*
Elle aussi.　　*So does she. So has she. So is she. She too.*
Moi non plus.　　*Me neither. Nor I.*

• with the suffix **-même(s)**

toi-même　　*yourself*　　**eux**-mêmes　　*themselves*

17 **Eux aussi.** La famille de Paul fait exactement ce qu'il fait *(what he does)*. Utilisez un pronom accentué pour répondre à la question. Si la première phrase est affirmative, répondez affirmativement. Si la première phrase est négative, répondez négativement.

MODÈLES: Paul a fait le ménage. Et sa sœur?
Elle aussi.

Paul n'a pas regardé la télévision. Et son frère?
Lui non plus.

1. Paul n'a pas lu le journal ce matin. Et ses sœurs?
2. Paul écrit des lettres. Et ses parents?
3. Paul ne se lève jamais tard. Et sa sœur?
4. Il a déjà mangé. Et son frère?
5. Paul n'aime pas les cigares. Et ses parents?
6. Il va souvent au cinéma le vendredi soir. Et sa sœur?

18 **À vous.** Répondez aux questions suivantes. Utilisez un pronom accentué dans chaque réponse.

1. Faites-vous la cuisine vous-même?
2. Déjeunez-vous d'habitude avec votre meilleur(e) ami(e)?
3. Avez-vous dîné chez cet(te) ami(e) hier soir?
4. Avez-vous passé les dernières vacances chez vos parents?
5. Vos amis et vous, allez-vous souvent au cinéma?
6. Faites-vous vos devoirs avec vos amis?

www **Réalités culturelles**

Comparison: Ask your students to compare their leisure activities with those of the students in this survey.

Les loisirs préférés des étudiants

Que font les étudiants français pendant le week-end et pendant leur temps libre? Voici les réponses à un questionnaire récent.

inviter des amis chez soi	46%
aller au cinéma	45%
faire du sport	40%
aller en boîte	29%
écouter de la musique	27%
aller au restaurant	27%
aller écouter un concert	20%
lire un livre	15%
regarder la télévision	12%

Vocabulaire: loisirs *leisure activities,* boîte *nightclub*

H. Les verbes *dormir, partir* et *sortir*

Je ne **dors** pas bien.   *I don't sleep well.*
Quand **partez-vous** en vacances?   *When are you leaving on vacation?*
Avec qui Annie **sort-elle** vendredi?   *With whom is Annie going out on Friday?*

dormir *(to sleep)*		**partir** *(to leave)*		**sortir** *(to go out)*	
je	**dors**	je	**pars**	je	**sors**
tu	**dors**	tu	**pars**	tu	**sors**
il/elle/on	**dort**	il/elle/on	**part**	il/elle/on	**sort**
nous	**dormons**	nous	**partons**	nous	**sortons**
vous	**dormez**	vous	**partez**	vous	**sortez**
ils/elles	**dorment**	ils/elles	**partent**	ils/elles	**sortent**

■ Note the pronunciation distinction between the third person singular and plural forms.

elle dort [dɔʀ]   il part [paʀ]   elle sort [sɔʀ]
elles dorment [dɔʀm]   ils partent [paʀt]   elles sortent [sɔʀt]

> **Partir** and **sortir** use **être** as the auxiliary in the passé composé and will be studied in the past tense in Ch. 7.

■ The past participle of **dormir** is **dormi**.

J'ai **dormi** pendant huit heures.

19 **Notre vie à l'université.** Complétez les phrases suivantes avec les verbes **dormir**, **partir** et **sortir**. Faites attention au choix du verbe et au choix entre le présent et l'infinitif.

1. Les étudiants de notre université _____ du campus chaque week-end pour aller chez leurs parents.
2. Mais ils ont envie de s'amuser et c'est pourquoi ils _____ avec leurs amis le jeudi soir.
3. Si on _____ le jeudi soir, on est naturellement fatigué le vendredi matin.
4. Si on ne _____ pas pendant huit heures, on ne se lève pas tôt.
5. Quelquefois, si on est très fatigué, on a envie de _____ en classe!
6. Si vous _____ en classe, les professeurs ne vont pas être très contents.
7. Alors, si vous allez _____ le jeudi soir, il faut faire la sieste le jeudi après-midi.

20 **La vie des étudiants.** Répondez aux questions suivantes.

1. Combien d'heures dormez-vous d'habitude par nuit?
2. Pendant combien de temps avez-vous dormi la nuit dernière?
3. Y a-t-il des étudiants qui ne dorment pas le samedi matin? Si oui, pourquoi?
4. Qui dort mal avant un examen important? Pourquoi?
5. Les étudiants sortent-ils quelquefois pendant la semaine? Si oui, où vont-ils? Si non, pourquoi pas?
6. Est-ce que la plupart des étudiants partent le week-end ou est-ce qu'ils restent sur le campus?
7. Quand allez-vous partir en vacances cette année?

I. Les verbes *nettoyer* et *envoyer*

Tu nettoies ta chambre ce matin?
Oui, mais d'abord **j'envoie** un
message électronique.

Are you cleaning your room this morning?
Yes, but first I'm sending an e-mail
message.

nettoyer *(to clean)*	
je	**nettoie**
tu	**nettoies**
il/elle/on	**nettoie**
nous	**nettoyons**
vous	**nettoyez**
ils/elles	**nettoient**
passé composé: j'**ai nettoyé**	

envoyer *(to send)*	
j'	**envoie**
tu	**envoies**
il/elle/on	**envoie**
nous	**envoyons**
vous	**envoyez**
ils/elles	**envoient**
passé composé: j'**ai envoyé**	

■ In the present tense, these verbs are conjugated like **parler,** except that **i** is used in place of **y** in the singular and the third-person plural.

21 **Un message à ma famille.** Complétez les phrases suivantes avec les verbes **envoyer** et **nettoyer.** Faites attention au choix du verbe et au choix entre le présent, le passé composé et l'infinitif.

1. Hier, j'ai _____ une lettre à ma famille.
2. J'ai parlé de mon camarade de chambre qui ne _____ jamais notre chambre.
3. J'ai écrit «Pourquoi est-ce que c'est toujours moi qui dois _____ la chambre?»
4. Lui, il s'amuse et il _____ des messages électroniques à ses amis.
5. Moi aussi, je voudrais _____ des messages et m'amuser.
6. Les bons camarades de chambre _____ leur chambre ensemble, n'est-ce pas?

22 **À vous.** Répondez aux questions suivantes.

1. Avez-vous envoyé une carte ou un message électronique récemment? Si oui, à qui?
2. Envoyez-vous des messages chaque jour? Si non, combien de fois par semaine envoyez-vous des messages?
3. Est-ce que vos amis envoient souvent des cartes ou des messages? Si oui, comment s'appellent ces amis?
4. Qui n'envoie jamais de lettres? Pourquoi pas?
5. Qui n'aime pas nettoyer sa chambre? Pourquoi pas?
6. Nettoyez-vous votre chambre chaque jour? Pourquoi ou pourquoi pas?

ENTRE AMIS

Le week-end

1. Ask your partner what s/he usually does on weekends.
2. Find out if s/he has fun.
3. Ask if s/he goes out with friends.
4. If so, find out where s/he goes.
5. Find out if s/he gets up early or late on Sunday morning.
6. Find out when s/he cleans her room.
7. What else can you find out?

Intégration

Révision

Communication (Presentational): Give students time to prepare. Then have individuals give short presentations followed by questions from the class.

A **Mon week-end.** Que faites-vous d'habitude le week-end? Avez-vous beaucoup de temps libre?

B **Notre vie à l'université.** Posez des questions. Votre partenaire va répondre. Attention au présent et au passé composé.

MODÈLE: parler français avec tes amis pendant le cours de français
> VOUS: **Est-ce que tu parles français avec tes amis pendant le cours de français?**
> VOTRE PARTENAIRE: **Oui, je parle français avec eux.** ou
> **Non, je ne parle pas français avec eux.**

1. dormir bien quand il y a un examen
2. aller souvent à la bibliothèque après le dîner
3. écouter la radio quelquefois pendant que tu étudies
4. être absent(e) le mois dernier
5. jouer aux cartes avec tes amis le week-end dernier
6. faire la vaisselle d'habitude après le dîner
7. sortir avec tes amis ce soir

C **Trouvez quelqu'un qui ...** Interviewez les autres étudiants pour trouver quelqu'un qui ...

1. écoute la radio pendant qu'il étudie
2. joue de la guitare
3. a eu le temps de lire un livre la semaine dernière
4. a déjà écrit une dissertation ce semestre
5. n'a rien mangé ce matin
6. a eu la grippe l'année dernière
7. a nettoyé sa chambre le week-end dernier
8. ne sort jamais le dimanche soir
9. envoie souvent des messages électroniques à ses professeurs

Communication (Presentational & Interpretive): If students present their descriptions to the class, others can be asked to recall information that was presented. Suggestion: Assign the *Rédaction* at the end of Ch. 6 in the Workbook.

Communication (Interpretive): Encourage students to use the practice test on the Lab Audio Program.

D **Début de rédaction.** Faites une liste de cinq activités que vous faites d'habitude pendant la semaine et/ou pendant le week-end. Indiquez, si possible, si vous faites ces activités le matin, l'après-midi ou le soir.

MODÈLE: **Le samedi matin je ne me lève pas très tôt. J'aime dormir et je ne travaille pas le samedi.**

E **À vous.** Répondez.

1. Que fait-on pour s'amuser le week-end sur votre campus?
2. Qu'est-ce que la plupart des étudiants font le dimanche soir?
3. Avez-vous regardé la télévision hier soir? Si oui, combien de temps avez-vous passé devant la télévision?
4. Quelle est la dernière fois que vous avez dîné au restaurant? Combien de temps avez-vous passé à table?
5. Combien de fois avez-vous été malade cette année?
6. Jouez-vous d'un instrument de musique? Si oui, de quel instrument jouez-vous?
7. Est-ce que vous êtes sportif (sportive)? Si oui, à quel sport jouez-vous?
8. Quelle est la dernière fois que vous avez nettoyé votre chambre?

Négociations:

Hier, d'habitude et pendant le week-end. Interviewez votre partenaire pour trouver les renseignements qui manquent (*missing information*). La copie de votre partenaire est dans l'appendice D.

For complete instructions on how to prepare for and to use this activity, see *Négociations* on the Class Prep CD-ROM.

MODÈLE: **Est-ce que Valérie va au cours de français d'habitude?**
Est-ce qu'Alain a fumé hier?

Be careful to choose between the past and the present.

A

nom	hier	d'habitude	pendant le week-end
Valérie	OUI	aller au cours de français _____	NON
Chantal	déjeuner avec ses amis _____	se lever tôt _____	OUI
Sophie	NON	OUI	faire ses devoirs _____
Alain	fumer _____	NON	lire des livres _____
David	nettoyer sa chambre _____	être absent _____	NON
Jean-Luc	NON	OUI	sortir avec ses amis _____

Réalités culturelles

Video for Chapter 6: A. Video worksheets *(Cahier)*; B. ACE Video practice test (WWW); C. CD-ROM

Le Maghreb

Le Maghreb est le nom donné à l'ensemble des trois pays du nord-ouest de l'Afrique: **le Maroc, l'Algérie** et **la Tunisie**. La France a colonisé l'Algérie en 1830. Plus tard, la Tunisie (1881) et le Maroc (1912) sont devenus des protectorats français. Ces deux pays sont indépendants depuis 1956. L'Algérie a eu son indépendance en 1962, après une guerre avec la France.

REPÈRES:	LE MAROC	L'ALGÉRIE	LA TUNISIE
Superficie:	710.850 km², comparable au Texas	environ 2.381.740 km², plus de trois fois le Texas	163.610 km²; un peu plus grand que la Géorgie
Population:	environ 30 millions	environ 32 millions	près de 9 millions
Ethnicité:	99% Arabes et Berbères; quelques Harratins (noirs) dans le sud	83% Arabes, 16% Berbères surtout dans les montagnes de l'Atlas, 1% Européens	98% Arabes, 2% Européens
Capitale:	Rabat	Alger	Tunis
Langues:	arabe, français, berbère, un peu d'espagnol	arabe, français, berbère	arabe, français

Vocabulaire: sont devenus *became*, guerre *war*, surtout *especially*

Lecture I

A **Étude du vocabulaire.** Étudiez les phrases suivantes et choisissez *(choose)* les mots anglais qui correspondent aux mots français en caractères gras *(bold print)*: saw, to move, the south of France, meals, knife, trees, fingers, all.

1. Je ne comprends pas **tous** les mots français.
2. Un homme attaque deux jeunes filles au **couteau.**
3. Quand on est paralysé, on n'est pas capable de **bouger.**
4. Les enfants comptent souvent sur les **doigts** pour faire une addition.
5. Marseille est dans le **Midi** de la France.
6. Nous avons **vu** un film intéressant le week-end dernier.
7. Il y a beaucoup d'**arbres** dans une forêt.
8. Le déjeuner et le dîner sont des **repas.**

B **Parcourez les deux articles.** Skim each of the following selections to find: (1) an example of personal charity and (2) the reward that was given.

Communities: Use this reading as a springboard to a discussion of immigration in France.

UN HOMME COURAGEUX

PARIS: Aziz Soubhane a 17 ans. Il est marocain, mais il habite en France depuis sept ans et fait ses études au Lycée d'enseignement professionnel privé de Notre-Dame, à la Loupe, en Eure-et-Loir.

Aziz a désarmé un homme qui attaquait au couteau deux jeunes filles anglaises dans le métro. Aziz a été le seul à bouger; les autres passagers n'ont pas levé le petit doigt.

Pour son courage, Aziz a reçu le «Prix servir» du Rotary-club de Paris et un chèque de 10.000 francs. C'est l'adjoint au maire de Paris qui a donné le prix à Aziz.

Ce jeune homme est un très bon exemple pour nous.

Les soldats ont planté des arbres

TOULON: L'été dernier, des feux ont détruit une grande partie de la forêt dans le Midi de la France. Le 29 décembre, on a vu des soldats américains aider tous les volontaires de la région à nettoyer la forêt et à replanter des arbres. En une journée, ils ont replanté 5.000 arbres près de la ville d'Hyères, dans la région du Var.

Le 2 janvier, le maire de la ville a donné un grand méchoui à tous les volontaires. Les 165 soldats américains sont en escale à Toulon en ce moment. Ils ont profité de leur temps libre pour aider les Français.

Adjoint au maire = *deputy mayor;* **feux** = *fires;* **méchoui** = *a North African specialty in which a whole lamb is roasted over an open pit of live coals for several hours.*

Connections: Point out the locations of Paris and Toulon on the map inside the front cover.

C **Vrai ou faux?** Si une phrase est fausse, corrigez-la.

1. Aziz n'est pas français.
2. Il étudie dans une école publique.
3. Les soldats américains ont aidé les Français.
4. Les soldats ont été obligés d'aider les Français.
5. Les soldats ont travaillé une semaine.

D **Questions.** Répondez.

1. Qui sont les «bons Samaritains» dans ces deux articles?
2. Qu'est-ce qu'Aziz a fait? Et les soldats américains?
3. Est-ce que les autres personnes dans le métro ont aidé Aziz?
4. Qui a travaillé avec les soldats américains?
5. Qu'est-ce qu'on a donné à Aziz après son acte de courage?
6. Qu'est-ce qu'on a donné aux soldats après leur travail?

E **Familles de mots.** Essayez de deviner le sens des mots suivants.

1. détruire, la destruction
2. donner, un don, un donneur, une donneuse
3. enseigner, l'enseignement *(m.)*, un enseignant, une enseignante
4. voir, vu, la vue, une vision

F **Discussion.**

1. Identify three aspects of French culture mentioned in these newspaper articles that are similar to or different from American culture.
2. Are North African people and their cultures viewed favorably or unfavorably in these articles? Explain your answer.

Lecture II

A **Étude du vocabulaire.** Étudiez les phrases suivantes et choisissez les mots anglais qui correspondent aux mots français en caractères gras: *neither… nor, sorrow, because, memories, swept up, it's all the same to me, love.*

1. J'ai **balayé** ma chambre et maintenant je vais nettoyer la cuisine.
2. L'**amour**, c'est quand on aime une personne.
3. Si elle est riche ou si elle est pauvre, **ça m'est bien égal**.
4. Elle est fille unique; elle n'a **ni** frère **ni** sœur.
5. Le **chagrin**, c'est quand on est triste.
6. J'ai de très bons **souvenirs** de mes grands-parents.
7. Le mot **car** est un synonyme de *parce que*.

B **Le contraire.** Lisez la chanson et ensuite choisissez les expressions de la colonne de droite qui sont le contraire des expressions de la colonne de gauche.

1. _____ le bien	a. hier	
2. _____ tout	b. le plaisir	
3. _____ aujourd'hui	c. c'est oublié	
4. _____ le passé	d. la mort	
5. _____ le chagrin	e. rien	
6. _____ mes souvenirs	f. le mal	
7. _____ la vie	g. le futur	

Une des plus célèbres chanteuses françaises, Édith Piaf est née le 19 décembre 1915. Quelques-unes de ses grandes chansons qu'il faut mentionner sont La vie en rose, L'hymne à l'amour, Jézébel, Mon manège à moi *et* Non, je ne regrette rien. *Le compositeur de cette dernière chanson s'appelle Charles Dumont. Piaf la chante pour la première fois deux ou trois ans avant sa mort, le 14 octobre 1963. Cette chanson est un peu la philosophie de sa vie. Piaf a dit «Je remercie le ciel* (heaven) *de m'avoir donné cette vie, cette possibilité de vivre, car j'ai vécu* (I lived) *à cent pour cent et je ne le regrette pas.»*

Comparison: 1. Point out that **je regrette** often has the meaning *I miss*. 2. Have students identify the cognates in the song. 3. Students have just studied the verb **partir**. Can they deduce the meaning of **je repars à zéro**? 4. Students have just studied stress pronouns. Have them identify the two that are used in this song.

Connections: The *Entre amis* web site contains a link to Édith Piaf and this song. If there are music majors in the class, have them describe what a tremolo is.

Non, je ne regrette rien

Non! Rien de rien
Non! Je ne regrette rien
Ni le bien qu'on m'a fait, ni le mal
Tout ça m'est bien égal.
Non! Rien de rien
Non! Je ne regrette rien
C'est payé, balayé, oublié
Je me fous du passé[1].

Avec mes souvenirs
J'ai allumé le feu[2].
Mes chagrins, mes plaisirs
Je n'ai plus besoin d'eux[3].
Balayés les amours
Et tous leurs trémolos[4]
Balayés pour toujours
Je repars à zéro.

Non! Rien de rien
Non! Je ne regrette rien
Ni le bien qu'on m'a fait, ni le mal
Tout ça m'est bien égal.
Non! Rien de rien
Non! Je ne regrette rien
Car ma vie, car mes joies
Aujourd'hui, ça commence avec toi.

1. *I don't give a darn about the past*   2. *lit the fire*   3. *I don't need them any more*   4. *tremors; emotions*

C **Vrai ou faux?** Décidez si les phrases suivantes sont vraies ou fausses. Ensuite cherchez dans la chanson quelque chose qui justifie chaque réponse *(answer)*.

1. Édith Piaf est triste parce qu'elle n'a pas été heureuse dans la vie.
2. Elle aime une personne maintenant.
3. Elle a oublié le passé.
4. Elle est pessimiste.

D **Discussion.** Research the life of Édith Piaf and then discuss whether her life reflects the words of this song.

VOCABULAIRE ACTIF

Practice this vocabulary with the flashcards on the *Entre amis* web site.

Instruments de musique
un accordéon *accordion*
une batterie *drums*
une flûte *flute*
une guitare *guitar*
un piano *piano*
un saxophone *saxophone*
une trompette *trumpet*
un violon *violin*

D'autres noms
un cigare *cigar*
une cigarette *cigarette*
une crêpe *crepe (pancake)*
un examen *test, exam*
un exercice *exercise*
la grippe *flu*
un robinet *faucet*
la valse *waltz*

Pronoms accentués
moi *I, me*
toi *you*
lui *he, him*
elle *she, her*
soi *oneself*
nous *we, us*
vous *you*
eux *they, them*
elles *they, them (female)*

Jeux
le basket-ball (le basket) *basketball*
le bridge *bridge*
les cartes *(f. pl.) cards*
les dames *(f. pl.) checkers*
les échecs *(m. pl.) chess*
le football (le foot) *soccer*
le football américain *football*
le golf *golf*
le hockey *hockey*
un jeu *game*
la pétanque *lawn bowling*
le rugby *rugby*
le tennis *tennis*

Choses à lire ou à écrire
une bande dessinée *comic strip*
une carte postale *postcard*

une dissertation *(term) paper*
un journal *newspaper*
une lettre *letter*
un magazine *magazine*
un message électronique *e-mail*
un mot *word*
une pièce *play*
un poème *poem*
un roman *novel*
un roman policier *detective story*

Divisions du temps
une année *year*
une fois *one time*
une journée *day*
un mois *month*
un semestre *semester*
le temps *time; weather*
les vacances *(f. pl.) vacation*

Prépositions
pendant *for; during*
sans *without*

Verbes
accompagner *to accompany*
s'amuser *to have fun*
se coucher *to go to bed*
décrire *to describe*
demander *to ask*
dormir *to sleep*
écrire *to write*
envoyer *to send*
être à *to belong to*
fermer *to close*
fumer *to smoke*
se lever *to get up*
lire *to read*
nettoyer *to clean*
oublier *to forget*
partir *to leave*
préparer (un cours) *to prepare (a lesson)*
remarquer *to notice*
sortir *to go out*
téléphoner (à qqn) *to telephone (someone)*

Expressions de temps
il y a ... ans (mois, etc.) ... *years (months, etc.) ago*
Je suis ici depuis ... mois (heures, etc.). *I've been here for ... months (hours, etc.).*
Pendant combien de temps ... ? *How long ... ?*
tout à l'heure *a little while ago; in a little while*

Adverbes de temps
déjà *already*
hier *yesterday*
hier soir *last night*
longtemps *a long time*
récemment *recently*
tard *late*
tôt *early*

D'autres adverbes
au moins *at least*
heureusement *fortunately*
rien (ne ... rien) *nothing, not anything*
tant *so much; so many*

D'autres expressions utiles
Aïe! *Ouch!*
à l'intérieur de *inside of*
À quoi jouez-vous? *What (game, sport) do you play?*
à table *at dinner, at the table*
Bonnes vacances! *Have a good vacation!*
C'est la vie! *That's life!*
chaque *each; every*
De quoi jouez-vous? *What (instrument) do you play?*
Eh bien *Well*
en vacances *on vacation*
faire du sport *to play sports*
faire du vélo *to go bike riding*
la plupart (de) *most (of)*
parce que *because*
par exemple *for example*
Pourquoi pas? *Why not?*
... veut dire ... ... *means ...*

Buts communicatifs
Relating past events (continued)
Describing your background
Stating what you just did

Structures utiles
Le passé composé avec **être**
Le pronom **y**
Le verbe **venir**
Les prépositions de lieu avec une ville ou un pays (suite)
Les mois de l'année, les saisons et le temps
Venir de + infinitif

Culture
• *À propos*
Une technologie de pointe
Le TGV
Le portable
La télécarte
L'amabilité

• *Il y a un geste*
Je vous en prie.

• *Lectures*
Vague de chaleur en Europe
«Il»

Coup d'envoi

Prise de contact **J'ai fait un voyage**

 Où es-tu allée l'été° dernier, Stéphanie?
Je suis allée en Europe.

    summer

Parle-moi de ce voyage, s'il te plaît.
    Eh bien! Je suis arrivée à Londres le 15
      juin°.

    June

    J'ai passé quinze jours à voyager en
      Angleterre.
    Puis je suis partie pour Paris le premier
      juillet°.

    July first

    Je suis restée chez des amis de mes
      parents qui habitent à Paris.
    Je me suis très, très bien amusée.
    Enfin je suis revenue° le 10 août°.
    Voilà!

    I came back / August

▶ **Et vous?** Qu'est-ce que vous avez fait pendant les vacances? Êtes-vous
parti(e) en voyage ou êtes-vous resté(e) chez vous?

Conversation

Les Smith sont arrivés à Angers

Monsieur et Madame Smith, amis de la famille de Lori Becker, sont partis pour Angers. Là, ils sont descendus du TGV° à la gare Saint-Laud. Monsieur Smith est entré dans une cabine téléphonique, a utilisé sa télécarte et a formé le numéro des Martin.

got off the high-speed train

Mme Martin:	Allô.
M. Smith:	Madame Martin?
Mme Martin:	Oui, qui est à l'appareil°?
M. Smith:	Bonjour, Madame. C'est Grayson Smith.
Mme Martin:	Ah! les amis de Lori. Vous êtes arrivés?
M. Smith:	Oui, nous sommes un peu en avance°. Nous venons de descendre° du train.
Mme Martin:	Mon mari et Lori sont déjà partis vous chercher. Restez là; ils arrivent.
M. Smith:	D'accord. Merci, Madame. À tout à l'heure.
Mme Martin:	À tout de suite°, Monsieur. Au revoir.

on the phone

early
we just got off

See you very soon

(Une demi-heure plus tard, chez les Martin)

Lori:	Madame Martin, je vous présente Monsieur et Madame Smith.
Mme Martin:	Bonjour, Madame. Bonjour, Monsieur. Vous devez être fatigués après votre voyage.
Mme Smith:	Bonjour, Madame. Non, pas trop.
M. Martin:	C'est la première fois que vous venez° en France?
Mme Smith:	Non, nous sommes déjà venus° il y a deux ans.
M. Smith:	Mais la dernière fois, nous n'avons pas beaucoup voyagé.
Mme Smith:	C'est gentil de vous occuper° de nous. Ça ne vous dérange pas trop?
Mme Martin:	Mais non! Je vous en prie.°

come

came

take care of

Don't mention it.

After practicing the conversation, have students complete ex. A in the Workbook.

 **Jouez ces rôles.** Répétez la conversation avec votre partenaire. Une personne joue le rôle des Smith et de Lori et l'autre joue le rôle des Martin. Utilisez vos propres *(own)* noms.

 This gesture is used in the video, *Module 2.*

Il y a un geste

Je vous en prie. With palm open and fingers spread, one hand (or both hands) is held at the waist level and the shoulders are shrugged. The lips are often rounded. This gesture indicates that you are pleased to be of service and that it is not worth mentioning.

Comparison: Have students describe public transportation in their own countries. Have them comment on their own use of "smart cards" and/or cell phones.

À propos

Pourquoi est-ce que Monsieur Smith utilise une télécarte?

a. Il n'a pas d'euros.
b. Il faut une carte pour utiliser les cabines téléphoniques à la gare Saint-Laud.
c. On peut utiliser des pièces de monnaie ou une carte pour téléphoner dans les cabines téléphoniques.

Une technologie de pointe

France is known worldwide for its leadership in art, fashion, perfume, food, and drink. France is also the world's fifth largest economy and fourth largest exporter. It is a leader in transportation (the TGV bullet train), aerospace (Airbus and the Ariane rocket), telecommunications (cell phones and wireless technology), and civil engineering (the Normandy bridge and the Channel tunnel).

Le TGV

France is also a world leader in public transportation *(les transports en commun)*. Buses, subways, and trains run well, are on time, and are widely used. Among the latter, the **TGV (train à grande vitesse)** is a spectacular technological achievement and a commercial success! The **TGV Atlantique** is a "bullet train" that serves the western part of France and transports over 40,000 customers per day. With a top speed of over 300 kilometers (200 miles) per hour, it offers exceptional comfort and service. **TGV Atlantique** passengers can even phone to all parts of the world.

Le portable

The use of cell phones (**le téléphone portable**) is widespread in France. Over 60 percent of the French have one, meaning that there are over 35 million cell phones in circulation. Under French law, it is illegal to use a cell phone while driving, even though many drivers admit to doing so.

La télécarte

The **télécarte** is an electronic smart card used throughout France for both local and long distance phone calls. It can be purchased in post offices, railroad stations, and tobacco shops in France. It can even be purchased in the TGV lounge. Tourists are often caught off guard believing that they will be able to use Euro coins to make a telephone call. Coin operated phones are becoming increasingly rare in France. In Angers, for example, none of the phone booths at the railroad station accept coins. For some useful expressions when using a **télécarte,** see the box on the next page.

 See video, *Module 2*, where the **télécarte** plays an important role.

CONTINUED →

L'amabilité *(Kindness)*

The Martins go out of their way to be helpful to Lori's friends. A warm welcome is the norm rather than the exception in Angers. Many *Angevins* serve as host families to foreign students who are enrolled at the *Centre international d'études françaises* or in one of the institutes organized on the campus of the *Université Catholique de l'Ouest*. Others, such as the Martins, employ a **jeune fille au pair** who often becomes a "member" of the family. The tourist who stays only a few days in Paris may not get to appreciate the generosity and the friendliness of the French.

V O C A B U L A I R E

Pour utiliser la télécarte

Connections: Teach students to associate a gesture with each command. Then have them perform the appropriate gesture when you read the sentences, occasionally changing the order.

Décrochez le téléphone.	*Pick up the phone.*
Introduisez votre télécarte.	*Put your telecarte in the slot.*
Composez le numéro.	*Dial the number.*
Attendez que quelqu'un réponde.	*Wait until someone answers.*
Quand vous avez fini, raccrochez le téléphone.	*When you've finished, hang up the phone.*
Reprenez votre télécarte.	*Take your telecarte.*

▶ **À vous.** Vous téléphonez à un(e) ami(e). Répondez.

VOTRE AMI(E):	Allô.
VOUS:	_____
VOTRE AMI(E):	Tu es arrivé(e)?
VOUS:	_____
VOTRE AMI(E):	Où es-tu?
VOUS:	_____
VOTRE AMI(E):	Reste là. J'arrive.
VOUS:	_____

ENTRE AMIS

Vous êtes arrivé(e) à la gare.

You are a foreign student at a French university and will be staying with a host family.

1. Call your host family and identify yourself.
2. Say that you are at the train station.
3. Reassure them that you are not too tired after your trip.
4. Express your thanks and say "See you very soon."

Prononciation

Les sons [ɔ] et [o]

■ French has an open [ɔ] sound and a closed [o] sound. The following words contain these sounds. Practice saying the words after your instructor, paying particular attention to the highlighted sound.

[ɔ] • **o**range, b**o**nne, c**o**mme, al**o**rs, s**o**mmes, c**o**nnaissez, enc**o**re, p**o**ste, per-s**o**nnes, acc**o**rdéon, h**o**ckey, p**o**stale, d**o**rmir, s**o**rtir, n**o**tre, n**o**te, j**o**gging

[o] • radi**o**, pian**o**, m**o**t, v**o**s, gr**o**s

  • ch**o**se, quelque ch**o**se, r**o**se

  • h**ô**tel, à la v**ô**tre, dr**ô**le

  • ch**au**d, f**au**x, **au** fait, d'**au**tres, **au** moins, à g**au**che, il f**au**t, f**au**x, f**au**sse, j**au**ne

  • **eau**, b**eau**coup, b**eau**, chap**eau**

▶ Now go back and look at how these sounds are spelled and in what kinds of letter combinations they appear. What patterns do you notice?

■ The sound [ɔ] is always followed by a pronounced consonant.

téléph**o**ne   ad**o**re   p**o**stale   n**o**te   d**o**rment   m**o**de   **o**ctobre

■ The sound [o] is used in several circumstances.

o as the word's final sound	pian**o**, m**o**t
o + [z]	ch**o**se, r**o**se
ô	h**ô**tel, v**ô**tre
au	**au** fait, il f**au**t
eau	l'**eau**, b**eau**coup

▶ Say the following pairs of words, making sure to pronounce the [ɔ] and [o] sounds correctly.

1. n**o**s / n**o**tre
2. r**o**binet / r**o**se
3. v**o**tre / v**ô**tre
4. ch**au**d / ch**o**colat
5. b**eau** / b**o**nne

Paris patchwork
édition révolutionnaire
COMMENT S'Y PERDRE, COMMENT S'Y RETROUVER

ALLEZ-Y EN MÉTRO

Buts communicatifs

1. Relating Past Events *(continued)*

Tu es sortie vendredi dernier, Nathalie?
    Oui, je suis sortie.
Où es-tu allée?
    Je suis allée au restaurant et chez des
        amis.
À quelle heure es-tu rentrée° chez toi?   *did you get back*
    Je suis rentrée à minuit.

*Communication
(Presentational):* Pair students
to practice the *Et vous?*, then
call on several to tell what they
did last weekend.

▶ **Et vous?** Vous êtes sorti(e) le week-end dernier?
              Si oui, où êtes-vous allé(e)?
              À quelle heure êtes-vous rentré(e)?

A. Le passé composé avec *être*

Review the formation of the
passé composé with **avoir,**
p. 160.

Êtes-vous **arrivée** en train?   *Did you arrive by train?*
Non, je **suis venue** en voiture.   *No, I came by car.*

Paul et Karine **sont sortis** hier soir?   *Did Paul and Karine go out last night?*
Oui, mais ils **sont rentrés** à neuf   *Yes, but they came home at nine o'clock.*
    heures.

Mon oncle **est né** à Paris en 1935.   *My uncle was born in Paris in 1935.*
Mais sa famille **est partie** aux États-   *But his family left for the United States*
    Unis avant la guerre.   *before the war.*
En 1985 il **est tombé** malade.   *He got sick in 1985.*
Il **est mort** en 1986.   *He died in 1986.*

Remember to consult
Appendix C at the end of
the book to review any
terms with which you are
not familiar.

■ While most verbs use **avoir** to form the passé composé (see Ch. 6), there are
a limited number that use **être**. These verbs are intransitive; that is, they do
not take a direct object. The most common are listed below.

VOCABULAIRE

Quelques verbes qui forment le passé composé avec être

You might want to point out that many of these verbs are general terms of movement or change of condition, but that more specific verbs of movement, such as **nager** or **danser**, take **avoir** in the passé composé. For the sake of simplicity, the use of **passer** as an intransitive verb and the use of **monter, descendre, rentrer,** and **sortir** as transitive verbs have been omitted here.

Infinitif		Participe passé
aller	to go	**allé**
venir	to come	**venu**
devenir	to become	**devenu**
revenir (ici)	to come back (here)	**revenu**
retourner (là)	to go back; to return (there)	**retourné**
rentrer (à la maison)	to go (come) back; to go (come) home	**rentré**
arriver (en retard)	to arrive (late)	**arrivé**
partir (à l'heure)	to leave (on time)	**parti**
rester (à la maison)	to stay, remain (at home)	**resté**
monter (dans une voiture)	to go up; to get into (a car)	**monté**
descendre (d'une voiture)	to go down; to get out (of a car)	**descendu**
tomber	to fall	**tombé**
entrer (dans la classe)	to enter (the classroom)	**entré**
sortir (de la classe)	to go out (of the classroom)	**sorti**
naître	to be born	**né**
mourir	to die	**mort**

Students will not have to use the present tense of **descendre** until Ch. 9, where regular **-re** verbs are introduced. The present tenses of **naître** and **mourir** are not required in this course.

Remember that if a plural subject is of mixed gender, the masculine plural form of the participle will be used.

■ Past participles used with **être** agree in gender and number with the subject, just as if they were adjectives. To show agreement, add **-e** (feminine singular), **-s** (masculine plural), or **-es** (feminine plural).

Masculin	**Féminin**
Je suis **né** à Paris.	Je suis **née** à Paris.
Tu es **né** à New York.	Tu es **née** à New York.
Il est **né** à Montréal.	Elle est **née** à Montréal.
Nous sommes **nés** à Boston.	Nous sommes **nées** à Boston.
Vous êtes **né(s)** à Angers.	Vous êtes **née(s)** à Angers.
Ils sont **nés** à Halifax.	Elles sont **nées** à Halifax.

■ Most of these verbs are followed by a preposition when they precede the name of a place.

Sandrine est entrée **dans** la salle de classe.

Sandrine went into the classroom.

Moi, je suis arrivé **au** cours de français à l'heure.

I arrived at the French class on time.

Mais Nicolas est retourné **chez** lui chercher son livre. Alors, il est arrivé en retard.

But Nicolas went back home for his book. So, he came late.

Review reflexive verbs, p. 169.

Note there is no accent on the first **-e-** of the past participle **levé(e)**.

The rules of past participle agreement with reflexive verbs will be learned in Ch.13. Until then, only verbs whose reflexive pronoun is a direct object are taught.

■ Reflexive verbs also use **être** to form the passé composé.

Les étudiants **se sont amusés** à la soirée.

Ils ne **se sont** pas **couchés** tôt.
Est-ce que Mélanie **s'est levée** tard le jour suivant?
Elle et sa sœur ne **se sont** pas **levées** avant midi.

Students had fun at the party.

They did not get to bed early.
Did Mélanie get up late the following day?
She and her sister didn't get up before noon.

Remember to choose the appropriate object pronoun.

se coucher *(to go to bed)*

je	**me** suis couché(e)	nous	**nous** sommes couché(e)s
tu	**t'**es couché(e)	vous	**vous** êtes couché(e)(s)
il	**s'**est couché	ils	**se** sont couchés
elle	**s'**est couchée	elles	**se** sont couchées

If this exercise is assigned for writing, remind students to make the agreement of the past participle.

1 **Thierry ne fait jamais rien comme les autres.** Expliquez d'après le modèle.

MODÈLE: Les autres (partir pour le Canada) / Et Thierry?
Les autres sont partis pour le Canada, mais Thierry n'est pas parti pour le Canada.

1. vous (aller au concert) / Et Thierry?
2. nous (sortir hier soir) / Et Thierry?
3. Marie et Monique (arriver à l'heure) / Et Thierry?
4. ses amis (tomber malades) / Et Thierry?
5. Madame Dubuque (monter dans un taxi) / Et Thierry?
6. les étudiants (rester sur le campus) / Et Thierry?
7. les étudiants (s'amuser) / Et Thierry?

2 **Le voyage.** Racontez la journée *(Tell about the day)* de Monsieur et Madame Smith. Attention à l'emploi des verbes **avoir** et **être**.

MODÈLES: se lever à 7 heures
Ils se sont levés à 7 heures.

chercher un taxi
Ils ont cherché un taxi.

Communication (Presentational): Follow up, books closed, by having students reiterate what the Smiths did.

1. voyager en train
2. arriver à Angers
3. descendre du train à la gare Saint-Laud
4. téléphoner aux Martin
5. monter dans la voiture de Monsieur Martin
6. parler avec Lori Becker
7. aller chez les Martin
8. déjeuner chez les Martin
9. s'amuser

3 **Qu'est-ce que tu as fait la semaine dernière?** Utilisez **tu** et les expressions suivantes pour interviewer votre partenaire.

MODÈLE: manger une pizza

VOUS: **Est-ce que tu as mangé une pizza la semaine dernière?**

VOTRE PARTENAIRE: **Oui, j'ai mangé une pizza.** ou
Non, je n'ai pas mangé de pizza.

Communication (Interpretive & Presentational): Follow up by asking students to tell 2 things they learned about their partners.

1. aller au cinéma
2. étudier à la bibliothêque
3. regarder la télévision
4. passer un examen
5. tomber malade
6. entrer dans un bistro
7. descendre en ville
8. lire un journal
9. se lever à 5 heures du matin

4 **La plupart des étudiants.** Qu'est-ce que la plupart des étudiants ont fait la semaine dernière? Utilisez les expressions suivantes pour la question et pour la réponse.

MODÈLE: manger une pizza — **Est-ce que la plupart des étudiants ont mangé une pizza la semaine dernière?**
— **Oui, ils ont mangé une pizza.** ou
Non, ils n'ont pas mangé de pizza.

1. aller aux cours
2. faire leurs devoirs
3. nettoyer leur chambre
4. sortir avec leurs amis
5. se coucher tard
6. se lever tôt
7. tomber malades

5 **À vous.** Répondez.

1. Êtes-vous resté(e) sur le campus le week-end dernier?
2. Qu'est-ce que vous avez fait le week-end dernier?
3. Quelle est la dernière fois que vous êtes sorti(e) avec vos amis? Où êtes-vous allés? Qu'est-ce que vous avez fait? À quelle heure êtes-vous rentrés?
4. Vos parents ont-ils déjà visité votre campus? Si oui, quand sont-ils venus?
5. Est-ce que vous arrivez à l'heure au cours, d'habitude?
6. Quelle est la dernière fois que vous êtes arrivé(e) en retard au cours?
7. Qui aime arriver en avance au cours de français? Pourquoi?

6 **Le voyage des Smith.** Racontez l'histoire suivante au passé composé.

Monsieur et Madame Smith passent la nuit à Paris. Ils se lèvent tôt. D'abord ils sortent de leur hôtel. Ensuite ils montent dans un taxi pour aller à la gare Montparnasse. Quand ils arrivent à la gare, ils trouvent leur train et ils cherchent leurs places. Enfin le train part. Ils ne mangent rien pendant le voyage. Après une heure et demie, leur train arrive à la gare Saint-Laud. Monsieur Smith s'occupe de leurs bagages et ils descendent du train.

Communication (Interpretive):
When presenting **y**, give lots of
personal examples: **Il y a un
cinéma au centre commercial.
J'y vais quelquefois. J'y suis
allé(e) samedi dernier,** etc.

B. Le pronom *y*

Ta sœur est **en France?**	Oui, elle **y** est.
Va-t-elle souvent **à Paris?**	Non, elle n'**y** va pas souvent.
Quand pars-tu **en France?**	J'**y** pars dans un mois.
Ton frère est resté **chez lui?**	Non, il n'**y** est pas resté.
Est-il allé **au cinéma?**	Oui, il **y** est allé.
Tu vas rester **dans ta chambre?**	Non, je ne vais pas **y** rester.

This use of **y** is restricted to
expressions of place. Point out to
students that in these examples
y answers the question **Où?**

■ **Y** *(There)* is very often used in place of expressions that tell where something is located (**à l'université, dans la voiture,** etc.). The pronoun **y** replaces both the preposition (**à, chez, dans, en, sur,** etc.) and the name of the place.

Nous allons **au cinéma.**   Nous **y** allons.

■ **Y** is placed directly before the conjugated verb. This means that in the passé composé, it goes in front of the auxiliary.

Nous **y** allons la semaine prochaine.	*We are going there next week.*
Nous n'**y** allons pas demain.	*We are not going there tomorrow.*
J'**y** suis allé.	*I went there.*
Ma mère n'**y** est jamais allée.	*My mother has never gone there.*

■ When there is more than one verb, **y** is placed directly in front of the verb to which it is related (usually the infinitive).

Je vais **y** aller.	*I am going to go there.*
Je ne vais pas **y** rester.	*I am not going to stay there.*
J'ai envie d'**y** passer un mois.	*I feel like spending a month there.*
Je n'ai pas l'intention d'**y** habiter.	*I don't plan to live there.*

Drill **j'y vais** and **je n'y vais pas**
first. Then do Ex. 7 in groups as
a chain exercise.

Review **Quelques endroits,**
p. 128.

7 **Non, je n'y vais pas.** Un(e) étudiant(e) demande **Vas-tu à la pharmacie?** Un(e) autre répond **Non, je n'y vais pas; je vais ...** (**au centre commercial, à l'église,** etc.). Inventez au moins 10 questions.

8 **Tu y vas souvent?** Demandez si votre partenaire fait souvent les choses suivantes. Votre partenaire va utiliser **y** dans chaque réponse.

MODÈLE: aller au cinéma
VOUS: **Tu vas souvent au cinéma?**
VOTRE PARTENAIRE: **Oui, j'y vais souvent.** ou
Non, je n'y vais pas souvent.

1. aller chez le médecin
2. étudier à la bibliothèque
3. dîner au restaurant
4. arriver en retard au cours
5. monter dans ta voiture
6. retourner chez tes parents
7. aller à la poste

9 **Tu y es allé(e) hier?** Refaites l'exercice 8, mais posez les questions au passé composé. Votre partenaire va utiliser **y** dans chaque réponse.

Suggestion: This
activity could be done in
the future: **Vas-tu aller
au cinéma demain?**

MODÈLE: aller au cinéma
VOUS: **Es-tu allé(e) au cinéma hier?**
VOTRE PARTENAIRE: **Oui, j'y suis allé(e).** ou
Non, je n'y suis pas allé(e).

10 **À vous.** Répondez. Utilisez **y** dans chaque réponse.

1. Êtes-vous sur le campus maintenant?
2. Êtes-vous allé(e) à la bibliothèque hier soir? Si oui, à quelle heure y êtes-vous entré(e)? Combien de temps y êtes-vous resté(e)?
3. Combien de fois par semaine allez-vous au cours de français? Y allez-vous demain?
4. Êtes-vous resté(e) chez vous pendant les dernières vacances?
5. La plupart des étudiants ont-ils dîné au restaurant hier soir?
6. Avez-vous envie d'aller un jour en France? Y êtes-vous déjà allé(e)? Si oui, combien de temps y avez-vous passé?
7. Allez-vous au cinéma ce soir? Si oui, avec qui y allez-vous?

ENTRE AMIS

Review the vocabulary on p. 128.

Devinez ce que j'ai fait.

Your partner will try to guess what you did last evening. Use **y**, if possible, when responding.

1. Tell your partner you went out last evening.
2. S/he will try to guess where (movies, library, gym, etc.)
3. S/he will try to guess what you did.
4. Finally, your partner will restate where you went and what you did. Verify his/her answers.

Communication (Interpretive): Prime this activity by first having students guess where you went and what you did.

2. Describing Your Background

 D'où viennent ces personnes?

Alain et Sylvie viennent de Nantes.

Tom vient d'Angleterre. Il vient de Londres.

Mike vient des États-Unis et Rose vient du Canada.

Il vient de l'état d'Iowa et elle vient de la province d'Ontario.

 Et vous? D'où venez-vous?

C. Le verbe *venir*

Est-ce que **Monique vient** de France?   *Does Monique come from France?*
Non, **elle vient** du Canada.   *No, she comes from Canada.*
Elle est devenue médecin.   *She became a doctor.*
Elle n'est pas ici mais **elle revient** à   *She isn't here but she's coming back*
    6 heures.   *at six o'clock.*

venir *(to come)*			
je	**viens**	nous	**venons**
tu	**viens**	vous	**venez**
il/elle/on	**vient**	ils/elles	**viennent**
passé composé: je **suis venu(e)**			

This is similar to the distinction between **américain** and **américaine**, pp. 93–94.

■ Note the pronunciation distinction between the third person singular and plural forms.

vien*t*   [vjɛ̃]   vienn*ent*   [vjɛn]

■ The verbs **revenir** *(to come back)* and **devenir** *(to become)* are conjugated like **venir**.

Ⅱ **Les gens partent.** Demandez quand ils reviennent. Votre partenaire va répondre.

MODÈLE: Marie-Dominique (à 15 h 30)
    VOUS: **Quand est-ce qu'elle revient?**
    VOTRE PARTENAIRE: **Elle revient à quinze heures trente.**

1. Stéphanie (ce soir)
2. Colette et Karine (à midi)
3. nous (la semaine prochaine)
4. vos amis (mercredi)
5. vous (dans une heure)
6. ta sœur et toi (tout de suite)

D. Les prépositions de lieu avec une ville ou un pays (suite)

You have already learned to use prepositions to express *to* or *at* with a city, state, province, or country (see Ch. 5).

D'où viennent vos parents?   *Where do your parents come from?*
Mon père est originaire **du** Canada.   *My father is a native of Canada.*
Ma mère vient **des** États-Unis.   *My mother comes from the United States.*
Je viens **de** Bruxelles.   *I come from Brussels.*
M. et Mme Luc viennent **de** France.   *M. and Mme Luc come from France.*

■ To tell where a person is *from*, some form of **de** is used.

• **de** with cities:
    de Paris, **d'**Angers

• **de** with feminine countries or countries that begin with a vowel sound:
    de France, **d'**Iran

• **du** with masculine countries:
    du Mexique, **du** Canada

• **des** with plural countries:
    des États-Unis

■ To say that someone is from a U.S. state or Canadian province, **de** is normally used before those that are feminine or that begin with a vowel sound. The preposition **du** is often used with masculine states and provinces that begin with a consonant.

de Géorgie	**d'**Iowa	**du** Kansas
de Terre-Neuve	**d'**Alberta	**du** Québec

NOTE — You may also use **de l'état de** or **de la province de** to say which U.S. state or Canadian province someone is from.

Mon meilleur ami vient **de l'état d'**Arizona.
Je viens **de la province d'**Ontario.

See Ch. 5 for a list of countries already studied, p. 144.

■ Use the expression **d'où** with **venir** to inquire where someone comes from.

D'où vient Guy—du Canada ou de France?

Synthèse: les prépositions de lieu

	Je viens ...	J'habite ... / Je vais ...
ville	de	à
pays féminin ou pays qui commence par une voyelle	de	en
pays masculin	du	au
pays pluriel	des	aux

Review prepositions of place, p. 143.

Comparison: Have students explain the choice of each preposition in these examples.

One can also say **la Hollande** for **les Pays-Bas.**

Je viens **d'**Atlanta. Je vais **à** New York.
María vient **d'**Espagne. Elle habite **en** France.
Emilio téléphone **du** Mexique **au** Canada.
Nous venons **des** États-Unis. Nous allons **aux** Pays-Bas en vacances.
John vient **de l'état de** Nebraska mais il habite **dans l'état d'**Arizona.
Denise vient **de la province d'**Ontario, mais elle habite **dans la province de** Québec.

12 André va voyager. Il a l'intention de donner de ses nouvelles (*keep in touch*) à ses parents et à ses amis. Qu'est-ce qu'il va faire?

MODÈLE: écrire / Italie
Il va écrire d'Italie.

1. téléphoner / Allemagne
2. poster une lettre / Moscou
3. écrire une carte postale / Japon
4. téléphoner / Mexique
5. écrire / état de New York
6. écrire un message / province d'Ontario
7. poster une cassette / Liverpool

13 **André est retourné chez lui.** Il a contacté ses parents et ses amis pendant son voyage. Qu'est-ce qu'il a fait?

MODÈLE: écrire / Rome
Il a écrit de Rome.

Culture & Comparison: Remind students that **le Mexique** is the country. The word **Mexico** is used only for *Mexico City*.

1. téléphoner / Berlin
2. poster une lettre / Russie
3. écrire une carte postale / Tokyo
4. téléphoner / Mexico

5. écrire / États-Unis
6. écrire un message / Canada
7. poster une cassette / Angleterre

14 **D'où viennent-ils?** La liste des passagers du vol *(flight)* Air France n° 0748 inclut des personnes de différents pays. Expliquez d'où viennent ces personnes et où elles habitent maintenant.

MODÈLE: Sandrine (Paris / New York)
Sandrine vient de Paris, mais elle habite à New York maintenant.

Habiter may be used with a direct object. In this text it is taught with a preposition.

1. Ralph (Canada / États-Unis)
2. Alice (Belgique / France)
3. Helmut et Ingrid (Allemagne / Italie)
4. William (Angleterre / Irlande)
5. José et María (Mexique / États-Unis)
6. Gertrude (Ontario / Manitoba)
7. Judy et Bill (Michigan / Allemagne)

15 **À vous.** Répondez.

1. De quelle ville venez-vous?
2. De quelle(s) ville(s) viennent vos parents?
3. D'où vient votre meilleur(e) ami(e)?
4. D'où viennent vos grands-parents?
5. D'où vient votre professeur de français? (Devinez.)
6. D'où viennent deux autres étudiants du cours de français?

Ils sont arrivés à la gare.

VOCABULAIRE

Les mois de l'année, les saisons, le temps

Les mois de l'année	Les saisons	Le temps
janvier	l'hiver	Il fait froid.
février		Il neige.
mars		Il fait du vent.
avril	le printemps	Il pleut.
mai		Il fait frais.
juin		
juillet	l'été	Il fait beau.
août		Il fait du soleil.
septembre		Il fait chaud.
octobre	l'automne	Il fait encore beau.
novembre		Il commence à faire froid.
décembre		Il fait mauvais.

Connections: See page 207.

The French also say **Il fait soleil.**

The opposite of **Il fait beau** is **Il fait mauvais.**

> NOTE — The negation of **il fait du vent** is **il ne fait pas *de* vent.**

E. Les mois de l'année, les saisons et le temps

■ Names of months begin with lowercase letters in French. Use the preposition **en** before the months to mean *in*.

en février

en août

en septembre

■ Use **en** also with all seasons except **le printemps**.

en été

en automne

en hiver

But: **au** printemps

Comparison: Point out that there are 2 ways of expressing dates in English *(May third, the third of May)* while there is only one way in French.

■ The French represent the date by giving the day first, then the month.

Amy est née **le premier mai.**	*Amy was born on the first of May.*
Mon anniversaire est **le dix février.**	*My birthday is the tenth of February.*
Le bébé est né **le vingt-cinq avril.**	*The baby was born on April twenty-fifth.*

> NOTE — Use **le premier** (... *first, the first of* ...), but then **le deux, le trois,** etc.
> La fête nationale suisse est **le premier** août.

www The dates of many religious holidays vary from year to year. Christian Easter (**Pâques**, *pl.*) falls in March or April, Jewish **Yom Kippour** generally occurs in October, and Moslem **Aïd El-Kébir** comes in February. See the ***Entre amis*** web site for examples of additional holidays.

V O C A B U L A I R E

Quelques dates

le premier janvier	le Jour de l'An
le premier juillet	la fête nationale canadienne
le quatre juillet	la fête nationale américaine
le quatorze juillet	la fête nationale française
le premier novembre	la Toussaint
le vingt-cinq décembre	Noël

www Réalités culturelles

Culture & Connections: Remind students of **le foulard islamique** (Ch. 4), **l'immigration** (Ch. 5), and **le Maghreb** (Ch. 6).

La diversité religieuse

De culture chrétienne, la France est aujourd'hui un pays de grande liberté religieuse. Les catholiques (46 millions), les musulmans (4 millions), les protestants (800 000), les juifs (700 000) et les bouddhistes (700 000) s'entendent bien, même si des guerres de religion, entre catholiques et protestants, ont marqué l'histoire de la France. L'immigration récente de musulmans, qui sont venus de l'Afrique du Nord, fait de l'Islam la deuxième religion de France.

Il y a plusieurs jours fériés en France qui sont aussi des fêtes religieuses catholiques. Récemment une commission française a proposé que la fête musulmane de l'Aïd El-Kébir et la fête juive de Yom Kippour soient aussi des jours fériés pour les élèves des écoles publiques de France. La commission désire préserver l'unité nationale et accepter la diversité de religions.

Vocabulaire: s'entendent *get along,* jours fériés *holidays,* soient *be*

D'après çasediscute.com et france2.fr

16 **En quelle saison sont-ils nés?** Expliquez quand et en quelle saison les personnes suivantes sont nées.

Communication (Presentational): Follow-up: Have students tell their own birthdays.

MODÈLE: Monique (15/4)
Elle est née le quinze avril. Elle est née au printemps.

1. Martin Luther King, fils (15/1)
2. Maureen (10/2) et Michel (23/9)
3. Anne (25/8) et Stéphanie (13/7)
4. George Washington (22/2)
5. vous

17 **Quelle est la date?** Votre partenaire va poser une question. Donnez la réponse.

MODÈLE: Noël

VOTRE PARTENAIRE: **Quelle est la date du jour de Noël?**
VOUS: **C'est le vingt-cinq décembre.**

1. ton anniversaire
2. l'anniversaire de ton (ta) meilleur(e) ami(e)
3. le Jour de l'An
4. le commencement du printemps
5. le commencement de l'été
6. le commencement de l'automne
7. le commencement de l'hiver
8. le commencement des vacances d'été à ton université
9. la fête nationale américaine
10. la fête nationale canadienne
11. la fête nationale française

18 **Quel temps fait-il?** Posez des questions. Si votre partenaire ne sait pas la réponse, il (elle) va deviner.

MODÈLE: février / chez toi

VOUS: **Quel temps fait-il en février chez toi?**
VOTRE PARTENAIRE: **Il fait froid et il neige.**

1. été / chez toi
2. hiver / Montréal
3. automne / Chicago
4. printemps / Washington, D.C.
5. août / Maroc
6. avril / Paris
7. décembre / Acapulco

DÉCEMBRE   25°   −3°   17°   11°   18°   11°

19 **À vous.** Répondez.

1. En quelle saison êtes-vous né(e)?
2. Quel mois êtes-vous né(e)?
3. Quel(s) mois les membres de votre famille sont-ils nés?
4. En quelle saison est-ce qu'il pleut chez vous?
5. En quelle saison est-ce qu'il commence à faire froid chez vous?
6. Quelle est votre saison préférée? Pourquoi?
7. Qu'est-ce que vous avez fait l'été dernier?

www Réalités culturelles

Les vacances d'été

One thousand French people 18 years of age or older responded to this phone survey. They were asked to choose the 2 things that best explain what vacation time means to them. Since most chose 2 items, the total percentage is greater than 100.

Les Français qui travaillent ont cinq semaines de vacances. Dans cette enquête, mille personnes ont répondu à la question «Sur la liste suivante, quelles sont les deux choses qui, pour vous, représentent le mieux les vacances?»

La vie de famille	52%
Visiter des endroits nouveaux	46%
Se reposer, bronzer	28%
Voir ses amis	23%
Visiter des monuments, des musées	14%
Faire du sport	11%
Lire, assister à des spectacles	10%
Faire des rencontres	9%

Vocabulaire: enquête *survey,* se reposer *to rest,* bronzer *to tan,* assister à *to attend,* faire des rencontres *to meet others*

D'après Madame Figaro

ENTRE AMIS

D'où viennent-ils?

1. Find out where your partner comes from.
2. Find out if that is where s/he was born.
3. Find out where your partner lives now.
4. Find out his/her birthdate.
5. Find out if your partner has ever gone to France, Canada, or some other French-speaking country.

3. Stating What You Just Did

Tu as déjà mangé, Thierry?

Oui, il y a une demi-heure. Je viens de manger.°   *I just ate.*

Tes amis ont téléphoné?

Oui, il y a dix minutes. Ils viennent de téléphoner.°   *They just called.*

▶ **Et vous?** Qu'est-ce que vous venez de faire?

Est-ce que vous venez de parler français?

F. *Venir de* + infinitif

■ **Venir de** followed by an infinitive means *to have just.*

Je **viens d'arriver.**	*I have just arrived.*
Ils **viennent de manger.**	*They just ate.*
Mon frère **vient de se coucher.**	*My brother just went to bed.*
Qu'est-ce que tu **viens de faire?**	*What did you just do?*

20 **Qu'est-ce qu'ils ont fait?** Chaque phrase est assez vague. Posez une question qui commence par **Qu'est-ce que** pour demander une précision. Ensuite votre partenaire va suggérer *(suggest)* une réponse à la question.

Point out that the question is in the **passé composé**.

MODÈLE: Mes amis viennent de manger quelque chose.

    VOUS: **Qu'est-ce qu'ils ont mangé?**

    VOTRE PARTENAIRE: **Ils ont mangé une pizza.**

1. Pierre vient de lire quelque chose.
2. Nous venons de regarder quelque chose.
3. Je viens d'étudier quelque chose.
4. Mon frère et ma sœur viennent de trouver quelque chose.
5. Je viens d'écrire quelque chose.
6. Nous venons de faire quelque chose.

21 **Elle vient de téléphoner.** Votre camarade de chambre vient de rentrer chez vous. Répondez **oui** à ses questions et utilisez **venir de** dans chaque réponse.

MODÈLE: Martine a téléphoné?

    Oui, elle vient de téléphoner.

1. Est-elle rentrée chez elle?
2. Est-ce qu'elle a déjà dîné?
3. Vous avez parlé de moi?
4. A-t-elle trouvé ma lettre?
5. Est-ce qu'elle a lu ma lettre?
6. Tu as expliqué pourquoi je n'ai pas téléphoné?

22 **La naissance** *(birth)* **de Vianney.** Vous êtes le frère de Brigitte et vos parents vous téléphonent de la maternité *(maternity hospital)*. Vous posez des questions au passé composé. Votre partenaire joue le rôle des parents et utilise **venir de** pour répondre.

MODÈLE: Vous / monter à la salle d'attente *(waiting room)*

LE FRÈRE: **Est-ce que vous êtes montés à la salle d'attente?**

LES PARENTS: **Oui, nous venons de monter à la salle d'attente.**

1. Brigitte / avoir son bébé
2. Vianney / naître
3. le médecin / partir
4. vous / entrer dans la chambre de Brigitte
5. Matthieu, Antoine et Julien / parler avec leurs parents
6. Chantal / téléphoner

Matthieu Monnier est né le 17 mai 1989. Ses frères s'appellent Antoine, Julien et Vianney. Antoine est né le 4 avril 1991, Julien le 29 mars 1993 et Vianney le 18 mai 1997. Ils habitent à Angers avec leurs parents, Brigitte et Jean-Philippe.

Connection & Communication (Presentational): Using this model, have students compose their own birth announcement.

Nous sommes heureux de vous annoncer la naissance de

VIANNEY

le dimanche 18 mai 1997

Bonjour ! Ça y est !! Bébé est né !!!

Culture: French birth announcements are often written from the point of view of older siblings.

ENTRE AMIS

Vous venez de rentrer d'un voyage.

You have just returned from a trip and you call a French-speaking friend to chat.

1. Call your friend and greet him/her.
2. Find out how s/he is doing.
3. Say that you have just returned and explain where you went.
4. Add that you had a good time.
5. Answer his/her questions about the trip.
6. Reassure him/her that you are not too tired after your trip.
7. Say goodbye and add that you will see him/her soon.

Intégration www ◎

Révision

A Les mois et les saisons.

1. Nommez les mois de l'année.
2. Nommez les saisons de l'année.
3. Parlez du temps qu'il fait pendant chaque saison.
4. Pour chaque saison, mentionnez une activité qu'on fait.

Partners should answer only **oui** or **non** to questions asked.

B Le week-end dernier. Faites une liste de vos activités du week-end dernier. Essayez ensuite de deviner ce que votre partenaire a écrit.

C Trouvez quelqu'un qui … Interviewez les autres étudiants pour trouver quelqu'un qui …

Modèle: s'est couché tard hier soir
Est-ce que tu t'es couché(e) tard hier soir?

1. vient de manger
2. est né dans un autre état ou dans une autre province
3. vient d'une grande ville
4. est arrivé au cours en retard aujourd'hui
5. s'est levé tôt ce matin
6. est resté sur le campus le week-end dernier
7. est sorti avec ses amis vendredi soir dernier
8. n'a pas regardé la télévision hier soir

Communication (Presentational & Interpretive): If students present their descriptions to the class, others can be asked to recall information that was presented. Suggestion: Assign the *Rédaction* at the end of Ch. 7 in the Workbook.

D Début de rédaction. Lisez d'abord les cinq activités que vous avez mentionnées dans votre début de rédaction pour le Chapitre 6 (page 177). Ensuite indiquez si vous avez fait ces activités le week-end dernier. Indiquez aussi, si possible, le jour et l'heure.

Modèle: **Samedi matin dernier je ne me suis pas levé(e) tôt. Je me suis levé(e) à neuf heures.**

Communication (Interpretive): Encourage students to use the practice test on the Lab Audio Program.

E À vous. Répondez.

1. Quelle est la date de votre anniversaire?
2. De quel pays venez-vous?
3. Dans quelle ville êtes-vous né(e)?
4. D'où viennent vos parents?
5. Quel temps fait-il en été chez vous?
6. Est-ce que vous êtes resté(e) chez vous l'été dernier?
7. Avez-vous déjà voyagé en train ou en avion? Où êtes-vous allé(e)?
8. Êtes-vous déjà allé(e) dans un pays où on parle français? Si oui, où, et avec qui?

Video for Chapter 7: A. Video worksheets *(Cahier)*; B. ACE Video practice test (WWW); C. CD-ROM

Négociations:

D'où viennent-ils? Interviewez votre partenaire pour trouver les renseignements qui manquent. La copie de votre partenaire est dans l'appendice D.

> MODÈLES: **D'où vient Sahibou?**
>
> **Où est-ce que Fatima est née?**
>
> **Quand est-ce que Cécile est partie?**

For complete instructions on how to prepare for and to use this activity, see *Négociations* on the Class Prep CD-ROM.

A

nom	pays d'origine	ville de naissance	départ	adresse
Sahibou	Sénégal		il y a 5 ans	
Fatima		Casablanca		France
Cécile		Bruxelles	il y a 10 ans	
Jean-Luc	France			Mexique
Marie			le mois dernier	Suisse

Lecture I

A **Étude du vocabulaire.** Étudiez les phrases suivantes et choisissez les mots anglais qui correspondent aux mots français en caractères gras: *up to, average for the season, sunstroke, heat wave, wave, lawns, for, reached, drought, ban, beat, vine(yard)*.

1. **Depuis** un mois l'Europe souffre de la **canicule**.
2. Un synonyme de «canicule» est «**vague** de chaleur».
3. En Italie la température a **atteint** 36 degrés.
4. Elle est montée **jusqu'à** 38 degrés à Trévise.
5. Ces températures sont supérieures aux **moyennes saisonnières**.
6. En France la canicule a **battu** des records.
7. Travailler dans une **vigne** est dangereux parce qu'on risque une **insolation**.
8. À cause de la **sécheresse**, il y a une **interdiction** d'utiliser l'eau pour les **pelouses**.

Connections: By inference, many students will be able to identify the 2 countries not mentioned in the reading, since the capitals are given.

B **Parcourez la lecture.** Lisez rapidement la lecture pour trouver, pour chaque pays de la liste, une ville et la température mentionnée pour cette ville.

	ville	*température*
L'Allemagne	_____	_____ degrés
L'Autriche	_____	_____ degrés
La Bulgarie	_____	_____ degrés
L'Espagne	_____	_____ degrés
La France	_____	_____ degrés
La Hongrie	_____	_____ degrés
L'Italie	_____	_____ degrés
La République tchèque	_____	_____ degrés
La Roumanie	_____	_____ degrés

NOTE CULTURELLE
Le Canada, la France et la plupart des pays utilisent les degrés Celsius (C) pour indiquer la température. Les États-Unis utilisent les degrés Fahrenheit (F).

Quelques comparaisons:
100°C/212°F: L'eau commence à bouillir (*boil*); 37°C/100°F: Il fait très chaud; 0°C/32°F: L'eau commence à geler (*freeze*).

Vague de chaleur en Europe

Les pays d'Europe souffrent d'une vague de chaleur où les températures ont atteint des records.

En Autriche, le mercure est monté jusqu'à 37,2 à Vienne, 36,4 à Linz (centre) et 36 à Salzbourg (centre), des records pour juin, qui s'accompagnent de pics de pollution à l'ozone.

Un record a été battu jeudi à Budapest pour un 12 juin, avec 34,5 degrés, tout comme à Prague où 32,6 degrés ont été enregistrés.

En Bulgarie, un record de 36 degrés a été enregistré à Sofia mercredi. Un homme de 34 ans est mort à Montana (nord-ouest), victime d'un coup de chaleur alors qu'il travaillait mercredi dans sa vigne.

En Roumanie, où la canicule sévit depuis plusieurs jours, un homme de 30 ans a succombé jeudi à une insolation à Alba Iulia (centre), par plus de 36 degrés de température.

L'Italie n'est pas en reste, avec des températures supérieures de 11 degrés aux moyennes saisonnières. Dans la plupart des grandes villes, le mercure a atteint vendredi les 35–36 degrés, grimpant même jusqu'à 38 degrés à Trévise (nord-est). Le pays est touché par une sécheresse sans précédent et les régions du Nord sont les plus affectées. À Rome, certains touristes se sont même baignés dans la célèbre fontaine de Trevi.

En France, dans l'est du pays il y a une période de canicule exceptionnellement longue, avec des records enregistrés notamment à Metz (33 degrés un 10 juin). Météo-France relève des températures maximales excédentaires de 10 à 12 degrés par rapport aux normales dans l'est et le centre-est de la France et souligne le caractère «exceptionnel» des nombreux records de chaleur déjà battus depuis le début du mois.

En Espagne et en Allemagne, les températures sont de 6 à 7 degrés supérieures à la normale.

Il a fait 40 degrés à Madrid (centre) ou à Séville (sud), mais le record pour la saison reste à battre (45 degrés en 1981). Ce pays a également battu son record de consommation d'électricité en raison d'un recours massif à l'air conditionné.

À Fribourg (sud-ouest de l'Allemagne), le mercure est monté jeudi à 36,5 degrés. Les élèves allemands, dispensés d'école, ont pris d'assaut les piscines de plein air.

À Berlin, les lacs de la capitale sont noirs de monde et dans les parcs, nombreux sont les gens qui bravent l'interdiction de griller des saucisses pour improviser sur les pelouses de gargantuesques barbecues familiaux.

D'après le site web de France 2

C **Vrai ou faux?** Décidez si les phrases suivantes sont vraies ou fausses d'après la lecture. Si une phrase est fausse, corrigez-la.

1. Les Allemands sont allés à la piscine.
2. Les Espagnols sont allés au lac.
3. Les températures mentionnées sont normales pour la saison.
4. Des gens sont morts en France et en Autriche.
5. L'air chaud et les voitures sont responsables de la pollution de l'air.
6. En Allemagne on a la permission de faire des barbecues dans les parcs.
7. Il ne pleut pas en Italie.

D **Discussion**

1. Quelles sont les «solutions» mentionnées au problème de la chaleur?
2. Que faites-vous quand il fait très chaud?

Lecture II

Comparison: Have students complete this activity before checking the *Vocabulaire* at the end of the book.

A **Parlons du genre** *(gender).* Identifiez les mots suivants qui sont masculins, féminins ou peuvent *(can)* être les deux.

	M	F	M/F
1. personne	____	____	____
2. enfant	____	____	____
3. professeur	____	____	____
4. artiste	____	____	____
5. victime	____	____	____
6. médecin	____	____	____
7. ingénieur	____	____	____

B **Faites une liste.** Faites une liste de toutes les expressions que vous connaissez *(that you know)* qui commencent par «Il».

Suggestion: Use the poem for a **Concours de prononciation** (see the Class Prep CD-ROM).

IL

Il pleut Il pleut

Il fait beau

Il fait du soleil

Il est tôt

Il se fait[1] tard

Il

Il

Il

toujours Il

Toujours Il qui pleut et qui neige

Toujours Il qui fait du soleil

Toujours Il

Pourquoi pas Elle

Jamais Elle

Pourtant[2] Elle aussi

Souvent se fait[3] belle!

Jacques Prévert, Éditions Gallimard

---

1. *is getting* 2. *However* 3. *makes herself*

C **Discussion.** Quel est le point de vue du poète? Êtes-vous d'accord avec lui? Pourquoi ou pourquoi pas?

Practice this vocabulary with the flashcards on the *Entre amis* web site.

VOCABULAIRE ACTIF

Les mois de l'année

janvier *(m.) January*
février *(m.) February*
mars *(m.) March*
avril *(m.) April*
mai *(m.) May*
juin *(m.) June*
juillet *(m.) July*
août *(m.) August*
septembre *(m.) September*
octobre *(m.) October*
novembre *(m.) November*
décembre *(m.) December*

Les saisons de l'année

le printemps *spring*
l'été *(m.) summer*
l'automne *(m.) fall*
l'hiver *(m.) winter*
une saison *season*

Expressions météorologiques

Il fait froid. *It's cold.*
Il fait chaud. *It's hot (warm).*
Il fait frais. *It's cool.*
It fait beau. *It's nice out.*
Il fait mauvais. *The weather is bad.*
Il fait (du) soleil. *It's sunny out.*
Il fait du vent. *It's windy.*
Il pleut. *It's raining.*
Il neige. *It's snowing.*

Il commence à faire froid. *It's starting to get cold.*

Expressions de temps

à l'heure *on time*
en avance *early*
en retard *late*
une demi-heure *half an hour*
puis *then; next*
tout de suite *immediately; right away*
À tout de suite. *See you very soon.*

D'autres noms

un anniversaire *birthday*
un avion *airplane*
un bébé *baby*
la fête nationale *national holiday*
une guerre *war*
le monde *world*
une place *seat*
le (téléphone) portable *cell phone*
un problème *problem*
une victime *victim (male or female)*

Expressions utiles

Ça ne vous dérange pas? *That doesn't bother you?*
D'où venez-vous? *Where do you come from?*
en voiture *by car*
être originaire de *to be a native of*

Je vous en prie. *Don't mention it; You're welcome; Please do.*
Parlez-moi de ce voyage. *Tell me about this trip.*
Qui est à l'appareil? *Who is speaking (on the phone)?*
suivant(e) *following; next*
y *there*

Verbes

arriver *to arrive*
commencer *to begin*
descendre *to go down; to get out of*
devenir *to become*
entrer *to enter*
monter *to go up; to get into*
mourir *to die*
naître *to be born*
poster *to mail*
rentrer *to go (come) back; to go (come) home*
retourner *to go back; to return*
revenir *to come back*
tourner *to turn*
venir *to come*
venir de … *to have just …*

Quelques fêtes

le Jour de l'An *New Year's Day*
Noël *Christmas*
la Toussaint *All Saints Day*

On mange bien en France

Coup d'envoi

Prise de contact   Quelque chose à manger?

This material is recorded on the Student Audio that accompanies your text. Practice with the recording as part of your homework.

See the Class Prep CD-ROM for detailed suggestions on how to teach this lesson.

Use the video, *Modules 4*, **La boulangerie,** & *10*, **Le marché,** to help set the scene for this chapter.

Tu as faim°, Bruno?   *You are hungry*
      Qu'est-ce qu'il y a?

Il y a ...
      du pain°.   *bread*
      des hors-d'œuvre°.   *appetizers*
      de la soupe.
      du poisson.
      de la viande°.   *meat*
      des légumes°.   *vegetables*
      de la salade.
      du fromage.

Qu'est-ce que tu vas prendre?°   *What are you going to have?*

▶ **Et vous?**

Qu'est-ce que vous allez prendre?
Je voudrais ...
Merci, je n'ai pas faim.
Je regrette° mais j'ai déjà mangé.   *I'm sorry*

Conversation

L'apéritif chez les Aspel

James Davidson est invité à prendre l'apéritif° chez Monsieur et Madame Aspel, les parents de Karine. Monsieur Aspel lui offre quelque chose à boire.

               have a before-dinner drink

M. ASPEL: Que voulez-vous boire, James? J'ai du vin, de la limonade, du jus de pomme°, de la bière ...   *apple*

JAMES: Quel choix!° Comment s'appelle ce vin?   *What a choice!*

M. ASPEL: C'est du beaujolais. Et voilà une bouteille° de bordeaux.   *bottle*

JAMES: Alors, un peu de beaujolais, s'il vous plaît.

M. ASPEL: Bien sûr°, voilà.   *Of course*
(*James lève° son verre et Monsieur Aspel verse° du vin.*)   *lifts / pours*

JAMES: Merci beaucoup.

M. ASPEL: Je vous en prie.
(*Un peu plus tard*)

M. ASPEL: Alors, que pensez-vous° de ce petit vin?   *what do you think?*

JAMES: Il est délicieux.

M. ASPEL: Encore à boire?°   *More to drink?*

JAMES: Non, merci.

M. ASPEL: C'est vrai?

JAMES: Oui, vraiment. Sans façon.°   *Honestly.*

M. ASPEL: Alors, je n'insiste pas.°   *I won't insist.*

▶ **Jouez ces rôles.** Répétez la conversation avec votre partenaire. Utilisez vos noms.

Remind students of the gesture for **Non, merci,** taught in Ch. 2.

After practicing the *Conversation*, have students complete ex. A in the Workbook.

Connection & Comparison: Have students compare the labels. The better wine's label shows (1) **appellation contrôlée,** (2) a date, and (3) an indication that it was bottled on the property.

À propos

Pourquoi est-ce que James lève son verre quand Monsieur Aspel va verser du vin?

   a. James est très poli. Cela fait partie *(is part)* du savoir-vivre *(code of good manners)*.
   b. C'est plus facile *(easier)* pour Monsieur Aspel.
   c. James ne veut pas renverser *(knock over)* son verre.

L'apéritif

A before-dinner drink is often offered. This might be **un kir, un porto** *(port wine),* **un jus de pomme,** etc.

L'art d'apprécier le vin

Wine is an integral part of French social life and there are a number of polite gestures, such as lifting one's glass when wine is to be poured, that are associated with wine appreciation.

Tout se fait autour d'une table
(Everything takes place around a table)

It does not take long in France to realize how much time is spent sitting around a table. Not only is a table the place to enjoy a meal or share a drink, it is also a primary spot for business deals, serious discussion, pleasant companionship, courtship, and child rearing! It is not surprising, therefore, to find that the table has a place of honor in France, whether it is in **la cuisine, la salle à manger, le restaurant, le resto U (restaurant universitaire), le café, le bistro,** or **la cafétéria.**

Sans façon

Refusing additional servings is often quite difficult in France. The French are gracious hosts and are anxious that their guests have enough to eat and drink. There is therefore a need to find ways to convey politely that you are full. Do not, incidentally, say **Je suis plein(e)** (literally, *I am full*), since this would convey that you

were either drunk or pregnant. When all else fails (e.g., **Merci; Non, merci; Vraiment; Je n'ai plus faim/soif; J'ai très bien mangé/bu,** etc.), the expression **Sans façon** *(Honestly; No kidding)* will usually work. Of course, if you feel like having a second serving, you may say **Volontiers!** or **Je veux bien.**

Relativité culturelle: Un repas français
(A French meal)

A good example of the presence of structure in French lives is the order of a French meal. There are not infrequently five separate courses at both lunch and dinner, although these are not necessarily heavy meals. After the **hors-d'œuvre,** the **plat principal** is served. There may be more than one **plat principal** (e.g., fish *and* meat). **La salade** normally comes next, followed by **le fromage** and **le dessert.** In a light meal, either the cheese or the dessert may be omitted.

   Any variation in the order of the French meal is almost always minor. The number of courses in a French meal reflects not only the French feeling for structure, but also the French appreciation of savoring each taste individually. A few contrasts between the structure of French and North American meals are shown in the chart on the next page.

CONTINUED →

In France

Eating several courses, even light ones, means that you have to stop after each course and wait for the next. Much more time is spent at the table.

A green salad is served *after* the **plat principal** (in a few places, such as Angers, at the same time). It is not eaten as a first course. Salad rarely includes any vegetable but lettuce.

There is only one type of dressing (oil and vinegar) served with a salad.

Bread is always served with the meal, usually without butter, and is bought fresh every day.

Coffee is not served during lunch or dinner. It is served, without cream, at the end of these meals.

Café au lait is served only at breakfast. This mixture of 1/2 coffee and 1/2 warm milk is often served in a bowl.

In North America

Everything may be served at once and, therefore, much less time is spent at the table.

Salad is often eaten at the start of the meal. Salads are usually mixed, including a variety of vegetables.

There is a variety of salad dressings available. What is referred to as *French dressing* is nothing like what is served with a salad in France.

Bread is not always served with the meal. When it is, butter is always provided.

Coffee is occasionally served right away at the start of the meal.

Many people put milk in their coffee at every meal.

Il y a un geste

Encore à boire? A fist is made with the thumb extended to somewhat resemble a bottle. Then the thumb is pointed toward a glass as an invitation or a request to have more to drink.

▶ **À vous.** Répondez.

1. Que voulez-vous? J'ai de la limonade, du jus de pomme, ...
2. Bien sûr, voilà.
3. Aimez-vous la limonade, le jus de pomme, ... ?
4. Encore à boire?

ENTRE AMIS

Tu as faim?

1. Find out if your partner is hungry. (S/he is.)
2. Ask if s/he wants something to eat.
3. S/he will ask what there is.
4. Tell what there is.
5. Find out what s/he is going to have.

www Use the ACE practice test on the *Entre amis* web site to review this *Coup d'envoi* section, pp. 210–213.

Prononciation

This pronunciation lesson is recorded on the Student Audio that accompanies your text. Use it to practice pronunciation at home.

Les sons [k], [s], [z], [ʃ], [ʒ] et [ɲ]

■ The following words contain some related French consonant sounds. Practice saying the words after your instructor, paying particular attention to the highlighted sound. As you pronounce the words for one sound, look at how that sound is spelled and in what kinds of letter combinations it appears. What patterns do you notice?

[k]
- **c**afé, en**c**ore, bi**c**yclette, chi**c**
- cin**q**, **qu**el**qu**efois
- **k**ir, vod**k**a

[s]
- **s**a, **s**ur, di**s**cret, **s**kier, conver**s**ation, val**s**e, fil**s**, mar**s**
- pre**ss**é, poi**ss**on
- **c**itron, exer**c**ice, bi**c**yclette
- **ç**a, fran**ç**ais, gar**ç**on
- si**x**, di**x**, soi**x**ante

[z]
- mai**s**on, va**s**e, poi**s**on, maga**s**in
- **z**éro, sei**z**e, maga**z**ine

[ʃ]
- **ch**aud, blan**ch**e, mé**ch**ant
- **sh**ort, sweat-**sh**irt

[ʒ]
- **j**ouer, tou**j**ours, dé**j**euner, dé**j**à
- oran**g**e, **g**énéral, gara**g**e, refri**g**érateur

[ɲ]
- espa**gn**ol, Allema**gn**e, rensei**gn**ement

■ In most situations, **-s-** is pronounced [s]. But when it appears between two vowels, it is pronounced as [z].

	soir	salade	seul	classe	considération
But:	vase	présente	raison	chose	musée

■ As in English, **-c-** is usually pronounced [k], but becomes [s] when it precedes the letters **-e, -i,** or **-y.** To create the [s] sound of **-c-** in some words where it is not followed by **e, i,** or **y,** it is written as **ç.**

	encore	cassis	comment	Maroc	crème
But:	France	voici	bicyclette	français	François

■ Finally, as in English, the letter **-g-** is usually pronounced [g], but becomes [ʒ] when it precedes the letters **-e, -i,** or **-y.** To create the [ʒ] sound of **-g-** in some words where it is not followed by **e, i,** or **y,** an **-e** is added after it.

re**g**arder	**g**olf	**g**uitare	**g**rippe	é**g**lise

But: **g**entil   oran**g**ina   **g**ymnase   man**g**eons   voya**g**eons

▶ Pronounce the following words correctly.

1. chocolat, commerce, chaussures, citron, bicyclette, ça, garçon, chercher, chance, avec
2. cinq, cinquante, quelques, pourquoi, Belgique, quart, chaque, question, banque
3. kir, vodka, skier, baskets, hockey
4. excellent, saxophone, examen, exercice, six, dix, soixante
5. Sénégal, orange, mangeons, voyageur, garage, gauche, âge, ménage, agent, gymnastique
6. surprise, Suisse, sous, semestre, saison, sieste, poisson, plaisir, ensuite
7. conversation, télévision, fonctionnaire, attention, provisions, dissertation
8. zéro, onze, magazine, douze
9. jupe, jeune, je, janvier, aujourd'hui, déjeuner, déjà
10. espagnol, Allemagne, accompagner, renseignement

Voici un des desserts préférés des Français. Ces gâteaux font venir l'eau à la bouche, n'est-ce pas?

Buts communicatifs

1. Ordering a French Meal

Garçon is the traditional way of referring to a waiter; however, the word **serveur** is increasingly used.

Point out the pronunciation of **oignon** [ɔɲɔ̃].

Client(e)	Serveur/Serveuse°	*waiter / waitress*
Qu'est-ce que vous avez comme ...	Il y a ...	
hors-d'œuvre?	des crudités°.	*raw vegetables*
	du pâté°.	*pâté (meat spread)*
	de la salade de tomates.	
soupes?	de la soupe de légumes.	
	de la soupe à l'oignon°.	*onion*
plats principaux?	de la truite°.	*trout*
	du saumon°.	*salmon*
	du bœuf°.	*beef*
	du porc.	
	du poulet°.	*chicken*
légumes?	des haricots verts°.	*green beans*
	des petits pois°.	*peas*
	des épinards°.	*spinach*
	des pommes de terre°.	*potatoes*
	des frites°.	*French fries*
	du riz°.	*rice*
fromages?	de l'emmental°.	*Swiss cheese*
	du camembert.	
	du chèvre°.	*goat cheese*
	du brie.	
desserts?	des fruits.	
	de la glace°.	*ice cream*
	des pâtisseries°.	*pastries*
	de la tarte°.	*pie*
	du gâteau°.	*cake*

Communication (Interpretive & Presentational): Before pairing students for practice, tell them they will have to remember 3 of their partner's choices for the follow-up activity.

▶ **Et vous?**   Avez-vous décidé? Qu'est-ce que vous allez commander°?   *to order*
Je vais prendre ...

REMARQUES

1. The words **hors-d'œuvre** and **haricot** begin with the letter **h-** but are treated as if they began with a pronounced consonant. Liaison does not take place after words like **les** and **des,** nor is the letter **-e** dropped in words like **le** and **de.**

   Nous aimons **les/hors-d'œuvre.**   Il n'y a pas **de haricots.**

2. **Hors-d'œuvre** is invariable in the plural.

   un **hors-d'œuvre**   des **hors-d'œuvre**

A. L'article partitif

Remember to consult Appendix C at the end of the book to review any terms with which you are not familiar.

Comparison: Give students 2 minutes to study the sentences above. Then (books closed), ask them to translate the English sentences into French. Check the choice of partitive article.

Apportez-moi **du** pain, s'il vous plaît.	*Bring me some bread, please.*
Vous voulez **de la** glace?	*Do you want (some) ice cream?*
Vous avez **de l'**eau minérale?	*Do you have (any) mineral water?*
Je vais manger **des** frites.	*I'm going to eat (some) French fries.*

■ You have already learned about definite articles and indefinite articles in French. There is a third type of article in French called **l'article partitif** *(the partitive article)* that is used when a noun represents a certain quantity, or a part, of a larger whole. In English, we sometimes use the words *some* or *any* to represent this idea, but sometimes we use no article at all.

Je voudrais **du** gâteau.	*I would like cake (but just some of it).*
Le professeur a **de la** patience.	*The professor has patience (not all the patience in the world, just a portion of it).*
Jean a **des** livres.	*Jean has books (but not all the books in the whole world).*

partitive article	when to use	examples
du	before a masculine singular noun	**du** pain
de la	before a feminine singular noun	**de la** salade
de l'	before a masculine or feminine singular noun that begins with a vowel sound	**de l'**eau
des	before all plural nouns, masculine or feminine	**des** frites

Write these sentences on the board, then drill: 1. **Est-ce qu'il y a du café?** (glace/légumes/eau/fromage/etc.) 2. **Il n'y a pas de café.** (glace/légumes/etc.)

■ Like the indefinite article, the partitive article usually becomes **de** after a negation.

Est-ce qu'il y a **de l'**eau minérale?	*Is there any mineral water?*
Non, il n'y a **pas d'**eau minérale.	*No, there isn't any mineral water.*
Il y a **des** légumes?	*Are there any vegetables?*
Non, il n'y a **pas de** légumes.	*No, there aren't any vegetables.*

NOTE — This rule does not apply after **être**.

Ce n'est pas **du** vin, ce n'est pas **de la** limonade.
Ce n'est pas **de l'**eau, c'est **du** lait.

■ In a series, the article must be repeated before each noun.

Vous voulez **de la** glace, **de la** tarte ou **du** gâteau?

Be sure to use the contractions **l'**, **de l'**, and **d'** before a vowel.

Synthèse: les articles

	définis	indéfinis	partitifs
masculin singulier	le	un	du
féminin singulier	la	une	de la
pluriel	les	des	des
dans une phrase négative	le/la/les	de	de

Review the definite article, p. 44, and the indefinite article, p. 63.

Follow-up: Use the items in the pictures to drill and contrast: **J'aime** *le* **pain,** / **Je voudrais** *du* **pain.**, etc.

1   Qu'est-ce que c'est? Identifiez les choses suivantes.

MODÈLES:

C'est du pain.

Ce sont des petits pois.

1.   2.   3.

4.   5.   6.

Communication (Interpretive & Presentational): Before pairing students for practice, tell them they will have to remember their partner's choices for the follow-up: **Qu'est-ce que votre partenaire va prendre?**

Remind students that the definite article is used to express a preference and that it does not change after a negation (see Ch. 2).

2   Qu'est-ce que vous commandez? Dites au garçon ou à la serveuse que vous aimez la catégorie indiquée. Ensuite demandez quels sont les choix. Il (elle) va mentionner deux choix. Décidez.

MODÈLE: vegetables

VOUS: **J'aime beaucoup les légumes. Qu'est-ce que vous avez comme légumes?**
SERVEUR/SERVEUSE: **Nous avons des petits pois et des épinards.**
VOUS: **Je voudrais des petits pois, s'il vous plaît.**

1. appetizers   3. fish   5. wine   7. desserts
2. meat   4. vegetables   6. cheese

3   Ils viennent de pique-niquer. Qu'est-ce qu'ils ont apporté *(brought)*? Qu'est-ce qu'ils n'ont pas apporté?

MODÈLE: Les Delille (pain, salade)
Les Delille ont apporté du pain, mais ils n'ont pas apporté de salade.

1. Séverine (salade, fromage)
2. Roland (haricots verts, petits pois)
3. Serge et Christelle (fromage, vin rouge)
4. Patricia (poisson, viande)
5. Vous (… , …)

4 **Un(e) touriste va au restaurant.** Jouez la scène suivante avec votre partenaire en complétant les phrases avec **du, de la, de l', des, de** ou **d'**.

—Vous avez décidé?
—Oui, je voudrais _____ pâté _____ truite, _____ frites et _____ épinards.
—Et comme boisson?
—Apportez-moi _____ café, s'il vous plaît.
—Mais c'est impossible! Il n'y a jamais _____ café avec le plat principal.
—Qu'est-ce qu'il y a?
—Nous avons _____ vin ou _____ eau minérale.
—Vous n'avez pas _____ orangina?
—Si, si vous insistez. Et comme dessert?
—Je crois que je voudrais _____ gâteau.
—Nous n'avons pas _____ gâteau. Il y a _____ glace et _____ fruits.
—Merci, je ne vais pas prendre _____ dessert.

B. *Ne ... plus*

■ The opposite of **encore** is **ne ... plus** (*no more, not any more, no longer*).

Avez-vous **encore** soif?	*Are you still thirsty?*
Non, je **n'**ai **plus** soif et je **n'**ai **plus** faim.	*No, I'm not thirsty any more and I'm no longer hungry.*

■ **Ne ... plus** works like the other negations you have learned; that is, **ne** and **plus** are placed around the conjugated verb. This means that in the passé composé, **ne** and **plus** surround the auxiliary verb and the past participle follows **plus**.

> Remember that the partitive article becomes **de** after a negation: **plus *de* glace, plus *de* dessert.**

Je regrette; nous **n'**avons **plus** de glace.	*I'm sorry; we have no more ice cream.*
Je **ne** vais **plus** manger de dessert.	*I am not going to eat any more dessert.*
Delphine **n'**a **plus** dîné dans ce restaurant-là.	*Delphine did not eat in that restaurant again.*

5 **Encore à manger ou à boire?** Offrez encore à manger ou à boire. Votre partenaire va refuser poliment.

MODÈLES: bière
—**Encore de la bière?**
—**Sans façon, je n'ai plus soif.**

glace
—**Encore de la glace?**
—**Merci, je n'ai plus faim.**

1. café	7. tarte
2. eau	8. poisson
3. limonade	9. légumes
4. pâté	10. beaujolais
5. viande	11. salade
6. frites	12. fromage

6 **Le restaurant impossible.** Il n'y a plus beaucoup à manger ou à boire. Le serveur (la serveuse) répond toujours **Je regrette** et suggère autre chose. Insistez! Expliquez que vous n'aimez pas ce qu'il (elle) propose.

MODÈLE: poisson (viande)

VOUS: **Avez-vous du poisson?**

SERVEUR/SERVEUSE: **Je regrette, nous n'avons plus de poisson; mais nous avons de la viande.**

VOUS: **Mais je voudrais du poisson! Je n'aime pas la viande.**

1. coca (vin)
2. soupe (hors-d'œuvre)
3. épinards (frites)
4. truite (saumon)
5. pâté (crudités)

6. pâtisseries (glace)
7. chocolat chaud (café)
8. haricots verts (petits pois)
9. orangina (limonade)

www **Réalités culturelles**

Review *Note Culturelle*, p. 127.

Le resto U

Tous les étudiants régulièrement inscrits dans un établissement d'enseignement supérieur français et qui ont droit à la sécurité sociale étudiante ont la possibilité de bénéficier des services des restos U. La carte d'étudiant est le seul document nécessaire pour acheter des tickets de repas. Pour un repas complet, avec des crudités, un plat chaud accompagné de légumes et un dessert, il faut

un ticket à 2,60 € . Un étudiant qui prend deux repas par jour dans un établissement de restauration rapide et bon marché doit quand même payer au moins 12 € par jour pour sa nourriture. Mais au resto U ces deux repas coûtent seulement 5,20 € par jour. Cela fait une économie de plus de 2.400 € par an.

Cinq cents établissements dans toute la France servent soixante millions de repas chaque année. Une méthode rigoureuse, créée par la NASA pour assurer la sécurité alimentaire des astronautes, est appliquée dans tous les restaurants. Elle garantit une qualité microbiologique optimale. L'hygiène de chaque resto U est soumise aux contrôles d'experts régionaux et nationaux.

Vocabulaire: acheter *to buy,* alimentaire *food,* inscrits *enrolled,* nourriture *food,* quand même *even so*

D'après cnous.fr

C. Le verbe *prendre*

Nous prenons souvent un repas ensemble.

We often have a meal together.

Je prends un café.

I'm having a cup of coffee.

Mes amis ne **prennent** pas le petit déjeuner.

My friends don't eat breakfast.

Qui a pris mon dessert?

Who took my dessert?

prendre *(to take; to eat, drink)*			
je	**prends**	nous	**prenons**
tu	**prends**	vous	**prenez**
il/elle/on	**prend**	ils/elles	**prennent**
passé composé: j'**ai pris**			

Drill: **Je ne prends pas le petit déjeuner. (Vous/Nous/Mes parents/**etc.**)**

■ Note the pronunciation distinction between the third person singular and plural forms.

il prend [prã]   ils prennent [prɛn]

■ The verbs **apprendre** *(to learn)* and **comprendre** *(to understand; to include)* are conjugated like **prendre.**

Quelle langue **apprenez-vous?**

What language are you learning?

J'apprends le français.

I'm learning French.

Peggy comprend bien le français.

Peggy understands French well.

Comprennent-ils toujours le professeur?

Do they always understand the teacher?

Pardon, **je** n'**ai** pas **compris.**

Excuse me, I didn't understand.

Le service est **compris.**

The service (tip) is included.

NOTE ⎯ To learn to do something is **apprendre à** + infinitive.

Nous **apprenons à parler** français.   *We are learning to speak French.*

7 **Les voyageurs.** Les personnes suivantes vont voyager. Expliquez quelle langue elles apprennent.

MODÈLE: Je vais en France.
Alors j'apprends à parler français.

Review **langues et pays,** in Ch. 5.

1. Mes parents vont en Italie.
2. Mon cousin va en Allemagne.
3. Ma sœur va au Mexique.
4. Mon oncle et ma tante vont en Russie.
5. Mes amis et moi allons en Belgique.
6. Vous allez en Chine.
7. Je vais au Maroc.

8 **La plupart des étudiants.** Interviewez votre partenaire à propos des étudiants de votre cours de français. Attention au présent et au passé composé.

MODÈLES: apprendre le français

—Est-ce que la plupart des étudiants apprennent le français?
—Bien sûr, ils apprennent le français.

apprendre le français à l'âge de quinze ans

—Est-ce que la plupart des étudiants ont appris le français à l'âge de quinze ans?
—Non, ils n'ont pas appris le français à l'âge de quinze ans.

1. prendre quelquefois un verre de vin au petit déjeuner
2. prendre le petit déjeuner ce matin
3. comprendre toujours le professeur de français
4. apprendre l'espagnol à l'âge de cinq ans
5. prendre souvent un taxi
6. prendre un taxi hier
7. comprendre cet exercice

9 **À vous.** Répondez.

1. Vos amis prennent-ils le petit déjeuner d'habitude? Si oui, qu'est-ce qu'ils prennent comme boisson?
2. D'habitude, qu'est-ce que vous prenez comme boisson au petit déjeuner? au déjeuner? au dîner?
3. Qu'est-ce que vous avez pris comme boisson ce matin?
4. Qu'est-ce que la plupart des Français prennent comme boisson au dîner?
5. Qu'est-ce que vous allez prendre si vous dînez dans un restaurant français?
6. Si vous commandez un dessert, que prenez-vous d'habitude?
7. Comprenez-vous toujours les menus qui sont en français?
8. Avez-vous appris à faire la cuisine?

Il y a un geste

L'addition, s'il vous plaît *(Check, please).* When the French want to signal to a waiter or waitress that they want the check, they pretend to be writing on the open palm of one hand. This is discreetly held up for the waiter to see.

ENTRE AMIS

L'addition, s'il vous plaît

Your partner is a waiter/waitress in a French restaurant.

1. After you have looked at the menu (see page 216), s/he will ask you what you are going to have.
2. Order from the menu.
3. Your partner will then ask what you want to drink.
4. Order something to drink.
5. When you have finished, ask for the bill.
6. Your partner will verify the items you ordered.
7. Confirm or correct what s/he says.

2. Discussing Quantities

Qu'est-ce que tu manges, Solange?
Je mange ...
    beaucoup de frites.
    un peu de gâteau.
    peu d'épinards.
    très peu de moutarde°.   *mustard*
Je mange ...
    un morceau° de pizza.   *piece*
    une tranche de jambon°.   *slice of ham*
    une assiette° de crudités.   *plate*
    une boîte de bonbons°.   *box of candy*

> The plural of **un morceau** is **des morceaux: Thomas a mangé cinq morceaux de pizza.**

▶ **Et vous?**   Qu'est-ce que vous mangez?
             Je mange ...
             Qu'est-ce que vous buvez°?   *you drink*
             Je bois° ...   *I drink*

D. Les expressions de quantité

■ You have already been using expressions of quantity throughout this course. There are two kinds of expressions of quantity: specific measures (**une tasse, un verre,** etc.) and indefinite expressions of quantity (**assez, beaucoup,** etc.).

■ To use these expressions of quantity with nouns, insert **de** (but no article) before the noun.

> **Un kilo** = 2.2 pounds.

Une bouteille de vin, s'il vous plaît.	*A bottle of wine, please.*
Il faut **un kilo de porc.**	*We need a kilo of pork.*
Trois kilos de pommes de terre aussi.	*Three kilos of potatoes also.*
Je voudrais **un morceau de pain.**	*I'd like a piece of bread.*
Ils n'ont pas **beaucoup d'amis.**	*They don't have a lot of friends.*
Combien de frères ou **de sœurs** avez-vous?	*How many brothers or sisters do you have?*

■ **Trop, beaucoup, assez,** and **peu** can be used with either singular or plural nouns. *Un* **peu** can only be used with singular nouns, those that cannot be counted. To express the idea of a small amount with a plural noun (which *can* be counted), use **quelques** *(a few, some)* without **de.**

	Voulez-vous **un peu de** fromage?	*Would you like a little cheese?*
But:	Voulez-vous **quelques** frites?	*Would you like a few French fries?*

■ The indefinite expressions of quantity can also be used with verbs, without the addition of **de.**

Je chante **beaucoup.**	*I sing a lot.*
Rip van Winkle a **trop** dormi.	*Rip van Winkle slept too much.*
Nous avons **assez** travaillé!	*We have worked enough!*

■ To express how much you like or dislike a thing, the definite article (not **de**) is used before the noun.

Je n'aime pas **beaucoup le** lait.	*I don't much like milk.*
Mon frère aime **trop la** glace.	*My brother likes ice cream too much.*

The expression of quantity, in such cases, is really modifying the verb.

■ **Peu de** can be introduced by the word **très** to make it more emphatic. **Très** cannot be used with the other expressions of quantity.

Je mange **très peu d'**épinards.	*I eat very little spinach.*

E. Le verbe *boire*

Quel vin **boit-on** avec du poisson?

Nous buvons un peu de thé.

Nos amis mangent de la salade et **ils boivent** de l'eau.

Hélène a trop **bu!**

boire *(to drink)*			
je	**bois**	nous	**buvons**
tu	**bois**	vous	**buvez**
il/elle/on	**boit**		
ils/elles	**boivent**		
passé composé: j'**ai bu**			

■ Note the pronunciation distinction between the third person singular and plural forms.

elle boi*t*   [bwa]

elles boi**v**e*nt*   [bwav]

10 **Dans un restaurant à Paris.** Complétez les phrases suivantes avec le verbe **boire**. Faites attention au choix entre le présent, le passé composé et l'infinitif.

1. (touriste) Je voudrais _____ de l'eau, s'il vous plaît.
2. (serveur) Mais vous avez _____ trois verres d'eau tout à l'heure.
3. (touriste) Oui, mais je _____ beaucoup d'eau.
4. Et si je viens de _____ de l'eau ou non, ça ne vous concerne pas.
5. Dans ma famille, nous _____ toujours de l'eau.
6. Vos clients _____ de l'eau, n'est-ce pas?
7. (serveur) Quelquefois, mais dans ce restaurant, on _____ aussi du vin.

www Réalités culturelles

La langue et la culture

En général, la richesse du vocabulaire pour décrire un phénomène est une indication de son rôle culturel. Il y a, par exemple, beaucoup de mots différents en français pour décrire le pain (baguette, flûte, etc.). La table joue un rôle énorme dans la culture française. Il est donc normal de trouver beaucoup d'expressions idiomatiques et de proverbes où on parle de la nourriture. Les exemples suivants aident à comprendre que la langue et la culture vont de pair.

L'appétit vient en mangeant.	The more you try it the more you'll like it.
Bon appétit!	Enjoy your meal!
avoir du pain sur la planche	to have a lot of work to do
avoir un appétit d'oiseau	to eat like a bird
avoir un bon coup de fourchette	to have a hearty appetite
être bon comme le pain	to have a heart of gold
mettre les petits plats dans les grands	to put on a wonderful meal
ne pas être dans son assiette	to feel ill
pour une bouchée de pain	for a ridiculously low price
se vendre comme des petits pains	to sell like hotcakes

Vocabulaire: bon coup de fourchette *handle a fork well*, bouchée *mouthful*, en mangeant *while eating*, mettre *to put*, planche *(bread) board*, vont de pair *go together*

Culture, Connection & Comparison: Point out that the expression «**Des goûts et des couleurs**» is a French idiomatic expression: "People have different tastes." Have students learn several of the expressions in the *Réalités culturelles* above.

Review pp. 58 and 213.

11 Des goûts et des couleurs *(Tastes and colors).* Donnez des précisions en utilisant *(by using)* les expressions de quantité entre parenthèses.

MODÈLES: Nous buvons du vin. (peu)
Nous buvons peu de vin.

Nous aimons les fruits. (beaucoup)
Nous aimons beaucoup les fruits.

1. Ma sœur boit de l'orangina. (trop)
2. Elle aime l'orangina. (beaucoup)
3. Nos parents prennent du café. (un peu)
4. Vous avez de la salade? (assez)
5. Jean n'aime pas le vin. (beaucoup)
6. Il boit de l'eau. (peu)
7. J'aime le poisson. (bien)
8. Du vin blanc, s'il vous plaît. (un verre)
9. Marie désire des hors-d'œuvre. (quelques)
10. Je voudrais de la viande et du vin. (quatre tranches / une bouteille)

12 Dans ma famille. Décrivez les habitudes de votre famille.

MODÈLES: **Nous mangeons beaucoup de glace.**
Ma sœur boit très peu de lait.

Do in pairs. Follow with a stand-up drill in which each student gives one true example.

			épinards
			fruits
mes parents		trop	limonade
ma sœur		beaucoup	lait
mon frère	manger	assez	glace
je	boire	peu	salade
nous		très peu	poisson
		jamais	eau
			chocolat chaud
			pommes de terre

13 Sur le campus. Utilisez une expression de quantité pour répondre à chaque question.

MODÈLE: Les étudiants ont-ils du temps libre?
Ils ont très peu de temps libre.

Communication (Interpretive): Poll students after doing ex. 13: **Combien ont des amis qui boivent du thé?**, etc.

1. Avez-vous des amis à l'université?
2. Est-ce que les étudiants de votre université boivent de la bière?
3. Aiment-ils le coca light?
4. Est-ce que vos amis boivent du thé?
5. Vos amis mangent-ils du fromage?
6. Les étudiants mangent de la pizza, n'est-ce pas?
7. Les étudiants ont-ils des devoirs?

14 **L'appétit vient en mangeant** *(Eating whets the appetite).*
Complétez les paragraphes avec **le, la, l', les, du, de la, de l', des, de** et **d'**.

1. Françoise est au restaurant. Elle va manger _____ hors-d'œuvre, _____ poisson, _____ viande, _____ salade, un peu _____ fromage et beaucoup _____ glace. Elle va boire _____ vin blanc avec _____ poisson et _____ vin rouge avec _____ viande et _____ fromage. Mais elle ne va pas manger _____ soupe parce qu'elle n'aime pas _____ soupe.

2. Monsieur et Madame Blanc ne boivent jamais _____ café. Ils détestent _____ café mais ils aiment beaucoup _____ thé. Quelquefois ils boivent _____ vin, mais jamais beaucoup. Leurs enfants adorent _____ orangina et _____ coca-cola classique. Mais il n'y a jamais _____ orangina ou _____ coca chez eux. Les parents pensent que _____ coca et _____ orangina ne sont pas bons pour les jeunes enfants. Alors leurs enfants boivent _____ lait ou _____ eau.

Le petit déjeuner à Paris

du pain
un croissant
du beurre
de la confiture
du café au lait
du thé
du chocolat chaud

Le petit déjeuner à Québec

du jus de fruits (orange, pomme, canneberge)
des céréales (froides ou chaudes)
un œuf
du jambon ou du bacon
du pain grillé
des crêpes
du beurre
de la confiture
du sirop d'érable
du café
du thé
du lait
du chocolat chaud

ENTRE AMIS

Tu prends le petit déjeuner d'habitude?

Use the breakfast menu on the previous page, if possible.

1. Find out if your partner usually has breakfast.
2. Find out if s/he had breakfast this morning.
3. If so, find out what s/he ate.
4. Ask what s/he drank.

3. Expressing an Opinion

NOTE CULTURELLE

Le croque-monsieur *(open-faced toasted ham and cheese sandwich):* Un des choix les plus populaires dans les cafés et les bistros de France. C'est une tranche de pain au jambon et au fromage qu'on fait griller.

Miam°, je trouve ce croque-monsieur délicieux!	*Yum*
Qu'en penses-tu°, René?	*What's your opinion?*
Je suis d'accord avec toi. Je le trouve très bon.°	*I think it's very good.*
Comment trouves-tu ces épinards?	
Ils sont bons. Je les aime bien.	
Que penses-tu de la pizza aux anchois°?	*anchovies*
Berk°, je la trouve affreuse°.	*Yuck / awful*

▶ **Et vous?** Que pensez-vous du thé au citron? Est-il … délicieux? bon? affreux?

Que pensez-vous des croissants français? Sont-ils … délicieux? bons? affreux?

Que pensez-vous de la glace au chocolat? Est-elle … délicieuse? bonne? affreuse?

Que pensez-vous des soupes froides? Sont-elles … délicieuses? bonnes? affreuses?

F. Les pronoms objets directs *le, la, les*

J'aime beaucoup mes amis.	*I like my friends a lot.*
Je **les** aime beaucoup.	*I like them a lot.*
Mes amis étudient le français.	*My friends study French.*
Ils **l'**étudient.	*They study it.*
Ils ne regardent pas souvent la télé.	*They don't watch TV often.*
Ils ne **la** regardent pas souvent.	*They don't watch it often.*

■ A direct object pronoun replaces a noun that is the direct object of a verb (where no preposition precedes the noun). Object pronouns are placed directly in front of the verb.

direct object pronouns	examples of nouns	examples of pronouns
le	Je déteste **le fromage.**	Je **le** déteste.
la	Je trouve **cette pâtisserie** affreuse.	Je **la** trouve affreuse.
l'	Je n'aime pas **la bière.**	Je ne **l'**aime pas.
les	J'adore **les croque-monsieur.**	Je **les** adore.

*NB: Use **l'** in place of **le** or **la** if the following word begins with a vowel sound.*

Other direct object pronouns will be studied in Ch. 10.

15 **Qu'en penses-tu?** *(What do you think of it/of them?)* Vous êtes à une soirée avec un(e) ami(e). Donnez votre opinion des choix indiqués et demandez l'opinion de votre ami(e). Suivez les modèles.

MODÈLES: hors-d'œuvre
VOUS: **Que penses-tu de ces hors-d'œuvre?**
VOTRE AMI(E): **Je les trouve très bons. Qu'en penses-tu?**
VOUS: **Je suis d'accord. Ils sont délicieux.**

pâtisserie
VOUS: **Que penses-tu de cette pâtisserie?**
VOTRE AMI(E): **Je la trouve affreuse. Qu'en penses-tu?**
VOUS: **Je ne suis pas d'accord. Elle est excellente.**

1. fromage	3. café	5. fruits *(m.)*	7. légumes *(m.)*	9. viande
2. bière	4. glace	6. poisson	8. croque-monsieur	10. salade

G. Quelques expressions avec *avoir*

Review the verb **avoir**, p. 64.

■ A number of idiomatic expressions in French use **avoir** with a noun where English would use *to be* with an adjective.

Use **très** with **faim, soif,** etc. to express the meaning *very.*

Feelings		Opinions/Judgments	
j'ai faim	*I am hungry*	j'ai raison	*I am right*
j'ai soif	*I am thirsty*		*I am wise*
j'ai froid	*I am cold*	j'ai tort	*I am wrong*
j'ai chaud	*I am hot*		*I am unwise*
j'ai sommeil	*I am sleepy*		
j'ai peur	*I am afraid*		

■ **Peur, raison,** and **tort** can be used alone, but are often followed by **de** and an infinitive. **Peur** can also be followed by **de** and a noun.

Paul **a tort de** fumer.	*Paul is wrong to smoke.*
Tu **as raison d'**étudier souvent.	*You are wise to study often.*
Nous **avons peur d'**avoir une mauvaise note.	*We are afraid of getting a bad grade.*
Je **n'ai pas peur des** examens.	*I am not afraid of tests.*

■ When an infinitive is negative, both **ne** and **pas** precede it.

Il a eu tort de **ne pas étudier.**	*He was wrong not to study.*

16 **Explications.** Donnez une explication ou exprimez votre opinion. Complétez les phrases suivantes avec une des expressions idiomatiques qui emploient le verbe **avoir.**

MODÈLE: Olivier ne porte pas de manteau en novembre. Il ...
Il a froid. ou **Il a tort.**

1. Je suis fatigué. J' ...
2. Ah! Quand nous pensons à une bonne pizza au fromage, nous ...
3. Christelle pense qu'on parle espagnol au Portugal. Elle ...
4. Mon frère ... des gros chiens.
5. Vous pensez que notre professeur est charmant? Ah! Vous ...
6. Nous allons boire quelque chose parce que nous ...
7. Cet après-midi je voudrais aller à la piscine. J' ...
8. C'est le mois de décembre et nous ...

17 **Si c'est comme ça** *(If that's the way it is).* Utilisez une ou deux expressions avec **avoir** pour compléter les phrases suivantes.

MODÈLE: Si on travaille beaucoup, on ...
Si on travaille beaucoup, on a faim et soif.

1. On a envie de manger quelque chose si on ...
2. Si on ne va pas aux cours, on ...
3. Si on ne porte pas de manteau en décembre, on ...
4. Si on pense que deux fois quatre font quarante-quatre, on ...
5. S'ils font leurs devoirs, les étudiants ...
6. Si on porte beaucoup de vêtements en été ...
7. Si on ne boit pas d'eau, on ...
8. Si on pense que les professeurs sont méchants, on ...

18 **À vous.** Répondez.

1. À quel(s) moment(s) de la journée avez-vous faim? Que faites-vous quand vous avez faim?
2. À quel(s) moment(s) de la journée avez-vous soif? Que faites-vous?
3. Où vont les étudiants de votre université quand ils ont soif?
4. À quel(s) moment(s) de la journée avez-vous sommeil? Que faites-vous?
5. Pendant quels cours avez-vous envie de dormir?
6. Quels vêtements portez-vous si vous avez froid?
7. Que faites-vous si vous avez chaud?
8. Avez-vous peur d'avoir une mauvaise note?
9. Avez-vous peur avant un examen? Si oui, de quels examens avez-vous peur?
10. Vos professeurs ont-ils toujours raison?

ENTRE AMIS

Que penses-tu de ... ?

1. Find out if your partner is hungry. (S/he is.)
2. Offer him/her something to eat.
3. Find out what s/he thinks of the food.
4. Find out if s/he is thirsty. (S/he is.)
5. Offer him/her something to drink.
6. Find out what s/he thinks of the drink you offered.
7. Find out when the next French test is.
8. Find out if your partner is afraid.
9. Ask what s/he thinks of French tests.

4. Expressing a Preference

Quelle sorte° de sandwichs préfères-tu, Valérie?   *type*
    Je préfère les sandwichs au fromage.
Quelle sorte de pizzas préfères-tu?
    Je préfère les pizzas aux champignons°.   *mushrooms*
Quelle sorte de glace préfères-tu?
    Je préfère la glace à la fraise°.   *strawberry*

▶ **Et vous?**   Que préférez-vous?

Moi, je préfère les sandwichs ...
     au beurre°   *with butter*
     au beurre d'arachide°   *with peanut butter*
     à la confiture°   *with jam*
     au fromage
     au jambon
     à la mayonnaise
     à la moutarde
     au pâté

Et je préfère les pizzas ...
     au fromage
     aux champignons
     aux oignons
     aux œufs°   *with eggs*
     aux anchois
     à l'ail°   *with garlic*

Et je préfère la glace ...
     au chocolat
     à la vanille
     à la fraise
     au café

Point out the French pronunciation of **pizza** [pidza].

Culture: You can point out to students that in France pizza is occasionally served with an egg on it.

Point out that the plural **œufs** is pronounced [ø]. The final **-fs** is silent.

Point out that **ail** is pronounced the same as **Aïe!** [aj].

Review the use of **à** with the definite article, p. 127.

REMARQUE — Use **à** and the definite article to specify ingredients.

une omelette **au fromage**	*a cheese omelet*
une crêpe **à la confiture**	*a crepe with jam*
une pizza **aux champignons**	*a mushroom pizza*
un croissant **au beurre**	*a croissant made with butter*

19 **Quel choix!** Vous êtes dans une pizzeria à Paris. Demandez à la serveuse ou au serveur le choix qu'elle (il) offre. Elle (il) va répondre. Ensuite commandez quelque chose.

MODÈLE: pizzas

> VOUS: **Quelles sortes de pizzas avez-vous?**
> SERVEUSE/SERVEUR: **Nous avons des pizzas au jambon, aux champignons et au fromage.**
> VOUS: **Je voudrais une pizza au fromage et au jambon, s'il vous plaît.**

1. sandwichs   4. crêpes
2. omelettes   5. croissants
3. pizzas   6. glaces

20 **Mes préférences.** Écrivez trois petits paragraphes pour décrire ...

Communication (Interpretive):
Have students guess each
other's choices. This activity can
serve as preparation for the
Début de rédaction, p. 234.

1. les choses que vous mangez souvent.
2. les choses que vous mangez si vous avez très faim.
3. les choses que vous ne mangez jamais.

H. Les verbes comme *préférer*

Vous préférez la glace ou la pâtisserie?	*Do you prefer ice cream or pastry?*
Je préfère la glace.	*I prefer ice cream.*
Espérez-vous aller en France un jour?	*Do you hope to go to France sometime?*
Oui, et **j'espère** aller au Canada aussi.	*Yes, and I hope to go to Canada also.*
Répétez, s'il vous plaît.	*Repeat, please.*
Les étudiants **répètent** après leur professeur.	*The students repeat after their teacher.*

■ The verbs **préférer** *(to prefer),* **espérer** *(to hope),* **répéter** *(to repeat; to practice),* and **exagérer** *(to exaggerate)* are all conjugated as regular **-er** verbs except that before a silent ending (as in the present tense of the **je, tu, il/elle/on,** and **ils/elles** forms), the **-é-** before the ending becomes **-è-**.

Préférer usually is followed
by **le, la, les,** when used with
a noun.

préférer *(to prefer)*			
silent endings		**pronounced endings**	
je	**préfère**	nous	**préférons**
tu	**préfères**	vous	**préférez**
il/elle/on	**préfère**		
ils/elles	**préfèrent**		
passé composé: j'**ai préféré**			

21 **Vos amis et vous.** Interviewez une autre personne d'après le modèle.

MODÈLE: la truite ou les anchois

> VOUS: **Est-ce que vos amis préfèrent la truite ou les anchois?**
> VOTRE PARTENAIRE: **Ils préfèrent la truite.**
> VOUS: **Et vous, qu'est-ce que vous préférez?**
> VOTRE PARTENAIRE: **Moi, je préfère les anchois.**
> VOUS: **Berk!**

Communication (Interpretive & Presentational): Have students report back to their partners as many of their partners' answers as they can remember. Then have them prepare a list of the items they agree on: **Nous préférons ...**

1. le samedi soir ou le lundi matin
2. faire la vaisselle ou faire la cuisine
3. New York ou Los Angeles
4. la politique ou les mathématiques
5. partir en vacances ou travailler
6. étudier ou jouer au tennis
7. le cinéma ou le théâtre
8. le petit déjeuner ou le dîner
9. voyager ou rester à la maison
10. les sandwichs ou les omelettes
11. le coca ou le coca light
12. apprendre les mathématiques ou apprendre le français
13. regarder la télévision ou écouter la radio

Review the choices on p. 216.

22 **Microconversation: Vous déjeunez au restaurant.** Qu'est-ce qu'il y a à manger et à boire? Il y a toujours un choix. Vous préférez autre chose, mais il faut choisir *(you have to choose)*. Suivez *(follow)* le modèle.

MODÈLE: le fromage

> VOUS: **Qu'est-ce que vous avez comme fromage?**
> SERVEUR: **Nous avons du brie et du camembert.**
> VOUS: **Je préfère le chèvre. Vous n'avez pas de chèvre?**
> SERVEUR: **Je regrette, mais le brie et le camembert sont très bons.**
> VOUS: **Très bien, je vais prendre du brie, s'il vous plaît.**

> *(Un peu plus tard)*
> SERVEUR: **Comment trouvez-vous le brie?**
> VOUS: **Je pense qu'il est excellent!**

1. les hors-d'œuvre   2. la viande   3. les légumes
4. le fromage   5. les desserts

ENTRE AMIS

Au snack-bar

1. Find out if your partner is hungry. (S/he is.)
2. Find out if s/he likes sandwiches, pizza, ice cream, etc.
3. Find out what kind of sandwich, etc., s/he prefers.
4. Tell your partner what you are going to order.

Intégration www ◎

Révision

Communication (Presenta-tional & Interpretive): If students do this in writing, they can then try to guess the items on their partner's list.

Communication (Presenta-tional & Interpretive): If students present their lists to the class, others can be asked to recall likes and dislikes. Suggestion: Assign the *Rédaction* at the end of Ch. 8 in the Workbook.

Communication (Interpretive): Encourage students to use the practice test on the Lab Audio Program.

A **À la carte.**

1. Nommez trois sortes de pizzas.
2. Nommez trois sortes de sandwichs.
3. Nommez trois sortes de légumes.
4. Nommez trois sortes de plats principaux.

B **Début de rédaction.** Faites deux listes: (1) les choses que vous aimez manger et boire, et (2) les choses que vous n'aimez pas manger et boire. Ensuite, pour chaque liste, expliquez pourquoi vous aimez/n'aimez pas les choses que vous mentionnez.

MODÈLE: **La pizza aux œufs: je ne l'aime pas beaucoup. Elle n'est pas très bonne. Je préfère la pizza sans œufs.**

C **À vous.** Répondez.

1. Où allez-vous si vous avez faim ou soif?
2. Aimez-vous les sandwichs? Si oui, quelle sorte de sandwich préférez-vous?
3. Qu'est-ce que vous préférez comme pizza? Qu'est-ce que vos amis préfèrent?
4. Si vous allez au restaurant, qu'est-ce que vous commandez d'habitude? Qu'est-ce que vous refusez de manger?
5. Avez-vous pris le petit déjeuner ce matin? Si oui, qu'est-ce que vous avez mangé? Qu'est-ce que vous avez bu?
6. Qu'est-ce que vous buvez le soir d'habitude? Qu'est-ce que vos amis boivent?
7. Qu'est-ce que vous pensez du vin de Californie? du vin de New York? du vin français?
8. Qu'est-ce que vous pensez du fromage américain? du fromage français?
9. Que pensez-vous des repas au restaurant universitaire?
10. À quel moment avez-vous sommeil? Pourquoi?
11. Qu'est-ce que vous espérez faire dans la vie?

ENTRE AMIS

Le menu, s'il vous plaît

You are a waiter (waitress). Use the menu that follows and wait on two cus-tomers. When you have finished taking their order, tell the chef (the teacher) what they are having.

The difference between **un menu** and **une carte** is explained in Ch. 13.

canard à l'orange = *duck in orange sauce*

omelette norvégienne = *baked Alaska*

Communication (Interpretive): Select an item that has sold out, e.g., **la truite.** When the waiter/waitress tells you (as chef) that someone has selected this item, tell him/her **il n'y a plus de ...** The waiter/waitress then has to inform the "customer."

Chez Jacques

Menu à 20 euros

assiette de crudités
soupe à l'oignon
pâté du chef
tarte à l'oignon
salade de tomates

bœuf bourguignon
truite aux amandes
canard à l'orange
steak-frites
poulet frites

salade

fromage

omelette norvégienne
mousse au chocolat
tarte maison
glace

Boisson non comprise; service compris

Négociations:

For complete instructions on how to prepare for and to use this activity, see *Négociations* on the Class Prep CD-ROM.

Video for Chapter 8: A. Video worksheets *(Cahier)*; B. ACE Video practice test (WWW); C. CD-ROM

Dînons-nous ensemble? Interviewez les autres étudiants pour trouver votre partenaire. C'est la personne qui a le même menu que vous. Les autres menus sont dans l'appendice D.

MODÈLE: **Qu'est-ce que tu prends comme hors-d'œuvre?**
Qu'est-ce que tu vas boire?

A

	votre partenaire	**VOUS**
hors-d'œuvre	crudités	salade de tomates
plat principal	truite	poulet
légume	haricots verts	petits pois
fromage	emmenthal	chèvre
dessert	glace	fruits
boisson	vin blanc	vin rouge

Lecture I

Ⓐ **Imaginez la scène.** Deux personnes prennent le petit déjeuner ensemble. Imaginez cette scène. Répondez aux questions suivantes.

1. Qu'est-ce qu'il y a sur la table?
2. Qui sont les deux personnes?
3. Que font-elles?
4. Que boivent-elles?
5. De quoi est-ce qu'elles parlent?
6. Quel temps fait-il?

Déjeuner du matin

Il a mis[1] le café
Dans la tasse
Il a mis le lait
Dans la tasse de café
Il a mis le sucre
Dans le café au lait
Avec la petite cuiller[2]
Il a tourné
Il a bu le café au lait
Et il a reposé[3] la tasse
Sans me parler

Il a allumé[4]
Une cigarette
Il a fait des ronds[5]
Avec la fumée
Il a mis les cendres[6]
Dans le cendrier[7]
Sans me parler
Sans me regarder

Il s'est levé
Il a mis
Son chapeau sur sa tête[8]
Il a mis
Son manteau de pluie[9]
Parce qu'il pleuvait[10]
Et il est parti
Sous la pluie
Sans une parole[11]
Sans me regarder
Et moi j'ai pris
Ma tête dans ma main[12]
Et j'ai pleuré.

Jacques Prévert

---

1. *He put*   2. *spoon*   3. *he set down*   4. *He lit*   5. *rings*   6. *ashes*   7. *ashtray*   8. *head*   9. *rain*
10. *it was raining*   11. *a word*   12. *hand*

Ⓑ **Questions.** Répondez.

1. Où sont ces personnes?
2. Qui sont les deux personnes? (Imaginez)
3. Quels problèmes y a-t-il? (Imaginez)
4. Est-ce que ce poème est triste? Expliquez votre réponse.

Communication (Presentational): Be prepared with props: a cup, a spoon, a cigarette and ashtray, etc.

Ⓒ **Jouez cette scène.** Faites tous les gestes nécessaires et présentez le poème *Déjeuner du matin* sans parler.

Lecture II →

A **Étude du vocabulaire.** Lisez la lecture suivante et essayez d'identifier les mots français qui correspondent aux mots anglais suivants.

1. *raw egg* _____
2. *soup spoon* _____
3. *bread crust* _____
4. *corn* _____
5. *olive oil* _____
6. *frying pan* _____
7. *peel* _____
8. *salt and pepper* _____

Comparison & Culture: Have students compare this with the Caesar salad with which they are familiar.

Salade Cæsar aux endives

Pour 4 personnes. Préparation: 20 minutes. Cuisson: 10 minutes

Ingrédients
endives: 8
maïs: 1 bocal
blancs de poulet: 3
pain de mie: 5 tranches
tomates: 2
huile
sel, poivre

Pour la sauce Cæsar:
ail: 1 gousse
œuf: 1
jus de citron: 2 cuillers à soupe
moutarde de Dijon: 5 cuillers à café
huile d'olive: 180 ml
parmesan: 30 gr

Préparation
Épluchez et émincez l'ail grossièrement.

Préparez la sauce dans un mixer en mettant l'ail, l'œuf cru, le jus de citron, la moutarde et le parmesan. Mixez le tout, ajoutez l'huile puis mixez à nouveau. Réservez au frais. Cette sauce ne doit pas être préparée plus d'une heure à l'avance.

Ôtez la croûte du pain de mie, puis coupez les tranches en petits carrés. Mettez un peu d'huile dans une poêle et faites frire les carrés de pain. Placez-les sur du papier absorbant.

Coupez les blancs de poulet en petits morceaux de la taille d'une bouchée et faites-les cuire à la poêle dans un peu d'huile d'olive. Réservez et laissez refroidir.

Coupez les endives en lamelles et les tomates en petits cubes. Versez dans un saladier, ajoutez les petits maïs, les croûtons et le poulet. Versez la sauce Cæsar, salez, poivrez et mélangez.

Servez.

D'après le site web de *CuizineAZ.com*

B **Identifiez les ingrédients.** Relisez la recette et ensuite faites une liste des ingrédients que vous reconnaissez d'après les catégories suivantes.

1. la viande
2. les légumes
3. les épices et assaisonnements
4. le fromage

C **Familles de mots.** Essayez de deviner le sens des mots suivants.

1. saler, le sel
2. poivrer, le poivre
3. la salade, le saladier

> Practice this vocabulary with the flashcards on the *Entre amis* web site.

VOCABULAIRE ACTIF

Boissons
un apéritif *before-dinner drink*
du beaujolais *Beaujolais*
du bordeaux *Bordeaux*

Hors-d'œuvre ou soupe
des crudités *(f. pl.) raw vegetables*
un hors-d'œuvre *appetizer*
du pâté *pâté (meat spread)*
de la salade de tomates *tomato salad*
de la soupe *soup*
de la soupe de légumes *vegetable soup*

Viandes
du bœuf *beef*
du jambon *ham*
du porc *pork*
du poulet *chicken*
de la viande *meat*

Poissons
des anchois *(m. pl.) anchovies*
du saumon *salmon*
de la truite *trout*

Légumes
de l'ail *(m.) garlic*
des épinards *(m. pl.) spinach*
des frites *(f. pl.) French fries*

des haricots verts *(m. pl.) green beans*
un légume *vegetable*
un oignon *onion*
des petits pois *(m. pl.) peas*
une pomme de terre *potato*
du riz *rice*

Fromages
du brie *Brie*
du camembert *Camembert*
du chèvre *goat cheese*
de l'emmental *(m.) Swiss cheese*

D'autres choses à manger
du beurre *butter*
du beurre d'arachide *peanut butter*
des céréales *(f. pl.) cereal*
des champignons *(m.) mushrooms*
de la confiture *jam*
un croissant *croissant*
un croque-monsieur *open-faced toasted ham and cheese sandwich*
de la mayonnaise *mayonnaise*
de la moutarde *mustard*
un œuf *egg*
une omelette *omelet*
du pain *bread*
du pain grillé *toast*
de la salade *salad*
un sandwich *sandwich*
une tomate *tomato*

Desserts
un bonbon *candy*
une crêpe *crepe, French pancake*
un dessert *dessert*
des fraises *(f.) strawberries*
un fruit *fruit*
du gâteau *cake*
de la glace (à la vanille) *(vanilla) ice cream*
des pâtisseries *(f.) pastries*
une pomme *apple*
de la tarte *pie*

Quantités et mesures
une assiette *plate*
une boîte *box; can*
une bouteille *bottle*
un kilo *kilogram*
un morceau *piece*
une tranche *slice*

D'autres noms
l'addition *(f.) (restaurant) bill, check*
un choix *choice*
un(e) client(e) *customer*
le déjeuner *lunch*
un garçon *waiter; boy*
le petit déjeuner *breakfast*
le plat principal *main course, main dish*
un repas *meal*

un serveur *waiter*
une serveuse *waitress*
le théâtre *theater*

Adjectifs
affreux (affreuse) *horrible*
délicieux (délicieuse) *delicious*
quelques *a few; some*

Verbes
apporter *to bring*
apprendre *to learn; to teach*
avoir chaud *to be hot*
avoir faim *to be hungry*
avoir froid *to be cold*
avoir peur *to be afraid*
avoir raison *to be right; to be wise*
avoir soif *to be thirsty*
avoir sommeil *to be sleepy*
avoir tort *to be wrong; to be unwise*
boire *to drink*
commander *to order*

comprendre *to understand*
décider *to decide*
espérer *to hope*
penser *to think*
préférer *to prefer*
prendre *to take; to eat, to drink*
répéter *to repeat; to practice*

Pronoms objets directs
le *him; it*
la *her; it*
les *them*

Adverbes
naturellement *naturally*
peu (de) *little; few*
plus (ne ... plus) *no more; no longer*

Expressions utiles
à propos de *regarding, on the subject of*
au contraire *on the contrary*
Berk! *Yuck! Awful!*
bien sûr *of course*
Encore à boire (manger)? *More to drink (eat)?*
Encore de ... ? *More ... ?*
Je n'insiste pas. *I won't insist.*
je regrette *I'm sorry*
Le service est compris. *The tip is included.*
Miam! *Yum!*
Quelle(s) sorte(s) de ... ? *What kind(s) of ... ?*
Qu'en penses-tu? *What do you think of it (of them)?*
Qu'est-ce que vous avez comme ... ? *What do you have for (in the way of) ... ?*
sans façon *honestly; no kidding*
si vous insistez *if you insist*

Où est-ce qu'on l'achète?

Buts communicatifs
Finding out where things are sold
Describing an illness or injury
Making a purchase

Structures utiles
Les verbes en **-re**
Depuis
Le verbe **acheter**
Les pronoms relatifs

Culture
• *À propos*
La pharmacie
Le tabac
Les petits magasins
On achète des fleurs

• *Il y a un geste*
Désolé(e)

• *Lectures*
«Il pleure dans mon cœur»
Hystérie anti-tabac;
Les mesures du président

Coup d'envoi

Prise de contact

Les achats

Où est-ce qu'on achète° des journaux?	*buy*
On peut° aller ...	*you can*
au bureau de tabac.	
à la gare.	
au kiosque°.	*newsstand*
Où est-ce qu'on achète des cadeaux°?	*gifts*
On peut aller ...	
chez un fleuriste°.	*florist's shop*
dans une boutique.	
dans un grand magasin°.	*department store*
au marché aux puces°.	*flea market*
Où est-ce qu'on achète quelque chose à manger?	
On peut aller ...	
au marché°.	*(open-air) market*
au supermarché.	
à l'épicerie.	

▶ **Et vous?** Qu'est-ce que vous voulez acheter?

Où allez-vous faire cet achat°?   *purchase*

Conversation

À la pharmacie

Grayson Smith est un touriste. Il désire acheter un journal américain et il pense qu'on achète les journaux à la pharmacie. Mais en France on n'y vend pas de journaux.

 This and all conversations are recorded, for your convenience, on the Student Audio. Use the Student Audio to help you learn this material.

GRAYSON SMITH:	Bonjour, Monsieur. Vous avez le *Herald Tribune?*	
PHARMACIEN:	Comment? Qu'est-ce que vous dites?°	*What are you saying?*
GRAYSON SMITH:	Je voudrais acheter le *Herald Tribune.*	
PHARMACIEN:	Qu'est-ce que c'est?	
GRAYSON SMITH:	C'est un journal.	
PHARMACIEN:	Mais on ne vend° pas de journaux ici, Monsieur.	*sell*
GRAYSON SMITH:	Vous n'en° avez pas?	*any*
PHARMACIEN:	Non, Monsieur. C'est une pharmacie. Nous vendons seulement des médicaments°.	*medicine*
GRAYSON SMITH:	Mais aux États-Unis on achète les journaux à la pharmacie.	
PHARMACIEN:	Désolé°, Monsieur, mais nous sommes en France.	*Sorry*
GRAYSON SMITH:	Pouvez-vous me dire° où on peut trouver des journaux, s'il vous plaît?	*Can you tell me*
PHARMACIEN:	Ça dépend°. Si vous cherchez un journal d'un autre pays, il faut aller au bureau de tabac qui est dans la rue° de la Gare.	*depends* / *street*
GRAYSON SMITH:	Merci, Monsieur. Vous êtes très aimable°.	*kind*

After practicing the *Conversation*, have students complete ex. A in the Workbook.

▶ **Jouez ces rôles.** Répétez la conversation avec votre partenaire. Utilisez le nom de votre journal préféré.

Il y a un geste

This gesture is used in the video, *Modules 1 & 4.*

Désolé(e). When saying **désolé(e)**, the shoulders are hunched and the upturned palms are often raised. Sarcasm is added to the gesture by also pursing one's lips and raising one's eyebrows.

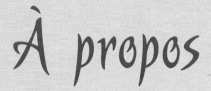
À propos

> **Comparison:** Have students share where and how often they shop for food or gifts. Ask them to try to describe (1) the role of bread in their diet: amount and type; (2) the giving of flowers in their culture.

Pourquoi le pharmacien ne vend-il pas de journal à Monsieur Smith?

a. Parce que Monsieur Smith est américain.
b. Parce que le pharmacien ne comprend pas Monsieur Smith quand il parle français.
c. Parce qu'on vend les journaux dans un magasin différent.

Quel est le meilleur cadeau si on est invité à dîner dans une famille française?

a. une boîte de bonbons
b. une bouteille de vin
c. un bouquet de fleurs

La pharmacie

Pharmacists in France don't sell magazines, newspapers, candy, drinks, or greeting cards. They will fill a prescription and are much less reticent than North American pharmacists to suggest treatments for nonserious illnesses, including a cold, a sore throat, and a headache. In this respect French pharmacies are a convenient and helpful solution for travelers who become ill.

> Use the video, *Modules 7*, **Les boutiques et les petits magasins,** and *11*, **Le tabac,** to help set the scene.

Le tabac

One can buy magazines, newspapers, and postcards at the tobacco shop. Among the most popular English language publications available in France are the *International Herald Tribune* and the international edition of *Time* magazine. Since **le bureau de tabac** is under state license, one can also purchase stamps and cigarettes. Smoking is more widespread in France than in North America. While there have been some efforts to suggest that smoking is bad for your health, the state monopoly on the sale of tobacco has meant that, until recently, little was done to restrict the purchase or the use of cigarettes. However, for several years smoking has been confined to specific areas in public places. Fines can be levied on those who refuse to obey.

Les petits magasins

Although supermarkets (**supermarchés**) and even larger, all-in-one **hypermarchés** are found in every French city, the tourist in France will readily discover a variety of shops that specialize in one type of food. **La boulangerie** *(bakery)*, **la pâtisserie** *(pastry shop)*, **la boucherie** *(butcher)*, **la charcuterie** *(pork butcher, delicatessen)*, and **l'épicerie** *(grocery store)* are found in many neighborhoods. Not only, for example, do the French buy fresh bread daily, they will also go out of their way and pay a bit more, if necessary, to get bread that they consider more tasty. The French often use the possessive adjective to refer to **mon boulanger** *(my baker)*, a phenomenon that is very rare or nonexistent in North America.

On achète des fleurs

Flower shops play an important role in French culture. More than any other gift, flowers are the number one choice when one is invited to dinner. Unless you plan on giving a dozen, choose an uneven (**impair**) number of flowers. Various reasons are given for the custom of offering three, five, or seven flowers rather than an even number. These include the implication that the donor has carefully selected them or that they may be more attractively arranged.

Brainstorm for examples before putting students in pairs.

▶ **À vous.** Entrez dans une pharmacie et essayez d'acheter *(try to buy)* un magazine—*Time, Paris Match, Elle,* etc. Répondez au pharmacien.

PHARMACIEN: Bonjour, Monsieur (Madame/Mademoiselle).
VOUS: _____

PHARMACIEN: Comment? Qu'est-ce que vous dites?
VOUS: _____

PHARMACIEN: Mais on ne vend pas de magazines ici.
VOUS: _____

COMMUNIQUÉ

conseils de saison

Pas de temps à perdre avec les états grippaux !

Déplacements professionnels, surcharge de travail, dossiers importants, obligations familiales... Les états grippaux ne s'embarrassent pas de votre emploi du temps, ni de vos impératifs professionnels et familiaux ! Alors, gérez-les... en vous tenant prêt à agir dès les premiers symptômes.

ÉTATS GRIPPAUX

oscillococcinum

BOIRON

ENTRE AMIS

Au tabac

Your partner will take the role of the proprietor of a tobacco shop.

1. Ask if s/he has a certain newspaper or magazine.
2. S/he will say s/he doesn't.
3. Ask if s/he has bread, milk, wine, etc.
4. S/he will say s/he is sorry, but s/he doesn't.
5. Find out where you can find the things you are looking for.
6. Get directions.

Prononciation

🎧 Use the Student Audio to help practice pronunciation.

Le son [ʀ]

■ The most common consonant sound in French is [ʀ]. While there are acceptable variations of this sound, [ʀ] is normally a friction-like sound made in roughly the same area of the mouth as [g] and [k]. Keeping the tongue tip behind the lower teeth, the friction sound is made when the back of the tongue comes close to the back part of the mouth (pharynx). Use the word **berk!** to practice several times. It might also be helpful to use the following process: (1) say "ahhh ... ," (2) change "ahhh ... " to "ahrrr ... " by beginning to gargle as you say "ahhh ... ," (3) add [g] at the beginning and say **gare** several times, (4) say **garçon.** Then practice the following words.

Culture & Comparison: The poem **Il pleure dans mon cœur** at the end of this chapter will provide further practice for the [R].

- pour
  sur
  bonjour
  bonsoir

- garçon
  merci
  parlez

- russe
  rien
  Robert
  rouge

- très
  trois
  crois
  droit
  frère
  écrire

- votre
  quatre
  notre
  propre
  septembre

 www **Réalités culturelles**

Le français en Afrique

See the map of francophone Africa on the inside back cover.

La colonisation a formé des liens contradictoires entre la France et l'Afrique. Dans la majorité des anciennes colonies d'Afrique, le français est la langue officielle ou la langue véhiculaire. Pour plusieurs intellectuels et hommes politiques africains, ce «décombre du régime colonial» est une source de malaise. Il faut, pensent-ils, s'exprimer dans la langue maternelle. Pour d'autres, comme le président du Sénégal, Abdoulaye Wade, la présence et l'universalité de la langue française, perpétuée et célébrée par l'institution de la francophonie, est un avantage commercial et politique. Le français représente un outil de modernité et une solution pratique à la communication dans les pays plurilingues de l'Afrique noire.

Culture & Communities: Review the *Réalités Culturelles* on pp. 5, 20, 68, 152, and 178.

Vocabulaire: liens *ties*, malaise *discontent*, outil *tool*

Buts communicatifs

1. Finding Out Where Things Are Sold

Qu'est-ce qu'on vend à la pharmacie?
　　On y vend ...
　　　　des médicaments.
　　　　des cachets d'aspirine°.
　　　　des pastilles°.
　　　　du dentifrice°.
　　　　des pilules°.
　　　　du savon°.
Qu'est-ce qu'on vend au bureau de tabac?
　　On y vend ...
　　　　du tabac°.
　　　　un paquet° de cigarettes.
　　　　des timbres°.
　　　　des télécartes.
　　　　des journaux.
　　　　des magazines.
　　　　des cartes postales.

aspirin tablets
lozenges
toothpaste
pills
soap

tobacco
pack
stamps

> Contrary to the general rule requiring a pronounced final **-c** (**avec, chic, Luc, Marc,** etc.), **tabac** has a silent final **-c.**

> Point out that this is true for **blanc** as well.

A. Les verbes en *-re*

J'**attends** mon amie avec impatience.	*I'm anxiously waiting for my friend.*
Entendez-vous son train?	*Do you hear her train?*
Elle **a répondu** «oui» à mon invitation.	*She responded "yes" to my invitation.*
Elle aime **rendre visite** à ses amis.	*She likes to visit her friends.*
La voilà. Elle **descend** du train.	*There she is. She's getting off the train.*
J'espère qu'elle n'**a** pas **perdu** sa valise.	*I hope she hasn't lost her suitcase.*

> Be careful to distinguish between the endings for **-re** verbs and those of **-er** verbs, p. 38.

vendre *(to sell)*		
je	**vend**	**s**
tu	**vend**	**s**
il/elle/on	**vend**	
nous	**vend**	**ons**
vous	**vend**	**ez**
ils/elles	**vend**	**ent**
passé composé: j'**ai vendu**		

■ A number of frequently used verbs are conjugated like **vendre**.

V O C A B U L A I R E

Be careful to avoid confusing **attendre** and **entendre**. Review the nasal vowels on p. 93. **Entendre** begins with a nasal vowel.

The verb **visiter** is normally reserved for use with *places*. **Rendre visite à** is used with *persons*.

Quelques verbes réguliers en -re

attendre (un ami)	*to wait (for a friend)*
descendre	*to go down; to get out of*
entendre (un bruit)	*to hear (a noise)*
perdre (une valise)	*to lose (a suitcase)*
rendre (les devoirs)	*to give back (homework)*
rendre visite à quelqu'un	*to visit someone*
répondre (à une question)	*to answer (a question)*

■ The singular (**je, tu, il/elle/on**) forms of each of these verbs are pronounced alike.

| je perds | tu perds | il perd | [pɛʀ] |
| je rends | tu rends | elle rend | [ʀɑ̃] |

■ There is no ending added to the stem in the **il/elle/on** forms of regular **-re** verbs. In inversion of the **il/elle/on** form, the **-d** is pronounced [t].

| | ven**d**ons | [vɑ̃dɔ̃] | ven**d**ent | [vɑ̃d] |
| *But:* | ven**d**-on | [vɑ̃tɔ̃] | ven**d**-elle | [vɑ̃tɛl] |

■ Past participles of regular **-re** verbs are formed by adding **-u** to the present tense verb stem.

ven**du**
per**du**
répon**du**

Comparison: Point out the differences in the use or nonuse of prepositions in the English verbs *to visit, to answer,* and *to wait for.*

■ **Rendre visite** and **répondre** are used with the preposition **à** before an object.

J'**ai rendu visite à** mon frère. *I visited my brother.*

Anne **répond** toujours **aux** questions du professeur. *Anne always answers the teacher's questions.*

■ **Attendre** does not use a preposition before an object.

J'**attends** mes amis. *I am waiting for my friends.*

■ In the expressions **perdre patience** and **perdre courage** the article or possessive adjective is omitted.

Le professeur a **perdu patience** avec moi.

But: J'ai **perdu** *mes* devoirs.

1 **Mes professeurs et moi.** Indiquez si *oui* ou *non* vos professeurs font les choses suivantes. Et vous, est-ce que vous les faites?

MODÈLE: perdre des livres
Mes professeurs ne perdent jamais de livres, mais moi, je perds quelquefois des livres.

Suggestion: Point out that since **perdre patience** has no article, students should not try to add **de** in the negative.

1. perdre patience
2. attendre les vacances avec impatience
3. répondre à beaucoup de questions
4. rendre visite à des amis
5. vendre des livres

2 **Un petit sketch: Au bureau de tabac.** Lisez ou jouez le sketch suivant et répondez ensuite aux questions.

M. SMITH: Madame, est-ce que vous avez le *Herald Tribune?*
LA MARCHANDE: Non, Monsieur. Je n'ai plus de journaux américains.
M. SMITH: Où est-ce que je peux acheter un journal américain, s'il vous plaît?
LA MARCHANDE: Il faut aller à la gare.
M. SMITH: Pourquoi à la gare?
LA MARCHANDE: Parce qu'on vend des journaux d'autres pays à la gare.
M. SMITH: Merci, Madame.
LA MARCHANDE: Je vous en prie, Monsieur.

QUESTIONS
1. Quelle sorte de journal Monsieur Smith cherche-t-il?
2. La marchande vend-elle des journaux?
3. A-t-elle le *Herald Tribune?* Expliquez.
4. Où Monsieur Smith va-t-il aller? Pourquoi?
5. Où vend-on des journaux dans votre ville?
6. Quel journal préférez-vous?

3 **À vous.** Répondez.

1. Où vend-on des cigarettes dans votre pays?
2. Qu'est-ce que les pharmaciens vendent dans votre pays?
3. À qui rendez-vous visite pendant les vacances?
4. Attendez-vous les vacances avec impatience? Pourquoi (pas)?
5. Dans quelles circonstances perdez-vous patience?
6. Est-ce que vous répondez rapidement aux lettres de vos amis?
7. À qui avez-vous répondu récemment?

ENTRE AMIS

À la pharmacie

Your partner will play the role of a pharmacist.

1. Find out if your partner sells stamps. (S/he doesn't.)
2. Ask if s/he sells postcards.
3. S/he will say that s/he is sorry, but s/he doesn't.
4. Ask where you can buy stamps and postcards.
5. Your partner will explain where these items are sold.
6. Ask your partner for directions.
7. Be sure to say thanks.

2. Describing an Illness or Injury

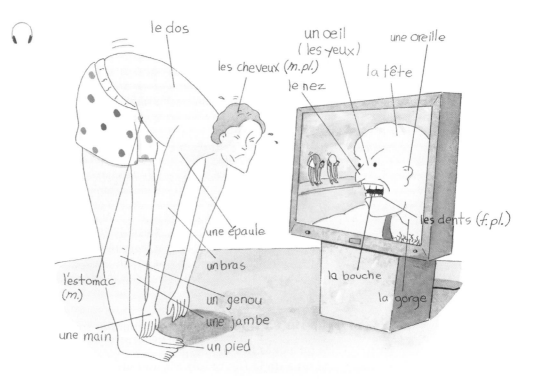

le dos

un œil (les yeux)   une oreille

les cheveux (*m.pl.*)   la tête

le nez

les dents (*f.pl.*)

une épaule

un bras

l'estomac (*m.*)

la bouche

un genou   la gorge

une jambe

une main

un pied

Jacques, qu'est-ce que tu as?° Tu as l'air° malade.   *what's the matter with you? /*
J'ai mal au dos° depuis° hier. J'ai trop fait   *You look / My back hurts /*
de gymnastique.   *since*
Oh là là! Moi aussi, mais j'ai mal aux jambes, moi!

▶ **Et vous?** Avez-vous eu la grippe cette année? Avez-vous souvent mal à
la tête?
Et les étudiants? S'ils étudient trop, ont-ils mal aux yeux?

REMARQUES

1. Like the word **tabac, estomac** has a silent final **-c.**
2. **Si** *(if)* becomes **s'** only before the words **il** and **ils.** Before other words
beginning with vowels, it does not elide.

    Si on a mal à la tête, on prend des cachets d'aspirine.
    Si elle est malade, elle doit rester au lit.
    But: **S'il** est malade, il doit rester au lit.

Review the contractions on
p. 127.

3. **Avoir mal à** is used with the definite article and a part of the body to
express that one has a sore hand, arm, etc.

    Mon fils **a mal au bras.**   *My son's arm hurts.*
    J'**ai mal à la gorge.**   *I have a sore throat.*
    Avez-vous **mal aux dents?**   *Do you have a toothache?*

The masculine form of the
adjective can also be used after
avoir l'air to make agreement
with the word **air.**

4. **Avoir l'air** *(to seem, appear, look)* is often followed by an adjective.

    Hélène **a l'air sportive.**   Jean-Yves **a l'air fatigué.**

VOCABULAIRE

Qu'est-ce que vous avez?

Je suis malade.	*I'm sick.*
J'ai de la fièvre.	*I have a fever.*
J'ai un rhume.	*I have a cold.*
J'ai la grippe.	*I have the flu.*
J'ai le nez qui coule.	*I have a runny nose.*
Je tousse.	*I am coughing.*

J'ai mal ...

à l'estomac.	*I have a stomachache. My stomach hurts.*
aux oreilles.	*My ears hurt.*
au pied.	*I have a sore foot. My foot hurts.*

Je suis ...

déçu(e).	*I'm disappointed.*
déprimé(e).	*I'm depressed.*
triste.	*I'm sad.*

4 Ça ne va pas. Complétez les phrases suivantes.

MODÈLE: Si on a de la fièvre, ...
Si on a de la fièvre, on est malade.
ou
Si on a de la fièvre, on a peut-être la grippe.

1. Si on regarde trop la télé-vision, ...
2. Si on danse trop souvent, ...
3. Si on boit trop, ...
4. Si on a le nez qui coule, ...
5. Si on tousse beaucoup, ...
6. Si on mange trop, ...
7. Si on fume trop, ...
8. Si on écrit trop, ...
9. Si on étudie trop, ...
10. Si on fait une trop longue pro-menade, ...
11. Si on entend trop de bruit, ...
12. Si on mange trop de bonbons, ..
13. Si on skie mal, ...
14. Si on passe trop d'examens, ...

5 Pauvres étudiants! Répondez aux questions suivantes.

1. Que prenez-vous si vous avez la grippe?
2. Est-ce que vous restez au lit si vous êtes malade?
3. Qu'est-ce que vous faites si vous avez un rhume?
4. Quand les étudiants ont-ils mal à la tête?
5. Quand les étudiants ont-ils mal aux pieds?
6. Quand les étudiants ont-ils mal à l'estomac?
7. Fumez-vous des cigarettes? Pourquoi ou pourquoi pas?

Communication (Interpretive): To review the parts of the body, play «**Jacques a dit**» *(Simon says)*, using **Touchez ...** Alternate: Play a game of charades in which students act out particular illnesses. The rest of the class has to guess what's wrong.

Culture: Encourage students to use **ça dépend** to show that some of their answers may not be clear-cut.

6 **Aïe!** Utilisez les expressions suivantes pour faire des phrases, mais ajoutez une explication *(add an explanation)* avec **si** ou **parce que.**

MODÈLES: **Les étudiants ont mal aux yeux s'ils étudient trop.**
J'ai mal à la tête parce que je passe trop d'examens.

		la tête
		le dos
		les bras
		les yeux
		la main
les étudiants		les jambes
je	avoir mal	les pieds	si ...
un(e) de mes ami(e)s		les dents	parce que ...
		la gorge
		l'estomac
		le nez
		l'épaule
		le genou

B. *Depuis*

Depuis combien de temps habites-tu ici?	*How long (for how much time) have you been living here?*
J'habite ici **depuis un an.**	*I've been living here for a year.*
Depuis quand étudies-tu le français?	*How long (since when) have you been studying French?*
J'étudie le français **depuis septembre.**	*I've been studying French since September.*

■ Use **depuis combien de temps** or **depuis quand** with the present tense to ask about something that has already begun but is *still continuing.* **Depuis combien de temps** asks for the length of time so far and **depuis quand** asks for the starting date.

verb (present tense) + **depuis** + { length of time / starting date }

Depuis combien de temps ... ?	*For how much time ... ?*
Depuis quand ... ?	*Since when ... ?*

Review expressions of time in Ch. 6, p. 162.

■ In the affirmative, the English translation of the present tense verb and **depuis** is usually *has (have) been … ing for* a certain length of time or *since* a certain date.

| Chantal **habite** à Chicago **depuis un an.** | *Chantal has been living in Chicago for a year.* |
| Chantal **habite** à Chicago **depuis février dernier.** | *Chantal has been living in Chicago since last February.* |

■ To state that something has *not* happened for a period of time, however, the negative of the passé composé is used with **depuis.**

| Je **n'ai pas été** malade **depuis** six mois. | *I haven't been sick for six months.* |
| Mes parents **n'ont pas écrit depuis** deux semaines. | *My parents haven't written for two weeks.* |

ATTENTION

Depuis is used to talk about situations that are still going on. To ask or state how much time was spent doing something that has already been *completed,* use **pendant** with the passé composé.

| **J'étudie depuis** deux heures. | *I've been studying for two hours (and I haven't finished yet).* |
| *But:* **J'ai étudié pendant** deux heures. | *I studied for two hours (and now I'm finished).* |

7 **Ils sont tous malades. Qu'est-ce qu'ils doivent faire?**
D'abord utilisez les expressions entre parenthèses pour indiquer depuis combien de temps chaque personne est malade. Ensuite répondez aux questions qui suivent.

MODÈLE: Virginie (pieds / deux jours)
Virginie a mal aux pieds depuis deux jours.
Qui doit changer de chaussures?
Virginie doit changer de chaussures.

1. Michel (gorge / deux heures).
2. Madame Matté (dents / une semaine).
3. Anne (yeux / un mois).
4. Monsieur Monneau (fièvre / ce matin).
5. Guy (genou / trois mois).

QUESTIONS

1. Qui doit changer de lunettes?
2. Qui doit se coucher et doit rester au lit?
3. Qui ne doit plus jouer au tennis?
4. Qui ne doit plus fumer et doit prendre des pastilles?
5. Qui doit aller chez le dentiste?

8 **Comment allez-vous?** Utilisez les expressions suivantes pour faire des phrases.

MODÈLES: **Mon frère est malade depuis trois mois.**

Je n'ai pas été malade depuis cinq ans.

Je n'ai pas eu mal à la tête depuis cinq ans.

		malade	
je		rhume	
ma sœur	(ne ... pas) avoir	fièvre	depuis ...
mon frère	(ne ... pas) être	déprimé(e)	
un(e) de mes ami(e)s		mal ...	
		fatigué(e)	

9 **Une interview.** Posez des questions logiques avec **depuis** ou **pendant**. Votre partenaire va répondre.

MODÈLES: parler français

VOUS: **Depuis combien de temps parles-tu français?**

VOTRE PARTENAIRE: **Je parle français depuis six mois.**

regarder la télé hier soir

VOUS: **Pendant combien de temps as-tu regardé la télé hier soir?**

VOTRE PARTENAIRE: **J'ai regardé la télé pendant une heure.**

1. étudier le français
2. étudier hier soir
3. habiter à l'adresse que tu as maintenant
4. écouter la radio ce matin
5. être étudiant(e) à cette université
6. faire cet exercice

ENTRE AMIS

Tu es malade depuis longtemps?

1. Greet your partner and inquire about his/her health. (S/he is sick.)
2. Find out what the matter is.
3. Find out how long s/he has been sick.
4. Suggest a remedy.

3. Making a Purchase

Où vas-tu Alain?

Je vais faire des achats.

De quoi as-tu besoin?°   *What do you need?*

J'ai besoin de toutes sortes de choses.°   *I need all kinds of things.*

J'ai besoin de pain, de bœuf, de saucisses°,   *sausages*
de légumes et de fruits.

J'ai besoin d'un livre et de fleurs° aussi.   *flowers*

Je vais acheter° ...   *to buy*

    du pain à la boulangerie,

    du bœuf à la boucherie,

    des saucisses à la charcuterie°,   *delicatessen*

    des légumes et des fruits à l'épicerie,

    des fleurs chez un fleuriste

    et un livre à la librairie.

Alors, j'ai besoin d'argent° pour payer   *money*
tout cela.°   *that*

▶ **Et vous?** De quoi avez-vous besoin?

NOTE CULTURELLE
Les deux premiers chiffres (*numbers*) dans un numéro de téléphone indiquent une région de France et les deux suivants représentent un département à l'intérieur de cette région. 02 ici représente la zone à l'ouest de Paris; 41 est le Maine-et-Loire où se trouve la ville d'Angers.

REMARQUES

1. **Avoir besoin** *(to need)* works much like **avoir envie**. It is used with **de** and an infinitive or a noun. If **avoir besoin** is used with a noun, the definite article is usually omitted.

J'**ai besoin d'**étudier.   *I need to study.*
Nous **avons besoin de** légumes et **d'**eau minérale.   *We need vegetables and mineral water.*

2. Use **un (une)** with **avoir besoin d'** to say that *one* item is needed.

Vous **avez besoin d'une** feuille de papier.   *You need a sheet of paper.*

Tu as besoin d'autre chose?

10 **Où faut-il aller?** Où est-ce qu'on trouve les produits suivants? Suivez *(follow)* le modèle.

MODÈLE: pâté **Si on a besoin de pâté, il faut aller à la charcuterie.**

1. épinards
2. médicaments
3. un kilo d'oranges
4. un rôti de bœuf
5. croissants
6. fleurs
7. jambon
8. un livre
9. cigarettes

After students have worked in pairs, have a stand-up drill. Each student has to say a sentence starting with **Si ...**

C. Le verbe *acheter*

Mon père va **acheter** une autre voiture.

Nous **achetons** nos livres à la librairie.

On **achète** un journal au bureau de tabac.

J'**ai acheté** cinq kilos de pommes de terre.

Review the formation of **préférer,** p. 232.

■ As you have already learned with **préférer,** certain verbs change their spelling of the verb stem of the present tense depending on whether or not the ending is pronounced.

Vous préf**é**rez le blanc ou le rouge?
Je préf**è**re le rouge.

Rules governing mute [ə] will be
presented in Ch. 15.

■ The verb **acheter** also contains a spelling change in the verb stem of the present tense. When the ending is not pronounced, the **-e-** before the **-t-** becomes **-è**.

acheter *(to buy)*			
silent endings		*pronounced endings*	
j'	**achète**	nous	**achetons**
tu	**achètes**	vous	**achetez**
il/elle/on	**achète**		
ils/elles	**achètent**		

passé composé: j'**ai acheté**

■ **Nous achetons tout ça.** On fait des achats. Utilisez les expressions suivantes pour faire des phrases. Utilisez la forme négative, si vous voulez.

MODÈLES: **J'achète de la glace pour mes amis.**

Nous n'achetons jamais de cigarettes pour nos amis.

Review the possessive
adjectives on p. 79.

		glace		
je		cigarettes		amis
nous		cachets d'aspirine		classe *(f.)*
le professeur		magazines		parents
mes amis	acheter	pommes	pour	professeur
ma mère		timbres		famille
mon père		pain		moi
les étudiants		bonbons		nous
		médicaments		
		fleurs		

Téléfleurs

Vos **émotions**, nos **créations**, voyageons ensemble

Have students redo this exercise in the **passé composé**.

12 **Pourquoi y vont-ils?** Demandez ce que ces personnes achètent. Votre partenaire va répondre.

MODÈLE: Je vais au bureau de tabac.
VOUS: **Qu'est-ce que tu achètes au bureau de tabac?**
VOTRE PARTENAIRE: **J'achète des timbres.**

1. Je vais à la boucherie.
2. Nous allons à la pharmacie.
3. Mon père va au supermarché.
4. Nous allons dans un grand magasin.
5. Les étudiants vont à la boulangerie.
6. Paul va à l'épicerie.
7. Ces deux femmes vont au bureau de tabac.
8. Marie va à la librairie près de l'université.
9. Je vais chez un fleuriste.

Both **un** and **une** may be used with fleuriste.

www Réalités culturelles

L'Union européenne

En 1957, six pays européens (la France, l'Allemagne, l'Italie, la Belgique, les Pays-Bas et le Luxembourg) signent le traité de Rome et une sorte de marché commun est né. Petit à petit, cette communauté économique européenne va s'élargir avec de nouveaux membres. En 1992, le traité de Maastricht donne le coup d'envoi d'une union économique et monétaire qui s'appelle l'Union européenne (UE). En 1995, il y a déjà quinze membres de l'UE et, en 2004, dix autres viennent se joindre au groupe. Le Parlement européen, qui se réunit à Strasbourg, et la Cour de Justice, qui est à Luxembourg, sont deux des grandes institutions de l'UE.

Depuis 2002, l'euro est la seule monnaie officielle de la France et de la plupart des pays de l'Union européenne. Il existe huit pièces de monnaie et sept billets, d'une pièce de 1 cent jusqu'à un billet de 500 euros. On peut les utiliser pour faire ses achats dans presque tous les pays de l'UE.

Vocabulaire: traité *treaty,* coup d'envoi *kickoff,* presque *almost,* se réunit *meets*

Consult the ***Entre amis*** web site to find the list of the current members of the European Union.

Communities: See the *Entre amis* web site for web search activities with links to up-to-date information concerning the euro and the European Union.

V O C A B U L A I R E

Pour payer les achats

de l'argent *(m.)*	*money*	une carte de crédit	*credit card*
un billet	*bill (paper money)*	un chèque	*check*
la monnaie	*change; currency*	un chèque de voyage	*traveler's check*
une pièce (de monnaie)	*coin*	coûter	*to cost*
un euro	*euro*	payer	*to pay*
un dollar	*dollar*	Environ combien?	*About how much?*

Comparison: You might wish to point out that **payer** takes a direct object, even when the object is a purchase: **Nous payons nos achats** = *We pay for our purchases.*

NOTE

Payer is often found with a spelling change. Before silent endings, the **-y-** becomes **-i-: je paie, tu paies,** etc. *But:* **nous pay**ons, **vous pay**ez.

13 **Un petit sketch: Au bureau de tabac de la gare.** Lisez ou jouez le sketch. Ensuite répondez aux questions.

Grayson Smith parle avec un marchand de journaux au bureau de tabac de la gare.

M. Smith: Vous vendez des journaux américains?
Le Marchand: Ça dépend du journal.
M. Smith: Avez-vous le *Herald Tribune?*
Le Marchand: Oui, nous l'avons.
M. Smith: Bien. Je vous dois combien?
Le Marchand: Un euro dix.
M. Smith: Voilà, Monsieur.
Le Marchand: C'est parfait, Monsieur. Merci.
M. Smith: Au revoir, Monsieur. Bonne journée.
Le Marchand: Merci. Vous aussi, Monsieur.

QUESTIONS

1. Où achète-t-il son journal?
2. Quel journal demande-t-il?
3. Est-ce que le marchand a ce journal?
4. Combien coûte le journal?
5. Est-ce que Monsieur Smith l'achète?

V O C A B U L A I R E

Mots utiles pour faire des achats

une barquette	*small box; mini crate*
une boîte	*box; can*
un bouquet	*bouquet*
une bouteille	*bottle*
un kilo	*kilogram (2.2 pounds)*
un litre	*liter*
une livre	*pound*
un paquet	*package*

14 **Ça coûte combien?** Demandez combien coûte l'objet. Votre partenaire va donner la réponse en euros.

MODÈLE: bonbons (3€ le paquet)
VOUS: **Combien coûte un paquet de bonbons?**
VOTRE PARTENAIRE: **Les bonbons coûtent environ trois euros le paquet.**

Notice the use of the *indefinite* article in the question and the *definite* article in the answer.

1. bordeaux (7€ le litre)
2. fromage Pont l'Évêque (3€ la livre)
3. fraises d'Espagne (1€ la barquette)
4. orangina (2€ la bouteille)
5. jambon de Bayonne (10€ le kilo)
6. cigarettes (5€ le paquet)
7. œufs (2€ la douzaine)
8. fleurs (8€ le bouquet)

15 **En ville.** Vous avez besoin de plusieurs *(several)* choses. Utilisez les deux listes suivantes pour trouver l'adresse et le numéro de téléphone des magasins nécessaires.

MODÈLE: pour acheter des médicaments
Pour acheter des médicaments, l'adresse est un, place de la Laiterie. Téléphonez au zéro deux/quarante et un/quatre-vingt-sept/cinquante-huit/trente-neuf.

1. pour acheter un kilo de bœuf
2. pour acheter un paquet de cigarettes
3. pour acheter du pain
4. pour demander à quelle heure le film va commencer
5. pour acheter un bouquet de fleurs
6. pour réserver une table pour dîner
7. pour acheter un pull ou un pantalon
8. pour acheter du saumon
9. pour acheter des euros si on a des dollars

Review numbers on pp. 3 & 66.

See the *Note Culturelle*, p. 254, regarding French telephone numbers.

Culture & Communication (Interpretive): Ask students to study the places listed and brainstorm with them to decipher the meaning.

Place de la Laiterie		Rue de la Gare	
1 PHARMACIE GODARD	02.41.87.58.39	1 PHOTO PLUS	02.41.87.67.31
4 CHEVALIER, Yves		2 MOD COIFFURE	02.41.88.00.03
bureau de tabac	02.41.87.48.37	3 CRÉDIT AGRICOLE	02.41.88.12.56
5 BANQUE NATIONALE DE PARIS	02.41.88.00.23	4 CATFISH	
7 ARMORIC POISSONNERIE	02.41.88.39.84	restaurant grill	02.41.87.14.87
9 BOUCHERIE DU RONCERAY	02.41.87.57.28	5 PHARMACIE DE LA GARE	02.41.87.66.67
11 FAÏENCERIE DU RONCERAY	02.41.87.40.29	6 LE FLORENTIN	
15 SALOUD, Gérard		fleuriste	02.41.87.41.72
assurances	02.41.87.50.27	7 LE RELAIS	
18 COLIN, Jean		hôtel	02.41.88.42.51
boulangerie-pâtisserie	02.41.88.01.62	8 CINÉMA LE FRANÇAIS	02.41.87.66.66
19 VERNAUDON, Michel		9 LE PEN DUICK	
vêtements	02.41.87.01.96	restaurant	02.41.87.46.59
21 DACTYL BURO ANJOU		10 BAR BRASSERIE LE SIGNAL	02.41.87.49.41
machines bureaux	02.41.88.59.52		

16 **Une révision des nombres.** Répondez.

1. Quelle est votre adresse?
2. Quel est votre code postal?
3. Quel est votre numéro de téléphone?
4. Quel est le numéro de téléphone de votre meilleur(e) ami(e)?
5. En quelle année êtes-vous né(e)?
6. Combien de jours y a-t-il dans une année?
7. Combien de pages y a-t-il dans ce livre de français?
8. Combien de minutes y a-t-il dans une journée?
9. En quelle année Christophe Colomb est-il arrivé au Nouveau Monde?
10. Combien d'étudiants y a-t-il sur ce campus?

Point out that students have already been using relative pronouns. See, for example, pp. 61 & 232, ex. 20. Relative pronouns will also be studied in Ch. 14.

D. Les pronoms relatifs

■ Relative pronouns like *who, whom, which,* and *that* relate or tie two clauses together. They refer to a word in the first clause.

Le cadeau est sur la table. Il est
  pour ma sœur.

La cadeau **qui** est sur la table est   *The gift (that is) on the table is for*
  pour ma sœur.   *my sister.*

Le cadeau est pour ma sœur. Je l'ai
  acheté ce matin.

Le cadeau **que** j'ai acheté ce matin   *The gift (that) I bought this morning is*
  est pour ma sœur.   *for my sister.*

■ The choice of the relative pronoun **qui** or **que** depends on its function as subject or object.

■ **Qui** *(who, that, which)* replaces a person or a thing that is the *subject* of a relative clause.

Une boulangerie est un magasin **qui** vend du pain.

■ **Que/qu'** *(whom, that, which)* replaces a person or a thing that is the *object* of a relative clause.

Le Monde est un journal **que** je lis avec intérêt.

Le Monde est un journal **qu'**on achète souvent.

Voilà un professeur **que** les étudiants aiment beaucoup.

■ Although the relative pronoun may be omitted in English, it is never omitted in French.

C'est le magasin **que** je préfère.   *It's the store (that) I prefer.*

FOR RECOGNITION ONLY

> The relative pronoun **dont** (*whose, of which, about which*) is normally used when the French expression would require the preposition **de**. In the following example, one needs to remember that **besoin** is used with **de**.
>
> C'est le livre **dont** j'ai besoin.   *It's the book (that) I need.*

17 **Identifications.** Identifiez la personne ou la chose qui correspond à la description.

MODÈLE: quelqu'un qui parle français depuis longtemps
Le professeur de français est quelqu'un qui parle français depuis longtemps.

1. un magasin qui vend des médicaments
2. quelque chose qu'on vend à l'épicerie
3. un restaurant que vous recommandez pour sa cuisine italienne
4. un livre que vous avez déjà lu et que vous recommandez
5. quelque chose que vous mangez souvent
6. quelque chose dont on a besoin pour payer ses achats au centre commercial
7. quelqu'un qui parle français avec vous
8. une personne qui vend des fleurs
9. quelque chose qu'on achète à la librairie
10. quelque chose dont les étudiants ont besoin pour être heureux

18 **Définitions.** Décrivez les personnes ou les choses suivantes.

MODÈLES: un McDo   **C'est un restaurant qui vend des Big Macs.**
un professeur **C'est une personne qui enseigne.**
ma mère   **C'est une personne que j'aime.**

Communication (Presentational): Have students work in pairs to create these definitions. Then brainstorm with the class to elicit as many definitions as possible for each item.

1. un bureau de tabac
2. une pizza aux anchois
3. une pharmacienne
4. la France
5. mon professeur de français
6. un francophone
7. un supermarché

ENTRE AMIS

Culture: Remind students to be polite when "breaking the ice." Tell them to review p. 10.

Je voudrais faire quelques courses.

You have recently arrived in France. Speak to a member of your host family (your partner) to find out where things are sold.

1. Greet your host and say, "Excuse me for bothering you."
2. Say that you are going shopping.
3. Tell him/her what you need.
4. Ask where to buy each item you need.
5. Add that you are also looking for the *New York Times*. Explain what this is.
6. Be sure to express your gratitude.

Intégration www ◎

Révision

Communication (Interpretive & Presentational): If students do this in writing, they can then try to guess the items on their partner's list.

A **Des renseignements.** Préparez une liste de cinq renseignements pour des touristes qui vont en France.

MODÈLE: **Si on a besoin de pain, on peut aller à la boulangerie.**

B **Je fais des achats.** En groupes de deux ou trois. Un membre du groupe fait une liste de cinq endroits différents où il va faire des achats et, pour chaque endroit, la chose qu'il va acheter. Les autres membres du groupe vont deviner *(guess)* 1. où il va faire ses achats, et 2. ce qu'il achète. Il répond seulement par oui ou par non.

MODÈLE: **Est-ce que tu achètes quelque chose à la librairie?**
Est-ce que tu achètes un livre?

Culture & Comparison: Tell students the current exchange rate between the euro and your currency. *Suggestion:* Assign the *Rédaction* at the end of Ch. 9 in the Workbook.

C **Début de rédaction.** Faites deux listes, dont une pour la France et une autre pour votre pays. Dans chaque liste indiquez cinq magasins différents et, pour chaque magasin, mentionnez une ou deux choses qu'on y achète. Indiquez aussi combien coûte chaque chose que vous mentionnez.

MODÈLE: **Le savon est une chose qu'on achète dans une pharmacie française. Il coûte environ 1 €.**

Communication (Interpretive): Encourage students to use the practice test on the Lab Audio Program.

D **À vous.** Répondez.

1. Êtes-vous souvent malade?
2. Que prenez-vous si vous avez la grippe?
3. Que faites-vous quand vous avez mal à la tête?
4. Aimez-vous les cigarettes? Fumez-vous? Si oui, depuis combien de temps? Si non, avez-vous déjà fumé? Pendant combien de temps?
5. Dans quel magasin faites-vous vos courses? Qu'est-ce que vous y achetez?
6. Quelle est votre adresse? Depuis quand y habitez-vous?
7. Comment s'appelle le magasin qui vend du pain?
8. Qu'est-ce que c'est qu'une épicerie?

Video for Chapter 9: A. Video worksheets *(Cahier);* B. ACE Video practice test (WWW); C. CD-ROM

Négociations:

Nos achats. Interviewez votre partenaire pour trouver les renseignements qui manquent. Il y a trois paires de cartes; les cartes B sont dans l'appendice D. Comme partenaires, A1 travaille avec B1, A2 avec B2, etc.

For complete instructions on how to prepare for and to use this activity, see *Négociations* on the Class Prep CD-ROM.

MODÈLE: **Qu'est-ce qu'on achète à la gare?**
Où est-ce qu'on achète des fleurs?

A1

achat	endroit
journal	
porc	
	épicerie
	pharmacie
pain	
	épicerie
livre	
	grand magasin
	kiosque
fruits	
cadeau	
	marché
pilules	
	supermarché

A2

achat	endroit
	supermarché
fleurs	
savon	
	librairie
	marché
cigarettes	
	gare
	pharmacie
bœuf	
croissants	
	marché
timbres	
	marché aux puces
carte postale	

A3

achat	endroit
	librairie
	marché
carte postale	
dentifrice	
	boutique
fromage	
	charcuterie
pain	
	bureau de tabac
porc	
	supermarché
bœuf	
	bureau de poste
cravate	

Lecture I

A **Étude du vocabulaire.** Étudiez les phrases suivantes et choisissez les mots anglais qui correspondent aux mots français en caractères gras: *grief, love, hate, rain, roofs, gentle, ground, heart.*

1. J'aime le son de la **pluie** qui tombe sur les **toits** des maisons.
2. L'**amour** et la **haine** sont deux émotions opposées. Quand on aime, c'est l'**amour** et quand on déteste, c'est la **haine**.
3. Le **cœur** fait circuler le sang dans les veines et les artères.
4. La **terre** noire de l'Iowa est très fertile.
5. La mort du président nous a plongés dans le **deuil**.
6. Une voix **douce** est agréable à entendre.

B **Anticipez le contenu.** Avant de lire le poème, répondez aux questions suivantes.

1. Aimez-vous la pluie?
2. Pleut-il souvent là où vous habitez?
3. Quand il pleut, êtes-vous content(e), triste ou indifférent(e)? Expliquez.

Communication (Presentational): Have students make a list of the words that rhyme. Have them make lists of words containing the sounds [R] or [l]. Give a prize to the first student who can recite the poem from memory. Have a **Concours de prononciation** (see Class Prep CD-ROM).

Il pleure dans mon cœur

Il pleure dans mon cœur
Comme il pleut sur la ville,
Quelle est cette langueur
Qui pénètre mon cœur?

Ô bruit doux de la pluie
Par terre et sur les toits!
Pour un cœur qui s'ennuie[1]
Ô le chant de la pluie!

Il pleure sans raison
Dans ce cœur qui s'écœure[2].
Quoi! nulle trahison[3]?
Ce deuil est sans raison.

C'est bien la pire peine[4]
De ne savoir[5] pourquoi,
Sans amour et sans haine,
Mon cœur a tant de peine.

Paul Verlaine

---

1. *is languishing*   2. *is heartsickened*   3. *no treason*   4. *the worst suffering*   5. *not to know*

C **Discussion**

1. Quelle est la réaction du poète à la pluie? Quelles expressions utilise-t-il pour exprimer cette émotion?
2. Est-ce que le poète sait pourquoi il a cette réaction à la pluie? Expliquez.

D **Familles de mots.** Essayez de deviner le sens des mots suivants.

1. pleuvoir, la pluie, pluvieux (pluvieuse)
2. aimer, l'amour, aimable, amoureux (amoureuse)
3. s'ennuyer, l'ennui, ennuyeux (ennuyeuse)
4. peiner, la peine, pénible

Lecture II

A **Étude du vocabulaire.** Étudiez les phrases suivantes et choisissez les mots anglais qui correspondent aux mots français en caractères gras: *flight, sponsoring, places, beat, billboard, sidewalks, samples, building.*

1. Nos joueurs de basket-ball espèrent **battre** leurs adversaires.
2. Un **vol** est un voyage en avion.
3. Un **immeuble** est un grand bâtiment où les gens travaillent ou habitent.
4. Les gens restent sur les **trottoirs** parce que les rues sont dangereuses.
5. Le mot **lieux** est souvent un synonyme pour le mot *endroits*.
6. Les représentants commerciaux donnent des **échantillons** pour encourager les gens à acheter leurs produits.
7. Sur le **panneau d'affichage** de la bande dessinée, on peut lire: «Le tabac tue».
8. Le **parrainage** d'une équipe de football coûte quelquefois très cher à une entreprise.

B **Devinez de quoi il s'agit.** Lisez rapidement le titre et la première phrase de chaque article pour identifier le sujet des articles et les deux pays dont il s'agit.

Hystérie anti-tabac

Le Canada est en train de battre les États-Unis en matière d'hystérie anti-tabac. Le conseil municipal de Toronto—la capitale économique et financière du pays—a adopté un règlement draconien contre les fumeurs: depuis le 1er janvier 1997, le Torontois a seulement sa maison, sa voiture ou la rue pour prendre sa bouffée[1] de nicotine. La croisade contre[2] la cigarette ne date pas d'hier. La compagnie aérienne nationale Air Canada a été la première à l'interdire[3] sur les vols transatlantiques. Dans les hôtels, le principe des chambres fumeurs et non fumeurs est en vigueur. Les immeubles du gouvernement fédéral sont des zones strictement non-fumeurs. On voit, sur les trottoirs des grandes villes, les fumeurs irréductibles faire la pause cigarette avant de regagner leur bureau[4].

Les mesures du président

Principales mesures annoncées par la Maison-Blanche, pour limiter l'accès des adolescents au tabac:
- les distributeurs automatiques sont interdits dans certains lieux fréquentés par les jeunes;
- les échantillons et paquets de moins de 20 cigarettes sont interdits;
- les publicités pour le tabac sont interdites dans un rayon[5] de 500 mètres autour des établissements scolaires et des terrains de jeux;
- sauf[6] dans les lieux interdits aux moins de 18 ans, et à condition qu'elles ne soient[7] pas visibles de l'extérieur, les publicités sur les panneaux d'affichage et les lieux de vente doivent se limiter à des textes en noir et blanc;
- la publicité dans les publications dont les lecteurs sont constitués en grande partie d'adolescents (plus de 15%) doit se limiter à des textes en noir et blanc;
- le parrainage d'événements sportifs est interdit.

D'après *Le Point*

---

1. *puff*   2. *crusade against*   3. *to forbid it*   4. *go back to their office*   5. *in a radius*   6. *except*
7. *provided that they are*

C **Dans quel article?** Relisez les deux articles et décidez si les idées suivantes se trouvent dans l'article sur le Canada ou dans l'article sur les États-Unis.

1. On n'accepte pas d'annonces publicitaires pour les cigarettes près des écoles.
2. Certains fumeurs continuent à fumer avant d'entrer dans le bâtiment où ils travaillent.
3. Il n'y a plus de publicité en couleur pour les cigarettes dans les magazines lus par les jeunes.
4. Cette mesure stricte a été appliquée juste après Noël.
5. On ne permet plus que les entreprises qui vendent du tabac sponsorisent les matchs de tennis, de base-ball, etc.
6. Dans les endroits où vont les jeunes, on ne vend plus de cigarettes dans des machines.
7. On n'accepte plus depuis longtemps que les gens fument dans les avions s'ils font un voyage dans un autre pays.
8. Il n'est plus permis de donner des cigarettes gratuites pour encourager les individus à fumer.

B **Familles de mots.** Essayez de deviner le sens des mots suivants.

1. interdire, interdit(e), une interdiction
2. vendre, la vente, un vendeur, une vendeuse
3. fumer, un fumeur, une fumeuse, la fumée
4. conseiller, le conseil, un conseiller, une conseillère
5. distribuer, un distributeur, la distribution

VOCABULAIRE ACTIF

Practice this vocabulary with the flashcards on the *Entre amis* web site.

Argent

l'argent *(m.) money*
un billet *bill (paper money)*
une carte de crédit *credit card*
un centime *centime*
un chèque *check*
un chèque de voyage *traveler's check*
un dollar *dollar*
un euro *euro*
la monnaie *change; currency*
une pièce (de monnaie) *coin*

Adjectifs

aimable *kind; nice*
déçu(e) *disappointed*
déprimé(e) *depressed*
désolé(e) *sorry*
long (longue) *long*

Magasins

une boucherie *butcher shop*
une boutique *(gift, clothing, etc.) shop*
une charcuterie *pork butcher's; delicatessen*
un grand magasin *department store*
un kiosque *newsstand*
un marché *(open-air) market*
un marché aux puces *flea market*
une pâtisserie *pastry shop; pastry*
un supermarché *supermarket*

À la pharmacie

un cachet d'aspirine *aspirin tablet*
du dentifrice *toothpaste*
un médicament *medicine*
une pastille *lozenge*

une pilule *pill*
un savon *bar of soap*

Parties du corps

la bouche *mouth*
un bras *arm*
une dent *tooth*
le dos *back*
une épaule *shoulder*
l'estomac *(m.) stomach*
un genou *knee*
la gorge *throat*
une jambe *leg*
une main *hand*
le nez *nose*
un œil *eye*
une oreille *ear*
un pied *foot*
la tête *head*

D'autres noms

un achat *purchase*
une barquette *small box*
un billet *ticket*
un bouquet *bouquet*
un bruit *noise*
un cadeau *gift*
un code postal *zip code*
un coin *corner*
une feuille *leaf; sheet (of paper)*
une fièvre *fever*
une fleur *flower*
un(e) fleuriste *florist*
l'impatience (f.) *impatience*
un litre *liter*
une livre *pound*
un(e) marchand(e) *merchant*
le papier *paper*
un paquet *package; pack*
un rhume *a cold*
une rue *street*
une sardine *sardine*
une saucisse *sausage*
le tabac *tobacco; tobacconist's shop*
un timbre *stamp*
une valise *suitcase*

Verbes

acheter *to buy*
attendre *to wait (for)*
avoir besoin de *to need*
avoir l'air *to seem, appear, look*
avoir mal (à) *to be sore, to have a pain (in)*
coûter *to cost*
dépendre *to depend*
entendre *to hear*
payer *to pay (for)*
perdre *to lose*
perdre patience *to lose (one's) patience*
rendre *to give back*
rendre visite à quelqu'un *to visit someone*
répondre (à) *to answer*
réserver *to reserve*
tousser *to cough*
vendre *to sell*

Préposition

depuis *for; since*

Expressions utiles

avec intérêt *with interest*
Ça dépend. *That depends.*
cela *that*
C'est bien simple. *It's quite simple.*
De quoi avez-vous besoin? *What do you need?*
Depuis combien de temps? *For how much time?*
Depuis quand? *Since when?*
Environ combien? *About how much?*
je peux *I can*
le nez qui coule *runny nose*
Oh là là! *Oh dear!*
on peut *one can*
Pouvez-vous me dire ... ? *Can you tell me ... ?*
Qu'est-ce que tu as? *What's the matter (with you)?*
Qu'est-ce que vous dites? *What are you saying?*
Vous n'en avez pas? *Don't you have any?*

Dans la rue et sur la route

Buts communicatifs
Giving reasons and
    making excuses
Expressing familiarity and
    judgment
Giving orders and advice
Describing ways of doing
    things

Structures utiles
Les verbes **vouloir** et
    pouvoir
Le verbe **connaître**
Les pronoms objets
    directs (suite)
L'impératif (suite)
Les pronoms à l'impératif
Les nombres ordinaux
Le verbe **conduire**
Les adverbes

Culture
• *À propos*
Conduire en France
Les expressions de
    tendresse
• *Il y a un geste*
Chut!
Tais-toi!
Mon œil!
Invitation à danser
À toute vitesse
• *Lectures*
«La France au volant»
Automobiles

Coup d'envoi

<u>**Prise de contact**</u>   **Les indications**

Use the video, *Module 7*, to help set the scene for this presentation. There are a number of examples for giving directions.

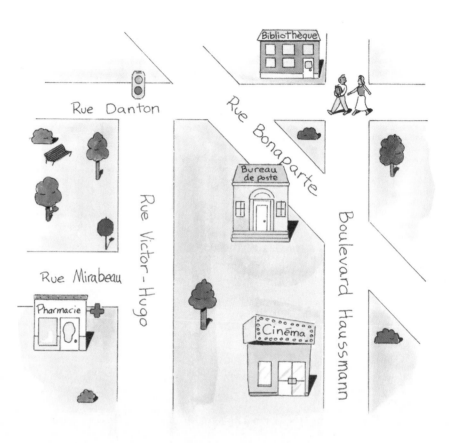

Culture: Remind students how to interrupt someone politely, p. 10.

Review the directions in Ch. 5, p. 138.

Comparison: Tell students to be careful when translating the English word "*on*". They should use *dans* with **rue**, but *sur* with **route/avenue/boulevard**.

Connections: Do this using local landmarks, streets, etc.

Pardon, pouvez-vous me dire où se trouve la pharmacie?

> Oui, c'est dans la rue Mirabeau.
> Prenez la rue Danton.
> Continuez jusqu'au feu°.   *until the traffic light*
> Puis, tournez à gauche. C'est la rue Victor-Hugo.
> Ensuite, la rue Mirabeau est la première rue à droite après le stop°.   *stop sign*

 Et vous?

Pouvez-vous me dire où se trouve la poste?
Où se trouve le cinéma, s'il vous plaît?
Pour la bibliothèque, s'il vous plaît?

Conversation

La leçon de conduite

Catherine apprend à conduire°. Son père, Michel, est nerveux et   to drive
parle continuellement pendant la leçon de conduite°.   driving lesson

CATHERINE: Papa, est-ce que je peux conduire?
MICHEL: Tu veux° conduire, ma chérie°?   You want/honey
Eh bien, attache ta ceinture de sécurité° et   seat belt
prends le volant°. Mais fais attention!   steering wheel
CATHERINE: Chut!° Pas de commentaires, s'il te plaît.   Shh!
Laisse-moi tranquille.°   Leave me alone.
MICHEL: D'accord, tu es prête°? Euh, démarre. Regarde   ready/start
à gauche, à droite et dans ton rétroviseur°.   rearview mirror
Avance lentement°, ma fille.   slowly
Change de vitesse.° Continue tout droit.   Shift; change speed.
Ne conduis pas si vite°.   so fast
(un peu plus tard)
Ne prends pas le sens interdit°.   one-way street
Prends la première rue à gauche.
Et ne regarde pas les garçons qui passent.
CATHERINE: Mais, tais-toi!° Tu n'arrêtes° pas de parler!   keep quiet!/stop
MICHEL: Excuse-moi, ma puce°. Je suis un   (lit.) flea
peu nerveux. C'est promis, plus un mot°.   not one more word
CATHERINE: Plus un mot, mon œil!° Je te connais° trop   my eye!/I know you
bien.

After practicing the
Conversation, have students
complete ex. A in the Workbook.

▶ **Jouez ces rôles.**   Répétez la conversation avec votre partenaire. Changez
ensuite de rôle: c'est un fils qui demande à sa maman s'il peut conduire.
Faites les changements nécessaires: par exemple, la mère appelle son fils
«mon chéri» et «mon grand».

Il y a un geste

Chut!   The index finger is raised to the lips to indicate that silence is in order.

Tais-toi!   The thumb and fingers are alternately opened and closed to tell someone to "shut up."

Mon œil!   There is a gesture meaning that one does not believe what was said. The index finger is placed under an eyelid and pulls down slightly on the skin.

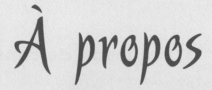

À propos

Pourquoi est-ce que Michel est nerveux?

a. Sa fille conduit très mal.
b. Tous les pères sont nerveux.
c. On conduit vite en France et il est important d'être prudent.

Michel appelle sa fille «ma puce». Pourquoi?

a. C'est une expression de tendresse *(term of endearment)*.
b. Il est sexiste. Les puces sont petites et il pense que sa fille est inférieure.
c. Les Français aiment beaucoup les insectes.

Conduire en France

One of the most unsettling discoveries one makes on a trip to France is the speed at which most people drive. Much has already been written about the French **appétit de la vitesse.** For example, Daninos's Major Thompson (see the **Lecture,** page 291) complains about the "peaceful citizen" who "can change in front of your eyes into a demonic pilot." That this can be the case, in spite of a very demanding driver's license test, a very elaborate and expensive training period in **l'auto-école,** the fact that one must be eighteen to get a license, and the fact that one must be at least sixteen years old to have a learner's permit and be accompanied by someone who is at least twenty-eight years old while learning to drive, may justify Major Thompson's comment that **Les Français conduisent plutôt bien, mais follement** *(The French drive rather well, but wildly).*

Les expressions de tendresse

Ma chérie, ma puce, mon chéri, and **mon grand** are common terms of endearment, but there are many others. Among couples, **mon chou** *(honey,* literally *my cabbage)* is very frequent. It is most likely a shortened form of **chou à la crème** *(cream puff).* In French families such expressions seem to be more frequently used than is the case among members of North American families. Terms of endearment are perhaps the verbal equivalent of the greater amount of physical contact found in France.

VOCABULAIRE

Quelques expressions de tendresse

femme	homme	femme ou homme
ma chérie	mon chéri	mon chou
ma puce *(flea)*	mon grand	mon cœur *(heart)*
ma biche *(deer)*	mon lapin *(rabbit)*	mon ange *(angel)*
		mon bijou *(jewel)*

▶ **À vous.** Votre ami(e) apprend à conduire. Répondez à ses questions.

1. Est-ce que je peux conduire?
3. Où allons-nous?
2. Tu vas attacher ta ceinture de sécurité?
4. Où se trouve cet endroit?

ENTRE AMIS

Communication (Interpretive): Instruct the student who is "driving" to respond each time with a gesture: Pretend to take the wheel, turn an imaginary key, etc.

Votre partenaire conduit.

1. Ask if your partner wants to drive. (S/he does.)
2. Tell your partner to take the wheel.
3. Tell him/her to start the car.
4. Tell him/her to look left and right.
5. Tell him/her to move ahead slowly.
6. Tell him/her to take the first street on the right.
7. Ask if s/he is nervous.

Prononciation

🎧

La lettre *h*

■ The letter **h** is never pronounced in French. There are, however, two categories of **h-** words:

1. Some **h-** words act *as if they began with a vowel:* These words are said to begin with **h muet** *(mute h).* Elision (dropping a final vowel and replacing it with an apostrophe) and liaison (pronouncing a normally silent final consonant and linking it to the next word) both occur before **h muet,** just as they would with a word beginning with a vowel.

d'habitude	**l'**heure	**j'**habite
un [n]homme	elle est [t]heureuse	deux [z]heures

2. Some **h-** words act *as if they began with a consonant:* These words are said to begin with **h aspiré** *(aspirate h).* Elision and liaison do not occur before **h aspiré.**

pas **de** haricots	**le** huit décembre	**le** hockey
un/hamburger	les/haricots	des/hors-d'œuvre

■ In addition, note that the combination **-th-** is pronounced [t].

thé	**Th**omas	a**th**lète
biblio**th**èque	ma**th**s	

NOTE CULTURELLE
Les jeunes Américains sortent souvent en couples. Il n'y a pas d'équivalent français pour le terme américain "dating." En effet, les jeunes Français sortent le plus souvent en groupes et n'ont pas besoin d'arriver à une boum avec une personne du sexe opposé.

Il y a un geste

Invitation à danser. When inviting someone to dance, the index finger is pointed toward the floor and makes a small circular motion.

Buts communicatifs

1. Giving Reasons and Making Excuses

Tu vas à la boum°, Brigitte?   *to the party*
    Oui, j'ai envie de danser.
    Oui, je veux m'amuser.
    Oui, je veux être avec mes amis.
    Je regrette. Je ne peux pas° sortir ce soir.   *I am unable to, I can't*

Et vous? Voulez-vous aller danser?
    Je veux bien! J'adore danser.
    Je regrette. Je ne sais pas danser.
    Merci, je suis trop fatigué(e).
    Je voudrais bien, mais j'ai besoin d'étudier.
    Voulez-vous sortir ce soir? Pourquoi ou pourquoi pas?

> Review the gesture for **Merci** on p. 30.

A. Les verbes *vouloir* et *pouvoir*

> The imperfect of **vouloir** and **pouvoir** will be taught in Ch. 11.

Mes amis veulent sortir tous les soirs.   *My friends want to go out every night.*

Mais ils ne peuvent pas.   *But they can't.*

As-tu pu parler avec Paul?   *Were you able to talk to Paul?*

J'ai voulu mais **je n'ai pas pu.**   *I wanted to (I tried to) but I wasn't able to.*

> *Comparison:* Contrast the sound [ø] in the singular with the [œ] sound in the 3rd person plural. This contrast will be the focus of the pronunciation section in Ch. 13.

> **Veux** and **peux** are pronounced like **deux.**

vouloir (to want; to wish)	
je	**veux**
tu	**veux**
il/elle/on	**veut**
nous	**voulons**
vous	**voulez**
ils/elles	**veulent**
passé composé: j'**ai voulu**	

pouvoir (to be able; to be allowed)	
je	**peux**
tu	**peux**
il/elle/on	**peut**
nous	**pouvons**
vous	**pouvez**
ils/elles	**peuvent**
passé composé: j'**ai pu**	

- **Vouloir** and **pouvoir** are frequently followed by an infinitive.

  Qui **veut sortir** ce soir?   *Who wants to go out tonight?*

  Je **ne peux pas sortir** ce soir.   *I can't go out tonight.*

- The passé composé of **vouloir, j'ai voulu,** means *I tried.* The passé composé of **pouvoir, j'ai pu,** means *I succeeded,* and the negative **je n'ai pas pu** means *I failed.*

■ **Vouloir** can also be used with a noun or pronoun, often to offer something or to make a request.

Voulez-vous **quelque chose** à boire? *Do you want something to drink?*

Culture: Remind students that the phrase **je veux bien** is often used when accepting an offer, p. 42.

NOTE ┤ When making requests, it is more polite to use **je voudrais** instead of **je veux**.

Je voudrais un verre d'eau. *I'd like a glass of water.*

■ **Pourquoi y vont-ils?** Expliquez où vont les personnes suivantes et pourquoi. Utilisez le verbe **aller** et le verbe **vouloir** dans chaque phrase.

Communication (Interpretive): As a follow-up, make up illogical sentences that students must correct, e.g., **On va au cinéma parce qu'on veut danser.**

MODÈLE: **Les étudiants vont à la boum parce qu'ils veulent danser.**

	à la résidence		étudier
	à la bibliothèque		acheter quelque chose
	à la boum		danser
	au restaurant		écouter un sermon
on	aux cours		dormir
je	à l'église		parler avec des amis
nous	dans la rue		manger
tu	aller Bourbon	vouloir	écouter du jazz
vous	à la piscine		prendre un avion
les étudiants	à la patinoire		patiner
	au cinéma		nager
	au centre		voir un film
	commercial		visiter des monuments
	en France		apprendre quelque
	à l'aéroport		chose

2 **Un petit sketch.** Lisez ou jouez le sketch suivant. Répondez ensuite aux questions.

Deux étudiants parlent de leurs activités.

JACQUES: Je peux porter ta veste grise?
CHRISTOPHE: Oui, si tu veux. Pourquoi?
JACQUES: Ce soir je sors.
CHRISTOPHE: Je vais être indiscret. Et tu vas où?
JACQUES: Les étudiants organisent une boum.
CHRISTOPHE: Tu y vas avec qui?
JACQUES: J'y vais seul, mais je crois que Sandrine a l'intention d'y aller aussi.
CHRISTOPHE: Et tu vas pouvoir l'inviter à danser, bien sûr?
JACQUES: Je voudrais bien danser avec elle. Mais elle a beaucoup d'admirateurs.
CHRISTOPHE: Tu as pu danser avec elle la dernière fois?
JACQUES: Non, elle n'a pas voulu. Mais cette fois, ça va être différent.

QUESTIONS ┤
1. Qui va à la boum?
2. Avec qui y va-t-il?
3. Quels vêtements veut-il porter?
4. Avec qui Jacques veut-il danser?
5. Pourquoi est-ce qu'il n'a pas pu danser avec Sandrine la dernière fois?

3 Pourquoi pas? Utilisez le verbe **pouvoir** à la forme négative et l'expression **parce que** pour expliquer pourquoi quelque chose n'est pas possible.

MODÈLE: **Tu ne peux pas sortir parce que tu es trop fatigué(e).**

tu		aller à un	avoir la grippe
vous		concert	avoir un rhume
mes amis		sortir	être malade(s)
mon ami(e)	ne pas	dîner	être trop fatigué(e)(s)
je	pouvoir	voyager	ne pas avoir d'argent
nous		jouer aux cartes	avoir sommeil
les étudiants		étudier	avoir besoin d'étudier
		venir au cours	être occupé(e)(s)
		danser	ne pas avoir le temps
		regarder la	avoir mal aux yeux
		télévision	avoir mal aux pieds
		skier	ne pas être libre(s)

4 Qu'est-ce qu'il a? Raymond répond toujours «non». Utilisez les expressions suivantes avec **vouloir** ou **pouvoir** pour expliquer quelle excuse il peut avoir.

MODÈLE: Si nous l'invitons à manger quelque chose, ...
Si nous l'invitons à manger quelque chose, Raymond va répondre qu'il ne veut pas manger parce qu'il n'a pas faim.

1. Si nous l'invitons à boire quelque chose, ...
2. Si nous l'invitons à chanter une chanson, ...
3. Si nous l'invitons à danser la valse, ...
4. Si nous l'invitons à la fête du mardi gras, ...
5. Si nous l'invitons à aller à un match de football, ...
6. Si nous l'invitons à faire du ski, ...
7. Si nous l'invitons à dîner chez nous, ...
8. Si nous l'invitons à étudier avec nous, ...

ENTRE AMIS

Pourquoi pas?

1. Ask if your partner can go to a movie with you. (S/he can't.)
2. Find out why not.
3. Suggest other activities. How many excuses can s/he find?

2. Expressing Familiarity and Judgment

Tu connais Éric, Céline?
>Oui, je le connais.

Tu connais ses parents?
>Je les connais mais pas très bien.

Tu connais la Nouvelle-Orléans?
>Non, je ne la connais pas.

▶ **Et vous?**   Vous connaissez l'histoire de la Louisiane?
Vous connaissez le Québec?

Le **Québec** refers to the province of Quebec. *Quebec City* is referred to simply as **Québec.** See p. 84.

B. Le verbe *connaître*

Est-ce que **vous connaissez** Paris?	*Do you know Paris?*
Anne ne **connaît** pas cette ville.	*Anne doesn't know that city.*
Je connais cet homme.	*I know that man.*
J'ai connu cet homme à Paris.	*I met that man in Paris.*

connaître
(to know, be acquainted with, be familiar with)

je	**connais**
tu	**connais**
il/elle/on	**connaît**
nous	**connaissons**
vous	**connaissez**
ils/elles	**connaissent**

passé composé: j'**ai connu**

Students already know the phrase **Je ne sais pas.** A clear distinction will be made between **je sais** and **je connais** in Ch. 12.

■ There is a circumflex accent on the **-i-** only in the verb stem of the **il/elle/on** form and in the infinitive.

>Je **connais** bien la mentalité américaine.
But: Il ne **connaît** pas l'histoire des Acadiens.

■ **Connaître** denotes familiarity and means *to know, be acquainted with (a person, a place, a concept, a thing).* It is always accompanied by a direct object and cannot stand alone.

The special meanings of **pouvoir** and **vouloir** in the passé composé were taught on p. 274.

Connaissez-vous **les parents de Thomas?**	*Do you know Thomas's parents?*
Non, mais je connais **leur maison.**	*No, but I'm familiar with their house.*

NOTE ─ In the passé composé, **connaître** denotes a first meeting.

J'**ai connu** Robert en janvier.   *I met Robert in January.*

The use of **savoir** in the passé composé will be taught in Ch. 12.

Review the direct object pronouns on p. 228.

C. Les pronoms objets directs (suite)

Connais-tu Christelle?	*Do you know Christelle?*
Non, je ne **la** connais pas personnellement.	*No, I don't know her personally.*
Est-ce qu'elle **te** connaît?	*Does she know you?*
Non, elle ne **me** connaît pas.	*No, she doesn't know me.*
Tu **nous** invites chez toi?	*Are you inviting us to your house?*
Non, ce soir je ne peux pas **vous** inviter.	*No, tonight I can't invite you.*
As-tu acheté ton livre?	*Did you buy your book?*
Je **l'**ai acheté mais je ne **l'**ai pas encore lu.	*I bought it but I haven't read it yet.*

See Appendix C to review the meaning of grammatical terms.

Pronoms objets directs

singulier		*pluriel*	
me (m')	*me*	**nous**	*us*
te (t')	*you*	**vous**	*you*
le (l')	*him; it*	**les**	*them*
la (l')	*her; it*		

■ Remember that object pronouns are placed directly in front of the verb.

Aimes-tu *les sandwichs?*	Oui, je **les** aime.
Connais-tu *ma mère?*	Non, je ne **la** connais pas.

■ When used with a verb followed by an infinitive, direct object pronouns are put directly in front of the verb to which they are related (usually the infinitive).

Pascale veut **me** connaître?	Oui, elle veut **vous** connaître.
Je vais demander *l'addition.*	Je vais **la** demander.
Nous ne pouvons pas regarder *la télévision.*	Nous ne pouvons pas **la** regarder.
J'ai envie d'écouter *la radio.*	J'ai envie de **l'**écouter.

■ Direct object pronouns can be used with **voici** and **voilà.**

Où est Robert? **Le** voilà!	*Where is Robert? There he is!*
Vous venez? **Nous** voilà!	*Are you coming? Here we are.*

■ In the passé composé, object pronouns are placed directly in front of the auxiliary verb.

Marc a acheté *son livre?*	Oui, il **l'**a acheté.
As-tu aimé *le film?*	Non, je ne **l'**ai pas aimé.

FOR RECOGNITION ONLY

The past participle agrees in gender and number with a *preceding* direct object.

Tu n'as pas **écouté** *la radio.*

> *But:* Tu ne *l*'as pas écouté**e**.

Nous avons **attendu** nos amis.

> *But:* Nous *les* avons attendu**s**.

5 **C'est vrai?** D'abord utilisez le verbe **connaître** pour faire des phrases à la forme affirmative. Ensuite utilisez un pronom objet dans une deuxième phrase pour dire si c'est vrai ou faux.

MODÈLE: je / la rue Bourbon
Je connais la rue Bourbon.
C'est faux. Je ne la connais pas.
ou
C'est vrai. Je la connais.

1. nos parents / notre professeur de français
2. notre professeur de français / nos parents
3. nous / l'avenue des Champs-Élysées
4. je / les amis de mes parents
5. mon ami(e) ... / le musée du Louvre
6. les étudiants / le (la) président(e) de l'université

6 **Qui les connaît?** Interviewez un(e) partenaire. Utilisez le verbe **connaître.** Employez un pronom objet dans votre réponse.

MODÈLES: tu / mes amis
VOUS: **Est-ce que tu connais mes amis?**
VOTRE PARTENAIRE: **Oui, je les connais.** ou
Non, je ne les connais pas.

tes amis / me
VOUS: **Est-ce que tes amis me connaissent?**
VOTRE PARTENAIRE: **Oui, ils te connaissent.** ou
Non, ils ne te connaissent pas.

1. tu / mes parents
2. tes parents / me
3. tes amis / le professeur de français
4. le professeur de français / tes amis
5. tu / les autres étudiants de notre cours de français
6. les autres étudiants de notre cours de français / te
7. le (la) président(e) de notre université / nous
8. nous / le (la) président(e) de notre université

⟨www⟩Réalités culturelles

Le français en Louisiane

Le français est la deuxième langue officielle de l'état de Louisiane et 21 pour cent de la population (899.000 personnes) se déclare d'ascendance française, dont 600.000 personnes d'origine acadienne. C'est du mot «acadien» qu'est venu le mot «cajun», pour désigner les francophones de la Louisiane. En plus, la Louisiane est le seul état américain qui utilise le Code Napoléon, le système légal créé par Napoléon Iᵉʳ et utilisé au dix-neuvième siècle dans la plupart des pays d'Europe et d'Amérique latine. Grâce à son héritage français et catholique, la Louisiane est aussi le seul état divisé en paroisses au lieu de comtés. À La Nouvelle-Orléans, la fête du mardi gras est un exemple célèbre des origines françaises de la ville.

Quelques dates

1682   Robert de la Salle descend le Mississippi et donne à cette région le nom de Louisiane en l'honneur du roi, Louis XIV.
1698   Des colons et de nombreux soldats arrivent de France.
1719   Environ 500 esclaves arrivent d'Afrique. Aujourd'hui, 31 pour cent de la population de cet état est afro-américain.
1755   Les Acadiens sont déportés de la Nouvelle-Écosse par les Anglais parce qu'ils refusent de prêter serment de fidélité au roi d'Angleterre. C'est ce qu'on appelle le Grand Dérangement.
1803   Napoléon Bonaparte vend la Louisiane aux États-Unis pour 15 millions de dollars.
1812   La Louisiane devient un état.

Vocabulaire: colons *colonists*, comtés *counties*, esclaves *slaves*, paroisses *parishes*, prêter serment *to swear an oath*, roi *king*

7 **Pourquoi ou pourquoi pas?** Répondez en utilisant un pronom objet direct. Ensuite expliquez votre réponse.

MODÈLES: Aimez-vous étudier le français?
Oui, j'aime l'étudier parce que j'ai envie de le parler.

Voulez-vous faire la vaisselle?
Non, je ne veux pas la faire parce que c'est ennuyeux.

1. Aimez-vous faire les courses?
2. Allez-vous regarder la télévision ce soir?
3. Voulez-vous connaître la ville de Shreveport?
4. Pouvez-vous chanter *la Marseillaise*?
5. Préférez-vous faire vos devoirs à la bibliothèque?
6. Comprenez-vous l'espagnol?
7. Me comprenez-vous?

8 **Une devinette** *(A riddle).* À quoi correspond le pronom? Devinez!

MODÈLE: On le trouve dans la classe de français.
On trouve le livre de français dans la classe de français. ou
On trouve Mike dans la classe de français.

Communication (Interpretive):
Do this first in pairs; then redo
as a teacher-led activity to elicit
as many answers as possible.

1. On le prend le matin.
2. On la regarde quelquefois.
3. On l'écoute souvent.
4. On peut les faire à la bibliothèque.
5. On le lit pour préparer ce cours.
6. On aime le parler avec le professeur.
7. Les étudiants l'adorent.
8. On la fait après le dîner.
9. On les achète à la librairie.

ENTRE AMIS

Tu connais … ?

Your partner should use an object pronoun whenever possible.

1. Ask if your partner knows a specific TV program. (Pick one that's on TV tonight.)
2. Find out if s/he is going to watch it this evening.
3. Ask if your partner is going to do the French homework this evening.
4. Depending on the answer, ask why or why not.
5. Inquire if s/he watches TV while s/he does homework.
6. Tell what you are going to do tonight. Explain why.

3. Giving Orders and Advice

Quelqu'un parle au chauffeur°:   *driver*

Démarrez!
Changez de vitesse!
Continuez tout droit!
Prenez à droite!
Arrêtez-vous au stop!
Reculez!°   *Back up!*
Faites attention aux voitures!

Remind students of the gesture
for **tais-toi (taisez-vous),**
p. 271.

Le chauffeur répond:

Taisez-vous is the **vous**
form of the imperative **tais-
toi,** used on p. 271.

Taisez-vous!°   *Keep quiet!*

▶ **Et vous?**   Parlez au chauffeur!

Communication (Interpretive): Pair students and tell the partners that
they should respond with a gesture to each command they are given.

D. L'impératif (suite)

Fais attention!	*Pay attention!*
Faites attention!	*Pay attention!*
Faisons attention!	*Let's pay attention!*

Ne sors pas!	*Don't go out!*
Ne sortez pas!	*Don't go out!*
Ne sortons pas!	*Let's not go out!*

Review the imperative on p. 141.

The use of pronouns with the imperative will be taught on p. 283.

■ The imperative is used to give commands and to make suggestions. The forms are usually the same as the present tense for **tu, vous,** and **nous.**

■ **Être** and **avoir** have irregular imperatives:

être	avoir
sois	aie
soyez	ayez
soyons	ayons

Sois gentil!	*Be nice!*
Soyons sérieux!	*Let's be serious!*
Ayez pitié de nous!	*Have pity on us!*
N'**aie** pas peur!	*Don't be afraid!*

Communication (Interpretive): Follow with two chain drills: A. One student gives an order to the next, who responds **Mais je ne veux pas ...** Tell students to try to avoid orders that have already been given. B. Reverse the process: the first student says **Je ne veux pas ...** and the next gives the order to do so.

9   Le pauvre professeur. Les étudiants refusent de faire ce qu'il veut. Utilisez **Mais je ne veux pas ...** et répondez.

MODÈLE: Écoutez!
    Mais je ne veux pas écouter.

1. Allez en classe!
2. Prenez ce livre!
3. Écrivez votre dissertation!
4. Lisez ce roman!
5. Parlez à votre professeur!
6. Soyez raisonnable!
7. Arrêtez de parler!
8. Ayez pitié de vos professeurs!
9. Faites attention!
10. Sortez de cette classe!

10   Un père exaspéré. Michel trouve que sa fille n'est pas raisonnable. Il décide que sa fille peut faire ce qu'elle veut.

MODÈLE: Je veux aller au cinéma.
    Alors, va au cinéma!

Remember that the final **-s** is omitted from the **tu** form of the imperative if the infinitive ends in **-er**.

1. Je ne peux rien manger.
2. Je ne veux pas faire la vaisselle.
3. Je veux regarder la télévision.
4. Je ne veux pas étudier.
5. Je ne peux pas écrire de rédaction.
6. Je ne veux pas avoir de bonnes notes en français.
7. Je ne veux pas être raisonnable.

11 **Des touristes.** Vous aidez des touristes francophones près de votre campus. Répondez et expliquez aux touristes où il faut aller.

MODÈLE: Où est le centre commercial, s'il vous plaît?
Prenez la rue Main. Ensuite tournez à gauche dans la rue Madison.

1. Pouvez-vous me dire où je peux trouver un supermarché?
2. Je voudrais trouver une pharmacie, s'il vous plaît.
3. Y a-t-il un bureau de poste dans cette ville?
4. Y a-t-il un arrêt d'autobus près d'ici?
5. Où sont les toilettes, s'il vous plaît?
6. Connaissez-vous un restaurant près d'ici?

E. Les pronoms à l'impératif

■ In an affirmative sentence, an object pronoun follows the imperative.

Je peux prendre la voiture?	**Prends-la!**	**Prenez-la!**
Je veux acheter ce livre.	**Achète-le!**	**Achetez-le!**
Je vais porter ces chaussures.	**Porte-les!**	**Portez-les!**
Je vais au cinéma.	**Vas-y!**	**Allez-y!**
Je m'amuse bien.	**Amuse-toi!**	**Amusez-vous!**
Je me lève.	**Lève-toi!**	**Levez-vous!**

> NOTE Used after a verb, **me** and **te** become **moi** and **toi**.
>
> Regardez-**moi!** *Look at me!* Écoute-**moi!** *Listen to me!*

■ If the sentence is negative, the object pronoun precedes the verb.

Je ne veux pas acheter ce livre.	**Ne l'achète pas!**	**Ne l'achetez pas!**
Je ne veux pas porter ces chaussures.	**Ne les porte pas!**	**Ne les portez pas!**
Vous me regardez tout le temps.	**Ne me regarde pas!**	**Ne me regardez pas!**
Je ne veux pas aller au cinéma.	**N'y va pas!**	**N'y allez pas!**
Je ne me lève pas.	**Ne te lève pas!**	**Ne vous levez pas!**

Sidebar notes
Allez-y and *Vas-y* are often used to mean *Go ahead*.

The imperative forms of reflexive verbs will be taught again in Ch. 13.

While the final *-s* of the **tu** form of verbs that end in *-er* is dropped in the imperative (see p. 141), it is retained when it is followed by a pronoun beginning with a vowel: **Vas-y!**

Point out that this is the same as the general rule for other forms of the verb.

12 **La voix de ma conscience (The voice of my conscience).** Qu'est-ce que votre conscience vous dit de faire ou de ne pas faire? Utilisez un pronom objet avec l'impératif.

MODÈLE: Je vais manger ces bonbons. **Mange-les!** ou **Ne les mange pas!**

Votre conscience est une bonne amie. Alors, quand elle vous parle, elle utilise **tu**.

1. Je ne vais pas faire mes devoirs.
2. Je veux prendre la voiture de mon ami(e).
3. Je ne veux pas attacher ma ceinture de sécurité.
4. Je vais boire cette bouteille de vin.
5. Je veux acheter ces vêtements.
6. Je veux faire la sieste.
7. Je ne veux pas me lever pour aller au cours.
8. Je vais regarder la télévision.
9. Je peux aller au cinéma?
10. Je vais m'amuser ce soir.

F. Les nombres ordinaux

Prends la **première** rue à gauche.
C'est la **deuxième** fois que je viens en France.
Elle habite dans la **quatrième** maison.
Victor Hugo est né au **dix-neuvième** siècle *(century)*.

■ To form most ordinal numbers, one simply adds **-ième** to the cardinal number. The abbreviated form is a numeral followed by a raised **e**.

deux ⟶ **deuxième**   **2e**
trois ⟶ **troisième**   **3e**

■ There are a few exceptions.

For cardinal numbers such as **vingt et un,** the ordinal number is formed according to the normal rule: **vingt et un → vingt et unième (21e).**

1. The ordinal number for **un (une)** is **premier (première).** It is the only ordinal number whose ending is altered to show gender agreement with the noun it modifies.

un (une) ⟶ **premier (première)**   **1er (1re)**

2. **Cinq** and numbers built on **cinq** add a **-u-** before the ending.

cinq ⟶ **cin*q*uième**   **5e**

3. **Neuf** and numbers built on **neuf** change the **-f-** to **-v-** before the ending.

neuf ⟶ **neu*v*ième**   **9e**

4. Cardinal numbers ending in **-e** drop the **-e** before the ending.

quatre ⟶ **quatrième**   **4e**
onze ⟶ **onzième**   **11e**
douze ⟶ **douzième**   **12e**

■ In dates, **le premier** is used, as in English, to express the meaning *the first,* but the cardinal numbers are used for the rest of the days in the month.

le **premier** mai   *But:* le **deux** mai, le **trois** mai

Remember that **Premier** agrees in the feminine: Elizabeth **Première.**

■ This is also true when talking about monarchs. **Premier (Première)** is used for *the First,* but the cardinal numbers are used thereafter. Note that the definite article is not used in French.

François **Premier**   *But:* Henri **Quatre**

13 **Prononcez et écrivez.** Lisez ces expressions et écrivez en toutes lettres.

MODÈLE: le 21e siècle
le vingt et unième siècle

1. Henri Ier
2. la 2e année consécutive
3. la 3e fois
4. le 1er mois de l'année
5. Louis XV
6. la 6e fois
7. le 20e siècle
8. la 1re rue à droite
9. le 25 décembre

14 **Le calendrier.** Répondez.

MODÈLE: Quelle est la date de Noël?
C'est le vingt-cinq décembre.

Review days, p. 134, and
months, p. 198.

1. Quelle est la date d'aujourd'hui?
2. Quelle est la date du Jour de l'An?
3. Quelles sont les dates de votre fête nationale et de la fête nationale française?
4. Quelle est la date de votre anniversaire?
5. Quelle est la date de l'anniversaire de mariage de vos parents?
6. Quel est le troisième mois de l'année?
7. Quel est le dernier jour de l'année?
8. Quel est le cinquième jour de la semaine en France?
9. Quel est le cinquième jour de la semaine pour vous?

ENTRE AMIS

Excusez-moi de vous déranger.

You are visiting a French-speaking city.

I. Stop a native and explain that you don't know the city.
2. Ask for directions to a good restaurant, a good hotel, and a post office.
3. Be sure to thank the native properly.

4. Describing Ways of Doing Things

À quelle vitesse conduisez-vous?

Moi, je conduis ...
    comme un escargot°.   *like a snail*
    lentement.
    tranquillement°.   *calmly*
    prudemment°.   *prudently*
    vite.
    à toute vitesse°.   *at top speed*
    comme un fou (une folle)°.   *like a crazy person*

▶ **Et vous?**
Comment est-ce que vous conduisez?
Comment est-ce que vos amis conduisent?

Il y a un geste

À toute vitesse.   A closed fist is held at chest level and moved horizontally away from the body and back in a few rapid motions. This suggests a rapid speed. It may also be used to describe someone who has a "hard-driving" personality.

G. Le verbe *conduire*

Est-ce que tu as peur de **conduire**?
Je conduis très souvent.
Hier, **nous avons conduit** une voiture de sport.

Communication (Presentational): Encourage students to describe the driving of friends, family, etc.

conduire *(to drive)*	
je	**conduis**
tu	**conduis**
il/elle/on	**conduit**
nous	**conduisons**
vous	**conduisez**
ils/elles	**conduisent**

passé composé: j'**ai conduit**

■ The verb **conduire** is not used to tell that you drive to a destination. It is used alone or with adverbs or direct objects. To tell *where* you are driving, use **aller en voiture.**

Il **conduit** une Ford.   *He drives a Ford.*

But: Il **va** en Louisiane **en voiture.**   *He is driving to Louisiana.*

15 **Comment ces gens conduisent-ils?** Votre partenaire va vous poser des questions. Répondez. Si vous ne savez pas, inventez une réponse.

MODÈLE: votre tante
VOTRE PARTENAIRE: **Comment votre tante conduit-elle?**
VOUS: **Ma tante conduit à toute vitesse.**

1. les étudiants de cette université
2. le professeur de français
3. les professeurs (en général)
4. les femmes
5. les hommes
6. les Français
7. les Américains
8. votre meilleur(e) ami(e)
9. vous

H. Les adverbes

Consult Appendix C to review the distinction between an adjective and an adverb.

■ While there are exceptions, most French adverbs end in **-ment**.

Avance **lentement!**

Tu vas trop **rapidement.**

■ If the masculine singular form of the adjective ends in a consonant, **-ment** is added to the feminine form.

premier (première)	⟶	**premièrement**	*first*
sérieux (sérieuse)	⟶	**sérieusement**	*seriously*
attentif (attentive)	⟶	**attentivement**	*attentively*
personnel (personnelle)	⟶	**personnellement**	*personally*

■ The suffix **-ment** is added to the masculine singular form of an adjective if it ends in a vowel.

vrai	⟶	**vraiment**	*truly*
facile	⟶	**facilement**	*easily*
absolu	⟶	**absolument**	*absolutely*

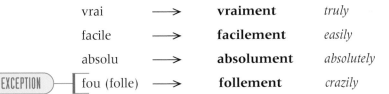 EXCEPTION — fou (folle) ⟶ **follement** *crazily*

Point out that this [a] is also found in the word **femme.**

■ For masculine adjectives ending in **-ant** or **-ent**, the adverbs will end in **-amment** or **-emment** respectively. The first vowel in both spellings is pronounced [a].

constant	⟶	**constamment**	*constantly*
patient	⟶	**patiemment**	*patiently*
prudent	⟶	**prudemment**	*prudently*

The comparative forms **meilleur(e)** and **mieux** will be taught in Ch. 11.

■ Several of the most common adverbs are completely different from their corresponding adjectives.

bon	⟶	**bien**	*well*	Loïc danse **bien.**
mauvais	⟶	**mal**	*poorly*	Il chante **mal.**
petit	⟶	**peu**	*little*	Et il mange très **peu.**

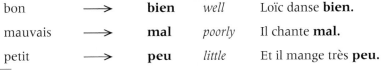 NOTE — **Rapide** has two corresponding adverbs: **rapidement** and **vite.**

16 **Tout le monde est chauffeur.** Décrivez les chauffeurs suivants. Pour chaque adjectif, faites une phrase avec le verbe **être** et un adjectif, et puis une autre phrase, avec le verbe **conduire** et un adverbe.

MODÈLE: ma tante/lent **Ma tante est lente. Elle conduit lentement.**

nous (les étudiants)	rapide
mon oncle	sérieux
ma tante	bon
mon père	prudent
ma mère	patient
je	nerveux
le professeur	admirable
les hommes	raisonnable
les femmes	parfait
	tranquille
	attentif
	fou

17 **Identification.** Identifiez des personnes qui correspondent aux questions suivantes.

Communication (Interpretive): Have students ask you the questions first. Then follow up, books closed, by asking them the questions.

MODÈLE: Qui conduit lentement?
Mes parents conduisent lentement. ou
Mon oncle conduit lentement.

1. Qui conduit nerveusement?
2. Qui parle rapidement le français?
3. Qui fait bien la cuisine?
4. Qui parle constamment?
5. Qui apprend facilement les maths?
6. Qui travaille sérieusement?
7. Qui écoute patiemment?
8. Qui étudie attentivement?
9. Qui chante mal?
10. Qui écrit peu?

ENTRE AMIS

Vous êtes journaliste.

Your partner will respond as factually as possible to your questions. However, if s/he doesn't know the answer, s/he should guess.

1. Find out if your partner speaks French.
2. Tell your partner that you are sorry to bother him/her.
3. Explain that you are a reporter for a magazine called *Marie-Claire*.
4. Say that you are studying French teachers.
5. Inquire if your partner knows a French teacher.
6. Ask how French teachers drive, sing, play golf, etc.
7. Verify answers you received by checking with your French teacher.

Intégration www ◉

Révision

A Des indications. Aidez un(e) touriste francophone qui cherche ...

1. un restaurant
2. un bureau de poste
3. une pharmacie

B Jacques a dit *(Simon says)*. Faites l'action ou le geste indiqué par le professeur, s'il commence par «Jacques a dit». Si le professeur n'utilise pas l'expression «Jacques a dit», ne faites pas l'action ou le geste décrit.

Frappez à la porte!	Mon œil!	Reculez!
Taisez-vous!	Comme ci, comme ça.	Prenez le volant!
Dites bonjour!	Comptez sur une main!	Conduisez!
Mangez!	Regardez à gauche!	Changez de vitesse!
Buvez!	Regardez à droite!	Asseyez-vous!
Invitez-moi à danser!	Avancez!	

C Les étudiants sérieux. Décidez si les étudiants sérieux font ou ne font pas les choses suivantes. Utilisez un pronom objet direct dans chaque réponse.

MODÈLE: regarder la télé pendant des heures
Ils ne la regardent pas pendant des heures.

1. oublier leurs livres dans leur chambre
2. conduire follement la voiture de leurs parents
3. pouvoir facilement apprendre le subjonctif
4. vouloir étudier le français
5. faire toujours leurs devoirs
6. passer la nuit à regarder la télévision

Communication (Presentational & Interpretive): If students present their lists of "driving tips" to the class, others can be asked to recall what was presented. Suggestion: Assign the *Rédaction* at the end of Ch. 10 in the Workbook.

Communication (Interpretive): Encourage students to use the practice test on the Lab Audio Program.

D Début de rédaction. Faites une liste d'au moins dix conseils que vous donnez aux chauffeurs prudents.

MODÈLE: **Ne parlez jamais au téléphone portable pendant que vous conduisez.**

E À vous. Répondez. Attention, si vous ne pouvez pas conduire, inventez des réponses pour une personne que vous connaissez.

1. Est-ce que vous conduisez prudemment?
2. À quelle vitesse est-ce que vous conduisez d'habitude?
3. Est-ce que vous attachez toujours votre ceinture de sécurité?
4. Est-ce que vous vous arrêtez toujours au stop?
5. Est-ce que vous parlez quelquefois au téléphone portable pendant que vous conduisez?
6. À quel âge avez-vous conduit une voiture pour la première fois?
7. Depuis combien de temps avez-vous votre permis de conduire?

Négociations:

La formule I. Interviewez votre partenaire pour trouver les renseignements qui manquent. La copie de votre partenaire est dans l'appendice D.

MODÈLE: **Quelle sorte de véhicule est-ce que mémé conduit? Comment conduit-elle?**

For complete instructions on how to prepare for and to use this activity, see *Négociations* on the Class Prep CD-ROM.

All of the vehicles in this activity are feminine.

NOTE CULTURELLE

Les francophones ont beaucoup d'expressions, utilisées principalement par les enfants ou par les adultes quand ils parlent aux enfants, pour désigner les membres d'une famille. Pour parler de ses parents on dit **maman** et **papa**. Pour sa grand-mère on dit souvent **mémé** ou **mamie** et pour son grand-père **pépé** ou **papi**. L'oncle et la tante deviennent **tonton** et **tatie** ou **tata**.

Video for Chapter 10: A. Video worksheets (*Cahier*); B. ACE Video practice test (WWW); C. CD-ROM

A

nom	conduire	comment?	pourquoi comme ça?
Michael Schumacher			C'est un pilote professionnel allemand.
Jacques Villeneuve	Honda	très rapidement	
Alain Prost			C'est un pilote professionnel français.
tonton Paul	Peugeot		Il veut toujours aller vite.
tatie Agnès			Elle apprend à conduire une moto.
papi	Mercedes	comme un escargot	
mémé		prudemment	
vous			
votre partenaire			

Lecture I

A **Étude du vocabulaire.** Étudiez les phrases suivantes et choisissez les mots anglais qui correspondent aux mots français en caractères gras: *more, convinced, rather, hates, approximately, those, latecomer, less, thus, bother.*

1. Un avion est **plus** rapide qu'un train.
2. L'état de Rhode Island est **moins** grand que le Texas.
3. Notre professeur **exècre** le tabac. Les cigarettes le rendent malade.
4. Pourquoi est-ce que vous me parlez **ainsi**? Qu'est-ce que je vous ai fait?
5. C'est un **retardataire.** Il n'arrive jamais à l'heure.
6. Est-ce que cela vous **dérange** si je fume?
7. **Ceux** qui étudient sont **ceux** qui ont les meilleures notes.
8. Christian chante **plutôt** mal, mais il aime chanter quand même.
9. Il y a **à peu près** trente personnes au restaurant.
10. Je suis **convaincu** que le professeur veut que j'étudie beaucoup.

B **Qu'en pensez-vous?** Quelle est la réputation des Français au volant? Quelle est la réputation des chauffeurs californiens? des chauffeurs new-yorkais? Et vous, comment conduisez-vous?

La France au volant

Il faut se méfier des[1] Français en général, mais sur la route en particulier. Pour un Anglais qui arrive en France, il est indispensable de savoir d'abord qu'il existe deux sortes de Français: les à-pied et les en-voiture. Les à-pied exècrent les en-voiture, et les en-voiture terrorisent les à-pied, les premiers passant instantanément dans le camp des seconds si on leur met un volant entre les mains. (Il en est ainsi au théâtre avec les retardataires qui, après avoir dérangé douze personnes pour s'asseoir, sont les premiers à protester contre ceux qui ont le toupet[2] d'arriver plus tard.)

Les Anglais conduisent plutôt mal, mais prudemment. Les Français conduisent plutôt bien, mais follement. La proportion des accidents est à peu près la même dans les deux pays. Mais je me sens[3] plus tranquille avec des gens qui font mal des choses bien[4] qu'avec ceux qui font bien de mauvaises choses.

Les Anglais (et les Américains) sont depuis longtemps convaincus que la voiture va moins vite que l'avion. Les Français (et la plupart des Latins) semblent encore vouloir prouver le contraire.

Pierre Daninos, *Les Carnets du Major Thompson*

Communities, Comparison & Culture: Use this reading as a springboard to discuss cultural stereotypes.

---

1. *watch out for*   2. *nerve*   3. *feel*   4. *do good things poorly*

C **Vrai ou faux?** Décidez si les phrases suivantes sont vraies ou fausses d'après la lecture. Si une phrase est fausse, corrigez-la.

1. Les Français sont dangereux quand ils conduisent.
2. Les Anglais sont de bons conducteurs *(drivers)* mais ils conduisent plutôt vite.
3. En France, ceux qui marchent n'apprécient pas beaucoup ceux qui sont au volant.
4. Ceux qui conduisent adorent les à-pied.
5. Les Anglais ont moins d'accidents que les Français.
6. L'avion va plus vite que la voiture mais les Américains ne le comprennent pas encore.

D **Questions.** Répondez.

1. Pourquoi dit-on qu'il y a deux sortes de Français?
2. Quelle transformation y a-t-il quand un Français prend le volant?
3. Les retardataires sont-ils hypocrites? Expliquez votre réponse.
4. Quelles différences y a-t-il entre les Anglais et les Français?
5. Qui sont les Latins?
6. Qui sont ceux qui font mal des choses qui sont bonnes?

E **Familles de mots.** Essayez de deviner le sens des mots suivants.

1. conduire, un conducteur, une conductrice, la conduite
2. exister, l'existence, l'existentialisme
3. retarder, un(e) retardataire, un retard
4. terroriser, un(e) terroriste, le terrorisme, la terreur

Lecture II

A **Les voitures françaises.** Lisez la lecture suivante et identifiez deux marques *(makes)* de voitures françaises.

AUTOMOBILES	
Vends Renault Espace RN 21 Turbo D, mod 96, 48.000 kms, bleue, climatisée, airbag, radio. Tél. 02.43.81.75.79 ap. 18h.	Vds Renault Twingo, 6 mois, noire, toit ouvrant, bag, 3.200 kms, 10.000€. Tél. 02.43.75.64.98.
Vends Renault 9 GTL, 68.000 kms, 5 vitesses, vitres teintées électriques, gris métallique, direction assistée, toit ouvrant. Tél. 02.41.34.63.23 après 20h.	Vends Laguna ii TD 2.2 RXE 7 cv, janvier 1999, 75.000 km, ABS, climatisation automatique, airbags, direction assistée, vitres électriques avant. Pare-brise athermique. Radio commande au volant. Etat neuf. 20.000€. Tél. 02.41.58.87.18 le soir.
Vds Mercedes C 250 D Élégance 95, 1ᵉ main, 94.000 kms, état neuf, clim, radio (Sony), alarme, radiocommandée, vert métal. Tél. 02.41.64.35.70.	Vds. Citroën C25 Camping car, 145.000 kms. Diesel, bon état moteur. Aménagement intérieur: 9 places assises, table et miroir maquillage, penderies, placards, wc, frigo, groupe électrogène 3.6 kw Honda; store extérieur dépliable. Tél. le soir au 02.41.19.53.66.
VDS R5 pour pièces détachées, roulante mais accidentée, petit prix. Tél. 02.41.32.51.61.	

B **Pouvez-vous décider?**

1. Quelle est probablement la plus vieille voiture?
2. Quelle voiture est probablement la plus chère?
3. Quelle voiture est probablement la moins chère?
4. Quelle voiture n'est pas française?
5. Dans quelle voiture est-ce qu'on peut dormir confortablement?
6. Quelles voitures sont confortables quand il fait chaud?
7. Quels propriétaires ne sont pas chez eux pendant la journée?

C **Une voiture à vendre.** Écrivez une petite annonce pour une voiture que vous voulez vendre.

VOCABULAIRE ACTIF

Sur la route

un arrêt (d'autobus) *(bus) stop*
(s')arrêter *to stop*
à toute vitesse *at top speed*
attacher *to attach; to put on*
avancer *to advance*
une ceinture de sécurité *safety belt, seat belt*
changer (de) *to change*
un chauffeur *driver*
comme un fou *like a crazy person*
conduire *to drive*
la conduite *driving*
démarrer *to start a car*
un feu *traffic light*
jusqu'au feu *until the traffic light*
un permis de conduire *driver's license*
reculer *to back up*
un rétroviseur *rearview mirror*
une route *highway*
le sens interdit *one-way street*
un stop *stop sign*
la vitesse *speed*
un volant *steering wheel*

D'autres noms

l'année scolaire *(f.) school year*
un anniversaire de mariage *wedding anniversary*
une boum *party*
un commentaire *commentary*
un conseil *(piece of) advice*
un escargot *snail*

un fou (une folle) *fool; crazy person*
une leçon *lesson*
un match *game*
une patinoire *skating rink*
un(e) propriétaire *owner*
un siècle *century*

Adjectifs

attentif (attentive) *attentive*
constant(e) *constant*
fou (folle) *crazy; mad*
lent(e) *slow*
neuf (neuve) *brand-new*
prêt(e) *ready*
prudent(e) *cautious*
raisonnable *reasonable*
rapide *rapid; fast*
sérieux (sérieuse) *serious*
tranquille *calm*

Verbes

avoir pitié (de qqn.) *to have pity (on s.o.); to feel sorry (for s.o.)*
connaître *to know; be acquainted with; be familiar with*
inviter *to invite*
laisser *to leave; to let*
pouvoir *to be able; to be allowed*
vouloir *to want; to wish*

Adverbes

absolument *absolutely*
constamment *constantly*

follement *in a crazy manner*
lentement *slowly*
patiemment *patiently*
personnellement *personally*
prudemment *prudently*
rapidement *rapidly*
sérieusement *seriously*
si *so*
vite *quickly; fast*

Pronoms objets directs

me *me*
te *you*
le *him; it*
la *her; it*
nous *us*
vous *you*
les *them*

Expressions utiles

C'est promis. *It's a promise.*
Chut! *Shh!*
je veux m'amuser *I want to have fun*
Laisse-moi (Laissez-moi) tranquille! *Leave me alone!*
(mon/ma) chéri(e) *(my) dear, honey*
Mon œil! *My eye!*
ma puce *honey (lit. my flea)*
Plus un mot. *Not one more word.*
Tais-toi! (Taisez-vous!) *Keep quiet!*

Coup d'envoi

Prise de contact   ## Quand vous étiez jeune

Qu'est-ce que tu faisais° quand tu avais seize ans°,   *used to do / were sixteen*
    Caroline?

> J'allais au lycée°.   *high school*
> J'étudiais l'anglais et les mathématiques.
> J'habitais une petite maison.
> Je sortais quelquefois avec mes amis.
> Nous allions au cinéma ensemble.
> Mais je n'avais pas encore mon permis de
>   conduire.

▶ **Et vous?**
Qu'est-ce que vous faisiez quand vous aviez seize ans?

Conversation

L'album de photos

Lori et son amie Denise sont en train de° regarder un album de photos.　　　　　　　　　　　　　　*in the process of*

LORI: C'est une photo de toi?

DENISE: Oui, c'était° au mariage de ma sœur. 　　*it was*

LORI: Elle est plus âgée que° toi? 　　*older than*

DENISE: Oui, de deux ans.

LORI: Ah! La voilà en robe de mariée°, n'est-ce pas? 　*wedding dress*
Comme elle était belle!° 　　*How beautiful she was!*

DENISE: Tu vois° la photo de ce jeune homme en 　*You see*
smoking°? C'est mon beau-frère. 　　*in a tuxedo*

LORI: Il avait l'air jeune.

DENISE: Il n'avait que vingt ans.° 　　*He was only twenty.*
À mon avis°, il en avait assez de° porter son 　*In my opinion / he was fed up*
smoking. 　　　　　　　　　　　　　　*with*

LORI: Il faisait chaud?

DENISE: Très! Et il avait déjà porté° son smoking 　*had already worn*
pour le mariage à la mairie°. 　　*town hall*

LORI: Quand est-ce que ce mariage a eu lieu°? 　*took place*

DENISE: Il y a deux ans.

LORI: Alors, c'est ton tour°. Quand est-ce que tu 　*turn*
vas épouser° ton petit ami? 　　*marry*
(Elles rient.°) 　　　　　　　　　　　*They laugh.*

DENISE: Lori, occupe-toi de tes oignons!° 　*mind your own business!*

▶ **Jouez ces rôles.** Répétez la conversation avec votre partenaire. Remplacez «mariage de ma sœur» par «mariage de mon frère». Faites tous les changements nécessaires.

Il y a un geste

J'en ai assez. The right hand is raised near the left temple. The hand is open but bent at a right angle to the wrist. The gesture is made by twisting the wrist so that the hand passes over your forehead, implying that you are "fed up to here."

À propos

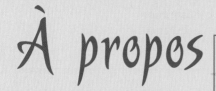

Pourquoi le beau-frère avait-il déjà porté son smoking à la mairie?

a. Il aimait beaucoup porter un smoking.
b. C'est normal. On porte toujours des vêtements élégants à la mairie.
c. Il y a eu deux cérémonies de mariage: à la mairie et à l'église.

Les jeunes

High unemployment (recently as high as 12 percent) and the increasing length of their studies have meant that few young adults are able to become financially independent of their families. At age twenty-two, 60 percent of French men and 45 percent of French women are still living with their parents. Very few students, for example, are able to have a part-time job or purchase a car. Fortunately public transportation is widely available and universities are inexpensive.

Le mariage en France

In order to be legally married in France, all couples are wed in a civil ceremony at the town hall. The mayor (**le maire**), or the mayor's representative, performs the ceremony and the couples express their consent by saying **oui.** Many couples choose to have a religious ceremony as well. This takes place at the church, temple, or mosque, after the civil ceremony.

Currently the average age for marriage is approximately 30 for men and 28 for women. (See **Lecture II, «Le Mariage, oui ou non?»**, page 317.) Since after marriage two women out of three continue to work and the birth rate has fallen to 1.8 children per family, attempts have been made by the government to help couples who have children. There are paid maternity (or paternity) leaves, public day care centers, and subsidies to families with more than two children.

Nursery schools accept children as young as two years of age and, if parents wish, will supervise the children, at school, from 7:30 A.M. until 7:00 P.M.

L'union libre

Today in France, an increasing number of couples live together without being married (**l'union libre** or **la cohabitation**), and many unmarried couples have had children. A recent law, the PACS (**le Pacte civil de solidarité**), confers legal status on unmarried couples, both heterosexual and homosexual, who choose to sign a contract guaranteeing them the same rights as married couples.

▶ **À vous.**   Répondez.

1. Où habitiez-vous quand vous aviez seize ans?
2. Comment s'appelaient vos amis?
3. À quelle école alliez-vous?
4. Qu'est-ce que vous étudiiez?

ENTRE AMIS

If they do not have a photo, give students a few seconds to draw stick figures of a group of people.

Une vieille photo

1. Show your partner an old photo of a group of people.
2. Tell who the people are.
3. Tell how old each one was in the photo.
4. Describe what they were wearing.
5. Tell where they lived.

Prononciation

🎧 Use the Student Audio to help practice pronunciation.

Comparison: Help students avoid pronouncing a short, English *i* [ɪ] in place of the French [i] in words such as **aspirine** and **visiter**.

Les sons [i] et [j]

■ Two related sounds in French are the pure vowel sound [i] (as in the English word *teeth*), and the semi-consonant/semi-vowel [j] (as in the English word *yes*). Practice saying the following words after your instructor, paying particular attention to the highlighted sound. As you pronounce the words for one sound, look at how that sound is spelled and in what kinds of letter combinations it appears. What patterns do you notice?

[i]
- **il**, **ici**, r**i**z, p**i**zza, pol**i**tique, asp**i**rine
- su**i**s, fru**i**t, depu**i**s, tru**i**te, condu**i**re, ju**i**llet
- br**i**e, am**i**e, Soph**i**e
- S**y**lvie, bic**y**clette, **y**

[j]
- mar**i**é, janv**i**er, h**i**er, m**i**am, k**i**osque, nat**i**onal, mons**i**eur, b**i**en
- déta**il**, somme**il**, œ**il**, trava**ill**e, Marse**ill**e, feu**ill**e
- gent**ill**e, f**ill**e, past**ill**e, van**ill**e, ju**ill**et
- **y**eux, essa**y**er, pa**y**er

■ The [i] sound is represented by written **-i-** or **-y-** in the following situations:

1. **i** not in combination with another vowel: merc**i**, avr**i**l, f**i**lle
2. **i** following a **u**: pu**i**s, bru**i**t, tru**i**te
3. final **-ie**: br**ie**, étud**ie**
4. **-y-** between two consonants: il **y** va, S**y**lvie

■ The [j] sound is required in the following circumstances:

The uses of [I] and [j] are further covered in Ch. 12.

1. **i-** before a pronounced vowel in the same syllable: p**i**ed, v**i**ande, mar**i**age
2. **-il, -ill** after a pronounced vowel in the same syllable: trava**il**, conse**ill**er, œ**il**
3. **-ll** after [i]: f**ill**e, ju**ill**et

EXCEPTIONS — million, milliard, mille, ville, village, tranquille

4. initial **y-** before a vowel, **-y-** between two vowels: **y**eux, essa**y**er.

NOTE — Between the sound [i] at the end of one syllable and another vowel at the beginning of the next syllable, [j] is pronounced even though there is no letter representing the sound.

quatrième [ka tRi jɛm]

Listen and repeat:

Point out that linking takes place before **yeux: les yeux.**

1. Sylvie, yeux, bicyclette, y, payer
2. télévision, brioche, nuit, addition, cuisine, principal, délicieux, insister, feuille
3. pitié, amie, papier, pièce, prier, pâtisserie, client, habitiez, impatient, oublier
4. milliard, juillet, ville, fille, bouteille, travail, travaille, conseil, allions, vanille, mille, œil, oreille, tranquille, gentil, gentille, million
5. entrions, entriez

Buts communicatifs

1. Describing Conditions and Feelings in the Past

Quand vous étiez jeune, ...

	oui	non
aviez-vous un chien ou un chat?	_____	_____
étiez-vous souvent malade?	_____	_____
habitiez-vous une grande ville?	_____	_____
aviez-vous beaucoup d'amis?	_____	_____
regardiez-vous beaucoup la télé?	_____	_____

Faisiez is pronounced [fəzje]; see also p. 110.

Que faisiez-vous après l'école?
Comment s'appelaient vos voisins°?   *neighbors*
À votre avis, quelle était la meilleure émission°   *best program*
    de télé?

A. L'imparfait

■ You have already been using one past tense, the passé composé, to relate what happened in the past. The imperfect (**l'imparfait**) is a past tense used to describe conditions and feelings and to express habitual actions.

1. Describing conditions

Ma sœur **était** belle.	*My sister was beautiful.*
Mon beau-frère **avait** l'air jeune.	*My brother-in-law seemed young.*
Léa **portait** une jolie robe.	*Léa was wearing a pretty dress.*
Anne **était** malade.	*Anne was sick.*
Il **pleuvait.**	*It was raining.*
Il y **avait** trois chambres dans notre maison.	*There were three bedrooms in our house.*

2. Describing feelings

Ma sœur **était** nerveuse.	*My sister was nervous.*
Mon beau-frère en **avait** assez.	*My brother-in-law was fed up.*
Je **détestais** les épinards.	*I used to hate spinach.*
Tout le monde **était** heureux.	*Everybody was happy.*

3. Expressing habitual past actions

Nous **regardions** des dessins
animés le samedi.

We used to watch cartoons on Saturday.

À cette époque, Marie **sortait**
avec Paul.

Back then, Marie used to go out with Paul.

Review uses of the passé composé, pp. 160–161.

But: Nous **avons regardé** des
dessins animés samedi.

We watched cartoons (last) Saturday. (once, not a repeated event)

Marie **est sortie** avec
Paul vendredi dernier.

Marie went out with Paul last Friday. (one day, not habitually)

■ To form the imperfect tense, take the **nous** form of the present tense, drop the **-ons** ending, and add the endings **-ais, -ais, -ait, -ions, -iez, -aient.**

jouer (jou~~ons~~)		
je	**jou**	**ais**
tu	**jou**	**ais**
il/elle/on	**jou**	**ait**
nous	**jou**	**ions**
vous	**jou**	**iez**
ils/elles	**jou**	**aient**

avoir (av~~ons~~)		
j'	**av**	**ais**
tu	**av**	**ais**
il/elle/on	**av**	**ait**
nous	**av**	**ions**
vous	**av**	**iez**
ils/elles	**av**	**aient**

aller (all~~ons~~)		
j'	**all**	**ais**
tu	**all**	**ais**
il/elle/on	**all**	**ait**
nous	**all**	**ions**
vous	**all**	**iez**
ils/elles	**all**	**aient**

■ Impersonal expressions also have imperfect tense forms.

infinitive	present	imperfect	
neiger	il neige	**il neigeait**	*it was snowing*
pleuvoir	il pleut	**il pleuvait**	*it was raining*
falloir	il faut	**il fallait**	*it was necessary*
valoir mieux	il vaut mieux	**il valait mieux**	*it was better*

■ **Être** is the only verb that has an irregular stem: **ét-.** The endings are regular.

J'**étais** malade.

Nous **étions** désolés.

■ The **je, tu, il/elle/on,** and **ils/elles** forms of the imperfect all sound alike because the endings are all pronounced the same.

je **jouais**   tu **jouais**   il **jouait**   elles **jouaient**

■ The **-ions** and **-iez** endings are pronounced as one syllable, with the letter **-i-** pronounced [j].

vous habit**iez**   [a bi tje]

nous all**ions**   [a ljɔ̃]

■ You have already learned that if the present tense stem of a verb ends in **-g,** an **-e-** is added before endings beginning with **-o-.** This is also true in other tenses before endings beginning with **-a-** or **-u-.**

present:	nous mang**e**ons			
imperfect:	je mang**e**ais	tu mang**e**ais	il mang**e**ait	ils mang**e**aient
But:	nous mangions vous mangiez			

■ Similarly, if the stem of a verb ends in **-c,** a **-ç-** is used instead before endings beginning with **-a-, -o-,** or **-u-.**

present:	nous commen**ç**ons		
imperfect:	je commen**ç**ais	tu commen**ç**ais	il commen**ç**ait
But:	nous commencions vous commenciez		

Do this activity in pairs. Follow with a stand-up drill.

I **Quand ils étaient jeunes.** Qu'est-ce que ces personnes faisaient ou ne faisaient pas quand elles étaient jeunes? Si vous ne savez pas, devinez. Utilisez **et** ou **mais** et la forme négative pour les décrire.

MODÈLE: mes amis / aller à l'école / conduire
Quand mes amis étaient jeunes, ils allaient à l'école mais ils ne conduisaient pas.

1. mes amis / regarder souvent des dessins animés / lire beaucoup
2. nous / aller à l'école / faire toujours nos devoirs
3. je / manger beaucoup de bonbons / avoir souvent mal aux dents
4. je / me coucher tôt / être toujours raisonnable
5. mes amis / jouer souvent aux jeux vidéo / regarder *Pokémon* à la télé
6. le professeur de français / avoir de bonnes notes / aller souvent à la bibliothèque

Les petits Français commencent l'école plus tôt que les petits Américains. Ils peuvent entrer à l'école maternelle à l'âge de deux ans.

2 **Ma grand-mère.** Transformez le paragraphe suivant à l'imparfait.

Ma grand-mère habite dans une petite maison qui est très jolie et qui a deux chambres. Dans cette région, il pleut souvent et en hiver, quand il neige, on reste à la maison. Ma grand-mère est fragile et elle travaille très peu. Elle est petite et assez vieille. Elle a soixante-quinze ans et elle est seule à la maison depuis la mort de mon grand-père. Mais quand je vais chez elle, nous parlons de beaucoup de choses et quelquefois nous chantons. Elle veut toujours nous préparer quelque chose à manger, mais je fais la cuisine moi-même. Ensuite nous mangeons ensemble. Je l'aime beaucoup et elle m'aime beaucoup aussi.

3 **Quand vous aviez quatorze ans.** Répondez.

Communication (Interpretive): Follow up by having the class interview first the teacher (with books open) and then another student (with books closed).

1. Qui était président des États-Unis quand vous aviez quatorze ans?
2. Quelles émissions regardiez-vous à la télé?
3. Quels acteurs et quelles actrices étaient populaires?
4. À quel jeu vidéo est-ce que vous jouiez?
5. Qu'est-ce que vous faisiez le vendredi soir?
6. Qu'est-ce que vous aimiez manger? Qu'est-ce que vous détestiez?
7. Qui faisait la cuisine pour vous?
8. À quelle école alliez-vous?
9. Comment s'appelaient vos voisins?

B. *Ne ... que*

Sylvie **n'**a **que** dix-huit ans.	*Sylvie is only eighteen.*
Ses parents **n'**ont **qu'**une fille.	*Her parents have only one daughter.*
Il **n'**y a **que** trois personnes dans la famille.	*There are only three people in the family.*

■ **Ne ... que,** a synonym of **seulement,** is used to express a limitation. **Ne** comes before the verb and **que** is placed directly before the expression that it limits.

Il **ne** sort **qu'**avec Renée.	*He goes out only with Renée.*
Il **ne** sort avec Renée **que** le vendredi soir.	*He goes out with Renée on Friday nights only.*

Review **il y a** + expressions of time, p. 162.

4 **Quel âge avaient-ils il y a cinq ans?** Décidez quel âge tout le monde avait il y a cinq ans. Si vous ne savez pas *(If you don't know),* devinez. Utilisez **ne ... que.**

Communication (Presentational): Follow up (books closed) by asking how old the people were *ten* years ago. Require **ne ... que** in each answer.

MODÈLE: votre frère
Il y a cinq ans, mon frère n'avait que seize ans.

1. vous
2. votre meilleur(e) ami(e)
3. votre mère ou votre père
4. les étudiants de cette classe
5. votre acteur préféré
6. votre actrice préférée
7. le professeur de français (Imaginez.)

ENTRE AMIS

Quand tu étais enfant.

1. Find out where your partner lived ten years ago.
2. Ask how old s/he was.
3. Ask what s/he did on Saturdays.
4. Find out what her/his school's name was.
5. Ask if s/he had a dog or a cat. If so, find out its name.
6. Find out who his/her neighbors were.

2. Setting the Scene in the Past

Quand vous êtes arrivé(e) sur ce campus pour la
première fois ...

> c'était en quelle saison?
> c'était quel mois?
> quel âge aviez-vous?
> étiez-vous seul(e) ou avec des amis?
> quel temps faisait-il?
> quels vêtements portiez-vous?

C. L'imparfait et le passé composé

Review the passé composé,
pp. 160 & 189–191.

■ The **imparfait** is often used to give background information that "sets the
scene" for some other verb in the past. This scene-setting information describes what was going on. It describes the conditions surrounding some other
action. If the other verb specifies what *happened*, it is in the **passé composé**.

J'étais en train de faire mes devoirs quand **Alain a téléphoné.**	*I was (busy) doing my homework when Alain telephoned.*
Il était huit heures quand **Renée est arrivée.**	*It was eight o'clock when Renée arrived.*
Jeanne avait quinze ans quand **elle a commencé** à fréquenter les garçons.	*Jeanne was fifteen when she started dating boys.*

■ For weather expressions:

• Use the **imperfect** when the weather sets the scene for another past action.

Il faisait beau quand **nous sommes sortis.**	*It was nice outside when we went out.*
Il pleuvait quand **nous sommes rentrés.**	*It was raining when we got home.*
Il neigeait. Alors **Karine a décidé** de porter ses bottes.	*It was snowing. So Karine decided to wear her boots.*

Connection: Point out that a
weather report would normally
use the passé composé.

• Use the **passé composé** when you simply state what the weather was
like at a specific time.

Hier, **il a plu** à Paris, mais **il a neigé** dans les montagnes. **Il a fait beau**
à Nice.

5 **Qu'est-ce qu'elle faisait?** Utilisez les expressions suivantes pour créer des phrases logiques.

MODÈLE: **Léa faisait du ski quand elle est tombée.**

Communication (Interpretive & Presentational): Follow up (with books closed) by asking students to try to recall some of the sentences other students created.

Léa

être en train d'étudier
regarder la télévision
être en train de lire
conduire
manger
boire
faire la sieste
écrire une lettre
prendre le petit déjeuner
descendre d'une voiture

quand

son fiancé
ses parents
je
elle
nous
ses amis

entrer
partir
arriver
tomber
avoir un accident
perdre patience
téléphoner

6 **Les Lauprête ont fait un voyage.** Quel temps faisait-il? Complétez les phrases suivantes.

*Do this activity in pairs. Then follow up (with books closed) by redoing the exercise as a teacher-led activity. Ask periodically **Comment est-ce qu'on écrit** pleuvait? (**pris, faisait,** etc.).*

MODÈLE: faire du vent / sortir de chez eux
Il faisait du vent quand les Lauprête sont sortis de chez eux.

1. pleuvoir / prendre le taxi
2. faire beau / arriver à l'aéroport
3. faire chaud / monter dans l'avion
4. faire froid / descendre de l'avion
5. neiger / commencer à faire du ski

7 **Dernière sortie au restaurant.** Décrivez la dernière fois que vous êtes allé(e) au restaurant.

Communication (Interpretive & Presentational): If done in pairs, follow up by asking students to share their partner's experience.

1. Quel jour est-ce que c'était?
2. Quel temps faisait-il?
3. Quels vêtements portiez-vous?
4. Quelle heure était-il quand vous êtes arrivé(e)?
5. Étiez-vous seul(e)? Si non, qui était avec vous?
6. Environ combien de personnes y avait-il au restaurant?
7. Quelle était la spécialité du restaurant?
8. Comment était le serveur (la serveuse)?
9. Aviez-vous très faim?
10. Qu'est-ce que vous avez commandé?
11. Comment était le repas?

8 **Renseignements.** Écrivez un petit paragraphe pour chaque numéro. Expliquez les conditions et ce qui est arrivé.

Alternate: Assign one question from each number per student. Then, as answers are dictated, write them on the board in the form of a paragraph. The result is usually quite comical.

Modèle: Quand je suis tombé(e), ...
(Qu'est-ce que vous faisiez? Avec qui étiez-vous? Qu'est-ce que vous avez dit?)
Quand je suis tombé(e), je faisais du ski. J'étais seul(e) et j'ai dit «Aïe!».

1. Quand j'ai trouvé mon ami, ...
(Qu'est-ce qu'il portait? Où allait-il? Avec qui était-il? Qu'est-ce que vous avez fait?)
2. Quand ma mère a téléphoné, ...
(Quelle heure était-il? Que faisiez-vous? Qu'est-ce qu'elle voulait? Qu'est-ce que vous avez répondu?)
3. Quand mon cousin (mon ami(e), mon frère, etc.) a eu son accident, ...
(Où était-il? Qu'est-ce qu'il faisait? Quel âge avait-il? Quel temps faisait-il? Qu'est-ce qu'il a fait après?)
4. Quand je suis entré(e) dans la classe, ...
(Quelles personnes étaient là? Qu'est-ce qu'elles portaient? Quelle heure était-il? Avec qui avez-vous parlé?)

ENTRE AMIS

Comparison: Before pairing students, have them identify the verb tense for each sentence.

Tu t'es bien amusé(e)?

1. Find out when the last time was that your partner went out.
2. Ask where s/he went and what s/he did.
3. Find out what s/he was wearing.
4. Find out what the weather was like.
5. Ask if s/he had fun.
6. Ask at what time s/he got home.
7. Find out if s/he was tired when s/he got home.

3. Making Comparisons

Est-ce que ta vie était différente quand tu avais seize ans, Christine?

Pas vraiment. À cette époque°, je   *Back then*
   travaillais autant° que maintenant.   *as much*
Et j'étudiais aussi° souvent que   *as*
   maintenant.
Mais j'étais plus° active.   *more*
J'étais moins stressée°,   *less stressed*
   parce que j'avais moins de soucis°.   *fewer worries*

Et vous?

Quand vous n'aviez que seize ans, …

> est-ce que vous étudiiez moins que maintenant?
> faisiez-vous autant de sport?
> aviez-vous plus de temps libre que maintenant?
> est-ce que vous aviez moins de soucis?
> étiez-vous plus heureux (heureuse) que maintenant?
> étiez-vous aussi grand(e)?
> sortiez-vous plus souvent que maintenant?

D. Le comparatif des adverbes

■ To make comparisons with adverbs, the French use the expressions **plus** (*more*), **moins** (*less*), and **aussi** (*as*). All comparisons may be followed by **que** (*than, as*) and a second term of comparison. When a personal pronoun is required after **que**, a stressed pronoun must be used.

Review the forms of stressed pronouns, p. 172.

Anne conduit **plus** lentement **que** Pierre.	*Anne drives slower than Pierre.*
Elle conduit **moins** rapidement **que lui.**	*She drives less fast than he (does).*
Il chante **aussi** bien **qu'elle.**	*He sings as well as she (does).*

■ The comparative forms of the adverb **bien** are **moins bien, aussi bien,** and **mieux.**

Je nage **moins bien** que ma sœur.	*I don't swim as well as my sister.*
Mais je danse **mieux** qu'elle.	*But I dance better than she (does).*
Elle patine **aussi bien** que moi.	*She skates as well as I (do).*

9   Une comparaison. Répondez aux questions suivantes. Si vous ne savez pas la réponse, devinez.

MODÈLE: Qui chante mieux, votre meilleur(e) ami(e) ou vous?
Je chante aussi bien que lui (qu'elle).   ou
Il (Elle) chante mieux que moi.

1. Qui conduit plus lentement, votre professeur de français ou vous?
2. Qui fait mieux la cuisine, votre mère ou votre père?
3. Qui travaille moins sérieusement, un bon étudiant ou un mauvais étudiant?
4. Qui danse mieux, les hommes ou les femmes?
5. Qui mange moins rapidement, votre meilleur(e) ami(e) ou vous?
6. Qui sort plus souvent le soir, votre meilleur(e) ami(e) ou vous?

E. Le comparatif des adjectifs

Encourage students to review the distinction between adjectives and adverbs in Appendix C.

■ You have already learned to use **plus**, **moins**, and **aussi** to make comparisons with adverbs. These words are also used to make comparisons with adjectives.

Haïti est **plus** pauvre que la République dominicaine.	*Haiti is poorer than the Dominican Republic.*
Ce pays est **moins** grand que la République dominicaine.	*This country is smaller than the Dominican Republic.*
Aïda est **aussi** belle que sa fille.	*Aïda is as beautiful as her daughter.*

■ The comparative forms of the adjective **bon(ne)** are **moins bon(ne), aussi bon(ne)**, and **meilleur(e)**.

Denise est **aussi bonne** que sa sœur?   *Is Denise as good as her sister?*
Non, comme étudiante, elle est **moins bonne**.   *No, as a student, she's worse.*
Sa sœur est **meilleure** qu'elle.   *Her sister is better than she (is).*

Synthèse: *bon* **et** *bien;* *mieux* **et** *meilleur*

adjectifs		adverbes	
bon(ne)	*good*	**bien**	*well*
meilleur(e)	*better*	**mieux**	*better*

In English, the comparative form of both *good* and *well* is the same word: *better*. In French there is a separate word for each.

Tom est un **meilleur** étudiant.   Tom parle **mieux** le français.
*Tom is a **better** student.*   *Tom speaks French **better**.*

---

10 **Est-ce que je suis d'accord avec le professeur?** Imaginez l'opinion du professeur. Ensuite donnez votre opinion. Attention aux adjectifs!

MODÈLE: la musique classique / la musique pop / beau
Le professeur pense que la musique classique est plus belle que la musique pop.
À mon avis, la musique pop est aussi belle que la musique classique.

Connection: Have students research the common origin of the monuments in #1.

1. la statue de la Liberté / la tour Eiffel / beau
2. le fromage français / le fromage américain / bon
3. la télévision / un livre / ennuyeux
4. les devoirs / les vacances / important
5. notre université / l'université de Paris / bon
6. les hommes / les femmes / travailleur

Follow-up: Have students compare themselves to a sibling. Alternate: Redo the exercise. Change **son frère David** to **sa sœur Stéphanie** and inform students that she is on a par with her brother (use **aussi bonne,** etc.).

11 **Deux frères.** Pauvre François! Son frère David fait toujours mieux que lui. Comparez-les.

MODÈLE: François est bon en anglais.
Oui, mais son frère David est meilleur que lui en anglais.

1. François parle bien l'anglais.
2. François a une bonne voiture.
3. François a une bonne note en anglais.
4. François joue bien au tennis.
5. François conduit attentivement.
6. François est un bon étudiant.
7. François chante bien.
8. François est intelligent.

12 **Nos meilleurs amis et nous.** D'abord faites une comparaison entre vous et votre meilleur(e) ami(e). Ensuite encouragez votre partenaire à faire la même chose.

MODÈLE: chanter bien

VOUS: Moi, je chante mieux que mon meilleur ami (ma meilleure amie). Et toi?

VOTRE PARTENAIRE: Moi, je chante moins bien que lui (qu'elle).

Communication (Presentational): Follow up by having students share 2 things they learned about their partner.

1. être bon(ne) en maths
2. parler bien le français
3. être patient(e)
4. conduire bien
5. être un(e) bon(ne) étudiant(e)
6. être grand(e)
7. danser bien
8. être bavard(e)

F. Le comparatif (suite)

■ To compare how much of a particular action people do, the words **plus, moins,** and **autant** (*as much, as many*) are used *after a verb.*

René **parle plus** que son père.	*René talks more than his father.*
Il **parle moins** que sa mère.	*He talks less than his mother.*
Il **parle autant** que moi.	*He talks as much as I (do).*

Review the use of expressions of quantity, Ch. 8, p. 223.

■ To compare how much of something one has, eats, drinks, etc., the expressions of quantity **plus de, moins de,** and **autant de** are used *before a noun.*

Haïti a **moins de** touristes que la Martinique.	*Haiti has fewer tourists than Martinique.*
Les Haïtiens ont **plus de** soucis que moi.	*Haitians have more worries than I (do).*
Ils n'ont pas **autant d'**argent que moi.	*They don't have as much money as I (do).*

13 **Une comparaison.** Répondez aux questions suivantes. Si vous ne savez pas la réponse, devinez.

MODÈLE: Qui a plus de soucis, un étudiant ou un professeur?
Un étudiant a plus de soucis qu'un professeur.
ou
Un étudiant a autant de soucis qu'un professeur.

1. Qui a moins d'argent, vous ou vos parents?
2. Qui a plus de responsabilités, un homme ou une femme?
3. Qui a moins de temps libre, un étudiant ou un professeur?
4. Qui a plus de travail, un pilote ou une hôtesse de l'air?

14 **Monique a quinze jours de vacances.** Décidez si Monique a plus, moins ou autant de vacances que les autres.

MODÈLE: Ses parents ont un mois de vacances.
Monique a moins de vacances qu'eux.

NOTE CULTURELLE
Les Français utilisent souvent l'expression **huit jours** comme synonyme d'**une semaine**. De la même manière, on utilise l'expression **quinze jours** à la place de **deux semaines**.

1. Alice a huit jours de vacances.
2. Nous avons deux mois de vacances.
3. Tu as un jour de vacances.
4. Son frère a deux semaines de vacances.
5. Vous avez trente jours de vacances.
6. Je n'ai pas de vacances.
7. Michel et Jean ont trois mois de vacances.
8. Philippe a une semaine de vacances.
9. Ses amies ont quinze jours de vacances.

G. Le superlatif

■ Superlatives normally use the definite article plus the words **plus** or **moins**. They may be used with an expression including **de** (*of, in*) plus a noun to make the extent of the superlative clear.

Mathusalem est la personne **la plus âgée** (**de** la Bible). — *Methuselah is the oldest person (in the Bible).*

Le Rhode Island est **le plus petit** état (**des** États-Unis). — *Rhode Island is the smallest state (in the United States).*

Les Canadiens sont **les meilleurs** joueurs de hockey. — *Canadians are the best hockey players.*

Be sure students understand that **le** modifies the adverb that follows it (which has no gender), not the subject of the sentence.

■ With the superlative of an adverb, **le** is always used.

C'est Anne qui danse **le mieux** (de toutes mes amies). — *Anne dances the best (of all of my friends).*

Point out that the possessive adjective can be used in place of the definite article. Students have already been using the superlative in the expression **votre meilleur(e) ami(e).**

■ With a superlative *adjective,* the definite article agrees with the adjective.

le plus petit   la plus petite
le moins grand   la moins grande

les plus petits   les plus petites
les moins grands   les moins grandes

NOTE | Superlative adjectives are placed either before or after the noun according to where they would be placed normally.

Review the adjectives that normally precede a noun, Ch. 4, p. 107.

1. If the adjective follows the noun, the definite article must be repeated.

Haïti est *le* **pays** *le* **plus pauvre** de l'Amérique latine.
Les romans policiers sont *les* **romans** *les* **plus intéressants.**
Sandrine est *l'*étudiante *la* **moins paresseuse.**

2. If the adjective precedes the noun, only one definite article is used.

Paris et Lyon sont *les* **plus grandes villes** de France.
Le français est *la* **plus belle langue** du monde.
C'est *le* **moins bon restaurant** de la ville.

15 **Quelle exagération!** Aimez-vous votre cours de français? Exagérez un peu. Utilisez le superlatif dans les phrases suivantes.

MODÈLE: C'est un cours important.
C'est le cours le plus important du monde!

> Try to use other endings besides **du monde.** For instance, **de l'université, des États-Unis,** etc.

1. C'est un cours intéressant.
2. C'est un bon cours.
3. C'est un professeur intelligent.
4. Ce sont des étudiants travailleurs.
5. Ce sont de bons étudiants.
6. Ce sont de belles étudiantes.
7. Ce sont de beaux étudiants.
8. C'est un livre bizarre.

16 **Quel est le plus ... ?** Répondez à ces questions. Si vous ne savez pas, devinez.

MODÈLE: Quel est le plus grand état des États-Unis?
L'Alaska est le plus grand état des États-Unis.

Answers: 1. New York, Toronto; 2. Montréal

1. Quelle est la plus grande ville des États-Unis? du Canada?
2. Quelle est la plus grande ville francophone du monde après Paris?
3. Qui est la meilleure actrice de votre pays?
4. Quel est le film le plus ennuyeux de cette année?
5. Quelle est la carte Pokémon la plus importante, à votre avis?
6. Qui est la personne la moins âgée de cette classe?
7. Quelle est l'émission de télévision la plus intéressante le jeudi soir?
8. Qui sont les meilleurs joueurs de hockey?

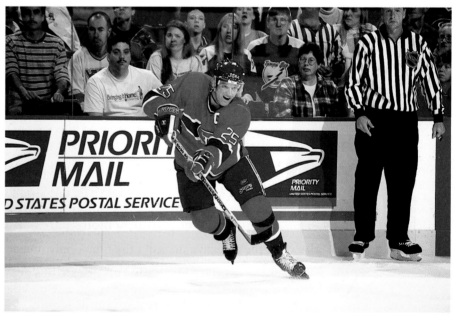

Les Canadiens de Montréal en action

17 **Rien que des superlatifs!** Donnez votre opinion personnelle. Faites des phrases au superlatif.

MODÈLES: un bon restaurant (de la ville)
Joe's Diner est le meilleur restaurant de la ville.

un sport intéressant (du monde)
Le golf est le sport le plus intéressant du monde.

1. une bonne actrice (de mon pays)
2. un professeur charmant (de cette université)
3. un film ennuyeux (de cette année)
4. un bel acteur (de mon pays)
5. une mauvaise chanson (de cette année)
6. une personne amusante (de ma famille)

18 **Microconversation: Tu n'es jamais d'accord** *(in agreement)* **avec moi.** Utilisez les expressions suivantes pour compléter la conversation.

MODÈLE: le meilleur restaurant

VOTRE PARTENAIRE: **Quel est le meilleur restaurant de la ville?**
VOUS: **C'est le restaurant qui s'appelle** *Chez Tony.*
VOTRE PARTENAIRE: **Mais non! C'est le plus mauvais restaurant.**
VOUS: **Tu n'es jamais d'accord avec moi!**

Review the gesture for **non**, Ch. 2, p. 30.

1. le meilleur bistro de la ville
2. le cours le plus intéressant de cette université
3. le bâtiment le plus laid de cette université
4. la plus belle ville du pays
5. le meilleur supermarché de la ville
6. le professeur le plus charmant de cette université

ENTRE AMIS

Comparaison des membres d'une famille

1. Find out how many people there are in your partner's family.
2. Find out who is the oldest, the tallest, the shortest, the youngest.
3. Find out who drives the best.
4. Find out who is the most generous, the most stingy.
5. Describe your own family.

Intégration www ⊙

Révision

A Quelles différences!

1. Nommez trois choses que vous faisiez quand vous étiez à l'école secondaire et que vous ne faites plus maintenant.
2. Nommez trois différences entre vous et un autre membre de votre famille.
3. Quelles différences y a-t-il entre un chien et un chat?
4. Quelles différences y a-t-il entre un avion et un train?

B Un sondage *(A poll).* Demandez aux autres étudiants d'identifier ...

Follow-up: Put students in pairs and have them try to guess each other's answers.

1. le plus bel homme du monde
2. la plus belle femme du monde
3. le meilleur groupe rock
4. le jeu vidéo le plus difficile
5. le jeu électronique que vous aimez le mieux
6. la meilleure émission de télévision
7. l'émission la moins intéressante
8. le meilleur film
9. le livre le plus intéressant
10. le sport que vous aimez le mieux
11. la personne que vous admirez le plus
12. le moment le plus ennuyeux de votre journée

Comparison & Communication (Interpretive): Have students read their lists out loud; brainstorm with the class to determine if information presented was placed in the correct list. Suggestion: Assign the *Rédaction* at the end of Ch. 11 in the Workbook.

C Début de rédaction. Vous êtes allé(e) à une boum. Faites deux listes.

Dans la première vous devez faire une description à l'aide de *l'imparfait.* Indiquez la date et l'endroit; décrivez les vêtements, etc. (C'était quel jour? Où se trouvait la boum? Que portiez-vous? Qui était là?)

Dans l'autre liste, vous devez utiliser *le passé composé.*
Expliquez à quelle heure vous êtes arrivé(e), avec qui vous avez parlé, ce que vous avez mangé et bu, à quelle heure vous êtes parti(e), etc.

Communication (Interpretive): Encourage students to use the practice test on the Lab Audio Program.

D À vous. Répondez.

1. Quel âge aviez-vous quand vous avez commencé vos études au lycée?
2. Où habitiez-vous à cette époque?
3. Avez-vous changé d'adresse depuis?
4. Combien de personnes y avait-il dans votre famille?
5. Quelle était votre émission de télévision préférée?
6. Comment s'appelait votre meilleur(e) ami(e)?
7. Quelle était la chanson la plus populaire quand vous étiez au lycée?
8. Quel cours aimiez-vous le moins quand vous étiez au lycée? Pourquoi?
9. Écoutiez-vous la radio aussi souvent que maintenant?

Négociations:

Hier et quand j'avais 10 ans. Interviewez autant d'étudiants que possible pour trouver des gens qui répondent *oui* aux questions.

Modèle: **Est-ce que tu as beaucoup étudié hier?**
Est-ce que tu étudiais beaucoup quand tu avais dix ans?

Be careful to choose between the passé composé and the imperfect. No *one* student's initials should be written more than twice.

For complete instructions on how to prepare for and to use this activity, see *Négociations* on the Class Prep CD-ROM. Since all students use the same form, it has not been reproduced in Appendix D.

Video for Chapter 11: A. Video worksheets (*Cahier*); B. ACE Video practice test (WWW); C. CD-ROM

regarder des dessins animés _____ hier _____ à 10 ans	téléphoner à des amis _____ hier _____ à 10 ans	lire des bandes dessinées _____ hier _____ à 10 ans
parler une autre langue _____ hier _____ à 10 ans	sortir avec des amis _____ hier _____ à 10 ans	nettoyer ta chambre _____ hier _____ à 10 ans
te lever tôt _____ hier _____ à 10 ans	étudier beaucoup _____ hier _____ à 10 ans	aller au cinéma _____ hier _____ à 10 ans
porter un jean _____ hier _____ à 10 ans	t'amuser beaucoup _____ hier _____ à 10 ans	perdre patience _____ hier _____ à 10 ans
te coucher tôt _____ hier _____ à 10 ans	boire du lait _____ hier _____ à 10 ans	faire du sport _____ hier _____ à 10 ans

www**Réalités culturelles**

Haïti

L'esclavage et la colonisation française continuent à marquer la structure sociale d'Haïti. Ce pays, qui était la plus riche des colonies françaises, est devenu un des pays les plus pauvres. Un héros, Toussaint Louverture, a inspiré son peuple et Haïti est devenu, en 1803, la première république des Amériques à pouvoir se libérer de son colonisateur. C'est ainsi que le 1er janvier 2004, jour de la fête nationale, Haïti a pu célébrer le bicentenaire de son independance. Mais l'instabilité politique, des rébellions, massacres et dictatures successives déchirent ce pays depuis longtemps. En 1990, une série d'élections démocratiques et l'arrivée au pouvoir d'un prêtre catholique, le père Jean-Bertrand Aristide, ont donné un nouvel espoir aux Haïtiens. Cependant, l'invasion de la drogue, des maladies infectieuses comme le SIDA et la tuberculose, des querelles politiques, la corruption, l'absence d'investisseurs étrangers et un embargo de l'aide financière promise font souffrir gravement ce pays. Le peuple haïtien, accueillant et croyant, mérite notre soutien moral, médical et économique.

Repères: Haïti

Statut politique:	république
Superficie:	27.750 km² (équivalente à celle du Maryland)
Population:	8.100.000
Langue officielle:	français et créole (depuis 1987); 20% de la population parle français
Religion:	catholique, protestant, vaudou
Capitale:	Port-au-Prince
Ressources:	tourisme, agriculture (bananes, canne à sucre, café, mangues), minéraux (bauxite, magnésium)

Vocabulaire: accueillant *hospitable,* cependant *however,* croyant *faith-filled,* déchirer *to tear apart,* esclavage *slavery,* espoir *hope,* mangues *mangoes,* prêtre *priest,* SIDA *AIDS,* soutien *help*

Lecture 1

Ⓐ Étude du vocabulaire. Étudiez les phrases suivantes et choisissez les mots anglais qui correspondent aux mots français en caractères gras: *especially, earth, when, rather, beyond, around, full, happiness.*

1. Quel **bonheur lorsque** les étudiants sont en vacances!
2. Elle était fatiguée **au-delà** des limites de ses forces.
3. Les tasses étaient **remplies** de café.
4. Il faisait froid? Non, il faisait **plutôt** chaud.
5. La **terre** de l'Iowa est fertile, **surtout** quand elle est noire.
6. Marc a regardé **autour** de lui pour voir s'il connaissait des gens.

Ⓑ Parcourez cette sélection. Lisez rapidement la lecture suivante pour trouver un ou deux exemples de l'amour et du courage d'Aïda.

La grand-mère Aïda

*Marie-Célie Agnant est née à Port-au-Prince, en Haïti, mais habite actuellement à Montréal. Dans **La Dot de Sara** (Sara's Dowry) elle raconte l'histoire de quatre générations de femmes haïtiennes.*

Grand-mère Aïda c'était comme la bonne terre. Amoureuse de la vie, généreuse et intelligente. Elle donnait, donnait, la femme Aïda, pour le plaisir de donner, pour l'amour de l'amour, l'amour de la tendresse, pour l'amour sans raison d'aimer, au-delà de la raison et de l'amour, cet amour de la vie pour ce qu'elle est véritablement: trésor, mystère, beauté, bonheur simple dans le

tourbillon[1] de l'existence, au milieu des siens[2]: enfants, petits-enfants, nièces et neveux. Aïda, les jupes toujours remplies d'enfants. Et lorsque j'y pense, au fait, qu'avait-elle d'autre, qu'avions-nous d'autre? ...

Grand-mère Aïda m'avait élevée au doigt et à la baguette[3], comme cela se faisait dans ce temps-là. Ma mère à moi, Man Clarisse, n'avait pas survécu à ma naissance[4]. Elle avait été emportée par une septicémie[5], dit-on, quelque temps après que je sois née et n'avait jamais voulu révéler le nom de celui qui l'avait mise en mal d'enfant[6]. Elle avait alors vingt ans. Comme tant d'autres, elle avait dû se dire que les enfants, c'est plutôt l'affaire des femmes. Il y avait autour de nous et avec nous cette communauté de commères, matantes et marraines[7], qui étaient pour moi comme autant de mamans. Elle avait tenu[8], grand-mère, à m'envoyer à l'école. À l'époque, c'était un grand pas[9], comme on dit, car les petites filles—et croyez-moi, cela n'a pas beaucoup changé—on les gardait surtout pour aider à la maison, ou à faire marcher le commerce. L'école, lorsqu'on le pouvait, on y envoyait plutôt les futurs messieurs. S'il y avait quelque argent à investir, mieux valait l'employer à garnir la caboche[10] des petits hommes, ceux qui, pensait-on, devaient par la suite sauver la famille de la faim en devenant agronomes[11], avocats, ingénieurs, et peut-être même médecins.

Envoyer les enfants à l'école, c'était, disait-on, comme mettre de l'argent en banque. J'y suis allée, moi, jusqu'à la deuxième année du secondaire, puis à l'école d'économie domestique du bourg, chez madame Souffrant. C'était énorme.

Marie-Célie Agnant, *La Dot de Sara*

---

1. *whirlwind*   2. *surrounded by her family*   3. *had raised me strictly*   4. *hadn't survived my birth*
5. *blood poisoning*   6. *the one who had made her pregnant*   7. *neighbors, aunts and godmothers*
8. *had insisted on*   9. *step*   10. *head*   11. *by becoming agricultural specialists*

C **Vrai ou faux?** Décidez si les phrases suivantes sont vraies ou fausses. Si une phrase est fausse, corrigez-la.

1. La narratrice est la fille d'Aïda.
2. On sait le nom du père de la narratrice.
3. Elle a sans doute appris à faire la cuisine dans une école spécialisée.
4. Sa mère était assez âgée quand elle est morte.
5. Les garçons devaient, plus tard, gagner de l'argent pour la famille.
6. Il était normal que les filles fassent des études.
7. Aïda s'occupait de beaucoup d'enfants.

D **Discussion.** Relisez la lecture et cherchez des exemples ...

1. pour comparer Aïda et les grands-mères que vous avez connues.
2. de généralisations/stéréotypes en ce qui concerne les hommes et les femmes.
3. de ressemblances ou de différences entre la culture haïtienne et la culture de votre pays.

E **Familles de mots.** Essayez de deviner le sens des mots suivants.

1. aimer, l'amour, aimable, amoureux (amoureuse)
2. naître, la naissance, né(e)
3. raisonner, la raison, raisonnable
4. la vérité, véritable, véritablement, vrai(e)

Lecture II

A **Étude du vocabulaire.** Étudiez les phrases suivantes et choisissez les mots anglais qui correspondent aux mots français en caractères gras: *live, birth, leave, out of, single-parent, close relatives, day care center, nanny, make easy.*

1. La **naissance** d'un enfant est une joie pour la famille.
2. Le **congé** de maternité vous permet de rester à la maison pendant plusieurs mois.
3. Les parents cherchent souvent une **crèche** pour garder leur enfant.
4. Il y a aussi des jeunes filles **au pair** qui **vivent** avec la famille.
5. Les enfants bien disciplinés **facilitent** le travail de leurs parents.
6. Les **parents proches** n'ont pas le droit de se marier.
7. Les familles **monoparentales** ne sont pas rares.
8. La machine ne marche pas; elle est **hors** service.

B **Parcourez la lecture.** Lisez rapidement la lecture qui suit pour trouver:

1. trois types de famille
2. les mots français pour *maternity leave*, *public day care*, et *nursery school*
3. ce que c'est qu'un PACS

Le mariage, oui ou non?

À quel âge se marient-ils? L'âge légal du mariage est fixé à dix-huit ans, et une jeune fille peut se marier à quinze ans avec l'accord de ses parents. Mais les jeunes se marient de plus en plus tard.

	hommes	*femmes*
en 1968	25 ans	23 ans
aujourd'hui	30 ans	28 ans

D'après le Quid

De nouveaux modèles de la famille. Le modèle traditionnel de la famille, avec un couple marié et des enfants issus du mariage, coexiste de plus en plus avec des modèles nouveaux. Avec le développement de la cohabitation il y a une augmentation du nombre des enfants hors mariage: près de 40% des naissances aujourd'hui. Le résultat des divorces (un divorce sur trois mariages en France et un sur deux à Paris) augmente le nombre des familles monoparentales: 9% des enfants vivent avec un seul de leurs parents. Les remariages multiplient les situations où des enfants vivent avec d'autres enfants issus d'un ou de plusieurs mariages précédents: 11% des enfants vivent dans des familles recomposées.

D'après Francoscopie

Si la mère travaille. Il y a, en France, des conditions qui facilitent la situation de la femme qui continue de travailler après la naissance de son enfant. La femme qui travaille peut avoir un congé de maternité où elle est rémunérée à 84% de son salaire. Elle peut rester à la maison pendant seize semaines: six semaines avant la naissance du bébé et dix semaines après. Pour une femme qui a trois enfants ou plus, la période du congé de maternité est plus longue: huit semaines avant et dix-huit semaines après la naissance.

Après son congé de maternité, quand la femme recommence à travailler, elle peut confier son enfant à une crèche collective publique ou choisir une autre solution comme le système des jeunes filles au pair. À deux ans, son enfant peut aller à l'école maternelle où il y a souvent un service de garderie le matin à partir de 7 heures 30 et le soir jusqu'à 19 heures.

Qu'est-ce que le PACS? Le PACS est un contrat conclu entre deux personnes majeures, de sexe différent ou de même sexe, pour organiser leur vie commune. Il crée des droits et obligations pour les partenaires, notamment «une aide mutuelle et matérielle». Deux personnes majeures peuvent signer un PACS, excepté dans les cas suivants :

- entre parents proches
- si l'une est déjà mariée
- si l'une a déjà conclu un PACS avec une autre personne
- si l'une est mineure

D'après www.france.diplomatie.fr et La Civilisation française en évolution II

C Questions. Répondez.

1. Quel est l'âge légal pour le mariage?
2. Y a-t-il des exceptions?
3. Quel est le pourcentage des divorces à Paris?
4. Est-ce que le nombre de familles avec un seul parent augmente ou diminue?
5. Quel pourcentage des enfants n'ont pas de parents mariés?
6. Quelle est la période du congé de maternité pour une femme qui a trois enfants?
7. Quel âge faut-il avoir pour aller à l'école en France?
8. Qui peut signer un PACS?

Comparison & Connection: Have students discuss or research these items with respect to their own country.

D Discussions. Relisez la lecture pour trouver les renseignements suivants.

1. the change in family structure in France
2. maternity leave and day care
3. the average age for marriage
4. the legal status of living together without being married

VOCABULAIRE ACTIF

Practice this vocabulary with the flashcards on the *Entre amis* web site.

Noms

un chanteur/une chanteuse *singer*
un dessin animé *cartoon*
une émission (de télé) *(TV) program*
une équipe *team*
une hôtesse de l'air *(female) flight attendant*
un lycée *senior high school*
le maire *mayor*
la mairie *town hall*
le mariage *marriage; wedding*
un pilote *pilot*
une responsabilité *responsibility*
une robe de mariée *wedding dress*
un smoking *tuxedo*
un souci *worry; care*
une statue *statue*
un tour *turn, tour*
une tour *tower*
un voisin/une voisine *neighbor*

Pour faire une comparaison

aussi ... *as ...*
autant *as much*
mieux *better*

moins *less*
plus *more*

Adjectifs

âgé(e) *old*
amusant(e) *amusing, funny; fun*
dangereux (dangereuse) *dangerous*
meilleur(e) *better*
pauvre *poor*
populaire *popular*
préféré(e) *favorite*
sincère *sincere*
stressé(e) *stressed*

Verbes

avoir lieu *to take place*
en avoir assez *to be fed up*
épouser (quelqu'un) *to marry (someone)*
être en train de *to be in the process of*
fréquenter (quelqu'un) *to date (someone)*
neiger *to snow*
pleuvoir *to rain*

Expressions utiles

à cette époque *at that time; back then*
à mon (ton, etc.) avis *in my (your, etc.) opinion*
Comme il (elle) était ... ! *How ... he (she) was!*
huit jours *one week*
il neigeait *it was snowing*
il pleuvait *it was raining*
j'aime le mieux (le plus) *I like best*
j'aime le moins *I like least*
ne ... que *only*
Occupe-toi de tes oignons! *Mind your own business!*
quinze jours *two weeks*
toute la famille *the whole family*
tu vois *you see*

Les réservations

Buts communicatifs
Making a request
Making a restaurant or
  hotel reservation
Making a transportation
  reservation

Structures utiles
Le verbe **savoir**
Les verbes réguliers en
  -ir (-iss-)
L'adjectif **tout**
Le futur
Le futur avec **si** et **quand**

Culture
• *À propos*
Pour répondre au
  téléphone
La politesse (rappel)
À l'hôtel
Mince!
• *Il y a un geste*
Qu'est-ce que je vais
  faire?
• *Lectures*
L'horaire des trains
  (Paris–Nantes)
Séjours organisés au
  Sénégal

Coup d'envoi

Au restaurant ou à l'hôtel

Puis-je° réserver une table?   *May I*
   Pour combien de personnes?
   Pour quel jour?
   Et pour quelle heure?
   À quel nom°, s'il vous plaît?   *In what name*

Puis-je réserver une chambre?
   Pour combien de personnes?
   Pour quelle(s) nuit(s)?
   À quel nom, s'il vous plaît?

Conversation

Une réservation par téléphone

Grayson Smith téléphone pour réserver une table pour demain soir dans un restaurant à Angers. Mais le restaurant sera° fermé demain.

will be

MME DUPONT:	Allô! Ici le restaurant La Pyramide. J'écoute.
M. SMITH:	Bonjour, Madame. Je voudrais réserver une table pour demain soir.
MME DUPONT:	Je regrette, Monsieur. Nous serons fermés demain.
M. SMITH:	Mince!° Je n'ai pas de chance°! Je ne savais pas° que vous fermiez le mardi. Qu'est-ce que je vais faire? Vous serez ouvert après-demain?°
MME DUPONT:	Mais oui, Monsieur.
M. SMITH:	Bien, alors puis-je réserver une table pour après-demain?
MME DUPONT:	Oui, c'est pour combien de personnes?
M. SMITH:	Cinq. Une table pour cinq personnes.
MME DUPONT:	À quel nom, s'il vous plaît?
M. SMITH:	Au nom de Smith.
MME DUPONT:	Pouvez-vous épeler° le nom, s'il vous plaît?
M. SMITH:	S-M-I-T-H.
MME DUPONT:	Et pour quelle heure?
M. SMITH:	Pour huit heures, si possible.
MME DUPONT:	Très bien, Monsieur. C'est entendu°. Une table pour cinq pour vingt heures.
M. SMITH:	Je vous remercie° beaucoup. Au revoir, Madame.
MME DUPONT:	Au revoir, Monsieur. À mercredi soir.

Darn it! / luck
I didn't know

You will be open the day after tomorrow?

spell

agreed

thank

Review the French alphabet on p. 4.

After practicing the *Conversation*, have students complete ex. A in the Workbook.

▶ **Jouez ces rôles.** Répétez la conversation avec votre partenaire. Utilisez vos propres *(own)* noms et demandez une réservation pour neuf heures. Faites tous les changements nécessaires.

This gesture is used in each video module. See especially *Modules 2 & 3*.

Il y a un geste

Qu'est-ce que je vais faire? The mouth is open, with a look of exasperation. An alternate gesture is to expel air through slightly pursed lips.

Comparison: Have students describe phone etiquette in their country. Elicit English-language euphemisms for less-than-polite expressions.

À propos

Comment dit-on «second floor» en français?

a. le premier étage
b. le deuxième étage
c. le troisième étage

Pourquoi est-ce que Monsieur Smith dit «Mince!»?

a. Il n'est pas gros.
b. Il mange trop et doit maigrir *(lose weight).*
c. Il regrette que le restaurant ferme le mardi.

Pour répondre au téléphone

Allô is only used, in French, when responding to the phone. Likewise, **J'écoute** *(lit. I'm listening)* and **Qui est à l'appareil?** *(Who is on the phone?)* are appropriate in this context.

La politesse (rappel)

Remember to use **je voudrais,** and not **je veux,** when making a polite request. Respect and politeness will not fail to make a good impression in France. Conversely, impatience and lack of courtesy will be met with similar treatment. Review the polite expressions on p. 10.

À l'hôtel

Most French hotels have private bathrooms, but there are exceptions. It is still possible to find hotels in which the toilet and the showers are located down the hall from the room. However, every room will have a sink of its own.

The first floor of any French building is called **le rez-de-chaussée** and the second floor is **le premier étage.** If your room is **au deuxième étage,** you will need to climb two flights of stairs, not one. In an elevator, you must remember to press **RC** and not **1** if you wish to get to the ground floor.

In order to conserve electricity, many French hotels have installed **minuteries.** These are hall lights that stay lit for only one minute. Unsuspecting tourists are

occasionally surprised to have the hall light go off before they can get their door key in the lock.

Mince!

This is one of a number of euphemisms used to avoid another "five-letter word." Other inoffensive expressions used to express disappointment are **zut!** and **flûte!** *(darn, shucks).*

▶ **À vous.** Vous avez téléphoné à l'hôtel de Champagne pour réserver une chambre. Parlez avec la réceptionniste.

RÉCEPTIONNISTE: Allô! Ici l'hôtel de Champagne.

Vous: _____

RÉCEPTIONNISTE: Ce soir?

Vous: _____

RÉCEPTIONNISTE: Pour combien de personnes?

Vous: _____

RÉCEPTIONNISTE: Et à quel nom?

Vous: _____

RÉCEPTIONNISTE: Épelez le nom, s'il vous plaît.

Vous: _____

RÉCEPTIONNISTE: Très bien. C'est entendu.

Vous: _____

ENTRE AMIS

Vous êtes hôte/hôtesse au restaurant.

You are speaking on the telephone to a customer. Your partner will take the role of the customer.

1. Ask if s/he wants to reserve a table.
2. Find out how many people there are.
3. Find out at what time s/he wishes to dine.
4. Find out his/her name.
5. Find out how to spell the name.
6. Repeat back the information you received.

Prononciation

Les sons [l] et [j]

■ You learned in Chapter 11 that the letter **l** in certain situations is pronounced [j], as in the English word *yes*. However, in many cases it is pronounced [l], as in the French word **la.**

■ While the [l] sound is somewhat close to the sound of *l* in the English word *like*, it is far from that in the English word *bull*. Special attention is therefore necessary when pronouncing [l], especially at the end of a word. To produce the [l] sound, the tongue must be in a curved, convex position. Practice saying the following words:

Use the Student Audio to help practice pronunciation.

la   pilote   bleu
quel   elle

▶ Now practice saying the following words after your instructor, paying particular attention to the highlighted sound. As you pronounce the words for one sound, look at how that sound is spelled and in what kinds of letter combinations it appears. What patterns do you notice?

[j]   • détail, sommeil, œil, soleil, travaille, oreille, feuille, meilleur

   • gentille, fille, pastille, vanille, famille, cédille, juillet, billet

[l]   • le, la, les, l'air, là, lycée, laisser, lent, lentement, longue

   • pilote, désolé, facile, populaire, fidèle, folie, volant, épaule, pilule

   • il, bal, postal, quel

   • pleut, plus, bleu, client

   • dollar, intelligent, allemand, appelle, elle, folle, mademoiselle

■ Remember that the [j] sound is required for the letter l in the following circumstances:

   1. **-il** or **-ill** after a pronounced vowel in the same syllable: travail, conseiller

   2. **-ll** after [i]: fille, juillet

(EXCEPTIONS)——| million, milliard, mille, ville, tranquille, village

Be sure to distinguish between **gentil** [ʒɑ̃ti] and **gentille** [ʒɑ̃tij].

■ In a few words, the letter l is silent: gentil, fils

■ In all other cases, the letter l or the combination ll is pronounced as [l]— that is, at the beginning or end of a word, between two vowels, or following a consonant.

   le   il   pilule   inutile   pleut   dollar

▶ **Listen and repeat:**

   1. Les lilas sont merveilleux.
   2. Il habite dans un village près de Marseille.
   3. Le soleil m'a fait mal aux yeux.
   4. Aïe! J'ai mal à l'oreille!
   5. Ma fille Hélène travaille au lycée.

Buts communicatifs

1. Making a Request

—C'est ici le bureau des renseignements°?   *information*
—Oui.
—Puis-je vous demander quelques renseignements?
—Mais certainement. Allez-y.
—Pourriez-vous me dire° où sont les toilettes?   *Could you tell me*
—Elles sont dans le couloir.
—Pouvez-vous m'indiquer où se trouve la gare?

—Oui, elle est tout près°. Quand vous sortirez,   *very near*
tournez à gauche dans la rue.
—Savez-vous° si le bureau de poste est ouvert toute   *Do you know*
la journée°?   *all day long*
—Oui, il reste ouvert. Il ne ferme pas à midi.
—Je voudrais savoir à quelle heure les banques ferment.
—Elles ferment à 17 heures.
—La pharmacie est ouverte jusqu'à quelle heure?
—Jusqu'à 19 heures.
—Merci, vous êtes très aimable.
—De rien.° Je suis là pour ça.   *You're welcome.*

<table>
<tr><td>

The final **-e** in
Puis-je ... is
silent: [pɥiʒ].
When inverted,
je does not
change before
a vowel.

</td><td>

REMARQUE

</td><td>

When asking permission to do something, you may use
Est-ce que je peux ... ? or **Puis-je ... ?**

Est-ce que je peux conduire?   *May I drive?*
Puis-je avoir un verre d'eau?   *May I have a glass of water?*

</td></tr>
</table>

VOCABULAIRE

Pour demander un service

faire une demande	*to make a request*
poser une question	*to ask a question*
demander un renseignement	*to ask for information*
réserver une place	*to reserve a seat*
louer une voiture	*to rent a car*
recommander un bon restaurant	*to recommend a good restaurant*
commander un repas	*to order a meal*
confirmer un départ	*to confirm a departure*
vérifier le numéro d'un vol	*to check a flight number*

Review possible answers before
doing the exercise: **Oui, allez-y!;**
Si vous voulez; etc.

Communication
(Presentational): Do the
exercise in pairs. Follow up with
a role-play: The teacher plays an
English-speaking tourist and
selects a student as
"interpreter" to translate his/her
questions and the "native's"
responses.

I   **Allez-y!** Utilisez la liste suivante pour faire une demande. Votre
partenaire va vous donner la permission.

MODÈLE: ask you for information
               VOUS: **Est-ce que je peux vous demander un**
                      renseignement, s'il vous plaît?
   VOTRE PARTENAIRE: **Mais certainement.** ou **Allez-y!**

1. speak with you
2. ask a question
3. ask something
4. read your newspaper
5. have a glass of water
6. order something
7. watch television

Communication (Interpretive):
A student answers one question and then addresses the next question to someone else.

2 Il n'y en a plus *(There are no more).* Utilisez les listes suivantes pour faire des demandes. Ensuite votre partenaire va expliquer qu'il n'y en a plus.

MODÈLE: VOUS: **Puis-je réserver une table?**
          VOTRE PARTENAIRE: **Je regrette. Il n'y a plus de tables.**

	réserver	un journal
	louer	un verre d'eau
	commander	une chambre
puis-je	avoir	un vélo
	acheter	une tasse de café
	demander	une voiture
	boire	une place

The word **carte** has various meanings depending on the context: **carte postale** *(postcard)*, **jouer aux cartes** *(cards)*, **carte** *(map)* **de France.** In Ch. 13, it will be used in a restaurant setting: **à la carte.**

3 Microconversation: Pour aller au château de Rigny.
Utilisez la carte *(map)* suivante pour expliquer quelles routes il faut prendre pour aller des villes indiquées au château de Rigny.

MODÈLE: la route de Paris au château de Rigny
    TOURISTE: **Puis-je vous demander un renseignement?**
       GUIDE: **Certainement. Allez-y.**
    TOURISTE: **Pouvez-vous m'indiquer la route de Paris au château de Rigny?**
       GUIDE: **Oui, regardez la carte. Prenez l'autoroute A6 et l'autoroute A38 jusqu'à Dijon et ensuite prenez la départementale D70 jusqu'au château de Rigny.**
    TOURISTE: **Je vous remercie. Vous êtes bien aimable.**

NOTE CULTURELLE
Les routes de France sont marquées **A** pour autoroute, **N** pour route nationale et **D** pour route départementale. On dit, par exemple, **l'autoroute A six, la nationale cinquante-sept** ou **la départementale quatre cent soixante-quinze.** Il faut payer pour utiliser l'autoroute.

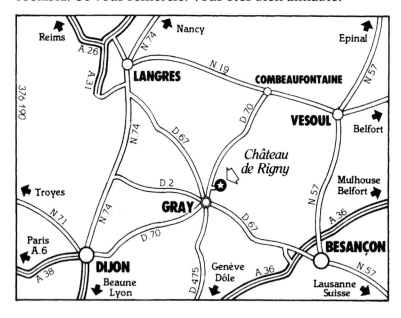

Communities & Communication (Presentational): Follow up (books closed) by having students give directions to places in their country.

1. la route de Besançon au château de Rigny
2. la route de Langres au château de Rigny
3. la route de Vesoul au château de Rigny
4. la route de Troyes au château de Rigny
5. la route de Belfort au château de Rigny
6. la route de Nancy au château de Rigny

A. Le verbe *savoir*

Cette femme **sait** bien **danser**.	*That woman really knows how to dance.*
Savez-vous **comment** elle s'appelle?	*Do you know her name?*
Je **sais que** son prénom est Sophie.	*I know her first name is Sophie.*
Je ne **sais** pas **si** elle est célibataire.	*I don't know if she is single.*

savoir (to know)

je	**sais**	nous	**savons**
tu	**sais**	vous	**savez**
il/elle/on	**sait**	ils/elles	**savent**

passé composé: j'**ai su** *(I found out, I learned)*

■ The verb **savoir** *(to know)* is used to express a skill or knowledge of a fact. It is used alone (**Je sais /Je ne sais pas**), or is followed by an infinitive, by the words **que** *(that)* or **si** *(if, whether),* or by question words such as **où, comment, combien, pourquoi, quand, quel.**

Je ne **savais** pas **que** tu venais.	*I didn't know that you were coming.*
Je ne **savais** pas **si** tu venais.	*I didn't know whether you were coming.*
Je ne **savais** pas **quand** tu venais.	*I didn't know when you were coming.*

NOTE

Followed by an infinitive, **savoir** means *to know how (to do something).*

Savez-vous parler espagnol?   *Do you know how to speak Spanish?*

Review the use of **connaître**, Ch. 10, p. 277.

■ The verbs **connaître** and **savoir** are used in different circumstances. Both are used with direct objects, but **connaître** (which means *to know* in the sense of *to be acquainted with, to be familiar with*) is used in general with people and places, while **savoir** is used with facts.

Vous **connaissez** ma sœur?	*Do you know my sister?*
Je ne **sais** pas son nom.	*I don't know her name.*

The special meanings of **vouloir** and **pouvoir** in the passé composé were learned in Ch. 10, p. 274.

■ The passé composé of **savoir** means *found out, learned.*

Je l'**ai su** hier.   *I found it out yesterday.*

4 **C'est inutile** *(It's useless).* On suggère que vous demandiez quelques renseignements. Répondez que c'est inutile. Ensuite utilisez le verbe **savoir** pour expliquer pourquoi c'est inutile.

Remind students of the pronunciation of **inutile**, [in], not [ɛ̃], where **in-** precedes a vowel. This was practiced on p. 93.

MODÈLE: Demandons à Jacques comment s'appelle cette jeune fille.
C'est inutile! Jacques ne sait pas comment elle s'appelle.

1. Demandons à Jacques si Jeanne va à la boum.
2. Demandons à nos amis où habite le professeur.
3. Demandons au professeur le nom de cette voiture.
4. Demandons à ces personnes quand le film va commencer.
5. Demandons à Jean-Michel où sont les toilettes.
6. Demandons à Françoise la date du concert.
7. Demandons à nos amis pourquoi ils sont déprimés.

5 **Une interview.** Interviewez votre partenaire. Attention aux verbes **savoir** et **connaître**.

MODÈLES: où j'habite

VOUS: **Sais-tu où j'habite?**

VOTRE PARTENAIRE: **Non, je ne sais pas où tu habites.**   ou
Oui, je sais où tu habites.

mes parents

VOUS: **Connais-tu mes parents?**

VOTRE PARTENAIRE: **Non, je ne les connais pas**.   ou
Oui, je les connais.

1. danser le tango
2. quelle heure il est
3. la famille du professeur
4. parler espagnol
5. la ville de Québec
6. mon adresse
7. pourquoi tu étudies le français
8. la différence entre **savoir** et **connaître**

6 **Un petit sketch: À la boum.** Lisez ou jouez le sketch suivant et ensuite répondez aux questions.

Georges parle avec son ami Thomas à la boum. Ils regardent une jeune fille.

GEORGES: Est-ce que tu connais cette jeune fille?

THOMAS: Oui, je la connais, mais je ne sais pas comment elle s'appelle.

GEORGES: Elle est jolie, n'est-ce pas?

THOMAS: Oui. Sais-tu si elle danse bien?

GEORGES: Je ne sais pas mais je vais l'inviter.

THOMAS: Bonne chance!

MOI, JE SAIS OÙ JE VAIS.

ÉCOLE SUPÉRIEURE D'INFORMATIQUE DE COMMERCE ET DE GESTION

ESIG

QUESTIONS — (Répondez à l'imparfait):

1. Qui connaissait la jeune fille?
2. Savait-il comment elle s'appelait?
3. Qu'est-ce que Thomas voulait savoir?
4. Qu'est-ce que Georges allait faire?

7 **Vous connaissez ce restaurant?** Complétez les phrases suivantes avec la forme convenable de **savoir** ou de **connaître**.

1. _____-vous s'il y a un bon restaurant près d'ici?
2. Oui, je _____ un restaurant qui est excellent, mais je ne _____ pas s'il est ouvert le mardi.
3. Je vais téléphoner à mon frère. Il_____ bien la ville et il va certainement _____ quel jour le restaurant est fermé. Est-ce que vous _____ mon frère?
4. Je le _____ un peu, mais je ne _____ pas comment il s'appelle.
5. Il s'appelle Paul. Vous _____ où nous habitons, n'est-ce pas?
6. Non, mais je _____ que ce n'est pas loin d'ici.

8 **À vous.** Répondez.

1. Connaissez-vous le président (la présidente) de votre université?
2. Savez-vous comment il (elle) s'appelle?
3. Vos parents savent-ils que vous étudiez le français?
4. Savent-ils à quelle heure vous allez au cours de français?
5. Connaissent-ils vos amis?
6. Vos amis savent-ils faire du ski?
7. Savez-vous s'ils étudient le français?
8. Connaissiez-vous ces amis quand vous étiez au lycée?
9. Est-ce qu'ils savent la date de votre anniversaire?
10. Saviez-vous parler français quand vous étiez au lycée?

ENTRE AMIS

Dans un magasin à Paris

You are a tourist, and your partner is Parisian.

1. Politely get permission to ask a question.
2. Ask if s/he knows how to speak English. (S/he doesn't.)
3. Tell who you are and where you are from.
4. Ask if there is a hotel nearby. (There is.)
5. Get directions to the hotel.
6. Ask if s/he knows if there's a restaurant nearby. (S/he does.)
7. Find out if s/he knows this restaurant well. (S/he does.)
8. Get directions to the restaurant.
9. Say thanks and tell your partner s/he is very kind.

2. Making a Restaurant or Hotel Reservation

Il vous reste° des chambres, s'il vous plaît?	*Do you still have*
Oui, pour combien de personnes?	
Non, je regrette. Nous sommes complets°.	*full*
Quel est le prix° d'une chambre avec salle de bain?	*price*
... euros par nuit.	
Est-ce que le petit déjeuner est compris dans le prix de la chambre?	
Oui, tout est compris.	
Non, il y a un supplément° de 3 euros.	*extra charge*
Puis-je demander d'autres serviettes°?	*towels*
Mais certainement.	
Je regrette. Il n'y en a plus.°	*There are no more.*

VOCABULAIRE

> Review the distinction between **les toilettes** and **la salle de bain**, p. 157.

À l'hôtel

une clé	*key*	une serviette	*towel*
un couloir	*hallway*	un supplément	*extra charge*
une douche	*shower*	les toilettes	*restroom, toilet*
le premier étage	*second floor*		
le rez-de-chaussée	*first floor*	complet (complète)	*full*
une salle de bain	*bathroom*	compris(e)	*included*

9 **Microconversation: Il vous reste des chambres?** Complétez la conversation avec les détails suivants. Décidez ensuite combien de chambres il vous faut.

MODÈLE: trois personnes / une nuit / 50€ (60€) / p.déj. (4€)

> TOURISTE: **Il vous reste des chambres?**
>
> HÔTELIER: **Oui, pour combien de personnes?**
>
> TOURISTE: **Pour trois personnes.**
>
> HÔTELIER: **Très bien. Pour combien de nuits?**
>
> TOURISTE: **Pour une seule nuit. Quel est le prix des chambres, s'il vous plaît?**
>
> HÔTELIER: **Cinquante euros pour une chambre pour une personne ou soixante euros pour une chambre pour deux personnes.**
>
> TOURISTE: **Est-ce que le petit déjeuner est compris?**
>
> HÔTELIER: **Non, il y a un supplément de quatre euros.**
>
> TOURISTE: **Très bien. Je vais prendre une chambre pour une personne et une chambre pour deux personnes.**

Communication (Presentational): Demonstrate the model with a student. Then have two students perform #1 for the class, before putting students in pairs. Follow-up (books closed): Have pairs of students ad-lib, choosing their own answers.

1. une personne / deux nuits / 40€ / p.déj. 5€
2. quatre personnes / une semaine / 45€ (60€) / tout compris
3. deux personnes / une nuit / 40€ (50€) / p.déj. 4€
4. vingt-cinq étudiants / un mois / 25€ (30€) / tout compris

10 **Si vous alliez à l'hôtel.** Posez des questions. Votre partenaire va donner une réponse appropriée.

MODÈLE: You want to know if there are any rooms left.
> VOUS: **Est-ce qu'il vous reste des chambres?**   ou
> **Avez-vous encore des chambres?**
> VOTRE PARTENAIRE: **Oui, certainement.**

Communication (Interpretive & Presentational): Do this exercise in pairs. Follow up with the teacher again playing an English-speaking tourist and selecting an "interpreter" from among the students.

You want to know ...

1. where the toilet is.
2. if there is a bathroom in the room.
3. if there is a shower in the bathroom.
4. if you can have extra towels.
5. how much the room costs.
6. if breakfast is included in the price.
7. at what time you can have breakfast.
8. if there is a television set in the room.

www**Réalités culturelles**

The title **France, mère des arts** comes from a famous poem by the 16th-century poet Joachim du Bellay.

Connections: Have students plan a trip to France, including hotel reservations, and include visits to some of the places mentioned in this note.

La France, mère des arts

La France est le premier pays touristique du monde. Ce n'est pas seulement dû à la richesse de son passé. C'est aussi grâce au talent de ses écrivains et de ses artistes et au génie de ses hommes et femmes illustres.

Pour certains, la France, c'est les «vieilles pierres», comme on dit. Ce sont des cathédrales comme Chartres, Reims et Notre-Dame de Paris. Il y a ensuite des palais somptueux, comme le château de Versailles, et des châteaux de la Renaissance, comme Chenonceau. Mais il y en a d'autres, plus massifs, qui servaient à la défense et qu'on appelle des châteaux forts, comme Angers.

La France, c'est aussi un pays de plus de mille musées qui contiennent des trésors inestimables d'art, de sculpture et d'objets qui nous

renseignent sur l'histoire des peuples du monde entier. Il faut d'abord mentionner, dans ce domaine, le musée du Louvre, un des plus célèbres du monde. Là, on peut admirer des collections d'œuvres qui datent de la naissance des grandes civilisations antiques du bassin méditerranéen jusqu'à la première moitié du dix-neuvième siècle. Viennent ensuite, à Paris, le musée d'Orsay, où on admire l'art de la seconde moitié du dix-neuvième siècle et du début du vingtième, dont les impressionnistes, et le Centre Georges-Pompidou, dit Beaubourg, qui est un musée d'art moderne. En 2004, on a inauguré le musée du quai Branly pour donner aux arts d'Afrique, d'Asie, d'Océanie et des Amériques leur juste place dans les musées français.

Vocabulaire: forts *strong*, génie *genius*, grâce à *thanks to*, moitié *half*, œuvres *works*, pierres *stones*

B. Les verbes réguliers en *-ir (-iss-)*

Qu'est-ce que vous **choisissez?**	*What do you choose?*
J'**ai** déjà **choisi** une pâtisserie.	*I have already chosen a pastry.*
Nous **finissons** à cinq heures.	*We finish at five o'clock.*
Obéis à ta mère!	*Obey your mother!*
Ralentissez, s'il vous plaît.	*Please slow down.*
Avez-vous **réussi** à votre examen?	*Did you pass your test?*

■ You have already learned several French verbs whose infinitives end in **-ir.**

sortir	je sors	nous sortons	ils sortent
partir	je pars	nous partons	ils partent
dormir	je dors	nous dormons	ils dorment

■ There is a larger group of French verbs that also have infinitives ending in **-ir** but that are conjugated differently.

choisir *(to choose)*		
je	**chois**	**is**
tu	**chois**	**is**
il/elle/on	**chois**	**it**
nous	**chois**	**issons**
vous	**chois**	**issez**
ils/elles	**chois**	**issent**

passé composé: j'**ai choisi**

■ Because there are a number of verbs formed in this way, these **-ir** verbs are said to be *regular*. The following verbs are conjugated like **choisir.**

V O C A B U L A I R E

Quelques verbes réguliers en *-ir (-iss-)*

finir	*to finish*
grossir	*to put on weight*
maigrir	*to take off weight*
obéir (à quelqu'un)	*to obey (someone)*
ralentir	*to slow down*
réussir (à un examen)	*to succeed; to pass (an exam)*

Drill **J'obéis toujours au professeur** with other subjects.

■ When used with an infinitive, **finir** and **choisir** are followed by **de,** and **réussir** is followed by **à.**

Nous **avons fini de** manger.   *We finished eating.*

Karine **a choisi d'**aller au centre   *Karine decided to go to the mall.*
    commercial.

Elle **a réussi à** trouver des   *She succeeded in finding delicious*
    desserts délicieux.   *desserts.*

■ The past participle of regular **-ir (-iss-)** verbs is formed by adding **-i** to the present tense verb stem.

choisi
fini
obéi

---

*Choisissez une orientation
    pour votre épargne.
Nos spécialistes feront le reste.*

---

11 **Qu'est-ce qu'ils choisissent d'habitude?** Posez la question et votre partenaire va répondre.

Review the partitive article, p. 217.

MODÈLE: tu / pâté ou soupe à l'oignon?
                   VOUS: **Est-ce que tu choisis du pâté ou de la soupe à
                            l'oignon, d'habitude?**
        VOTRE PARTENAIRE: **D'habitude je choisis du pâté.**

1. tu / crudités, soupe ou pâté?
2. les végétariens / viande ou poisson?
3. les enfants / épinards ou frites?
4. le professeur de français / camembert ou fromage américain?
5. tes amis / glace, fruits, tarte ou gâteau?
6. tu / café ou thé?

12 **À vous.** Répondez.

1. Est-ce que vous choisissez un dessert d'habitude?
2. Qu'est-ce que vous avez choisi comme dessert la dernière fois que vous avez dîné au restaurant?
3. Qu'est-ce que vos amis choisissent comme dessert?
4. Est-ce que vous avez tendance à grossir?
5. Réussissez-vous à maigrir quand vous voulez?
6. Que peut-on choisir au restaurant si on veut grossir?
7. Que peut-on choisir au restaurant si on veut maigrir?
8. Finissez-vous toujours votre repas?
9. Finissiez-vous toujours votre repas quand vous étiez jeune?

C. L'adjectif *tout*

Il y a des toilettes dans **toutes** les chambres.	*There are toilets in all the rooms.*
Je parle avec mes amis **tous** les jours.	*I speak with my friends every day.*
Nous regardons la télévision **tous** les soirs.	*We watch television every evening.*
J'ai passé **toute** la journée à la bibliothèque.	*I spent the whole day at the library.*
Tout le monde aime dîner au restaurant.	*Everybody likes to dine out.*

■ **Tout** *(all, every, each, the whole)* is often used as an adjective. In those cases it is usually followed by one of the determiners: **le, un, ce,** or **mon, ton, son, notre, votre, leur.** Both **tout** and the determiner agree with the noun they modify.

	masculin	féminin
singulier	**tout**	**toute**
pluriel	**tous**	**toutes**

■ In the singular, the meaning of **tout** is usually *the whole* or *all . . . (long).*

toute la journée	*all day (long)*
toute l'année	*all year*
toute la classe	*the whole class*
tout le temps	*all the time*
tout le monde	*everybody* (literally, *the whole world*)

■ In the plural, the meaning of **tout** is usually *all* or *every.*

tous mes amis	*all my friends*
tous les hommes et **toutes** les femmes	*all (the) men and all (the) women*
tous les deux	*both (masc.)*
toutes les deux	*both (fem.)*
toutes ces personnes	*all these people*
toutes sortes de choses	*all sorts of things*
tous les jours	*every day*
toutes les semaines	*every week*
tous les ans	*every year*

■ Only when **tous** is used as a pronoun is the final **-s** pronounced.

Mes amis sont **tous** ici.   [tus]   *My friends are all here.*

13 **Toute la famille Jeantet.** Complétez les phrases avec la forme convenable de l'adjectif **tout**.

1. Monsieur et Madame Jeantet parlent anglais, _____ les deux.
2. _____ le monde dit qu'ils sont très gentils.
3. _____ leurs filles ont les yeux bleus.
4. Elles passent _____ leur temps à regarder la télévision.
5. _____ la famille va en Angleterre _____ les ans.
6. Ils achètent _____ sortes de choses.
7. Les filles Jeantet écrivent une carte postale à _____ leurs amis.
8. Elles sont contentes de voyager, _____ les trois.

14 **À votre avis.** Ajoutez **tout** et posez une question. Votre partenaire va décider ensuite si la généralisation est vraie ou fausse.

MODÈLE: Les hommes sont beaux.
                  VOUS: **Est-ce que tous les hommes sont beaux?**
VOTRE PARTENAIRE: **Oui, à mon avis tous les hommes sont beaux.** ou
                              Non, à mon avis tous les hommes ne sont pas beaux.

1. Les femmes sont belles.
2. Les repas au restaurant universitaire sont délicieux.
3. Les professeurs sont gentils.
4. Le campus est très beau.
5. Tes amis adorent parler français.
6. Ta famille chante bien.
7. Tes cours sont intéressants.

ENTRE AMIS

Communication (Interpretive):
Put students' chairs
back-to-back when they
are "telephoning."

La Pyramide

Call the restaurant La Pyramide and ask if the restaurant is open every day. Then make a reservation.

Restaurant LA PYRAMIDE

**Cuisine française traditionnelle
Recommandé par les meilleurs guides**

Réservation: 02-41-83-15-15

Restaurant non fumeur
Ouvert tous les jours

3. Making a Transportation Reservation

Use video, *Module 5*, to help set the scene. Alissa and Bruno are going to purchase train tickets.

Point out that **aller simple** is two separate words, while **aller-retour** is one word containing a hyphen.

seconde: [səgɔ̃d]

NOTE CULTURELLE

Les billets de train peuvent être utilisés pendant quelques mois. Il est donc nécessaire de composter le billet le jour où on prend le train. Si on oublie de le composter, on peut être obligé de payer une amende *(fine)*.

Culture: Explain that tickets are stamped or punched by inserting them into a machine in the railroad station.

Bonjour, Madame.
   Bonjour, Monsieur. Puis-je avoir un billet° *ticket*
      pour Strasbourg, s'il vous plaît?
Un aller simple°?   *one way*
   Oui, un aller simple.
   Non, un aller-retour°.   *round trip*
En quelle classe?
   En première.
   En seconde.
Fumeur° ou non fumeur?   *Smoking*
   Fumeur.
   Non fumeur.
Quand partirez-vous?°   *When will you leave?*
   Tout de suite.°   *Right away.*
   Bientôt.
   Dans quelques jours.
Très bien. N'oubliez pas de composter° votre billet.   *punch, stamp*

REMARQUE

Second(e) is normally used in place of **deuxième** when there are only two in a series. Note that the **c** is pronounced [g].

Un billet en **seconde** classe, s'il vous plaît.

15 **Microconversation: Nous prenons le train.** Réservez des places dans le train. Complétez la conversation avec les catégories suivantes.

MODÈLE: 1 / Paris 17 h / ven. / 1ʳᵉ / vous ne fumez pas

Communication (Presentational): Do in pairs. Follow up with the teacher playing the **guichetier** (**guichetière**) and having students line up at the "ticket window."

VOUS: Puis-je réserver une place?
EMPLOYÉ(E): Dans quel train, s'il vous plaît?
VOUS: Le train pour Paris qui part à 17 heures.
EMPLOYÉ(E): Quel jour, s'il vous plaît?
VOUS: Vendredi.
EMPLOYÉ(E): Et en quelle classe?
VOUS: En première.
EMPLOYÉ(E): Fumeur ou non fumeur?
VOUS: Non fumeur.
EMPLOYÉ(E): Très bien, une place en pre-
      mière classe non fumeur dans
      le train pour Paris qui part à
      17 heures vendredi.

1. 1 / Marseille 11 h / lun. / 2ᵉ / vous ne fumez pas
2. 4 / Dijon 18 h / dim. / 2ᵉ / vous fumez
3. 15 / Biarritz 8 h / sam. / 2ᵉ / vous ne fumez pas
4. 2 / Madrid 23 h / merc. / 1ʳᵉ / vous ne fumez pas

Bonjour, Madame. Puis-je avoir un billet?

D. Le futur

Nous **aurons** notre diplôme en juin.	*We will get our diplomas in June.*
Nous **irons** en France l'été prochain.	*We will go to France next summer.*
Nous **prendrons** l'avion pour Paris.	*We will take the plane to Paris.*
J'espère qu'il ne **pleuvra** pas.	*I hope it won't rain.*
Nous **passerons** une nuit à l'hôtel Ibis.	*We will spend a night at the Ibis Hotel.*

Review the formation of the near future, Ch. 5, p. 130.

■ You have already learned to express future time by using **aller** plus an infinitive.

Ils **vont sortir** ensemble.　　*They are going to go out together.*

■ Another way to express what will take place is by using the future tense.

Ils **sortiront** ensemble.　　*They will go out together.*

The future has only three different pronounced endings: [e] **-ai, -ez;** [a] **-as, -a;** and [ɔ̃] **-ons, -ont.**

■ To form the future tense for most verbs, take the infinitive and add the endings **-ai, -as, -a, -ons, -ez, -ont.** For infinitives ending in **-e,** drop the **-e** before adding the endings. Note that the future endings are similar to the present tense of the verb **avoir.**

finir		
je	**finir**	**ai**
tu	**finir**	**as**
il/elle/on	**finir**	**a**
nous	**finir**	**ons**
vous	**finir**	**ez**
ils/elles	**finir**	**ont**

vendre		
je	**vendr**	**ai**
tu	**vendr**	**as**
il/elle/on	**vendr**	**a**
nous	**vendr**	**ons**
vous	**vendr**	**ez**
ils/elles	**vendr**	**ont**

Review the formation of **acheter,** Ch. 9, p. 256.

■ Verbs like **acheter** keep their spelling change in the future, even for the **nous** and **vous** forms.

J'achèterai une voiture l'année prochaine.

Nous achèterons une Renault.

Les étudiants **se lèveront** tard pendant les vacances.

You may wish to point out that verbs like **préférer** do *not* have a spelling change in the future.

■ All future stems end in **-r** and the future endings are always the same. There are, however, a number of verbs with irregular stems.

infinitive	stem	future
être	**ser-**	je **serai**
avoir	**aur-**	j'**aurai**
faire	**fer-**	je **ferai**
aller	**ir-**	j'**irai**
venir (devenir)	**viendr- (deviendr-)**	je **viendrai** (je **deviendrai**)
pouvoir	**pourr-**	je **pourrai**
savoir	**saur-**	je **saurai**
vouloir	**voudr-**	je **voudrai**

■ Here are the future forms of two impersonal expressions.

infinitive	present	future
pleuvoir	il pleut	**il pleuvra**
falloir	il faut	**il faudra**

For the future of verbs not mentioned here, tell students to see the Appendix. This includes **mourir** and **payer**, as well as many regular verbs students have learned actively.

16 **Pendant les vacances.** Qu'est-ce que tout le monde fera? Utilisez le futur au lieu *(in place)* du verbe **aller** plus l'infinitif.

MODÈLE: Nous n'allons pas étudier.   **Nous n'étudierons pas.**

Le château de Chenonceau

1. Joe va voyager avec ses parents.
2. Ils vont faire un voyage en France.
3. Ils vont visiter le château de Chenonceau.
4. Je vais les accompagner.
5. Nous allons prendre un avion.
6. Nous allons partir bientôt.
7. Une semaine à l'hôtel à Paris va coûter cher.
8. Je vais acheter des souvenirs.
9. Il va falloir que j'achète une autre valise.
10. Il ne va pas pleuvoir.

Follow-up: Students use the questions to interview first the instructor (with books open) and then another student (with books closed).

17 **À vous.** Répondez.

1. Est-ce que vous resterez sur le campus l'été prochain?
2. Est-ce que vous travaillerez? Si oui, où? Si non, pourquoi pas?
3. Est-ce que vous ferez un voyage? Si oui, où?
4. Qu'est-ce que vous lirez?
5. Qu'est-ce que vous regarderez à la télévision?
6. À qui rendrez-vous visite?
7. Sortirez-vous avec des amis? Si oui, où irez-vous probablement?
8. Serez-vous fatigué(e) à la fin des vacances?

E. Le futur avec *si* et *quand*

■ When a main clause containing a *future* tense verb is combined with a clause introduced by **si** *(if)*, the verb in the **si**-clause is in the *present* tense. English works the same way.

Nous ferons un pique-nique demain **s'il fait beau.**	*We will have a picnic tomorrow if it is nice out.*
Si tu veux, nous sortirons vendredi soir.	*If you want, we will go out on Friday night.*
Si tu travailles cet été, est-ce que tu gagneras beaucoup d'argent?	*If you work this summer, will you earn a lot of money?*

■ However, when a main clause with a future tense verb is combined with a clause introduced by **quand,** the verb in the **quand** clause is in the *future.* Be careful not to allow English to influence your choice of verb tense. English uses the present in this case.

NOTE LEXICALE
Faites attention aux différents sens du mot **gagner.** Ce verbe veut dire *to earn* et *to win.*

Marie a travaillé pour **gagner de l'argent.** *Marie worked to earn money.*

Anne a **gagné à la loterie.** *Anne won the lottery.*

Quand il fera beau, nous ferons un pique-nique.	*When it is nice out, we will have a picnic.*
Aurez-vous beaucoup d'enfants **quand vous serez marié(e)?**	*Will you have a lot of children when you are married?*
Quand j'aurai le temps, j'écrirai.	*When I have time, I will write.*
Quand je gagnerai à la loterie, je ferai un long voyage.	*When I win the lottery, I will take a long trip.*

Beaucoup d'étudiants feront les vendanges *(grape harvest)* en automne. Ils veulent gagner de l'argent.

18 **Si nous gagnons beaucoup d'argent.** Utilisez **si** avec l'expression **gagner beaucoup d'argent** et complétez les phrases suivantes.

MODÈLE: moi / acheter des vêtements
Si je gagne beaucoup d'argent, j'achèterai des vêtements.

1. mes amis / être très contents
2. le professeur de français / habiter dans un château
3. les étudiants du cours de français / aller en France
4. nous / dîner dans les meilleurs restaurants
5. moi / arrêter de travailler
6. ma meilleure amie / faire un long voyage

19 **Quand ferons-nous tout cela?** Combien de phrases logiques pouvez-vous faire? Chaque phrase commence par **quand**.

Follow work in pairs with a stand-up drill. Each student must give one sentence before sitting down.

MODÈLE: **Quand j'aurai faim, j'irai au restaurant.**

| quand | mes amis
je
mon ami(e)
nous
les étudiants | réussir aux examens
avoir faim
avoir un diplôme
être riche(s)
parler bien le français
avoir soif
finir d'étudier
gagner de l'argent | avoir … ans
boire …
acheter …
(ne … pas) travailler
aller …
chanter
être fatigué(e)(s)
manger …
faire un voyage … |

20 **Qu'est-ce que tu feras?** Utilisez les expressions suivantes pour interviewer votre partenaire.

Suggestion: Brainstorm with students to elicit all the questions before pairing students.

MODÈLE: quand / avoir le temps / écrire à tes parents
VOUS: **Quand tu auras le temps, écriras-tu à tes parents?**
VOTRE PARTENAIRE: **Oui, quand j'aurai le temps, j'écrirai à mes parents.**

1. si / être libre / écrire à tes parents
2. quand / finir tes études / avoir quel âge
3. quand / travailler / gagner beaucoup d'argent
4. si / être marié(e) / faire la cuisine
5. quand / faire la cuisine / préparer des spécialités françaises
6. si / avoir des enfants / être très content(e)
7. quand / parler français / penser à cette classe

21 **Un petit sketch: On confirme un départ.** Lisez ou jouez le sketch et ensuite répondez aux questions.

Un touriste téléphone à la compagnie Air France.

L'EMPLOYÉ: Allô, Air France. J'écoute.
LE TOURISTE: Bonjour, Monsieur. Je voudrais confirmer un départ, s'il vous plaît.
L'EMPLOYÉ: Très bien, Monsieur. Votre nom, s'il vous plaît?
LE TOURISTE: Paul Schmitdz.
L'EMPLOYÉ: Comment? Pouvez-vous épeler votre nom, s'il vous plaît?
LE TOURISTE: S-C-H-M-I-T-D-Z.
L'EMPLOYÉ: Très bien. Votre jour de départ et le numéro de votre vol?
LE TOURISTE: Mardi prochain, et c'est le vol 307.
L'EMPLOYÉ: Très bien, Monsieur Schmitdz. Votre départ est confirmé.
LE TOURISTE: Merci beaucoup.
L'EMPLOYÉ: À votre service, Monsieur.

QUESTIONS (Répondez au passé.)

1. Pour quelle compagnie l'employé travaillait-il?
2. Quelle était la première question de l'employé?
3. Quand le vol partait-il?
4. Quel était le numéro du vol?

ENTRE AMIS

Confirmez votre départ.

1. Call Air Canada.
2. State that you wish to confirm your departure.
3. Identify yourself and your flight number.
4. Verify the time of departure.
5. Find out at what time you need to arrive at the airport.
6. End the conversation appropriately.

Intégration

Révision

Communication (Presentational): Have partners sit back-to-back for activity A.

A **Au téléphone.** «Téléphonez» à votre partenaire et jouez les rôles suivants.

1. Réservez une table au restaurant.
2. Réservez une place dans un train.
3. Confirmez un départ en avion.
4. Réservez une chambre d'hôtel.

Communication (Interpretive): Role-play activity B with one student before beginning. You could "ham this up" by putting a bandana on your head and pretending to read the student's palm.

Have individual students read their predictions out loud. Can the class guess whom they are describing?

B **Diseur (diseuse) de bonne aventure** *(fortuneteller).* Écrivez cinq phrases pour prédire l'avenir *(predict the future)* d'un(e) de vos camarades de classe.

MODÈLE: **Tu parleras français comme un Français.**

Communication (Presentational & Interpretive): In activity C, if students read their lists to the class, others can be asked to recall information that was presented. Suggestion: Assign the *Rédaction* at the end of Ch. 12 in the Workbook.

C **Début de rédaction.** Vous êtes au Sénégal. Faites deux listes: une pour une chambre d'hôtel et une seconde pour une table de restaurant. Dans chaque liste vous devez donner toutes les précisions possibles (au moins 10 pour chaque liste). Par exemple, indiquez la date, l'heure d'arrivée, le nombre de personnes, etc.

Communication (Interpretive): Encourage students to use the practice test on the Lab Audio Program.

D **À vous.** Répondez.

1. En quelle année avez-vous fini vos études au lycée?
2. Saviez-vous déjà parler français?
3. Est-ce que vous réussissiez toujours à vos examens quand vous étiez au lycée?
4. Quand finirez-vous vos études universitaires?
5. Qu'est-ce que vous ferez quand vous aurez votre diplôme?
6. Où irez-vous si vous faites un voyage?
7. Quelles villes visiterez-vous si vous avez le temps?
8. Qui fera le ménage quand vous serez marié(e)?

Négociations: **Savoir ou connaître?** Interviewez autant d'étudiants que possible pour trouver des gens qui répondent **oui** aux questions.

MODÈLE: **Est-ce que tu sais conjuguer le verbe** *connaître?*

Be careful when choosing between **savoir** and **connaître**. No one student's initials should be written more than twice.

For complete instructions on how to prepare for and to use this activity, see *Négociations* on the Class Prep CD-ROM. Since all students use the same form, it has not been reproduced in Appendix D.

où se trouve la tour Eiffel	faire du ski	danser la valse
comment s'appelle notre professeur	le prix d'un billet de cinéma	le musée d'Orsay
l'avenue des Champs-Élysées	conduire une moto	tous les étudiants de ce cours
à quelle heure ce cours finit	la musique de Céline Dion	jouer à la pétanque
s'il va faire beau demain	mon (ma) meilleur(e) ami(e)	une famille française
le Premier ministre de France	parler espagnol	conjuguer le verbe **connaître**

Lecture 1

Video for Chapter 12: A. Video worksheets *(Cahier)*; B. ACE Video practice test (WWW); C. CD-ROM

A **Étude du vocabulaire.** Étudiez les phrases suivantes et choisissez les mots anglais qui correspondent aux mots français en caractères gras: *holiday, until, schedule, except, beginning on, run.*

1. J'ai téléphoné à l'aéroport pour savoir l'**horaire** des vols.
2. Nous serons en France **à partir du** 10 juin.
3. Certains trains ne **circulent** pas le week-end.
4. Tout le monde est venu **sauf** Christian. Pourquoi est-ce qu'il n'est pas venu?
5. Le magasin est ouvert **jusqu'à** dix-huit heures.
6. Le quatorze juillet est la **fête** nationale en France.

B **Parcourez l'horaire.** Lisez rapidement pour trouver le nom de la gare d'Angers et le nombre de trains qui vont de Montparnasse à Angers.

L'horaire des trains (Paris–Nantes)

Numéro de train		3741	3741	8849	8955	8957	13557	86743	6816/7	8859	86745	86745	86745	3789	8863	8967	8869	8975	8879	566/7
Notes à consulter		1	2	3	4	5	6	7	8	9	10	11	12	13	4	14	9	15	16	9
				TGV	TGV	TGV			TGV						TGV	TGV	TGV	TGV	TGV	TGV
Paris-Montparnasse 1-2	D	16.43	16.43	16.50	17.25	17.30			17.50					18.10	18.25	18.40	18.45	19.25	19.50	
Massy	D																			21.02
Versailles-Chantiers	D																			
Chartres	D	17.30	17.30																	
Le Mans	A	18.27	18.27	17.44					18.44					19.55			19.39			
Le Mans	D			17.46			17.53	18.27	18.46	18.54	18.54	19.21	19.57				19.41			
Sablé	A						18.16	19.00		19.29	19.29	19.56	20.21				20.00			
Angers-St-Laud	A		18.24						19.02	19.23		20.02		20.46			20.21			22.28
Ancenis	A												21.20				20.45			
Nantes	A			19.01	19.27	19.29			19.43	20.01				21.39	20.27	20.39	21.03	21.27	21.49	23.04

Notes :

1. Circule : jusqu'au 3 juil : les ven;les 4, 11, 18 et 25 sept - Départ de Paris Montp 3 Vaug.- ⅌ 🛗 assuré certains jours.
2. Circule : du 10 juil au 28 août : les ven- ⅌.
3. Circule : tous les jours sauf les sam, dim et fêtes et sauf le 13 juil - ⅌- ♿.
4. Circule : les ven- ⅌- ♿.
5. Circulation périodique- ⅌- ♿.
6. Circule : les lun, mar, mer, jeu sauf le 8 juin, 13 et 14 juil - 🚲.
7. Circule : tous les jours sauf les sam, dim et fêtes- 🚲.
8. Circule : jusqu'au 3 juil : les ven, dim et fêtes sauf le 7 juin ;Circule du 4 juil au 6 sept : tous les jours;à partir du 11 sept : les ven et dim- ⅌- ♿.
9. ⅌- ♿.
10. Circule : tous les jours sauf les ven, dim et fêtes- 🚲.
11. Circule : les dim et fêtes- 🚲.
12. Circule : les ven- 🚲.
13. Circule : les ven- ⅌.
14. Circule : tous les jours sauf les ven, dim et fêtes;Circule les 7 juin, 12 juil et 15 août - ◻1reCL assuré certains jours-⅌- ♿.
15. Circule : les ven- ◻1reCL- ⅌- ♿.
16. Circulation périodique- ◻1reCL assuré certains jours-⅌- ♿.

C **Questions.** Répondez.

1. Quel est le train le plus rapide entre Paris-Montparnasse et Angers?
2. Quel est le train le moins rapide entre Paris-Montparnasse et Angers? Pourquoi?
3. Combien d'arrêts y a-t-il pour ce train?
4. Combien de temps le TGV prend-il entre Massy et Angers?
5. Quels sont les trains qui offrent des facilités aux handicapés?
6. Quels trains ne circulent pas le samedi?
7. Si on est au Mans, quels trains peut-on prendre pour Angers?
8. Si on part de Paris-Montparnasse, quels trains peut-on prendre si on veut arriver pour dîner à Angers à vingt heures?

www Réalités culturelles

Le Sénégal

République indépendante depuis 1960, le Sénégal est situé à l'extrême ouest du continent africain. Ce pays a un climat tropical caractérisé par deux saisons: une saison sèche de novembre à juin et une saison des pluies de juillet à octobre. La grande ville de Dakar, qui compte une population de deux millions, est devenue en 1958 la capitale du Sénégal. Presqu'île située sur la côte atlantique, Dakar est aujourd'hui un véritable carrefour de routes maritimes et aériennes. Tout près de Dakar se trouve l'île de Gorée, de triste mémoire, où on détenait des esclaves avant de les embarquer pour un voyage sans retour.

La population du Sénégal est de 10 millions et représente des ethnies diverses, parmi lesquelles on peut citer les Wolofs, les Peuls, et les Sérers. Le français est la langue officielle, mais on entend parler aussi plusieurs langues nationales, dont le wolof. Quatre-vingt-quatorze pour cent de la population pratiquent l'islam, cinq pour cent le christianisme et un pour cent des religions traditionnelles.

Mais on ne peut pas parler du Sénégal sans parler de son premier président, Léopold Sédar Senghor (1906–2001). Poète, professeur, membre de l'Académie française, Senghor a créé, avec d'autres écrivains comme Aimé Césaire, le mouvement de la francophonie et le mouvement de la négritude.

Vocabulaire: carrefour *crossroads*, esclaves *slaves*, parmi lesquelles *among which*, sèche *dry*

Connections & Communities: Have students research Senegal through the ***Entre amis*** web site.

Lecture II

A Étude du vocabulaire. Étudiez les phrases suivantes et choisissez les mots anglais qui correspondent aux mots français en caractères gras: *full board, huts, dugout canoe, housing, mattress, bush country, river, water skiing, wind surfing, beach.*

1. Les Sénégalais circulent beaucoup en **pirogue** le long de leurs rivières.
2. Un **fleuve** est une grande rivière qui rejoint la mer.
3. La **brousse** est une région qui se trouve loin des villes.
4. Les habitants des villages africains vivent dans des **cases.**
5. Sur le lac, les plus sportifs peuvent faire du **ski nautique** ou, quand il y a du vent, de la **planche à voile.**
6. L'**hébergement** pendant le séjour peut se faire dans un hôtel ou dans des bungalows près de l'hôtel.
7. À l'hôtel, on peut choisir la **pension complète** ou prendre ses repas dans les restaurants de la ville.
8. En vacances, de nombreux touristes aiment passer leur temps au bord de la mer à la **plage.**
9. Si on ne veut pas avoir mal au dos, il vaut mieux avoir un **matelas** sur son lit.

B **Parcourez la lecture.** Lisez rapidement la lecture pour trouver ...

1. quatre types de transport.
2. cinq endroits à visiter qui se trouvent sur la carte.

Séjours organisés au Sénégal

Brousse et plage

Une semaine: 3 nuits en brousse en pension complète à l'hôtel Le Pélican/4 nuits à l'hôtel Village Club Les Filaos.

L'hôtel Le Pélican à 2 h 30 de Dakar au bord du fleuve Saloum joint le confort aux charmes de la vie africaine. Un site géographique exceptionnel, la province du Siné Saloum est réputée pour la richesse de sa faune et de sa flore.

L'hôtel Village Club Les Filaos se trouve à 73 kilomètres au sud de Dakar, en bordure de plage. Ses bungalows sont entièrement équipés, notamment avec salle de bain et toilettes privées. Restaurants, piscines. Sports et loisirs gratuits: tennis, planche à voile, volley-ball, pétanque. Sports et loisirs payants: ski nautique, excursions.

Le Circuit Cap Vert

Deux semaines. Ce circuit traverse une très belle région du Sénégal, sauvage et peu fréquentée par les touristes: le pays Bassari. Le déplacement se fait en minibus. Ce type de voyage vous fera côtoyer en permanence les habitants du pays et favorisera les contacts avec une population toujours accueillante. Il procure un confort limité. Les voyageurs sont hébergés dans des cases, des écoles ou en bivouac. Un sac de couchage et un petit matelas de mousse sont indispensables. Une réunion de préparation avec votre accompagnateur aura lieu deux à trois semaines avant le départ.

Itinéraire type: Visite de Dakar et de l'île de Gorée, descente en taxi-brousse sur Thiès (visite du marché), Saint-Louis (marché), Mlomp (cases à étages), Elinkine (promenade en pirogue), île de Karabane (baignade), parc de Basse Casamance, Gambie, région du Siné Saloum (promenade en pirogue), Toubakouta, Kaolack, M'Bour-Dakar.

Le prix comprend:

- l'assistance à l'aéroport
- les transports au Sénégal, la nourriture et l'hébergement (petits hôtels, chez l'habitant)
- un accompagnateur
- l'assurance

Le prix ne comprend pas:

- le transport aérien
- les boissons

C Vrai ou faux? Décidez si les phrases suivantes sont vraies ou fausses. Si une phrase n'est pas vraie, corrigez-la.

1. L'hôtel Le Pélican se trouve à Dakar.
2. Il y a beaucoup d'animaux et de plantes dans la région du Siné Saloum.
3. Il ne sera pas nécessaire de payer pour faire usage de la planche à voile.
4. Les participants seront hébergés dans des hôtels de luxe pour toute la durée du circuit Cap Vert.
5. Beaucoup de touristes ont déjà fait ce voyage et connaissent le pays Bassari.
6. Il est peu probable qu'on doive passer la nuit dans des cases pendant le circuit.
7. Le voyage en avion est compris dans le prix du circuit.
8. Les repas sont compris dans le prix du circuit, mais pour les boissons il faudra payer un supplément.

D Discussion. Lequel des deux séjours préférez-vous? Expliquez votre réponse.

VOCABULAIRE ACTIF

Practice this vocabulary with the flashcards on the *Entre amis* web site.

Les voyages
un aller-retour *round-trip ticket*
un aller simple *one-way ticket*
l'autoroute (f.) *turnpike, through-way, highway*
un billet *ticket*
une carte *map*
composter (un billet) *to punch (a ticket)*
confirmer (un départ) *to confirm (a departure)*
le départ *departure*
en première *in first class*
en seconde *in second class*
fumeur *smoking (car)*
non fumeur *non-smoking (car)*
ralentir *to slow down*
un renseignement *item of information*
la route *route, way, road*
le vol *flight*

Adjectifs
complet (complète) *full; complete*
inutile *useless*
ouvert(e) *open*
riche *rich*
tout (toute/tous/toutes) *all; every; the whole*

D'autres noms
la chance *luck*
une demande *request*
un diplôme *diploma*
un pique-nique *picnic*

Expressions utiles
Allez-y. *Go ahead.*
Allô! *Hello! (on the phone)*
après-demain *day after tomorrow*
À quel nom ... ? *In whose name ... ?*
avoir tendance à *to tend to*
Comment je vais faire? *What am I going to do?*
De rien *You're welcome*
entendu *agreed; understood; O.K.*
Il n'y en a plus. *There is (are) no more.*
Il vous reste ... ? *Do you still have ... ?*
Mince! *Darn it!*
Pourriez-vous me dire ... ? *Could you tell me ... ?*
Puis-je ... ? *May I ... ?*
tous (toutes) les deux *both*
tout de suite *right away*
tout près *very near*

À l'hôtel
une clé *key*
une douche *shower*

un étage *floor*
le prix *price*
le rez-de-chaussée *ground floor*
une serviette *towel*
un supplément *extra charge; supplement*

Verbes
choisir *to choose*
épeler *to spell*
faire une demande *to make a request*
finir *to finish*
gagner (à la loterie) *to win (the lottery)*
gagner (de l'argent) *to earn (money)*
grossir *to put on weight*
indiquer *to tell; to indicate; to point out*
louer *to rent*
maigrir *to lose weight*
obéir *to obey*
poser une question *to ask a question*
recommander *to recommend*
remercier *to thank*
réussir *to succeed; to pass*
savoir *to know*
vérifier *to check*

Buts communicatifs
Describing a table setting
Describing one's day
Describing past activities
Expressing one's will

Structures utiles
Le verbe **mettre**
Les verbes pronominaux (suite)
Les verbes **se promener, s'inquiéter, s'appeler et s'asseoir**
Le passé des verbes pronominaux
Le subjonctif

Culture
• *À propos*
Au menu ou à la carte?
Relativité culturelle: L'étiquette à table

• *Il y a un geste*
Il n'y a pas de quoi

• *Lectures*
«Les feuilles mortes»
Une lettre du Burkina Faso

Coup d'envoi

Prise de contact   Bon appétit!

Avant de manger

Culture: You may wish to tell students that French monograms are placed *on the back* of spoons and forks. Thus, they traditionally face down when set on a table.

Mettez° une nappe° sur la table.   *Put / tablecloth*
Mettez des assiettes sur la nappe.
Mettez un verre et une cuiller° devant chaque   *spoon*
   assiette.
Mettez une fourchette° à gauche de l'assiette.   *fork*
Mettez un couteau° à droite de l'assiette.   *knife*

À table

You learned in Ch. 9 that **genou** means *knee.* In the plural, it can refer to either *lap* or *knees.*

Asseyez-vous.
Mettez une serviette° sur vos genoux°.   *napkin / lap*
Coupez° le pain.   *Cut*
Mettez un morceau de pain sur la nappe à côté de
   l'assiette.
Versez° du vin dans le verre.   *Pour*
Levez° votre verre et admirez la couleur du vin.   *Lift*
Humez° le vin.   *Smell*
Goûtez-le.°   *Taste it.*
Bon appétit!

Conversation

Nous nous mettons à table

Monsieur et Madame Smith et Monsieur et Madame Martin sont arrivés au restaurant, mais Lori n'est pas encore là.

MAÎTRE D'HÔTEL:	Bonsoir, Messieurs, Bonsoir, Mesdames. Vous avez réservé?	
M. SMITH:	Oui, Monsieur, au nom de Smith.	
MAÎTRE D'HÔTEL:	Très bien, un instant, s'il vous plaît. *(Il vérifie sa liste.)* C'est pour cinq personnes, n'est-ce pas?	
MME SMITH:	C'est exact.°	*That's right.*
MAÎTRE D'HÔTEL:	Vous voulez vous asseoir°?	*to sit down*
M. SMITH:	Volontiers, notre amie ne va pas tarder°.	*won't be long*
MAÎTRE D'HÔTEL:	Par ici, s'il vous plaît. *(ensuite)* Voici votre table. *(Ils s'asseyent.°)*	*They sit down.*
M. SMITH:	Merci beaucoup, Monsieur. *(Le maître d'hôtel sourit° mais ne répond pas. Il s'en va°.)*	*smiles* *leaves*
MME MARTIN:	C'est très gentil à vous de nous inviter.	
MME SMITH:	Mais c'est un plaisir pour nous.	
M. MARTIN:	Voilà Lori qui arrive. Bonsoir, Lori. *(Lori serre la main à Monsieur et Madame Martin et fait la bise à Monsieur et Madame Smith.)*	
LORI BECKER:	Excusez-moi d'être en retard.	
MME MARTIN:	Ne vous inquiétez pas°, Lori. Nous venons d'arriver.	*Don't worry*

After practicing the *Conversation*, have students complete Ex. A in the Workbook.

▶ **Jouez ces rôles.** Répétez la conversation avec vos partenaires. Ensuite imaginez une excuse pour Lori. Pourquoi est-elle arrivée en retard?

Il y a un geste

This gesture is used in video, *Modules 2, 6, & 7.*

Comparison: While perhaps not an obvious gesture, this is culturally pertinent to our students, who may expect a verbal response every time they say **merci.**

Il n'y a pas de quoi. Although the French have numerous spoken formulae that convey the idea of *You're welcome* (**Il n'y a pas de quoi, De rien, Je vous en prie,** etc.), they frequently respond with only a discreet smile. This smile is often unnoticed by North Americans, who may interpret the lack of a verbal response to their "thank you" as less than polite.

À propos

Quelle est la différence entre un menu et une carte dans un restaurant?

a. C'est la même chose, mais un menu est plus élégant qu'une carte.

b. C'est la même chose, mais une carte est plus élégante qu'un menu.

c. Un menu propose deux ou trois repas à prix fixe. Une carte donne la liste de tous les plats.

Au menu ou à la carte?

La carte lists all of the dishes that the restaurant prepares. Customers can choose any combination of items they wish (**à la carte**). **Le menu** has one or more set (complete) lunches or dinners at a set price. There might, for example, be **le menu à 15€** and **le menu à 20€**. Each **menu** will include three or more courses, with or without beverage. Menus are usually by far the less expensive way to order food in France.

Relativité culturelle: L'étiquette à table

When the Smiths and the Martins arrive at their table in the restaurant, the table is set, as in North America, with the forks to the left and the knives to the right. But there are differences: forks are often turned tines down; glasses are above the plate rather than to one side; teaspoons are placed between the glass and the plate. If

En France, on boit beaucoup d'eau minérale.

soup is served, the soup spoon is not held sideways but rather placed tip first in the mouth.

The French do not pick up a slice of bread and bite off a piece. Rather, they break off a small bite-sized piece and may even use this as a utensil to guide food onto the fork. From time to time, this piece is eaten and another piece broken off.

A few contrasts between table customs in France and North America are shown in the chart below.

In France	In North America
Ice cubes are not readily available at restaurants.	Ice water is often served automatically with meals. Cold drinks are very common.
Dinner is often at 8:00 P.M. or later.	Dinner is sometimes at 6:00 P.M. or even earlier.
Meals may last two hours or more.	Meals may last only 20 or 25 minutes.
Bread is placed on the tablecloth instead of on a plate.	Bread is not always served with a meal. When it is served, it is always kept on the plate.
People keep both hands on the table while eating.	People put one hand in their lap while eating.
The service charge, or tip, is already included in the bill (**le service est compris**).	The tip is often not included in the bill.

Review *Relativité culturelle: Un repas français*, pp. 212–213.

▶ **À vous.**   Répondez au maître d'hôtel.

1. Bonsoir, Monsieur (Madame / Mademoiselle). Vous avez réservé?
2. Pour deux personnes?
3. Vous voulez vous asseoir?
4. Par ici, s'il vous plaît. Voici votre table.

ENTRE AMIS

Au restaurant

You are the maître d'hôtel at a restaurant. Your partner is a customer.

1. Ask if s/he has made a reservation. (S/he has.)
2. Find out for how many people.
3. Ask if the others have already arrived.
4. Ask him/her if s/he wants to sit down.
5. Tell him/her "This way, please."

Prononciation

Les voyelles arrondies [ø] et [œ]

■ Lip rounding plays a much greater role in the accurate pronunciation of French than it does in English. French has rounded vowels that are produced in the front part of the mouth, a combination that does not exist in English. Use the word **euh** to practice. This word is prevalent and is very characteristic of the normal position for French pronunciation: the lips are rounded and the tongue is behind the lower teeth.

■ For the [ø] sound in **euh,** round your lips and then try to say **et.** For the [œ] sound in **neuf,** the lips are more open than for **euh.** There is, moreover, always a pronounced consonant after the vowel sound in words like **neuf, sœur,** etc.

[ø]   • **euh,** d**eu**x, v**eu**t, p**eu**t
      bl**eu,** ennuy**eu**x, pl**eu**t

[œ]   • n**eu**f, s**œu**r
      b**eu**rre, profess**eu**r
      h**eu**re, v**eu**lent
      p**eu**vent, pl**eu**re

▶ **Listen and repeat:**

1. Est-ce que je peux vous aider?
2. La sœur du professeur arrive à neuf heures.
3. Ils veulent du beurre sur leur pain.
4. Les deux portent un pull bleu.
5. «Il pleure dans mon cœur comme il pleut sur la ville.» *(Verlaine)*

Connection: Remind students that this poem is in Ch. 9.

Buts communicatifs

1. Describing a Table Setting

Où est-ce qu'on met la nappe?	On la met sur la table.
Où est-ce qu'on met l'assiette?	On la met sur la nappe.
Où est-ce qu'on met le couteau?	On le met à droite de l'assiette.
Où est-ce qu'on met la cuiller?	On la met entre l'assiette et le verre.
Où est-ce qu'on met la serviette?	On la met sur ses genoux.
Où est-ce qu'on met les mains?	On les met sur la table.
Où est-ce qu'on met le pain?	On le met sur la nappe, à côté de l'assiette.

Use video, *Module 10* to help introduce the table setting.

▶ **Et vous?** Chez vous, qu'est-ce qu'on met à gauche de l'assiette?
Chez vous, où est-ce qu'on met les verres?

A. Le verbe *mettre*

Je vais **mettre** mon pyjama.	*I'm going to put on my pajamas.*
Nous **mettons** un maillot de bain pour aller à la piscine.	*We put on a bathing suit to go to the pool.*
J'**ai mis** le sel, le poivre et le sucre sur la table.	*I put the salt, pepper, and sugar on the table.*

Notice that, like the **-re** verbs, p. 246, the endings for **mettre** are **-s, -s, –, -ons, -ez, -ent.** The plural stem, however, has **-tt-.**

mettre *(to put, place, lay; to put on)*

je	**mets**	nous	**mettons**
tu	**mets**	vous	**mettez**
il/elle/on	**met**	ils/elles	**mettent**

passé composé: j'**ai mis**

■ **Mettre** can also mean *to turn on* (the radio, the heat, etc.) and is used in the expression **mettre la table** to mean *to set the table.*

Qui **a mis** la table ce soir?	*Who set the table this evening?*
Mets le chauffage; j'ai froid.	*Turn on the heat; I'm cold.*
Mais je viens de **mettre** la climatisation.	*But I just turned on the air conditioning.*

VOCABULAIRE

Des choses à mettre

mettre un maillot de bain / un pyjama	*to put on a swimsuit / pajamas*
mettre le chauffage / la climatisation	*to turn on the heat / the air conditioning*
mettre la table	*to set the table*

1 Qu'est-ce qu'ils mettent? Indiquez les vêtements que mettent les personnes suivantes.

MODÈLES: Qu'est-ce que vos amis mettent pour nager?
Ils mettent un maillot de bain.

Review articles of clothing on pp. 90 & 99.

1. Qu'est-ce que les étudiants mettent pour aller à leurs cours?
2. Qu'est-ce que le professeur de français met pour aller au cours de français?
3. Qu'est-ce que vous mettez s'il neige?
4. Qu'est-ce que vous mettez s'il fait chaud?
5. Qu'est-ce qu'on met pour faire du jogging?
6. Qu'est-ce que vos amis mettent s'ils vont à une boum?
7. Que mettez-vous si vous allez dîner dans un restaurant très chic?

2 Un petit test de votre savoir-vivre. Choisissez une réponse pour chaque question et ensuite lisez l'analyse de vos réponses.

Communication (Interpretive):
Do this first with books closed. The teacher reads the question and students suggest answers before they see the answers in the book.

1. Que mettez-vous quand vous allez dîner au restaurant?
   a. des vêtements chic
   b. un jean et des baskets
   c. un bikini
   d. rien

2. Que buvez-vous pendant le repas?
   a. du vin ou de l'eau
   b. du lait ou du café
   c. du whisky
   d. de l'eau dans un bol

3. Où mettez-vous le pain pendant le repas?
   a. sur la nappe à côté de l'assiette
   b. dans mon assiette
   c. dans l'assiette de mon (ma) voisin(e)
   d. sous la table

4. Où est votre main gauche pendant que vous mangez?
   a. sur la table
   b. sur mes genoux
   c. sur le genou de mon (ma) voisin(e)
   d. sous la table

Remember that you learned in Ch. 8 *not* to say **Je suis plein(e),** literally *I am full,* because in French it can mean either *I am drunk* or, referring to an animal, *pregnant.*

5. Combien de temps passez-vous à table?
   a. entre une et deux heures
   b. entre 25 et 45 minutes
   c. Ça dépend du charme de mon (ma) voisin(e).
   d. cinq minutes

6. Que dites-vous à la fin du repas?
   a. C'était très bon.
   b. Je suis plein(e).
   c. Veux-tu faire une promenade, chéri(e)?
   d. Oua! oua! *(bow-wow!)*

RÉSULTATS

a. Si vous avez répondu **a** à toutes les questions, vous êtes peut-être français(e) ou vous méritez de l'être.
b. Si vous avez répondu **b,** vous êtes probablement américain(e), comme la personne qui a écrit ce questionnaire.
c. Si votre réponse est **c,** vous êtes trop entreprenant(e) *(forward, bold)* et vous dérangez beaucoup votre voisin(e).
d. Si votre réponse est **d,** vous vous identifiez beaucoup aux chiens.

www**Réalités culturelles**

Le vocabulaire de la cuisine

La langue anglaise a beaucoup d'expressions qui viennent du français. Cela est surtout vrai dans le domaine de la cuisine. Il est utile de connaître les expressions suivantes parce qu'on pourra les trouver sur les menus et les cartes anglophones.

au gratin	topped with cheese or breadcrumbs and then baked
au jus	with meat juice
bisque	seasoned shellfish purée, white wine, cognac, and cream; used to make soup
casserole	a baking dish of glass or pottery
chocolat fondu	a dessert: melted chocolate with fruit to dip
coq au vin	chicken in red wine sauce
crème brûlée	rich custard topped with caramelized sugar
croissant	a dinner or breakfast roll of leavened bread shaped in a crescent
croûtons	small pieces of fried or toasted bread, used in soups or as a garnish
éclair	finger-shaped cream puff, filled with whipped cream or custard, usually topped with icing
flambé	flamed with alcohol
fondue	melted cheese and seasonings, served with pieces of bread for dipping
julienne	a way to cut meat or vegetables into thin strips
mousse	dessert of flavored custard or fruit purée, mixed with whipped cream
parfait	a dessert of layered ice cream, fruit, dessert sauce, and whipped cream
pâté	cooked meat, usually duck or goose liver, made into a spread
purée	cooked and strained food
quiche	a pie of cheese and custard, with ham, bacon, or spinach sometimes added
roquefort	strongly flavored cheese, veined with mold; ripens in a cave in the town of Roquefort in southern France
salade niçoise	salad with tomatoes, garlic, oil, and dark olives
sauter	to cook quickly in a hot pan, tossing the food so that it "jumps"
tarte	French pie

Vocabulaire: brûler *to burn,* croûton *crust,* fondre *to melt,* gratter *to scratch,* niçoise *in the style of Nice,* parfait *perfect,* sauter *to jump*

3 **À vous.** Répondez.

Communication (Interpretive): With books open, the class interviews the teacher, then (books closed) they interview another student.

1. Mettez-vous du sucre ou de la crème dans votre café?
2. Que mettez-vous dans une tasse de thé?
3. Où met-on le pain quand on mange à la française?
4. Que faut-il faire pour mettre la table?
5. À quel moment de l'année met-on le chauffage dans la région où vous habitez? À quel moment de l'année met-on la climatisation?
6. En quelle saison met-on un gros manteau?
7. Quels vêtements les étudiants mettent-ils d'habitude sur votre campus?
8. Quels vêtements avez-vous mis hier? Pourquoi avez-vous décidé de porter ces vêtements-là?

ENTRE AMIS

L'éducation d'un(e) enfant

You are a French parent instructing your child (your partner) on table manners. Remember to use **tu.**

1. Tell your child to put the napkin on his/her lap.
2. Tell him/her to put a piece of bread on the table.
3. Tell him/her not to play with the bread.
4. Tell him/her to put water in his/her glass.
5. Find out what s/he did at school today.

2. Describing One's Day

You may wish to teach **se doucher** as well. It seems to be used less frequently than **prendre une douche.**

Le matin

7 h	Je me réveille tôt et je me lève.
7 h 10	Je me lave ou je prends une douche.
7 h 25	Je m'habille.
7 h 35	Je me brosse les cheveux.
7 h 50	Après avoir mangé°, je me brosse les dents.

After eating

L'après-midi

3 h	Je me repose.
5 h	Je m'amuse avec mon chien.

Le soir

11 h	Je me couche assez tard et je m'endors.

▶ **Et vous?** À quelle heure vous réveillez-vous?
Que faites-vous le matin? l'après-midi? le soir?

REMARQUE

Review pp. 168 & 190.

Tôt and **tard** mean *early* and *late* in the day. They should not be confused with **en avance** and **en retard,** which mean *early* and *late* for a specific meeting, class, etc.

Il se lève **tard!** (à midi)
Il est **en retard.** (pour son cours de français)

V O C A B U L A I R E

Quelques verbes pronominaux

se réveiller	*to wake up*
se laver	*to get washed*
se brosser (les dents, les cheveux)	*to brush (one's teeth, one's hair)*
s'habiller	*to get dressed*
s'amuser	*to have fun*
se souvenir (de)	*to remember*
s'inquiéter	*to worry*
s'asseoir	*to sit down*
se promener	*to take a walk, ride*
se dépêcher	*to hurry*
s'appeler	*to be named*
s'endormir	*to fall asleep*
se reposer	*to rest*

The conjugations of **se promener, s'inquiéter,** and **s'appeler**, which have spelling changes in their stems, and the conjugation of **s'asseoir,** are given on p. 359.

Review **Les verbes pronominaux**, Ch. 6, p. 169.

B. Les verbes pronominaux (*suite*)

■ Remember that the reflexive pronouns are **me, te, se, nous, vous,** and **se.**

se laver *(to get washed, to wash oneself)*

je	**me** lave	nous	**nous** lavons
tu	**te** laves	vous	**vous** lavez
il/elle/on	**se** lave	ils/elles	**se** lavent

s'endormir *(to fall asleep)*

je	**m'**endors	nous	**nous** endormons
tu	**t'**endors	vous	**vous** endormez
il/elle/on	**s'**endort	ils/elles	**s'**endorment

NOTE

The reflexive pronoun always changes form as necessary to agree with the subject of the verb, even when it is part of an infinitive construction.

Je vais **m'**amuser.   **Tu** vas **t'**amuser aussi.   **Nous** allons **nous** amuser!

■ Many verbs can be used reflexively or nonreflexively, depending on whether the object of the verb is the same as the subject or not.

Jean **se lave** avant de manger. (*Jean* is the subject *and* the object.)

Mais: Jean **lave sa voiture.** (*Jean* is the subject but *sa voiture* is the object.)

Noëlle adore **se promener.** (*Noëlle* is the subject *and* the object.)

Mais: Noëlle refuse de **promener le chien.** (*Noëlle* is the subject but *le chien* is the object.)

■ Like all other object pronouns, the reflexive pronoun is always placed immediately before the verb (except in an affirmative command). This rule is true no matter whether the verb is in an affirmative, interrogative, negative, or infinitive form.

Past tenses of reflexive verbs are covered on pp. 191 & 361.

Comment **vous** appelez-vous?	*What is your name?*
Tu veux **t'**asseoir?	*Do you want to sit down?*
Ne **s'**amusent-ils pas en classe?	*Don't they have fun in class?*
Je ne **m'**appelle pas Aude.	*My name is not Aude.*
Roman ne **se** réveille jamais très tôt.	*Roman never wakes up very early.*
Nous allons **nous** promener.	*We are going to take a walk.*
J'ai décidé de ne pas **me** lever.	*I decided not to get up.*

Review the imperative with pronouns, Ch. 10, p. 283. Remember that when **me** and **te** follow the verb they become **moi** and **toi**.

■ As you have already seen (see Ch. 10), when the imperative is affirmative, the object pronoun is placed after the verb. This is true even when the object pronoun is a reflexive pronoun.

Dépêche-**toi**!	*Hurry (up)!*
Dépêchez-**vous**!	*Hurry (up)!*
Dépêchons-**nous**!	*Let's hurry!*

Remind students not to use the imperative of reflexive verbs when they mean to use an interrogative: **Lavez-vous!** vs. **Vous lavez-vous?**

■ You also know that if the imperative is negative, normal word order is followed and the object pronoun precedes the verb.

Ne **te** dépêche pas.	*Don't hurry.*
Ne **vous** dépêchez pas.	*Don't hurry.*
Ne **nous** dépêchons pas.	*Let's not hurry.*

4 **Vrai ou faux?** Décidez si les phrases suivantes sont vraies. Si elles ne sont pas vraies, corrigez-les.

MODÈLE: Vous vous réveillez toujours tôt le matin.
C'est faux. Je ne me réveille pas toujours tôt le matin.

1. Vous vous brossez les dents avant le petit déjeuner.
2. On se lave avec de l'eau froide normalement.
3. Les étudiants de votre université se douchent une fois par semaine.
4. Ils s'habillent avant la douche.
5. Vous vous endormez quelquefois en classe.
6. Vous vous reposez toujours après les repas.
7. D'habitude, on se brosse les cheveux avec une brosse à dents.
8. Les professeurs se souviennent toujours des noms de leurs étudiants.

5 **Nos activités de chaque jour.** Faites des phrases logiques. Vous pouvez utiliser la forme négative.

Communication (Interpretive): Follow up by creating "illogical" sentences. Have students correct them.

MODÈLE: **Ma sœur se brosse les cheveux trois fois par jour.**

	se laver	tôt
	s'amuser	tard
	se dépêcher	le matin
nous	se coucher	le soir
les étudiants	prendre une douche	dans un fauteuil
mon père	s'habiller	dans la salle de bain
ma mère	s'endormir	avec de l'eau chaude
je	se réveiller	avec de l'eau froide
ma sœur	se brosser les cheveux	une (deux, etc.) fois par jour
mon frère	se brosser les dents	avec une brosse à cheveux
	se mettre à table	avec une brosse à dents
	se reposer	

6 **Fais ce que tu veux.** Utilisez l'impératif et l'expression **Eh bien, ...** pour encourager les autres à faire ce qu'ils veulent.

MODÈLES: Je voudrais m'asseoir.
Eh bien, assieds-toi.

Je ne voudrais pas me lever.
Eh bien, ne te lève pas.

Remind students that the **-s** is not written in the **tu** form of the imperative of **-er** verbs.

1. Je voudrais me coucher.
2. Je ne voudrais pas me dépêcher.
3. Je ne voudrais pas me brosser les dents.
4. Je voudrais m'amuser.
5. Je ne voudrais pas me lever à 7 heures.
6. Je ne voudrais pas étudier.
7. Je voudrais sortir avec mes amis.
8. Je voudrais m'endormir en classe.

C. Les verbes *se promener, s'inquiéter, s'appeler* et *s'asseoir*

■ Some reflexive verbs contain spelling changes in the verb stem of the present tense.

Review **se lever**, p. 169, **préférer**, p. 232, & **acheter**, p. 256.

■ Like **se lever** and **acheter**, **se promener** changes **-e-** to **-è-** before silent endings.

se promener *(to take a walk, ride)*			
je	me prom**è**ne	nous	nous promenons
tu	te prom**è**nes	vous	vous promenez
il/elle/on	se prom**è**ne		
ils/elles	se prom**è**nent		

■ Like **préférer**, **s'inquiéter** changes **-é-** to **-è-** before silent endings.

s'inquiéter *(to worry)*			
je	m'inqui**è**te	nous	nous inquiétons
tu	t'inqui**è**tes	vous	vous inquiétez
il/elle/on	s'inqui**è**te		
ils/elles	s'inqui**è**tent		

You may wish to point out that, like **acheter**, the spelling change occurs in the future for **se lever**, **se promener**, and **s'appeler**: **Je me lèverai tôt. Elle s'appellera Dubois.** However, like **préférer**, there is no change in the future for **s'inquiéter**: **Je ne m'inquiéterai plus.**

■ **S'appeler** changes **-l-** to **-ll-** before silent endings.

s'appeler *(to be named)*			
je	m'appe**ll**e	nous	nous appelons
tu	t'appe**ll**es	vous	vous appelez
il/elle/on	s'appe**ll**e		
ils/elles	s'appe**ll**ent		

NOTE — **S'asseoir** is irregular and is conjugated as follows:

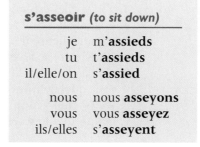

s'asseoir *(to sit down)*	
je	m'**assieds**
tu	t'**assieds**
il/elle/on	s'**assied**
nous	nous **asseyons**
vous	vous **asseyez**
ils/elles	s'**asseyent**

7 **La journée des étudiants.** Utilisez les verbes pronominaux **s'amuser, se coucher, se dépêcher, s'endormir, s'habiller, s'inquiéter, se lever** et **se réveiller** pour compléter les phrases suivantes.

MODÈLE: Nous ＿＿＿ à nos places.
Nous nous asseyons à nos places.

1. Le soir, les étudiants ne ＿＿＿ pas avant minuit parce qu'ils ont beaucoup de travail.
2. S'ils sont en retard pour un cours, ils ＿＿＿.
3. Ils ＿＿＿ s'il y a un examen.
4. Le week-end, les étudiants ＿＿＿.
5. Le samedi matin, ils restent au lit; ils ne ＿＿＿ pas avant 10 heures.
6. Ils ＿＿＿ très tard et ils ＿＿＿ tard aussi.
7. Ils ＿＿＿ en jean normalement parce que les jeans sont confortables.

8 **Pour avoir du succès à l'université.** Vous êtes très docile et vous répondez systématiquement que vous êtes d'accord. Utilisez le futur.

MODÈLE: Ne vous couchez pas trop tard.
D'accord, je ne me coucherai pas trop tard.

Review the future on p. 337.

1. Ne vous endormez pas pendant le cours de français.
2. Ne vous lavez pas avec de l'eau froide.
3. Amusez-vous bien pendant le week-end.
4. Dépêchez-vous pour ne pas être en retard.
5. Levez-vous avant 8 heures.
6. Ne vous inquiétez pas quand vous avez un examen.
7. Ne vous promenez pas après 22 heures.

9 **Un petit sondage (A small poll).** Vous êtes journaliste. Interviewez une autre personne (votre partenaire). Demandez ...

MODÈLE: s'il (si elle) se lève tôt
VOUS: **Est-ce que vous vous levez tôt le samedi matin?**
VOTRE PARTENAIRE: **Non, je me lève assez tard.**

Communication (Interpretive): Follow up by having the class interview the teacher (with books open) and then another student (with books closed).

1. s'il (si elle) parle français
2. comment il (elle) s'appelle
3. comment il (elle) va
4. s'il (si elle) est fatigué(e)
5. à quelle heure il (elle) se lève en semaine
6. à quelle heure il (elle) se couche
7. s'il (si elle) se lève tôt ou tard le samedi matin
8. s'il (si elle) s'endort à la bibliothèque
9. avec quel dentifrice il (elle) se brosse les dents
10. s'il (si elle) s'inquiète quand il y a un examen
11. depuis quand il (elle) étudie le français

ENTRE AMIS

Communication (Presentational): Follow-up by calling on a few students to tell the class about their partners' typical days.

Et ta journée?

Interview your partner about his/her typical day.

1. Find out at what time your partner wakes up.
2. Find out what s/he does during the day.
3. Find out at what time your partner goes to bed.
4. Double-check the information by repeating what your partner has told you.

3. Describing Past Activities

La dernière fois que j'ai dîné au restaurant avec des amis ...

	oui	non
ils y sont arrivés avant moi.	____	____
je me suis dépêché(e) pour arriver à l'heure.	____	____
mes amis s'inquiétaient parce que j'étais en retard.	____	____
nous nous sommes mis à table à huit heures.	____	____
je me suis bien amusé(e).	____	____
nous nous sommes promenés après le repas.	____	____
je me suis couché(e) assez tôt.	____	____

D. Le passé des verbes pronominaux

■ The imperfect tense of reflexive verbs is formed in the same way as that of simple verbs. The reflexive pronoun precedes the verb.

There are no spelling changes in the imperfect for stem-changing verbs; **s'appeler: Il s'appelait Pierre; se lever: Je me levais tôt.**

s'inquiéter (inquiétons)				
je	**m'inquiétais**	nous	**nous inquiétions**
tu	**t'inquiétais**	vous	**vous inquiétiez**
il/elle/on	**s'inquiétait**	ils/elles	**s'inquiétaient**

Review the passé composé of **se coucher** in Ch. 7, p. 191.

■ All reflexive verbs use the auxiliary **être** to form the passé composé. The past participle agrees in gender and number with the preceding direct object (usually the reflexive pronoun).

The past participle of stem changing verbs is not affected by spelling changes; it is based on the infinitive: **promené, inquiété, appelé.**

se reposer			
je	me	suis	reposé(e)
tu	t'	es	reposé(e)
il/on	s'	est	reposé
elle	s'	est	reposée
nous	**nous**	sommes	reposé(e)s
vous	**vous**	êtes	reposé(e)(s)
ils	se	sont	reposés
elles	se	sont	reposées

Delphine **s'est couchée** tôt parce qu'elle était fatiguée.

Nous **nous sommes** bien **amusé(e)s** le week-end dernier.

NOTE

Except for **s'asseoir,** the past participles of reflexive verbs are formed by the normal rules. The past participle of **s'asseoir** is **assis.**

Les deux femmes se sont **assises** à côté de moi.

■ In the negative, **ne ... pas** (**jamais,** etc.) are placed around the reflexive pronoun and the auxiliary verb.

Les enfants **ne** se sont **pas** couchés.
Je **ne** me suis **jamais** endormi(e) en classe.

■ In questions with inversion, as in all cases of inversion, the *subject* pronoun is placed after the auxiliary verb. The *reflexive* pronoun always directly precedes the auxiliary verb.

À quelle heure **t'es-tu** couchée, Christelle?
Vos amies **se** sont-**elles** reposées?

Reflexive pronouns are object pronouns, just like **le, la, les.** They follow the same general placement rules. See Ch. 10, p. 278.

FOR RECOGNITION ONLY

The past participle of a reflexive verb agrees with a preceding direct object. In most cases, the direct object is the reflexive pronoun, which precedes the past participle.

Claire **s'**est lavée.   *Claire washed **herself.***
Nous **nous** sommes amusés.   *We had a good time. (We amused **ourselves.**)*

However, with some reflexive verbs (such as **se laver** and **se brosser**), the direct object often follows the verb and the reflexive pronoun is not the direct object. The past participle *does not agree* with a reflexive pronoun that is not a direct object.

Claire s'est lavé **les cheveux.**   *Claire washed **her hair.***
Elle s'est brossé **les dents.**   *She brushed **her teeth.***

Indirect object pronouns will be presented in Ch. 14.

Comparison: Ask students: *What did Claire wash? (her hair); What did she brush? (her teeth).*

Le professeur et ses étudiants
s'amusent après le cours.

10 Mais oui, Maman. Madame Cousineau pose beaucoup de questions à sa fille. Utilisez l'expression entre parenthèses pour répondre à ces questions.

MODÈLE: Tu t'es réveillée à 7 heures? (mais oui)
Mais oui, je me suis réveillée à 7 heures.

1. Est-ce que tu t'es lavée ce matin? (mais oui)
2. Tu ne t'es pas dépêchée? (mais si!)
3. As-tu pris le petit déjeuner? (mais oui)
4. À quelle heure es-tu partie pour l'école? (à 7 heures 45)
5. Est-ce que tu t'es amusée à l'école? (non)
6. Tu ne t'es pas endormie en classe? (mais non)
7. À quelle heure es-tu rentrée de l'école? (à 5 heures)
8. Est-ce que tu as fait tes devoirs? (euh … non)

11 Vous aussi? Décidez si les phrases suivantes sont vraies pour vous. Utilisez **Moi aussi, Moi non plus** ou **Pas moi** pour répondre. Si vous choisissez **Pas moi,** ajoutez une explication.

MODÈLE: Les professeurs se sont bien amusés le week-end dernier.
Pas moi, je ne me suis pas amusé(e). J'ai étudié pendant tout le week-end.

1. Les professeurs se sont couchés avant minuit hier.
2. Ils se sont réveillés à 8 heures ce matin.
3. Ils ont pris le petit déjeuner.
4. Ils ont pris une douche ensuite.
5. Ils sont allés à leur premier cours à 9 heures.
6. Ils ne se sont pas assis pendant leurs cours.
7. Ils se sont bien amusés en classe.
8. Ils ont bu du café après le cours.

12 Votre vie sur le campus. Vous êtes journaliste. Interviewez un(e) étudiant(e). Demandez …

MODÈLES: s'il (si elle) s'est levé(e) tôt ce matin.
Vous êtes-vous levé(e) tôt ce matin?

ce qu'il (elle) a mangé.
Qu'est-ce que vous avez mangé?

1. s'il (si elle) arrive quelque fois en retard en classe.
2. s'il (si elle) s'est dépêché(e) ce matin.
3. où il (elle) va pour s'amuser.
4. ce qu'il (elle) a fait hier soir.
5. s'il (si elle) s'est amusé(e) hier soir.
6. à quelle heure il (elle) s'est couché(e).
7. s'il (si elle) s'est endormi(e) tout de suite.
8. combien d'heures il (elle) a dormi.
9. s'il (si elle) se repose d'habitude l'après-midi.
10. s'il (si elle) s'inquiète avant un examen.

ENTRE AMIS

Hier

1. Find out at what time your partner got up yesterday.
2. Find out what clothing s/he put on.
3. Ask if s/he took a walk.
4. Find out what else s/he did.
5. Ask if s/he had fun.
6. Find out at what time s/he went to bed.

4. Expressing One's Will

Que voulez-vous que le professeur fasse°?   *What do you want the teacher to do?*

Je voudrais que le professeur ...

	vrai	faux
donne moins de devoirs.	_____	_____
soit plus patient.	_____	_____
fasse la cuisine pour la classe.	_____	_____
s'amuse moins en classe.	_____	_____
chante avec ses étudiants.	_____	_____
parle plus lentement.	_____	_____
me donne une bonne note.	_____	_____

E. Le subjonctif

■ You have learned to use the infinitive after a number of verbal expressions. This happens when both verbs have the same subject or when the first verb is an impersonal expression with no specific subject.

Je veux parler français.   *I want to speak French.*

Il faut étudier.   *One (You, We, etc.) must study.*

■ Expressions that are used to express one's will, however, are frequently followed by **que** plus the subject and its verb in a form called **le subjonctif** (the subjunctive).

Je veux **que vous parliez** français.   *I want you to speak French.*

Il faut **qu'on étudie.**   *One (You, We, etc.) must study.*

■ The stem of the subjunctive is usually the same as the stem of the **ils/elles** form of the present tense. Except for **avoir** and **être,** the endings of the subjunctive are the same for all verbs.

-e	-ions
-es	-iez
-e	-ent

■ For regular **-er** verbs, the subjunctive forms for **je, tu, il/elle/on,** and **ils/elles** look and sound the same as the present tense.

Je veux que les professeurs **donnent** moins de devoirs.	*I want teachers to give less homework.*
Il faut que je **parle** avec eux.	*I must speak to them.*

■ The **nous** and **vous** forms of the subjunctive look and sound different from the present tense because of the **-i-** in their endings.

Je veux **que vous donniez** moins de devoirs.	*I want you to give less homework.*
Il faut **que nous parlions.**	*We need to speak.*

chanter (ils chant**ent**)		
que je	chant	**e**
que tu	chant	**es**
qu'il/elle/on	chant	**e**
que nous	chant	**ions**
que vous	chant	**iez**
qu'ils/elles	chant	**ent**

vendre (ils vend**ent**)		
que je	vend	**e**
que tu	vend	**es**
qu'il/elle/on	vend	**e**
que nous	vend	**ions**
que vous	vend	**iez**
qu'ils/elles	vend	**ent**

choisir (ils choisiss**ent**)		
que je	choisiss	**e**
que tu	choisiss	**es**
qu'il/elle/on	choisiss	**e**
que nous	choisiss	**ions**
que vous	choisiss	**iez**
qu'ils/elles	choisiss	**ent**

> **NOTE** — Even many irregular verbs follow the two basic rules above.
>
> | | | |
> |---|---|---|
> | **écrire** | (ils écriv**ent**) | que j'**écrive,** que nous **écrivions** |
> | **lire** | (ils lis**ent**) | que je **lise,** que nous **lisions** |
> | **partir** | (ils part**ent**) | que je **parte,** que nous **partions** |
> | **connaître** | (ils connaiss**ent**) | que je **connaisse,** que nous **connaissions** |
> | **conduire** | (ils conduis**ent**) | que je **conduise,** que nous **conduisions** |
> | **mettre** | (ils mett**ent**) | que je **mette,** que nous **mettions** |

Suggestion: Have students supply the **je** and **nous** forms for the verbs named here.

■ Some verbs have one stem for **je, tu, il/elle/on,** and **ils/elles** forms and another stem for **nous** and **vous.** Many of these are the same verbs that have two stems in the present tense. Some verbs of this type that you have already learned are **venir, prendre, boire, devoir, préférer, acheter,** and **se lever.**

venir					
	(ils	vienn**ent**)		(nous	ven**ons**)
que je	vienn	**e**	que nous	ven	**ions**
que tu	vienn	**es**	que vous	ven	**iez**
qu'il/elle/on	vienn	**e**			
qu'ils/elles	vienn	**ent**			

NOTE

Aller also has two stems (**aill-,** which is irregular, and **all-**).

Aille, ailles, aille, and **aillent** are pronounced like **aïe!** *(ouch!)* and **ail** *(garlic):* [aj].

aller

	(aill-)			(nous	allons)	
que j'	aill	e	que nous	all	ions	
que tu	aill	es	que vous	all	iez	
qu'il/elle/on	aill	e				
qu'ils/elles	aill	ent				

You might also want to mention that **vouloir** is also of this type, having **veuill-** and **voul-** as its two stems.

■ Some verbs have totally irregular stems. Their endings, however, are regular.

You might also want to mention that **pouvoir** is also of this type, having **puiss-** as its stem.

faire *(fass-)*

que je	fass	e
que tu	fass	es
qu'il/elle/on	fass	e
que nous	fass	ions
que vous	fass	iez
qu'ils/elles	fass	ent

savoir *(sach-)*

que je	sach	e
que tu	sach	es
qu'il/elle/on	sach	e
que nous	sach	ions
que vous	sach	iez
qu'ils/elles	sach	ent

■ Only **être** and **avoir** have irregular stems *and* endings.

Aie, aies, ait, and **aient** are pronounced [ɛ], like **est** *(is).*

Point out that the subjunctive forms of **avoir** and **être** are similar to the imperative, p. 282.

être

que je	sois
que tu	sois
qu'il/elle/on	soit
que nous	soyons
que vous	soyez
qu'ils/elles	soient

avoir

que j'	aie
que tu	aies
qu'il/elle/on	ait
que nous	ayons
que vous	ayez
qu'ils/elles	aient

VOCABULAIRE

La volonté

il est essentiel que	*it is essential that*
il est important que	*it is important that*
il est indispensable que	*it is essential that*
il est nécessaire que	*it is necessary that*
il faut que	*it is necessary that; (someone) must*
il ne faut pas que	*(someone) must not*
il vaut mieux que	*it is preferable that; it is better that*
je désire que	*I want*
j'exige que	*I demand that*
je préfère que	*I prefer that*
je souhaite que	*I wish that; I hope that*
je veux que	*I want*
je voudrais que	*I would like*

Communication (Presentational): Put students in pairs. Tell them to brainstorm to see how many sentences they can create beginning with **Le professeur veut que ...** Follow up by calling on students to share their sentences with the class.

■ With the above expressions, it is important to remember that, if there is no change of subjects, the infinitive is used. The preposition **de** is, however, required after **il est essentiel/important/indispensable/nécessaire.**

Je ne veux pas **perdre** mon temps.   *I don't want to waste my time.*
Il est important d'**étudier** beaucoup.   *It's important to study a lot.*

■ When the above expressions are followed by **que** and a change of subjects, the subjunctive must be used.

Ma mère ne veut pas **que je perde**   *My mother doesn't want me to*
mon temps.   *waste my time.*
Il est important **que j'étudie**   *It's important that I study a lot.*
beaucoup.

Il faut qu'elles se dépêchent parce qu'elles vont bientôt se mettre à table.

13 Ils veulent que je fasse tout ça? Tout le monde vous demande de faire quelque chose. Décidez si vous êtes d'accord.

MODÈLE: Votre père veut que vous étudiiez beaucoup.
Très bien, je vais étudier beaucoup. ou
Mais je ne veux pas étudier beaucoup.

1. Vos parents veulent que vous restiez à la maison.
2. Votre mère veut que vous rendiez visite à vos grands-parents.
3. Vos parents ne veulent pas que vous vendiez vos livres.
4. Vos parents ne veulent pas que vous sortiez tous les soirs.
5. Votre professeur veut que vous ayez «A» à votre examen de français.
6. Vos parents ne veulent pas que vous fumiez.
7. Vos professeurs ne veulent pas que vous perdiez vos devoirs.
8. Vos parents veulent que vous attachiez votre ceinture de sécurité.

14 Nos professeurs sont si exigeants! *(Our teachers are so demanding!)* Utilisez les expressions suivantes pour faire des phrases.

MODÈLE: les professeurs / vouloir / les étudiants / venir aux cours
Les professeurs veulent que les étudiants viennent aux cours.

1. les professeurs / désirer / les étudiants / faire leurs devoirs
2. les professeurs / vouloir / les étudiants / avoir de bonnes notes
3. les professeurs / exiger / les étudiants / être à l'heure
4. notre professeur / vouloir absolument / nous / parler français en classe
5. notre professeur / désirer / nous / réussir
6. notre professeur / souhaiter / nous / aller en France
7. notre professeur / préférer / nous / habiter chez une famille française
8. notre professeur / souhaiter / nous / savoir parler comme les Français

15 Que veulent-ils que je fasse? Tout le monde veut que vous fassiez quelque chose. Faites des phrases pour expliquer ce qu'ils veulent. Vous pouvez utiliser la forme négative si vous voulez.

MODÈLES: **Mes amis désirent que je sorte tous les soirs.**
Ma mère ne veut pas que je conduise vite.
Mon père préfère que je n'aie pas de voiture.

			étudier beaucoup
			sortir tous les soirs
			aller au bistro
	exiger		tomber malade
mes amis	vouloir		être heureux/heureuse
mon père	désirer	que je	avoir une voiture
ma mère	souhaiter		conduire vite
	préférer		faire la cuisine
			partir en vacances
			m'amuser beaucoup
			m'inquiéter quand il y a un examen
			acheter moins de vêtements

16 **Un petit sketch: Une fille au pair.** Lisez ou jouez le sketch suivant et répondez ensuite aux questions.

MME MARTIN: Je serai absente toute la journée.

LORI: Très bien, Madame. Que voulez-vous que je fasse aujourd'hui?

MME MARTIN: Je préparerai le dîner, mais je voudrais que vous alliez au marché.

LORI: D'accord.

MME MARTIN: Vous pouvez aussi y envoyer les enfants. J'ai laissé ma liste sur la table de la cuisine.

(Elle regarde sa montre.)
Aïe! Il faut que je parte. Au revoir, Lori. Au revoir, les enfants.

(après le départ de Mme Martin)

LORI: David! Sylvie! Dépêchez-vous! Votre mère veut que vous achetiez six tomates et un kilo de pommes de terre. Et n'oubliez pas de dire «s'il vous plaît» et «merci» à la dame au marché.

DAVID ET SYLVIE: Mais Lori!

LORI: Dépêchez-vous! Et mettez vos manteaux! Il pleut.

DAVID ET SYLVIE: Où est l'argent?

LORI: Attendez, le voilà. *(Elle donne l'argent aux enfants.)* Allez-y! Il ne faut pas que vous oubliiez la monnaie.

Point out **-ii-** in the subjunctive of **oublier.** Can students recall another verb in **-ier** (e.g., **étudier**)?

 QUESTIONS
1. Que faut-il que Lori fasse?
2. Est-il nécessaire qu'elle aille au marché elle-même?
3. Pourquoi veut-elle que les enfants mettent leurs manteaux?
4. Pourquoi les enfants ne partent-ils pas tout de suite?

17 **Fais comme il faut.** Madame Martin donne des conseils à sa fille Céline. Utilisez un verbe de volonté avec **que** et le subjonctif. Qu'est-ce qu'elle dit?

MODÈLES: ne pas t'endormir en classe
Je souhaite que tu ne t'endormes pas en classe.

conduire lentement
J'exige que tu conduises lentement.

1. prendre le petit déjeuner
2. ne pas boire de bière
3. mettre un chapeau s'il fait froid
4. aller aux cours tous les jours
5. savoir l'importance d'une bonne éducation
6. ne sortir avec tes amis que le week-end
7. être prudente
8. rentrer tôt
9. ne pas te lever tard

www**Réalités culturelles**

Le Burkina Faso

Situé au cœur de l'Afrique occidentale, le Burkina Faso est un peu plus grand que l'état de Colorado. Sa capitale est Ouagadougou. Il y a environ 12.200.000 Burkinabè, comme on appelle ses habitants. La langue officielle du pays est le français, mais il y a beaucoup de langues régionales. Les religions principales sont l'islam, le catholicisme, le protestantisme et des croyances traditionnelles. Quatre-vingt-douze pour cent des Burkinabè travaillent dans le domaine de l'agriculture.

Ce pays est devenu une colonie française au dix-neuvième siècle. Il s'appelait la Haute-Volta lorsqu'en 1960 il a gagné son indépendance. Mais en 1984 il a changé de nom pour devenir le Burkina Faso, nom qui signifie la «terre des hommes intègres». La devise du pays, «Unité, Progrès, Justice», semble bien décrire les Burkinabè parce que, pour eux, les qualités humaines les plus importantes sont l'hospitalité, l'humilité, la loyauté, la politesse et le respect du bien commun. Ces traits sont souvent célébrés dans leurs contes, leurs chants, leurs danses, leurs films et leurs représentations théâtrales. C'est d'ailleurs à Ouagadougou qu'a lieu le FESPACO, le plus grand festival du film africain.

Vocabulaire: contes *tales,* croyances *beliefs,* d'ailleurs *besides,* devise *motto,* intègres *honest,* lorsque *when*

Use the map on the inside back cover to locate this country.

The word **Burkinabè** does not add 's' in the plural. **FESPACO** is **le Festival Panafricain du Cinéma de Ouagadougou.**

18 **À vous.** Répondez.

1. Que voulez-vous que vos parents fassent pour vous?
2. Qu'est-ce qu'ils veulent que vous fassiez pour eux?
3. Où voulez-vous que vos amis aillent avec vous?
4. Que voulez-vous que vos amis vous donnent pour votre anniversaire?
5. Quels vêtements préférez-vous mettre pour aller à vos cours?
6. Quels vêtements préférez-vous que le professeur mette?
7. Qu'est-ce que le professeur veut que vous fassiez?

ENTRE AMIS

Un voyage d'études au Burkina Faso

1. Tell your partner that your teacher wants you to go to Burkina Faso with the class.
2. Tell your partner that you want him/her to come too.
3. Explain that you have to speak French there.
4. Explain why you want to visit that country.

Intégration

Révision

A **Pour mettre la table.** Que faut-il qu'on fasse pour mettre la table à la française? Donnez une description complète.

MODÈLE: **Il faut qu'on mette une nappe sur la table.**

B **Ma journée.** D'abord décrivez votre journée habituelle. Ensuite décrivez votre journée d'hier.

C **Trouvez quelqu'un qui...** Interviewez les autres étudiants pour trouver quelqu'un qui …

MODÈLE: se lève avant 7 heures du matin
Est-ce que tu te lèves avant 7 heures du matin?

1. s'inquiète s'il y a un examen
2. ne s'endort jamais en classe
3. s'est couché après minuit hier soir
4. veut que le professeur donne moins de devoirs
5. se promène le matin
6. promène souvent son chien
7. s'assied toujours à la même place au cours de français

D **Début de rédaction.** Faites une liste de dix choses qu'il faut que vous fassiez la semaine prochaine.

MODÈLE: **Lundi il faut que je me lève tôt.**

E **À vous.** Répondez.

1. Que font les étudiants de votre université pour s'amuser?
2. Qu'est-ce que les professeurs veulent que leurs étudiants fassent?
3. Qu'est-ce que vos parents ne veulent pas que vous fassiez?
4. Dans quelles circonstances vous dépêchez-vous?
5. À quel(s) moment(s) de la journée vous brossez-vous les dents?
6. Avez-vous quelquefois envie de vous endormir en classe? Pourquoi ou pourquoi pas?

Est-ce que vos parents ne veulent pas que vous alliez au café?

Négociations: **Il manque quelque chose.** Interviewez les autres étudiants pour trouver les choses qui manquent. Il y a sept cartes différentes en tout. Les autres cartes sont dans l'appendice D.

For complete instructions on how to prepare for and to use this activity, see *Négociations* on the Class Prep CD-ROM.

You should be able to identify a specific classmate for each of the missing items.

Video for Chapter 13: A. Video worksheets (*Cahier*); B. ACE Video practice test (WWW); C. CD-ROM

MODÈLE: **Est-ce que tu as un(e) ... sur ta table?**
Moi, j'ai un(e) ..., mais je n'ai pas de (d') ...

A

Lecture I

A **Étude du vocabulaire.** Étudiez les phrases suivantes et choisissez les mots qui correspondent aux mots français en caractères gras: *sand, those, burning, gently, shovel, lived, erased, pick up, sea.*

1. Le professeur a écrit une phrase au tableau et ensuite il a **effacé** la phrase.
2. Marie, regarde ta chambre! Tu as laissé tes vêtements sur ton lit. **Ramasse**-les tout de suite!
3. **Ceux** qui habitent près de la **mer** peuvent souvent s'amuser dans l'eau.
4. Quand nous étions jeunes, nous **vivions** heureux avec notre famille.
5. En été, les enfants aimaient bien nager dans la **mer** ou jouer avec une **pelle** dans le **sable.**
6. Quand il faisait très chaud, le **sable** était **brûlant.** On ne pouvait pas marcher sans chaussures.
7. Parlez **doucement!** Les enfants dorment.

B **Pensez à la saison.** À quelle saison pensez-vous quand vous entendez les expressions suivantes?

1. la mer et le sable
2. le soleil brûlant
3. les feuilles mortes
4. le vent du nord
5. la belle vie
6. la nuit froide
7. les jours heureux

Les feuilles mortes

Connection: If you have a
recording of **Les feuilles
mortes** (there are several
available), play it for your
students. See the *Entre amis*
Web site.

Oh! Je voudrais tant que tu te souviennes
Des jours heureux où nous étions amis.
En ce temps-là la vie était plus belle
Et le soleil plus brûlant qu'aujourd'hui.
Les feuilles mortes se ramassent à la
    pelle,
Tu vois, je n'ai pas oublié.
Les feuilles mortes se ramassent à la
    pelle,
Les souvenirs et les regrets aussi
Et le vent du nord les emporte[1]
Dans la nuit froide de l'oubli.
Tu vois, je n'ai pas oublié
La chanson que tu me chantais.

Comparison: If students do not
recognize *"Autumn Leaves,"*
ask them to give the poem an
English title. Have students
brainstorm to suggest songs
they know that have a similar
theme.

C'est une chanson qui nous ressemble,
Toi, tu m'aimais, et je t'aimais.
Nous vivions tous les deux ensemble,
Toi, qui m'aimais; moi, qui t'aimais.
Mais la vie sépare ceux qui s'aiment
Tout doucement, sans faire de bruit
Et la mer efface sur le sable
Les pas des amants désunis.[2]

Jacques Prévert

*Communication (Presenta-
tional):* Use the poem for a
Concours de prononciation
(see the Class Prep CD-ROM).

---

1. *carries away* 2. *the footprints of separated lovers*

C **À votre avis.** Relisez le poème et faites deux listes: (1) des expressions qui vous semblent tristes ou nostalgiques et (2) des expressions qui vous semblent plus heureuses.

Lecture II

A **Étude du vocabulaire.** Étudiez les phrases suivantes et choisissez les mots qui correspondent aux mots français en caractères gras: *corn, dry, dust, maid, rooms, harvest.*

1. C'était une maison avec quatre **pièces:** deux chambres, une cuisine et une salle de séjour.
2. Il y a longtemps que j'ai nettoyé cette chambre. Les meubles sont couverts de **poussière.**
3. Sans pluie, toute la région était **sèche.**
4. L'automne est la saison de la **récolte** du **maïs** dans l'Iowa.
5. Quelquefois les familles ont une **bonne** pour les aider au ménage.

B **Situez ces expressions.** Étudiez les expressions suivantes qui sont utilisées dans la lettre que Madame Nabi a envoyée du Burkina Faso. Ensuite cherchez-les dans sa lettre.

barrage *dam*, bouillie de mil *millet porridge*, dolo *a type of punch*, ignames *yams*, marmite *large pot*, occasions de rencontre *chances to meet others*, oseille *sorrel*, pagne *(grass) skirt*, Pâques *Easter*, prière *prayer*, tamarin *tamarind fruit*, tarissent *dry up*, tuteurs, *legal guardians*, volaille *poultry*

Une lettre du Burkina Faso

Madame Nabi adresse une lettre à son amie américaine où elle lui parle de sa vie au Burkina Faso. Madame Nabi et son mari s'occupent d'un CSPS, Centre de santé et de promotion sociale, pour procurer à leurs compatriotes aide et conseils au point de vue santé.

Zitenga, le 3 avril 2005

À Madame Baer

Je suis ravie de vous écrire cette lettre. Vous avez le bonjour de mon mari, M. Nabi, et de mon bébé, Wen Danga Benaja (puissance de Dieu, en mooré), qui a quatre mois. Mon bonjour également à toute votre famille et à tous ceux et celles qui vous sont chers. Nous vous ferons découvrir le Burkina par notre correspondance.

Nous habitons à Zitenga, qui est à 53 km au nord de la ville d'Ouagadougou, capitale du Burkina Faso. Ce village se trouve dans la province d'Oubritenga, une des 45 provinces du pays. Nous avons un climat sahélien[1]: il pleut de juin à octobre, il fait froid de novembre à janvier et chaud de février à mai. Pendant la saison froide, le vent, qu'on appelle le Harmattan et qui vient du désert, couvre tout de poussière. Les villageois sont des cultivateurs, surtout de mil, d'arachides et de riz, et des éleveurs de moutons, de bœufs et de volailles. En saison sèche, on fait du jardinage et du commerce.

Le village respecte la hiérarchie traditionnelle. Le chef est généralement le plus vieux de la tribu et c'est lui qui est gardien de la tradition. Parmi les principales religions, l'animisme, la plus ancienne, est en voie de disparaître. Les gens qui la pratiquent adorent des idoles et placent leur confiance dans les ancêtres. Il y a aussi des catholiques, des protestants et des musulmans; ces derniers sont les plus nombreux. Les ethnies existantes sont les Mossis, qui sont en majorité, et les Peuhls qui sont nomades. On parle le mooré, le foulfouldé (peuhl) et le français.

Les occasions de rencontre sont surtout les fêtes traditionnelles mossis, dont le Basga, fête des récoltes où les vieux animistes préparent des boissons comme le dolo

Les notables du village habillés pour la fête

fait à base de sorgho rouge. Il y a aussi la fête musulmane du Ramadan et la Tabaski, fête des moutons. Les Chrétiens fêtent Noël et Pâques. Après un décès dans le village, on se réunit pour fêter le mort et demander à Dieu de l'accepter dans sa maison. On prépare un repas avec poulet et mouton, on boit le dolo, et on assiste à la danse des masques, exécutée au rythme des tams-tams. Ces masques sont des objets sacrés qui ne sortent que pour les funérailles et certaines fêtes mossis. Les jours de grands marchés, tous les 21 jours, le vendredi, les jeunes organisent des fêtes, les Damandassés, qui sont l'occasion pour eux de montrer leurs beaux habits, leurs belles robes et pagnes. C'est l'occasion aussi pour garçons et filles de se lier d'une amitié qui peut souvent aller jusqu'au mariage. Les Damandassés commencent après les récoltes à quatre heures de l'après-midi et durent jusqu'au petit matin.

Mme Nabi et sa petite sœur dans les champs

   Les maisons sont construites en "banco" ou terre séchée au soleil. Notre maison a deux pièces et un salon. J'y habite avec mon mari, mon bébé, ainsi que la femme d'un grand frère de mon mari, trois élèves (ma petite sœur qui fait la sixième, et une fille et un garçon qui font la cinquième, dont nous sommes les tuteurs), deux garçons qui nous aident pour les travaux domestiques et la construction, une bonne et un homme de 45 ans qui est chez nous depuis trois mois. En tout nous sommes onze dans la famille.

   Nous commençons chaque journée par une prière protestante de 6h à 6h30. Puis, mon mari et moi, nous allons au Centre de santé et de promotion sociale[2], où nous sommes agents de santé. À 12h30 c'est le déjeuner, et de 15h à 17h nous repartons au CSPS. Vers 19h c'est le dîner. Nous nous couchons chaque soir vers 22h, si nous n'avons pas de malade à surveiller au dispensaire. Quand on a un peu de temps, on lit un bon roman.

   Le repas du matin, c'est la bouillie de mil préparée avec le jus de tamarin, cuite avec du sucre. Très rarement, on prend du café, du lait ou du pain. À midi, on prépare du riz avec sauce ou haricots; ou bien des ignames avec sauce tomate ou simplement salées, avec de l'huile d'arachide. Le soir, on mange du tô. Le tô est fait avec de la farine de maïs ou de mil, de l'eau et du jus de tamarin. On y ajoute une sauce faite avec des légumes tels que de l'oseille, des oignons, des tomates, ou de la viande ou du poisson fumé. On utilise aussi l'huile ou la pâte d'arachide. On mange assis par terre autour de la marmite et on prend la nourriture avec la main droite. Les femmes et les hommes mangent séparément.

   Nous cherchons l'eau de boisson à un forage (une pompe) assez loin de chez nous, parce que le forage du dispensaire est en panne et nous n'avons pas les moyens suffisants pour le réparer. En plus des forages, les habitants puisent l'eau des puits, des mares ou des marigots[3]. Malheureusement ces sources d'eau tarissent *très vite. Les femmes portent l'eau sur leur tête. Ceux qui ont les moyens vont à l'eau avec des charrettes. Les légumes frais, qu'on achète au marché, viennent des villages environnants où il y a des barrages et donc des terres irriguées. Le problème de l'eau est crucial à Zitenga.*

Je remercie Madame Baer des cadeaux qu'elle a offerts à mon bébé. Si vous voulez d'autres détails, vous pouvez nous écrire. Nous vous souhaitons courage dans votre travail et surtout bonne réception de cette lettre.

Madame Nabi, née Ouedraogo Abzèta, Zitenga

1. *climate of transition between the desert and damper regions*   2. *M. Nabi is head of the Center, but not a doctor. His wife has nursing skills. Two midwives do pre-natal and post-natal counseling, including family planning. A second man does vaccination tours, and a third is a fix-it person and also gives shots and does circumcisions.*
3. *dead branch of a river bed*

C Vrai ou faux? Décidez si les phrases suivantes sont vraies ou fausses d'après la lecture. Si une phrase est fausse, corrigez-la.

1. Madame Nabi habite une grande maison.
2. Il y a plus de protestants que de membres d'autres religions.
3. On ne parle que le français au Burkina Faso.
4. La famille se met à table pour manger.
5. On utilise une fourchette, un couteau et une cuiller et on mange «à la française».
6. Les légumes frais viennent du jardin des Nabi.
7. Madame Nabi et son mari travaillent dans une sorte de clinique.
8. Ils se lèvent avant six heures du matin.
9. Pour avoir de l'eau, on doit simplement ouvrir le robinet dans la cuisine.

D Questions. Répondez.

1. Combien d'hommes et combien de femmes habitent la maison de Madame Nabi?
2. D'après cette lettre, combien de langues est-ce qu'on parle au Burkina Faso?
3. Quelles sont les quatre religions dont parle Madame Nabi?
4. Quelles sont les différentes sortes de viande mentionnées dans cette lettre?
5. Quels sont les besoins essentiels pour les gens du village?

E Cherchez des exemples. Relisez la lettre et cherchez des exemples ...

1. qui indiquent que le Burkina Faso se trouve en Afrique.
2. qui prouvent que le Burkina Faso est un pays pauvre.
3. qui montrent l'influence de l'Islam au Burkina Faso.
4. qui révèlent la foi *(faith)* et la charité des Nabi.

VOCABULAIRE ACTIF

À table
un bol *bowl*
un couteau *knife*
une cuiller *spoon*
une fourchette *fork*
une nappe *tablecloth*
le poivre *pepper*
le sel *salt*
une serviette *napkin*
le sucre *sugar*

Au restaurant
une carte *(à la carte) menu*
un menu *(fixed price) menu*

D'autres noms
une brosse à cheveux (à dents) *hairbrush (toothbrush)*
le chauffage *heat*
la climatisation *air conditioning*
une dame *lady*
les genoux *(m. pl.) lap; knees*
un maillot de bain *bathing suit*
un pyjama *(pair of) pajamas*
des skis *(m.) skis*
une soirée *evening party*
un sourire *smile*

La routine quotidienne
se brosser (les dents) *to brush (one's teeth)*
se coucher *to go to bed*
s'endormir *to fall asleep*
s'habiller *to get dressed*
se laver *to get washed; to wash up*
se lever *to get up; to stand up*
se mettre à table *to sit down to eat*
se promener *to take a walk, ride*
se reposer *to rest*
se réveiller *to wake up*

La volonté
il est essentiel que *it is essential that*
il est important que *it is important that*
il est indispensable que *it is essential that*
il est nécessaire que *it is necessary that*
il faut que *it is necessary that; (someone) must*
il ne faut pas que *(someone) must not*
il vaut mieux que *it is preferable that; it is better that*
je désire que *I want*
j'exige que *I demand that*
je préfère que *I prefer that*
je souhaite que *I wish that; I hope that*
je veux que *I want*
je voudrais que *I would like*

Expressions utiles
à la française *in the French style*
Bon appétit! *Have a good meal!*
C'est exact. *That's right.*
de rien *you're welcome; don't mention it; not at all*
Excusez-moi (nous, etc.) d'être en retard. *Excuse me (us, etc.) for being late.*
Il n'y a pas de quoi. *Don't mention it.; Not at all.*
il sourit *he smiles*

Verbes
s'appeler *to be named; to be called*
s'asseoir *to sit down*
couper *to cut*
se dépêcher *to hurry*
goûter *to taste*
s'inquiéter *to worry*
laver *to wash*
lever *to lift; to raise*
mettre *to put; to place; to lay*
mettre le chauffage *to turn on the heat*
mettre la table *to set the table*
se souvenir (de) *to remember*
tarder *to be a long time coming*
verser *to pour*

Quelle histoire!

Buts communicatifs
Describing interpersonal relationships
Describing television programs
Expressing emotion

Structures utiles
Le verbe **dire**
Les pronoms objets indirects
Les verbes **voir** et **croire**
Les interrogatifs **quel** et **lequel**
Les pronoms relatifs (suite)
Le subjonctif (suite)
Le pronom **en**

Culture
• *À propos*
La télévision française
Les faux amis

• *Il y a un geste*
Je te le jure
Quelle histoire!

• *Lectures*
À la télévision
Au cinéma

Coup d'envoi

Prise de contact

Une histoire d'amour

David et Marie sortent ensemble.

Ils s'entendent° très bien.	*get along*
Ils s'embrassent°.	*kiss*
Ils s'aiment.	
Il lui° a demandé si elle voulait l'épouser.	*her*
Elle lui° a répondu que oui.	*him*
Il lui a acheté une très belle bague de fiançailles°.	*engagement ring*
Ils vont se marier.	

▶ **Et vous?**

Connaissez-vous des couples célèbres° qui sont fiancés?	*famous*
Connaissez-vous des couples célèbres qui sont mariés?	
Connaissez-vous des couples célèbres qui sont divorcés?	

M. et Mme Jean-Pierre Delataille

M. et Mme Émile Baron

ont l'honneur de vous annoncer le mariage de leurs enfants

Marie et David

et vous prient d'assister ou de vous unir d'intention à la Messe de Mariage

qui sera célébrée le samedi 16 juillet 2005 à 17 heures, en l'Église St-Gervais.

27, rue des Tournelles-75004 Paris

27, rue Mahler-75004 Paris

Conversation

Je te le jure

Lori et son amie Denise sont assises à la terrasse d'un café.
Denise lui demande si elle a regardé le feuilleton° d'hier soir.   soap opera, series

DENISE:	Encore à boire, Lori?
LORI:	Non, vraiment, sans façon.
DENISE:	Au fait, tu as regardé le feuilleton hier à la télé?
LORI:	Lequel?°
DENISE:	*Nos chers enfants.*
LORI:	Non. Qu'est-ce qui est arrivé?°
DENISE:	David et Marie ne s'aiment plus. Marie a un petit ami maintenant.
LORI:	Eh! ça devient sérieux.
DENISE:	Tu ne sais pas tout. Ils vont divorcer. David lui a dit qu'il allait partir.
LORI:	Il est sans doute très malheureux°, n'est-ce pas?
DENISE:	Bien sûr. Il dit que le mariage est une loterie. Pour se consoler le plus vite possible, il a mis une annonce° dans le journal local.
LORI:	Ça, c'est original°. Et il y a des candidates?
DENISE:	Oui, trois femmes lui ont répondu et veulent le rencontrer°.
LORI:	Sans blague?°
DENISE:	Je te le jure.° C'est passionnant!
LORI:	Quelle histoire!

Right margin glosses:
Which one?
What happened?
unhappy
advertisement
a novel idea
meet
No kidding?
I swear.

After practicing the Conversation, have students complete ex. A in the Workbook.

▶ **Jouez ces rôles.** Répétez la conversation avec votre partenaire. Remplacez ensuite *David* par *Marie* et *Marie* par *David,* par exemple: **Elle lui a dit qu'elle allait partir.** Faites tous les changements nécessaires.

Il y a un geste

Comparison: Point out the relationship between **jurer** and the English word *jury.*

The **Quelle histoire!** gesture is used in the video, *Modules 1 & 6.*

Je te le jure.   An outstretched hand, palm down, means *I swear,* perhaps originally meaning "I would put my hand in the fire (if it were not true)."

Quelle histoire!   To indicate that something is amazing, exaggerated, or far-fetched, the French hold the hand open with fingers pointing down and shake the wrist several times. Other expressions used with this gesture are **Oh là là!** *(Wow!, Oh dear!)* and **Mon Dieu!** *(My goodness!).*

À propos

> ***Comparison:*** Have students describe their TV viewing. What do they watch and how much time do they spend watching TV? How do their viewing habits compare with those of the French?

Comment dit-on «passionnant» en anglais?

    a. passionate b. amazing c. exciting

Que veut dire «sans doute»?

    a. certainement b. probablement c. peut-être

En France il y a cinq chaînes *(channels)* de télévision nationales. Sur ces cinq, _____ sont des chaînes publiques.

    a. deux b. trois c. quatre

For more information on French TV, see also the Note culturelle, p. 392.

La télévision française

Until recently, commercials **(la publicité),** if allowed at all, were grouped into relatively lengthy segments and shown between programs. Today, however, commercials often interrupt programs, especially on the private channels. As in North America, many viewers cope by channel "surfing" **(zapper).**

  Of the five major channels available to all, only two **(TF1** and **M6)** are private. The others **(France 2, France 3,** and **Arte/La 5)** are public. In addition to commercials and government subsidies, public television is financed in France (and in most European countries) by a user tax. Everyone who has a color TV set, currently 96 percent of French households, must pay well over 100 euros per year.

  France 2 programming, especially the evening news **(le Journal de vingt heures),** is made available throughout the francophone world and in most other countries. It may be found on the French-language channels in Canada and on SCOLA and the International channel in the United States.

  Recently, Internet use has increased considerably in France. French has become, after English, the second language of the World Wide Web.

Les faux amis *(False cognates)*

It is estimated that as much as 50 percent of our English-language vocabulary comes from French. Most of these words are true cognates and facilitate comprehension. There are, however, a number of false cognates whose meaning *in a given context* is quite different from what we might expect. Some examples are given below.

Review the concepts of *cognate,* p. 25, and *false cognate,* p. 52.

VOCABULAIRE

Quelques faux amis

actuellement	*now*	une histoire	*story*
une annonce	*advertisement*	un journal	*newspaper*
arriver	*to happen*	original(e)	*novel, odd; different*
assister (à)	*to attend*	par hasard	*by chance*
attendre	*to wait for*	passer un examen	*to take a test*
un avertissement	*warning*	passionnant(e)	*exciting, fascinating*
compréhensif (-ve)	*understanding*	des plaisanteries	*jokes*
un conducteur	*driver*	rester	*to stay*
confus(e)	*ashamed, embarrassed*	sans doute	*probably*
demander	*to ask*	sensible	*sensitive*
une émission	*program*	un smoking	*a tuxedo*
formidable	*wonderful*		

▶ **À vous.** Répondez.

1. Avez-vous un feuilleton préféré? Si oui, lequel?
2. Que pensez-vous des feuilletons en général?
3. Quel feuilleton aimez-vous le moins?

ENTRE AMIS

Ton émission préférée

1. Find out if your partner watches TV.
2. If so, ask what his/her favorite TV program is.
3. Find out if your partner listens to the radio.
4. If so, ask what his/her favorite radio program is.
5. If your partner has responded affirmatively, find out the date and time of his/her favorite programs.
6. If your partner has responded no, find out why s/he doesn't watch TV or listen to the radio.

Prononciation

La tension

■ There is much more tension in the facial muscles when speaking French than when speaking English. Two important phenomena result from this greater tension.

1. *There are no diphthongs (glides from one vowel sound to another) in French.* French vowels are said to be "pure." The positions of mouth and tongue remain stable during the pronunciation of a vowel, and therefore one vowel sound does not "glide" into another as often happens in English.

▶ **Contrast:**

English	French
d**ay**	d**es**
aut**o**	aut**o**

■ Notice that in the English word *day,* the **a** glides into an **ee** sound at the end, and that in the English word *auto,* the **o** glides to **oo.**

▶ Now practice "holding steady" the sound of each of the vowels in the following French words.

étudiant, am**é**ricain
sant**é**, soir**ée**
dans**er**, parl**ez**
l**es**, j'**ai**

ch**o**se, styl**o**
tr**o**p, z**é**ro
aussi, ch**au**d
b**eau**, mant**eau**

2. *Final consonants are completely released.* The pronunciation of final French consonants is much more "complete" than is the case for those of American English.

■ Note that in American English, the final consonants are often neither dropped nor firmly enunciated. In similar French words, the final consonants are all clearly pronounced.

▶ **Contrast:**

English	French
ro**b**	rob**e**
gran**d**	gran**d**e
ba**g**	ba**gu**e
be**ll**	be**ll**e
ho**m**e	ho**mm**e
America**n**	américai**n**e
gri**p**	gri**pp**e
intelligen**t**	intelligen**t**e

▶ Now practice "releasing" the highlighted final consonant sounds below so that you can hear them clearly.

1. une gran**d**e fille

2. Elle s'appe**ll**e Michèle.

3. un pi**qu**e-ni**qu**e

4. une ba**gu**e de fiançailles

5. un ho**mm**e et une fe**mm**e

6. sa ju**p**e verte

In #5, be sure there is liaison after **un** but not after **et.**

L'homme qu'on interviewe parle au micro.

www Réalités culturelles

Les Petites Antilles françaises

Situées en zone tropicale, les Petites Antilles françaises sont un archipel en forme d'arc de cercle où se trouvent la Martinique (mot qui veut dire «île aux fleurs») et la Guadeloupe («île aux belles eaux»). Cette dernière est composée de deux îles principales, qui forment un papillon, Basse-Terre et Grande-Terre. C'est à la Martinique, au village des Trois-Îlets, que la future impératrice Joséphine, femme de Napoléon Ier, est née.

Culture & Connections: One part of the video is dedicated to Guadeloupe.

Mais ces îles de rêve ont leur côté sombre. Chaque année, des ouragans violents frappent la région. Ces îles volcaniques sont à la merci d'éruptions, comme celle qui en 1902 a détruit Saint-Pierre à la Martinique. Elles sont aussi menacées de tremblements de terre qui peuvent faire disparaître des portions d'île entières. Au cours de leur histoire, ces îles ont connu l'exploitation, la violence et la misère. Aujourd'hui encore, le chômage est très élevé: 23,5 pour cent à la Martinique, plus élevé encore en Guadeloupe. Certains Antillais voudraient se séparer de la France. Aimé Césaire, célèbre poète de la négritude, qui est devenu maire de Fort-de-France, a déclaré que la Martinique «perdait son âme» en restant française et dépendante de la France. Par contre, une séparation de la France serait un désastre économique.

Communities: Review the *Réalités culturelles* on p. 68.

Repères:	La Martinique	La Guadeloupe
Statut politique:	départements français d'outre-mer	
Superficie:	1.106 km²	1.780 km²
Population:	385.000	426.000
Langue officielle:	français	français
Religion:	catholique	catholique
Chef-lieu:	Fort-de-France	Pointe-à-Pitre
Ressources:	subvention de l'État français, tourisme, industrie (rhum, sucre), agriculture (canne à sucre, bananes, ananas)	

Vocabulaire: âme *soul,* chômage *unemployment,* ouragan *hurricane,* papillon *butterfly,* par contre *on the other hand,* rêve *dream,* tremblement de terre *earthquake*

Buts communicatifs

1. Describing Interpersonal Relationships

L'histoire d'un divorce

David et Marie ne s'entendent plus très bien.
Ils se fâchent°.   *get angry*
Ils se disputent°.   *argue; fight*
Il ne lui envoie plus de fleurs.
Elle ne lui parle plus.
Il lui a dit° qu'il ne l'aime plus.   *He told her*
Ils vont se séparer.
Ils ont même° l'intention de divorcer.   *even*

▶ **Et vous?**   Choisissez un couple (de Hollywood, de Washington, de vos amis, etc.) que vous connaissez. Comment s'appellent-ils? Est-ce qu'ils s'entendent bien? Est-ce qu'ils se disputent quelquefois? Décrivez ce couple.

A. Le verbe *dire*

David **dit** qu'il va partir.   *David says (that) he's going to leave.*
Dites à Marie de faire attention.   *Tell Marie to watch out.*

dire *(to say; to tell)*			
je	**dis**	nous	**disons**
tu	**dis**	vous	**dites**
il/elle/on	**dit**	ils/elles	**disent**
passé composé: j'**ai dit**			

■ The verb **dire** should not be confused with the verb **parler**. Both can mean *to tell*, but they are used differently.

• **Dire** can be followed by a quote or by an item of information (sometimes contained in another clause introduced by **que**).

Bruno **dit bonjour** à Alissa.   *Bruno **says hello** to Alissa.*
Il **lui dit un secret.**   *He **tells her a secret.***
Il **dit qu'il l'aime.**   *He **says that he loves** her.*
Il **dit** toujours **la vérité.**   *He always **tells the truth.***

• **Parler** can stand alone or can be followed by an adverb, by **à** (or **avec**) and the person spoken to, or by **de** and the topic of conversation.

Bruno **parle** (lentement).   *Bruno **is speaking** (slowly).*
Il **parle à** Alissa.   *He **is talking to** Alissa.*
Il **parle de** lui-même.   *He **is telling about** himself.*

NOTE — When the meaning is *to tell (a story)*, the verb **raconter** is used.

Raconte-nous une histoire.   *Tell us a story.*

1 **Qu'est-ce qu'ils disent?** Quelles sont les opinions de chaque personne? Utilisez le verbe **dire** et le verbe **être** dans chaque phrase.

MODÈLE: Ma grand-mère / le rap / facile ou difficile à comprendre
Ma grand-mère dit que le rap est difficile à comprendre.

1. je / la publicité à la télé / très bonne ou très mauvaise
2. nos grands-parents / nous / charmants ou désagréables
3. nous / le cours de français / formidable ou ennuyeux
4. le professeur de français / nous / travailleurs ou paresseux
5. mes professeurs / je / intelligent(e) ou stupide
6. mes amis / le football à la télé / passionnant ou affreux

2 **À vous.** Répondez.

1. Que dites-vous quand vous avez une bonne note à un examen?
2. Que dit votre professeur de français quand vous entrez en classe?
3. Que dites-vous quand vous êtes en retard à un cours?
4. Que dites-vous à un(e) ami(e) qui vous téléphone à 6 heures du matin?
5. De quoi parlez-vous avec vos amis?
6. Vos professeurs racontent-ils quelquefois des histoires en classe? Si oui, quelle sorte d'histoires?
7. Comment dit-on «Oh dear!» en français?
8. Dites-vous toujours la vérité?

Communication (Interpretive & Presentational): Follow up, books closed, by asking students to recall their partners' answers.

3 **Le perroquet et la fourmi** *(the parrot and the ant).* **Quelle histoire!** Utilisez les verbes **dire, parler** et **raconter** pour compléter le paragraphe suivant.

Mon frère _____ qu'il adore les histoires drôles. Hier soir, par exemple, il m'a _____ l'histoire d'une femme anglaise qui achète un perroquet qui ne _____ que le français. Mais la pauvre dame ne peut rien _____ en français et ne peut pas _____ avec lui. Un jour, la dame va boire un verre de lait mais dans le verre il y a une fourmi. Le perroquet veut _____ à la dame de ne pas boire le lait; il _____ FOURMI!! parce qu'il ne _____ pas anglais. La dame pense que le perroquet a _____ «For me!» et elle part chercher un verre de lait pour son perroquet. J'ai _____ à mon frère que je n'apprécie pas beaucoup les histoires qu'il _____.

B. Les pronoms objets indirects

David parle *à Marie.*	*David is speaking to Marie.*
Il **lui** dit qu'il l'aime.	*He tells **her** that he loves her.*
Il **lui** demande de l'épouser.	*He asks **her** to marry him.*
Il **lui** achète une bague de fiançailles.	*He buys **her** an engagement ring.*
Ils écrivent *à leurs parents.*	*They write to their parents.*
Ils **leur** disent qu'ils vont se marier.	*They tell **them** that they are going to get married.*

Il lui a demandé si elle voulait
se promener.

■ Indirect object nouns in French are preceded by the preposition **à.** Many
verbs take indirect objects, either in addition to a direct object or with no
direct object.

VOCABULAIRE

Quelques verbes qui prennent un objet indirect

acheter		*to buy*
demander		*to ask*
dire		*to say; to tell*
donner		*to give*
écrire		*to write*
emprunter		*to borrow*
envoyer	quelque chose **à quelqu'un**	*to send*
montrer		*to show*
prêter		*to lend*
raconter		*to tell*
rendre		*to give back*
vendre		*to sell*
obéir		*to obey*
parler		*to speak, talk*
répondre	**à quelqu'un**	*to respond, answer*
téléphoner		*to telephone*

> Two additional expressions that you have already learned take a specific direct object plus an indirect object: **poser une question à quelqu'un; rendre visite à quelqu'un.** J'ai posé une question **au professeur.** *(I asked the teacher a question.)* Vas-tu rendre visite **à tes parents?** *(Are you going to visit your parents?)*

NOTE — Do not be confused by verbs that take an indirect object in French but a
direct object in English.

Paul obéit **à ses parents.** *Paul obeys his parents.*

Je téléphone **à Brigitte.** *I call Brigitte.*

Marc rend visite **à ses amis.** *Marc visits his friends.*

■ Indirect object nouns can be replaced in sentences by indirect object pronouns.

Review the direct object pronouns on pp. 228 & 278.

me (m')	(to) me	nous	(to) us
te (t')	(to) you	vous	(to) you
lui	(to) him; (to) her	leur	(to) them

NOTE

Point out that the indirect object pronouns are *personal* pronouns. Remind students that they have already learned (Ch. 7) to substitute the pronoun **y** for **à** + an object, place, etc.

The indirect object pronouns **me, te, nous,** and **vous** are identical to the direct object pronouns. But unlike direct objects, **lui** is used for both *(to) him* and *(to) her,* and **leur** is used for *(to) them.*

Alain a-t-il téléphoné **à Pierre?**	Oui, il **lui** a téléphoné.
A-t-il téléphoné aussi **à Anne?**	Oui, il **lui** a téléphoné aussi.
A-t-il téléphoné **à Guy et à Ariel?**	Oui, il **leur** a téléphoné après.
Vous a-t-il parlé de tout ça?	Non, il ne **m'**a pas parlé de ça. Ariel **m'**a dit ça.

NOTE

Point out that in the passé composé there is no agreement with preceding *indirect* objects.

Often in English, the preposition *to* is omitted. Also, in some contexts indirect object pronouns may mean *for someone, from someone,* etc.

Est-ce que je **t'**ai donné de l'argent?	*Did I give **you** some money? (= to you)*
Mais non, tu **m'**as emprunté 5 dollars!	*No, you borrowed 5 dollars **from me!***
Alors, je **t'**achèterai quelque chose.	*Then I'll buy **you** something. (= for you)*

■ Like a direct object pronoun, an indirect object pronoun is almost always placed directly *before* the verb.

Remind students that an object pronoun normally precedes the infinitive if it is the second of two verbs.

Nous **lui** répondons tout de suite.	*We answer him (her) right away.*
Ils ne **nous** ont pas téléphoné.	*They didn't telephone us.*
Vous dit-elle la vérité?	*Is she telling you the truth?*
Elle va **leur** rendre visite.	*She is going to visit them.*
Ne **m'**écris pas.	*Don't write to me.*

NOTE

Review the use of pronouns with the imperative, Ch. 10, p. 283.

Also like direct object pronouns, indirect object pronouns follow the verb *only* in affirmative commands, and in that case **me** and **te** become **moi** and **toi.**

Écris-**lui** immédiatement!	*Write to him immediately!*
Donne-**moi** de l'eau, s'il te plaît.	*Give me some water, please.*

Synthèse: object pronouns

direct:	me	te	le/la	nous	vous	les
indirect:	me	te	lui	nous	vous	leur
reflexive:	me	te	se	nous	vous	se

4 **Le professeur et les étudiants.** Utilisez les expressions suivantes pour faire des phrases. Utilisez un pronom objet indirect dans chaque phrase et utilisez la forme négative si vous voulez.

Follow with a stand-up drill. Each student must give one example.

MODÈLES: **Le professeur leur parle toujours en français.**

Les étudiants ne lui rendent jamais visite.

*In this activity **lui** refers to **le professeur,** and **leur** refers to **les étudiants.***

		dire bonjour	
		parler en français	
		écrire des lettres	toujours
		téléphoner	d'habitude
le professeur	leur	rendre visite	souvent
les étudiants	lui	poser des questions	quelquefois
		demander un conseil	rarement
		raconter des histoires	jamais
		obéir	
		donner des tests faciles	
		envoyer des messages	

5 **Vrai ou faux?** Décidez si les phrases suivantes sont vraies ou fausses. Ensuite répondez chaque fois avec un pronom objet indirect. Si une phrase est fausse, corrigez-la.

MODÈLES: Le professeur dit toujours bonjour aux étudiants.
C'est vrai. Il leur dit toujours bonjour.

Le président vous a téléphoné.
C'est faux. Il ne m'a pas téléphoné.

1. Le professeur de français ne donne pas beaucoup de devoirs aux étudiants.
2. Le professeur vous pose beaucoup de questions.
3. Les étudiants répondent toujours correctement au professeur.
4. Vous écrivez quelquefois des lettres à vos amis.
5. Vos amis vous répondent chaque fois.
6. Vous téléphonez souvent à votre meilleur(e) ami(e).
7. Vous ne rendez jamais visite à vos cousins.
8. Vous montrez toujours vos notes à vos parents.
9. Vos parents vous prêtent souvent leur voiture.

6 **Faites-le donc!** *(Then do it!)* Encouragez la personne d'après les modèles. Utilisez des pronoms objets indirects.

MODÈLES: Je vais rendre visite à Jean.
Eh bien, rendez-lui donc visite!

Je voudrais poser une question au professeur.
Eh bien, posez-lui donc une question!

1. Je vais parler à Claire.
2. Je voudrais répondre au professeur.
3. Je vais rendre visite à mes grands-parents.
4. Je vais prêter ma voiture à mon amie.
5. J'ai envie de vous poser une question.
6. Je voudrais dire bonjour à Thierry.
7. J'ai envie de téléphoner à mes parents.

7 **Non, ne le faites pas!** Employez encore les phrases de l'activité 6 pour dire à la personne de *ne pas* faire ce qu'elle veut faire. Utilisez des pronoms objets indirects.

MODÈLES: Je vais rendre visite à Jean.
Mais non, ne lui rendez pas visite!

Je voudrais poser une question au professeur.
Mais non, ne lui posez pas de question!

8 **La voiture de Paul.** Remplacez chaque expression en italique par un des pronoms suivants:
le, la, les, lui ou **leur.**

MODÈLES: Les parents de Paul ont acheté une voiture *à leur fils.*
Les parents de Paul lui ont acheté une voiture.

Ils aiment beaucoup *leur fils.*
Ils l'aiment beaucoup.

1. Il a dit merci *à ses parents.*
2. Georges a demandé *à Paul* s'il pouvait conduire *la voiture.*
3. Paul a prêté sa voiture *à Georges.*
4. Georges rend visite *à sa petite amie.*
5. Elle aime beaucoup *la voiture.*
6. Elle demande *à Georges* si elle peut conduire *la voiture.*
7. Il prête la voiture *à sa petite amie.* Elle dit merci *à Georges.*
8. Il dit *à son amie* de prendre *le volant.*
9. Elle va rendre la voiture *à Georges* la semaine prochaine.

9 **Je vais le faire.** Répondez affirmativement à chaque ordre par l'expression **Je vais** + un infinitif. Remplacez les expressions en italique par un pronom objet direct ou indirect.

MODÈLES: Il faut que vous téléphoniez *à Léa!*
D'accord, je vais lui téléphoner.

Il faut que vous écriviez *votre nom.*
D'accord, je vais l'écrire.

1. Il faut que vous obéissiez *à vos parents!*
2. Il faut que vous prêtiez votre livre *à votre voisine!*
3. Il faut que vous regardiez *cette émission!*
4. Il faut que vous écriviez une lettre *à vos grands-parents!*
5. Il faut que vous disiez *la vérité!*
6. Il ne faut pas que vous demandiez *à Agnès* quel âge elle a!
7. Il ne faut pas que vous buviez *ce verre de vin!*
8. Il faut que vous posiez une question *au professeur!*
9. Il faut que vous *me* répondiez!

Remind students of the expression **Occupez-vous de vos oignons!**, p. 296, and allow them to use this answer if the questions are too personal.

10 **À vous.** Répondez.

1. Téléphonez-vous souvent à vos amis?
2. À qui avez-vous parlé récemment?
3. Qu'est-ce que vous lui avez dit?
4. Qu'est-ce que vous lui avez demandé?
5. Qu'est-ce qu'il ou elle vous a répondu?
6. Allez-vous rendre visite à des amis bientôt?
7. Si oui, quand est-ce que vous leur rendrez visite? Si non, comment les contacterez-vous?
8. Que prêtez-vous à vos amis?
9. Qu'est-ce que vous empruntez à vos parents?

ENTRE AMIS

Votre meilleur(e) ami(e)

Talk to your partner about his/her best friend. Use indirect object pronouns where appropriate.

1. Find out the name of your partner's best friend.
2. Ask if your partner wrote to him/her this week.
3. Ask if your partner visited him/her this week.
4. Ask if your partner called him/her this week.
5. If so, try to find out what your partner said to his/her friend.

2. Describing Television Programs

NOTE CULTURELLE
Si on ne considère que les chaînes nationales TF1, France 2, France 3, Arte/La Cinquième et M6, les Français regardent plus de 1.050 heures de programmes par an, dont 272 h. de fiction (feuilletons, etc.); 151 h. d'informations; 99 h. de publicité; 86 h. de jeux; 71 h. de sport; 31 h. d'émissions pour enfants (dessins animés).
D'après le Quid

Quelles émissions y a-t-il à la télévision?
Il y a ...

les informations, par exemple, *le Journal du soir.*
la météorologie, par exemple, *le Bulletin météo.*
les sports, par exemple, *le Tour de France.*
les films, par exemple, *Tous les matins du monde.*
les pièces, par exemple, *L'Avare* de Molière.
les feuilletons, par exemple, *Le Fond du problème.*
les dessins animés, par exemple, *Popeye.*
les jeux, par exemple, *la Roue de la fortune.*
la publicité, par exemple, les spots publicitaires pour Perrier, Coca-Cola.

▶ **Et vous?** Qu'est-ce que vous regardez à la télévision?

À vous. Répondez.

1. Combien de temps par jour passez-vous à regarder la télévision?
2. Que regardez-vous à la télévision?
3. Quelles sont les émissions que vous ne regardez presque *(almost)* jamais?
4. Quelle émission trouvez-vous la plus drôle?
5. Quelle émission trouvez-vous la plus ennuyeuse?
6. Regardez-vous quelquefois des feuilletons? Si oui, quel feuilleton préférez-vous?
7. Que pensez-vous de la publicité à la télévision?
8. Voudriez-vous qu'il y ait plus, autant ou moins de sports à la télévision? Pourquoi?

Students have already learned **je voudrais.**

⦿ **www Réalités culturelles**

A total of 907 French people, with an average age of 19, responded to this Internet survey. They were asked to check the programs that they prefer to watch on TV. Many chose more than one type of program.

Comparisons: Have students compare this list with (1) the list in the **Note culturelle** above and (2) their own preferences.

Qu'est-ce que les Français regardent à la télé?

En général, les Français regardent beaucoup la télévision. Dans cette enquête, 907 personnes ont choisi un ou plusieurs types d'émissions pour répondre à la question «La télé: Tu regardes surtout . . . ?»

1. des films (825)
2. des séries (718)
3. des clips (555)
4. les divertissements (351)
5. les informations (323)
6. les feuilletons (315)
7. les dessins animés (306)
8. les jeux télévisés (300)
9. les émissions de variétés (291)
10. le sport (256)
11. les documentaires (229)
12. la météo (227)
13. les émissions culturelles (185)
14. les émissions occasionnelles (36)
15. les pubs (23)
16. les émissions de télé achat (15)

D'après *membres.lycos.fr/maxisondages*

C. Les verbes *voir* et *croire*

Je **crois** qu'il va neiger. Qu'en pensez-vous?	*I think it's going to snow. What do you think?*
On **verra**.	*We'll see.*
Je **crois** que je **vois** nos amis.	*I think (that) I see our friends.*
Avez-vous déjà **vu** ce film?	*Did you already see this film?*
Je **crois** que oui.	*I believe so.*
Non, je ne **crois** pas.	*No, I don't believe so.*

Note the use of **que** in the expression **Je crois que oui.**

Comparison: Point out that **voir** means *to see* and **regarder** means *to look at.* You may also wish to point out that **croire** and **penser** often have the same meaning, but that there are differences, e.g., **je le crois** *(I believe him),* **je pense à lui** *(I think about him).*

■ The verbs **voir** and **croire** have similar present tense conjugations.

voir *(to see)*	
je	**vois**
tu	**vois**
il/elle/on	**voit**
nous	**voyons**
vous	**voyez**
ils/elles	**voient**
passé composé: j'**ai vu**	

croire *(to believe, think)*	
je	**crois**
tu	**crois**
il/elle/on	**croit**
nous	**croyons**
vous	**croyez**
ils/elles	**croient**
passé composé: j'**ai cru**	

■ The future tense verb stem for **voir** is irregular: **verr-.** The future of **croire** is regular.

Je vous **verrai** demain.	*I will see you tomorrow.*
Mes amis ne me **croiront** pas.	*My friends won't believe me.*

■ The subjunctive forms of **voir** and **croire** have two stems just like other verbs that have two present tense stems.

Il faut que je le **voie**.	Il faut que vous le **voyiez** aussi.
Je veux qu'il me **croie**.	Je veux que vous me **croyiez**.

12 **Que croient-ils?** Tout le monde a son opinion. Utilisez le verbe **croire** et identifiez ce qui, à votre avis, correspond à la description donnée.

Communication (Interpretive & Presentational): Follow up by having students tell you where they agreed or disagreed with their partner.

Modèle: mon père / la meilleure équipe de football
Mon père croit que les New York Giants sont la meilleure équipe de football.

1. je / l'émission la plus intéressante le jeudi soir
2. nous / le cours le plus ennuyeux
3. le professeur de français / les étudiants les plus travailleurs
4. mes parents / la chose la plus importante de ma vie
5. mes amis / le feuilleton le plus passionnant
6. je / le plus mauvais film de cette année

13 **Que croyez-vous?** Est-ce que la phrase est vraie pour la plupart des étudiants de votre cours de français? Si oui, répondez **Je crois que oui.** Si non, répondez **Je ne crois pas** et corrigez la phrase.

MODÈLE: La plupart des étudiants croient que le professeur de français est méchant. **Je ne crois pas. Ils croient que le professeur est très gentil.**

1. La plupart des étudiants voient leurs parents tous les jours.
2. La plupart des étudiants verront un film le week-end prochain.
3. La plupart des étudiants ont déjà vu un film français.
4. La plupart des étudiants veulent voir un pays où on parle français.
5. La plupart des étudiants verront la tour Eiffel un jour.
6. La plupart des étudiants croient que les femmes conduisent mieux que les hommes.
7. La plupart des étudiants croyaient au Père Noël quand ils étaient petits.
8. La plupart des étudiants croient actuellement au Père Noël.

14 **À vous.** Répondez.

1. Quel film avez-vous vu la dernière fois que vous êtes allé(e) au cinéma?
2. Qui voyez-vous tous les jours?
3. Qui avez-vous vu hier?
4. Quelle note croyez-vous que vous aurez en français?
5. Quand croyez-vous que vous irez en Europe?
6. Qu'est-ce que vous verrez si vous y allez?
7. Qui croit au Père Noël?

D. Les interrogatifs *quel* et *lequel*

Review **quel,** p. 114.

■ You have already learned to use the adjective **quel** *(which? what?)*. **Quel** always occurs with a noun and agrees with that noun.

Quel feuilleton avez-vous vu?

De **quelle** actrice parlez-vous?

Quels acteurs préférez-vous?

Quelles sont vos émissions préférées?

■ **Lequel** *(which one)* replaces **quel** and the noun it modifies. Both parts of **lequel** show agreement.

Vous avez vu le feuilleton?	**Lequel?** (Quel feuilleton?)
Que pensez-vous de cette actrice?	**Laquelle?** (Quelle actrice?)
Ces acteurs sont formidables.	**Lesquels?** (Quels acteurs?)
Ce sont vos émissions préférées?	**Lesquelles?** (Quelles émissions?)

	singulier	pluriel
masculin	**lequel**	**lesquels**
féminin	**laquelle**	**lesquelles**

■ Do not use the indefinite article (**un, une, des**) when **quel** is used in an exclamation.

Quelle histoire!   *What a story!*
Quel cours!   *What a course!*
Quels étudiants!   *What students!*

■ **Lequel** is often followed by the preposition **de** to name the group from which the choice is to be made.

Laquelle *de vos amies* s'appelle Mimi?   *Which of your friends is named Mimi?*

Lesquels *de vos professeurs* parlent français?   *Which of your teachers speak French?*

FOR RECOGNITION ONLY

When **lequel, lesquels,** and **lesquelles** are preceded by the prepositions **à** or **de,** the normal contractions are made. No contraction is made with **laquelle.**

à + lequel	→	**auquel**	de + lequel	→	**duquel**
à + lesquels	→	**auxquels**	de + lesquels	→	**desquels**
à + lesquelles	→	**auxquelles**	de + lesquelles	→	**desquelles**

Alexis parle d'un film, mais **duquel** parle-t-il?
Il parle aussi des émissions de télé, mais **desquelles?**
Auxquelles de ces émissions vous intéressez-vous?

15 **Dans une salle bruyante** *(In a noisy room)*. On fait du bruit et vous n'entendez pas bien les réponses de votre partenaire. Demandez-lui de répéter. Utilisez une forme de **quel** dans la première question et une forme de **lequel** dans la deuxième.

MODÈLE: ville
                    VOUS: **Quelle ville préfères-tu?**
        VOTRE PARTENAIRE: **Je préfère Québec.**
                    VOUS: **Laquelle?**
        VOTRE PARTENAIRE: **Québec.**

1. émission
2. ville
3. dessin animé
4. film
5. voiture
6. acteurs
7. actrices
8. chanson
9. feuilleton
10. cours
11. dessert
12. sports

16 **Microconversation: Non, je n'ai pas pu.** Interviewez votre partenaire d'après le modèle. Faites tous les changements nécessaires.

MODÈLE: regarder le feuilleton

> VOUS: **As-tu regardé le feuilleton hier?**
> VOTRE PARTENAIRE: **Lequel?**
> VOUS: **«Mes chers enfants».**
> VOTRE PARTENAIRE: **Non, je n'ai pas pu le regarder.**

1. voir le match (de basket-ball, de base-ball, etc.)
2. regarder les informations
3. voir la pièce
4. regarder l'émission
5. regarder les dessins animés
6. voir le film

17 **À vous.** Répondez.

1. Y a-t-il des mois de l'année plus agréables que les autres? Lesquels?
2. Quel est le mois le moins agréable, à votre avis?
3. Lequel des membres de votre famille est le plus jeune?
4. Laquelle des actrices célèbres trouvez-vous la plus belle?
5. Lequel des acteurs célèbres trouvez-vous le plus beau?
6. Lesquels de vos amis voyez-vous tous les jours?
7. Auxquels envoyez-vous des messages électroniques?

E. Les pronoms relatifs (suite)

Review relative pronouns on p. 260.

■ Relative pronouns like *who, whom,* and *which* relate or tie two clauses together. They refer to a word in the first clause.

(J'ai des amis. Ils habitent en France.)
J'ai des amis **qui** habitent en France. *I have friends who live in France.*
(J'ai des amis. Vous les connaissez bien.)
J'ai des amis **que** vous connaissez bien. *I have friends whom you know well.*

■ The choice of the relative pronoun **qui** or **que** depends on its function as subject or object.

• **Qui** *(who, that, which)* replaces a person or a thing that is the *subject* of a relative clause.

«La Roue de la fortune» est une émission **qui** est très populaire.

• **Que** *(whom, that, which)* replaces a person or a thing that is the *object* of a relative clause.

Le film **que** j'ai vu était très intéressant.

Review agreement on p. 279.

■ Past participles conjugated with **avoir** agree with a preceding direct object. Therefore, a past participle will agree with **que** in a relative clause.

la pièce que j'ai vu**e**	*the play I saw*
la robe qu'elle a mis**e**	*the dress she put on*
les fleurs que tu as achet**ées**	*the flowers you bought*

■ Although the relative pronoun may be omitted in English, it is never omitted in French.

C'est l'émission **que** je préfère.   *It's the program (that) I prefer.*

■ Preceded by a preposition, **qui** is normally used with persons and **lequel, laquelle,** etc., is used with things.

la personne **avec qui** j'ai dansé   *the person with whom I danced*
la question **à laquelle** j'ai déjà répondu   *the question I already answered*

■ **Dont** *(whose, of which, about which)* is normally used to replace a relative pronoun and the preposition **de** that precedes it.

l'émission **de laquelle** nous avons parlé   *the program we spoke about*
l'émission **dont** nous avons parlé

l'annonceur **de qui** je me souviens bien   *the announcer I remember well*
l'annonceur **dont** je me souviens bien

NOS PARTENAIRES
buzz™
AEROPORT DE BORDEAUX
Chambre de Commerce et d'Industrie de Bordeaux
La compagnie qui, sur Bordeaux-Londres, vous offre l'essentiel

18 **Identifiez-les.** Quelles sont les personnes ou les choses suivantes?

MODÈLE: une personne que vous avez vue à la télé
Jay Leno est une personne que j'ai vue à la télé.

1. une émission qui est très populaire à la télé
2. une émission que vous refusez de regarder à la télé
3. le dernier film que vous avez vu
4. une personne que vous connaissez qui n'aime pas regarder la télé
5. la publicité qui est la plus ennuyeuse de la télé
6. le dessin animé que vous trouvez le plus drôle
7. l'actrice ou l'acteur que vous préférez
8. une émission de télévision dont vous avez parlé avec vos amis
9. une personne avec qui vous êtes allé(e) au cinéma

ENTRE AMIS

À la télé

1. Find out if your partner likes soap operas.
2. If so, find out which one(s) and ask your partner to describe one of the soap operas.
3. If not, ask why not and inquire if there are other programs your partner watches on TV.
4. If so, choose one and ask your partner to describe what that program is about.

3. Expressing Emotion

Êtes-vous d'accord avec les sentiments exprimés dans les phrases suivantes? Qu'en pensez-vous?[1]

	oui	non
Je suis fâché(e) que les professeurs donnent tant de devoirs!	____	____
Je regrette que mes notes ne soient pas meilleures.	____	____
C'est dommage qu'il y ait tant d'émissions sportives à la télévision.	____	____
C'est ridicule qu'il y ait tant de publicité à la télévision.	____	____
Je suis désolé(e) que tant de gens n'aient pas assez à manger.	____	____
Le professeur est ravi que je fasse des progrès.	____	____

1. *What's your opinion (about them)?*

Review the forms and uses of the subjunctive in Ch. 13.

F. Le subjonctif (suite)

■ The subjunctive forms for **vouloir** and **pouvoir** are as follows:

vouloir

	(veuill-)				(nous	voulóns)
que je	veuill	e	que nous		voul	ions
que tu	veuill	es	que vous		voul	iez
qu'il/elle/on	veuill	e				
qu'ils/elles	veuill	ent				

pouvoir (puiss-)

que je	puiss	e	que nous	puiss	ions
que tu	puiss	es	que vous	puiss	iez
qu'il/elle/on	puiss	e	qu'ils/elles	puiss	ent

■ In addition to expressing necessity and will, the subjunctive is also used to express emotion.

Je suis content(e) que vous **soyez** ici. *I am happy (that) you are here.*
Je regrette que Luc ne **puisse** pas venir. *I am sorry Luc can't come.*

■ If there is no change of subjects, the preposition **de** plus the infinitive is used instead of the subjunctive.

Je suis content(e) **d'être** ici. *I am happy to be here.*
Luc regrette **de ne pas pouvoir** venir. *Luc is sorry he can't come.*

VOCABULAIRE

Pour exprimer un sentiment

Comparison: You may wish to point out that **chouette** is familiar speech. Also, the expressions with **C'est** reflect informal, spoken usage.

Je suis ravi(e) que	*I am delighted that*
C'est formidable que	*It's great that*
C'est chouette que	*It's great that*
Je suis content(e) que	*I am happy that*
Ce n'est pas possible que	*It's not possible that*
C'est incroyable que	*It's unbelievable that*
C'est dommage que	*It's too bad that*
C'est ridicule que	*It's ridiculous that*
Je suis triste que	*I am sad that*
Je regrette que	*I am sorry that*
Je suis désolé(e) que	*I am very sorry that*
Je suis fâché(e) que	*I am angry that*

19 **Des réactions différentes.** Décidez si votre professeur est content et si vous êtes content(e) aussi.

MODÈLE: J'ai beaucoup de devoirs.
Mon professeur est content que j'aie beaucoup de devoirs.
Mais moi, je ne suis pas content(e) d'avoir beaucoup de devoirs.

Communication (Presentational): Follow up with books closed by having students give 2 sentences each: **Je suis content(e) de ...** and **Mon professeur est content que ...**

1. Je vais souvent à la bibliothèque.
2. Je sais parler français.
3. Je lis *Entre amis* tous les soirs.
4. Je suis un(e) bon(ne) étudiant(e).
5. J'ai «A» à mon examen.
6. Je sors tous les soirs.
7. Je fais régulièrement des rédactions.
8. Je peux aller en France cet été.
9. Je veux étudier le français en France.

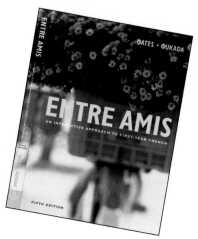

20 **Votre réaction, s'il vous plaît.** Choisissez une expression pour réagir *(react)* aux phrases suivantes.

MODÈLE: Véronique va en Floride. Mais il pleut.
C'est formidable qu'elle aille en Floride. Mais c'est dommage qu'il pleuve.

1. Les vacances commencent bientôt. Mais les examens vont avoir lieu avant les vacances.
2. Tous les professeurs sont généreux et charmants. Mais ils donnent beaucoup de devoirs.
3. Les étudiants de cette classe font toujours leurs devoirs. Mais ils sont fatigués.

21 **Test psychologique.** Expliquez les causes de vos réactions. Faites deux ou trois phrases chaque fois.

MODÈLE: Je suis triste ...

Je suis triste que mon petit ami (ma petite amie) ne m'aime plus.
Je suis triste que tout le monde me déteste.
Je suis triste de ne pas avoir de bons amis.

Communication (Presentational): Follow up, books closed, by asking students to share sentences they created.

1. C'est ridicule ...   3. Je suis ravi(e) ...   5. C'est chouette ...
2. Nous regrettons ...   4. C'est dommage ...

Communication (Interpretive): Follow up, books closed, with a chain drill in which students have to listen and then react to others.

22 **En groupes (*3 ou 4 étudiants*).**   Une personne dira une phrase au présent ou au futur (par exemple: **J'ai chaud** ou **Je sortirai ce soir**). Une autre personne réagira (par exemple: **C'est dommage que tu aies chaud** ou **Je suis content(e) que tu sortes ce soir**). Combien de phrases pouvez-vous former?

G. Le pronom *en*

On vend des journaux ici?	*Do you sell newspapers here?*
Non, on n'**en** vend pas. Vous **en** trouverez à la gare.	*No, we don't sell any. You will find some at the station.*
Vous avez du brocoli?	*Do you have any broccoli?*
Oui, j'**en** ai.	*Yes, I have some.*
Il y a beaucoup de fruits cette année?	*Is there a lot of fruit this year?*
Oui, il y **en** a beaucoup.	*Yes, there is a lot (of it).*
Vous avez des oranges?	*Do you have any oranges?*
Oui. Combien **en** voulez-vous?	*Yes. How many (of them) do you want?*
J'**en** voudrais six.	*I would like six (of them).*

■ The pronoun **en** takes the place of a noun that is preceded by some form of **de** (e.g., **de, du, de la, de l', des**) or by a number (e.g., **un, une, deux, trois**), or by an expression of quantity (e.g., **beaucoup de, trop de**).

Vous avez **du** camembert?	Oui, j'**en** ai.
Noël a **une** voiture?	Oui, il **en** a une.
Nous avons **assez de** livres?	Oui, nous **en** avons assez.

■ When a noun is preceded by a number or a quantity word, the number or quantity word must be included in a sentence with **en**.

Vous avez **une** maison?	*Do you have a house?*
Oui, j'**en** ai **une**.	*Yes, I have one.*

Vous avez **deux** valises?	*Do you have two suitcases?*
Non, je n'**en** ai pas **deux**.	*No, I don't have two (of them).*
Je n'**en** ai qu'**une**.	*I have only one.*
Mon père **en** a **beaucoup**.	*My father has a lot (of them).*

NOTE — To say *I don't have any*, use **Je n'en ai pas.**

■ **En** is also used to replace **de** plus an infinitive or **de** plus a noun with expressions of emotion.

Hervé est triste **de partir?**	Oui, il **en** est triste.
Es-tu contente **de tes notes?**	Oui, j'**en** suis ravie.

23 **Sondage** *(Poll).* Utilisez les expressions suivantes pour interviewer votre partenaire. Il (elle) va utiliser **en** dans chaque réponse.

MODÈLE: voitures

VOUS: **Combien de voitures as-tu?**
VOTRE PARTENAIRE: **J'en ai une.** ou **Je n'en ai pas.**

1. frères
2. sœurs
3. enfants
4. camarades de chambre
5. professeurs
6. voitures
7. cours
8. cartes de crédit

24 **Quelles réactions!** Composez deux phrases affirmatives ou négatives. La première peut être au présent, à l'imparfait ou au passé composé. Utilisez **en** dans la deuxième.

MODÈLE: **Mes amis n'ont pas gagné à la loterie.**
Ils en sont désolés.

	être fiancé(e)(s)	
	se marier	ravi
je	attendre un bébé	content
mes amis	réussir à un examen	triste
un(e) de mes ami(e)s	avoir une mauvaise note	désolé
	divorcer	fâché
	gagner à la loterie	confus
	arriver en retard	

> Remember that **confus** is a false cognate, p. 381.

25 **À vous.** Répondez. Utilisez **en** dans chaque réponse.

1. Combien de tasses de café buvez-vous par jour?
2. Buvez-vous du thé?
3. Voulez-vous du chewing-gum?
4. Êtes-vous content(e) de vos notes?
5. Combien de personnes y a-t-il dans votre famille?
6. Combien de maillots de bain avez-vous?
7. Quelle est votre réaction quand vous avez «A» à l'examen?

ENTRE AMIS

Les examens finals

Use **en** whenever possible.

1. Find out how many courses your partner has this semester.
2. Ask if s/he is pleased (happy) with his/her courses.
3. Ask if s/he is pleased (happy) with his/her grades.
4. Find out how many final exams s/he will have.
5. Ask if s/he is afraid of them.

Intégration www ◎

Révision

Communication (Presentational): Review pp. 379 & 385. Have students describe famous couples.

A **Décrivez-les.** Inventez une description pour les couples suivants:

1. un couple qui va se marier.
2. un couple qui divorce.
3. un couple qui habite chez les parents du mari.

B **Un feuilleton.** Choisissez un feuilleton que vous connaissez. Décrivez-le à votre partenaire.

C **Mes réactions.** Quelles sont vos réactions aux circonstances suivantes?

MODÈLE: Le professeur vous annonce qu'il n'y aura pas de cours demain.
J'en suis ravi(e)! Je lui dis «Merci beaucoup!». C'est chouette qu'il n'y ait pas de cours.

1. Le professeur vous dit qu'il y aura un examen demain.
2. On vous téléphone pour vous annoncer que vous venez de gagner à la loterie.
3. Vous vous êtes disputé(e) avec votre ami(e) et il (elle) vous envoie un message électronique pour vous demander pardon.
4. Vos parents veulent vous parler de vos études et de ce que vous allez faire dans la vie.
5. Une amie vous annonce que son petit ami ne veut plus la voir.
6. Vous dormez et le téléphone sonne à trois heures du matin. Vous y répondez et une personne que vous ne connaissez pas vous demande si vous voulez acheter une encyclopédie.

Communication (Presentational & Interpretive): If students present their lists to the class, others can be asked to recall information presented. Suggestion: Assign the **Rédaction** at the end of Ch. 14 in the Workbook.

D **Début de rédaction.** Faites d'abord une liste de cinq émissions de télé de votre pays. Essayez de varier votre liste et de ne pas choisir le même type d'émission pour toutes les cinq. Ensuite, pour chaque émission que vous avez choisie, donnez une petite description en français.

Communication (Interpretive): Encourage students to use the practice test on the Lab Audio Program.

E **À vous.** Utilisez un pronom objet indirect dans chaque réponse.

MODÈLE: Qu'est-ce que vos amis vous envoient pour votre anniversaire?
Ils m'envoient une carte (des fleurs, un cadeau, des bonbons, etc.).
ou
Ils ne m'envoient rien.

1. Qu'est-ce que vous envoyez à vos amis pour leur anniversaire?
2. Qu'est-ce que vous dites à votre professeur de français quand vous arrivez au cours?
3. Qu'est-ce que votre professeur vous répond?
4. Posez-vous beaucoup de questions au professeur de français?
5. Est-ce que vous téléphonez quelquefois à vos amis?
6. Est-ce que vos amis vous écrivent souvent?

Négociations:

Qu'est-ce qu'il (elle) en pense? Interviewez votre partenaire pour trouver les renseignements qui manquent. La copie de votre partenaire est dans l'appendice D.

For complete instructions on how to prepare for and to use this activity, see *Négociations* on the Class Prep CD-ROM.

MODÈLE: **Quelle est la réaction de Catherine?**
Pourquoi est-elle triste?

A

	Ce qui arrive	Sa réaction
Catherine	Son mari ne lui envoie pas de fleurs.	
Éric		Il en est content.
Alain		Il croit que c'est ridicule.
Chantal	Ses professeurs ne sont pas compréhensifs.	
Monique		Elle en est contente.
Jacques	Ses meilleurs amis divorcent.	
Christophe	Ses notes ne sont pas très bonnes.	
Nathalie		Elle en est désolée.
Véronique		Elle en est ravie.
Pierre	Sa petite amie et lui ne s'entendent pas très bien.	

Lecture I

Connections: Ask students to try to identify **Le maillon faible** (*The Weakest Link*), **Qui veut gagner des millions?,** and **Urgences.** Inform them that **ovni** means **objet volant non identifié** and ask them their opinion about flying saucers. Point out that three episodes of **Urgences** (*ER*) are shown back-to-back, which is typical in France.

A **Parcourez les listes d'émissions.** Lisez rapidement les listes d'émissions pour identifier (1) le jour de la semaine et (2) les différents sports qui sont mentionnés.

B **À vous de juger.** Relisez la lecture qui suit. Lesquelles des émissions intéresseront probablement une personne qui ...

1. pratique sa religion?
2. aime le sport?
3. aime l'émission américaine *ER*?
4. veut gagner de l'argent?
5. veut savoir le temps qu'il fera demain?
6. veut savoir ce qui se passe dans le monde?
7. aime les films?

À la télévision

Les deux colonnes suivantes sont tirées du site web de Yahoo! France.

TF1	
08h10	Disney! (dessin animé)
09h57	Météo
10h00	Motocross: Championnat du Monde 250cc
11h00	Téléfoot: Championnat de France
12h15	Le juste prix (jeu)
12h50	À vrai dire: Aménager la cuisine
12h55	Météo
13h00	Le journal
13h15	Au nom du sport
13h55	Formule 1: Grand Prix d'Italie
15h40	Dingue de toi (série, comédie)
17h00	Dawson: La nouvelle Ève (série, comédie)
17h55	Le maillon faible
18h55	Qui veut gagner des millions?
19h55	Être heureux comme (magazine, culturel)
20h00	Le journal
20h35	Au nom du sport (magazine, sportif)
20h40	Le résultat des courses (magazine, sportif)
20h45	Le temps d'un tournage (magazine, cinéma)
20h50	Météo
20h55	Boomerang (film, comédie)
23h00	Les films dans les salles (magazine, cinéma)
23h05	Rob Roy (film historique)

France 2	
08h30	Les voix bouddhistes
08h45	Connaître l'Islam
09h15	À bible ouverte
09h30	Orthodoxie
10h00	Présence protestante
10h30	Le jour du Seigneur
11h00	Messe célébrée en la cathédrale St.-Michel
12h00	Chanter la vie
13h00	Le journal de treize heures
13h25	Météo 2
13h30	Rapport du Loto
13h35	Ni vue ni connue
15h35	Ovnis, le secret américain
16h35	Boston public
17h20	Un gars, une fille
18h15	Stade 2
19h25	Championnat du monde
20h00	Le journal de vingt heures
20h45	Météo 2
20h55	Urgences
21h45	Urgences
22h35	Urgences
23h20	New York 911

C **Inférence.** Relisez la lecture et cherchez des exemples qui aident à identifier une des chaînes comme privée et l'autre comme publique.

Lecture II

A **Étude du vocabulaire.** Étudiez les phrases suivantes et choisissez les mots qui correspondent aux mots français en caractères gras: *operation, healer, very attractive, wage a fierce struggle, lover, producer, although.*

1. Cet homme est gentil **quoiqu'**un peu bizarre.
2. Le **réalisateur** dirige toutes les opérations de préparation et de réalisation d'un film.
3. On a dû transporter le malade à l'hôpital et on lui a fait subir une **intervention chirurgicale.**
4. Un **amant** est un homme qui a des relations sexuelles avec une femme à laquelle il n'est pas marié.
5. Une **guérisseuse** fait profession de guérir sans avoir les qualités officielles d'un médecin.
6. L'armée va **mener une lutte acharnée** contre l'ennemi.
7. La jeune femme était **séduisante,** pleine de charme.

Video for Chapter 14: A. Video worksheets *(Cahier);* B. ACE Video practice test (WWW); C. CD-ROM

B **Avant de lire.** Répondez d'après les films que vous avez vus.

1. À votre avis, quel est le meilleur film de cette année?
2. Quel film trouvez-vous le plus bizarre?
3. Quel film trouvez-vous le plus comique?
4. Quel est le film le plus violent?
5. Combien de fois êtes-vous allé(e) au cinéma le mois dernier?
6. Quel est le dernier film que vous avez vu?

C **Parcourez la liste des films.** Lisez rapidement pour identifier les films et les acteurs que vous connaissez.

Comparison: Remind students that **sensible** and **hasard** in *La Petite Lili* are false cognates (p. 381).

AU CINÉMA

«PÈRE ET FILS»: Léo, un vieux père de famille, ancien représentant de commerce, est prêt à tout pour retrouver l'affection de ses trois fils, David, Max et Simon. Il va même jusqu'à invoquer une maladie et une intervention chirurgicale pour les convaincre de l'accompagner dans un voyage au Canada, où il a l'intention de refaire l'unité du clan familial. Les quatre Français y feront la rencontre d'une guérisseuse et de sa fille. Avec Philippe Noiret, Charles Berling, Marie Tifo.

«TERMINATOR 3: LE SOULÈVEMENT DES MACHINES»: Dix ans ont passé depuis «Le Jugement dernier». Maintenant âgé de 22 ans, John Connor vit sans domicile, sans travail et sans identité. Mais les machines de Skynet parviennent à retrouver sa trace. Elles envoient alors vers le passé la T-X, une androïde nouvelle génération quasi-invulnérable, capable de disparaître, de se métamorphoser ou de devenir de la pure énergie, pour éliminer le futur leader de la résistance humaine mais également Kate Brewster, une jeune vétérinaire. Un autre Terminator, le T-101, est venu protéger la vie de John Connor. Ensemble, l'homme et la machine vont mener une lutte acharnée contre la T-X: de l'issue de ce combat dépendra le futur de l'humanité ... Avec Arnold Schwarzenegger, Kristanna Loken.

«LA PETITE LILI»: Mado, une actrice célèbre, passe ses vacances d'été dans sa propriété en Bretagne, en compagnie de son frère Simon, de son fils Julien qui veut devenir cinéaste et de Brice, son amant du moment, réalisateur de ses derniers films. Les relations de Julien avec sa mère sont très tumultueuses. Ce dernier est amoureux de Lili, une jeune fille de la région qui ambitionne d'être actrice. Celle-ci considère Julien avec tendresse mais elle est fascinée par Brice, qui semble sensible à sa grâce. Un jour, Lili lui propose de tout quitter pour l'emmener à Paris. Cinq ans plus tard, Lili est une actrice célèbre. Elle n'est plus avec Brice. Elle apprend par hasard que Julien va tourner son premier long métrage et qu'il parle d'elle ... Avec Ludivine Sagnier, Nicole Garcia.

«LA COUPE D'OR»: L'intrigue: au début du vingtième siècle, un beau prince italien follement amoureux d'une séduisante Américaine se voit dans l'obligation d'épouser la fille d'un richissime collectionneur new-yorkais. Mais la maîtresse, pugnace, parvient, pour ne pas s'éloigner de son amant, à se faire épouser du père de la mariée, compatriote fortuné et ... veuf bien conservé! Le jeu est dangereux et les quatre protagonistes ont beaucoup à perdre. Un drame britannique de James Ivory avec Kate Beckinsale, James Fox, Anjelica Huston et Nick Nolte.

«APPARENCES»: C'est une belle maison, près d'un lac du Vermont, quoiqu'un peu isolée. C'est un beau couple: lui, brillant et séduisant, mais un peu obsédé par le travail; elle, une belle femme qui-a-tout-pour-être-heureuse. Une porte qui s'ouvre seule, un visage apparu dans l'eau du bain et quelques murmures dans une pièce doivent-ils suffire à vous faire croire que votre nouvelle voisine est morte assassinée? Oui, dans ce film à suspense où le spectateur nage en plein mystère et en fausses déductions ... Un film de Robert Zemeckis avec Harrison Ford, Michelle Pfeiffer, Miranda Otto et James Remar.

«ENDURANCE»: C'est l'histoire incroyable mais authentique d'Haile Gebreselassie, ce jeune Éthiopien, pratiquement inconnu du grand public jusqu'aux Jeux Olympiques d'Atlanta, où il a remporté la course du 10.000 mètres, pulvérisant le précédent record. Derrière cet hommage au champion, interprété par lui-même, il y a un portrait de la vie en Afrique de l'Est. Une comédie dramatique de Leslie Woodhead avec Yonas Zergaw, Shawanness Gebreselassie et Tedesse Haile.

Connections & Communication (Presentational): Whenever possible, have students give reasons to justify their answers.

 Questions. Relisez la lecture et ensuite répondez aux questions suivantes.

1. Dans quel film est-ce que le personnage principal est un champion sportif?
2. Dans lequel est-ce que le personnage principal veut que ses enfants l'aiment?
3. Dans lequel est-ce que le héros est recherché par des machines?
4. Lesquels des films peuvent vous faire peur? Justifiez votre réponse.
5. Lequel a l'air le plus intéressant? Justifiez votre réponse.
6. Lequel a l'air le plus violent? Justifiez votre réponse.

VOCABULAIRE ACTIF

Practice this vocabulary with the flashcards on the *Entre amis* web site.

À propos de la télévision
une annonce *advertisement*
une chaîne (de télé) *(TV) channel*
un feuilleton *soap opera; series*
les informations (f. pl.) *news*
la météo(rologie) *weather forecast*
la publicité *publicity; commercial*

D'autres noms
un avertissement *warning*
un revenant *ghost*
la vérité *truth*

Adjectifs
célèbre *famous*
chouette *great (fam.)*
confus(e) *ashamed; embarrassed*
drôle *funny*
fâché(e) *angry*
formidable *terrific*
incroyable *unbelievable, incredible*
malheureux (malheureuse) *unhappy*
original(e) *different, novel; original*
passionnant(e) *exciting*
ravi(e) *delighted*
ridicule *ridiculous*

Relations personnelles
s'aimer *to love each other*
une bague (de fiançailles) *(engagement) ring*

un couple *couple*
se disputer *to argue*
un divorce *divorce*
divorcer *to get a divorce*
s'embrasser *to kiss*
s'entendre (avec) *to get along (with)*
se fâcher *to get angry*
se faire des amis *to make friends*
se marier (avec) *to marry*
rencontrer *to meet*
se séparer *to separate (from each other)*

D'autres verbes
assister (à) *to attend*
se consoler *to console oneself*
croire *to believe, think*
dire *to say; to tell*
emprunter *to borrow*
s'intéresser à *to be interested in*
montrer *to show*
prêter *to lend*
raconter (une histoire) *to tell (a story)*
regretter *to be sorry*
voir *to see*

Adverbes
actuellement *now*
même *even*
presque *almost*

Pronoms objets indirects
me *(to) me*
te *(to) you*
lui *(to) him; (to) her*
nous *(to) us*
vous *(to) you*
leur *(to) them*

D'autres pronoms
en *some; of it (them); about it (them)*
dont *whose, of which*
lequel/laquelle/lesquels/lesquelles *which*

Expressions utiles
C'est dommage. *That's (It's) too bad.*
Je crois que oui. *I think so.*
Je ne crois pas. *I don't think so.*
Je te le jure. *I swear (to you).*
Quelle histoire! *What a story!*
Qu'est-ce qui est arrivé? *What happened?*
Sans blague! *No kidding!*

Qu'est-ce que je devrais faire?

Buts communicatifs
Seeking and providing information
Making basic hypotheses

Structures utiles
L'imparfait, le passé composé (suite) et le plus-que-parfait
Le verbe **devoir** (suite)
Les pronoms interrogatifs
Ne ... personne et **ne ... rien**
Le conditionnel
Si hypothétique

Culture
• *À propos*
Les agents et les gendarmes
Les contraventions

• *Il y a un geste*
J'ai eu très peur
Quel imbécile!
Ivre

• *Lectures*
Deux accidents
«Le jardin»

Coup d'envoi

Prise de contact

Use the video, *Module 8,* **La voiture,** to help set the scene.

Qu'est-ce qui est arrivé?

Qu'est-ce qui est arrivé, Emmanuelle?

J'ai eu un accident.

L'autre conducteur (conductrice)° n'a pas vu ma voiture. *driver*

Il (elle) a freiné° trop tard. *braked*

Sa voiture a dérapé°. *skidded*

Il (elle) a heurté° ma voiture. *struck; hit*

Pourquoi l'accident a-t-il eu lieu?

Le conducteur (la conductrice) ne faisait pas attention.

Il (elle) croyait que personne° ne venait. *nobody*

Il (elle) ne regardait pas à droite.

Il (elle) roulait° trop vite. *was going*

Il (elle) avait trop bu°. *had had too much to drink*

Il (elle) était ivre°. *drunk*

▶ **Et vous?** Avez-vous déjà eu un accident?

Avez-vous déjà vu un accident?

Si oui, qu'est-ce qui est arrivé?

Connections: Ask students to read this information; it will help familiarize them with lexical and cultural content.

VOTRE SÉCURITÉ

Sur route, sur mer, en montagne, la majorité des accidents sont dus à des imprudences caractérisées.

Alors soyez attentifs aux conseils que vous rappelleront la Sécurité Routière et la Gendarmerie Nationale.

Sur route

Méfiez-vous de la conduite en plein soleil après un repas, des routes de nuit après une journée d'activité. Bouclez votre ceinture, respectez les limitations de vitesse :

– pas plus de 60 km/h en agglomération,

– pas plus de 90 km/h sur route,

– pas plus de 130 km/h sur autoroute.

Minitel : 36 15 ROUTE.

Conversation

Un accident a eu lieu

James Davidson vient d'avoir un accident de voiture. Il en parle avec son voisin Maurice.

MAURICE: Mais qu'est-ce que tu as? Tu es tout pâle!

JAMES: C'est que j'ai eu très peur ce matin.

MAURICE: Qu'est-ce qui est arrivé?

JAMES: J'ai eu un accident de voiture.

MAURICE: Mon Dieu!

JAMES: J'allais au travail quand l'accident a eu lieu. L'autre ne faisait pas attention. Ce chauffard° *bad driver* avait brûlé un stop° parce qu'il allait trop vite. *had run through a stop sign*

MAURICE: Quel imbécile!

JAMES: Oui, et nous sommes entrés en collision.

MAURICE: Quel idiot! Et personne n'a vu l'accident?

JAMES: Si! Heureusement il y avait deux témoins° *witnesses* et puis un gendarme qui était juste derrière moi.

MAURICE: Quelle chance! Qu'est-ce que le gendarme a fait?

JAMES: Il m'a assuré° qu'il avait tout vu° et que *assured / had seen everything* c'était la faute° de l'autre. *fault*

MAURICE: J'espère que le gendarme lui a donné une bonne contravention°! *ticket*

Comparison: Explain that the pejorative term **chauffard** comes from **chauffeur**.

Use the video, *Module 11,* to show an example of someone who has received a **contravention.**

After practicing the *Conversation,* have students complete ex. A in the Workbook.

▶ **Jouez ces rôles.** Répétez la conversation avec votre partenaire. Ensuite Maurice parle avec deux personnes (James et Karine étaient dans la voiture). Faites tous les changements nécessaires, par exemple **nous** à la place de **je.**

Il y a un geste

J'ai eu très peur. To indicate fear, the open hand is held fingers facing up; the hand is lowered with the fingers "trembling."

Quel imbécile! To indicate that someone has done something stupid, touch your index finger to your temple. The finger is either tapped on the temple or twisted back and forth.

Ivre. To indicate that someone has had too much to drink, one hand is cupped in a fist, and placed loosely on the nose and rotated.

À propos

Essayez de classer les infractions *(violations)* **suivantes d'après leur fréquence.**

a. Ne pas s'arrêter à un feu rouge ou à un stop.
b. Dépasser le degré légal d'alcool dans le sang *(blood)*.
c. Dépasser la limite de vitesse.
d. Ne pas porter de ceinture de sécurité.

Les agents et les gendarmes

The **agent de police** is often found directing traffic at major intersections in French cities. Since the **agents** are normally on foot, they are often stopped by tourists in need of information. The **gendarme**, often found in the countryside and in small towns, is actually part of the French military and is stationed in separate quarters in the **gendarmerie**. **Gendarmes** are similar to state police in that they are usually on motorcycles or in patrol cars. They would therefore normally be the ones to investigate an accident.

Les contraventions

There are approximately 15 million traffic tickets given in France per year. Of these, 9 million are for illegal parking and 1 million for exceeding the speed limit. The record for a speeding ticket is 243 KPH (over 150 MPH) for which the speeder received a year in prison and a 100,000 franc fine. In addition, approximately 660,000 tickets for not wearing a seat belt and 100,000 for drunken driving are given in an average year. Besides the parking tickets, the following were the most frequent traffic violations in France in a recent year: (1) speeding (43%), (2) not wearing a seat belt while riding in a car or a helmet when on a motorcycle (24%), (3) failure to give right of way or to stop at a light or a stop sign (13%), (4) failure to pass the alcohol test (7%). Eighty-one percent of those committing a traffic violation were men.

Reread **Votre Sécurité** on p. 408 to determine the speed limits in France.

▶ **À vous.** Répondez.

1. Quand avez-vous eu peur?
2. Pour quelle raison avez-vous eu peur?
3. Qu'est-ce que vous avez fait?

ENTRE AMIS

C'était la faute du professeur.

 1. Tell your partner that you had an accident.
 2. Explain that you hit the teacher's car.
 3. Say that it was the teacher's fault.
 4. Explain that s/he was going too slowly.

Prononciation

La voyelle [ə]

■ As you have already learned, the letter **-e-** can stand for any one of the sounds [e], [ɛ], [ɑ̃], and [ɛ̃], depending on the spelling combinations of which it is a part. You have also seen, however, that the letter **-e-** sometimes represents the sound [ə]. The symbol [ə] stands for a vowel called "unstable **e**" or "mute **e**." It is called unstable because it is sometimes pronounced and sometimes not.

▶ Look at the following pairs of examples and then read them aloud. A highlighted **-e-** represents a pronounced [ə]. An **-e-** with a slash through it represents a silent [ə]. Compare especially changes you find in the same word from one sentence of the pair to the other.

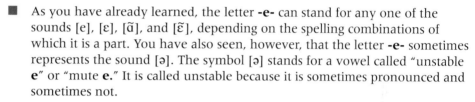

L**e** voilà!	Mais l¢ voilà!
C**e** film est très bon.	Moi, j¢ n'aim¢ pas c¢ film.
D**e**main, vous l¢ trouv¢rez.	Vous l¢ trouv¢rez d**e**main.
Denis¢ est américain¢?	Ell¢ est français¢.
R**e**gardez cett¢ femm¢.	Vous r¢gardez cett¢ femm¢?

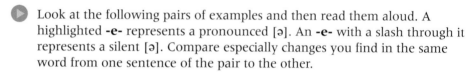

Nous pr**e**nons l¢ train vendr**e**di.	Nous arriv¢rons sam**e**di.
Votr**e** pèr¢ est charmant.	Votr¢ ami¢ est charmant¢.
Voilà un¢ tass¢ d**e** café.	Nous n¢ voulons pas d¢ café.
C'est un¢ bagu¢ d**e** fiançaill¢s.	Mais il n'y aura pas d¢ mariag¢.
Qu'est-c¢ qu**e** tu veux?	Elle a dit qu¢ tu voulais m¢ voir.

d**e** rien	Il finit d¢ rir¢.
vous s**e**riez	vous s¢rez

You may wish to explain the change from **votre** to **vot'** before a consonant in familiar French.

Comparison: Have students identify examples of each circumstance in the sentences above.

■ In general, [ə] is *silent* in the following circumstances.

 1. at the end of a sentence

 2. before or after a pronounced vowel

 3. when it is preceded by only one pronounced consonant sound

■ In general, [ə] is *pronounced* in the following circumstances.

1. when it is in the first syllable of a sentence
2. when it is preceded by two pronounced consonant sounds (even if there is an intervening silent [ə]) and followed by at least one pronounced consonant
3. when it precedes the combination [Rj]

You may wish to point out that
ex- + vowel = [ɛgz-] and
ex- + consonant = [ɛks-].

> **NOTE**
>
> When the letter **-e-** is followed *in the same word* by two consonants or by **-x,** it is normally pronounced [ɛ].
>
> **e**lle   av**e**rtissement   c**e**tte   pr**e**nnent   v**e**rser   m**e**rci
> **e**xiger   **e**xcusez-moi   **e**xact   **e**xamen

▶ **Listen and repeat:**

Remind students that the first syllable of **faisait** has an unstable **e:** [fəzɛ]. See p. 299.

1. L'autre conducteur ne faisait pas attention.
2. Qu'est-ce que votre frère a fait?
3. Est-ce que tu regardes des feuilletons le vendredi ou le samedi?
4. De quelle ville venez-vous?
5. Vous venez de Paris, n'est-ce pas?

Buts communicatifs

1. Seeking and Providing Information

Avez-vous entendu parler d'un accident?
Avez-vous vu un accident?

Est-ce que quelqu'un a été blessé°?	*wounded*
Est-ce que quelqu'un a été tué°?	*killed*
Est-ce qu'il y a eu beaucoup de morts°?	*deaths*
Où est-ce que l'accident a eu lieu?	
Quelle heure était-il?	
De quelle couleur étaient les voitures?	
De quelle marque° étaient les voitures?	*make; brand*

De quelle année étaient les voitures?
Est-ce qu'il avait plu?°   *Had it rained?*
La chaussée° devait être glissante°,   *pavement / slippery*
     n'est-ce pas?
Y avait-il d'autres témoins?

A. L'imparfait, le passé composé (*suite*) et le plus-que-parfait

Review the comparison of the passé composé and imperfect, Ch. 11, p. 303.

■ It is perhaps helpful, when trying to remember whether to use the imperfect or the passé composé, to think of the analogy with a stage play.

• In a play, there is often scenery (trees, birds singing, the sun shining, etc.) and background action (minor characters strolling by, people playing, working, etc.). This scenery and background action are represented by the imperfect.

Il **était** tôt.	*It was early.*
Il **faisait** froid.	*It was cold out.*
James **allait** au travail.	*James was going to work.*
Un autre conducteur ne **faisait** pas attention.	*Another driver wasn't paying attention.*

• Likewise, in a play, there are main actors upon whom the audience focuses, if even for a moment. They speak, move, become aware, act, and react. The narration of these past events requires the passé composé.

Qu'est-ce qui lui **est arrivé?**	*What happened to him?*
Il **a eu** un accident.	*He had an accident.*
Ils **sont entrés** en collision.	*They collided.*
Un gendarme lui **a donné** une contravention.	*A policeman gave him a ticket.*

■ The pluperfect (**le plus-que-parfait**) is used to describe a past event that took place prior to some other past event. This tense normally corresponds to the English *had* plus a past participle.

Il **avait plu** (avant l'accident).	*It had rained (before the accident).*
La dame **était arrivée** (avant moi).	*The lady had arrived (before me).*

■ To form the **plus-que-parfait,** use the **imparfait** of **avoir** or **être** and the past participle.

étudier	arriver	se lever
j'avais étudié	j'étais arrivé(e)	je m'étais levé(e)
tu avais étudié	tu étais arrivé(e)	tu t'étais levé(e)
il/on avait étudié	il/on était arrivé	il/on s'était levé
elle avait étudié	elle était arrivée	elle s'était levée
nous avions étudié	nous étions arrivé(e)s	nous nous étions levé(e)s
vous aviez étudié	vous étiez arrivé(e)(s)	vous vous étiez levé(e)(s)
ils avaient étudié	ils étaient arrivés	ils s'étaient levés
elles avaient étudié	elles étaient arrivées	elles s'étaient levées

Que faisaient les acteurs dans la pièce?

1 **Voilà pourquoi.** Répondez aux questions suivantes. Essayez de trouver des raisons logiques.

MODÈLE: Pourquoi Laurent a-t-il téléphoné à Mireille?
Il lui a téléphoné parce qu'il voulait sortir avec elle.   ou
Il lui a téléphoné parce qu'il la trouvait gentille.

1. Pourquoi Laurent et Mireille sont-ils sortis samedi soir?
2. Pourquoi ont-ils mis leur manteau?
3. Pourquoi sont-ils allés au restaurant?
4. Pourquoi n'ont-ils pas pris de dessert?
5. Pourquoi ont-ils fait une promenade après?

2 **Pourquoi pas, Amélie?** Utilisez la forme négative. Expliquez pourquoi Amélie n'a pas fait les choses suivantes.

MODÈLE: prendre le petit déjeuner
Amélie n'a pas pris le petit déjeuner parce qu'elle n'avait pas faim.   ou
Amélie n'a pas pris le petit déjeuner parce qu'elle a oublié.

Brainstorm with the class to find as many reasons as possible for each thing Amélie did not do.

1. aller au cinéma
2. étudier dans sa chambre
3. regarder son émission préférée
4. danser avec Gérard
5. nager
6. avoir un accident
7. boire du vin

3 **Quel chauffard!** Utilisez le plus-que-parfait pour indiquer ce que le mauvais chauffeur avait fait avant l'accident.

MODÈLE: ne pas être prudent
Il n'avait pas été prudent.

1. aller au bistro
2. boire de la bière
3. ne pas attacher sa ceinture
4. oublier de faire attention
5. brûler un stop
6. se regarder dans le rétroviseur

www**Réalités culturelles**

La Croix-Rouge

Créé en 1863 par le Suisse Henri Dunant, le Comité International de la Croix-Rouge (CICR) est à l'origine du mouvement international de la Croix-Rouge et du Croissant-Rouge (pour les pays musulmans).

La première conférence internationale du CICR a eu lieu à Genève. Seize nations y ont participé, dont la France. Elles ont décidé de créer, dans chaque pays, des comités de secours et ont choisi un emblème: une croix rouge sur fond blanc. Les États ont adopté des règles internationales qui définissaient comment on devait traiter les gens non-combattants aux mains de l'ennemi. Ce sont les Conventions de Genève dont la première date du 22 août 1864.

Aujourd'hui la Croix-Rouge est présente dans 181 pays et regroupe 97 millions d'hommes et de femmes. C'est la plus importante organisation humanitaire du monde.

Vocabulaire: croix *cross,* fond *background,* secours *help*

D'après *croix-rouge.fr*

Review **devoir**, Ch. 5, p. 138.

B. Le verbe *devoir (suite)*

Où est Céline?	*Where is Céline?*
Je ne sais pas. Elle **doit** être malade.	*I don't know. She **must** be sick.*
Mais elle **devait** apporter des fleurs pour le prof!	*But she **was supposed to** bring flowers for the teacher!*
Oui, je sais. Puisqu'elle n'est pas venue, j'**ai dû** aller les acheter.	*Yes, I know. Since she didn't come, I **had to** go buy them.*
Maintenant tout le monde me **doit** un euro pour le bouquet.	*Now everybody **owes** me one euro for the bouquet.*

- The past participle of **devoir** is **dû.** When it has a feminine agreement, however, it loses the circumflex: **due.** This often occurs when the past participle is used as an adjective.

  l'argent **dû** à mon frère   la pollution **due** à l'industrie

- The future tense verb stem for **devoir** is irregular: **devr-.**

  Elle **devra** travailler dur.   *She **'ll have** to work hard.*

- Like other verbs with two stems in the present tense, **devoir** has two stems in the subjunctive.

  que je **doive**   que nous **devions**

■ The passé composé and the imperfect can both mean *had to* or *probably (must have)*. The choice of tense depends, as usual, on whether the verb is a specific action or a description or habitual condition.

Hier j'**ai dû** aller voir ma tante.	*Yesterday, I **had to** go see my aunt.*
En général, je **devais** faire mes devoirs avant de sortir.	*In general, I **had to** do my homework before going out.*
Il **a dû** oublier notre rendez-vous!	*He **probably** forgot our date! (He **must have** forgotten our date!)*
Il **devait** être très occupé.	*He was **probably** very busy. (He **must have** been very busy.)*

> **NOTE**
>
> When **devoir** means *was supposed to,* the imperfect is always used.
>
> | | |
> |---|---|
> | Nous **devions** dîner chez les Gilbert. | *We **were supposed to** have dinner at the Gilberts'.* |

4 C'est probable. Utilisez **devoir** au passé composé d'après le modèle pour modifier les phrases suivantes.

MODÈLE: Delphine n'a probablement pas fait ses devoirs.
Elle n'a pas dû faire ses devoirs.

Remember that **sans doute** and **probablement** are synonyms. See p. 381.

1. Elle est sans doute sortie avec ses amis.
2. Elle n'a probablement pas étudié.
3. Elle a probablement eu une mauvaise note.
4. Elle a probablement pleuré.
5. Elle a sans doute parlé avec son professeur.
6. Elle a sans doute réussi la semaine d'après.

5 Toutes ces obligations! Traduisez *(translate)* la forme verbale anglaise entre parenthèses pour compléter la phrase.

MODÈLE: Chantal _____ étudier pendant le week-end. *(was supposed to)*
Chantal devait étudier pendant le week-end.

1. Mes parents _____ venir nous chercher il y a 30 minutes. *(were supposed to)*
2. Ils _____ oublier. *(must have)*
3. Non, ils _____ être déjà en route. *(must)*
4. Nous _____ leur téléphoner, s'ils n'arrivent pas bientôt. *(will have to)*
5. Il commence à faire froid. Tu _____ mettre ton manteau. *(must)*
6. Il est déjà midi. Je _____ être chez moi avant onze heures. *(was supposed to)*

C. Les pronoms interrogatifs

Review **qui, que,** and **quel,** Ch. 4, p. 114.

■ Interrogative pronouns are used to ask questions. You have already learned to use several interrogative pronouns.

Qui est-ce?	*Who is that?*
Qu'est-ce que c'est?	*What is that?*

■ As in English, interrogative pronouns in French change form depending on whether they refer to people or to things.

> **Qui** voyez-vous? *Whom do you see?*
>
> **Que** voyez-vous? *What do you see?*

■ In addition, French interrogative pronouns change form depending on their function in the sentence. For example, the word *what* in English can take three different forms in French depending on whether it is the subject, the direct object, or the object of a preposition.

> **Qu'est-ce qui** est à droite? *What is on the right?*
>
> **Qu'est-ce que** tu vois? *What do you see?*
>
> À **quoi** penses-tu? *What are you thinking about?*

People

Subject

Qui	Qui parle?	*Who is speaking?*
Qui est-ce qui	Qui est-ce qui parle?	

Object

Qui (+ inversion)	Qui avez-vous vu?	*Whom did you see?*
Qui est-ce que	Qui est-ce que vous avez vu?	

After a preposition

... qui (+ inversion)	À qui écrivez-vous?	*To whom are you writing?*
... qui est-ce que	À qui est-ce que vous écrivez?	

Things

Subject

Qu'est-ce qui	Qu'est-ce qui fait ce bruit?	*What's making that noise?*

Object

Que (+ inversion)	Qu'avez-vous fait?	*What did you do?*
Qu'est-ce que	Qu'est-ce que vous avez fait?	

After a preposition

... quoi (+ inversion)	De quoi avez-vous besoin?	*What do you need?*
... quoi est-ce que	De quoi est-ce que vous avez besoin?	

■ If the question involves a person, the pronoun will always begin with **qui.** If it is a question about a thing, the pronoun will begin with **que** or **quoi.** There is no elision with **qui** or **quoi,** but **que** becomes **qu'** before a vowel.

Qui a parlé?   *Who spoke?*

De **quoi** a-t-il parlé?   *What did he talk about?*

Qu'est-ce **qu'**il a dit?   *What did he say?*

■ As shown in the charts above, there are two forms of each of these interrogative pronouns, except the subject pronoun **qu'est-ce qui.**

■ When interrogative pronouns are used as subjects, the verb is normally singular.

Mes parents ont téléphoné.   Qui **a** téléphoné?

QUOI DE NEUF, DOC?
SAVEZ-VOUS QUE BUGS BUNNY PARLE FRANÇAIS?

6 **Quelqu'un ou quelque chose?** Utilisez un pronom interrogatif pour poser une question.

MODÈLES: Quelqu'un m'a téléphoné.
Qui vous a téléphoné?

Quelque chose m'intéresse.
Qu'est-ce qui vous intéresse?

J'ai téléphoné à quelqu'un.
À qui avez-vous téléphoné?

J'ai acheté quelque chose.
Qu'est-ce que vous avez acheté?

1. J'ai fait quelque chose le week-end dernier.
2. Quelque chose m'est arrivé.
3. J'ai vu quelqu'un.
4. Quelqu'un m'a parlé.
5. J'ai dansé avec quelqu'un.
6. Nous avons bu quelque chose.
7. J'ai dû payer pour quelqu'un.
8. J'ai dit au revoir à quelqu'un.

7 **Comment? Je n'ai pas compris.** Votre partenaire vous a parlé mais vous n'avez pas bien entendu. Demandez qu'il (elle) répète. Remplacez l'expression en italique par un pronom interrogatif.

MODÈLES: *Mon frère* a acheté une voiture.

VOUS: **Comment? Qui a acheté une voiture?**
VOTRE PARTENAIRE: **Mon frère.**

J'ai lu *deux livres.*

VOUS: **Comment? Qu'est-ce que tu as lu?**
VOTRE PARTENAIRE: **Deux livres.**

1. *Sophie* a écrit une lettre à ses parents.
2. Elle avait besoin *d'argent.*
3. *Ses parents* ont lu la lettre.
4. Ils ont répondu *à Sophie.*
5. Ils lui ont envoyé *l'argent.*
6. Sa mère *lui* a téléphoné hier soir.
7. Elle lui a dit *que son frère était malade.*
8. Sophie aime beaucoup *son frère.*
9. *Sa maladie* lui fait peur.

D. *Ne ... personne* et *ne ... rien*

Qui avez-vous rencontré?	Je **n'**ai rencontré **personne.**
Qu'est-ce que vous avez fait?	Je **n'**ai **rien** fait.
Avec qui avez-vous dansé?	Je **n'**ai dansé avec **personne.**
De quoi avez-vous besoin?	Je **n'**ai besoin de **rien.**
Qui est venu?	**Personne n'**est venu.
Qu'est-ce qui est arrivé?	**Rien n'**est arrivé.

■ You have already learned that the opposite of **quelque chose** is **ne ... rien** *(nothing, not anything)*. The opposite of **quelqu'un** is **ne ... personne** *(no one, nobody, not anyone)*.

Review **ne ... rien**, Ch. 6, p. 165.

■ When used as a *direct object,* **ne ... personne,** like **ne ... rien,** is placed around the conjugated verb.

Entendez-vous quelque chose?	Non, je **n'**entends **rien.**
Voyez-vous quelqu'un?	Non, je **ne** vois **personne.**

Remind students that all other negatives they have learned (**ne ... pas/plus/jamais**) are placed *before* the past participle.

NOTE

Unlike **ne ... rien,** however, **ne ... personne** surrounds both the auxiliary verb *and* the past participle in the passé composé.

	Avez-vous entendu quelque chose?	Non, je **n'**ai **rien** entendu.
But:	Avez-vous vu quelqu'un?	Non, je **n'**ai vu **personne.**

■ Both **rien** and **personne** can be used as the *object of a preposition.*

Avez-vous besoin de quelque chose?	Non, je **n'**ai besoin *de* **rien.**
Parlez-vous avec quelqu'un?	Non, je **ne** parle *avec* **personne.**

■ **Personne** and **rien** can also serve as the *subject* of a verb. In this case, **personne** and **rien** come before **ne. Ne** still comes before the conjugated verb.

Personne n'a téléphoné.	*Nobody telephoned.*
Personne ne va à cet endroit.	*No one goes to that place.*
Rien ne m'intéresse.	*Nothing interests me.*

■ Like **jamais** and **rien, personne** can be used alone to answer a question.

Qui est venu?   **Personne.**
Qui avez-vous rencontré?   **Personne.**

Si vous ne faites rien pour
votre pension, que ferez-vous
pendant votre pension?

Plans de pension.

8 **Je n'ai rien fait à personne!** Utilisez **rien** ou **personne** pour répondre aux questions suivantes.

MODÈLES: Qui avez-vous vu?   Qu'avez-vous entendu?
Je n'ai vu personne.   Je n'ai rien entendu.

1. Avec qui êtes-vous sorti(e)?
2. Qu'est-ce que vous avez fait?
3. Qu'est-ce que vous avez bu?
4. Qui est-ce que vous avez vu?
5. De quoi aviez-vous besoin?
6. À qui pensiez-vous?
7. À quoi pensiez-vous?
8. À qui est-ce que vous avez téléphoné?
9. Qu'avez-vous dit?

9 **Personne n'a rien fait.** Utilisez **rien** ou **personne** pour répondre aux questions suivantes.

MODÈLES: Qui a vu l'accident?   Qu'est-ce qui vous intéresse?
Personne n'a vu l'accident.   Rien ne m'intéresse.

1. Qui a pris ma voiture?
2. Qu'est-ce qui est arrivé hier soir?
3. Qui a écrit à Sylvie?
4. Qui lui a téléphoné?
5. Qu'est-ce qui lui est arrivé?
6. Qui est-ce qui est sorti avec elle?
7. Qui va faire ses devoirs ce soir?
8. Qu'est-ce qui va mal?
9. Qui a brûlé un stop?

10 **Ni rien ni personne.** Utilisez **rien** ou **personne** pour répondre aux questions suivantes.

Tell students to play the role of a person who never does anything.

1. Vous avez fait quelque chose le week-end dernier?
2. Quelque chose vous est arrivé?
3. Vous avez rencontré quelqu'un?
4. Quelqu'un vous a invité(e) à danser?
5. Vous avez dansé avec quelqu'un?
6. Après le bal quelqu'un vous a accompagné(e) au café?
7. Vous avez bu quelque chose?
8. Quelqu'un a payé pour vous?
9. Vous avez dit au revoir à quelqu'un?

ENTRE AMIS

Ma journée d'hier

1. Find out from your partner what happened yesterday.
2. Ask what s/he did.
3. Find out where s/he went and who was there.
4. Ask with whom s/he spoke.
5. What else can you find out?

2. Making Basic Hypotheses

Que feriez-vous[1] ...

	oui	non
... si vous n'aviez pas de devoirs?		
Je resterais dans ma chambre.	_____	_____
Je sortirais avec mes amis.	_____	_____
J'irais au cinéma.	_____	_____
Je m'amuserais.	_____	_____
... si, par hasard[2], vous gagniez à la loterie?		
J'achèterais une voiture.	_____	_____
Je paierais mes dettes[3].	_____	_____
Je donnerais de l'argent aux pauvres.	_____	_____
Je mettrais de l'argent à la banque.	_____	_____
... si vous n'étiez pas étudiant(e)?		
Je chercherais du travail.	_____	_____
Je gagnerais de l'argent.	_____	_____
Je voyagerais.	_____	_____
J'irais en France.	_____	_____

---

1. *What would you do*   2. *by chance*   3. *debts*

E. Le conditionnel

Je pourrais apporter quelque chose?	*Could I bring something?*
J'aimerais inviter les Martin.	*I would like to invite the Martins.*
Ils viendraient si tu leur téléphonais maintenant.	*They would come if you called them now.*

■ The conditional is used to express hypotheses and also politely stated requests or wishes.

■ The conditional is formed by adding the imperfect endings **(-ais, -ais, -ait, -ions, -iez, -aient)** to the future stem (see Ch. 12).

aimer				**vendre**		
j'	**aimer**	**ais**		je	**vendr**	**ais**
tu	**aimer**	**ais**		tu	**vendr**	**ais**
il/elle/on	**aimer**	**ait**		il/elle/on	**vendr**	**ait**
nous	**aimer**	**ions**		nous	**vendr**	**ions**
vous	**aimer**	**iez**		vous	**vendr**	**iez**
ils/elles	**aimer**	**aient**		ils/elles	**vendr**	**aient**

■ Remember that a number of verbs have irregular future stems (see Ch. 12). These verbs use the same irregular stem in the conditional. The endings, however, are always regular.

être	**ser-**	je **serais**	*I would be*
avoir	**aur-**	j'**aurais**	*I would have*
faire	**fer-**	je **ferais**	*I would do*
aller	**ir-**	j'**irais**	*I would go*
venir	**viendr-**	je **viendrais**	*I would come*
devenir	**deviendr-**	je **deviendrais**	*I would become*
vouloir	**voudr-**	je **voudrais**	*I would like*
pouvoir	**pourr-**	je **pourrais**	*I could; I would be able*
devoir	**devr-**	je **devrais**	*I should; I ought to*
savoir	**saur-**	je **saurais**	*I would know*

■ Impersonal expressions also have conditional forms.

infinitive	present	conditional
pleuvoir	il pleut	**il pleuvrait**
falloir	il faut	**il faudrait**
valoir mieux	il vaut mieux	**il vaudrait mieux**

Review p. 411.

■ Since **-e-** is *pronounced* as [ə] before the sound combination [Rj], it is never dropped in the **nous** and **vous** forms of the conditional of **-er** verbs and of irregular verbs such as **vous feriez** and **nous serions**.

future	conditional
nous dans*e*rons	nous dans**e**rions
vous chant*e*rez	vous chant**e**riez
nous s*e*rons	nous s**e**rions
vous f*e*rez	vous f**e**riez

In formal French (literature, speeches, etc.) **savoir** is often used in the conditional with the negative in place of **pouvoir**, with the meaning *would not be able; could not.* Normally the word **pas** is omitted in the negative in this literary usage: **La princesse ne saurait avoir de meilleur guide** *(The princess could not have a better guide).*

■ The conditional is used to make a polite request or suggestion because the present is often considered rather harsh or brusk. **Devoir** is often the verb used to make a polite suggestion.

Je **veux** une tasse de café.	*I **want** a cup of coffee.*
Je **voudrais** une tasse de café.	*I **would like** a cup of coffee.*
Vous **devez** faire attention.	*You **must** pay attention.*
Vous **devriez** faire attention.	*You **should** (ought to) pay attention.*

11 **Quelle audace!** *(What nerve!)* Mettez le verbe au conditionnel pour être plus poli(e).

Connections: Point out this use of **savoir** in the poem *Le Jardin*, p. 429.

MODÈLE: Vous devez parler plus fort *(loudly)*.
Vous devriez parler plus fort.

1. Je peux vous poser une question?
2. Avez-vous l'heure?
3. Pouvez-vous me dire votre nom?
4. Faites-vous la cuisine ce soir, par hasard?
5. C'est très gentil de m'inviter.
6. Je veux un steak-frites.

12 **Quel conseil donneriez-vous?** Utilisez le verbe **devoir** au conditionnel pour suggérer ce qu'il faudrait faire. Pourriez-vous donner deux suggestions pour chaque phrase?

MODÈLE: Nous n'avons pas de bonnes notes.
Vous devriez étudier.
Vous ne devriez pas sortir tous les soirs.

1. Marc a très faim.
2. Nos amis ont soif.
3. Nous sommes en retard.
4. Robert et Anne sont malades.
5. Gertrude est fatiguée.
6. Je n'ai pas envie de sortir ce soir.
7. Notre professeur donne beaucoup de devoirs.

F. *Si* hypothétique

Review **si** + present, Ch. 12, p. 339.

Si je gagne à la loterie, **j'irai** en Europe et en Asie.

Si je ne gagne pas à la loterie, **je resterai** ici.

REVIEW

Hypothetical statements about the future can be made by using **si** plus the present tense in conjunction with a clause in the future. Such a hypothesis will become a virtual certainty *if* the event described in the **si** clause actually occurs.

Si ma mère me **téléphone** ce soir, je lui **raconterai** cette histoire.
Je n'**irai** pas avec toi **si** tu **continues** à me parler comme ça.

■ To *suggest* what someone *might* do, **si** can be used with the imperfect as a question.

Si vous veniez à 8 heures?	*How about coming at 8 o'clock?*
Si j'allais au supermarché?	*What if I went to the supermarket?*
Si nous jouions aux cartes?	*How about a game of cards?*

■ Hypothetical statements referring to what would happen if something else were also to take place can be made by using **si** + imperfect with a clause in the conditional. Such hypotheses are not as certain actually to occur as those expressed by **si** + present with a clause in the future.

Si j'étais libre, **je sortirais** avec mes amis.	*If I were free, I would go out with my friends.*
Que **feriez-vous si vous étiez** riche?	*What would you do, if you were rich?*

Synthèse: *si* clauses used with the future or the conditional

Si + *le présent,*	→	*le futur*	**S'il pleut, nous ne sortirons pas.**
Si + *l'imparfait,*	→	*le conditionnel*	**S'il pleuvait, nous ne sortirions pas.**

---

13 **Deux solutions.** Pour chaque «problème» vous devez suggérer deux solutions.

MODÈLE: Nous avons faim.
   Si vous mangiez quelque chose?
   Si nous allions au restaurant?

1. Nous avons un examen demain.
2. Je suis malade.
3. Paul a besoin d'argent.
4. Je dois contacter mes amis.
5. J'ai soif.
6. Nous devons faire de l'exercice physique.
7. Nos amis sont tristes.

14 **Que ferais-tu?** Lisez ce questionnaire et répondez à chaque question. Interviewez ensuite votre partenaire en mettant les phrases à la forme interrogative avec **tu.** Comparez vos réponses.

MODÈLE: VOUS: **Si tu avais besoin d'argent, est-ce que tu écrirais à tes parents?**

VOTRE PARTENAIRE: **Non, je n'écrirais pas à mes parents. Et toi?**

1. Si j'avais besoin d'argent, ...

	oui	non
j'écrirais à mes parents.	___	___
je chercherais du travail.	___	___
je vendrais mon livre de français.	___	___
j'irais voir mes amis.	___	___
je pleurerais.	___	___

2. Si j'avais «F» à l'examen, ...

je pleurerais.	___	___
je serais fâché(e).	___	___
je serais très triste.	___	___
je téléphonerais à mes parents.	___	___
je resterais dans ma chambre.	___	___
j'arrêterais mes études.	___	___

3. Si on m'offrait une Mercédès, ...

je l'accepterais.	___	___
je la garderais.	___	___
je la vendrais.	___	___
je la donnerais à mes parents.	___	___

15 **À vous.** Répondez.

1. Si vous étiez professeur, qu'est-ce que vous enseigneriez?
2. Donneriez-vous beaucoup de devoirs à vos étudiants? Pourquoi ou pourquoi pas?
3. Quels vêtements est-ce que vous porteriez en classe?
4. Que feriez-vous pendant les vacances?
5. Quelle marque de voiture auriez-vous?
6. Où iriez-vous dans cette voiture?

ENTRE AMIS

Des châteaux en Espagne *(Daydreams)*

1. Find out what your partner would do if s/he had a lot of money.
2. Ask where s/he would live.
3. Find out what s/he would buy.
4. Suggest two things your partner could do with the money.

Intégration

Révision

Communication (Interpretive):
Activity A: Have students work in pairs to try to guess each other's questions.

Communication (Presentational): Activity B: Give students 3–4 minutes. Who will have the longest list?

Have students review **si** + imperfect, p. 424.

Communities & Communication (Presentational & Interpretive):
Encourage students to choose some of their 5 places from the *Réalités culturelles* notes in this text. If students present their list of places to the class, others can be asked to guess what they want to do in each of the places. Suggestion: Assign the *Rédaction* at the end of Ch. 15 in the Workbook.

Communication (Interpretive):
Encourage students to use the practice test on the Lab Audio Program.

A **Le témoin.** Un ami francophone a vu un accident. Faites une liste de questions que vous pourriez lui poser.

B **Un remue-méninges** (*Brainstorming*). Faites une liste de choses que vous pourriez faire avec cinquante dollars.

C **Quelques suggestions.**

1. Citez trois choses qu'on pourrait donner à un(e) ami(e) pour son anniversaire.
2. De quoi les étudiants ont-ils besoin pour être heureux sur votre campus? (trois choses)
3. Faites trois suggestions pour les prochaines vacances.
4. Quelles sont trois choses que vous feriez si vous étiez en France?

D **Début de rédaction.** Faites une liste de cinq endroits que vous aimeriez visiter. Pour chaque endroit que vous choisissez, indiquez aussi trois choses que vous voudriez faire à cet endroit.

MODÈLE: **J'aimerais visiter Paris. Là, je voudrais voir la tour Eiffel et visiter le musée du Louvre et la cathédrale Notre-Dame de Paris.**

E **À vous.** Répondez.

1. Quelle serait votre réaction si vous gagniez à la loterie?
2. À qui est-ce que vous téléphoneriez?
3. Qu'est-ce que vous lui diriez?
4. Que feriez-vous de cet argent?
5. Qu'est-ce que vous ne feriez pas de cet argent?
6. Où iriez-vous?

PAR TELEPHONE

Négociations:

Vous êtes témoin d'un accident. Vous jouerez le rôle de témoin. Complétez le formulaire suivant avant de répondre aux questions posées par le «gendarme». Votre partenaire jouera ce rôle et utilisera le formulaire dans l'appendice D.

Video for Chapter 15: A. Video worksheets (*Cahier*); B. ACE Video practice test (WWW); C. CD-ROM

A (témoin)

Date: _____   Lieu: _____

For complete instructions on how to prepare for and to use this activity, see *Négociations* on the Class Prep CD-ROM.

Heure: _____   Nombre de véhicules: _____

Conditions météorologiques: _____ beau temps _____ neige _____ pluie _____ brouillard (*fog*)

Chaussée: _____ glissante _____ sèche (*dry*)

Description du/des chauffeur(s):

Type(s) de véhicule(s):

_____ voiture(s) _____ camion(s) _____ vélo(s) _____ moto(s) _____ monospace(s) (*minivans*)

_____ mobylette(s) _____ autre (expliquer)

Numéro(s) de plaque d'immatriculation (*license plate*): _____

Marque(s): _____ Renault _____ Peugeot _____ Citroën _____ autre (expliquer)

Qu'est-ce que vous avez vu?

À votre avis, pourquoi cet accident a-t-il eu lieu?

Lecture I

NOTE CULTURELLE
Environ huit mille personnes sont tuées tous les ans dans des accidents de la circulation (*traffic*) en France. Avec près de 150 décès par million d'habitants, la France a la quatrième place des pays de l'Union européenne, après le Portugal, la Grèce et le Luxembourg. (*D'après Francoscopie*)

A **Étude du vocabulaire.** Étudiez les phrases suivantes et choisissez les mots anglais qui correspondent aux mots français en caractères gras: *unavoidable, when, chase, darted out, stone throwing, was astonished, lived, young girls, imprisoned, right away, around, court, cross, district.*

1. Il y avait plusieurs **fillettes** qui jouaient et riaient dans la cour de l'école.
2. Avant son mariage, Mme Dupont **demeurait** chez ses parents dans un **quartier** résidentiel.
3. Paul **s'est étonné** de ne pas voir beaucoup de gens dans les magasins **aux environs de** Noël.
4. Il fallait **traverser** la rue pour rentrer chez nous.
5. Après tous ses accidents, il était **inévitable** que cet homme perde son permis de conduire.
6. Le gendarme **s'est élancé** à la poursuite du criminel dont la voiture s'est écrasée contre un arbre. Le passager a été tué **sur le coup.**
7. **Lorsque** le **tribunal** a condamné le criminel, on l'a **écroué** dans une cellule de la prison.
8. Après une longue **course-poursuite** en voiture, les gendarmes ont réussi à arrêter le criminel.
9. Les **jets de pierre** sont formellement interdits par la police.

B **Une interrogation.** Vous êtes gendarmes et vous devez questionner deux automobilistes. Lisez d'abord les articles qui suivent et ensuite composez huit questions qui commencent par des mots interrogatifs (**Qui?**, **Qu'est-ce qui?**, etc.) dont quatre questions pour Madame Walther et quatre pour Monsieur Martin.

Deux accidents

Mulhouse. Sortie d'école tragique, hier, en fin de journée, à Habsheim, près de Mulhouse. Une fillette de onze ans a perdu la vie en rentrant à son domicile. Il était aux environs de 16 h 45. Monique Schoenhoffen se promenait le long de la route, lorqu'elle s'est subitement élancée pour traverser la chaussée, devant la maison où elle demeurait, juste à l'entrée de la commune. Elle n'avait pas vu venir une voiture, qui arrivait de Mulhouse, et qui était pilotée par Mme Georgette Walther, domiciliée dans cette ville. Le choc était inévitable. La fillette a été tuée sur le coup. À l'arrivée des gendarmes, il n'y avait malheureusement plus rien à faire. À 20 h, la gendarmerie n'avait pas encore déterminé les circonstances exactes de ce drame.

Roanne. Un automobiliste de 25 ans, sans permis de conduire, qui avait engagé une course-poursuite avec la police à plus de 110 km/heure dans les rues de Roanne (Loire) et qui avait frappé les policiers après son arrestation, a été condamné mercredi à six mois de prison ferme par le tribunal correctionnel de la ville. M. Djaffar Martin, déjà condamné en mars dernier à quatre mois de prison, avait été reconnu, mardi après-midi, par une patrouille de police qui l'avait aussitôt pris en chasse. Le chauffard avait alors pris une rue du centre en sens interdit, à plus de 110 km/heure, puis brûlé cinq feux rouges, forçant les automobilistes à s'immobiliser, sans cependant provoquer d'accident. Il avait été finalement intercepté par la police dans son quartier. Il a alors violemment attaqué les policiers qui le questionnaient sous les jets de pierre d'une dizaine de jeunes du quartier. Le chauffard a été écroué à la prison de la Talaudière.

C **Une analyse des faits.** Relisez les deux articles et comparez-les. Ensuite choisissez l'accident (Mulhouse ou Roanne) qui correspond le mieux à chacune des descriptions suivantes.

1. L'automobiliste n'avait sans doute rien fait de mauvais.
2. L'automobiliste avait déjà été en prison.
3. Une personne est morte dans cet accident.
4. D'autres ont voulu aider l'automobiliste.
5. L'automobiliste allait trop vite.
6. L'automobiliste n'avait pas pu s'arrêter à temps.

D **À votre avis.** Relisez les deux articles. Ensuite décidez ce que vous feriez si vous étiez le juge (1) au procès *(lawsuit)* de Madame Walther; (2) au procès de Monsieur Martin.

Lecture II

A **Étude du vocabulaire:** Étudiez les phrases suivantes. Essayez de deviner le sens des mots en caractères gras.

1. Des **milliers** de personnes viennent écouter ce concert de musique pop.
2. Est-ce que cette grande salle de concert va **suffire** pour tous ces gens?
3. Avec toute la **lumière** beaucoup porteraient des lunettes de soleil.
4. Un **parc** est une sorte de grand **jardin** public, avec des fleurs et beaucoup d'arbres.

Le jardin

Des milliers et des milliers d'années

Ne sauraient suffire

Pour dire

La petite seconde d'éternité

Où tu m'as embrassé

Où je t'ai embrassée

Un matin dans la lumière de l'hiver

Au parc Montsouris à Paris

À Paris

Sur la terre

La terre qui est un astre[1].

Jacques Prévert, *Paroles*

Review the use of **savoir** on p. 423.

---

1. *star*

B **Questions**

1. À votre avis, qui sont ces gens?
2. À quel moment de la journée et en quelle saison se sont-ils embrassés?
3. Qui a embrassé le premier, l'homme ou la femme? Expliquez votre réponse.
4. Quel endroit le poète a-t-il choisi pour cette scène? Que pensez-vous de ce choix?
5. Pourquoi le poète appelle-t-il cette scène «une seconde d'éternité»? Que pensez-vous de cette description?
6. À votre avis, est-ce que le poète est triste, heureux ou les deux à la fois? Expliquez votre réponse.

VOCABULAIRE ACTIF

À propos d'un accident

un accident *accident*
un agent de police *police officer*
un(e) automobiliste *driver*
blessé(e) *wounded*
brûler un stop *to run a stop sign*
un chauffard *bad driver*
la chaussée *pavement*
un conducteur *driver (male)*
une conductrice *driver (female)*
une contravention *traffic ticket*
déraper *to skid*
entrer en collision *to hit; to collide*
freiner *to brake*
un gendarme *policeman*
glissant(e) *slippery*
heurter *to hit; to run into (something)*

ivre *drunk*
la mort *death*
rouler *to go; to roll*
un témoin *witness*
tuer *to kill*

Expressions utiles

juste derrière *right behind*
par hasard *by chance*
parler plus fort *to speak more loudly*
puisque *since*

Noms

une dette *debt*
les études *(f. pl.) studies*
une faute *fault; mistake*
un(e) idiot(e) *idiot*

un(e) imbécile *imbecile*
une marque *make, brand*

Adjectifs

pâle *pale*
physique *physical*

Verbes

accepter *to accept*
assurer *to assure; to insure*
entendre parler de *to hear about*

Pronom

personne (ne ... personne) *no one; nobody; not anyone*

Préposition

contre *against; (in exchange) for*

Références

Verbes

Infinitif	Présent		Passé Composé		Imparfait	
1. parler	je	parle	j'	ai parlé	je	parlais
	tu	parles	tu	as parlé	tu	parlais
	il/elle/on	parle	il/elle/on	a parlé	il/elle/on	parlait
	nous	parlons	nous	avons parlé	nous	parlions
	vous	parlez	vous	avez parlé	vous	parliez
	ils/elles	parlent	ils/elles	ont parlé	ils/elles	parlaient
2. finir	je	finis	j'	ai fini	je	finissais
	tu	finis	tu	as fini	tu	finissais
	il/elle/on	finit	il/elle/on	a fini	il/elle/on	finissait
	nous	finissons	nous	avons fini	nous	finissions
	vous	finissez	vous	avez fini	vous	finissiez
	ils/elles	finissent	ils/elles	ont fini	ils/elles	finissaient
3. attendre	j'	attends	j'	ai attendu	j'	attendais
	tu	attends	tu	as attendu	tu	attendais
	il/elle/on	attend	il/elle/on	a attendu	il/elle/on	attendait
	nous	attendons	nous	avons attendu	nous	attendions
	vous	attendez	vous	avez attendu	vous	attendiez
	ils/elles	attendent	ils/elles	ont attendu	ils/elles	attendaient
4. se laver	je	me lave	je	me suis lavé(e)	je	me lavais
	tu	te laves	tu	t'es lavé(e)	tu	te lavais
	il/on	se lave	il/on	s'est lavé	il/on	se lavait
	elle	se lave	elle	s'est lavée	elle	se lavait
	nous	nous lavons	nous	nous sommes lavé(e)s	nous	nous lavions
	vous	vous lavez	vous	vous êtes lavé(e)(s)	vous	vous laviez
	ils	se lavent	ils	se sont lavés	ils	se lavaient
	elles	se lavent	elles	se sont lavées	elles	se lavaient

Impératif	Futur		Conditionnel		Subjonctif	
parle	je	parlerai	je	parlerais	que je	parle
parlons	tu	parleras	tu	parlerais	que tu	parles
parlez	il/elle/on	parlera	il/elle/on	parlerait	qu'il/elle/on	parle
	nous	parlerons	nous	parlerions	que nous	parlions
	vous	parlerez	vous	parleriez	que vous	parliez
	ils/elles	parleront	ils/elles	parleraient	qu'ils/elles	parlent
finis	je	finirai	je	finirais	que je	finisse
finissons	tu	finiras	tu	finirais	que tu	finisses
finissez	il/elle/on	finira	il/elle/on	finirait	qu'il/elle/on	finisse
	nous	finirons	nous	finirions	que nous	finissions
	vous	finirez	vous	finiriez	que vous	finissiez
	ils/elles	finiront	ils/elles	finiraient	qu'ils/elles	finissent
attends	j'	attendrai	j'	attendrais	que j'	attende
attendons	tu	attendras	tu	attendrais	que tu	attendes
attendez	il/elle/on	attendra	il/elle/on	attendrait	qu'il/elle/on	attende
	nous	attendrons	nous	attendrions	que nous	attendions
	vous	attendrez	vous	attendriez	que vous	attendiez
	ils/elles	attendront	ils/elles	attendraient	qu'ils/elles	attendent
lave-toi	je	me laverai	je	me laverais	que je	me lave
lavons-nous	tu	te laveras	tu	te laverais	que tu	te laves
lavez-vous	il/on	se lavera	il/on	se laverait	qu'il/on	se lave
	elle	se lavera	elle	se laverait	qu'elle	se lave
	nous	nous laverons	nous	nous laverions	que nous	nous lavions
	vous	vous laverez	vous	vous laveriez	que vous	vous laviez
	ils	se laveront	ils	se laveraient	qu'ils	se lavent
	elles	se laveront	elles	se laveraient	qu'elles	se lavent

VERBES RÉGULIERS AVEC CHANGEMENTS ORTHOGRAPHIQUES

Infinitif	Présent		Passé Composé	Imparfait
1. manger	je mange	nous mangeons	j'ai mangé	je mangeais
	tu manges	vous mangez		
	il/elle/on mange	ils/elles mangent		
2. avancer	j' avance	nous avançons	j'ai avancé	j'avançais
	tu avances	vous avancez		
	il/elle/on avance	ils/elles avancent		
3. payer	je paie	nous payons	j'ai payé	je payais
	tu paies	vous payez		
	il/elle/on paie	ils/elles paient		
4. préférer	je préfère	nous préférons	j'ai préféré	je préférais
	tu préfères	vous préférez		
	il/elle/on préfère	ils/elles préfèrent		
5. acheter	j' achète	nous achetons	j'ai acheté	j'achetais
	tu achètes	vous achetez		
	il/elle/on achète	ils/elles achètent		
6. appeler	j' appelle	nous appelons	j'ai appelé	j'appelais
	tu appelles	vous appelez		
	il/elle/on appelle	ils/elles appellent		

Impératif	Futur	Conditionnel	Subjonctif	*Autres verbes*
mange mang**e**ons mangez	je mangerai	je mangerais	que je mange que nous mangions	exiger nager neiger voyager
avance avan**ç**ons avancez	j'avancerai	j'avancerais	que j'avance que nous avancions	commencer divorcer
pa**ie** payons payez	je pa**ie**rai	je pa**ie**rais	que je pa**ie** que nous payions	essayer
préf**è**re préférons préférez	je préférerai	je préférerais	que je préf**è**re que nous préférions	espérer exagérer s'inquiéter répéter
ach**è**te achetons achetez	j'ach**è**terai	j'ach**è**terais	que j'ach**è**te que nous achetions	lever se lever se promener
appe**ll**e appelons appelez	j'appe**ll**erai	j'appe**ll**erais	que j'appe**ll**e que nous appelions	s'appeler épeler jeter

VERBES IRRÉGULIERS

To conjugate the irregular verbs on the top of the opposite page, consult the verbs conjugated in the same manner, using the number next to the verbs. The verbs preceded by a bullet are conjugated with the auxiliary verb **être**. Of course, when the verbs in this chart are used with a reflexive pronoun (as reflexive verbs), the auxiliary verb **être** must be used in compound tenses.

Infinitif	Présent		Passé Composé	Imparfait
1. aller	je vais tu vas il/elle/on va	nous allons vous allez ils/elles vont	je suis allé(e)	j'allais
2. s'asseoir	je m'assieds tu t'assieds il/elle/on s'assied	nous nous asseyons vous vous asseyez ils/elles s'asseyent	je me suis assis(e)	je m'asseyais
3. avoir	j' ai tu as il/elle/on a	nous avons vous avez ils/elles ont	j'ai eu	j'avais
4. battre	je bats tu bats il/elle/on bat	nous battons vous battez ils/elles battent	j'ai battu	je battais
5. boire	je bois tu bois il/elle/on boit	nous buvons vous buvez ils/elles boivent	j'ai bu	je buvais
6. conduire	je conduis tu conduis il/elle/on conduit	nous conduisons vous conduisez ils/elles conduisent	j'ai conduit	je conduisais
7. connaître	je connais tu connais il/elle/on connaît	nous connaissons vous connaissez ils/elles connaissent	j'ai connu	je connaissais
8. croire	je crois tu crois il/elle/on croit	nous croyons vous croyez ils/elles croient	j'ai cru	je croyais
9. devoir	je dois tu dois il/elle/on doit	nous devons vous devez ils/elles doivent	j'ai dû	je devais

apprendre 25
comprendre 25
couvrir 21
découvrir 21
décrire 11

détruire 6
• devenir 28
dormir 22
élire 16
• s'endormir 22

offrir 21
permettre 17
promettre 17
réduire 6

• repartir 22
• revenir 28
revoir 29
sentir 22

• sortir 22
sourire 26
traduire 6
valoir mieux 15

Impératif	Futur	Conditionnel	Subjonctif
va allons allez	j'irai	j'irais	que j'aille que nous allions
assieds-toi asseyons-nous asseyez-vous	je m'assiérai	je m'assiérais	que je m'asseye que nous nous asseyions
aie ayons ayez	j'aurai	j'aurais	que j'aie que nous ayons
bats battons battez	je battrai	je battrais	que je batte que nous battions
bois buvons buvez	je boirai	je boirais	que je boive que nous buvions
conduis conduisons conduisez	je conduirai	je conduirais	que je conduise que nous conduisions
connais connaissons connaissez	je connaîtrai	je connaîtrais	que je connaisse que nous connaissions
crois croyons croyez	je croirai	je croirais	que je croie que nous croyions
dois devons devez	je devrai	je devrais	que je doive que nous devions

Infinitif	Présent				Passé Composé	Imparfait
10. dire	je	dis	nous	disons	j'ai dit	je disais
	tu	dis	vous	dites		
	il/elle/on	dit	ils/elles	disent		
11. écrire	j'	écris	nous	écrivons	j'ai écrit	j'écrivais
	tu	écris	vous	écrivez		
	il/elle/on	écrit	ils/elles	écrivent		
12. envoyer	j'	envoie	nous	envoyons	j'ai envoyé	j'envoyais
	tu	envoies	vous	envoyez		
	il/elle/on	envoie	ils/elles	envoient		
13. être	je	suis	nous	sommes	j'ai été	j'étais
	tu	es	vous	êtes		
	il/elle/on	est	ils/elles	sont		
14. faire	je	fais	nous	faisons	j'ai fait	je faisais
	tu	fais	vous	faites		
	il/elle/on	fait	ils/elles	font		
15. falloir		il faut			il a fallu	il fallait
16. lire	je	lis	nous	lisons	j'ai lu	je lisais
	tu	lis	vous	lisez		
	il/elle/on	lit	ils/elles	lisent		
17. mettre	je	mets	nous	mettons	j'ai mis	je mettais
	tu	mets	vous	mettez		
	il/elle/on	met	ils/elles	mettent		
18. mourir	je	meurs	nous	mourons	je suis mort(e)	je mourais
	tu	meurs	vous	mourez		
	il/elle/on	meurt	ils/elles	meurent		
19. naître	je	nais	nous	naissons	je suis né(e)	je naissais
	tu	nais	vous	naissez		
	il/elle/on	naît	ils/elles	naissent		
20. nettoyer	je	nettoie	nous	nettoyons	j'ai nettoyé	je nettoyais
	tu	nettoies	vous	nettoyez		
	il/elle/on	nettoie	ils/elles	nettoient		
21. ouvrir	j'	ouvre	nous	ouvrons	j'ai ouvert	j'ouvrais
	tu	ouvres	vous	ouvrez		
	il/elle/on	ouvre	ils/elles	ouvrent		

Impératif	Futur	Conditionnel	Subjonctif
dis disons dites	je dirai	je dirais	que je dise que nous disions
écris écrivons écrivez	j'écrirai	j'écrirais	que j'écrive que nous écrivions
envoie envoyons envoyez	j'enverrai	j'enverrais	que j'envoie que nous envoyions
sois soyons soyez	je serai	je serais	que je sois que nous soyons
fais faisons faites	je ferai	je ferais	que je fasse que nous fassions
—	il faudra	il faudrait	qu'il faille
lis lisons lisez	je lirai	je lirais	que je lise que nous lisions
mets mettons mettez	je mettrai	je mettrais	que je mette que nous mettions
meurs mourons mourez	je mourrai	je mourrais	que je meure que nous mourions
nais naissons naissez	je naîtrai	je naîtrais	que je naisse que nous naissions
nettoie nettoyons nettoyez	je nettoierai	je nettoierais	que je nettoie que nous nettoyions
ouvre ouvrons ouvrez	j'ouvrirai	j'ouvrirais	que j'ouvre que nous ouvrions

Infinitif	Présent				Passé Composé	Imparfait
22. partir*	je	pars	nous	partons	je suis parti(e)*	je partais
	tu	pars	vous	partez		
	il/elle/on	part	ils/elles	partent		
23. pleuvoir		il pleut			il a plu	il pleuvait
24. pouvoir	je	peux**	nous	pouvons	j'ai pu	je pouvais
	tu	peux	vous	pouvez		
	il/elle/on	peut	ils/elles	peuvent		
25. prendre	je	prends	nous	prenons	j'ai pris	je prenais
	tu	prends	vous	prenez		
	il/elle/on	prend	ils/elles	prennent		
26. rire	je	ris	nous	rions	j'ai ri	je riais
	tu	ris	vous	riez		
	il/elle/on	rit	ils/elles	rient		
27. savoir	je	sais	nous	savons	j'ai su	je savais
	tu	sais	vous	savez		
	il/elle/on	sait	ils/elles	savent		
28. venir	je	viens	nous	venons	je suis venu(e)	je venais
	tu	viens	vous	venez		
	il/elle/on	vient	ils/elles	viennent		
29. voir	je	vois	nous	voyons	j'ai vu	je voyais
	tu	vois	vous	voyez		
	il/elle/on	voit	ils/elles	voient		
30. vouloir	je	veux	nous	voulons	j'ai voulu	je voulais
	tu	veux	vous	voulez		
	il/elle/on	veut	ils/elles	veulent		

*__Dormir, sentir,__ and **servir** are conjugated with **avoir** in the passé composé. **Partir, sortir,** and the reflexive **s'endormir** are conjugated with **être.**

The inverted form of **je peux is **puis-je ... ?**

Impératif	Futur	Conditionnel	Subjonctif
pars partons partez	je partirai	je partirais	que je parte que nous partions
—	il pleuvra	il pleuvrait	qu'il pleuve
— — —	je pourrai	je pourrais	que je puisse que nous puissions
prends prenons prenez	je prendrai	je prendrais	que je prenne que nous prenions
ris rions riez	je rirai	je rirais	que je rie que nous riions
sache sachons sachez	je saurai	je saurais	que je sache que nous sachions
viens venons venez	je viendrai	je viendrais	que je vienne que nous venions
vois voyons voyez	je verrai	je verrais	que je voie que nous voyions
veuille veuillons veuillez	je voudrai	je voudrais	que je veuille que nous voulions

Appendices

A list of International Phonetic Alphabet symbols

Voyelles

Son	Exemples	Pages: *Entre amis*
[i]	il, y	93, 298
[e]	et, parlé, aimer, chez	33, 39, 60, 382
[ɛ]	mère, neige, aime, tête, chère, belle	33, 60, 412
[a]	la, femme	60
[wa]	toi, trois, quoi, voyage	60
[ɔ]	folle, bonne	188
[o]	eau, chaud, nos, chose	188, 382
[u]	vous, août	158
[y]	une, rue, eu	158, 160
[ø]	deux, veut, bleu, ennuyeuse	351
[œ]	heure, veulent, sœur	351
[ə]	le, serons, faisons	60, 325, 411
[ɑ̃]	an, lent, chambre, ensemble	93
[ɔ̃]	mon, nom, sont	39, 93
[ɛ̃]	main, faim, examen, important, vin, chien, symphonie, brun*, parfum*	93

*Some speakers pronounce written **un** and **um** as [œ̃].

Consonnes

Son	Exemples	
[p]	père, jupe	383
[t]	toute, grand ami, quand est-ce que …	67, 107, 145, 383
[k]	comment, qui	214
[b]	robe, bien	383
[d]	deux, rendent	383
[g]	gare, longue, second	336, 383
[f]	fou, pharmacie, neuf	67
[s]	merci, professeur, français, tennis, démocratie	67, 214
[ʃ]	chat, short	214
[v]	vous, neuf ans	67
[z]	zéro, rose	67, 107, 214

[ʒ]	**j**e, â**g**e, na**ge**ons	39, 214
[l]	**l**ire, vi**ll**e	323
[R]	**r**ue, sœu**r**	244
[m]	**m**es, ai**m**e, co**mm**ent	93
[n]	**n**on, américai**n**e, bo**nn**e	93
[ɲ]	monta**gn**e	214

Semiconsonnes

Son	Exemples	
[j]	fi**ll**e, trava**il**, ch**i**en, vo**y**ez, **y**eux, h**i**er	298, 323
[w]	**ou**i, **w**eek-end	
[ɥ]	h**ui**t, t**u**er	325

APPENDICE B

Professions

The following professions are in addition to those taught in Ch. 4, p. 112.

agent *m.* **d'assurances** insurance agent
agent *m.* **de police** police officer
agent *m.* **de voyages** travel agent
agent *m.* **immobilier** real-estate agent
artisan *m.* craftsperson
assistant(e) social(e) social worker
avocat(e) lawyer
banquier *m.* banker
boucher/bouchère butcher
boulanger/boulangère baker
caissier/caissière cashier
chanteur/chanteuse singer
charcutier/charcutière pork butcher, delicatessen owner
chauffeur *m.* driver
chercheur/chercheuse researcher
chirurgien(ne) surgeon
commerçant(e) shopkeeper
conférencier/conférencière lecturer
conseiller/conseillère counsellor; advisor
cuisinier/cuisinière cook
dentiste *m./f.* dentist
douanier/douanière customs officer
électricien(ne) electrician
épicier/épicière grocer
expert-comptable *m.* CPA
facteur/factrice letter carrier
femme de ménage *f.* cleaning lady
fleuriste *m./f.* florist
garagiste *m./f.* garage owner; mechanic
homme/femme politique politician
hôtelier/hôtelière hotelkeeper
hôtesse de l'air *f.* stewardess

informaticien(ne) data processor
instituteur/institutrice elementary-school teacher
jardinier/jardinière gardener
joueur/joueuse (de golf, etc.) (golf, etc.) player
maire *m.* mayor
mannequin *m.* fashion model
mécanicien(ne) mechanic
ménagère *f.* housewife
militaire *m.* serviceman/servicewoman
moniteur/monitrice (de ski) (ski) instructor
musicien(ne) musician
opticien(ne) optician
PDG *m./f.* CEO (chairperson)
pasteur *m.* (Protestant) minister
peintre *m./f.* painter
photographe *m./f.* photographer
pilote *m.* pilot
plombier *m.* plumber
pompier *m.* firefighter
prêtre *m.* priest
psychologue *m./f.* psychologist
rabbin *m.* rabbi
religieuse *f.* nun
reporter *m.* reporter
représentant(e) de commerce traveling salesperson
restaurateur/restauratrice restaurant owner
savant *m.* scientist; scholar
sculpteur *m.* sculptor
serveur/serveuse waiter/waitress
traducteur/traductrice translator
vétérinaire *m./f.* vet

Reference: Robert–Collins dictionary.

A P P E N D I C E   C

Glossary of Grammatical Terms

Term	Definition	Example(s)
accord *(agreement)* 16, 22–23, 71	Articles, adjectives, pronouns, etc. are said to agree with the noun they modify when they "adopt" the gender and number of the noun.	*La voisine de Patrick est allemande. C'est une jeune fille très gentille. Elle est partie en vacances.*
adjectif *(adjective)* 16, 22, 96	A word that describes or modifies a noun or a pronoun, specifying size, color, number, or other qualities. (See **adjectif démonstratif, adjectif interrogatif, adjectif possessif.**)	*Lori Becker n'est pas mariée. Nous sommes américains. Le professeur a une voiture noire. C'est une belle voiture.*
adjectif démonstratif *(demonstrative adjective)* 103	A noun determiner (see **déterminant**) that identifies and *demonstrates* a person or a thing.	*Regarde les couleurs de cette robe et de ce blouson!*
adjectif interrogatif *(interrogative adjective)* 114, 394	An adjective that introduces a question. In French, the word **quel** *(which or what)* is used as an interrogative adjective and agrees in gender and number with the noun it modifies.	*Quelle heure est-il? Quels vêtements portez-vous?*
adjectif possessif *(possessive adjective)* 71, 78	A noun determiner that indicates *possession* or *ownership*. Agreement depends on the gender of the noun and not on the sex of the possessor, as in English *(his/her)*.	*Où est mon livre? Comment s'appelle son père?*
adverbe *(adverb)* 97, 287	An invariable word that describes a verb, an adjective, or another adverb. It answers the question *when?* (time), *where?* (place), or *how? how much?* (manner).	*Mon père conduit lentement.* (how?) *On va regarder un match de foot demain.* (when?) *J'habite ici.* (where?)
adverbe interrogatif *(interrogative adverb)* 145	An adverb that introduces a question about time, location, manner, number, or cause.	*Où sont mes lunettes? Comment est-ce que Lori a trouvé le film? Pourquoi est-ce que tu fumes?*

Term	Definition	Example(s)
article *(article)* 44, 63, 217	A word used to signal that a noun follows, and to specify the noun as to its *gender* and *number,* as well as whether it is general, particular, or part of a larger whole. (See **article défini, article indéfini,** and **article partitif.**)	
article défini *(definite article)* 44, 46, 309	The definite articles in French are **le, la, l',** and **les.** They are used to refer to a specific noun, or to things in general, in an abstract sense.	*Le professeur est dans la salle de classe. Le lait est bon pour la santé. J'aime les concerts de jazz.*
article indéfini *(indefinite article)* 63	The indefinite articles in French are **un, une,** and **des.** They are used to designate unspecified nouns.	*Lori Becker a un frère et une sœur. J'ai des amis qui habitent à Paris.*
article partitif *(partitive article)* 217	The partitive articles in French are **du, de la, de l',** and **des.** They are used to refer to *part* of a larger whole, or to things that cannot be counted.	*Je vais acheter du fromage. Tu veux de la soupe?*
comparatif *(comparison)* 306–308	When comparing people or things, these comparative forms are used: **plus** *(more),* **moins** *(less),* **aussi** *(as … as),* and **autant** *(as much as).*	*Le métro est plus rapide que le bus. Il neige moins souvent en Espagne qu'en France. Ma sœur parle aussi bien le français que moi. Elle gagne autant d'argent que moi.*
conditionnel *(conditional)* 422	A verb form used when stating hypotheses or expressing polite requests.	*Tu devrais faire attention. Je voudrais une tasse de café.*
conjugaison *(conjugation)* 38	An expression used to refer to the various forms of a verb that reflect *person* (1st, 2nd, or 3rd person), *number* (singular or plural), *tense* (present, past, or future), and *mood* (indicative, subjunctive, imperative, conditional). Each conjugated form consists of a *stem* and an *ending.*	Présent: *Nous parlons français en classe.* Passé composé: *Je suis allé à Paris l'année dernière.* Imparfait: *Quand il était jeune, mon frère s'amusait beaucoup.* Futur: *Je ferai le devoir de français ce soir.* Impératif: *Ouvrez vos livres!* Subjonctif: *Il faut qu'on fasse la lessive tout de suite.* Conditionnel: *Je voudrais un verre de coca.*

Term	Definition	Example(s)
contraction *(contraction)* 76, 125, 395	The condensing of two words to form one.	*C'est une photo **du** professeur* [de + le]. *Nous allons **au** café* [à + le].
déterminant *(determiner)* 333	A word that precedes a noun and *determines* its quality *(definite, indefinite, partitive,* etc.). In French, nouns are usually accompanied by one of these determiners.	Article *(**le** livre)*; demonstrative adjective *(**cette** table)*; possessive adjective *(**sa** voiture)*; interrogative adjective *(**Quelle** voiture?)*; number *(**trois** crayons)*.
élision *(elision)* 14, 20, 44, 249	The process by which some words drop their final vowel and replace it with an apostrophe before words beginning with a vowel sound.	*Je **m'**appelle Martin et **j'**habite près de **l'**église.*
futur *(future)* 36, 130, 337	A tense used to express what *will* happen. The construction **aller** + *infinitive* often replaces the future tense, especially when referring to more immediate plans.	*Un jour, nous **irons** en France. Nous **allons partir** cet après-midi.*
genre *(gender)* 4, 14, 44	The term used to designate whether a noun, article, pronoun, or adjective is masculine or feminine. All nouns in French have a grammatical *gender*.	***la** table, **le** livre, **le** garçon, **la** mère*
imparfait *(imperfect)* 299, 413	A past tense used to describe a setting (background information), a condition (physical or emotional), or a habitual action.	*Il **faisait** beau quand je suis parti. Je **prenais** beaucoup de médicaments quand j'**étais** jeune.*
impératif *(imperative)* 141, 282	The verb form used to give commands or to make suggestions.	***Répétez** après moi! **Allons** faire une promenade.*
indicatif *(indicative)* 14, 160, 299, 337	A class of tenses used to relate facts or supply information. **Le présent, le passé composé, l'imparfait,** and **le futur** all belong to the indicative mood.	*Je ne **prends** pas le petit déjeuner. Le directeur **partira** en vacances le mois prochain. Il **faisait** beau quand je **suis parti**.*
infinitif *(infinitive)* 36, 38, 246, 332, 337	The plain form of the verb, showing the general meaning of the verb without reflecting *tense, person,* or *number*. French verbs are often classified according to the last two letters of their infinitive forms: **-er** verbs, **-ir** verbs, or **-re** verbs.	*étud**ier**, chois**ir**, vend**re***

Term	Definition	Example(s)
inversion *(inversion)* 49, 66, 145, 161	An expression used to refer to the reversal of the subject pronoun-verb order in the formation of questions.	*Parlez-vous français? Chantez-vous bien?*
liaison *(liaison)* 12, 15, 39, 63–64, 126	The term used to describe the spoken linking of the final and usually silent consonant of a word with the beginning vowel sound of the following word.	*Vous [z]êtes américain? Ma sœur a un petit [t]ami.*
mot apparenté *(cognate)* 25, 92, 381	Words from different languages that are related in origin and that are similar are referred to as *cognates*.	***question*** [Fr.] = *question* [Eng.]; ***semestre*** [Fr.] = *semester* [Eng.]
négation *(negation)* 20, 97, 161, 283, 419	The process of transforming a positive sentence into a negative one. In negative sentences the verb is placed between two words, **ne** and another word defining the nature of the negation.	*On **ne** parle **pas** anglais ici. Il **ne** neige **jamais** à Casablanca. Mon grand-père **ne** travaille **plus**. Il n'y a **personne** dans la salle de classe. Mon fils n'a **rien** dit.*
nom *(noun)* 16	The name of a person, place, thing, idea, etc. All nouns in French have a grammatical gender and are usually preceded by a determiner.	*le **livre**, la **vie**, les **étudiants**, ses **parents**, cette **photo***
nombre *(number)* 14, 16, 44	The form of a noun, article, pronoun, adjective, or verb that indicates whether it is *singular* or *plural*. When an adjective is said to agree with the noun it modifies in *number*, it means that the adjective will be singular if the noun is singular, and plural if the noun is plural.	***La** voiture de James **est** très petite. **Les** livres de français ne **sont** pas aussi chers que **les** livres de biologie.*
objet direct *(direct object)* 228, 278, 388	A thing or a person bearing directly the action of a verb. (See **pronom objet direct.**)	*Thierry écrit **un poème**. Il aime **Céline**.*

Term	Definition	Example(s)
objet indirect *(indirect object)* 385	A person (or persons) to or for whom something is done. The indirect object is often preceded by the preposition **à** because it receives the action of the verb *indirectly*. (See **pronom objet indirect.**)	*Thierry donne une rose **à Céline**.* *Le professeur raconte des histoires drôles **aux étudiants**.*
participe passé *(past participle)* 157, 189, 243	The form of a verb used with an auxiliary to form two-part (compound) past tenses such as the **passé composé.**	*Vous êtes **allés** au cinéma. Moi, j'ai **lu** un roman policier.*
passé composé 157, 188, 417	A past tense used to narrate an event in the past, to tell what happened, etc. It is used to express actions *completed* in the past. The **passé composé** is composed of two parts: an auxiliary **(avoir** or **être)** conjugated in the present tense, and the past participle form of the verb.	*Le président **a parlé** de l'économie. Nous **sommes arrivés** à 5h.*
personne *(person)* 13	The notion of *person* indicates whether the subject of the verb is speaking *(1st person)*, spoken to *(2nd person)*, or spoken about *(3rd person)*. Verbs and pronouns are designated as being in the singular or plural of one of the three persons.	First person singular: *Je n'ai rien compris.* Second person plural: *Avez-**vous** de l'argent?* Third person plural: ***Elles** sont toutes les deux sénégalaises.*
plus-que-parfait *(pluperfect)* 412	A past tense used to describe an event that took place prior to some other past event. The **plus-que-parfait** is composed of two parts: an auxiliary **(avoir** or **être)** conjugated in the imperfect tense, and the past participle form of the verb.	*Il était ivre parce qu'il **avait** trop **bu**.*
préposition *(preposition)* 138, 142, 195	A word (or a small group of words) preceding a noun or a pronoun that shows position, direction, time, etc. relative to another word in the sentence.	*Mon oncle qui habite **à** Boston est allé **en** France. L'hôtel est **en face de** la gare.*
présent *(present)* 14, 38	A tense that expresses an action taking place at the moment of speaking, an action that one does habitually, or an action that began earlier and is still going on.	*Il **fait** très beau aujourd'hui. Je me **lève** à 7h tous les jours.*

Term	Definition	Example(s)
pronom *(pronoun)* 13, 114, 193, 228, 278, 388, 400	A word used in place of a noun or a noun phrase. Its form depends on the *number* (singular or plural), *gender* (masculine or feminine), *person* (1st, 2nd, 3rd), and *function* (subject, object, etc.) of the noun it replaces.	*Tu aimes les fraises? Oui, **je les** adore. / Irez-**vous** à Paris cet été? Non, **je** n'**y** vais pas. / Prenez-**vous** du sucre? Oui, **j'en** prends. / Qui t'a dit de partir?* **Lui.**
pronom accentué *(stress pronoun)* 172, 306	A pronoun that is separated from the verb and appears in different positions in the sentence.	*Voilà son livre à **elle**. Viens avec **moi**!*
pronom interrogatif *(interrogative pronoun)* 114, 394–395, 416–418	Interrogative pronouns are used to ask questions. They change form depending upon whether they refer to people or things and also whether they function as the subject, the direct object, or the object of a preposition of a sentence.	***Qui** est là? **Que** voulez-vous faire dans la vie? **Qu'est-ce que** vous faites? **Qu'est-ce qui** est arrivé?*
pronom objet direct *(direct object pronoun)* 228, 278, 388	A pronoun that replaces a direct object noun (a noun object not preceded by a preposition).	*Thierry aime Céline et elle **l'**aime aussi.*
pronom objet indirect *(indirect object pronoun)* 386	A pronoun that replaces an indirect object noun (a noun object preceded by the preposition **à**).	*Thierry **lui** a donné une rose.*
pronom relatif *(relative pronoun)* 61, 232, 260, 396	A pronoun that refers or "relates" to a preceding noun and connects two clauses into a single sentence.	*Le professeur a des amis **qui** habitent à Paris. J'ai lu le livre **que** tu m'as donné.*
pronom sujet *(subject pronoun)* 13	A pronoun that replaces a noun subject.	***Ils** attendent le train. **On** parle français ici.*
sujet *(subject)* 13	The person or thing that performs the action of the verb. (See **pronom sujet**.)	***Les étudiants** font souvent les devoirs à la bibliothèque. **Vous** venez d'où?*
subjonctif *(subjunctive)* 364, 398	A class of tenses, used under specific conditions: (1) the verb is in the second (or subordinate) clause of a sentence; (2) the second clause is introduced by **que**; and (3) the verb of the first clause expresses advice, will, necessity, emotion, etc.	*Mon père préfère que je n'**aie** pas de voiture. Le professeur veut que nous **parlions** français. Ma mère est contente que vous **soyez** ici.*

Term	Definition	Example(s)
superlatif *(superlative)* 309	The superlative is used to express the superior or inferior degree or quality of a person or a thing.	*Le TGV est le train le plus rapide du monde. L'eau minérale est la boisson la moins chère.*
temps *(tense)* 38, 160, 299, 337	The particular form of a verb that indicates the time frame in which an action occurs: present, past, future, etc.	*La tour Eiffel est le monument le plus haut de Paris. Nous sommes arrivés à 5h à la gare. Je ferai de mon mieux.*
verbe *(verb)* 14, 38, 246, 332	A word expressing action or condition of the subject. The verb consists of a *stem* and an *ending*, the form of which depends on the *subject* (singular, plural, 1st, 2nd, or 3rd person), the *tense* (present, past, future), and the *mood* (indicative, subjunctive, imperative, conditional).	
verbe auxiliaire *(auxiliary verb)* 160, 189	The two auxiliary (or helping) verbs in French are **avoir** and **être.** They are used in combination with a past participle to form the **passé composé** and the **plus-que-parfait.**	*Nous sommes allés au cinéma hier. Nous avons vu un très bon film.*
verbes pronominaux *(reflexive verbs)* 168, 191, 356	Verbs whose subjects and objects are the same. A reflexive pronoun will precede the verb and act as either the direct or indirect object of the verb. The reflexive pronoun has the same *number, gender,* and *person* as the subject.	*Lori se réveille. Elle et James se sont bien amusés hier soir.*

A P P E N D I C E   D

Négociations

The *Révision* part of the *Intégration* section of each chapter ends with an activity called **Négociations**. In this activity you will exchange information with a partner. Partner A uses the version of the activity shown in the chapter. In most cases, Partner B (and occasionally C, D, etc.) uses the version of the activity given in this appendix.

For the last two blanks you should choose adjectives that describe the person, e.g., *tall*.

Chapitre I (p. 25)

Identifications. Work with your partner to prepare a new identity. First, decide with your partner whether you are describing a man or a woman. Then, complete the second half of the following form. Ask questions of your partner, who will complete the first half of the form. Your partner will ask you other questions about the person you are describing. Answer only **oui** or **non**.

MODÈLE: **Comment vous appelez-vous? Quel est votre nom de famille?
Êtes-vous français(e)? Êtes-vous jeune?**

A   **B**

Nom de famille: _____   État civil: _____

Prénom: _____   Description 1: _____

                                                            _____

Nationalité: _____   Description 2: _____

                                                            _____

Chapitre 2 (p. 52)

Les activités. Use one of the forms below to interview as many students as possible. Try to find people who answer the questions affirmatively; then write their initials in the appropriate boxes. No student's initials should be used more than twice.

MODÈLE: **Est-ce que tu détestes les hot-dogs?**

B

regarder la télé le soir	aimer étudier le français	chanter une chanson française
détester les hot-dogs	parler espagnol	aimer patiner
pleurer quelquefois	être marié(e)	travailler beaucoup
étudier l'anglais	adorer skier	jouer au golf

C

danser souvent le week-end	adorer skier	parler espagnol
jouer au ping-pong	chanter une chanson française	étudier l'anglais
travailler beaucoup	être célibataire	tomber quelquefois
pleurer quelquefois	détester les hot-dogs	aimer patiner

Chapitre 3 (p. 82)

C'est la voiture de son frère? Work with your partner to complete the forms. Ask questions to determine the information that is missing.

MODÈLE: **C'est la voiture du frère de David?**
C'est le vélo de ses grands-parents?

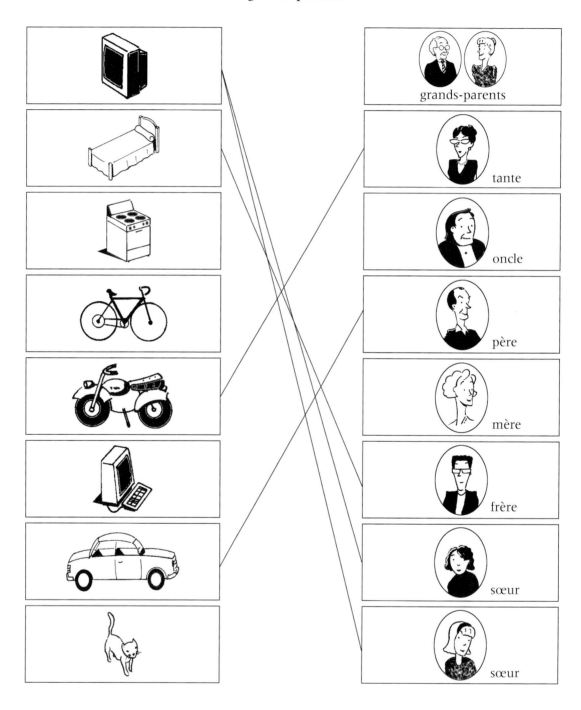

Chapitre 4 (p. 117)

Nos amis. Work with your partner to complete the forms. Ask questions to determine the information that is missing.

MODÈLE: **Est-ce que Marie a les yeux bleus?**

B

nom	yeux	cheveux	description	à la maison	dans la vie	vêtement
Marie		noirs	bavarde			short
Alain	marron			courses		
Chantal		roux		lessive	journaliste	
Éric	bleus		charmant		cuisinier	
Karine	gris		pessimiste	liste	médecin	chapeau
Pierre		bruns				blouson
Sylvie		blonds	patiente	provisions	cadre	
Jean	verts					ceinture

Chapitre 5 (p. 148)

L'emploi du temps de Sahibou. Interviewez votre partenaire pour trouver les renseignements qui manquent *(missing information)*.

MODÈLE: **Est-ce qu'il a un cours le mercredi à onze heures?**
Est-ce que c'est un cours de mathématiques?

B

	lundi	mardi	mercredi	jeudi	vendredi	samedi	dimanche
9h							
10h		gestion		gestion			église
11h	français		français		français		
12h	cafétéria		cafétéria		cafétéria	cafétéria	déjeuner avec ses parents
1h		cafétéria		cafétéria			
2h							
7h		bibliothèque		informatique			bibliothèque
8h	résidence	bibliothèque		informatique	cinéma		bibliothèque

Chapitre 6 (p. 177)

Hier, d'habitude et pendant le week-end. Interviewez votre partenaire pour trouver les renseignements qui manquent *(missing information)*.

Modèle: **Est-ce que Valérie va au cours de français d'habitude?**
Est-ce qu'Alain a fumé hier?

B			
nom	hier	d'habitude	pendant le week-end
Valérie	écrire une dissertation _____	OUI	nettoyer sa chambre _____
Chantal	NON	NON	rester dans sa chambre _____
Sophie	être malade _____	étudier seule _____	OUI
Alain	NON	travailler après les cours _____	OUI
David	NON	OUI	jouer au basket-ball _____
Jean-Luc	passer un examen _____	envoyer des messages électroniques _____	NON

Chapitre 7 (p. 205)

D'où viennent-ils? Interviewez votre partenaire pour trouver les renseignements qui manquent.

Modèles: **D'où vient Sahibou?**
Où est-ce que Fatima est née?
Quand est-ce que Cécile est partie?

B				
nom	pays d'origine	ville de naissance	départ	adresse
Sahibou		Dakar		Canada
Fatima	Maroc		en juin dernier	
Cécile	Belgique			États-Unis
Jean-Luc		Nantes	en avril dernier	
Marie	Canada	Québec		

Chapitre 8 (p. 235)

Dînons-nous ensemble? Interviewez les autres étudiants pour trouver votre partenaire. C'est la personne qui a le même menu que vous.

MODÈLES: **Qu'est-ce que tu prends comme hors-d'œuvre?**
Qu'est-ce que tu vas boire?

B

	votre partenaire	vous
hors-d'œuvre	soupe de légumes	pâté
plat principal	saumon	bœuf
légume	épinards	riz
fromage	camembert	brie
dessert	gâteau	pâtisseries
boisson	eau minérale	eau

C

	votre partenaire	vous
hors-d'œuvre	soupe à l'oignon	crudités
plat principal	porc	truite
légume	frites	riz
fromage	brie	chèvre
dessert	tarte	gâteau
boisson	eau	vin blanc

D

	votre partenaire	vous
hors-d'œuvre	salade de tomates	soupe à l'oignon
plat principal	bœuf	poulet
légume	petits pois	frites
fromage	chèvre	emmenthal
dessert	fruits	gâteau
boisson	vin rouge	eau

E

	votre partenaire	vous
hors-d'œuvre	pâté	salade de tomates
plat principal	saumon	bœuf
légume	épinards	haricots verts
fromage	camembert	brie
dessert	fruits	glace
boisson	eau minérale	eau minérale

F

	votre partenaire	vous
hors-d'œuvre	crudités	soupe de légumes
plat principal	truite	poulet
légume	riz	petits pois
fromage	camembert	emmenthal
dessert	tarte	pâtisseries
boisson	vin blanc	eau

G

	votre partenaire	vous
hors-d'œuvre	soupe de légumes	pâté
plat principal	porc	bœuf
légume	frites	épinards
fromage	emmenthal	brie
dessert	tarte	glace
boisson	vin rouge	eau minérale

H

	votre partenaire	vous
hors-d'œuvre	soupe à l'oignon	crudités
plat principal	saumon	porc
légume	haricots verts	riz
fromage	chèvre	camembert
dessert	pâtisseries	glace
boisson	vin blanc	vin rouge

I

	votre partenaire	vous
hors-d'œuvre	salade de tomates	crudités
plat principal	poulet	truite
légume	petits pois	haricots verts
fromage	chèvre	emmenthal
dessert	fruits	glace
boisson	vin rouge	vin blanc

J

	votre partenaire	vous
hors-d'œuvre	pâté	soupe de légumes
plat principal	bœuf	saumon
légume	riz	épinards
fromage	brie	camembert
dessert	pâtisseries	gâteau
boisson	eau	eau minérale

K

	votre partenaire	vous
hors-d'œuvre	crudités	soupe à l'oignon
plat principal	truite	porc
légume	riz	frites
fromage	chèvre	brie
dessert	gâteau	tarte
boisson	vin blanc	eau

L

	votre partenaire	vous
hors-d'œuvre	soupe à l'oignon	salade de tomates
plat principal	poulet	bœuf
légume	frites	petits pois
fromage	emmenthal	chèvre
dessert	gâteau	fruits
boisson	eau	vin rouge

M

	votre partenaire	vous
hors-d'œuvre	salade de tomates	pâté
plat principal	bœuf	saumon
légume	haricots verts	épinards
fromage	brie	camembert
dessert	glace	fruits
boisson	eau minérale	eau minérale

N

	votre partenaire	vous
hors-d'œuvre	soupe de légumes	crudités
plat principal	poulet	truite
légume	petits pois	riz
fromage	emmenthal	camembert
dessert	pâtisseries	tarte
boisson	eau	vin blanc

O

	votre partenaire	vous
hors-d'œuvre	pâté	soupe de légumes
plat principal	bœuf	porc
légume	épinards	frites
fromage	brie	emmenthal
dessert	glace	tarte
boisson	eau minérale	vin rouge

P

	votre partenaire	vous
hors-d'œuvre	crudités	soupe à l'oignon
plat principal	porc	saumon
légume	riz	haricots verts
fromage	camembert	chèvre
dessert	glace	pâtisseries
boisson	vin rouge	vin blanc

Chapitre 9 (p. 262)

Nos achats. Interviewez votre partenaire pour trouver les renseignements qui manquent. Il y a trois paires de cartes. Comme partenaires, A1 travaille avec B1, A2 avec B2, etc.

MODÈLE: **Qu'est-ce qu'on achète à la gare?**
Où est-ce qu'on achète des fleurs?

B I

achat	endroit
	gare
	supermarché
légumes	
médicaments	
	supermarché
fromage	
	librairie
chapeau	
magazine	
	épicerie
	boutique
fleurs	
	pharmacie
savon	

B2

achat	endroit
coca	
	fleuriste
	pharmacie
livre	
légumes	
	bureau de tabac
magazine	
pastilles	
	boucherie
	boulangerie
pommes	
	bureau de tabac
cadeau	
	supermarché

B3

achat	endroit
journal	
fruits	
	bureau de tabac
	pharmacie
cadeau	
	marché
saucisses	
	boulangerie
magazine	
	charcuterie
fleurs	
	boucherie
timbres	
	grand magasin

Chapitre 10 (p. 290)

All of the vehicles in this activity are feminine.

La formule 1. Interviewez votre partenaire pour trouver les renseignements qui manquent.

MODÈLE: **Quelle sorte de véhicule est-ce que mémé conduit?**
Comment conduit-elle?

B

nom	conduire	comment?	pourquoi comme ça?
Michael Schumacher	Ferrari	à toute vitesse	
Jacques Villeneuve			C'est un pilote professionnel canadien.
Alain Prost	Renault	très vite	
tonton (*oncle*) Paul		comme un fou	
tatie (*tante*) Agnès	Harley	tranquillement	
papi (*grand-père*)			Il ne peut pas changer de vitesse.
mémé (*grand-mère*)	mobylette		Elle a peur des accidents.
votre partenaire			
vous			

Chapitre 11 (p. 313)

Hier et quand j'avais 10 ans. Since all students use the same form, it has not been reproduced here. Use the form on p. 313.

Chapitre 12 (p. 342)

Savoir ou connaître? Since all students use the same form, it has not been reproduced here. Use the form on p. 342.

Chapitre 13 (p. 372)

Il manque quelque chose. Interviewez les autres étudiants pour trouver les choses qui manquent. Il y a sept cartes différentes en tout.

MODÈLE: **Est-ce que tu as un(e) … sur ta table?**
Moi, j'ai un(e) …, mais je n'ai pas de (d') …

Chapitre 14 (p. 403)

Qu'est-ce qu'il (elle) en pense? Interviewez votre partenaire pour trouver les renseignements qui manquent.

MODÈLE: **Quelle est la réaction de Catherine?**
Pourquoi est-elle triste?

B

	ce qui arrive	sa réaction
Catherine		Elle en est triste.
Éric	Une jolie femme veut le rencontrer.	
Alain	Il y a trop de publicité à la télé.	
Chantal		Elle en est fâchée.
Monique	Sa sœur va avoir un bébé.	
Jacques		Il le regrette.
Christophe		Il en est confus.
Nathalie	Son amie se dispute avec elle.	
Véronique	Son petit ami lui achète une bague de fiançailles.	
Pierre		Il croit que c'est dommage.

Chapitre 15 (p. 426)

Vous êtes témoin d'un accident. Vous jouerez le rôle de gendarme. Interviewez votre partenaire qui joue le rôle de témoin d'un accident. Ensuite, complétez le formulaire suivant.

B (gendarme)

Nom du témoin: _____

Adresse du témoin: _____

Numéro de téléphone du témoin: _____

Observations (date, heure, lieu, conditions météorologiques, chaussée, véhicules, chauffeur(s), description de l'accident, cause de l'accident, autres ...):

Vocabulaire

This vocabulary list includes all of the words and phrases included in the *Vocabulaire actif* sections of *Entre amis*, as well as the passive vocabulary used in the text. The definitions given are limited to the context in which the words are used in this book. Entries for active vocabulary are followed by the number of the chapter in which they are introduced for the first time. If a word is formally activated in more than one chapter, a reference is given for each chapter. Some entries are followed by specific examples from the text. Expressions are listed according to their key word. In subentries, the symbol ~ indicates the repetition of the key word.

Regular adjectives are given in the masculine form, with the feminine ending in parentheses. For irregular adjectives, the full feminine form is given in parentheses.

The gender of each noun is indicated after the noun. Irregular feminine and plural forms are also noted.

The following abbreviations are used:

CP   Chapitre préliminaire

adj.	adjective	*f.*	feminine	*n.*	noun
adv.	adverb	*f.pl.*	feminine plural	*pl.*	plural
art.	article	*inv.*	invariable	*prep.*	preposition
conj.	conjunction	*m.*	masculine	*pron.*	pronoun
fam.	familiar	*m.pl.*	masculine plural	*v.*	verb

à at, in, to   1
   ~ côté next door; to the side   5
   ~ côté de next to, beside   5
   ~ droite (de) to the right (of)   7
   ~ gauche (de) to the left (of)   7
   ~ ... heure(s) at ... o'clock   1
   ~ la vôtre! (here's) to yours!   2
   ~ l'heure on time   7
   ~ l'intérieur de inside   6
   ~ midi at noon   5
   ~ minuit at midnight   5
   ~ toute vitesse at top speed   10
   ~ travers throughout
   être ~ to belong to   6
abord: d'~ at first   5
absolument absolutely   10
accepter to accept   15
accident *m.* accident   15
accompagner to accompany   6
accord *m.* agreement
   d'~ okay   5
   être d'~ (avec) to agree (with)   1, 11

accordéon *m.* accordion   6
accueillant(e) friendly
achat *m.* purchase   9
acheter to buy   9
acteur/actrice *m./f.* actor/ actress   1
activité *f.* activity   11
actuellement now   14; nowadays
addition *f.* (restaurant) bill, check   8; addition
adieu *m.* (*pl.* **adieux**) farewell
adjoint au maire *m.* deputy mayor
adorer to adore; to love   2
adresse *f.* address   4
aéroport *m.* airport   5
affaires *f.pl.* business   4
   homme/femme d'~ *m./f.* businessman/woman   4
affreux (affreuse) horrible   8
âge *m.* age   3
   quel ~ avez-vous? how old are you?   3

âgé(e) old   11
agent (de police) *m.* (police) officer   15
agglomération *f.* urban area
agir: il s'agit de it's (*lit.* it's a matter of)
agrumes *m.pl.* citrus fruits
aider to help   4
aïe! ouch!   6
ail *m.* garlic   8
aimable kind; nice   9
aimer to like; to love   2
   s' ~ to love each other   14
ainsi thus, for that reason
air: avoir l'~ to seem; to appear, to look   9
album *m.* album   11
alcool *m.* alcohol
Allemagne *f.* Germany   5
allemand(e) German   1
aller to go   2, 5
   ~ en ville to go into town   5
   ~ -retour *m.* round-trip ticket   12

~ simple *m.* one-way (ticket) 12

allez à la porte! go to the door! CP

allez-y! go ahead; let's go 12

je vais très bien I'm fine 2

allô! hello! *(on the phone)* 12

alors then, therefore, so 2

amant *m.* lover

amener to bring

américain(e) American 1

ami/amie *m./f.* friend 2

amour *m.* love

amusant(e) amusing, funny; fun 11

s'amuser to have fun; to have a good time 6

je veux m'amuser I want to have fun 10

an *m.* year 3

Jour de l'~ *m.* New Year's Day 7

ananas *m.* pineapple

anchois *m.* anchovy 8

ancien (ancienne) former; old 4

anglais(e) English 1

Angleterre *f.* England 5

année *f.* year 6

~ scolaire *f.* school year 10

anniversaire *m.* birthday 7

~ de mariage wedding anniversary 10

annonce *f.* advertisement 14

petites annonces want ads

annuler to cancel

août *m.* August 7

apéritif *m.* before-dinner drink 8

appareil *m.* appliance; phone 7

appartement *m.* apartment 3

s'appeler to be named, be called 13

comment vous appelez-vous? what is your name? 1

je m'appelle … my name is … 1

appétit *m.* appetite

Bon ~! Have a good meal! 13

apporter to bring 8

apprendre to learn; to teach 8

après after 5

après-demain day after tomorrow 12

après-midi *m.* afternoon 2

de l'~ in the afternoon 5

Bon ~. Have a good afternoon.

arabe *m.* Arabic 5; Arab

arachide *f.* peanut

arbre *m.* tree

argent *m.* money 9

armée *f.* army

arrêt (d'autobus) *m.* (bus) stop 10

(s')arrêter to stop 10

arrière- great- 3

arriver to arrive 7

qu'est-ce qui est arrivé? what happened? 14

artiste *m./f.* artist 4

aspirine *f.* aspirin 9

s'asseoir to sit down 13

Asseyez-vous! Sit down! CP

assez sort of, rather, enough 1

~ bien fairly well 2

~ mal rather poorly 2

en avoir ~ to be fed up 11

assiette *f.* plate 8

assister (à) to attend 14

assurer to assure; to insure 15

attacher to attach; to put on 10

attendre to wait (for) 9

attentif (attentive) attentive 10

attention: faire ~ to pay attention 4

au contraire on the contrary 4

au moins at least 5

au pair au pair

jeune fille ~ *f.* nanny 4

au revoir good-bye 1

aujourd'hui today 4

aussi also, too 1; as 11

~ … que as … as … 11

autant (de) as much 11

autocar *m.* tour bus 12

automne *m.* fall 7

automobiliste *m./f.* driver 15

autoroute *f.* turnpike; throughway, highway 12

autour de around 5

autre other 3

avance *f.* advance

en ~ early 7

avancer to advance 10

avant before 5

avare miserly, stingy 4

avec with 2

avenir *m.* future

avertissement *m.* warning 14

avion *m.* airplane 7

avis *m.* opinion, advice

à mon (à ton, etc.) ~ in my (your, etc.) opinion 11

avoir to have 3

~ besoin de to need 9

~ chaud to be hot 8

~ envie de to want to; to feel like 5

~ faim to be hungry 8

~ froid to be cold 8

~ l'air to seem, to appear, to look 9

~ lieu to take place 11

~ l'intention de to plan to 5

~ mal (à) to be sore, to have a pain (in) 9

~ peur to be afraid 8

~ pitié (de) to have pity (on), to feel sorry (for) 10

~ raison to be right 8

~ rendez-vous to have an appointment, meeting 4

~ soif to be thirsty 8

~ sommeil to be sleepy 8

~ tendance à to tend to 12

~ tort to be wrong; to be unwise 8

en ~ assez to be fed up 11

qu'est-ce que tu as? what's the matter with you? 9

avril *m.* April 7

bagages *m.pl.* luggage 7

bague *f.* ring 14

bain: salle de ~ bathroom 3

balayer to sweep

bande dessinée *f.* comic strip 6

banque *f.* bank 5

barquette *f.* small box; mini crate 9

basket-ball (basket) *m.* basketball 6

baskets *f.pl.* high-top sneakers 4

bâtiment *m.* building 5

batterie *f.* drums 6

bavard(e) talkative 4

beau/bel/belle/beaux/belles handsome, beautiful 1

il fait ~ it's nice out CP, 7

beau-frère *m.* brother-in-law 3

beau-père *m.* (*pl.* **beaux-pères**) stepfather (or father-in-law) 3

beaucoup a lot 2; much, many

beaujolais *m.* Beaujolais *(wine)* 8

beaux-parents *m.pl.* stepparents (or in-laws) 3

bébé *m.* baby 7
beige beige 4
belge Belgian 1
Belgique *f.* Belgium 5
belle-mère *f.* (*pl.* **belles-mères**) stepmother (or mother-in-law) 3
belle-sœur *f.* sister-in-law 3
berk! yuck! awful! 8
besoin *m.* need
   avoir ~ de to need 9
beurre *m.* butter 8
   ~ d'arachide *m.* peanut butter 8
bibliothèque *f.* library 5
bien *m.* good 6
bien *adv.* well; fine 2
   ~ que although
   ~ sûr of course 8
bientôt soon
   À bientôt. See you soon. 5
Bienvenue! Welcome! 3
bière *f.* beer 2
billet *m.* bill (*paper money*) 9; ticket 12
bise *f.* kiss 5
bistro *m.* bar and café; bistro 5
bizarre weird; funny looking 4
blague *f.* joke
   sans ~! no kidding! 14
blanc (blanche) white 4
blessé(e) wounded 15
bleu(e) blue 4
bleuet *m.* blueberry (*French-Canadian*)
blond(e) blond 4
blouson *m.* windbreaker, jacket 4
bœuf *m.* beef 8
boire to drink 8
   voulez-vous ~ quelque chose? do you want to drink something? 2
boisson *f.* drink, beverage 2
boîte *f.* box, can 8
bol *m.* bowl 13
bon (bonne) good 2
   bon marché *adj. inv.* inexpensive 4
   bonne journée have a good day 1
bonbon *m.* candy 8
bonjour hello 1
bonnet de nuit *m.* party pooper
bonsoir good evening 2
bordeaux *m.* Bordeaux (*wine*) 8
bottes *f.pl.* boots 4

bouche *f.* mouth 9
bouchée *f.* mouthful
boucherie *f.* butcher shop 9
boulangerie *f.* bakery 5
boum *f.* party 10
bouquet *m.* bouquet 9
bout *m.* end, goal
bouteille *f.* bottle 8
boutique *f.* (gift, clothing) shop 9
bras *m.* arm 9
bridge *m.* bridge (*game*) 6
brie *m.* Brie (*cheese*) 8
brocoli *m.* broccoli 8
brosse *f.* brush
   ~ à cheveux *f.* hairbrush 13
   ~ à dents *f.* toothbrush 13
se brosser (les dents) to brush (one's teeth) 13
bruit *m.* noise 9
brûler to burn; to run through (light) 15
brun(e) brown(-haired) 4
bureau *m.* (*pl.* **bureaux**) desk; office 3
   ~ de poste *m.* post office 5
   ~ de tabac *m.* tobacco shop 5
but *m.* goal

ça (cela) that 4
   ~ dépend It depends 9
   ~ m'est égal It's all the same to me
   ~ ne vous concerne pas That's no concern of yours
   ~ va? How's it going? 2
   ~ va bien (I'm) fine 2
   ~ veut dire … it means … CP
cachet (d'aspirine) *m.* (aspirin) tablet 9
cadeau *m.* gift 9
cadre *m.* executive 4
café *m.* coffee 2; café 5
   ~ crème *m.* coffee with cream 2
cafétéria *f.* cafeteria 5
calculatrice *f.* calculator 3
calme calm 4
camarade de chambre *m./f.* roommate 3
camembert *m.* Camembert (*cheese*) 8
campagne *f.* country(side)
campus *m.* campus 5
Canada *m.* Canada 5
canadien(ne) Canadian 1

canicule *f.* heat wave
car because
carte *f.* map 12; menu 13
   ~ de crédit *f.* credit card 9
   ~ postale *f.* postcard 4
cartes *f.pl.* cards (*game*) 6
cas: en tout ~ in any case
cassis *m.* blackcurrant
ce/cet/cette/ces this, that, these, those 4
ce sont they are, there are 3
ceinture *f.* belt 4
   ~ de sécurité *f.* safety belt, seat belt 10
cela (ça) that 9
célèbre famous 14
célibataire single, unmarried 1
celle *f.* this (that) one
celles *f.pl.* these; those
celui *m.* this (that) one
cendre *f.* ash 8
cent one hundred 3
centime *m.* centime (1/100 of a euro) 3
centre commercial *m.* shopping center, mall 5
cependant however
céréales *f.pl.* cereal; grains 8
certainement surely, of course 1
c'est it is, this is 1
   c'est-à-dire that is to say
   ~ gentil à vous that's nice of you 2
   ~ pour vous it's for you 1
ceux *m.pl.* these; those
CFA (=Communauté financière africaine) African Financial Community
chacun(e) each
chagrin *m.* sorrow
chaîne (de télé) *f.* (TV) channel 14
chaise *f.* chair 3
chaleur *f.* heat
chambre *f.* bedroom 3; room
   camarade de ~ *m./f.* roommate 3
champignons *m.pl.* mushrooms 8
chance *f.* luck 12
   Bonne ~! Good luck! 12
changer (de) to change 10
chanson *f.* song 2
chanter to sing 2
chanteur/chanteuse *m./f.* singer 11

chapeau *m.* (*pl.* **chapeaux**) hat   4
chaque each, every   6
charcuterie *f.* pork butcher's; delicatessen   9
charmant(e) charming   3
chat *m.* cat   3
château *m.* castle   5
chaud(e) hot   2
  avoir ~ to be hot   8
  il fait ~ it's hot (warm)   CP, 4, 7
chauffage *m.* heat   13
chauffard *m.* bad driver   15
chauffeur *m.* driver   10
chaussée *f.* pavement   15
chaussettes *f.pl.* socks   4
chaussures *f.pl.* shoes   4
chauve bald   4
chef *m.* head (*person in charge*); boss; chef
chemise *f.* shirt   4
chemisier *m.* blouse   4
chèque *m.* check   9
  ~ de voyage *m.* traveler's check   9
cher (chère) dear   2; expensive   4
chercher to look for   2
chéri(e) *m./f.* dear, honey   10
cheveux *m.pl.* hair   4
chèvre *m.* goat cheese   8
chewing-gum *m.* chewing gum   9
chez at the home of   3
  ~ moi at my house   3
  ~ nous at our house; back home   3
  ~ vous at your house   3
chic *adj. inv.* chic; stylish   4
chien *m.* dog   3
chiffre *m.* number
chimie *f.* chemistry   5
Chine *f.* China   5
chinois(e) Chinese   1
chocolat chaud *m.* hot chocolate   2
choisir to choose   12
choix *m.* choice   8
chose *f.* thing   4
  pas grand-~ not much   5
  quelque ~ *m.* something   2
chouette great (*fam.*)   14
chut! shh!   10
cigare *m.* cigar   6
cimetière *m.* cemetery
cinéma *m.* movie theater   5
cinq five   CP
cinquante fifty   3

circulation *f.* traffic   15
citron pressé *m.* lemonade   2
classe *f.* class
  en ~ in class; to class   4
clé *f.* key   12
client/cliente *m./f.* customer   8
climatisation *f.* air conditioning   13
coca *m.* Coca-Cola   2
code postal *m.* zip code   9
coin *m.* corner
collège *m.* Jr. high school
combien (de) how many, how much   3
commander to order   8
comme like, as   2; how; since
  ~ ci, ~ ça so-so   2
  ~ il (elle) était …! how … he (she) was!   11
  ~ si … as if …
commencer to begin   7
  commencez! begin!   CP
comment how; what   3
  ~? what (did you say?)   CP, 2
  ~ allez-vous? how are you?   2
  ~ ça va? how is it going?   2
  ~ dit-on …? how do you say …?   CP
  ~ est (sont) …? what is (are) … like?   4
  ~ est-ce qu'on écrit …? how do you spell …?   2
  ~ je vais faire? what am I going to do?   12
  ~ trouvez-vous …? what do you think of …?   2
  ~ vous appelez-vous? what is your name?   1
commentaire *m.* commentary   10
commerce *m.* business   5
communication *f.* communication
  votre ~ de … your call from …   1
complet *m.* suit   4
complet (complète) full; complete   12
composter (un billet) to punch (a ticket)   12
compréhensif/compréhensive understanding   4
comprendre to understand; to include   8
  je ne comprends pas I don't understand   CP

compris(e) included; understood   8
comptabilité *f.* accounting   5
compter to count
condamner: être condamné(e) to be sentenced
conducteur/conductrice driver   15
conduire to drive   10
conduite *f.* driving   10
confirmer to confirm   12
confiture *f.* jam   8
confortable comfortable   4
confus(e) ashamed; embarrassed   14
congé *m.* leave, holiday
connaître to know; to be acquainted with, to be familiar with   10
conseil *m.* (piece of) advice   10
se consoler to console oneself   14
constamment constantly   10
constant(e) constant   10
content(e) happy   4
continuer to continue
  continuez continue   CP
contraire *m.* contrary, opposite
  au ~ on the contrary   4, 8
contravention *f.* traffic ticket   15
contre against; in exchange for   15
  par ~ on the other hand
corps *m.* body   9
côté *m.* side
  à ~ next door; to the side   5
  à ~ de next to, beside   5
se coucher to go to bed   6
couci-couça so-so
couleur *f.* color   4
  de quelle ~ est (sont) …? what color is (are) …?   4
couloir *m.* hall; corridor   5
coup *m.*: **~ d'envoi** kick-off
couper to cut   13
couple *m.* couple   14
cour *f.* court
couramment fluently
coureur/coureuse runner; cyclist
courir to run
cours *m.* course; class   5
course *f.* race
courses *f.pl.* errands, shopping   4
cousin/cousine *m./f.* cousin   3
couteau *m.* (*pl.* **couteaux**) knife   13
coûter to cost   9

coutume *f.* custom
craie *f.* chalk   CP
cravate *f.* tie   4
crèche *f.* daycare center
crédit: carte de ~ *f.* credit card   9
crème *f.* cream   2
crêpe *f.* crepe; French pancake   8
croire to believe, to think   14
   je crois que oui I think so   14
   je ne crois pas I don't think
     so   14
croissance *f.* increase, growth
croissant *m.* croissant   8
croque-monsieur *m.* grilled ham
  and cheese sandwich   8
croûte *f.* crust
crudités *f.pl.* raw vegetables   8
cuiller *f.* spoon   13
cuisine *f.* cooking; food   4;
  kitchen   3
cuisinière *f.* stove   3

d'abord at first   5
d'accord okay   5
   être ~ (avec) to agree (with)   5
dame *f.* lady   13
dames *f.pl.* checkers   6
dangereux (dangereuse)
  dangerous   11
dans in   2
   ~ une heure one hour from
     now   5
danser to dance   2
d'après according to
davantage additional, more
de (d') from, of   1
de rien you're welcome   12
décalage horaire *m.* time
  difference   5
décembre *m.* December   7
décider to decide
décombres *m.pl.* ruins
décrire to describe   6
déçu(e) disappointed   9
dehors outside
déjà already   6
déjeuner *m.* lunch   8
   petit ~ breakfast   8
déjeuner *v.* to have lunch   5
délicieux (délicieuse) delicious   8
demain tomorrow   5
   après-~ day after tomorrow   12
demande *f.* request   12
   faire une ~ to make a
     request   12

demander to ask   6
démarrer to start   10
demi(e) half
   et ~ half past (the hour)   5
demi- (frère, sœur) step (brother,
  sister)   3
demi-heure *f.* half hour   7
dent *f.* tooth   9
dentifrice *m.* toothpaste   9
départ *m.* departure   12
départementale *f.* departmental
  (local) highway   12
dépasser to pass
se dépêcher to hurry   13
dépendre to depend   9
   ça dépend (de ...) it (that)
     depends (on ...)   9
déprimé(e) depressed   9
depuis for   6; since   9
déranger to bother   1
   Excusez-moi de vous ~ Excuse
     me for bothering you   1
déraper to skid   15
dernier (dernière) last   6
   la dernière fois the last time   6
derrière behind   5
   juste ~ right behind   15
des some; any   3; of the
désagréable disagreeable   4
descendre to go down, get out
  of   7
désirer to want   2
désolé(e) sorry   9
dessert *m.* dessert   8
dessin animé *m.* cartoon   11
se détendre to relax   9
détester to hate, to detest   2
détruire to destroy
dette *f.* debt   15
deux two   CP, 1
   tous (toutes) les ~ both   12
devant in front of   5
devenir to become   7
deviner to guess
devoir *m.* obligation
   devoirs *m.pl.* homework   4
devoir *v.* must, to have to, to
  probably be, to be supposed to;
  to owe   5
d'habitude usually   4
Dieu *m.* God
   Mon Dieu! My goodness!   2
dimanche *m.* Sunday   5
dîner *m.* dinner   4
dîner *v.* to eat dinner   4

diplôme *m.* diploma   12
dire to say; to tell   14
   ... veut ~ ... ... means ...   6
   vous dites you say   3
discret (discrète) discreet,
  reserved   4
se disputer to argue   14
dissertation *f.* (term) paper   6
divorce *m.* divorce   14
divorcé(e) divorced   1
divorcer to get a divorce   14
dix ten   CP
dix-huit eighteen   CP
dix-neuf nineteen   CP
dix-sept seventeen   CP
doigt *m.* finger
dollar *m.* dollar   9
**DOM (=Département d'outre-
mer)** overseas department
  (equivalent of a state)
dommage *m.* pity, shame
   c'est ~ that's (it's) too bad   14
donc then; therefore
donner to give   4
   donnez-moi ... give me ...   CP
dont about/of which (whom);
  whose   14
dormir to sleep   6
dos *m.* back   9
d'où: vous êtes ~? where are
  you from?   2
douche *f.* shower   12
   prendre une douche to
     shower
doute *m.* doubt
   sans ~ probably   3
doux (douce) mild
douzaine *f.* dozen
douze twelve   CP
droit *m.* right *(entitlement)*
droit(e) *adj.* right
   à droite (de) to the right (of)   5
   tout droit straight ahead   5
drôle funny   14
durcir to harden
durée *f.* duration; length

eau *f.* (*pl.* **eaux**) water   2
   ~ minérale mineral water   2
échanger (contre) to trade
  (for)   15
échecs *m.pl.* chess   6
éclater to burst
école *f.* school   5

écouter to listen (to)   2
  écoutez! listen!   CP
écrire to write   6
  comment est-ce qu'on écrit…? how do you spell … ?   2
  écrivez votre nom! write your name!   CP
  … s'écrit … … is spelled …   2
écrivain *m.* writer   4
égal(e) (*m.pl.* **égaux**) equal
  cela (ça) m'est ~ I don't care   5
église *f.* church   5
Eh bien … Well then …
élève *m./f.* pupil   4
élire to elect
elle she, it   1; her   6
elles they   1; them   6
s'éloigner to move away
s'embrasser to kiss   14
émission (de télé) *f.* (TV) show   11
emmenthal *f.* Swiss cheese   8
emploi du temps *m.* schedule   5
employé/employée *m./f.* employee   4
emprunter to borrow   14
en *prep.* in   1; by, through
  ~ avance early   7
  ~ première (seconde) in first (second) class   12
  ~ retard late   7
  ~ tout cas in any case
  ~ voiture by car   7
en *pron.* some, of it (them); about it (them)   14
  je vous ~ prie don't mention it; you're welcome; please do   7
  vous n'~ avez pas? don't you have any?   9
enchanté(e) delighted (to meet you)   1
encore again   CP; still, more   3
  ~ à boire (manger)? more to drink (eat)?   8
  ~ de …? more …?   8
  pas ~ not yet   2
s'endormir to fall asleep   13
endroit *m.* place   5
enfant *m./f.* child   3
enfin finally   5
ennuyeux (ennuyeuse) boring   4
enseigne *f.* sign
enseigner to teach   2
ensemble together   CP, 2
ensoleillé(e) sunny

ensuite next, then   5
entendre to hear   9
  s'~ (avec) to get along (with)   14
  ~ parler de to hear about   15
  entendu agreed; understood   12
entre between, among   5
  ~ amis between (among) friends   1
entrée *m.* first course, appetizer
entreprise *f.* business
entrer to enter   7
  ~ en collision to hit, collide   15
  entrez! come in!   CP
envie: avoir ~ de to want to; to feel like   5
environ approximately   9
envoyer to send   6
épaule *f.* shoulder   9
épeler to spell   12
épicerie *f.* grocery store   5
épinards *m.pl.* spinach   8
époque *f.* time, period   11
  à cette ~ at that time; back then   11
épouser to marry   11
équilibré(e) stable
équipe *f.* team   11
escale *f.* stop(over)
escargot *m.* snail   10
esclave *m./f.* slave
Espagne *f.* Spain   5
espagnol(e) Spanish   1
espérer to hope   8
essayer to try
essentiel: il est ~ que it is essential that   13
est *m.* east
est-ce que (*question marker*)   2
estomac *m.* stomach   9
et and   1
étage *m.* floor   12
état *m.* state   5
  ~ civil marital status   1
États-Unis *m.pl.* United States   5
été *m.* summer   7
étranger/étrangère *m./f.* foreigner
étranger (étrangère) foreign   12
étroit(e) narrow; close
études *f.pl.* studies   15
étudiant(e) *m./f.* student   3
étudier to study   2
être to be   1
  ~ à to belong to   6

  ~ d'accord (avec) to agree (with)   5
  ~ en train de to be in the process of   11
  ~ originaire de to be a native of   7
  vous êtes d'où? where are you from?   2
Europe *f.* Europe
eux *m.pl. pron.* they, them   6
exact(e) exact, correct
  c'est ~ that's right   13
exagérer to exaggerate   2
examen *m.* test, exam   6
  à un ~ on an exam   6
excellent(e) excellent   2
excuser to excuse
  excusez-moi excuse me   1
  excusez-moi (-nous, etc.) d'être en retard excuse me (us, etc.) for being late   13
exemple *m.* example
  par ~ for example   6
exercice *m.* exercise   6
exiger (que) to demand (that)   13
expédier to send
extroverti(e) outgoing   4

fâché(e) angry   14
se fâcher to get angry   14
facile easy   9
façon *f.* way, manner   8
  sans ~ honestly, no kidding   8
faculté *f.*: **~ des lettres** College of Liberal Arts
faim *f.* hunger
  avoir ~ to be hungry   8
faire to do, to make   4
  ~ attention to pay attention   4
  ~ du pouce to hitchhike (*French-Canadian*)
  ~ du sport to play sports   6
  ~ la cuisine to cook   4
  ~ la lessive to do laundry
  ~ la sieste to take a nap   4
  ~ des provisions to do the grocery shopping   4
  ~ un voyage to take a trip   5
  ~ une demande to make a request   12
  ~ une promenade to take a walk; to take a ride   4
  il fait chaud it's hot out   CP, 4, 7

se ~ **des amis** to make friends 14

fait *m.* fact

au ~ ... by the way ... 2

falloir (il faut) to be necessary 4, 10

famille *f.* family 3

fatigué(e) tired 2

faut: il ~ ... it is necessary ... 4

il ~ que it is necessary that, (someone) must 13

il ne ~ pas que (someone) must not 13

faute *f.* fault; mistake 15

fauteuil *m.* armchair 3

faux (fausse) false; wrong 2

femme *f.* woman 1; wife 3

~ **d'affaires** businesswoman 4

~ **politique** (female) politician 4

fermé(e) closed 6

fermer to close 6

fermez le livre! close the book! CP

fermez la porte! close the door! CP

fermier/fermière *m./f.* farmer 4

fête *f.* holiday; party 7

feu *m.* (*pl.* **feux**) traffic light 10; fire

feuille *f.* leaf/sheet (of paper) 9

feuilleton *m.* soap opera; series 14

février *m.* February 7

fiançailles *f.pl.* engagement 14

fiancé(e) engaged 1

fier (fière) proud

fièvre *f.* fever 9

fille *f.* girl 3; daughter 3

film *m.* film, movie 5

fils *m.* son 3

fin *f.* end

finir to finish 12

flamand *m.* Flemish 5

fleur *f.* flower 9

fleuriste *m./f.* florist 9

fleuve *m.* river

flûte *f.* flute 6

~! darn!; shucks! 12

fois *f.* one time 6; times, multiplied by

à la ~ at the same time

deux ~ twice

la dernière ~ the last time 6

follement in a crazy manner 10

fonctionnaire *m./f.* civil servant 4

football (foot) *m.* soccer 6

~ **américain** *m.* football 6

formidable great, fantastic 14

fort *adv.* loudly, with strength 15

fou/folle *m./f.* fool; crazy person 10

fou (folle) (*m.pl.* **fous**) crazy 10

foulard *m.* scarf 4

fourchette *f.* fork 13

frais: il fait ~ it's cool 7

fraises *f.pl.* strawberries 8

franc *m.* franc 9

français(e) French 1

à la française in the French style 13

en français in French CP

France *f.* France 5

francophone French-speaking

frapper to knock

Frappez à la porte! Knock on the door! CP

freiner to brake 15

fréquenter (quelqu'un) to date (someone) 11

frère *m.* brother 3

frire to fry

frites *f.pl.* French fries 8

steak-~ *m.* steak with French fries 15

froid(e) cold 2

avoir ~ to be cold 8

il fait ~ it's cold CP, 7

fromage *m.* cheese 5

frontière *f.* border

fruit *m.* a piece of fruit 8

fumer to smoke 6

fumeur/fumeuse *m./f.* smoker

non-~ nonsmoker

fumeur *m.* smoking car 12;

non ~ nonsmoking car 12

fumeur/fumeuse *adj.* smoking 12

gagner to win; to earn

~ **(à la loterie)** to win (the lottery) 12

gants *m.pl.* gloves 4

garage *m.* garage 3

garçon *m.* boy 3; waiter 8

garder to keep; to look after 4

gare *f.* (train) station 3

gâteau *m.* (*pl.* **gâteaux**) cake 8

petit ~ cookie

gauche *adj.* left

à ~ (de) to the left (of) 5

gendarme *m.* (state) policeman 15

général: en ~ in general 2

généralement generally 4

généreux (généreuse) generous

genou *m.* knee 9

genoux *m.pl.* lap, knees 13

gens *m.pl.* people 4

gentil(le) nice 3

c'est ~ à vous that's nice of you 2

gestion *f.* management 5

glace *f.* ice cream 8

glissant(e) slippery 15

golf *m.* golf 6

gorge *f.* throat 9

goudron *m.* tar

goûter to taste 13

grand(e) big, tall 1

~ **magasin** *m.* department store 9

pas grand-chose not much 5

grand-mère *f.* (*pl.* **grands-mères**) grandmother 3

grand-père *m.* (*pl.* **grands-pères**) grandfather 3

grands-parents *m.pl.* grandparents 3

gras (grasse) fat

faire la grasse matinée to sleep in, to sleep late

gratuit(e) free

grippe *f.* flu 6

gris(e) grey 4

gros(se) fat; large 1

grossir to put on weight 12

guerre *f.* war 7

en temps de ~ in wartime

guitare *f.* guitar 6

gymnase *m.* gymnasium 5

gymnastique *f.* gymnastics 5

An asterisk indicates that no liaison or élision is made at the beginning of the word.

habile skilful

s'habiller to get dressed 13

habiter to live; to reside 2

où habitez-vous? where do you live? 1

habitude *f.* habit
  avoir l'~ de to be used to 5
  d'~ usually 4
*haricots verts *m.pl.* green beans 8
*hasard *m.* chance, luck
  par ~ by chance 15
heure *f.* hour CP, 1; (clock) time 5
  à l'~ on time 7
  dans une ~ one hour from now 5
  il est … heure(s) it is … o'clock CP, 5
  tout à l'~ in a little while 5; a little while ago 6
heureusement fortunately 6
heureux (heureuse) happy 4
*heurter to hit, run into 15
hier yesterday 6
histoire *f.* story 14
  quelle ~! what a story! 14
hiver *m.* winter 7
*hockey *m.* hockey 6
homme *m.* man 1
  ~ d'affaires businessman 4
  ~ politique politician 4
horaire *m.* timetable 12
*hors except; out of
*hors-d'œuvre *m. inv.* appetizer 8
hôtel *m.* hotel 1
hôtesse de l'air *f.* (female) flight attendant 11
huile (d'olive) *f.* (olive) oil
*huit eight CP
hypermarché *m.* giant supermarket 9

ici here 4
  par ~ this way, follow me 13
idiot/idiote *m./f.* idiot 15
il he, it 1
il y a there is (are) 3
  il n'y a pas de quoi you're welcome 13
  il n'y en a plus there is (are) no more 12
  ~ … jours … days ago 6
  qu'est-ce qu'~ ? what's the matter? 3
île *f.* island
ils they 1
imbécile *m./f.* imbecile 15
immeuble *m.* building

impair: nombre ~ *m.* odd number
impatience *f.* impatience 9
impatient(e) impatient 4
imperméable *m.* raincoat 4
important(e) important
  il est ~ que it is important that 13
incroyable *adj.* unbelievable, incredible 14
indications *f.pl.* directions 10
indiquer to tell; to indicate; to point out 12
indispensable indispensable, essential
  il est ~ que it is essential that 13
infirmier/infirmière *m./f.* nurse 4
informations *f.pl.* news 14
informatique *f.* computer science 5
ingénieur *m.* engineer 4
inondation *f.* flood
s'inquiéter to worry 13
insister to insist
  je n'insiste pas I won't insist 8
  si vous insistez if you insist 8
s'installer to move (into)
instrument *m.* instrument 6
intelligent(e) intelligent 4
intellectuel(le) intellectual 4
intention: avoir l' ~ de to plan to 5
interdiction *f.* ban
interdit(e) forbidden
  sens ~ *m.* one-way street 10
intéressant(e) interesting 4
s'intéresser à to be interested in 14
intérêt *m.* interest 9
intérieur *m.* inside
  à l'~ de inside of 6
interprète *m./f.* interpreter 4
intolérant(e) intolerant 4
inutile useless 12
inviter to invite 10
Irak *m.* Iraq 5
Irlande *f.* Ireland 5
Israël *m.* Israel 5
Italie *f.* Italy 5
italien(ne) Italian 1
ivre drunk 15

jamais ever, never
  ne … ~ never 4

jambe *f.* leg 9
jambon *m.* ham 8
janvier *m.* January 7
Japon *m.* Japan 5
japonais(e) Japanese 1
jardin *m.* garden
jaune yellow 4
je I 1
jean *m.* jeans 4
jeu *m.(pl.* **jeux)** game 6
jeudi *m.* Thursday 5
jeune young 1
jogging *m.* jogging 2
joli(e) pretty 1
jouer to play 2
  à quoi jouez-vous? what (game) do you play? 6
  de quoi jouez-vous? what (instrument) do you play? 6
jour *m.* day 2
  ~ de l'An New Year's Day 7
  quinze jours two weeks 11
journal *m.* newspaper 6
journée *f.* day
  bonne ~! have a nice day! 1
juillet *m.* July 7
juin *m.* June 7
jupe *f.* skirt 4
jurer to swear
  je te le jure I swear (to you) 14
jus *m.* juice
  ~ d'orange orange juice 2
jusqu'à *prep.* until 10
  jusqu'au bout right up till the end
juste *adv.* just; right
  ~ derrière moi right behind me 15

kilo *m.* kilogram 8
kiosque *m.* newsstand 9
kir *m.* kir 2

la (*see* **le**)
là there 4
laid(e) ugly 1
laisser to leave; to let 10
  laisse-moi (laissez-moi) tranquille! leave me alone! 10
lait *m.* milk 2
lamelle *f.* strip
langue *f.* language 5
laquelle (*see* **lequel**)

las(se) tired
lave-linge *m.* washing machine 3
lave-vaisselle *m.* dishwasher 3
laver to wash 13
　se ~ to get washed; to wash up 13
le/la/l'/les *art.* the 2; *pron.* him, her, it, them 8
leçon *f.* lesson 10
légume *m.* vegetable 8
lent(e) slow 10
lentement slowly 10
lequel/laquelle/lesquels/ lesquelles which? which one(s)? 14
les (*see* **le**)
lesquel(le)s (*see* **lequel**)
lessive *f.* wash; laundry 4
lettre *f.* letter 6
leur *pron.* (to) them 14
leur(s) *adj.* their 3
lever to lift; to raise 13
　se ~ to get up; to stand up 6
　Levez-vous! Get up! CP
librairie *f.* bookstore 5
libre free 5; vacant
lien *m.* tie; bond
lieu *m.* (*pl.* **lieux**) place 5
　avoir ~ to take place 11
limonade *f.* lemon-lime soda 2
lire to read 6
　lisez! read! CP
lit *m.* bed 3
litre *m.* liter 9
littérature *f.* literature 5
livre *f.* pound 9
livre *m.* book CP, 3
loi *f.* law
loin (de) far (from) 5
loisir *m.* leisure activity
long (longue) long 9
longtemps a long time 6
louer to rent 12
lui he, him 6; (to) him; (to) her 14
lumière *f.* light
lundi *m.* Monday 5
lunettes *f.pl.* eyeglasses 4
lycée *m.* high school

ma (*see* **mon**)
machine à laver *f.* washing machine

Madame (Mme) Mrs., ma'am 1
Mademoiselle (Mlle) Miss 1
magasin *m.* store 4
　grand ~ department store 9
magazine *m.* magazine 6
Maghreb *m. the three North African countries of Algeria, Morocco, and Tunisia*
mai *m.* May 7
maigrir to lose weight 12
maillot de bain *m.* bathing suit 13
main *f.* hand 9
maintenant now 5
maire *m.* mayor 11
　adjoint au ~ deputy mayor
mairie *f.* town (city) hall 11
mais but 2
maison *f.* house 3
mal *m.* harm; pain; evil
　avoir ~ (à) to be sore, to have a pain (in) 9
mal *adv.* poorly 2; badly
malade sick 2
maladie *f.* illness, disease
malgré in spite of
manger to eat 2
manquer to miss
manteau *m.* (*pl.* **manteaux**) coat 4
marchand/marchande *m./f.* merchant 9
marché *m.* (open-air) market 9
　~ aux puces flea market 9
mardi *m.* Tuesday 5
mari *m.* husband 3
mariage *m.* marriage; wedding 11
marié(e) married 1
se marier (avec) to marry 14
marine *f.* navy
Maroc *m.* Morocco 5
marocain(e) Moroccan 1
marque *f.* make, brand 15
marron *adj. inv.* brown 4
mars *m.* March 7
match *m.* game 10
matin *m.* morning 2
matinée: faire la grasse ~ to sleep in late
mauvais(e) bad 4
　il fait ~ the weather is bad 7
mayonnaise *f.* mayonnaise 8
me me 10; (to) me 14

méchant(e) nasty; mean 4
méchoui *m.* roast lamb (*North-African specialty*)
médecin *m.* doctor 4
médicament *m.* medicine 9
se méfier de to watch out for
meilleur(e) better 11
　Avec mon ~ souvenir With my best regards 4
　le/la ~ the best 11
　~ ami(e) *m./f.* best friend 1
membre *m.* member 3
même even 14; same
　-~(s) -self (-selves) 2
ménage *m.* housework 4
ménagère *f.* housewife 4
menu *m.* (fixed price) menu 13
merci thank you 1; (no) thanks 2
　non, ~ no, thank you 2
mercredi *m.* Wednesday 5
mère *f.* mother 2, 3
mes (*see* **mon**)
mesdames *f.pl.* ladies 13
message *m.* message
　~ électronique e-mail 6
messieurs *m.pl.* gentlemen 13
mesure *f.* (unit of) measure
météo(rologie) *f.* weather 14
météorologique *adj.* weather
mettre to put; to place; to lay 13
　Mettez …! Put …! CP
　~ la table to set the table 13
　~ le chauffage to turn on the heat 13
　se ~ à table to sit down to eat 13
mexicain(e) Mexican 1
Mexico Mexico City
Mexique *m.* Mexico 5
miam! yum! 8
midi noon 5
le mien/la mienne mine 5
mieux better 11
　il vaut ~ que it is preferable that, it is better that 10
　j'aime le ~ I like best 11
militaire *m.* serviceman/ servicewoman 4
mille *inv.* one thousand 3
milliard *m.* billion 3
millier *m.* thousand
million *m.* million 3
mince thin 1
　~! darn it! 12

minuit midnight   5
minute *f.* minute   5
mobylette *f.* moped, motorized bicycle   3
moi me   1; I, me   6
  ~ aussi me too   2
  ~ non plus me neither   2
moins less   11
  au ~ at least   6
  j'aime le ~ I like least   11
  ~ le quart quarter to (the hour)   5
mois *m.* month   6
moment *m.* moment; time   2
  à quel ~ (de la journée)? at what time (of day)?
mon, ma, mes my   3
monde *m.* world   7
  tout le ~ everybody   4
monnaie *f.* change, coins   9
Monsieur (M.) Mr., Sir; man   1
monter to go up; to get into   7
montre *f.* watch   4
montrer to show   14
morceau *m.* (*pl.* **morceaux**) piece   8
mort *f.* death   15
mort(e) dead
mot *m.* word   6
  plus un ~ not one more word   10
moto *f.* motorcycle   3
mourir to die   7
moutarde *f.* mustard   8
moyenne *f.* average
musée *m.* museum   5
musique *f.* music   6
myrtille *f.* blueberry

nager to swim   2
naïf (naïve) naive   4
naissance *f.* birth
naître to be born   7
  je suis né(e) I was born   3
  né(e) born
nappe *f.* tablecloth   13
nationalité *f.* nationality   1
naturellement naturally   8
navire *m.* ship
ne (n') not   1
  ~ ... jamais never   4
  ~ ... pas not   1
  ~ ... personne no one, nobody, not anyone   15
  ~ ... plus no more, no longer   8

  ~ ... que only   11
  ~ ... rien nothing, not anything   6
n'est-ce pas? right?; are you?; don't they?; etc.   2
nécessaire: il est ~ que it is necessary that   13
négritude *f.* negritude *(system of black cultural and spiritual values)*
neiger to snow   7
  il neige it's snowing   CP, 7
nerveux (nerveuse) nervous   4
nettoyer to clean   6
neuf nine   CP
neuf (neuve) brand-new   10
  quoi de neuf? what's new?   5
neveu *m.* (*pl.* **neveux**) nephew   3
nez *m.* nose   9
  le ~ qui coule runny nose   9
ni ... ni neither ... nor
nièce *f.* niece   3
Noël *m.* Christmas   7
  le père ~ Santa Claus   1
noir(e) black   4
nom *m.* name   CP, 1
  à quel ~ ...? in whose name ...?   12
  ~ de famille last name   1
nombre *m.* number   1
nommer to name
non no   1
non plus neither   6
nord *m.* north
note *f.* note; grade, mark   4
notre, nos our   3
nourrir to feed, to nourish
nous we   1; us   10; (to) us   14
nouveau/nouvel (nouvelle) (*m.pl.* **nouveaux**) new   4
novembre *m.* November   7
nuit *f.* night   2
  Bonne ~ Pleasant dreams.   5
numéro (de téléphone) *m.* (telephone) number   4

obéir to obey   12
occidental(e) western
occupé(e) busy   6
s'occuper de to be busy with, to take care of   7
  occupe-toi de tes oignons! mind your own business!   11
octobre *m.* October   7
œil *m.* (*pl.* **yeux**) eye   9

  mon ~! my eye!, I don't believe it!   10
œuf *m.* egg   8
œuvre *f.* work
offrir to offer
oh là là! oh dear!, wow!   9
oignon *m.* onion   8
  occupe-toi de tes oignons! mind your own business!   11
oiseau *m.* bird   5
omelette *f.* omelet   8
on one, people, we, they, you   1
oncle *m.* uncle   3
onze eleven   CP
optimiste optimistic   4
or *m.* gold
orange *f.* orange *(fruit)*   4
  jus d'~ *m.* orange juice   2
orange *adj. inv.* orange   4
orangina *m.* orange soda   2
ordinaire ordinary, everyday   4
ordinateur *m.* computer   3
ordre *m.* order
oreille *f.* ear   9
oriental(e) eastern
original(e) (*m.pl.* **originaux**) different; novel; original   14
ou or   1
où where   1
oublier to forget   6
ouest *m.* west
oui yes   1
ouvert(e) open   12
ouverture *f.* opening
  heures d'~ hours of business
ouvrier/ouvrière *m./f.* laborer   4
ouvrir to open
  ouvrez la porte! open the door!   CP

pain *m.* bread   8
  ~ de mie *m.* sandwich bread
  ~ grillé toast   8
pâle pale   15
pantalon *m.* (pair of) pants   4
papier *m.* paper   9
paquet *m.* package   9
par by; through   5
  ~ contre on the other hand
  ~ exemple for example   6
  ~ ici (come) this way, follow me
  ~ jour per day   5
parce que because   6

pardon: ~? pardon?, what did you say? CP
  je vous demande ~ please excuse me; I beg your pardon 9
parents *m.pl.* parents; relatives 3
paresseux (paresseuse) lazy 4
parfait(e) perfect 5
parking *m.* parking lot 5
parler to speak 2
  ~ de to tell about 7
  ~ fort to speak loudly 15
part *f.* behalf, portion
  de ma ~ for me; on my behalf
partie *f.* part
partir (de) to leave (from) 6
  à partir de from that time on
pas no, not
  ne … ~ not 1
  ~ du tout! not at all! 1
  ~ encore not yet 2
  ~ grand-chose not much 5
  ~ trop bien not too well 2
passé *m.* past
passer to pass
  ~ un an to spend a year 3
  ~ un test to take a test 5
se passer to happen; to take place
passionnant(e) exciting 14
pastille *f.* lozenge 9
pâte dentifrice *f.* toothpaste 9
pâté *m.* pâté *(meat spread)* 8
patiemment patiently 10
patient(e) patient 4
patiner to skate 2
patinoire *f.* skating rink 10
pâtisserie *f.* pastry shop; pastry 9
patrie *f.* homeland
patron/patronne *m./f.* boss 4
pauvre poor 4, 11
payer to pay (for) 9
pays *m.* country 5
Pays-Bas *m.pl.* Netherlands 5
pêche *f.* fishing
pédagogie *f.* education, teacher preparation 5
pelouse *f.* lawn
pendant for; during 6
  ~ combien de temps …? how long …? 6
  ~ que while 6
penser to think 8
  qu'en penses-tu? what do you think of it (of them)? 8
perdre to lose 9
  ~ patience to lose (one's) patience 9

père *m.* father 2
père Noël *m.* Santa Claus 1
permettre to allow
  permettez-moi de me présenter allow me to introduce myself 1
  vous permettez? may I? 1
permis de conduire *m.* driver's license 10
personnage *m.* character; individual
personne *f.* person *(male or female)* 1
  ne … ~ no one, nobody, not anyone 15
personnellement personally 10
pessimiste pessimistic 4
pétanque *f.* lawn bowling 6
petit(e) small, short 1
  ~ ami(e) *m./f.* boyfriend/ girlfriend 3
  ~ déjeuner *m.* breakfast 8
  ~-fils *m.* (*pl.* **petits-fils**) grandson 3
  petite-fille *f.* (*pl.* **petites-filles**) granddaughter 3
  petits-enfants *m.pl.* grandchildren 3
  petits pois *m.pl.* peas 8
peu (de) little, few 8
  un ~ a little bit 2
peuple *m.* people
peur *f.* fear
  avoir ~ to be afraid 8
peut-être maybe; perhaps 2
pharmacie *f.* pharmacy 5
pharmacien/pharmacienne *m./f.* pharmacist
photo *f.* photograph 3
  sur la ~ in the picture 3
physique physical 15
piano *m.* piano 6
pièce *f.* room 3; play 6
  ~ (de monnaie) coin 9
pied *m.* foot 9
pilote *m.* pilot 11
pilule *f.* pill 9
pique-nique *m.* picnic 12
piscine *f.* swimming pool 5
pitié *f.* pity
  avoir ~ (de) to have pity, to feel sorry (for) 10
pizza *f.* pizza 2
place *f.* seat; room; place 7
plaire to please

s'il vous plaît please 2
plaisanterie *f.* joke 14
plaisir *m.* pleasure
  au ~ see you again 5
  avec ~ with pleasure 2
plan *m.* map (city; house)
plancher *m.* floor 13
plat *m.* course, dish 8
plein(e) full
pleurer to cry 2
pleuvoir to rain 7
  il pleut it's raining CP, 7
  il pleuvait it was raining 11
  il pleuvra it will rain 12
plupart *f.* majority
  la ~ (de) most (of) 6
plus more 11
  il n'y en a ~ there is (are) no more 12
  le/la/les ~ … the most … 11
  moi non ~ nor I, me neither 6
  ne … ~ no more, no longer 8
plusieurs several
poêle *f.* frying pan
poème *m.* poem 6
pois *m.pl.:* **petits ~** peas 8
poisson *m.* fish 2
poivre *m.* pepper 13
police *f.* police (force)
  agent de ~ police officer 15
politique *f.* politics 2; policy
politique: homme/femme ~ *m./f.* politician 4
pomme *f.* apple 8
pomme de terre *f.* potato 8
populaire popular 11
porc *m.* pork 8
portable *m.* cell phone 7
porte *f.* door 1
porter to wear; to carry 4
portugais(e) Portuguese 5
poser une question to ask a question 12
possession *f.* possession 3
postale: carte ~ *f.* postcard 4
poste *f.* post office; mail
  bureau de ~ *m.* post office 5
poster to mail 7
pouce *m.* thumb
  faire du ~ to hitchhike *(French-Canadian)*
poulet *m.* chicken 8
pour for, in order to 2
  ~ ce qui est de with respect to
pourquoi why 2
  ~ pas? why not? 6

pourvoir to provide
pouvoir *m.* power
pouvoir *v.* to be able; to be
  allowed   10; can
  je peux I can   9
  on peut one can   9
  pourriez-vous …? could
    you …?   12
  pouvez-vous me dire …? can
    you tell me …?   9
  puis-je …? may I …?   12
préciser to specify
préféré(e) favorite   5
préférence *f.:* **de ~** preferably
préférer to prefer   8
  je préfère que I prefer that   13
premier (première) first   5
  en première in first class   12
prendre to take; to eat, to drink   8
  prenez …! take …!   CP
prénom *m.* first name   1
préparer (un cours) to prepare
  (a lesson)   6
près (de) near   1
  tout ~ very near   12
présenter to introduce
  je vous présente … let me
    introduce you to …   3
presque almost   14
prêter to lend   14
prie: je vous en ~ you're
  welcome   7
printemps *m.* spring   7
prise de conscience *f.* awareness
prix *m.* price   12
problème *m.* problem
  Pas de problème! No problem!
prochain(e) next   5
  À la prochaine. Until next
    time.   5
proche near; close
produit *m.* product; article
professeur (prof) *m.* (secondary
  or college) teacher   1
profession *f.* profession, occupation
progrès *m.* progress   14
promenade *f.* walk; ride   4
  faire une ~ to take a walk; to
    take a ride   4
se promener to take a walk,
  ride   13
promettre to promise
  c'est promis it's a promise   10
propos: à ~ de regarding, on the
  subject of   8

propre clean   4; specific; own
propriétaire *m./f.* owner   10
provisions *f.pl.* groceries   4
  faire des ~ to do the grocery
    shopping   4
provoquer to cause
prudemment carefully   10
prudent(e) cautious   10
publicité *f.* publicity;
  commercial   14
puis then; next   4
puis-je …? may I …?   12
puisque since
pull-over (pull) *m.* sweater   4
pyjama *m.* (pair of) pajamas   13

quand when   4
quantité *f.* quantity
quarante forty   3
quart quarter
  et ~ quarter past, quarter
    after   5
  moins le ~ quarter to, quarter
    till   5
quatorze fourteen   CP
quatre four   CP, 1
quatre-vingt-dix ninety   3
quatre-vingt-onze ninety-one   3
quatre-vingt-un eight-one   3
quatre-vingts eighty   3
que that
  ne … ~ only   11
  ~ …? what …?   4
quel(le) …? which …?   4
  quel âge avez-vous? how old
    are you?   3
  quel jour est-ce? what day is
    it?   5
  quelle …! what a …!   2
  quelle est votre nationalité?
    what is your nationality?   1
  quelle heure est-il? what time
    is it?   5
quelque chose *m.* something   2
quelquefois sometimes   4
quelques a few; some   8
quelqu'un someone   2
qu'est-ce que/qui what?   4
  qu'est-ce que c'est? what is
    this? what is it?   4
  qu'est-ce que tu aimes? what
    do you like?   2
  qu'est-ce que vous avez

comme …? what do you have
  for (in the way of) …?   8
  qu'est-ce que vous voulez?
    what do you want?   2
  qu'est-ce qu'il y a …? what is
    there …? what's the matter?   3
qui who   1
  qu'est-ce ~ …? what …?   4
quinze fifteen   CP
  ~ jours two weeks   11
quoi what
  il n'y a pas de ~ don't mention
    it, you're welcome   13
  ~ de neuf? what's new?   5
quoique although

raconter to tell   14
radio *f.* radio   2
raison *f.* reason
  avoir ~ to be right   8
raisonnable reasonable   10
ralentir to slow down   12
rapide rapid, fast   10
rapidement rapidly   10
rarement rarely   4
ravi(e) delighted   14
récemment recently   6
recette *f.* recipe
recommander to recommend   12
reculer to back up   10
récuser to exclude; to challenge
réduire to reduce
réfrigérateur *m.* refrigerator   3
refuser to refuse
regarder to watch; to look at   2
regretter to be sorry   14
  je regrette I'm sorry   8; I miss
relief *m.* relief, hilly area
remarquer to notice   6
remercier to thank   12
remplacer to replace
rencontrer to meet   5, 14
rendez-vous *m.* meeting; date   5
  avoir ~ to have an
    appointment, meeting
rendre to give back   9
  ~ visite à qqn to visit
    someone   9
renseignement *m.* item of
  information   12
(se) renseigner to inform
  (oneself); to find out about

rentrer to go (come) back; to go (come) home   7

repas *m.* meal   8

répéter to repeat; to practice   8
   répétez, s'il vous plaît please repeat   CP

répondre (à) to answer   9
   répondez answer   CP

réponse *f.* answer

se reposer to rest   13

RER *m. train to Paris suburbs*   2

réserver to reserve   9

résidence (universitaire) *f.* dormitory   5

responsabilité *f.* responsibility   11

restaurant *m.* restaurant   5

rester to stay   5; to remain
   il vous reste …? do you still have …?   12

résultat *m.* result; outcome

retard *m.* delay
   en ~ late   7

retour *m.* return
   aller-~ round-trip ticket   12

retourner to go back, to return   7

rétroviseur *m.* rearview mirror   10

réunion *f.* meeting   13

réussir (à) to succeed; to pass (a test)   12

se réveiller to wake up   13

revenant *m.* ghost   14

revenir to come back   7

revoir to see again
   au ~ good-bye   1

rez-de-chaussée *m.* ground floor   12

rhume *m.* cold *(illness)*   9

riche rich   12

ridicule ridiculous   14

rien nothing
   de ~ you're welcome; don't mention it, not at all   12
   ne … ~ nothing, not anything   6

riz *m.* rice   8

robe *f.* dress   4
   ~ de mariée wedding dress   11

robinet *m.* faucet   6

roi *m.* king

roman *m.* novel   6
   ~ policier detective story   6

rose *adj.* pink   4

rôti (de bœuf) *m.* (beef) roast   9

rouge red   4

rouler to roll; to move *(vehicle)*; to go   15

route *f.* route, way, road   10, 12

roux (rousse) red(-haired)   4

rue *f.* street   9

rugby *m.* rugby   6

russe Russian   1

Russie *f.* Russia   5

sa *(see* **son***)*

s'agir to be about
   il s'agit de it's a matter of

saison *f.* season   7

salade *f.* salad   8
   ~ verte green salad   8

sale dirty   4

salle *f.* room
   ~ à manger dining room   3
   ~ de bain bathroom   3
   ~ de classe classroom   P, 5
   ~ de séjour living room; den   3

salon *m.* living room   3

salut! hi!   2; bye (-bye)   5

salutation *f.* greeting

samedi *m.* Saturday   5

s'amuser to have a good time; to have fun   6

sandwich *m.* sandwich   8

sans without   6
   ~ blague! no kidding   14
   ~ doute probably   3
   ~ façon honestly, no kidding   8

santé *f.* health
   à votre ~! (here's) to your health!; cheers!   2

sardine *f.* sardine   9

saucisse *f.* sausage   9

saumon *m.* salmon   8

savoir to know   12
   je ne sais pas I don't know   2

saxophone *m.* saxophone   6

sciences *f.pl.* science   5
   ~ économiques economics   5

scolaire *adj.* school
   année ~ *f.* school year   10

se oneself   6

sec (sèche) dry

sécheresse *f.* drought

second(e) second
   en seconde in (by) second class   12

seize sixteen   CP

séjour *m.* stay

sel *m.* salt   13

semaine *f.* week   5

semestre *m.* semester   6

Sénégal *m.* Senegal   5

sénégalais(e) Senegalese   1

sens interdit *m.* one-way street   10

se séparer to separate (from each other)   14

sept seven   CP

septembre *m.* September   7

sérieusement seriously   10

sérieux (sérieuse) serious   10

serveur/serveuse *m./f.* waiter/waitress   8

service *m.* service
   à votre ~ at your service

serviette *f.* towel   12; napkin   13

ses *(see* **son***)*

seul(e) alone; only   5
   un ~ a single

seulement only   2

short *m.* (pair of) shorts   4

si *conj.* if   3
   s'il vous plaît please   2

si *adv.* so   10
   ~! yes!   3

siècle *m.* century   10

sieste *f.* nap   4
   faire la ~ to take a nap   4

simple simple, plain   4
   aller ~ one-way ticket   12
   c'est bien ~ it's quite easy

sincère sincere   11

se situer to be situated

six six   CP

skier to ski   2

skis *m.pl.* skis   13

smoking *m.* tuxedo   11

SNCF *f. French railroad system*   2

sœur *f.* sister   3

sofa *m.* sofa   3

soi oneself   6

soif: avoir ~ to be thirsty   8

soir *m.* evening   2
   ce ~ tonight   5
   tous les soirs every night   6

soirée *f.* party   13; evening

soixante sixty   3

soixante-dix seventy   3

soixante-douze seventy-two   3

soixante et onze seventy-one   3

soleil *m.* sun   7
  Il fait (du) ~ It's sunny.   CP
son, sa, ses his, her, its   3
sorte *f.* kind   8
  quelle(s) ~(s) de …? what kind(s) of …?   8
  toutes sortes de choses all kinds of things   9
sortir to go out   6
  je vais ~ I'm going to go out   5
  sortez! leave!   CP
souci *m.* worry; care   11
souffler to blow
souhaiter (que) to wish; to hope (that)   13
soupe *f.* soup   8
sourire *m.* smile   13
sourire *v.* to smile   13
souris *f.* mouse   5
sous under   5
  ~-sol *m.* basement   3
souvenir *m.* memory; recollection   4
se souvenir (de) to remember   13
souvent often   2
sportif (sportive) athletic   4
statue *f.* statue   11
steak *m.* steak
  ~-frites steak with French fries   15
stéréo *f.* stereo   3
stop *m.* stop sign   10
stressé(e) stressed   11
stupide stupid   4
sucre *m.* sugar   13
sud *m.* south
Suède *f.* Sweden   5
suédois(e) Swedish   1
Suisse *f.* Switzerland   5
suisse *adj.* Swiss   1
suite: tout de ~ right away   1
suivant(e) following, next   5
superficie *f.* area
supermarché *m.* supermarket   9
supplément *m.* extra charge; supplement   12
sur on   3
sûr(e) sure
  bien ~ of course   8
sûrement surely, definitely   14
surveiller to watch
sweat-shirt *m.* sweatshirt   4

TGV *m.* *very fast train*   7
tabac *m.* tobacco; tobacco shop   9
  bureau de ~ tobacco shop   5
table *f.* table   CP, 1
  à ~ at dinner, at the table   6
tableau *m.* chalkboard   CP
taille *f.* size, height
se taire to be quiet
  tais-toi! (taisez-vous!) keep quiet!   10
tant so much; so many   6
tante *f.* aunt   3
tard late   6
tarder to be a long time coming   13
tarte *f.* pie   8
tasse *f.* cup   2
taux *m.* rate
tchao bye   5
te you   10; (to) you   14
tee-shirt *m.* tee-shirt   4
téléphone *m.* telephone   1
  au ~ on the telephone   6
  ~ portable *m.* cell phone   7
téléphoner (à) to telephone   6
télévision (télé) *f.* television   2
témoin *m.* witness   15
temps *m.* time   6; weather   4
  emploi du ~ *m.* schedule   4
  quel ~ fait-il? what is the weather like?   4
tendance *f.* tendency, trend
  avoir ~ à to tend to   12
tennis *m.* tennis   2
  jouer au ~ to play tennis   2
  ~ *f.pl.* tennis shoes   4
tentation *f.* temptation
terre *f.* earth, land   9
tête *f.* head   9
thé *m.* tea   2
théâtre *m.* theater
Tiens! Well! Gee!   3
timbre *m.* stamp   9
toi you   4
toilettes *f.pl.* restroom   3
toit *m.* roof   5
tomate *f.* tomato   8
tomber to fall   2
ton, ta, tes your   3
tort *m.* wrong
  avoir ~ to be wrong; to be unwise   8
tôt early   6
toujours always   4; still

toupet *m.* nerve
tour *f.* tower   11
tour *m.* turn, tour   11
tourner to turn   7
tous *pron. m.pl.* all   4
Toussaint *f.* All Saints' Day
tousser to cough   9
tout/toute/tous/toutes *adj.* all; every; the whole   12
  tous les deux (toutes les deux) both   12
  tous les soirs every night
  tout le monde everybody   CP, 12
  tout le week-end all weekend (long)   5
  toute la famille the whole family   11
tout *adv.* completely; very   12
  À ~ de suite See you very soon
  ~ à l'heure a little while ago, in a little while   5
  ~ de suite right away   12
  ~ près very near   7
tout *pron. inv.* all, everything
  pas du ~ ! not at all!   1
train *m.* train   3
  être en ~ de to be in the process of   11
tranche *f.* slice   8
tranquille calm   10
travail (manuel) *m.* (manual) work   4
travailler to work   2
travailleur (travailleuse) hardworking   4
travers: à ~ throughout
treize thirteen   CP
tremblement de terre *m.* earthquake
trente thirty   3
très very   1
tricot *m.* knitting; sweater
triste sad   4
trois three   CP, 1
trompette *f.* trumpet   6
trop (de) too much, too many   3
trouver to find, to be of the opinion   2
  se ~ to be located
  où se trouve (se trouvent) …? where is (are) …?   5
  vous trouvez? do you think so?   2

truite *f.* trout   8
tu you *(familiar)*   1
tuer to kill   15

un(e) one   CP, 1; one, a, an   3
union *f.*: **~ douanière** customs union
unique unique
  enfant ~ *m./f.* only child
université *f.* university   1
universitaire *(adj.)* university   5

vacances *f.pl.* vacation   6
  bonnes ~! have a good vacation!   6
  en ~ on vacation   6
vague *f.* wave
vaisselle *f.* dishes   4
valeur *f.* value
valise *f.* suitcase
valoir mieux (il vaut mieux) to be better   10
valse *f.* waltz
vanille *f.*: **glace à la ~** *f.* vanilla ice cream   8
vaut: il ~ mieux que it is preferable that, it is better that   13
véhicule *m.* vehicle   10
vélo *m.* bicycle   3
  faire du ~ to go bike riding   6
vendeur/vendeuse *m./f.* salesman/saleswoman   4
vendre to sell   9
vendredi *m.* Friday   5
venir to come   7
  d'où venez-vous? where do you come from?   7
  je viens de ... I come from ...   2
  ~ de ... to have just ...   7
vent *m.* wind

  il fait du ~ it's windy   CP, 7
véranda *f.* porch   3
vérifier to verify; to check   12
vérité *f.* truth   14
verre *m.* glass   2
vers toward   5
  ~ (8 heures) approximately, around (8 o'clock)   5
verser to pour   13
vert(e) green   4
veste *f.* sportcoat   4
vêtement *m.* article of clothing   4
veuf/veuve *m./f.* widower/widow   1
veux *(see* **vouloir***)*
viande *f.* meat   8
victime *f.* victim   7
vie *f.* life   4
  c'est la ~ that's life   6
  gagner sa ~ to earn one's living
vieux/vieil (vieille) old   1
vigne *f.* vine; vineyard
ville *f.* city   4; town
vin *m.* wine   2
vingt twenty   CP
vingt-deux twenty-two   CP
vingt et un twenty-one   CP
violet(te) purple   4
violon *m.* violin   6
visite: rendre ~ à to visit (a person)   9
visiter to visit (a place)
vite quickly   10
vitesse *f.* speed   10
  à toute ~ at top speed   10
vivement eagerly
vivre to live
voici here is; here are   3
voilà there is; there are   1
voir to see   14
  tu vas ~ you're going to see   5
  tu vois you see   11

voisin/voisine *m./f.* neighbor   11
voiture *f.* automobile   3
  en ~ by car   7
voix *f.* voice   7
vol *m.* flight   12
volant *m.* steering wheel   10
volontiers gladly   2
votre, vos your   1
vôtre: à la ~! (here's) to yours!, to your health!   2
vouloir to want, to wish   10
  je veux bien gladly; yes, thanks   2
  je veux que I want   13
  je voudrais I would like   2, 13
  ... veut dire ... ... means ... CP, 6
vous you *(formal; familiar pl.)*   1; (to) you   14
voyage *m.* trip, voyage   5
  chèque de ~ *m.* traveler's check   9
  faire un ~ to take a trip   5
voyager to travel   2
vrai(e) true   2
vraiment really   2

week-end *m.* weekend   5
  tout le ~ all weekend (long)   5
wolof *m.* Wolof *(language)*   5

y there   7
  allez- ~ go ahead   12
  il y a there is (are)   3
yeux *m.pl.* eyes   4

zéro zero   CP, 3
Zut! Darn!   12, 15

Vocabulaire

This vocabulary list includes only the active words and phrases listed in the *Vocabulaire actif* sections. Only those French equivalents that occur in the text are given. Expressions are listed according to the key word. The symbol ~ indicates repetition of the key word.

The following abbreviations are used:

adj.	adjective	*m.*	masculine
adv.	adverb	*m.pl.*	masculine plural
conj.	conjunction	*n.*	noun
fam.	familiar	*pl.*	plural
f.	feminine	*prep.*	preposition
f.pl.	feminine plural	*pron.*	pronoun
inv.	invariable	*v.*	verb

a, an un(e)
able: be ~ pouvoir
about de; environ
  ~ 8 o'clock vers 8 heures
  ~ it (them) en
  hear ~ entendre parler de
absolutely absolument
accept accepter
accident accident *m.*
accompany accompagner
according to d'après
accordion accordéon *m.*
accounting comptabilité *f.*
acquainted: be ~ with connaître
activity activité *f.*
actor/actress acteur/actrice *m./f.*
address *n.* adresse *f.*
adore adorer
advance *v.* avancer
advertisement annonce *f.*
advice (piece of) conseil *m.*
afraid: be ~ avoir peur
after après
afternoon après-midi *m.*
  in the ~ de l'après-midi
again encore
against contre
age âge *m.*
ago il y a …
agree (with) être d'accord (avec)
  agreed entendu

ahead: go ~ allez-y
  straight ~ tout droit
air conditioning climatisation *f.*
airplane avion *m.*
airport aéroport *m.*
all *pron./adj.* tout
  (toute/tous/toutes)
  ~ weekend (long) tout le
  weekend
  not at ~! pas du tout!
allow permettre
  ~ me to introduce myself
  permettez-moi de me présenter
almost presque
alone seul(e)
  leave me ~! laisse-moi (laissez-
  moi) tranquille!
already déjà
also aussi
always toujours
  not ~ pas toujours
American *adj.* américain(e)
amusing *adj.* amusant(e)
anchovy anchois *m.*
and et
angry fâché(e)
  get ~ se fâcher
answer *n.* réponse *f.*
answer *v.* répondre (à)
anyone quelqu'un
  not ~ ne … personne

anything quelque chose *m.*
  not ~ ne … rien
apartment appartement *m.*
appear avoir l'air
appetizer hors-d'œuvre *m.inv.*
apple pomme *f.*
appointment rendez-vous *m.*
  have an ~ avoir rendez-vous
approximately environ; vers
  (time)
April avril *m.*
Arabic arabe *m.*
argue se disputer
arm bras *m.*
armchair fauteuil *m.*
around environ; vers *(time)*;
  autour de *(place)*
  ~ (8 o'clock) vers (8 heures)
arrive arriver
artist artiste *m./f.*
as aussi, comme
  ~ … ~ aussi … que
  ~ much autant (de)
ashamed confus(e)
ask demander
  ~ a question poser une
  question
asleep: fall ~ s'endormir
aspirin tablet cachet
  d'aspirine *m.*
assure assurer

at à
- **~ first** d'abord
- **~ least** au moins
- **~ midnight** à minuit
- **~ noon** à midi
- **~ ... o'clock** à ... heure(s)
- **~ the home of** chez
- **~ what time (of day)?** à quel moment (de la journée)?

athletic sportif (sportive)
attach attacher
attend assister (à)
attention: pay ~ faire attention
attentive attentif (attentive)
August août *m.*
aunt tante *f.*
automobile voiture *f.*
autumn automne *m.*
away: right ~ tout de suite
awful! berk!

baby bébé *m.*
back *n.* dos *m.*
back *adv.:* **go ~** retourner; rentrer
- **~ then** à cette époque
- **come ~** revenir, rentrer
- **give ~** rendre

back up reculer
bad mauvais(e)
- **~ driver** chauffard *m.*
- **that's (it's) too ~** c'est dommage
- **the weather is ~** il fait mauvais

badly mal
bakery boulangerie *f.*
bald chauve
ball (dance) bal *m.*
bank banque *f.*
bar and café bistro *m.*
basement sous-sol *m.*
basketball basket-ball (basket) *m.*
bathing suit maillot de bain *m.*
bathroom salle de bain *f.*
be être
- **~ a long time coming** tarder
- **~ able** pouvoir
- **~ acquainted with, familiar with** connaître
- **~ afraid** avoir peur
- **~ born** naître
- **~ cold** avoir froid
- **~ fed up** en avoir assez
- **~ hot** avoir chaud
- **~ hungry** avoir faim
- **~ in the process of** être en train de
- **~ interested in** s'intéresser à

~ located se trouver
~ necessary falloir (il faut)
~ of the opinion trouver
~ probably, supposed devoir
~ right avoir raison
~ sleepy avoir sommeil
~ sore avoir mal (à)
~ sorry regretter
~ thirsty avoir soif
~ wrong, unwise avoir tort

beans haricots *m.pl.*
Beaujolais *(wine)* beaujolais *m.*
beautiful beau/bel/belle/beaux/belles
because parce que
become devenir
bed lit *m.*
- **go to ~** se coucher

bedroom chambre *f.*
beef bœuf *m.*
beer bière *f.*
before avant
begin commencer
behind derrière; en retard
- **right ~** juste derrière

beige beige
Belgian belge
Belgium Belgique *f.*
believe (in) croire (à)
- **I don't ~ it!** mon œil!

belong to être à
belt ceinture *f.*
- **safety ~, seat ~** ceinture de sécurité *f.*

beside à côté (de)
best *adv.* mieux; *adj.* le/la meilleur(e)
- **~ friend** meilleur(e) ami(e) *m./f.*
- **~ regards** avec mon meilleur souvenir
- **I like ~** j'aime le mieux (le plus); je préfère

better *adv.* mieux; *adj.* meilleur(e)
- **it is ~ that** il vaut mieux que

between entre
- **~ friends** entre amis

beverage boisson *f.*
bicycle vélo *m.*
big grand(e), gros(se)
bill *n.* *(paper money)* billet *m.*; *(restaurant check)* addition *f.*
billion milliard *m.*
bird oiseau *m.*
birthday anniversaire *m.*
bistro bistro *m.*

black noir(e)
- **~ currant liqueur** crème de cassis *f.*

blond blond(e)
blouse chemisier *m.*
blue bleu(e)
body corps *m.*
book livre *m.*
bookstore librairie *f.*
boots bottes *f.pl.*
Bordeaux *(wine)* bordeaux *m.*
boring ennuyeux (ennuyeuse)
born né(e)
- **be ~** naître

borrow emprunter
boss patron (patronne) *m./f.*
both tous (toutes) les deux
bother déranger
bottle bouteille *f.*
bowl *n.* bol *m.*
bowling: lawn ~ pétanque *f.*
box boîte *f.*
boy garçon *m.*
boyfriend petit ami *m.*
brake *v.* freiner
brand *n.* marque *f.*
brand-new neuf (neuve)
bread pain *m.*
breakfast petit déjeuner *m.*
bridge *(game)* bridge *m.*
Brie *(cheese)* brie *m.*
bring apporter
broccoli brocoli *m.*
brother frère *m.*
brother-in-law beau-frère *m.* (*pl.* beaux-frères)
brown brun(e); marron *inv.*
brush *n.* brosse *f.*
- **tooth ~** brosse à dents *f.*

brush *v.* se brosser
building bâtiment *m.*
burn brûler
business affaires *f.pl.,* commerce *m.*
- **mind your own ~!** occupe-toi de tes oignons!

businessman/woman homme/femme d'affaires *m./f.*
busy occupé(e)
- **be ~ with** s'occuper de

but mais
butcher shop boucherie *f.*
- **pork butcher's** charcuterie *f.*

butter beurre *m.*
- **peanut ~** beurre d'arachide *m.*

buy acheter

by par
  ~ **car** en voiture
  ~ **chance** par hasard
  ~ **the way ...** au fait ...
bye salut; tchao

café café *m.*, bistro *m.*
cafeteria cafétéria *f.*
cake gâteau *m.* (*pl.* gâteaux)
calculator calculatrice *f.*
call appeler, téléphoner
  your ~ from ... votre communi-
    cation de ...
called: be ~ s'appeler
calm calme, tranquille
Camembert (*cheese*) camembert *m.*
campus campus *m.*
can *n.* boîte *f.*
can (be able to) *v.* pouvoir
Canada Canada *m.*
Canadian canadien(ne)
candy bonbon *m.*
car voiture *f.*
  by ~ en voiture
card carte *f.*
  credit ~ carte de crédit
  post ~ carte postale
cards (*game*) cartes *f.pl.*
care *n.* souci *m.*
  take ~ of s'occuper de
care *v.*: **I don't ~** cela (ça) m'est
  égal
carefully prudemment
carry porter
cartoon dessin animé *m.*
cat chat *m.*
cautious prudent(e)
cell phone portable *m.*
centime centime *m.*
century siècle *m.*
cereal céréales *f.pl.*
certain sûr(e)
certainly tout à fait; certainement
chair chaise *f.*
chalk craie *f.*
chalkboard tableau *m.*
chance hasard *m.*
  by ~ par hasard
change *n.* monnaie *f.*
change *v.* changer (de)
channel: TV ~ chaîne (de télé) *f.*
charge: extra ~ supplément *m.*
charming charmant(e)
cheap bon marché *adj. inv.*

check chèque *m.*
  ~ (*restaurant bill*) addition *f.*
  traveler's ~ chèque de voyage *m.*
check *v.* vérifier
checkers dames *f.pl.*
cheese fromage *m.*
chemistry chimie *f.*
chess échecs *m.pl.*
chewing gum chewing-gum *m.*
chic chic *adj. inv.*
chicken poulet *m.*
child enfant *m./f.*
China Chine *f.*
Chinese chinois(e)
chocolate: hot ~ chocolat chaud *m.*
choice choix *m.*
choose choisir
Christmas Noël *m.*
church église *f.*
cigar cigare *m.*
cigarette cigarette *f.*
city ville *f.*
civil servant fonctionnaire *m./f.*
class cours *m.*, classe *f.*
  in ~ en classe
  in first ~ en première classe
classroom salle de classe *f.*
clean *adj.* propre
clean *v.* nettoyer
close *adj.* près (de)
close *v.* fermer
closed fermé(e)
clothing (article of) vêtement *m.*
coat manteau *m.* (*pl.* manteaux)
Coca-Cola coca *m.*
coffee café *m.*
coin pièce (de monnaie) *f.*
cold (*illness*) *n.* rhume *m.*
cold *adj.* froid(e)
  be ~ avoir froid
  it's ~ il fait froid
collide entrer en collision
color couleur *f.*
  what ~ is (are) ...? de quelle
    couleur est (sont) ...?
come venir
  ~ **back** revenir, rentrer
  ~ **in!** entrez!
  where do you ~ from? d'où
    venez-vous?
comfortable confortable
comic strip bande dessinée *f.*
commentary commentaire *m.*
commercial *n.* publicité *f.*
complete complet (complète)

completely tout *inv. adv.*;
  complètement
computer ordinateur *m.*
  ~ **science** informatique *f.*
confirm confirmer
console oneself se consoler
constant constant(e)
constantly constamment
contrary contraire *m.*
  on the ~ au contraire
cooking cuisine *f.*
cool: it's ~ il fait frais
corner coin *m.*
corridor couloir *m.*
cost *v.* coûter
cough *v.* tousser
could you ...? pourriez-vous ...?
country pays *m.*
course (*classroom*) cours *m.*; (*meal*)
  plat *m.*
  of ~ certainement, bien sûr
cousin cousin/cousine *m./f.*
crazy fou (folle)
  ~ **person** fou/folle *m./f.*
  in a ~ manner follement
cream crème *f.*
credit card carte de crédit *f.*
croissant croissant *m.*
cry *v.* pleurer
cup tasse *f.*
custom coutume *f.*
customer client/cliente *m./f.*
cut *v.* couper
cyclist coureur (cycliste) *m.*

dance *n.* bal *m.*
dance *v.* danser
dangerous dangereux
  (dangereuse)
darn it! mince!; zut!
date *n.* date *f.*; rendez-vous *m.*
date (someone) *v.* fréquenter
  (quelqu'un)
daughter fille *f.*
day jour *m.*
  ~ **after tomorrow** après-demain
  have a good ~ bonne journée
  New Year's ~ Jour de l'An *m.*
  what ~ is it? quel jour est-ce?
dead mort(e)
dear *n.* chéri/chérie *m./f.*
dear *adj.* cher (chère)
death mort *f.*
debt dette *f.*

December décembre *m.*
definitely sûrement, certainement
delicatessen charcuterie *f.*
delicious délicieux (délicieuse)
delighted ravi(e)
  ~ to meet you enchanté(e)
demand (that) exiger (que)
department store grand
  magasin *m.*
departmental (local) highway
  départementale *f.*
departure départ *m.*
depend dépendre
  it (that) depends ça dépend
depressed déprimé(e)
describe décrire
desk bureau *m.* (*pl.* bureaux)
dessert dessert *m.*
detective story roman policier *m.*
detest détester
die mourir
different original(e) (*m.pl.*
  originaux); différent(e)
dining room salle à manger *f.*
dinner dîner *m.*
  at ~ à table
  have ~ dîner *v.*
diploma diplôme *m.*
directions indications *f.pl.*
dirty sale
disagreeable désagréable
disappointed déçu(e)
discreet discret (discrète)
dish plat *m.*
dishes vaisselle *f.*
  do the ~ faire la vaisselle
dishwasher lave-vaisselle *m.*
divorce *n.* divorce *m.*
divorce *v.* divorcer
divorced divorcé(e)
do faire
  ~ the grocery shopping faire
    les provisions
  what am I going to ~?
    comment je vais faire?
doctor médecin *m.*, docteur *m.*
dog chien *m.*
dollar dollar *m.*
door porte *f.*
dormitory résidence
  (universitaire) *f.*
dozen douzaine *f.*
dress *n.* robe *f.*
  wedding ~ robe de mariée *f.*
dressed: get ~ s'habiller

drink *n.* boisson *f.*
  before-dinner ~ apéritif *m.*
drink *v.* boire, prendre
  do you want to ~ something?
    voulez-vous boire quelque
    chose?; quelque chose à boire?
drive *n.*: **to take a ~** faire une
  promenade en voiture   4
drive conduire
driver automobiliste *m./f.*,
  conducteur/conductrice *m./f.*,
  chauffeur *m.*
  ~ 's license permis de
    conduire *m.*
driving *n.* conduite *f.*
drums batterie *f.*
drunk *adj.* ivre
during pendant

each *adj.* chaque
  ~ (one) chacun(e)
ear oreille *f.*
early tôt; en avance
earn one's living gagner sa vie
earth terre *f.*
easy facile; simple
eat manger; prendre
  ~ dinner dîner
  ~ lunch déjeuner
economics sciences économiques
  f.pl.
education pédagogie *f.*
egg œuf *m.*
eight huit
eighteen dix-huit
eighty quatre-vingts
eighty-one quatre-vingt-un
eleven onze
embarrassed confus(e)
employee employé/employée *m./f.*
end *n.* fin *f.*
engaged fiancé(e)
engagement fiançailles *f.pl.*
engineer ingénieur *m.*
England Angleterre *f.*
English anglais(e)
enough assez
enter entrer
errands courses *f.pl.*
essential essentiel(le)
  it is ~ that il est essentiel que
even même
evening soir *m.*
  good ~ bonsoir

ever jamais
every chaque; tout (toute/tous/
  toutes)
  ~ night tous les soirs
everybody tout le monde
everything tout *pron. inv.*
exaggerate exagérer
exam examen *m.*
  on an ~ à un examen
example exemple *m.*
  for ~ par exemple
excellent excellent(e)
exciting passionnant(e)
excuse: ~ me je vous demande
  pardon; excusez-moi
executive cadre *m.*
exercise exercice *m.*
expensive cher (chère)
eye œil *m.* (*pl.* yeux)
  my ~! mon œil!
eyeglasses lunettes *f.pl.*

fall *n.* automne *m.*
fall *v.* tomber
  ~ asleep s'endormir
false faux (fausse)
familiar: be ~ with connaître
family famille *f.*
famous célèbre
fantastic formidable
far (from) loin (de)
farmer fermier/fermière *m./f.*
fast rapide
fat gros(se), gras(se)
father père *m.*
father-in-law beau-père *m.* (*pl.*
  beaux-pères)
faucet robinet *m.*
fault faute *f.*
favorite préféré(e)
fear peur
February février *m.*
fed up: be ~ en avoir assez
feel sentir, se sentir
  ~ like avoir envie de
  ~ sorry (for someone) avoir
    pitié (de)
fever fièvre *f.*
few peu (de)
  a ~ quelques
fifteen quinze
fifty cinquante
film film *m.*
finally enfin

find *v.* trouver
fine bien
  I'm ~ je vais très bien; ça va bien
finish *v.* finir
first premier (première)
  at ~ d'abord
  ~ name prénom *m.*
  in ~ class en première classe
fish *n.* poisson *m.*
five cinq
flea market marché aux puces *m.*
Flemish flamand *m.*
flight vol *m.*
flight attendant *(female)* hôtesse de l'air *f.*
floor *(of a building)* étage *m.*; *(of a room)* plancher *m.*
  ground ~ rez-de-chaussée *m.*
florist fleuriste *m./f.*
flower fleur *f.*
flu grippe *f.*
fluently couramment
flute flûte *f.*
follow: ~ me par ici
following suivant(e)
food cuisine *f.*
fool fou/folle *m./f.*
foot pied *m.*
football football américain *m.*
for depuis; pendant; pour
foreign étranger (étrangère)
forget oublier
fork fourchette *f.*
fortunately heureusement
forty quarante
four quatre
fourteen quatorze
franc franc *m.*
France France *f.*
free libre
French français(e)
  ~ fries frites *f.pl.*
  in ~ en français
  in the ~ style à la française
  steak with ~ fries steak-frites *m.*
Friday vendredi *m.*
friend ami/amie *m./f.*
  make friends se faire des amis
from de
front: in ~ of devant
fruit fruit *m.*
fun *adj.* amusant(e)
  have ~ s'amuser
funny amusant(e), drôle

game jeu *m.* *(pl.* jeux); match *m.*
garage garage *m.*
garlic ail *m.*
Gee! Tiens!
general: in ~ en général
generally généralement
generous généreux (généreuse)
German allemand(e)
Germany Allemagne *f.*
get obtenir, recevoir
  ~ along (with) s'entendre (avec)
  ~ angry se fâcher
  ~ dressed s'habiller
  ~ into monter
  ~ out of descendre
  ~ up, stand up se lever
  ~ washed, wash up se laver
ghost revenant *m.*
gift cadeau *m.*
girl fille *f.*
girlfriend petite amie *f.*
give donner
  ~ back rendre
gladly volontiers; je veux bien
glass (drinking) verre *m.*
glasses (eye) lunettes *f.pl.*
gloves gants *m.pl.*
go (in a vehicle) aller, rouler
  ~ across traverser
  ~ ahead allez-y
  ~ back retourner, rentrer
  ~ down descendre
  ~ into town aller en ville
  ~ out sortir
  ~ to bed se coucher
  ~ up monter
goat cheese chèvre *m.*
golf golf *m.*
good bon (bonne)
  ~ evening bonsoir
  ~ morning bonjour
  have a ~ day bonne journée
  have a ~ time s'amuser
good-bye au revoir
grade note *f.*
grains céréales *f.pl.*
grandchildren petits-enfants *m.pl.*
granddaughter petite-fille *f.* *(pl.* petites-filles)
grandfather grand-père *m.* *(pl.* grands-pères)
grandmother grand-mère *f.* *(pl.* grands-mères)
grandparents grands-parents *m.pl.*
grandson petit-fils *m.* *(pl.* petits-fils)

great formidable; chouette *(fam.)*
great-grandfather arrière-grand-père *m.*
green vert(e)
  ~ beans haricots verts *m.pl.*
grey gris(e)
groceries provisions *f.pl.*
  do the grocery shopping faire les provisions
grocery store épicerie *f.*
guess deviner
guitar guitare *f.*
gymnasium gymnase *m.*
gymnastics gymnastique *f.*

hair cheveux *m.pl.*
  hairbrush brosse à cheveux *f.*
half *adj.* demi(e)
  ~ past ... il est ... heure(s) et demie
hall couloir *m.*
ham jambon *m.*
hand main *f.*
handsome beau/bel/belle/beaux/belles
happen arriver, se passer
happy heureux (heureuse); content(e)
hardworking travailleur (travailleuse)
hat chapeau *m.*
hate *v.* détester
have avoir
  do you still ~ ...? il vous reste ...?
  ~ a pain (in) avoir mal (à)
  ~ an appointment, date avoir rendez-vous
  ~ dinner dîner
  ~ fun s'amuser
  ~ just venir de
  ~ lunch déjeuner
  ~ pity avoir pitié (de)
  ~ to devoir
  what do you ~ for (in the way of) ...? qu'est-ce que vous avez comme ...?
he *pron.* il; lui
head tête *f.*
health: (here's) to your ~! à votre santé!
hear entendre
  ~ about entendre parler de
heat chauffage *m.*

hello bonjour; bonsoir; salut
  ~ ! *(on the phone)* allô!
help *v.* aider
her *pron.* elle; la; (**to ~** lui)
her *adj.* son, sa, ses
here ici
  ~ is, ~ are voici
hi! salut!
high-top sneakers baskets *f.pl.*
highway autoroute *f.*
  departmental (local) ~ départementale *f.*
him *pron.* le; (**to~**) lui
his *adj.* son, sa, ses
hockey hockey *m.*
holiday fête *f.*
home maison *f.*
  at the ~ of chez
  go (come) ~ rentrer
homework devoirs *m.pl.*
honestly sans façon
hope *v.* espérer; souhaiter (que)
horrible affreux (affreuse)
hot chaud(e)
  be ~ avoir chaud
  ~ chocolate chocolat chaud *m.*
  it is ~ il fait chaud
hotel hôtel *m.*
hour heure *f.*
  one ~ ago il y a une heure
  one ~ from now dans une
  heure
house maison *f.*
  at your ~ chez toi
housewife ménagère *f.*
housework ménage *m.*
  do ~ faire le ménage
how comment
  ~ are you? comment allez-
  vous?; (comment) ça va?
  ~ do you say ...? comment
  dit-on ...?
  ~ do you spell ...? comment
  est-ce qu'on écrit ...?
  ~ ... he (she) was! comme il
  (elle) était ...!
  ~ long? pendant combien de
  temps ...?
  ~ many, much combien (de)
  ~ old are you? quel âge
  avez-vous?
hundred cent
hungry: be ~ avoir faim
hurry se dépêcher
husband mari *m.*

I *pron.* je; moi
ice cream glace *f.*
  vanilla ~ glace à la vanille *f.*
idiot idiot/idiote *m./f.*
if si
imbecile imbécile *m./f.*
impatience impatience *f.*
impatient impatient(e)
important important(e)
  it is ~ that il est important que
in à; dans; en
  ~ a crazy manner follement
  ~ a little while tout à l'heure
  ~ exchange for contre
  ~ general en général
  ~ order to pour
  ~ the afternoon de l'après-midi
included compris(e)
incredible incroyable
indeed tout à fait
indicate indiquer
indispensable indispensable
inexpensive bon marché *inv.*
inform (se) renseigner
information renseignement *m.*
inside intérieur *m.*
  ~ of à l'intérieur de
insist insister
instrument instrument *m.*
insure assurer
intellectual *adj.* intellectuel(le)
intelligent intelligent(e)
interest intérêt *m.*
interested: be ~ in s'intéresser à
interesting intéressant(e)
interpreter interprète *m./f.*
introduce présenter
  allow me to ~ myself
  permettez-moi de me
  présenter
invite inviter
Ireland Irlande *f.*
Israel Israël *m.*
it *pron.* cela, ça; il, elle
it is il est, c'est
  is it ...? est-ce (que) ...?
  ~ better that il vaut mieux que
  ~ cold il fait froid
  ~ cool il fait frais
  ~ essential il est essentiel
  ~ nice out il fait beau
  ~ preferable il vaut mieux
  ~ raining il pleut
  ~ snowing il neige
  ~ windy il fait du vent

Italian italien(ne)
Italy Italie *f.*
its *adj.* son, sa, ses

jacket blouson *m.*
jam confiture *f.*
January janvier *m.*
Japan Japon *m.*
Japanese japonais(e)
jeans jean *m.*
jogging jogging *m.*
juice jus *m.*
  orange ~ jus d'orange *m.*
July juillet *m.*
June juin *m.*
just: to have ~ ... venir de ...
just *adv.* juste

keep garder
key clé *f.*
kidding: no ~ sans façon; sans
  blague!
kilogram kilo *m.*
kind *n.* sorte *f.*
  all ~s of things toutes sortes de
  choses
  what ~(s) of ... quelle(s) sorte(s)
  de ...
kind *adj.* aimable; gentil(le)
kir kir *m.*
kiss *v.* s'embrasser
kitchen cuisine *f.*
knee genou *m.* (*pl.* genoux)
knife couteau *m.* (*pl.* couteaux)
knock frapper
know connaître, savoir
  I don't ~ je ne sais pas

laborer ouvrier/ouvrière *m./f.*
lady dame *f.*
language langue *f.*
lap *n.* genoux *m.pl.*
last dernier (dernière)
  ~ name nom de famille *m.*
  the ~ time la dernière fois
late tard, en retard
  be ~ être en retard
  it is ~ il est tard
lawn bowling pétanque *f.*
lay mettre
lazy paresseux (paresseuse)
leaf *(of paper)* feuille *f.*
learn apprendre (à)

least le/la/les moins
  at ~ au moins
  I like ~ j'aime le moins
leave laisser, partir
  ~ from partir (de)
  ~ me alone! laisse-moi
    (laissez-moi) tranquille!
  there's one left il en reste un(e)
left: to the ~ (of) à gauche (de)
leg jambe *f.*
leisure activity loisir *m.*
lemon-lime soda limonade *f.*
lemonade citron pressé *m.*
lend prêter
length *(of time)* durée *f.*
less moins
lesson leçon *f.*
let laisser
  let's go allez-y, allons-y
letter lettre *f.*
library bibliothèque *f.*
license: driver's ~ permis de
  conduire *m.*
life vie *f.*
  that's ~ c'est la vie
lift *v.* lever
like *v.* aimer
  I would ~ je voudrais
like *conj.* comme
listen (to) écouter
liter litre *m.*
literature littérature *f.*
little *adj.* petit(e)
  ~ girl petite fille *f.*
little *adv.* peu (de)
  a ~ un peu (de)
live *v.* habiter
living room salon *m.*
long long (longue)
  a ~ time longtemps
  be a ~ time coming tarder
  how ~ ...? pendant combien de
    temps ...?
  no longer ne ... plus
look regarder; *(seem)* avoir l'air
  ~ after garder
  ~ for chercher
lose perdre
  ~ (one's) patience perdre
    patience
  ~ weight maigrir
lot: a ~ (of) beaucoup (de)
love *v.* adorer; aimer
  ~ each other s'aimer
lozenge pastille *f.*

luck chance *f.*
  good ~! bonne chance!
  what ~! quelle chance!
lunch déjeuner *m.*
  have ~ déjeuner

magazine magazine *m.*
mail *v.* poster
make *n.* marque *f.*
make *v.* faire
  ~ a request faire une demande
  ~ friends se faire des amis
mall centre commercial *m.*
man homme *m.*; monsieur *m.*
management gestion *f.*
manner façon *f.*
manners étiquette *f.*
many beaucoup
  how ~ combien
  so ~ tant
  too ~ trop (de)
map carte *f.*; *(city)* plan *m.*
March mars *m.*
market marché *m.*
  flea ~ marché aux puces *m.*
  super ~ supermarché *m.*
marriage mariage *m.*
married marié(e)
marry se marier (avec); épouser
matter: what's the ~ with you?
  qu'est-ce que tu as?
May mai *m.*
may (be able to) pouvoir
  ~ I? vous permettez?; puis-je?
maybe peut-être
mayonnaise mayonnaise *f.*
mayor maire *m.*
me *pron.* me, moi
  ~ neither, nor I moi non plus
meal repas *m.*
  have a good ~! bon appétit!
mean *v.* vouloir dire
mean *adj.* méchant(e)
meat viande *f.*
medicine médicament *m.*
meet rencontrer
  to have met avoir connu
meeting réunion *f.*; rendez-
  vous *m.*
  have a ~ avoir rendez-vous
member membre *m.*
mention: don't ~ it il n'y a pas
  de quoi; de rien
menu *(à la carte)* carte *f.*; *(fixed price)* menu *m.*

merchant marchand/marchande
  m./f.
Mexican mexicain(e)
Mexico Mexique *m.*
midnight minuit
milk lait *m.*
million million *m.*
mind your own business!
  occupe-toi de tes oignons!
mine *pron.* le mien/la mienne
minute minute *f.*
mirror: rearview ~
  rétroviseur *m.*
miserly avare
Miss Mademoiselle (Mlle)
mistake faute *f.*
Monday lundi *m.*
money argent *m.*
month mois *m.*
moped mobylette *f.*
more encore, plus
  ~ ...? encore de ...?
  ~ to drink (eat)? encore à boire
    (manger)?
  there is no ~ il n'y en a plus
morning matin *m.*
Moroccan marocain(e)
Morocco Maroc *m.*
most (of) la plupart (de);
  the ~ le/la/les plus
mother mère *f.*
mother-in-law belle-mère
  (*pl.* belles-mères)
motorcycle moto *f.*
motorized bicycle mobylette *f.*
mouse souris *f.*
mouth bouche *f.*
movie film *m.*
  ~ theater cinéma *m.*
Mr. Monsieur (M.)
Mrs. Madame (Mme)
much beaucoup
  as ~ autant (de)
  how ~ combien
  not ~ pas grand-chose
  so ~ tant (de)
  too ~ trop (de)
museum musée *m.*
mushrooms champignons *m.pl.*
music musique *f.*
must devoir; il faut
  (someone) ~ not il ne faut pas
mustard moutarde *f.*
my *adj.* mon, ma, mes

naive naïf (naïve)
name *n.* nom *m.*
  family (last) ~ nom de famille
  in whose ~ ...? à quel nom ...?
  my ~ is ... je m'appelle ...
  what is your ~? comment vous appelez-vous?
named: be ~ s'appeler
nap sieste *f.*
  take a ~ faire la sieste
napkin serviette *f.*
nasty méchant(e)
nationality nationalité *f.*
  what is your ~? quelle est votre nationalité?
naturally naturellement
near près (de)
  very ~ tout près
necessary nécessaire
  it is ~ il faut, il est nécessaire (que)
need *v.* avoir besoin de
neighbor voisin/voisine *m./f.*
neither: me ~ moi non plus
  ~ ... nor ni ... ni
nephew neveu *m.* (*pl.* neveux)
nervous nerveux (nerveuse)
never jamais (ne ... jamais)
new nouveau/nouvel (nouvelle) (*m.pl.* nouveaux); neuf (neuve)
  ~ Year's Day Jour de l'An *m.*
  what's ~? quoi de neuf?
news informations *f.pl.*
newspaper journal *m.*
newsstand kiosque *m.*
next *adv.* ensuite, puis; *adj.* prochain(e); suivant(e)
  ~ door à côté
  ~ to à côté de
nice aimable; gentil(le)
  have a ~ day bonne journée
  it's ~ out il fait beau
  that's ~ of you c'est gentil à vous
niece nièce *f.*
night nuit *f.*
nine neuf
nineteen dix-neuf
ninety quatre-vingt-dix
ninety-one quatre-vingt-onze
no non
  ~ kidding! sans blague!; sans façon
  ~ longer ne ... plus
  ~ more ne ... plus
  ~ one ne ... personne

nobody ne ... personne
noise bruit *m.*
noon midi
nor: ~ I moi non plus
  neither ... ~ ni ... ni
nose nez *m.*
  runny ~ le nez qui coule
not ne (n') ... pas
  ~ anyone ne ... personne
  ~ anything ne ... rien
  ~ at all il n'y a pas de quoi, de rien; pas du tout
  ~ much pas grand-chose
  ~ yet pas encore
note note *f.*
nothing ne ... rien
notice remarquer
novel *n.* roman *m.*
novel *adj.* original(e) (*m.pl.* originaux)
November novembre *m.*
now maintenant, actuellement
number nombre *m.*, numéro *m.*; chiffre *m.*
  telephone ~ numéro de téléphone *m.*
nurse infirmier/infirmière *m./f.*

obey obéir (à)
o'clock heure(s)
  at ... ~ à ... heure(s)
  it is ... ~ il est ... heure(s)
October octobre *m.*
of de
  ~ course bien sûr
office bureau *m.* (*pl.* bureaux)
  post ~ bureau de poste *m.*
officer: police ~ agent de police *m.*
often souvent
oh dear! oh là là!
okay d'accord
  if that's ~ si ça va
old âgé(e), vieux/vieil (vieille)
  how ~ are you? quel âge avez-vous?
omelet omelette *f.*
on sur
one *pron.* on
  no ~ ne ... personne
one (*number*) un (une)
one-way: ~ street sens interdit *m.*
  ~ ticket aller simple *m.*
onion oignon *m.*
only *adj.* seul(e); *adv.* seulement; ne ... que

open *v.* ouvrir
open *adj.* ouvert(e)
opening ouverture *f.*
opinion avis *m.*
  be of the ~ trouver; penser
  in my (your, etc.) ~ à mon (à ton, etc.) avis
opposite contraire *m.*
optimistic optimiste
or ou
orange *n.* orange *m.*
  ~ juice jus d'orange *m.*
  ~ soda orangina *m.*
orange *adj.* orange *inv.*
order *v.* commander
order: in ~ to pour
ordinary *adj.* ordinaire
original original(e) (*m.pl.* originaux)
other autre
ouch! aïe!
our notre, nos
outgoing extroverti(e)
outside dehors
owe devoir
owner propriétaire *m./f.*

package paquet *m.*
pain: have a ~ (in) avoir mal (à)
pajamas (pair of) pyjama *m.*
pale pâle
pants (pair of) pantalon *m.*
paper papier *m.*
  (news)paper journal *m.*
  term ~ dissertation *f.*
pardon: I beg your ~ je vous demande pardon; excusez-moi
parents parents *m.pl.*
parents-in-law beaux-parents *m.pl.*
party boum *f.*; soirée *f.*; fête *f.*
pass (*an exam*) réussir
pass (*a car*) dépasser
pastry pâtisserie *f.*
  ~ shop pâtisserie *f.*
patience: lose (one's) ~ perdre patience
patient *adj.* patient(e)
patiently patiemment
pavement chaussée *f.*
pay (for) payer
  ~ attention faire attention
peanut arachide *f.*
  ~ butter beurre d'arachide *m.*
peas petits pois *m.pl.*

people gens *m.pl.;* on
pepper poivre *m.*
per par
perfect parfait(e)
perhaps peut-être
period *(time)* époque *f.*
person *(male or female)*
  personne *f.*
personally *adv.* personnellement
pessimistic pessimiste
pharmacy pharmacie *f.*
photograph photo *f.*
physical physique
piano piano *m.*
picnic pique-nique *m.*
pie tarte *f.*
piece morceau *m. (pl.* morceaux)
pill pilule *f.;* cachet *m.*
pilot pilote *m.*
pink rose
pity pitié *f.*
pizza pizza *f.*
place *n.* endroit *m.;* lieu *m.*
  take ~ avoir lieu
place *v.* mettre
plain simple
plan to avoir l'intention de
plate assiette *f.*
play *n.* pièce *f.*
play *v.* jouer
  ~ a game jouer à
  ~ an instrument jouer de
  ~ sports faire du sport
  ~ tennis jouer au tennis
please s'il vous (te) plaît
  ~ do je vous (t')en prie
pleasure plaisir *m.*
  with ~ avec plaisir
poem poème *m.*
point out indiquer
police officer agent de police *m.;*
  gendarme *m.*
politician homme/femme
  politique *m./f.*
politics politique *f.*
poor *adj.* pauvre
poorly mal
popular populaire
porch véranda *f.*
pork porc *m.*
  ~ butcher's charcuterie *f.*
post office bureau de poste *m.*
postcard carte postale *f.*
potato pomme de terre *f.*

pound *n.* livre *f.*
pour verser
practice répéter
prefer préférer
  I ~ that je préfère que
preferable: it is ~ that il vaut
  mieux que
prepare (a lesson) préparer (un
  cours)
pretty joli(e)
price prix *m.*
probably sans doute
process: be in the ~ of être en
  train de
program programme *m.*
  TV ~ émission (de télé) *f.*
promise *v.* promettre
  it's a ~ c'est promis
publicity publicité *f.*
punch (a ticket) composter (un
  billet)
pupil élève *m./f.*
purchase achat *m.*
purple violet(te)
put mettre
  ~ on attacher; mettre *(clothes)*
  ~ on weight grossir

quarter *m.* quart
  ~ past, ~ after et quart
  ~ to, ~ till moins le quart
question question *f.*
  ask a ~ poser une question
quickly vite; rapidement
quiet: keep ~! tais-toi!
  (taisez-vous!)

race course *f.*
radio radio *f.*
rain pleuvoir
  it's raining il pleut
raincoat imperméable *m.*
raise *v.* lever
rapid rapide
rapidly rapidement
rare *(undercooked)* saignant(e)
rarely rarement
rather assez
  ~ poorly assez mal
read lire
really vraiment; sans façon
reasonable raisonnable

recently récemment
recommend recommander
red rouge
  ~ -haired roux (rousse)
refrigerator réfrigérateur *m.*
regarding à propos de
relatives parents *m.pl.*
remain rester
remember se souvenir (de)
rent *v.* louer
repeat répéter
request *n.* demande *f.*
  make a ~ faire une demande
reserve réserver
reside habiter
responsibility responsabilité *f.*
rest se reposer
restaurant restaurant *m.*
restroom toilettes *f.pl.*
return *v.* retourner, revenir, rentrer
rice riz *m.*
rich riche
ride: take a ~ se promener; faire
  une promenade en voiture
  ~ a bike faire du vélo
ridiculous ridicule
right *n.* droit *m.*
right *adj.* droit(e); exact(e)
  be ~ avoir raison
  ~ ? n'est-ce pas?
  ~ away tout de suite
  ~ behind juste derrière
  that's ~ c'est exact
  to the ~ (of) à droite (de)
ring *n.* bague *f.*
road route *f.*
roast (of beef) rôti (de bœuf) *m.*
roll *v.* rouler
roof toit *m.*
room chambre *f.;* salle *f.;* pièce *f.*
  bath~ salle de bain *f.*
  bed~ chambre *f.*
  class~ salle de classe *f.*
  dining~ salle à manger *f.*
roommate camarade de chambre *m./f.*
round-trip ticket aller-retour *m.*
rugby rugby *m.*
run courir
  ~ a stop sign brûler un stop
  ~ into heurter
runner coureur/coureuse
Russia Russie *f.*
Russian russe

sad triste
salad salade *f.*
  (green) ~ salade (verte) *f.*
salesman/saleswoman
  vendeur/vendeuse *m./f.*
salmon saumon *m.*
salt sel *m.*
sandwich sandwich *m.*
Santa Claus *m.* père Noël
sardine sardine *f.*
Saturday samedi *m.*
sausage saucisse *f.*
saxophone saxophone *m.*
say dire
scarf foulard *m.*
schedule emploi du temps *m.*
school école *f.*
  high ~ lycée *m.*
science sciences *f.pl.*
  computer ~ informatique *f.*
season saison *f.*
seatbelt ceinture de sécurité
second second(e), deuxième
  in ~ class en seconde
see voir
seem avoir l'air
-self(-selves) -même(s)
sell vendre
semester semestre *m.*
send envoyer
Senegal Sénégal *m.*
Senegalese sénégalais(e)
separate *v.* séparer
  ~ from each other se séparer
September septembre *m.*
series *(TV)* feuilleton *m.*
serious sérieux (sérieuse)
seriously sérieusement
service: at your ~ à votre
  service
serviceman/woman militaire *m.*
set: ~ the table mettre la table
seven sept
seventeen dix-sept
seventy soixante-dix
seventy-one soixante et onze
seventy-two soixante-douze
she *pron.* elle
sheet (of paper) feuille *f.*
shh! chut!
shirt chemise *f.*
shoes chaussures *f.pl.*
shop *(clothing)* boutique *f.*
  tobacco ~ (bureau de) tabac *m.*

shopping courses *f.pl.*
  ~ center centre commercial *m.*
short petit(e)
shorts (pair of) short *m.*
shoulder épaule *f.*
show *v.* montrer
shower *n.* douche *f.*
shower *v.* se doucher
sick malade
since depuis
sincere sincère
sing chanter
singer chanteur/chanteuse *m./f.*
single célibataire
Sir Monsieur (M.)
sister sœur *f.*
sister-in-law belle-sœur *f.*
  (pl. belles-sœurs)
sit down s'asseoir
  ~ to eat se mettre à table
six six
sixteen seize
sixty soixante
skate patiner
skating rink patinoire *f.*
ski skier
skid déraper
skirt jupe *f.*
skis skis *m.pl.*
sleep dormir
sleepy: be ~ avoir sommeil
slice tranche *f.*
slippery glissant(e)
slow *adj.* lent(e)
slow down ralentir
slowly lentement
small petit(e)
smile *n.* sourire *m.*
smile *v.* sourire
smoke fumer
smoking (car) fumeur
  non- ~ non-fumeur
snail escargot *m.*
snow *v.* neiger
  it's snowing il neige
so alors, si
  ~ many tant
  ~ much tant
so-so comme ci, comme ça
soap opera feuilleton *m.*
soccer football (foot) *m.*
socks chaussettes *f.pl.*
soda: lemon-lime ~ limonade *f.;*
  orange ~ orangina *m.*

sofa sofa *m.*
some *adj.* des, quelques; *pron.* en
someone quelqu'un
something quelque chose *m.*
sometimes quelquefois
son fils *m.*
song chanson *f.*
soon bientôt
sore: be ~ avoir mal (à)
sorry désolé(e)
  be ~ regretter
  feel ~ (for) avoir pitié (de)
sort of assez
soup soupe *f.*
Spain Espagne *f.*
Spanish espagnol(e)
speak parler
specify préciser
speed vitesse *f.*
  at top ~ à toute vitesse
spell épeler
  how do you ~ …? comment
    est-ce qu'on écrit …?
  … is spelled … … s'écrit …
spend (a year) passer (un an)
spinach épinards *m.pl.*
spoon cuiller *f.*
sportcoat veste *f.*
spring *n.* printemps *m.*
stamp timbre *m.*
stand up se lever
start commencer; démarrer
  it's starting to get cold il
    commence à faire froid
state état *m.*
statue statue *f.*
stay rester
steak steak *m.*
  ~ with French fries steak-
    frites *m.*
steering wheel volant *m.*
stepbrother demi-frère *m.*
stepfather beau-père *m.*
  (pl. beaux-pères)
stepmother belle-mère *f.*
  (pl. belles-mères)
stepparents beaux-parents *m.pl.*
stepsister demi-sœur *f.*
stereo stéréo *f.*
still encore; toujours
stomach estomac *m.*
stop *n.* arrêt *m.*
  bus ~ arrêt d'autobus *m.*
  ~ sign stop *m.*

stop *v.* (s')arrêter
store magasin *m.*
  department ~ grand magasin *m.*
  grocery ~ épicerie *f.*
story histoire *f.*
  detective ~ roman policier *m.*
stove cuisinière *f.*
straight ahead tout droit
strawberries fraises *f.pl.*
street rue *f.*
  one-way ~ sens interdit *m.*
stressed stressé(e)
student étudiant/étudiante *m./f.*
studies *n.* études *f.pl.*
study *v.* étudier
stupid stupide
stylish chic *adj. inv.*
succeed réussir
sugar sucre *m.*
suit *n.* complet *m.*
  bathing ~ maillot de bain *m.*
suitcase valise *f.*
summer été *m.*
sun soleil *m.*
Sunday dimanche *m.*
supermarket supermarché *m.*
  giant ~ hypermarché *m.*
supplement supplément *m.*
supposed: be ~ to devoir
surely certainement, sûrement
surprise surprise *f.*
  what a good ~! quelle bonne surprise!
swear jurer
  I ~ (to you) je te le jure
sweater pull-over (pull) *m.*
sweatshirt sweat-shirt *m.*
Sweden Suède *f.*
Swedish suédois(e)
swim nager
swimming pool piscine *f.*
swimsuit maillot de bain *m.*
Swiss suisse
  ~ cheese emmenthal *m.*
Switzerland Suisse *f.*

table table *f.*
  at the ~ à table
  set the ~ mettre la table
tablecloth nappe *f.*
tablet cachet *m.*
  aspirin ~ cachet d'aspirine *m.*

take prendre
  ~ a nap faire la sieste
  ~ a test passer (un examen)
  ~ a trip faire un voyage
  ~ a walk, a ride faire une promenade
  ~ place avoir lieu
talkative bavard(e)
tall grand(e)
taste *v.* goûter
tea thé *m.*
teach enseigner
teacher professeur *m.*
  ~ preparation pédagogie *f.*
team équipe *f.*
tee-shirt tee-shirt *m.*
telephone *n.* téléphone *m.*
  on the ~ au téléphone
  ~ number numéro de téléphone *m.*
telephone *v.* téléphoner (à)
television télévision (télé) *f.*
tell indiquer, raconter, dire, parler
  can you ~ me ...? pouvez-vous me dire ...?
  ~ a story raconter une histoire
ten dix
tend to avoir tendance à
tennis tennis *m.*
  ~ shoes tennis *f.pl.*
  play ~ jouer au tennis
term paper dissertation *f.*
test examen *m.*
thank *v.* remercier
thanks merci
  yes, ~ je veux bien
that *adj.* ce/cet, cette, ces; *conj.* que; *pron.* ce, cela, ça; *relative pron.* qui, que
the le/la/les
theater théâtre *m.*
their leur(s)
them elles, eux; les, leur
then alors, ensuite, puis
there là, y
  over ~ là-bas
  ~ is (are) il y a; voilà
therefore alors; donc
they *pron.* ils, elles, on, eux
  ~ (these) are ce sont
thin mince
thing chose *f.*
think croire, penser, trouver
  do you ~ so? vous trouvez?
  I don't ~ so je ne crois pas

what do you ~ of ...? comment trouvez-vous ...?
what do you ~ of it (of them)? qu'en penses-tu?
thirsty: be ~ avoir soif
thirteen treize
thirty trente
this *adj.* ce/cet, cette, ces
  ~ way par ici
those *adj.* ces
thousand mille *inv.*
three trois
throat gorge *f.*
throughway autoroute *f.*
Thursday jeudi *m.*
ticket billet *m.*
  one-way ~ aller simple *m.*
  round-trip ~ aller-retour *m.*
  traffic ~ contravention *f.*
tie *n.* cravate *f.*
time temps *m.*; heure *f.*; fois *f.*
  a long ~ longtemps
  at that ~ à cette époque
  on ~ à l'heure
  the last ~ la dernière fois
  ~ difference décalage horaire *m.*
  what ~ is it? quelle heure est-il?
tired fatigué(e)
to à
  ~ the side à côté
toast pain grillé *m.*
tobacco tabac *m.*
  ~ shop (bureau de) tabac *m.*
today aujourd'hui
together ensemble
tomato tomate *f.*
tomorrow demain
  day after ~ après-demain
tonight ce soir
too aussi
  ~ many trop (de)
  ~ much trop (de)
  you ~ vous aussi
tooth dent *f.*
toothbrush brosse à dents *f.*
toothpaste dentifrice *m.*
tour tour *m.*
  ~ bus autocar *m.*
towel serviette *f.*
tower tour *f.*
town ville *f.*
  ~ hall mairie *f.*
trade ... for échanger ... contre
traffic circulation *f.*
traffic light feu *m.* (*pl.* feux)

train train *m.*
   ~ station gare *f.*
travel voyager
traveler's check chèque de
   voyage *m.*
trip voyage *m.*
trout truite *f.*
true vrai(e)
truly vraiment
   yours ~ amicalement
trumpet trompette *f.*
truth vérité *f.*
try essayer
   may I ~ ...? puis-je ...?
Tuesday mardi *m.*
turn *n.* tour *m.*
turn *v.* tourner
   ~ on *(the TV)* mettre
   ~ on the heat mettre le
      chauffage
turnpike autoroute *f.*
tuxedo smoking *m.*
twelve douze
twenty vingt
twenty-one vingt et un
twenty-two vingt-deux
two deux

ugly laid(e)
unbelievable incroyable
uncle oncle *m.*
under sous
understand comprendre
understanding compréhensif/
   compréhensive
United States États-Unis *m.pl.*
university université *f.*
unmarried célibataire
until *prep.* jusqu'à
unwise: be ~ avoir tort
up: get ~ se lever
us nous
useless inutile
usually d'habitude

vacation vacances *f.pl.*
   have a good ~! bonnes vacances!
   on ~ en vacances
vanilla vanille *f.*
   ~ ice cream glace à la vanille *f.*
vegetable légume *m.*
   raw vegetables crudités *f.pl.*

very très; tout
violin violon *m.*
visit visiter
   ~ someone rendre visite à qqn
voyage voyage *m.*

wait (for) attendre
waiter garçon *m.;* serveur *m.*
waitress serveuse *f.*
wake up se réveiller
walk *n.* promenade *f.*
   take a ~ se promener; faire une
      promenade
walk *v.* se promener
waltz valse *f.*
want vouloir, désirer, avoir
   envie de
war guerre *f.*
warning avertissement *m.*
wash laver; se laver
washing machine lave-linge *m.;*
   machine à laver *f.*
watch *n.* montre *f.*
watch *v.* regarder
water eau *f.* *(pl.* eaux)
   mineral ~ eau minérale
way route *f.;* façon *f.*
   by the ~ au fait
we nous
wear porter
weather météo(rologie) *f.;*
   temps *m.*
   the ~ is bad il fait mauvais
   what is the ~ like? quel temps
      fait-il?
wedding mariage *m.*
   ~ anniversary anniversaire de
      mariage *m.*
   ~ dress robe de mariée *f.*
Wednesday mercredi *m.*
week semaine *f.*
   per ~ par semaine
   two weeks quinze jours
weekend week-end *m.*
weight: put on ~ grossir
   lose ~ maigrir
welcome: you're ~ de rien; je
   vous en prie; il n'y a pas de quoi
Welcome! Bienvenue!
well *adv.* bien
   are you ~? vous allez bien?
   fairly ~ assez bien
   not very ~ pas très bien

Well! Tiens!
Well then ... Eh bien ...
what *pron.* qu'est-ce que/qu'est-ce
   qui, que; *adj.* quel(le)
   ~? comment?
   ~ am I going to do? comment
      je vais faire?
   ~ day is it? quel jour est-ce?
   ~ (did you say)? comment?
   ~ is (are) ... like? comment est
      (sont) ...?
   ~ is there ...? qu'est-ce qu'il y
      a ...?
   ~ is this? qu'est-ce que c'est?
   ~ is your name? comment vous
      appelez-vous?
   ~ time is it? quelle heure
      est-il?
   ~'s new? quoi de neuf?
   ~'s the matter? qu'est-ce qu'il
      y a?
wheel: steering ~ volant *m.*
weird bizarre
when quand
where où
   ~ are you from? vous êtes
      d'où?; d'où venez-vous?
   ~ is (are) ...? où se trouve (se
      trouvent) ...?
which *adj.* quel(le); *pron.*
   lequel
while pendant que
   in a little ~ tout à l'heure
white blanc (blanche)
who qui
why pourquoi
   ~ not? pourquoi pas?
widower/widow veuf/veuve *m./f.*
wife femme *f.*
win gagner
   ~ the lottery gagner à
      la loterie
wind vent *m.*
   it's windy il fait du vent
windbreaker blouson *m.*
wine vin *m.*
winter hiver *m.*
wish *v.* vouloir; souhaiter
with avec
without sans
witness témoin *m.*
Wolof *(language)* wolof *m.*
woman femme *f.;* dame *f.*
word mot *m.*

work *n.* travail *m.*
  manual ~ travail manuel *m.*
work *v.* travailler
world monde *m.*
worry *n.* souci *m.*
worry *v.* s'inquiéter
wounded *adj.* blessé(e)
wow! oh là là!
write écrire
wrong faux (fausse)
  be ~ avoir tort

year an *m.;* année *f.*
  school ~ année scolaire
yellow jaune
yes oui; si!
yesterday hier
yet encore
  not ~ pas encore
you *pron.* tu, vous; te, vous; toi, vous
young jeune

your *adj.* ton, ta, tes; votre, vos
  (here's) to yours! à la vôtre!
yuck! berk!
yum! miam!

zero zéro
zip code code postal *m.*

Index

In the following index, the symbol (v) refers to lists of vocabulary within the lessons. The symbol (g) refers to the sections titled *Il y a un geste* that explain gestures used with the indicated phrase.

Permissions and Credits

The authors and editors wish to thank the following persons and publishers for permission to include the works or excerpts mentioned.

Text credits

Chapter 4:

p. 118: Jacques Prévert, «Familiale», from *Paroles*. Copyright © Editions Gallimard. Reprinted with permission.

Chapter 5:

p. 151: Jean-Louis Dongmo, «Village natal». Reprinted by permission of Jean-Louis Dongmo from *Neaf Camerounais: Anthologie* par Lilyan Kesteloot, deuxième edition, (Yaoundé: Editions Clé, 1971).

Chapter 6:

p. 179: © L'Alsace: Le Journal des enfants; p. 181: «Non, Je Ne Regrette Rien». Music by Charles Dumont. French Lyric by Michel Vaucaire. Copyright © 1960 Éditions Musicales Eddie Barclay, Paris, France. Publisher for USA and Canada: Shapiro, Bernstein & Co., Inc./ The Barclay Music Division, New York. Publisher outside USA and Canada: S.E.M.I./Peer Music, France. International Copyright Secured. All Rights Reserved. Used by Permission.

Chapter 7:

p. 207: Jacques Prévert, «Refrains enfantins», from *Paroles*. Copyright © Editions Gallimard. Reprinted with permission.

Chapter 8:

p. 236: Jacques Prévert, «Déjeuner du matin», from *Paroles*. Copyright © Editions Gallimard. Reprinted with permission.

Chapter 9:

p. 266: «Hystérie anti-tabac,» *Le Point*, 31 Août 1996, p. 15; p. 266: «Les mesures du président,» *Le Point*, 31 Août 1996, p. 60.

Chapter 10:

p. 291: «La France au volant», Pierre Daninos, *Les Carnets du Major Thompson*, © Hachette, 1954.

Chapter 11:

p. 315: Marie-Célie Agnant, *La Dot de Sara*, (Montréal: Remue-ménage, 1995). By permission of Les Éditions du Remue-ménage.

Chapter 13:

p. 373: Copyright © 1997 Enoch et Cie, Paris, France. Reprinted with permission.

Images; p. 336, © Beryl Goldberg; p. 339, © Owen Franken; p. 343, © Jeremy Hartley/Panos Pictures.

Chapter 13:
p. 347, © Richard Kalvar/Magnum; p. 362, © Beryl Goldberg; p. 367, © Chad Ehlers/Stone/Getty Images; p. 370, © Crispin Hughes/Panos Pictures; p. 371, © Jean-Marc Truchet/Stone/Getty Images; p. 373, © Michael Busselle/Stone.

Chapter 14:
p. 378, Digital Vision/Getty Images; p. 383, © Beryl Goldberg; p. 384, © Rose Hartman/Corbis; p. 387, © Charles Nes.

Chapter 15:
p. 407, © Kevin Galvin; p. 410, © Mark Burnett/David R. Frazier Photolibrary; p. 414, © Andrew Brilliant; p. 415, © Mahmud Hams/AFP/Getty Images.

Realia
Chapter 1:
p. 9, Hotel Ibis brochure: Accorhotels

Chapter 2:
p. 29, Orangina: Cadbury Schweppes PLC; p. 29, Perrier: Courtesy of Nestlé Waters North America; p. 53, Simulated personal ad: Paru Vendu

Chapter 4:
p. 92, Catfish Steakhouse: Courtesy David Whitsett

Chapter 5:
p. 149, Advertisement for Angers: Office de Tourisme Angers; p. 149, Angers Tourism ad: Office de Tourisme Angers

Chapter 8:
p. 211, Jurancon wine label: Domaine Nigri; p. 211, Vieux Fagots wine label: Société Marjolaine; p. 225, Photograph taken by Rosalee Briner

Chapter 9:
p. 256, Téléfleurs

Chapter 11:
p. 304, © Léon de Bruxelles S. A.

Chapter 12:
p. 328, ESIG ad: www.ESIG-EST.com; p. 333, Société Générale

Chapter 13:
p. 370, Courtesy Kristina Baer; p. 375, Courtesy Kristina Baer

Chapter 14:
p. 399, Getty Images

Chapter 15:
p. 420, Swiss Life

Cartoon Credits
Chapter 9:
p. 265, Le tabac tue!: Courtesy Hoviv and *L'illustré*, Lausanne.

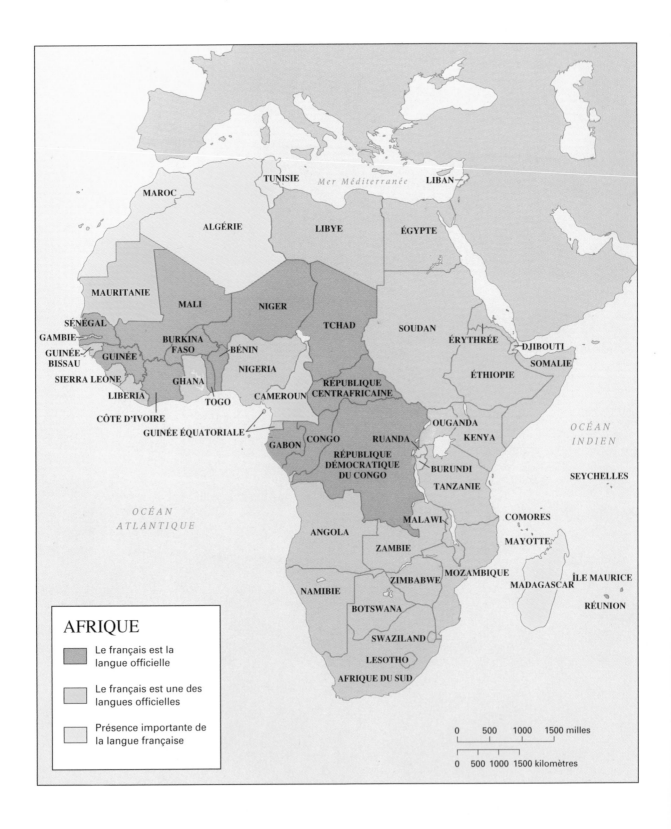

MAROC

TUNISIE

Mer Méditerranée

LIBAN

ALGÉRIE

LIBYE

ÉGYPTE

MAURITANIE

MALI

NIGER

TCHAD

SOUDAN

ÉRYTHRÉE

DJIBOUTI

SÉNÉGAL

GAMBIE

BURKINA
FASO

BÉNIN

SOMALIE

GUINÉE-
BISSAU

GUINÉE

ÉTHIOPIE

SIERRA LEONE

GHANA

NIGERIA

LIBERIA

TOGO

CAMEROUN

RÉPUBLIQUE
CENTRAFRICAINE

CÔTE D'IVOIRE

GUINÉE ÉQUATORIALE

OUGANDA

KENYA

OCÉAN
INDIEN

GABON

CONGO

RUANDA

RÉPUBLIQUE
DÉMOCRATIQUE
DU CONGO

BURUNDI

SEYCHELLES

TANZANIE

OCÉAN
ATLANTIQUE

MALAWI

COMORES

ANGOLA

ZAMBIE

MAYOTTE

MOZAMBIQUE

ÎLE MAURICE

NAMIBIE

ZIMBABWE

MADAGASCAR

RÉUNION

BOTSWANA

SWAZILAND

LESOTHO

AFRIQUE DU SUD

AFRIQUE

Le français est la
langue officielle

Le français est une des
langues officielles

Présence importante de
la langue française

0   500   1000   1500 milles

0   500 1000 1500 kilomètres